The ILLUSTRATED HISTORY *of the* JEWISH PEOPLE

The ILLUSTRATED HISTORY *of the* JEWISH PEOPLE

WITH ESSAYS BY JANE S. GERBER, ODED IRSHAI,
ORA LIMOR, MICHAEL R. MARRUS, DEREK J. PENSLAR,
SETH SCHWARTZ, DAVID SORKIN
AND BERNARD WASSERSTEIN

EDITED BY NICHOLAS DE LANGE

AURUM PRESS

First published in Great Britain 1997 by Aurum Press Limited, 25 Bedford Avenue, London WC1B 3AT.

Published in Canada in 1997 by Key Porter Books Limited and in the United States in 1997 by Harcourt Brace & Company.

A catalogue reference for this book is available from The British Library.

ISBN 1 85410 530 2.

Design: Jack Steiner
Cartography: Stuart Daniel, Starshell Maps
Picture research: Patricia Buckley

Printed and bound in Canada

CONTENTS

Acknowledgments

This book originated, several years ago, in a suggestion from Malcolm Lester and Kathy Lowinger. I hope they are pleased with the results.

I am grateful to Anna Porter for her confidence in me and the project.

Barbara Berson made sure it happened. She has earned heartfelt thanks from the editor and all the contributors.

Finally, a number of people gave to this project their time and expertise: Patricia Buckley, Doris Cowan, Bernice Eisenstein, Professor David Novak, Lisa Rampton, Alison Reid and Cy Strom—for which my sincere thanks.

Introduction

Nicholas de Lange

The Jews have always been a wandering people. They have had many homes, and all have proved, sooner or later, to be temporary. The frail booths of the autumn festival of Sukkot, Tabernacles, originally harvesters' huts, have come to symbolize the wandering life of the Jewish people, at home nowhere, always prepared to move on. So deep is this sense of transitoriness that it has permeated their existential value system: the whole of life, in Jewish thought, has come to seem like a wandering in the wilderness. The true home is elsewhere.

In this present world, only one place has been seen as the authentic home of the Jews: the holy city of Jerusalem, "God's previous address," as the contemporary Jerusalem poet Yehudah Amichai has put it.

The foundation document of the Jewish people, the Torah, tells the story of the formation of the people from early beginnings in Mesopotamia and Egypt, the giving of the law at Mount Sinai and the forty-year wanderings in the wilderness before the entry into the Promised Land. The other books of the Hebrew Bible tell of the settlement of the land, the building of Jerusalem and the Temple, the exile in Babylon and the return and reconstruction. The city of Jerusalem plays a central role in this story, yet much of the narrative unfolds elsewhere, in the Fertile Crescent, on the banks of the Nile or in great cities like Babylon and Nineveh. The symbolism of wandering and displacement, of exile and return, is inscribed in the earliest writings of the people.

The festival of Pesach, or Passover, reenacts this history from nomadic origins to Egypt, then through the wilderness to Jerusalem, then on to the recognition that the Temple is destroyed and the Jews live under the constant threat of annihilation, of which the biblical story of Pharaoh is a potent symbol. History and present existence merge. "In each and every generation one must consider himself as though he himself came out of Egypt." And the liberation from Egyptian slavery is used as an image and guarantee of a future liberation from the shackles of the present world order, encapsulated in the seder celebration's concluding exclamation: "Next year in Jerusalem!"

The history of the Jewish people is constantly being rewritten. No two versions are the same. In part, the reasons are personal: each author has a different perspective. Advances in our knowledge, due, for example, to discoveries of new documents, play a large part too. But the most significant differences result from the changing needs of the times.

Recent research has underlined the distance that exists between the real beginnings of the Jewish people and the story as it is recounted in the Bible. The biblical books rewrite the past to make sense of it and pass on a message to the people. Every generation of Jewish historians has faced the same task: to retell and adapt the story to meet the needs of its own situation.

This constant reinvention of the past demands a balance between the conflicting forces of continuity and change. The changes from the Bible to the present day have been spectacular. It could well be claimed that nothing has remained the same: the Jewish people today, in their life, thought and worship, are not the same people who came out of Egypt. But without a sense of continuity there is no history. It is the task of the historian to discern the continuity amid the change.

The present history, like all its predecessors, attempts to do just this: to trace the continuous history of the Jewish people from their remote beginnings to our own time. We do not underestimate the momentous changes that have taken place, but we do not let them have the final word. A history is a story, and the story of the Jewish people is unbroken, even by the most dramatic interruptions.

Every generation needs its own version of history. The same events, narrated in different times and circumstances, take on a different meaning. We can see this clearly if we look back at the way the history of the Jewish people was perceived at key moments in the past.

The conquest of the Kingdom of Judah (from which the Jews take their name) by a Babylonian army in the early sixth century B.C.E. was a traumatic event that might have led to the people's annihilation. The earlier example of the fate of the northern Kingdom of Israel pointed in this direction: "The Lord said: I shall remove Judah too from my sight, as I removed Israel. I shall reject this city, Jerusalem, which I chose, and the house where I said my name would be" (2 Kings 23:27).

The destruction and the subsequent exile and return gave rise to important historical reflections that are preserved in the Hebrew Bible. They center on the role of God in history and his relationship with his people. The God whose home is in Jerusalem keeps a close watch on his people. He has given them commandments to live by, and has warned them of the consequences of disobedience. Righteousness is rewarded and wickedness punished. It follows from this theological system that if disaster strikes the people, it must be a punishment for sin. Yet the survival of the Jews proves that God's love is stronger than his justice: he will punish his people, but he will never destroy them.

This view of Jewish history, shaped by the Babylonian conquest, was still prevalent at the time of the Roman conquest of Jerusalem in 70 C.E. As Josephus, the main historian of the event, puts it: "Reflecting on such things one will find that God cares for humankind, and indicates to his people the way to salvation by all kinds of portents, but that they destroy themselves by their own self-willed stupidity and wickedness" (*The Jewish War* 6:310).

This is a thoroughly biblical view of history, yet what Greek reader of Josephus could avoid recalling, however obliquely, the fateful words of Zeus from the beginning of Homer's *Odyssey*, which was in a sense the Greek equivalent of the Bible? "Alas, how mortals blame the gods! They say that evil comes from us, yet they bring undue woes upon themselves by their own wickedness" (1:32–4).

Josephus, a proud Jew and the first real historian of the Jews in the modern sense of the word, modeled himself on Greek historians such as Thucydides and Polybius. His work, in common with that of other contemporary Jewish writers, represents a fusion of biblical and Greek ideas. His books were accessible to a mixed readership of Jews and gentiles, and this knowledge determined the way he wrote.

While Josephus applied his mind to writing calmly and professionally about the greatest catastrophe to afflict the Jewish people, others were totally crushed by the burden of grief:

> Our sanctuary is in ruins, our altars are demolished, our Temple destroyed; our worship has been suppressed, our singing silenced, our praises hushed; the light has been extinguished in our sacred lamp, the ark of the covenant has been carried away, our holy vessels have been besmirched; our leaders have been tortured, our Levites taken captive, our virgins have been defiled and our wives raped, our pious men imprisoned and our saints scattered, our children enslaved and our fighting men enfeebled (4 Ezra 10:19ff).

These words have a special resonance today, in the aftermath of the Shoah (the Holocaust).

A thousand years ago, in the tenth century, the Jewish people were divided fairly equally between the lands of Islam and Christendom. (The "Jewish empire" of the Khazars was a marginal and little-known entity.) There was a widespread sense of stability and continuity. Institutions such as the yeshivot (academies) of Israel and Iraq looked back on a history of centuries. The misfortunes of dispersion, subjugation and occasional oppression were accepted as part of a divine dispensation that would end in God's good time. The gaon Saadia (882–942) could read the book of Job as a philosophical treatise expounding God's justice and goodness, without the need to relate the suffering of Job directly to the suffering people of Israel. There was order in the world, and if the destiny of Israel was in temporary eclipse there was a strong hope that God, in his own good time, would give a further and definitive turn to the wheel of fortune. It is interesting that at this time there was no explicit historical writing by Jews: such historical reflections as we have are contained in commentaries and liturgies that, attributing all history to God, sidestep the need to analyze human motivation.

The new millennium brought a change to the destiny of the Jews. Violent upheavals shook Christian and Muslim society alike, and at each turn the powerless Jewish minorities suffered. The religious fanaticism of Muslim Almoravids and Almohads and of Christian crusaders spelled destruction for whole communities of Jews. The theologian poet Judah Halevi (d. after 1141) went so far as to portray the relationship between Israel and God as the relationship between a battered wife and the violent husband she cannot abandon. She revels in the blows inflicted on her by others because they remind her of the blows of her former lover:

Since you have ever been the home of love,
My love encamps where'er you pitch your tent.
Foes' taunts I bear with relish for your sake:
They do but harry one whom you torment.
I love my foes: they imitate your rage,
And chase the body your dear blows have bent!
Do you despise me?— I despise myself:
What self-respect can weather your contempt?
Oh when will you return, like days gone by,
And liberate your own, all fury spent?

The last line of the poem invokes the one consolation of this dark history: the memory of the liberation from Egypt offers a hope that God will act again to save his people. In another poem, Judah encapsulates the predicament of Israel in the powerful phrase "prisoner of hope." "Is there any redeemer like you?" he asks God, "or any prisoner of hope like me?" The Jew appears to be trapped within his history, in a persistent sequence of violence and oppression tempered by a hope that always proves illusory. If the relationship of the people to their God is painted in conventional colors as a love relationship, it is a love that has become bitter, if not indeed pathological.

Five hundred years ago, the situation of the Jews was even bleaker. In Western Europe and elsewhere, Christian intolerance had led to their forcible conversion or expulsion. The Byzantine Empire had fallen to the Ottoman Turks, and its once-flourishing Jewish life was in ruins. The fate of the proud Jewries of Spain, now Christianized or exiled in cruel conditions, was perceived as a catastrophe of epoch-making dimensions. The shadow of this disaster can be perceived in all the voluminous Jewish literature of the ensuing century. Significantly, this literature contains a number of genuine historical works, composed in response to recent events in Jewish and world history. Jewish history had not been a subject of serious study since the destruction of the Temple by the Romans, chronicled and analyzed by Josephus.

The Jewish historians of the sixteenth century shared a common assumption that history had taken a fateful step forward. There was even a sense that the coming of the long-awaited Messiah was at hand. And, indeed, there were signs of hope even amid the destruction. The decline of the West was accompanied by the rise of the East. In Poland, a golden age was dawning that would rival that of Spain. The Ottoman Empire offered a hospitable welcome to Jewish refugees from Christian lands. Istanbul and Salonica became major centers of Sephardi Jewry, and it was even made possible for Jews to settle once again in the Land of Israel. Safed (Tsfat) became the home of a brilliant and fascinating coterie of mystically inspired scholars. One of these, Joseph Caro, drafted a new code of law for the survivors of the destruction. Another, Isaac Luria, devised a mystical theology indicating new ways in which the world might be redeemed. The Lurianic Kabbalah fueled the messianic pretensions of Shabbetai Zvi, which first excited, then disappointed, the Jewish world in the mid-seventeenth century. Meanwhile, in Amsterdam, his older contemporary Menasseh Ben Israel, responding to claims that the lost tribes of Israel had been discovered in the New World, pointed in his book *The Hope of Israel* to various signs that the redemption of the world was at hand. *The Hope of Israel* made a contribution to the decision to readmit the Jews to England after an absence of three and a half centuries. The title of the book was borrowed from the biblical prophecies of Jeremiah, where it is an appellation for God.

The hope that was kindled after the Spanish catastrophe and that glowed more brightly in the seventeenth and eighteenth centuries was a hope for progress and change. In part, this hope expressed itself in traditional terms, in the classical yearning for divine redemption that can be traced through the biblical prophets through the rabbinic Midrash to Judah Halevi and all other medieval Jewish authors. But the contrast between the blazing supernaturalism of Shabbetai Zvi and the cautious and reasoned supernaturalism of Menasseh Ben Israel was to become more marked with time, and led toward the alternative versions of Jewish messianism that were to emerge in the course of the nineteenth century. These rivals to the hope of redemption through a personal Messiah took various forms. The most extreme was an untraditional pursuit of the salvation of the individual at the expense of the survival of the community: in other words, assimilation into the surrounding society. But even the proponents of less total reforms had as their target some kind of normalization of the condition of the Jews, which would bade farewell to the "difference" that had once been the glory of the "holy people." The Jewish category of holiness indicates being set apart for a special purpose. The political and religious reformers of the nineteenth century aimed to rid the Jews of this holiness, and of the troubles that they perceived accompanied it. Political compromises were espoused that turned the Jewish community into just another religious or ethnic minority among others within the nation-state. The Jewish religion was modernized to resemble a version of Christianity. Those who refused to part company with the idea of a Jewish nation allied themselves to the romantic nationalism of the period and sought a national solution to the problem of Jewish uniqueness.

Once again Jewish history was rewritten. The nineteenth-century religious reformers applied the methods of historical research to the Bible and Talmud, and used the findings to support their reforms. The Zionists discovered ancient and persistent seams of Jewish nationalism, and sang of "the two-thousand-year-old hope to be a free people in our own land." The biblical prophets were read as social and political reformers, and Judah Halevi, that subtle medieval theologian, enjoyed a new vogue as a proto-Zionist bard.

A hundred years ago, the dominant mood in Jewish historiography was one of hope. Despite the menace of the Russian pogroms and the spread of antisemitic politics, there was a real confidence in progress. As the 1885 Pittsburgh Platform of American Reform Judaism put it:

> We recognize in the modern era of universal culture of heart and intellect the approach of the realization of Israel's great Messianic hope for the establishment of the kingdom of truth, justice and peace among all men.

Even if the Jewish past was commonly portrayed as a catalog of woes, there was an underlying assumption that that gloomy past was approaching its end. Political emancipation, intellectual enlightenment, social openness, technological progress and a commitment to understanding and cooperation between peoples signaled the dawning of a rosier future.

As we now confront the history of the Jewish people at the end of another century, and indeed of another millennium, the general mood is in marked contrast to that which prevailed a hundred years ago. There is a confidence in progress, to be sure, but it is a cautious and hesitant confidence. The earlier faith was shattered by the great events of European history in the twentieth century: the horrors of two World Wars, antisemitism, Stalinism and, above all, the Nazi nightmare.

The Shoah is a catastrophe for the Jews on a level with the expulsion from Spain or the destruction of the Jerusalem Temple. In some respects it is worse, not only in the sense that whatever is nearer is bound to bulk larger, but because it appears like a narrow escape from annihilation. As we now survey Jewish history, everything we observe is colored by the knowledge of the Shoah. Even the great achievements of the past are poisoned by this perspective, and the calamities take on a more ominous hue. As we read of the optimism and real progress of the last century, we are aware of how hollow and temporary were the gains. We see how easily the emancipation and social integration of the Jews were undone by a few decrees. When we study the rich and wonderful history of the Jews in Poland, we cannot banish thoughts of death marches and cattle trucks. The history of relations between Jews and gentiles cannot be read in innocence.

The Shoah has put paid to the widespread belief in a divine purpose for the Jewish people that could be relied on even in adversity. The biblical idea, already under threat in the nineteenth century, that history is the arena in which God's inscrutable but reliable plan for humankind is played out, appears to many as untenable. Those who do attempt to maintain it, like the German theologian Ignaz Maybaum, are dismissed because the implication that God was in some sense on the side of the Nazis seems intolerable. Others who insist soothingly on God's inscrutability encounter agonized impatience. The book of Job offers no answers. The American writer Richard Rubenstein has more support when he argues that God is no longer an operative concept for the Jewish people, whatever its role in the past. History in any case has become divorced from theology: most histories of the Nazi genocide, or of anything else for that matter, look exclusively to human factors and pay no attention to the divine dimension so important in medieval interpretations.

Contemporary Jewish historians focus on the creation of the state of Israel as a sign of real hope, an antidote to post-Holocaust despair and a token of vigorous national recovery. Israel has reopened old questions about the meaning of the Diaspora and the relationship between the two. It has also reappropriated aspects of Jewish history within the Land of Israel that had become submerged. We are more aware now of the continuity of Jewish life in the Land of Israel, and the important contributions that Israel has made to Judaism worldwide. Archaeological exploration has brought buried treasures to light. The history of the Jews when written in Israel can seem very different from perspectives evolved in diaspora. The unity of the Jewish people and the various definitions of Jewish identity have also become vital issues in Israel, as has the conflict between religious traditionalism and godless secularism, two extreme ideologies nurtured in the East whose clash seems to leave little room for the various modernist denominations developed in the West.

As contributors to the present history, we write from the perspective of our own time. We have endeavored to reflect present-day concerns, and indeed to anticipate certain trends that are just now becoming apparent. This book is not a chronicle, a blow-by-blow account of everything that has happened to the Jews. It is a carefully focused study of key aspects. Each of the eight chapters examines a topic of the Jewish past that is of direct relevance to the present. The account of Jewish origins makes use of the latest research to tell a story that is in some respects quite unfamiliar: it has a direct bearing on contemporary questions such as the limits of cultural compromise and the relations between Jews and non-Jews in Jewish-ruled Israel. The story of the Diaspora delves back beyond the myth that this crucial feature of Jewish experience began in 70 C.E., and it also shows how long a real struggle persisted between Israel and the Diaspora. In surveying the relations between Church and Synagogue, we try to move beyond the purely conflictual model to appreciate the richness and subtlety of the relationship and the positive contribution that each religion made to the other. The Jewish experience under Muslim rule is being studied in a new light too, as befits a period when Jewish-Muslim relations are assuming a renewed significance. We give prominence to the encounter with modernity, and the reintegration of the Jews into the societies from which they were excluded by majority intolerance, as a prelude to studying the resurgence of medieval segregation and intolerance in the Nazi period. The reestablishment of a self-governing Jewish state in the Land of Israel is of central importance, and is treated with the seriousness it deserves. We end with an analysis of the Jewish world today, trying to look forward, however tentatively, to likely developments as we enter a new millennium.

As we survey Jewish history as a whole from the vantage point of the late twentieth century, Judah Halevi's phrase "prisoner of hope" seems entirely apposite. The prisoner of hope is sustained and encouraged by his hope, even as he is confined by it. At the dawn of Jewish history, during the Babylonian captivity, the prophet Ezekiel had a vision of a valley full of dry bones. The heavenly voice explained: "These bones are the whole house of Israel. They say: our bones are dried up and our hope is lost. . . . But I shall bring you up out of your graves, my people, and lead you back to the soil of Israel." Twenty-five centuries later, another Hebrew writer, N. H. Imber, penned these lines:

> Our hope is not lost,
> The two-thousand-year-old hope,
> To be a free people in our own land,
> Land of Zion, Jerusalem.

The poem, titled "The Hope" (*Hatikvah*), eventually became the national hymn of the restored Jewish state. Who could have foreseen in Babylon that the hope would last so long? The Babylonian Empire, like so many other powerful empires, has perished, and the Jewish people live on in perennial hope.

The ILLUSTRATED HISTORY *of the* JEWISH PEOPLE

1

Beginnings

Seth Schwartz

When to begin our story? The origins of the Jewish people are lost in antiquity. The earliest record is the Hebrew Bible, but the Bible begins with the creation of the world and the origin of the human race. It fails to make explicit when Jewish history began, even though it indicates a number of crucial moments: Abraham's arrival in the Land of Canaan, the Exodus from Egypt, the giving of the Torah at Sinai, the entry into the Promised Land. In fact, the very term Jew *is found only in one of the later biblical books, Esther. So when can we say this Jewish history began, and what can we discover about its real beginnings?*

Opposite: King David dancing before the Lord (see 2 Samuel 6). This marble relief, which perhaps served originally as a table-top, is thought to have been carved in Egypt in the second or early third century C.E. It illustrates the enduring power of biblical motifs, coupled with the strong influence of Hellenistic art.

We need first of all to face a problem shared by all who are interested in the distant past: the lack of information. For the period down to the destruction of Jerusalem by the Babylonians, in 586 B.C.E. (see page 5), most of our information comes from the Hebrew Bible. The Bible tells us a great deal about its own authors, the scribes, prophets and priests who wrote it between about 800 and 400 B.C.E. (some parts are earlier or later than these dates). We can learn much about their religious beliefs and practices, their view of the past, their attitudes to Israelites and non-Israelites, Jews and non-Jews (see page 5 on these terms). This is important because these writers eventually shaped Judaism. But the biblical books cannot adequately answer our questions because their authors were not interested in history in our sense of the term. The stories they told, the laws they prescribed, the prophecies and hymns they recorded, can be made to yield only a fragmentary and one-sided account, and that only by means of the

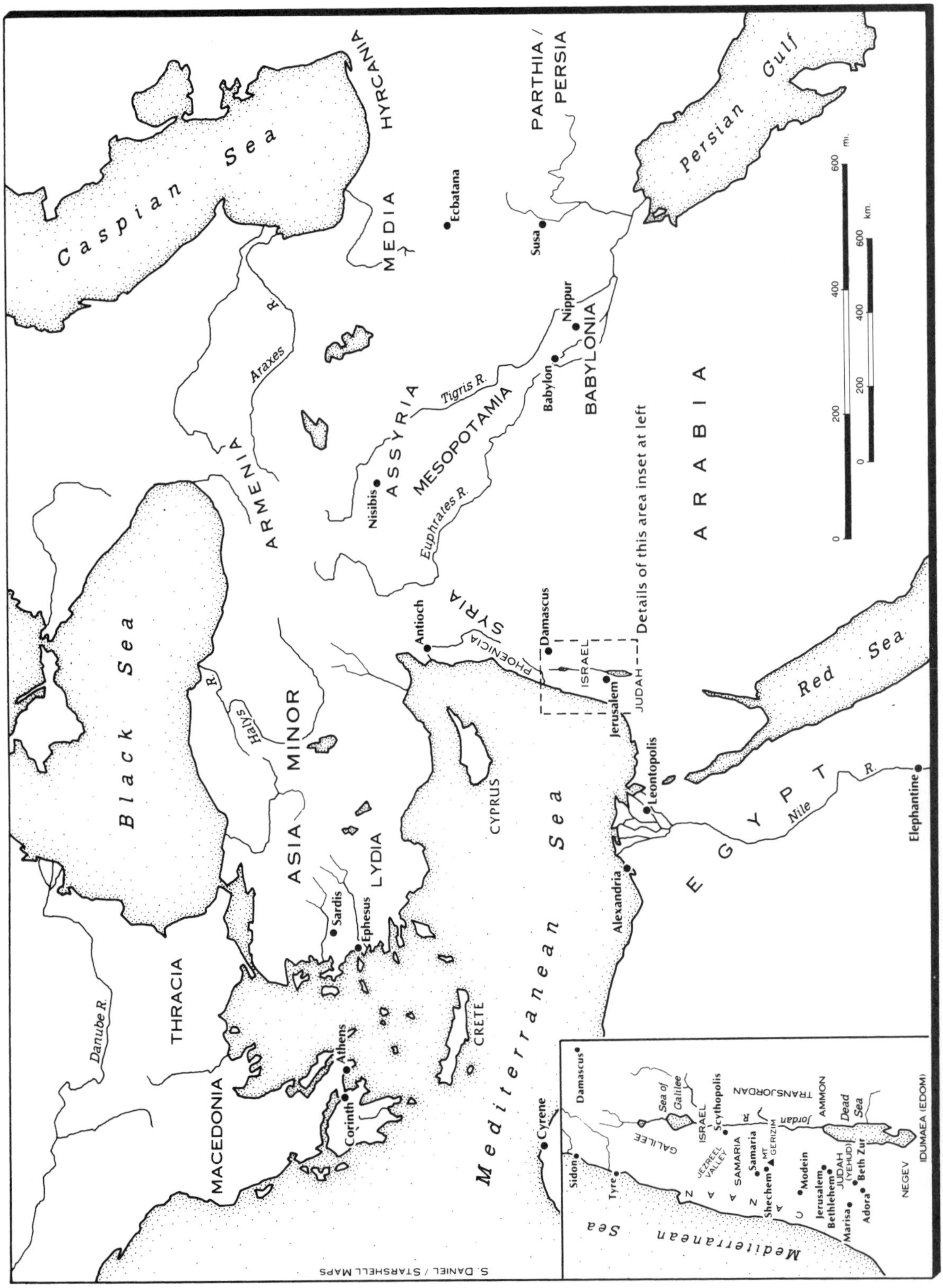

The Ancient World

most careful and skeptical reading of the texts, informed as much as possible by the findings of archaeologists and of experts on the history of Israel's neighbors in Egypt, Phoenicia and Mesopotamia.

The situation is only slightly better for the second half of the first millennium B.C.E. The Bible is silent about events after 430 B.C.E., but a few of the books, like Esther, Ecclesiastes and Daniel, were probably composed as late as the early second century B.C.E. Furthermore, various Christian churches preserved translations of a number of Jewish books written between the third century B.C.E. and the first century C.E. These books, like those of the Bible, paint for us a picture mainly of religious developments—a sketchy one, to be sure, but better than nothing.

Only at the very end of the millennium does the information become richer. This is principally because we possess two extensive narrative histories of the Jews from 170 B.C.E. to 70 C.E., *The Jewish Antiquities* and *The Jewish War*. Both of these works were written in the late first century C.E. by Flavius Josephus (c. 38–c. 100 C.E.), a priest of the Temple of Jerusalem who participated briefly in the Jewish revolt against the Romans that led to the Temple's destruction in 70 C.E., defected to his enemies and wrote his books in Greek while residing in Rome and benefiting from the protection of the emperors. Josephus' past, and his situation at the time he wrote, surely affected his presentation of the history of the Jews; he was no more immune to bias, self-interest and selective ignorance than any other historian, ancient or modern. Nevertheless, the *Antiquities* and the *War* do provide us with a rough framework of political history within which we can place information mainly about religion derived from the other sources.

All these considerations necessarily influence the chapter that follows. Since it is impossible to write a narrative history of the ancient Jews for more than a small part of the period covered in this chapter, I will not try to do so; rather, I will integrate discussion of a series of questions about ancient Jewish society and religion in an unavoidably fragmented narrative. Since information of any sort is scarce and the connections between the isolated pieces of information are a matter of (one hopes) educated guesswork and debate, I often refer to sources and use expressions of caution. Such expressions should in fact be understood even when not stated.

Can we, then, with all due caution, provide an answer to the question with which this chapter started? When did Jewish history begin? Let us first of all explore the implications of a change in terminology.

ISRAELITES AND JEWS

Strictly speaking, *Jewish* history began only after the destruction of Jerusalem by the Babylonians in 586 B.C.E. Ancient writers were generally careful to speak of Israelites or Hebrews before this date and Jews afterward. Josephus even stated explicitly in *The Jewish Antiquities*, book 11.173, that the Jews were properly known as such only after their gradual return from the Babylonian Exile in the sixth and fifth centuries B.C.E. Does this shift in terminology have a deeper significance? Does it reflect a well-founded view of the ancient Jews that despite acknowledged continuities between their ancestors and themselves, there remained essential differences?

This question is difficult to answer because the history of the pre-exilic Israelites, and in particular the character of their religion, are the subjects of unflagging controversy. The emergence of the Israelites themselves is unrecoverable, lost in the obscurity of the early Iron Age (beginning c. 1200 B.C.E.). By the eighth century B.C.E., some Israelites had come to believe that their ancestors had been enslaved in Egypt, had been led out by Moses and, already a discrete and powerful nation, had taken the Land of Canaan by storm, uprooting the previous inhabitants in the process. Such is the story the biblical book of Joshua tells. The so-called Deuteronomic History (Judges, 1 and 2 Samuel and 1 and 2 Kings, apparently a unitary composition of the sixth century B.C.E.) tells a different story. It abandons the idea of swift and total conquest in favor of gradual infiltration and slow conquest by the twelve Israelite tribes separately; according to the Deuteronomic History, the Israelites dealt with the previous inhabitants of Canaan by accommodation and intermarriage. Although this account seems more realistic to us than that of Joshua, it proves on closer examination to be no less theologically motivated: the Deuteronomic Historian, living as he did after the destruction of the Kingdom of Judah in 586 B.C.E., had to explain in theological terms why the Israelite kingdoms had failed. He did so by imagining that the Israelites had never conquered the Land of Canaan as completely as they should have, and so had never freed themselves from the idolatrous influence of the Canaanite tribes with whom they had sinfully allowed themselves to mingle. And so their God first subjected the Israelites to foreign rulers and then sent them into exile. It is unlikely that this theologizing really provides a better account of the emergence of the Israelite nation than the differently tendentious account in Joshua.

Nor has archaeology solved the problem of the Israelites' origin. The twelfth century B.C.E., when the Israelites were most likely first identifiable as a unique people, was a period of radical change throughout the eastern Mediterranean basin. Empires yielded to city-states and small kingdoms, bronze weapons to iron, and ideographic writing, like Egyptian hieroglyphics, gave way to syllabic and alphabetic script, like Hebrew and Greek writing. The emergence of the Israelites was just one rather small-scale episode in this general transformation, and the physical remains of the general transformation obscure almost completely the interpretation of the specific case.

It is in fact difficult to tell how seriously to take the belief commonly expressed in the biblical books that the Israelites had always been in some measure distinct from their Canaanite milieu, and had entered, whether gradually or not, the Land of Canaan from the outside. Given the persistence of this belief among the Israelites themselves, it may be unwise to ignore it completely. Nevertheless, some modern scholars replace the biblical story with one of their own, that "Israel" was simply a league of the indigenous inhabitants of the Palestinian hill country, formed to throw off the domination of the interior by the coastal cities. For all the once-attractive modern resonances of this hypothesis, it has little more to recommend it than the biblical story of invasion.

With the rise of the Kingdom of Israel in the eleventh century, the fog begins to thin, if not quite lift. It is true that our main source of information about the kingdom, the Deuteronomic History, was composed only after its fall. It is also obvious that the stories about the first three kings, Saul, David and Solomon, found in the books of Samuel and 1 Kings, are free literary compositions—in the case of the David cycle, of uncanny brilliance—rather than sober chronicles. Nevertheless, it is possible that the Historian had access to some more or less reliable, if fragmentary, information. At any rate, few modern scholars doubt that these kings actually ruled the Israelites in the eleventh and tenth centuries B.C.E., and it may also be true that David decisively defeated the Philistines, the prosperous and technologically relatively advanced cousins of the Mycenaean Greeks, who ruled the Palestinian interior from their base in the cities of the southern part of the coast. David (c. 1000–c. 960 B.C.E.) is likely also to have established Jerusalem as his royal city, and his son Solomon (c. 961–c. 920 B.C.E.) to have constructed there a great palace and a temple (someone must have done so). There is consensus, however, about little else.

Nevertheless, it seems likely that until the eighth century, the northern Kingdom of Israel and the southern Kingdom of Judah (Solomon's kingdom split after his death) were with respect to their religious life typical small states of the eastern Mediterranean. They had a chief national god, Yahweh, but worshiped other deities as well: inscriptions seem to indicate that Yahweh was thought to have had a consort, "his Asherah," and other members of the general Canaanite pantheon, and the gods and goddesses of neighboring peoples, were beneficiaries of public worship as well.

King Ahab ruled the northern Kingdom of Israel in the ninth century B.C.E. He built a famous palace at Samaria, decorated with ivory carvings. This sphinxlike cherub is one of a rich collection of ivories discovered there by archaeologists. The cherubim figure prominently in biblical mythology: God is often described as "enthroned upon the cherubim," and cherubim decorated Solomon's Temple in Jerusalem.

Be that as it may, the Israelite religion began to change in the eighth century. The earliest preserved prophetic discourses, those of Amos and Hosea, from the middle of the century, boldly imagine that Yahweh is no mere tribal god, but from his home on Mount Zion, in Jerusalem, controls the fate of humanity, or some part of it. He rules, furthermore, not by whim but with justice. For the prophets, Yahweh alone is Israel's Ba'al, its master/husband (an allusion to Ba'al, the chief god of the Canaanite pantheon), and Israel's worship of other gods is therefore adulterous. This new religious ideology, which, it must be emphasized, is almost but not quite monotheistic, was part of a general process of social, religious and political change in the eastern Mediterranean of the high Iron Age. The emphasis on divine justice, closely paralleled in the works of the eighth-century Greek poet Hesiod, may be connected to the region-wide rise of an ideology of the self-regulating, basically egalitarian citizen community ("Israel," "the *polis*"—that is, the classical Greek city-state). In the eighth century this notion began to replace an older feudal ideology, in which the gods ruled arbitrarily.

Whatever the explanation may be, the eighth and seventh centuries were certainly a period of transformation for the Israelite religion. Some kings, like Manasseh (c. 686–640 B.C.E.), were pious traditionalists who continued to patronize the old gods in addition to Yahweh, but others, like Hezekiah (c. 715–686 B.C.E.), are said to have taken the prophetic reformers seriously. The Yahwist prophets, for all their erratic behavior and countercultural attitudes, came largely from the Judahite upper classes, and though not all their peers shared their views completely, they may have been somewhat representative of their class. Most suggestive in this regard is the evidence from an unlikely source, Judahite personal names.

Most Semitic names, like Greek but unlike Latin or English names, are obviously meaningful and often make brief religious statements—for example, Yehoyishma', Yahweh-will-hear, or Ba'alnatan, Ba'al-has-given. It is thus reasonable to suppose that personal names can provide a rough index (rough because names were often given because they were traditional within families and for other reasons unconnected with their meaning) of the religious attitudes of those who bestowed them. Recent archaeological discoveries mainly in Jerusalem have yielded an abundant corpus of personal names stamped on pieces of clay used to seal papyrus documents; the documents themselves have not survived. Most of these come from the late eighth and seventh centuries, and thus provide important evidence for the growing importance of bureaucracy in the Judahite kingdom. The seals also demonstrate the near disappearance of such divine elements as Ba'al, 'Ashtart, As (the Egyptian goddess Isis, who was widely worshiped throughout the Near East) from the personal names of Judahite bureaucrats, officials and prosperous landowners and the predominance of Yahweh, El and Shaddai. The latter two were old Semitic gods who had come to be identified with Yahweh. This change of onomastic habit does not prove that the other gods were no longer worshiped (see page 9 on Elephantine), but it does suggest declining interest in them at least among wealthier Judahites, and may thus provide some of the social context of the preaching of such prophets as Isaiah (c. 700 B.C.E.) and Jeremiah (c. 600 B.C.E.). Interestingly, the same sort of evidence suggests a similar development in the neighboring kingdom of Ammon: wealthy Ammonites, too, were becoming increasingly devoted to their national god Milkom, and increasingly uninterested in other gods, in precisely the same period.

The reforms reached their culmination in the reign of King Josiah (639–609 B.C.E.), the hero of the Deuteronomic History. Hilkiah, the chief priest of the Jerusalem Temple, "discovered"—modern scholars would say caused to be written—a Book of the Law of Moses, which apparently resembled the biblical book of Deuteronomy, and had it read out to the king (c. 621 B.C.E.). The king was convinced that this book contained the genuine laws God had given to the Israelites through Moses, laws long since forgotten, and at once set about putting them into practice. The central point of the new law code was that, following the precepts of the Yahwist prophets, it unambiguously forbade worship of gods other than Yahweh, regarding such indiscriminate worship as the source of all the Israelites' woes. It also forbade all sacrifice, even to Yahweh, outside the Temple of Jerusalem—a blatant manifestation of Jerusalemite priestly self-interest, as are also the laws requiring payment of taxes to the priests and declaring them the leading judicial authorities. And it (re-?)introduced such novel ritual observances as Passover, and transformed into law the prophetic ethical exhortations against oppressing the poor, widows, orphans and strangers.

But the reforms were short-lived. In 612 B.C.E. the king of Babylon, Nabopolassar, a vassal of the Assyrian emperor, overthrew his lord, destroyed his city, Nineveh, and took over his empire. In 609 Josiah, the new emperor's loyal

King Jehu ruled Israel in the second half of the ninth century. Here, he is shown paying homage to the Assyrian king Shalmaneser III, during the Assyrian invasion of Syria in 841 B.C.E. The accompanying inscription names him as "Jehu son of Omri": in fact, Jehu had overthrown the house of Omri and founded a dynasty of his own.

vassal, tried to stop the army of the other great imperial power of the region, Egypt, from invading Mesopotamia, and was defeated and killed in the process. Whether his reforms survived his ignominious defeat—in itself a contradiction of a central canon of the Deuteronomic theology, that Yahweh assures that the righteous will prosper—is uncertain, but seems unlikely.

The Kingdom of Judah survived Josiah by only two decades. The last kings were sporadically rebellious against their Babylonian masters, despite the repeated warnings of the prophet Jeremiah. The Babylonians, under Nebuchadnezzar II (ruled 605–561 B.C.E.), responded first with deportations of the most prominent Judahites, including the king, Jeconiah, to Mesopotamia (596), and then with wholesale destruction (586), accompanied and followed, in 582, by further deportations. In 539, Cyrus, king of Persia, conquered Babylon and thereby established himself as ruler of the largest Near Eastern empire yet, incorporating three great predecessors, the Median Empire (in Iran and points north and east), the Babylonian Empire (in Mesopotamia and the Fertile Crescent) and the Lydian Empire (in Asia Minor—modern Turkey).

THE ELEPHANTINE PAPYRI: EVIDENCE FOR ISRAELITE RELIGION

A cache of papyrus documents provides us with a precious glimpse of pre-Jewish Israelite religious life, unmediated by the hostile rhetoric of the prophets or the Deuteronomic writers. The documents were written in the fifth century B.C.E. in

Aramaic, the official scribal language of the Persian Empire, and were found at Elephantine, called Yeb in Aramaic and Egyptian, an island in the Nile near Aswan, at the southern border of ancient Egypt. These documents were the legal and personal papers of members of a fortified military settlement at the south-western border of the Persian Empire. The settlement seems to have been in continuous existence from the seventh century B.C.E., when Egypt was ruled by the Saite Dynasty, until the beginning of the fourth, when a native Egyptian dynasty expelled the Persians who had ruled the country since 525 B.C.E., and destroyed or replaced the garrison. The settlement was an ethnic patchwork, with the different groups constituting separate military units. One of these groups was Judahite. Though the religious life of Judah proper had by the fifth century been transformed into something readily recognizable as Jewish (see below), the Judahite colony of Elephantine carefully preserved the Israelite religion of its seventh-century founders—a religion increasingly under attack by the end of the fifth century.

The colony had at its religious center "the house, or temple, of Yaho-who-is-in-Yeb-the-Fortress" (that is, a local version of Yahweh), staffed by priests (*kahanaya*, in the Aramaic documents, translating the Hebrew *kohanim*, as in the Bible) and assistants (*lahanaya*—not the biblical "Levites"). The colonists thus ignored or were unaware of the prohibition of sacrifice outside the Jerusalem Temple, imposed by Josiah's version of the Law of Moses and our version of Deuteronomy. In the colonists' temple, which by the fifth century was already ancient, the Judahites offered incense, meal offerings, libations and sacrifices of sheep and goats, as the Israelites had done in the Jerusalem Temple. Probably they sang hymns that resembled the biblical Psalms. The names of the Judahites, unlike the documents, are all Hebrew, and Yahweh is overwhelmingly the most common divine element in them. The religious sentiments that the names express, "Yah is my protection," "Yah will judge," "Yah is my trust," "Yah will sustain," "Yah has heard," "aided," "delivered," and so on, can all be paralleled in the Psalms and in other biblical books.

Yet the Judahites intermarried freely with their Egyptian neighbors; as far as we can tell, the offspring of these marriages were normally given Yahwist names and counted as members of the Judahite unit. The Judahites' oaths by various Egyptian gods in their court cases we might have dismissed as legal convention, but their invocations of the same gods in addition to Yaho in their personal letters cannot be so dismissed. Some of the Judahite donors to the temple of Yaho earmarked their gifts for Anathbethel and Eshembethel, obscure Syro-Palestinian gods, with no opposition from the *kahanaya*. The documents mention few distinctively Jewish observances. The Sabbath is mentioned, without any hint of how it was celebrated. The one mention of Passover indicates, if the document has been correctly interpreted, that it was a private voluntary observance not tied to a specific date, unlike the biblical Passover. Another document, to be discussed presently, suggests that the Feast of the Unleavened Bread, in this period still distinct from Passover, was unknown to the colony until the end of the fifth century B.C.E. We may recall that according to 2 Kings, Passover was not observed in Jerusalem until the Josianic reforms. In sum, the religious life of the colony is strongly reminiscent of biblical religion, especially that variety of it denounced by the prophets and attacked by Josiah. But it cannot be called Jewish in any way that does not stretch the sense of the term to its breaking point.

The colony's Israelite religion came under attack in the late fifth century mainly from the local Egyptian priests, employed in the main temple of Elephantine, dedicated to the god Khnum. There must always have been tension. The Egyptian priests considered the sacrifice of sheep and goats, as practiced in the Judahite temple, as indeed in all Semitic temples, sacrilege. But they acted only in 411 B.C.E., when they bribed local officials (so the Judahites claimed) to turn a blind eye while they destroyed the temple of Yaho-who-is-in-Yeb. The Judahite colonists mourned this destruction with fasting, sackcloth and ashes, just as their compatriots had mourned the destruction of the Jerusalem Temple in 586 B.C.E. They then wrote the authorities in the homeland appealing for help in rebuilding their temple. The Jerusalem authorities, by now committed to upholding the Deuteronomic legislation, failed to respond.

This was not the colonists' first encounter with the new religious situation in Judah. Eight years earlier, in 419, a Judahite official wrote to the colony informing them that Darius, the Persian emperor, wished them to observe the Feast of the Unleavened Bread; he continued by explaining when and how the feast was to be observed, in terms strongly reminiscent of the Bible: from the fifteenth to the twenty-first of the month of Nisan (March-April) the colonists were to remain pure and abstain from eating and drinking any leavened or fermented substances—beer was the most common drink in ancient Egypt—which were to be locked up over the holiday. This last prescription conforms with much later Jewish practice, but contradicts the biblical commandment to destroy all leavened food. Why should the Persian king have issued such a command to the little Judahite colony of Elephantine and, we must suppose, to other such scattered settlements of Judahites as well? And what accounts for the changes in Jerusalem, to which the Egyptian documents indirectly testify?

EXILE AND RECONSTRUCTION: ONE TEMPLE FOR THE ONE GOD

The Babylonian Exile is thought by many scholars to have been the formative experience in the transformation of Israelite religion into Judaism. It is commonly supposed that it was in the community of deportees that the Pentateuch (the first five books of the Bible) began to assume something like its present form, and that the deportees began to internalize the message of the prophets. This may well be so, but it must be said that next to nothing is actually known about the activities of the deported Judahites, or for that matter about those of the numerous poorer Judahites left behind in Judah. There is an exception: one deportee, the brilliant author of Isaiah, chapters 40–55, who lived through the transition from Babylonian to Persian rule, was the most radical prophet yet. He claimed that the God of Israel was in fact the ruler of the universe, not merely the only god worth worshiping, but the only god. He also regarded the Persian king Cyrus as God's anointed. He was probably not alone, either in his theology or his politics, but it would be unfounded to regard him as typical.

We are informed in the book of Ezra that Cyrus permitted a group of deportees to return to Judah, led by a certain Sheshbazzar. In comparison to the Assyrians and Babylonians, who were mainly interested in collecting tribute from their subjects, and punished brutally those who failed to pay, the Persians were mild but interventionist. Cyrus posed as a liberator, a restorer of gods and peoples following the depredations and deportations of the Babylonians, and this pose became a fixture of Persian imperial rhetoric. What this often amounted to in practice was that the Persians tended to patronize native oligarchies, preferably those with strong connections to temples, and encouraged them to try to regulate the legal and economic activities of their provinces. The desired and sometimes attained result was a smoothly running, peaceful and consistently profitable empire, which depended on the loyalty of the hand-picked oligarchs, a royal provincial administration more elaborate than anything the Babylonians had had and mild intimidation produced by the presence everywhere of small numbers of Persian-commanded garrison troops. Persian policy thus contrasted with Babylonian, with its alternating periods of complete laissez-faire and brutal terror. In some cases, then, Persian interventionism practically created the nations the Persians ruled. It is in the light of these practices that the return under Sheshbazzar and the other events reported in the biblical books of Ezra, Nehemiah, Haggai and Zechariah, which are discussed in what follows, should be seen.

In any case, nothing came of the group under Sheshbazzar, which is likely to have met opposition from the Judahite *'am ha'aretz* (literally, "people of the land")—that is, the common folk who had stayed behind. In 522 B.C.E., the emperor Darius I appointed the deportee Zerubbabel, a grandson of the Judahite king Jeconiah, governor of the new province of Yehud (Judah), and authorized a large number of deportees, reportedly over 40,000, to return to the province under the leadership of Zerubbabel and of Joshua, descendant of the chief priests of the old Jerusalem Temple. Many of the returnees were members of the former ruling class, with priests especially prominent among them.

According to the biblical book of Ezra, the returnees began to rebuild the Temple, barring some or all of the *'am ha'aretz* from the process. According to the biblical book of Zechariah, Joshua, who was to be high priest, was compelled to purify himself and submit to "the law" as a condition for his service. Both of these episodes are enigmatic, but hint at religious tensions between the returnees and the *'am ha'aretz*, and within the group of returnees. Nevertheless, the Second Temple was completed in 515 B.C.E., by which time Zerubbabel was off the scene—still another enigma. Whatever the precise character of the tensions, it is significant that the two Yahwist prophets who participated in the dedication of the Temple, Haggai and Zechariah, nowhere suggest in their books that any god other than the God of Israel was worshiped in the new Temple; nor do they denounce shrines or temples in the countryside of Judah.

Josiah, who just over a century earlier had tried to outlaw the worship of all gods but Yahweh and to restrict his worship to Jerusalem, had won a posthumous victory, and this time the change endured. Except at the time of the Maccabean

Revolt, no Jew would ever again suggest that it was appropriate for the Jews to worship any god but the God of Israel, nor would anyone succeed in building a temple or shrine to that God in Judah outside Jerusalem (there were a few temples elsewhere, one of which, at Leontopolis in Egypt, continued to function into the first century C.E.). Two of the elements that distinguished the Jews both from their neighbors and from their Israelite ancestors, that, in other words, made the Jews Jews—worship of one god, in a single temple—were thus firmly established.

EZRA, NEHEMIAH AND THE TORAH OF MOSES

About the sixty years that followed the dedication of the Second Temple our sources are silent. The silence ends in 458 B.C.E., the seventh year of the reign of the Persian king Artaxerxes I, who appointed Ezra (fifth century B.C.E.) to lead a new group of Jews back to Judah and to establish there the Torah as the authoritative law of the province, but apparently not to serve as provincial governor. Ezra was a descendant of Judahite priests and also a "skillful scribe," that is, a high-ranking Persian bureaucrat. Scholars continue to argue about the relationship between Ezra's Torah and the Pentateuch. They may well have differed in some details. Most important, Ezra's Torah may have forbidden marriages between Jews

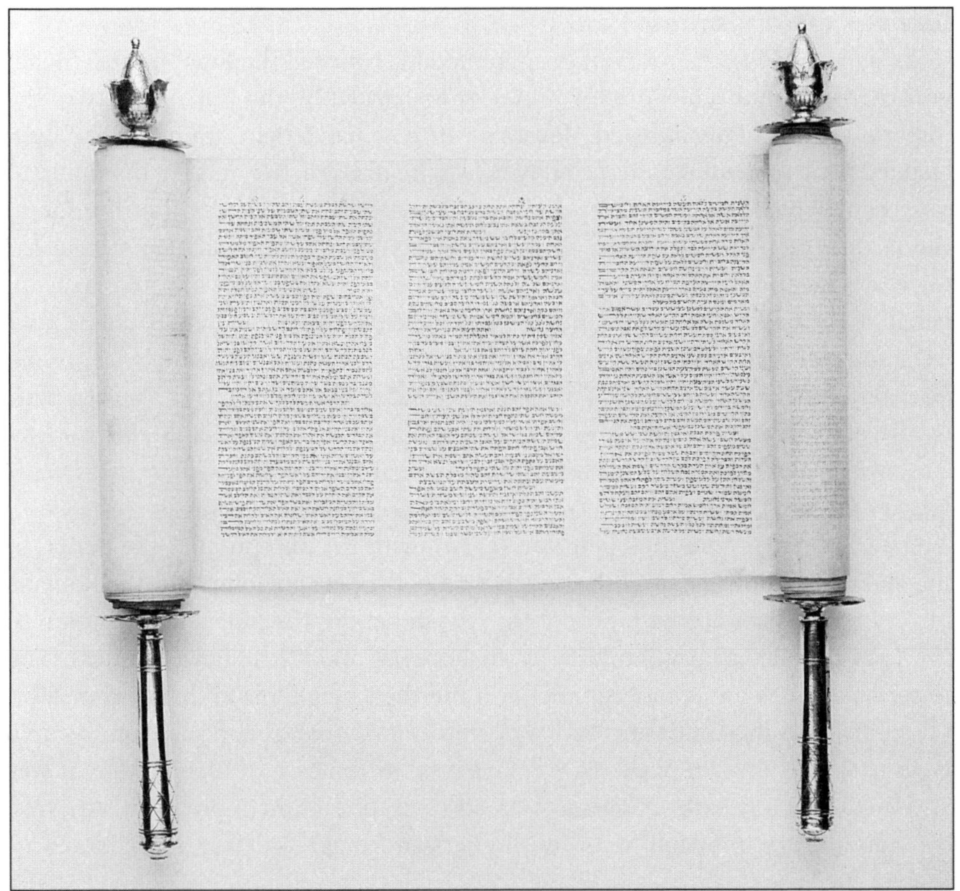

The precise origins of the Torah are obscure, but it has remained the most sacred text of Judaism since ancient times. This scroll, copied in mid-nineteenth-century Germany but similar to those in use in synagogues today, illustrates the power of religious tradition: it is written by hand on parchment, in a Hebrew script that can be traced back to antiquity.

and pagans far more unambiguously than the Pentateuch does. At any rate, it is not in doubt that Ezra's Torah bore a strong resemblance to the Pentateuch.

Why should the king have been interested in imposing the Torah on the Judahites? Probably, in keeping with standard Persian practice, he wished to have the legal life of the province well regulated. The Torah, though in fact probably mainly the work of reformists and radicals, claimed to be the traditional law of the Israelites and was the only Jewish law code available. An Egyptian text informs us that the king Darius I had created a committee of Egyptian priests to compile an authoritative code of Egyptian law, and Artaxerxes, in authorizing the Torah, may have been doing the same sort of thing for the Jews. The Pentateuch, with its long stretches of narrative, is unlikely to have been compiled at the king's request *for the purpose* of serving as a law code, as some scholars have suggested, but it is reasonable to suppose that it could have been appropriately pressed into service as one.

Ezra failed in his mission, primarily because of his demand that Judahites divorce their foreign spouses. Interethnic marriages were common among the upper classes throughout the ancient eastern Mediterranean and Near East, mainly because they served to create and maintain important social and economic ties between the elites of the little ethnic and tribal groups who populated the region. Ezra's demand thus met opposition not only from prominent Judahites, including priests and members of the community of returnees, but also from the upper classes of the surrounding peoples, with whom the wealthy Judahites were intermarried.

In 445 or 444 B.C.E., Artaxerxes appointed his courtier, the Judahite Nehemiah, governor of Yehud. The Torah would now be backed by the full authority of the imperial throne. This allowed Nehemiah a freer hand than Ezra had had, and enabled him to act with more political sophistication. He rebuilt the walls of Jerusalem, which had fallen into disrepair. This was an important contribution to the security of a district where, as in Greek city-states, the inhabitants preferred to seek refuge in the main city during invasions or raids. He collected taxes on behalf of the Levites, temple staff who ranked below the priests and could be used to counteract their influence. He won the support of poorer farmers by canceling all debts, ending the practice of debt-slavery and redistributing land. He was thus finally able to impose the law of the Torah in full—compelling the wealthy landowners and prominent priests to dismiss their foreign wives, closing the markets on the Sabbath and instituting the characteristic biblical festivals.

The Torah was from this point on (again, with the exception of the period of the Maccabean Revolt), until the destruction of the Second Temple by the Romans in 70 C.E. and the deconstitution of the Jewish nation, the official constitution of the Jews of Palestine, authorized by all imperial and native Jewish rulers. The third major distinction between the Jews and their neighbors and ancestors, after the conviction that only one god was worthy of worship and only one temple legitimate, was thus in place. As we have seen in the case of Elephantine, it was also imposed on Jewish settlements outside Palestine, though probably only very sporadically, and probably only by the Persian kings, not their Macedonian or Roman successors.

JUDAEA UNDER THE PERSIANS AND THEIR SUCCESSORS

The regime initiated in Judaea by Darius and Artaxerxes and their Jewish vassals Zerubbabel, Ezra and Nehemiah lasted with a few interruptions down to the middle of the second century B.C.E. Though the history of Yehud/Judaea (the province acquired its Greek name after its conquest by Alexander the Great, in 332 B.C.E.) in much of this period is very obscure indeed, we have enough information to provide at least a general and impressionistic account of some aspects of life in the district under this regime. (The two issues discussed in this section are priestly interpretation of the Torah and intermarriage.) The institutional stability of Judaea in this period suggests that the impression of calm created by the silence of the sources, preceding the well-attested dynamism and disorder of the two and a half centuries beginning in 170 B.C.E., is no mere mirage.

Yehud/Judaea was in the main a self-governing district. Though Nehemiah had taken measures to reduce the power of the priesthood, by the beginning of the fourth century the high priests, descendants of Zerubbabel's colleague Joshua, were in effect the rulers of the district. There was a Persian governor, but though the evidence is poor, it is likely that the Persians often appointed the high priests to the position. The high priests were thus responsible, in addition to the running of the Jerusalem Temple, for the collection of taxes, the administration of civil law and for keeping the peace in the province. The common priests constituted an important part of the aristocracy, and filled the main magistracies, in accordance with the laws of the Torah. Though the same laws denied the priests the right to own land (their lot was to serve God, not to till the soil), they seem nevertheless to have been important landowners, having found a way to interpret the biblical prohibition out of existence.

Similarly, the silver coins of the province of Yehud and later of Judaea (starting c. 400 B.C.E.), minted under the authority of the largely priestly provincial administration, are engraved with images, including images of a god. This seems to be a direct violation of the second of the Ten Commandments, prohibiting the making of images of living things, yet it must be supposed that as in the case of land ownership here, too, the priests had some way of interpreting the biblical prohibition to permit the engraving of images on the coins. Thus, though the law of the Torah was unambiguously the constitution of the province of Yehud, the actual established practice of the priestly administrators of the law remained in important ways in tension with the prescriptions of the law. The priests, therefore, inescapably became experts in interpretation—sometimes highly creative interpretation—of the Torah, a privilege the Torah itself yielded to them.

A silver coin struck in Jerusalem under Persian rule (fourth century B.C.E.). The inscription reads "Yehud," the official name of the province of Judah at the time.

It is worth emphasizing that the laws of the Torah, though related to earlier Israelite and Jewish practice, were still new to many Jews and were thus often in conflict with established norms of behavior, and not just among the priests. Furthermore, like any law code, the Torah contained many laws that were vague or contradictory. For the Torah to work as a constitution/law code, it *needed* creative interpretation. Thus, the priests fulfilled two critically important roles: they conducted the sacrificial cult of the Jerusalem Temple, which secured God's goodwill toward Israel, and they administered and interpreted the native laws of the province as embodied in the Torah. It is possible, however, that some nonpriests worked as judges, scribes and teachers, especially outside Jerusalem.

There were limits to how far the priests' interpretative creativity could be pressed, even when their self-interest was involved. The first-century C.E. Jewish historian Josephus reports that in the middle of the fourth century B.C.E. a certain Manasses, brother of the high priest, married the daughter of the Persian governor of the neighboring province of Samaria to the north. Though the Samarians regarded themselves as Israelites, Josephus or his source, or the Judaean authorities in the fourth century, apparently considered them foreigners. The marriage thus violated Ezra's and Nehemiah's interpretation of Torah law. Manasses was therefore expelled from Judaea, together with a group of priestly fellow miscreants. They fled to Samaria, where they became the chief priests of the new Samarian temple on Mount Gerizim near Shechem (present-day Nablus).

This story has aroused the suspicions of many modern scholars, and rightly so. The relations between Judaeans and Samarians in ancient times were often competitive and sometimes hostile. The information, preserved in the work of Josephus, who was a Judaean priest, that the Samarian temple was staffed by descendants of Judaean outlaws sounds too much like a salvo in a propaganda war to be taken seriously as history. Furthermore, archaeological excavations on Mount Gerizim conducted in the 1980s suggest that the temple there was built no earlier than about 200 B.C.E., almost 150 years after the dramatic date of Josephus' story. Nevertheless, the story does contain elements that ring true.

The political and economic pressures that had always made marriage alliances between the Judaean elites and their counterparts in neighboring districts common obviously did not disappear with Nehemiah's prohibition of the practice. In the early second century B.C.E., Judaean aristocrats who wished to restore foreign marriages, in violation of Torah law, argued that the Judaeans had paid a high price for the separatist behavior of their upper class (1 Maccabees 1:11). It is thus perfectly reasonable to suppose that some aristocrats continued contracting marriage alliances with foreigners, despite the prohibition, and that the common punishment for this crime was expulsion.

But other scenarios were possible too. Josephus also informs us that in the third century B.C.E. the high priests of Jerusalem were intermarried with the Tobiad family of Transjordan. This family was descended from Tobiah, Persian governor of the province of Ammon in the fifth century B.C.E. (in the vicinity of Amman, Jordan) and one of the villains of the book of Nehemiah. Though of Ammonite origin, the family seems at an early date to have adopted the worship of Yahweh and somehow to have become Jewish (*Tobiah* means "Yahweh is good"). Nehemiah had expelled a priest who married into Tobiah's family, but there is no hint that anyone considered the priests' later marriage alliances with the Tobiads problematic. Though there is no clear reference in the sources to the ritual of conversion to Judaism before the middle of the second century B.C.E., perhaps in the case of the Tobiads we are dealing with something very much like it. Thus, elite intermarriages, which helped to integrate the Jews into the larger economic and political world of the eastern Mediterranean, could also help to integrate some elements of that larger world into Judaism. Thereby the leading Judaeans satisfied both their practical need to retain social and economic ties outside Judaea, and the requirement of separation from their neighbors enjoined by the Torah.

HELLENIZATION

The second-century critics of the Torah were no doubt right to think that the nation of the Jews was less integrated into eastern Mediterranean society than many of their neighbors. But as we have seen, enduring integrative pressures forced them to find ways to circumvent the separatist requirements of Jewish law; the same pressures also encouraged them to embrace aspects of the common culture of the eastern Mediterranean that Jewish law did not prohibit.

The most significant cultural development in the eastern Mediterranean in the fifth century B.C.E. and following was the process modern historians call Hellenization (there is no precise ancient equivalent for the word). This vague term is used to denote a confusing variety of phenomena, ranging from use by non-Greeks of imported Greek tableware, to development of a taste for Greek and imitation Greek painted vases and sculptures, to worship of Greek gods, to adoption of the Greek language and reading of Greek literature, to, finally, the acquisition of citizenship in Greek cities—that is, becoming "Greek" (for citizenship, at least as much as descent, was an essential requirement for Greekness). The extent to which the Jews were "Hellenized" in antiquity is highly controversial, and one reason for this is precisely the sloppiness with which the term is commonly used. It may, then, be worth introducing some precision, by separating Hellenization in the sense of "acting Greek" while maintaining one's own cultural identity, from Hellenization in the sense of "becoming Greek" and so necessarily abandoning one's previous cultural identity. Hellenization in the first sense might culminate in Hellenization in the second sense, but need not do so—in fact it might even function to preserve a native non-Greek culture; and Hellenization in the second sense need not presuppose, rather surprisingly, prior Hellenization in the first sense. For the time being, it is the first type of Hellenization that concerns us.

Though until 332 B.C.E. the Judaeans and their neighbors were subject to Persia, far in the east, they remained part of the cultural and economic world of the eastern Mediterranean, which included not only the cities and nations of the Syro-Palestinian coast and Egypt, but also the old Greek cities of western Asia Minor and, at its western fringe, Greece itself. There had been trade and other contacts between Greece and the east coast of the Mediterranean, including Israel, for as long as there had been boats. The Philistines, who infiltrated the coastal cities of Palestine about 1200 B.C.E., probably came from the Aegean and had close ties to the Mycenaean Greeks. Greeks served as mercenaries in the armies of the kings of Judah and Israel, and Greek traders were not unknown in the region in the same period. Presumably, though, there was nothing noteworthy about these people—they were just part of the general eastern Mediterranean ethnic stew, alongside Egyptians, Phoenicians and various groups of Asians.

The Greek victory over Persia in 478 B.C.E., the subsequent rise of the Athenian Empire, the consolidation of classical Greek culture (which was among other things an important item for export, like American popular culture in the later twentieth century) and of Athenian economic dominance, which survived the decline of their empire, changed matters. By the fifth century, Greek goods predominated over all other imports in the cities of the Syro-Palestinian coast. The well-to-do there had always liked nicely decorated imported goods, but the trickle of Greek imports now turned into a flood—a development of profound cultural significance but one that is frustratingly difficult to interpret: why, apart from the commercial strength of Athens, should Greek products and the Greek style have acquired such prestige in coastal Syria, Phoenicia and Palestine in the fifth century B.C.E., and what are the implications of this development? In the absence of written sources, it is almost impossible to say.

By the fourth century B.C.E., the flood of Greek goods reached the Palestinian interior, including Judaea. The coins of Persian Judaea, for example, are all modeled on Greek, especially Athenian, coins. Indeed, the practice of stamping pieces of preweighed silver, though it originated in the seventh century B.C.E. in the kingdom of Lydia, in western Turkey, spread in the eastern Mediterranean in the sixth and fifth centuries primarily because of Greek influence; the minting of coins itself was thus in some measure an aspect of Hellenization. The coinage of Judaea's northern neighbor, Samaria, is similar to that of Judaea, but remarkably enough, some of these tiny coins bear inscriptions in Greek. These coins were almost all of very small denomination, and so intended for local use, not interstate trade. They thus reflect the tastes and interests of Judaeans and Samarians, not their foreign commercial partners. When the Macedonian king Alexander the Great conquered the east coast of the Mediterranean in 332 B.C.E., he found there a world that was not completely foreign to him, in which certain aspects, at least, of Greek culture already enjoyed widespread acceptance.

THE MACEDONIAN CONQUEST

Josephus recounts that when Alexander marched down the Palestinian coast, he detoured to Jerusalem to meet the high priest Jaddus (Yaddu'a). When he saw that venerable figure, he at once realized that Jaddus had appeared in his dreams, foretelling his victory over the Persians; so the great conqueror prostrated himself at the old man's feet. This is surely a folk tale. In reality, Alexander never left the coastal road but entrusted the reduction of the Palestinian interior to a subordinate. The following decades, down to 301, were chaotic. Alexander died in 323, and his immense empire, stretching from Greece to India, fell into several pieces, each ruled by one of Alexander's generals initially eager to seize the whole. (This ambition soon became unrealistic.) Palestine was especially controversial, since it was claimed by Ptolemy, son of Lagos, whose base was Egypt; Seleucus, the ruler of Mesopotamia and Syria; and Antigonus the One-Eyed, the greatest of all of

Alexander's generals. Ptolemy's conquest of the region in 301 B.C.E. was decisive, and Palestine remained part of Ptolemy's kingdom until 200 B.C.E., when Seleucus' descendant Antiochus III (the Great) wrested it from Ptolemy V. And though coastal Palestine and Phoenicia were in this century the scenes of near-constant warfare between the two dynasties, Judaea, which was a poor hill-country district off the main roads and of little strategic interest, remained at peace.

Alexander and his successors retained much of the administrative structure set in place by the Persians, and tended, like the Persians, to grant subject nations, like the Jews, limited autonomy. And like the Persians, they nowhere actively forced their own language or culture on their subjects. However, the rulers themselves were adamantly Greek, instinctively assumed the superiority of Greek culture and seem to have preferred Greeks as administrators, friends and courtiers. These preferences were consequential enough in inducing wealthier, politically ambitious natives to adopt elements of Greek culture, but Alexander had in addition introduced an unprecedented practice that had profound though probably unintended consequences in all the lands he conquered. In order to secure his empire, he founded throughout the Near East cities to be settled by his mainly Greek or Greco-Macedonian veterans and other Greek immigrants. These cities were "Greek"—that is, they had constitutions and a public life loosely modeled on those of Athens, were legally autonomous (because "freedom" was an essential characteristic of Greekness—in reality, of course, as opposed to self-aggrandizing rhetoric, the cities were subjected to the kings) and had assigned to them a rural territory. These territories were farmed not like those of the cities of Old Greece, by citizen farmers, but by native peasants who were subjected to the citizens and enjoyed very few civil rights.

Thereafter, foundation of new Greek cities became a normal activity for all of the so-called Hellenistic kings who succeeded Alexander, and even for the Romans who eventually succeeded them, so that the entire eastern Mediterranean and Near East was in short order linked by a web of Greek cities. These cities enjoyed no more legal rights than autonomous non-Greek nations did, but they were unquestionably prestigious and prosperous, their self-confidence enhanced by royal patronage and friendship. They were thus soon joined by ancient non-Greek cities, like Sardis in Asia Minor, or Tyre and Sidon in Phoenicia, which in the third century B.C.E. succeeded in transforming themselves into Greek cities, though few of their citizens were of Greek descent.

Given the omnipresence of Greek cities in the Fertile Crescent, and the pressures especially on better-off natives to adopt Greek culture wholesale, and even become Greek—pressures, it bears emphasizing, not consciously imposed by the rulers but rather built into their system of rule—the stakes in Hellenization changed dramatically after Alexander the Great. It was now not unthinkable that nations long in existence or established by the Persians might simply be willed out of existence by their upper classes' desire to be Greek, to reconstitute themselves as the citizen body of a Greek city. And even where the upper classes apparently had no such desire, as for example in parts of Mesopotamia, they could not fail to be affected by Greek culture. For the Jews, the tensions created by Macedonian rule reached a boiling point in the 170s B.C.E.

THE BACKGROUND TO THE MACCABEAN REVOLT (300–175 B.C.E.)

The Tobiads

Little is known about the history of Judaea in the third century B.C.E., the peaceful century when the country was ruled by the Ptolemies. Josephus records but a single story for the third century; in fact, he believed it occurred in the early second century, but the contents of the episode make it clear that Josephus was mistaken. In Josephus' account, Joseph, son of Tobias, a member of the Tobiad family mentioned previously and nephew of the Judaean high priest Onias II, succeeded in wresting the tax-farming contract for Judaea from his ineffectual uncle. (The Ptolemies collected taxes by auctioning tax-farming contracts district by district, often to wealthy natives; the tax farmers were then left to raise what they could. They had to pay for shortfalls out of their own pockets, but could keep profits.) Josephus embroidered Joseph's exploits and those of his son and heir, Hyrcanus, with so many swashbuckling details that it is tempting to dismiss the entire tale as a fabrication produced by an adventure writer. Nevertheless, the story is not wholly devoid of value. It suggests that Ptolemaic policies created important opportunities for men with capital, even if they were not exactly members of the traditional ruling classes. The story also portrays the Tobiads as Jewish heroes who take a kind of accountants' revenge on the Judaeans' traditional enemies in the Greek cities of Palestine by exacting taxes from them with special rigor. The Tobiads' assertive Judaism is striking in light of their non-Judaean ancestry; but their Judaism is of a peculiarly modern-seeming secular-"nationalist" kind. The story portrays Joseph and Hyrcanus as persistent and unselfconscious violators of Jewish law. And for all their alleged hostility to the Greek cities, they are entirely comfortable in the Hellenic environment of the Ptolemaic royal court in Alexandria, Egypt. The family's ease around high government officials, at least, is confirmed by some papyri written in the 250s B.C.E. concerning the business and political arrangements of Joseph's father, Tobias, a large landowner whose private army had been integrated into the Ptolemaic forces, and the royal agent Zenon. Thus, despite the dubious details of Josephus' story, it introduces us to an element of the Judaean elite in the process of transformation, in the form of a wealthy, marginally Jewish but Jewishly well-connected family. This family had greatly benefited both economically and politically from the Ptolemies' preference for capital-rich subjects, and it participated in the common Greek culture of eastern Mediterranean elite society, yet resisted actually becoming Greek, and by successfully walking this tightrope came to play an important role in Judaean society.

The New Wisdom

There are several pieces of Judaean literature that most scholars agree were composed in the third century B.C.E., and these works introduce us to a different segment of Judaean society from that which is the subject of Josephus' stories. The priestly and/or scribal circles who produced the literature were no less affected by the new conditions created by Macedonian rule than Josephus' Tobiads were, but they changed at first in more subtle ways. For despite the ascendancy of people like the Tobiads, the Temple and the Torah remained the centrally important institutions in Judaea, and the priests and scribes who administered them continued to play the same sort of role in Judaean society in the third century as they had in the fifth and fourth. They now presumably needed to be literate in Greek, but acquisition of this skill can have posed little challenge to a class whose main characteristic had always been linguistic talent.

Despite the essential stability of the scribal and priestly classes in the third century, things were changing for them. We can see this clearly if we look at the way they transformed the classical Israelite/Jewish wisdom tradition, the recording of which was one of this class's chief literary activities. In the earliest complete example, the biblical book of Proverbs (seventh to sixth centuries B.C.E.?), wisdom is an adjunct of official Jewish piety. Here fear of God is identified with wisdom, the righteous with the wise. Like the Deuteronomic History and some of the Psalms, Proverbs supposes that wisdom/righteousness is the key to prosperity. Though Proverbs has an undeniable worldliness, its central themes are specifically and conventionally Israelite.

This bureaucratic piety was soon subjected to criticism. The book of Job (fifth century B.C.E.?) had already drawn on 2 Isaiah's transcendental monotheism (see above) to reject, in a rhetorical tour de force, the traditional Deuteronomic piety, which supposed that a powerful but immanent God could be counted on to reward the righteous and punish the wicked. Jewish writers of the third century produced even more radical revisions of the wisdom tradition. The author of Ecclesiastes, who came closer than any other ancient writer in Hebrew to producing a Greek-style philosophical treatise, as opposed to the loose collection of sayings typical of Israelite-Jewish wisdom, was practically a nihilist. He went well beyond Job in taking for granted God's total withdrawal from the world, the unchanging character of nature and the futility of all human endeavor, including righteous behavior and the seeking of wisdom. If Ecclesiastes recommended pious behavior at all, it was only for pragmatic reasons: conformity with the laws of the Torah was likely to be less painful than nonconformity.

Another Jewish book written in the third century B.C.E., known as 1 Enoch, is preserved not in the Hebrew Bible but only in translation into Ge'ez, the holy language of the Ethiopian Church, which regards 1 Enoch as a canonical book. Fragmentary manuscripts of the work in the original Aramaic have been found among the Dead Sea Scrolls. This book, too, like Ecclesiastes and Job, is much concerned with the presence of evil in the world, but its explanation may be the most radical of all. Chapters 1–36 of 1 Enoch are based on the brief and enigmatic biblical story, which immediately precedes the story of Noah's flood, of the Sons of God who descended to earth and took for themselves the daughters of man (Genesis 6:1–4). Enoch follows Job in imagining that God's ways are mysterious, though in contrast to Job, Enoch seems to imply that some humans actually have access to God's mysteries. Chief among these mysteries is that God, having created the universe, quickly relinquished control over it, allowing humanity to fall into the hands of wicked deities (the Sons of God of Genesis). These deities were God's servant-angels, who had successfully rebelled against their master. God responded by withdrawing to the remotest part of heaven, but promised that one day he and the angels who had remained loyal to him, together with a selected part of humanity, would overthrow the forces of evil and restore God's sole rule over the universe.

Enoch thus responds to the claim of traditional Israelite wisdom that the one God is both good and powerful—a claim made problematic by the presence of evil in the world—not by reducing the reader to awed and uncomprehending silence, like Job, or by dismissing the claim with a resigned and world-weary shrug, like Ecclesiastes. Enoch solves the problem of evil by infusing the biblical cosmology with myth, by restoring to his rewriting of Genesis 1–11 the divine drama and tension that the biblical author was so careful to omit. The result is a worldview that is closer to dualism than to monotheism, and that certainly supposes that many divine beings aside from God can act independently and are extremely powerful. Enoch is also deterministic: the human characters are more or less pawns to be manipulated by the divine protagonists.

For all the radicalism of these books, there is little in them that is demonstrably Greek. Israelite wisdom tradition is transformed in these works but remains recognizably itself—the books are motivated by traditional Israelite-Jewish concerns and in every verse betray their authors' familiarity with earlier biblical literature. Apparently, Palestinian Jews were not yet composing books in the Greek language and in Greek genres (at least no such works have been preserved), as their co-religionists in Egypt had already begun to do (though in content such works were often far more conservative than the more formally traditional Palestinian books). Thus, though it is overwhelmingly likely that there is some connection between the intellectual crisis of priestly and scribal classes and the new conditions created by Macedonian rule, it is very difficult to say precisely what this connection may have been.

Judaea under the Seleucids (200–175 B.C.E.)

In 200 B.C.E., following the Battle of Panion (the modern Banyas, on the Golan Heights), in the course of the Fifth Syrian War, Antiochus III, the Seleucid king, at last succeeded in taking Phoenicia and Palestine from Egypt. Far from producing any radical change in the government of Judaea, the Seleucid conquest seems in the short term to have confirmed, or even significantly strengthened, the status quo there. The high priest, Simon, and a segment of the Judaean aristocracy had evidently helped Antiochus in the war, and the king responded generously, in a series of decrees. He made a large contribution to the Temple, recognized the Judaeans' right to conduct their lives according to their own laws (those of the Torah), granted tax exemptions to the members of the aristocratic council, the priests, the Temple scribes and the Temple singers. The last two groups were Levites. The king also specifically confirmed the priests' strict interpretation of the biblical laws forbidding access to the Temple precinct to gentiles and ritually impure Jews (Josephus, *Antiquities* 12:138–46). Antiochus III thus affirmed for the Judaeans the centrality of the Temple and Torah, and the political and economic privilege of their priestly and Levitical guardians.

In the decrees of Antiochus III, there is no acknowledgment of the burgeoning class of lay landowners whom, if we may judge from the story of the Tobiads, the Ptolemies had promoted. Nor is there any hint that among the priests themselves whatever consensus had once existed about important aspects of the Israelite tradition was breaking down. It may be no coincidence that one of the major literary artifacts of this brief period of conservative restoration is the Wisdom of Jesus ben Sira (written in Hebrew, c. 190–180 B.C.E.; in the Christian tradition it is called Ecclesiasticus). This book is excluded from the Hebrew canon, but was read by Jews down into the later Middle Ages and is frequently quoted in the Talmud.

The Wisdom of Ben Sira is unique among ancient Hebrew books written after the biblical books of the Prophets in that the author reveals his identity and tells something of himself—a characteristic the book shares with Greek literature. Ben Sira had been a government official, and taught wisdom to the well-to-do youth of Jerusalem. He was a great admirer of Simon, the high priest, and was perhaps a priest himself. His book constitutes a ringing reassertion of the views of the author of Proverbs and of the Deuteronomic Historian. In what is very likely to be an intentional rejection of the radicalism of Job and Ecclesiastes, Ben Sira repeatedly emphasizes the traditional identification of wisdom and fear of the Lord. Like all wisdom writers, Ben Sira, too, contemplated the meaning of nature. But although for Job nature proved God's inscrutability, and for Ecclesiastes it proved the fundamental amorality of the world, for Ben Sira, as for the Psalmist, nature demonstrates only God's majesty. Ben Sira doubts not for a moment that the righteous prosper, and, in an apparent rejection of the views of 1 Enoch, eschews the pursuit of hidden wisdom. Ben Sira did not react against inner-Jewish developments alone. Though his own wisdom, like that of Proverbs, is heavily borrowed from Egyptian and perhaps even some Archaic Greek sources, his insistent identification of righteousness, or Torah, as the font of all wisdom has plausibly been understood as a reaction against a growing vogue for Greek literature among the wealthy youth of Jerusalem.

THE MACCABEAN REVOLT (175–134 B.C.E.)

Sources

With the events immediately preceding the Maccabean Revolt, it becomes possible, for the first time in Jewish history, to provide a more or less detailed narrative of a long series of events. Of the revolt itself there survive two primary ancient accounts, both written in the later second century B.C.E., known as the First and Second Books of Maccabees. (The books are unrelated to each other.) The First Book, 1 Maccabees, composed in Hebrew but surviving only in Greek translation, covers events from about 170 to 134 B.C.E. It is written in a spare style, in conscious imitation of the Deuteronomic History. Its author was a great admirer of the Maccabean, or Hasmonean, dynasty (the latter term is the more correct, but both are in common use, and are interchangeable), regarding them as the family "in whose hands was entrusted the salvation of Israel" (1 Maccabees 5:62). The Second Book was composed in Greek in a rather overwrought rhetorical style; its gruesome descriptions of the Jews' sufferings and martyrdoms are the source of the word *macabre*. An abbreviation of a much longer work that has not survived, composed by one Jason of Cyrene, 2 Maccabees covers events from about 175 to 161 B.C.E. Its governing concerns are moral rather than political. The book argues that God subjected the Jews to tribulations in order to test them, that he never relaxed his vigilant care for them and always continued to protect his Temple. The author of 2 Maccabees thought of the Maccabean Revolt as a struggle between "Judaism" and "Hellenism"—words that he is the first author, Jew or Greek, to have used, and that he may conceivably have invented. By contrast, the author of 1 Maccabees regarded the revolt as a rising of pious, Torah-observant Jews, against the Seleucid king, Antiochus IV, who had tried to eradicate their special lifestyle, and the sinful Jews who supported the king.

The Events

When Antiochus IV ascended the throne, in 175 B.C.E., Jason, brother of Onias III, high priest of Jerusalem, promised the king a large sum of money if he would appoint him high priest in place of his brother, allow him to construct a gymnasium in Jerusalem and establish in the city a citizen body with a Greek constitution. A gymnasium was an essential component of a Greek city, the institution in which the youth received their training to become full-fledged citizens. The king, who perhaps felt he had more use for cash than for the stability of a tiny, strategically trivial district, agreed, and Onias was deposed. Jason transformed Judaea from an autonomous nation centered on its Temple and ruled by its priests into a Greek city-state, named Antioch in honor of the king, ruled by its citizens (part of the priesthood, and other members of the old city elite). The Temple cult was unchanged and though the constitutional role of the Torah in the new state is unclear, it is certain that no one attempted to interfere with the observance of its prescriptions. Though Jason's reforms were radical in their implications, if not in their immediate results, it is striking that they aroused no public opposition.

There was an inherent instability in Jason's reforms. The Hellenization of Jerusalem was in principle no different from the slightly earlier Hellenization of the cities of coastal Phoenicia. These cities, too, had become Greek while retaining their traditional religion and some elements of their traditional culture. But the Phoenicians were not separatist and exclusivist; they could call their gods Ba'al and Melqart by the Greek names Zeus and Herakles, and participate fully in the general Greek culture of the area without significant internal conflict. But the Torah demanded that the Jews worship the God of Israel alone, and that they conduct their lives in rigorous separation from their idolatrous neighbors. How then could Jerusalem be a Greek city, yet remain Jewish? What would its Hellenism consist of, what its Judaism? Jason wanted Jerusalem to participate in a Panhellenic festival at Tyre, which involved gestures of reverence toward the Tyrian city god, Herakles. How could the Jerusalemite, probably priestly, envoys visit the pagan festival and then return to Jerusalem to serve in the Temple of the God who tolerated "no other gods before him"? (In this case we happen to know that they refrained from full participation in the festival.) Perhaps Jason succeeded in working out some sort of compromise. In any case, he seems to have held Judaea together for four or five years, down to about 170.

In that year, Antiochus replaced Jason with a certain Menelaus, who had offered the king a larger bribe than Jason. Menelaus may not have been of priestly descent, and was certainly not a member of the legitimate high-priestly family. He may have been prepared to move further from Judaism than Jason had done. What next occurred is obscure. Antiochus conducted either one or two humiliatingly unsuccessful campaigns in Egypt, and marched home to Antioch through Jerusalem, which may have been in a state of rebellion. The king plundered the Temple, tore down the walls of the city and settled a garrison there, in a section of the city called the Akra—that is, the acropolis (site uncertain). Thus, it was Antiochus himself who brought Jason's experiment to an end. Then or perhaps later, in 168–87 B.C.E., the king, possibly acting with the encouragement of Menelaus, ordered the Temple of Jerusalem to be rededicated to Zeus Olympius–Ba'al Shamim (chief god of the Syrian pantheon) and outlawed the practice of Judaism on pain of death. Government agents were sent into the countryside to oversee the introduction of Greek or Greco-Syrian religious practices there.

The King's Motives and the Initial Jewish Reaction

Religious persecution of such blatant character was extremely rare in Greco-Roman antiquity. Small religious organizations might be expelled from cities if they were deemed threatening, as the devotees of Bacchus were expelled from Rome in 186 B.C.E. But it is difficult to find an ancient pagan parallel to Antiochus IV's intention to extirpate an established, hitherto fully licit, ethnic religion. It is true that some Greek intellectuals regarded Judaism as prescribing a misanthropic and antisocial lifestyle. But there is no more reason that this should have led to its being outlawed than that some Greek intellectuals' contempt for the traditional Egyptian worship of animals should have caused the Ptolemaic kings to try to outlaw it. The writer of 1 Maccabees believed that the king sought to impose a unitary religion on all his domain, but this is incorrect. Some modern scholars have sought the key to the king's behavior in the obscure events of the two years that preceded his decree: perhaps the persecution was a response to a Jewish revolt that had somehow drawn on the Temple and the Torah for its strength? Others suppose that Jason was a relatively moderate member of a larger group of Jewish reformers, the more radical of whom wished to eliminate all obstacles placed by Judaism in the path of Judaean integration into the Hellenistic world. It was they, in their reformist zeal, who encouraged the king to persecute Judaism.

Whatever the case may be, it is clear that the reaction of the Judaeans to the reforms and the persecution was not uniform. Many Judaeans embraced them and happily collaborated with royal agents. Some fled, to Egypt or to the desert—both traditional places of refuge. Some resisted passively and paid with their lives. Various groups moved haltingly toward active resistance. But the overwhelming majority of Judaeans conformed with the state's demands, most but surely not all unwillingly.

The Maccabees (or Hasmoneans)

The scattered resistance meanwhile began to coalesce under the leadership of Mattathias, a locally prominent priest from the village of Modein, in the far northwestern corner of Judaea. The resisters soon began to engage in guerrilla activities and what can only be described as acts of terrorism, at this stage directed mainly against Jewish collaborators. They threw down altars in villages, circumcised children, thereby forcing the villagers into outlawry, and so collaboration with the revolt, and tried in other ways to stir up resistance. When Mattathias died in 166 or 165 B.C.E., his son Judah, known as Maccabee, took over.

The resistance movement had attracted the notice of the government, and although the king paid little attention to Judaean affairs, hemmed in as he was by the Romans and their clients to the west, and the Parthian Empire to the east, he did nevertheless entrust his minister Lysias with the responsibility, and resources, for quelling the revolt. The king himself went off to fight in Parthia. Lysias was surprised at the ferocity of the opposition his small detachments encountered in Judaea. Judah and his men consistently defeated the royal troops, who like all Macedonian armies depended mainly on the phalanx, a line of heavily armed infantry in tight formation, and the cavalry charge—neither of much use in the Judaean hill country against the flexible, light-armed and enthusiastic Jewish troops.

Whatever had motivated the Seleucids' persecution of Judaism, their commitment to it proved fragile. Early in 164 B.C.E., Lysias in effect canceled the persecution and offered amnesty to rebels who laid down their arms. Later in the year, Judah and his men managed to seize the Temple Mount in Jerusalem, chase out the reformist Jews who controlled it, who now probably took refuge in the Akra, and purify the Temple. The Temple was rededicated to the God of Israel on 25 Kislev (November/December), 164 B.C.E., on the third anniversary of its dedication to Zeus Olympius. The festival of dedication (Hanukkah in Hebrew) lasted eight days and was established as an annual holiday, celebrated by the lighting of lamps. Judah then conducted a series of raids on Seleucid military settlements in the districts surrounding Judaea, and began to besiege the garrison in the Akra of Jerusalem. All this went on without the intervention of the government, which was now fully occupied in Parthia.

But when several inhabitants of the Akra, including a group of reformist Jews, went to Lysias to complain about Judah's activities, Lysias, who was now in full control in Antioch since Antiochus IV had died in the east and Antiochus V was still a little boy, brought a large army and the child king to Judaea. There he decisively defeated Judah and was on the verge of seizing the Temple Mount when he received word from Antioch that another royal minister, Philip, had taken the city

Children in Israel celebrating Hanukkah. This midwinter festival of lights has ancient historical roots: it commemorates the rededication of the Jerusalem Temple by the Maccabees in 164 B.C.E.

and was claiming to be the legitimate regent of Antiochus V. So Lysias was compelled to abandon his siege of Jerusalem after coming to terms with the rebels (in 162). He overturned all the changes of the previous decade and restored the *status quo ante*. Specifically, Lysias restored the Jews' right to conduct their lives according to the laws of the Torah and granted approval to the traditional cult of the God of Israel in the Jerusalem Temple. He did not name Judah high priest, though; in fact, Judah had no claim on the position. Rather, the high priesthood was soon afterward granted to a certain Alcimus, or Yakim in Hebrew (d. 159 B.C.E.), apparently a member of the legitimate high-priestly family, whom even some members of Judah's faction found entirely acceptable.

Nevertheless, Judah continued fighting. He was aiming either at expelling the Seleucids altogether or at his own advancement, or both. When Alcimus complained to the new king Demetrius I (a nephew of Antiochus IV who had seized the throne after killing his young cousin Antiochus V), the king sent his general Nicanor to Judaea with the largest army yet, and Judah was resoundingly victorious. The victory, on 13 Adar (February/March), 161 B.C.E., was celebrated with a festival, Nicanor's Day, which apparently fell out of fashion by the second century C.E. Judah also sent an embassy to secure the friendship and alliance of the Roman Republic, fellow enemies of the Seleucids. But Demetrius immediately sent another army, and this time Judah and his faction were routed; Judah himself was killed and what was left of his faction fled across the Jordan, where, under the leadership of Judah's brother Jonathan, they had to resort to brigandage in order to survive. Meanwhile, Judaea was controlled by Alcimus and his faction, who were, it must be emphasized, by no means "Hellenizers" or reformists, but rather continuators of the pre-175 status quo.

Jonathan (Reigned 152–142 B.C.E.)

After the death of Antiochus IV in 164 B.C.E., the Seleucid Empire began a decline from which it would never emerge. Great slabs of territory fell away east and west, while competition over the center intensified. The war of succession that erupted soon after Antiochus' death lasted with a few interruptions precisely a century, until in 63 B.C.E. the Roman general Pompey the Great marched in and conquered the entire region, turning what little was left of the Seleucid Empire into the Roman province of Syria. It was in these circumstances that the successors of Judah Maccabee transformed themselves first into vassals and courtiers of the Seleucids and, by the very end of the second century, into kings of a short-lived independent kingdom.

In 160 B.C.E. the high priest Alcimus died, and the next thing our primary source, 1 Maccabees, tells us is that in 152 the two rival claimants to the Seleucid throne, Demetrius I and Alexander Balas, who claimed to be a son of Antiochus IV, were competing for Jonathan's support. Clearly in the intervening period Jonathan had gone from being a brigand chief to the most powerful man in Judaea, though he lacked an official position. Jonathan decided to throw his support behind Balas in return for appointment to the high priesthood, which had been vacant since Alcimus' death. Though a priest, Jonathan was not a descendant of the legitimate high-priestly family. His appointment must have been controversial, especially among the more conservative Judaeans who constituted an important part of his faction. The controversy would have been intensified by Jonathan's military activities in the service of his Seleucid overlord, which were doubly unlawful for a high priest: the high priest is forbidden by the Torah to leave the vicinity of the Temple; he may also not subject himself to the risk of contracting ritual impurity by touching a corpse—inescapable for an ancient general who led his troops into battle. Some scholars believe that Jonathan's appointment caused the pietistic, ascetic sect that wrote the Dead Sea Scrolls to withdraw to the desert. This is at least a reasonable guess. It is interesting that though 1 Maccabees has much to say about Jonathan's military triumphs and successful entanglements in international politics, it is silent about his activities as high priest and governor of Judaea (a position Balas officially granted him in 150 B.C.E.; Jonathan's brother Simon was appointed governor—perhaps chief tax collector—of the Palestinian coast). Jonathan may have enjoyed only limited popularity among the Jews.

Simon (Reigned 142–134 B.C.E.)

In 142, Jonathan was assassinated by Tryphon, a pretender to the Seleucid throne, and was succeeded by Simon, the last surviving brother of Judah Maccabee. Simon naturally threw his support behind Tryphon's rival, Demetrius II, son of Demetrius I. The weak Demetrius was so grateful that he not only confirmed Simon's high priesthood and governorship of the province of Judaea, but also exempted the Judaeans from tribute (which he may in any case have been in no position to exact). Though these were merely standard royal concessions, Simon represented them to the Judaeans as tokens of their independence—a claim convincing only as long as the Seleucid throne remained weak and contested, as it did for several years. Nevertheless, Simon exploited this window of opportunity by at once conquering the port city of Joppa (modern Yaffo), providing Judaea with an outlet to the sea for the first time in centuries, and then the ancient fortress of Gezer, which controlled access to the Judaean hills from the coast. Finally, in the summer of 141 B.C.E., Simon expelled the garrison from the Akra of Jerusalem—an act of some symbolic significance, since the Akra garrison was the last visible sign of Seleucid rule in Judaea. The day of the expulsion was established as a festival.

Having won these real and symbolic victories, Simon convened in September 140 B.C.E. an assembly of the priests, the nation and the leaders and elders of the Judaeans. This assembly recognized Simon as high priest, military commander and political ruler of the Judaeans "for ever until a trustworthy prophet should arise" (1 Maccabees 14:41)—that is, either until Simon's death, or until his descendants, not explicitly mentioned in the decree of the assembly, were replaced by divine intervention. The decree constituted the legal basis for the high-priestly and temporal authority of the Hasmonean dynasty. It was engraved on bronze tablets that were displayed in the Temple. Soon afterward, the Roman senate renewed its friendship and alliance with the Judaean nation, first established in 161 B.C.E., and recognized Simon as the legitimate authority in Judaea, simultaneously ordering its allies in the eastern Mediterranean, the most important being Egypt, Pergamum and Cappadocia (in central and eastern Turkey respectively), to do the same.

Despite all these developments, Judaea remained a province of the Seleucid Empire. When Antiochus VII Sidetes, the vigorous brother of Demetrius II, who died in Parthia in 139, arrived in Syria in 138, he recognized Simon as his vassal and "friend" (that is, subordinate), and expected Simon to provide him with troops, which Simon did. As soon as Antiochus eliminated his rival Tryphon, he demanded that Simon give up the towns and fortresses he had conquered, or pay a large fine. When Simon refused, Antiochus sent an army to recover the territory, which Simon defeated. After Simon was murdered, in 134, by his son-in-law Ptolemy, son of Habub, Antiochus VII attacked again and this time conquered the entire district of Judaea. Though he reduced Simon's heir, John Hyrcanus I, to subjection, he refrained from attacking the Temple or interfering with the constitutional status of the Torah and so acquired among the Jews a reputation for piety. Judaea was freed from the Seleucids only by Antiochus' death in Parthia in 129, and the renewal of the Seleucid war of succession.

THE MEANING OF THE MACCABEAN REVOLT

Why the Maccabees Fought

The pivotal moment in the Maccabean Revolt was Lysias' withdrawal from Jerusalem in 162 B.C.E., when he restored to the Judaeans the status that Antiochus III had granted them in 200 B.C.E. Until that moment Judah Maccabee

"Here were brought the bones of Uzziah, King of Judah. Not to be opened." Uzziah reigned from 807 to 754 B.C.E. This inscription, found on the Mount of Olives in Jerusalem, marks the reburial of his bones during the Herodian period.

and his followers plausibly claimed that they were fighting on behalf of the Judaean nation and its main institutions, the Temple and the Torah, which had been altered by Jason the high priest and abolished by Antiochus IV. With Judah's decision to continue fighting after the restoration of the Temple and the Torah, the Maccabees lost much of their support. They may have claimed that they now wished to secure the independence of Judaea. This at least is the view of the author of 1 Maccabees, whose understanding of events may have been affected by the fact that he was writing shortly after the reign of Simon, who did indeed endeavor to secure Judaea's independence from the Seleucids. Be that as it may, it is worth emphasizing the difficulty of determining how attractive notions like "independence" or "self-determination" would have been to Judaeans in the second century B.C.E. Some Jews may well have been nostalgic for the mythic glories of the Davidic and Solomonic kingdoms, but the same biblical books that told moving stories of these ancient heroes also recommended obedience to the Babylonian Empire, and declared the Persian king Cyrus to be God's anointed. The fact was that Judaism had been established and maintained in Judaea through the patronage of the Persian and Macedonian kings, and this fact was acknowledged without apology in the biblical books themselves. If some Jews were attracted by such slogans as "independence" or "freedom," their attraction may paradoxically have had more to do with the influence of the ideals of the Greek city, in which "freedom" was the highest value, than with the more ambiguous message of the Hebrew Bible.

Why the Maccabees Won

If in the final analysis the Maccabees did not enjoy unqualified popular support in Judaea, why then did they succeed? The Roman historian Tacitus, who wrote at the beginning of the second century C.E., argued that the Maccabees succeeded primarily because they had the good fortune to have lived in the century of Seleucid decline, before the Romans arrived in the eastern Mediterranean. Despite Tacitus' hostility to the Jews, there is a hard core of truth in his analysis. The Hasmoneans were one of many native dynasties that rose up at the unraveling fringes of the Seleucid Empire in the second century B.C.E. The Hasmoneans had the disadvantage of having come from an obscure family in an obscure village on the periphery of Judaea. But there were several cases in ancient Judaea, among them also the Tobiads, who have already been encountered, and the Herodian family in the following century, of marginal families endowed with ambition, flexibility and above all ruthlessness, who managed to exploit the periodic regional disorder and establish themselves in power at the center. The common characteristic of these families was their willingness to advance on all fronts: the

Maccabees, for instance, were not just heroic guerrilla fighters and brave generals, working as they claimed for the restoration of Judaism, but were also savvy politicians talented at making their way through the complexities of late-Seleucid palace intrigue, and capable builders of inner-Jewish coalitions. They had, furthermore, a keen sense of how most effectively to present themselves to different and sometimes opposed groups of constituents, allies and superiors.

What the Maccabees Stood For: The Torah and Hellenism

Mattathias may have been a zealously pious and learned priest, as 1 Maccabees says he was. But his sons were primarily warriors and politicians, not Torah scholars, and their precise religious inclinations are difficult to recover. They certainly behaved in untraditional ways, and introduced innovations in law and temple procedure. Their very assumption of the high priesthood and secular authority, without possession of either Zadokite (legitimate high-priestly) or Davidic descent was at very least problematic. Their constant exposure to corpse impurity was a more or less blatant violation of biblical law. There were surely other changes, too, about which less is known. (One especially striking case, their decision to regard vast numbers of non-Judaean Palestinians as Jews, will be discussed presently.) Many Judaean traditionalists quickly developed reservations about the Hasmoneans, and some became open opponents of the dynasty, while others, less willing to incur the dangers of open opposition, unhappily reached a *modus vivendi*. Nevertheless, there can be no doubt that the Hasmoneans were in general terms traditionalists, who may have engaged in a rather different sort of creative interpretation of the Torah than their Zadokite predecessors, but still upheld the Torah's validity as the constitution of Judaea. This may have been enough to satisfy most Judaeans.

Despite the Hasmoneans' essential traditionalism, in some respects in their rise Jason won a posthumous victory, for they stood for integration as surely as Jason did, though on slightly different terms. Every Judaean leader living under Persian, Macedonian or Roman rule had to mediate between the integrative pressures of the eastern Mediterranean environment and the separatist pressure exerted by the Jews' gradually deepening devotion to the Torah. The Hasmoneans demonstrated that it was possible for Judaea to participate politically and economically in an increasingly tightly knit eastern Mediterranean world without surrendering that which made it distinctively Judaean. Embrace of elements of Greek culture by the Hasmoneans themselves facilitated their integration with their neighbors.

For though the author of 2 Maccabees believed Judah Maccabee was engaged in a battle against Hellenism, he was surely wrong, if by Hellenism we mean the adoption of elements of Greek culture by non-Greeks. The evidence is unambiguous. Even Judah had counted the most culturally Hellenized Judaeans among his partisans. One of these was an aristocratic priest named Eupolemus, who in 161 B.C.E. led Judah's embassy to the Roman senate, which permitted easterners to address it in Greek. Furthermore, in 159 B.C.E., Eupolemus published a *History of the Judaean Kings*, of which only brief excerpts survive. This book was composed in the Greek language according to the canons of Greek historiography. The excerpts concern David and Solomon, and one wonders whether the point of the book might not have been to argue that Judah and his brothers were worthy heirs of the ancients, notwithstanding their deficient ancestry. It is in any case surely significant that the earliest Palestinian Jewish book to have been written in Greek was published by a partisan of Judah Maccabee at the height of the Maccabean Revolt, and may well have been addressed to a mainly local Jewish audience.

The Maccabean brothers themselves at a fairly early date necessarily acquired facility in the Greek language, if they did not have it from childhood, and must have learned, like the Tobiads before them, how to behave when in the presence of royal officials. In their political behavior in Judaea, too, they depended heavily on Greek norms, demonstrating that Hellenizing pressures came not only from the eastern Mediterranean environment but from within Judaea itself. The engraving of the resolution of the assembly convened by Simon in 140 B.C.E. on tablets, and their display in the Temple, conforms with practices that originated in the Greek cities of the later sixth and fifth centuries B.C.E. In the same period in Judaea, the public assemblies convened by Ezra and Nehemiah produced not inscribed resolutions but oral oaths. When Simon's son John Hyrcanus I wished to give material expression to Judaea's independence, he minted coins—another practice derived from the cities of Old Greece. Like the much earlier coins of Persian Yehud, these coins, too, were almost all of very small denomination and so intended only for local use. (The coins lacked the customary portrait of the ruler, presumably in deference to the Second Commandment.) In the case both of Simon's resolution and of John's coinage, it is apparent that it was the Jews themselves, or some section of them, whose expectations about the behavior of their rulers were under strong Greek influence.

THE HASMONEAN DYNASTY (134–37 B.C.E.)

The Hasmoneans ruled as a stable dynasty for only two generations, from the death of Antiochus VII Sidetes in 129 B.C.E. until the outbreak of a war of succession in 67 B.C.E., followed quickly by the Roman conquest of 63, which had the effect of transforming the war of succession into a civil war, and greatly lengthening it. Despite its brief duration, the Hasmoneans' reign was of momentous significance. It was the Hasmoneans, chiefly John Hyrcanus I and his sons Judah Aristobulus I and Alexander Yannai (Jonathan), who made Palestine Jewish by conquering the non-Judaean districts of the country and forcing or encouraging (the ancient accounts are ambiguous) the inhabitants to convert to Judaism. It is also under the Hasmoneans that we hear of the rise of the main Jewish sects, the Pharisees, Sadducees and Essenes (these issues are discussed in more detail beginning on page 40).

The sects had a crucial impact on the later history of Judaism. After the destruction in 70 C.E. and the decline in importance of the Temple staff, it was the remnants of the sects, especially the Pharisees, who gradually came to control the religious life of the Jews. All modern varieties of Judaism were shaped by the teachings of the rabbis, as these postdestruction authorities came to be known.

The precise role of the rulers in bringing about the development of sectarianism is unclear, though controversy about the Hasmoneans' high priesthood may have been a factor, as already suggested. Before we consider these issues, though, a brief account of the history of the Hasmonean rulers is provided, courtesy of Josephus, who has in his *Jewish Antiquities* books 13 and 14 and in the first book of his *Jewish War* a fairly detailed if occasionally confused report.

John Hyrcanus I (Reigned 134–104 B.C.E.)

When John was freed of Seleucid domination by the death of Antiochus VII in Parthia, in 129 B.C.E., he undertook a series of campaigns. For this purpose he had the help of a large number of foreign mercenaries. According to Josephus, he marched against the Judaeans' northern neighbors, the Samaritans, conquered their main city, Shechem, and destroyed their temple on Mount Gerizim, just outside Shechem. Evidently, the Samaritans, who were Israelites, were expected to switch their religious loyalties to the Jerusalem Temple, and in return were regarded by the Judaean authorities as Jews.

John next conquered the Judaeans' southern neighbors, the Idumaeans, and their main cities, Marisa (Mareshah, in Hebrew; now Tell Sandahanna, near Qiryat Gat, Israel) and Adora (Adoraim in Hebrew; Dura, southwest of Hebron, on the West Bank). These people were descendants of the biblical Edomites. Like the Samaritans, the Edomites/Idumaeans had a centuries-long history of close relations with the Judaeans, the earliest stages of which are reflected in the biblical stories about the ambivalent relationship between Jacob, ancestor of the Israelites, and his twin brother, Esau, ancestor of the Edomites. As the biblical stories suggest, the Idumaeans were not Israelites but shared many customs with them, not least important of which was the practice of circumcision. John is said to have demanded that the Idumaeans adopt the customs and laws of the Judaeans or leave their country. Many of the Idumaeans acceded to John's demand, and from that time on began to regard themselves and to be regarded as Jews. Since circumcision was evidently an inescapable requirement for entry of males into the community of Israel, the fact that the Idumaeans already practiced it obviously facilitated their conversion. Nevertheless, some Idumaeans did in fact flee to Egypt and some of those who stayed behind remained secretly devoted to their ancestral religion.

John's final conquests, apparently in the last years of his reign, were of Greek cities in central Palestine. These were the city of Samaria, a heavily fortified Macedonian military colony several miles northwest of Shechem, and the extremely ancient city of Scythopolis–Beth Shean, the chief settlement of the Jezreel Valley, which separates the district of Samaria from Galilee, and is the most productive grain-growing region in Palestine. These cities John treated differently from the territories of the Samaritans and Idumaeans. He "destroyed" them, which almost certainly means that he threw down their walls, deconstituted them, enslaved part of their inhabitants, reduced the remainder to subjection and perhaps installed Jewish colonies. John's treatment of the Greek cities thus forms a sharp contrast to his treatment of the non-Greek ethnic territories, which he apparently recognized as partly autonomous components of his state, provided that the inhabitants became Jewish. The Hasmoneans' promotion of cultural Hellenism did not prevent them from regarding Greek cities as their enemy—an attitude they shared with Josephus' Tobiads and very likely also with the upper classes of the Idumaeans and Samaritans as well.

Josephus also mentions an apparently small-scale rebellion, whose cause is uncertain, but which serves to remind us that the Hasmoneans had and always retained many Jewish enemies. And we also know that he gave his three sons two sets of names: they all had Hebrew names—Judah, Mattathias, Jonathan (Yannai)—commemorating their Maccabean ancestry, and also Greco-Macedonian names—Aristobulus, Antigonus, Alexander—derived from those of Alexander the Great and his successors, evidently emphasizing their legitimacy as Hellenistic rulers.

Judah Aristobulus I (Reigned 104–103 B.C.E.)

Aristobulus was the first of the Hasmonean rulers, indeed, the first Judaean ruler since the Babylonians crushed the revolt of Zedekiah in 586 B.C.E., to take the title *king*. Hellenistic rulers conventionally assumed the royal title after a military victory. Aristobulus seems to have conquered all or part of the district of Galilee, hitherto a pagan area with a small Jewish minority partly (?) ruled by an Arab tribe called the Ituraeans. Like the other non-Greek inhabitants of Palestine, the Galilaeans were forced/encouraged to convert to Judaism. It is a minor historical puzzle that Aristobulus is reported to have assumed the title Philhellene (lover of the Greeks).

Alexander Yannai (Reigned 103–76 B.C.E.)

The only relatives who survived Aristobulus' reign were his wife, Salome Alexandra, and his brother, Alexander Yannai, whom Salome now married. Once in power, Yannai greatly extended the Hasmonean conquests, concentrating on the Greek cities of coastal Palestine and the mainly Greek cities east of the Jordan River. It is likely that his normal treatment of these cities was to "destroy" them in much the same way that his father had destroyed Samaria and Scythopolis, but it is not impossible that he judaized some of the cities and simply reduced others to subjection and tribute. He was not invariably successful in his campaigns, especially in Transjordan, where he came up against the Nabataeans. After one of his failures, about 96 B.C.E., a massive domestic rebellion erupted, about whose causes our sources report their usual potpourri of legends and gossip. The rebels appealed to the Seleucid king, Demetrius III, part-ruler of a kingdom in its death throes, to come to their aid, and Demetrius and the Jewish rebels inflicted a resounding defeat on Yannai, illustrating yet again the fragility of the Hasmonean kingdom, even at the peak of its power. But a large contingent of the rebels now felt sorry for their king and defected to his side. Demetrius withdrew in confusion, and Yannai easily quelled the revolt and punished the perpetrators Roman-style, by crucifying them in the public marketplace of Jerusalem.

Salome Alexandra (Reigned 76–67 B.C.E.)

Though Yannai had two sons, he named his wife his heir—a common enough act for a Hellenistic king but unprecedented in Jewish history. Salome Alexandra's reign was a peaceful interlude between the continuous violence of her husband's reign and the thirty-year-long civil war that broke out between her sons even before her death. Yannai had been a harsh opponent of the Pharisees, for reasons that are unclear; but allegedly while he was on his deathbed, he instructed his wife to make peace with them. This is, once again, evidently a piece of gossip, but it does seem to be the case that Alexandra began to patronize the Pharisees at the cost of losing the support of many of Yannai's partisans—whom the Pharisees in fact now persecuted. Under Alexandra, the conquests came to an end, largely because there was nothing available to conquer: to the east and the south were the Nabataeans and the desert, and to the north the Seleucid kingdom had fallen to the powerful Armenian king, Tigranes. Alexandra sensibly maintained cordial relations with Tigranes, bribing him when necessary.

The Civil War (67–37 B.C.E.)

Salome's elder son, Hyrcanus II (d. 31 B.C.E.), had served as high priest during her reign, and was named heir to the kingdom, but at their mother's death was immediately attacked and defeated by his brother Aristobulus II (king of Judea 67–63 B.C.E.). Aristobulus now took the high priesthood and royal throne and allowed his brother to live in retirement, which, our sources suggest, was an entirely suitable role for this mild and peaceful man. However, Hyrcanus had a friend, an Idumaean called Antipater (d. 42 B.C.E.), whose father had been a friend of Alexander Yannai and had governed Idumaea on the king's behalf, and had also prudently maintained ties of friendship or marriage in the Nabataean royal court. This Antipater convinced Hyrcanus that if he went to war against Aristobulus, he would secure the support of the Nabataean king, Aretas. For his part, Aristobulus seems to have enjoyed the support of some Ituraean dynasts who ruled the land just north of the Hasmonean kingdom in what is now Lebanon, and also a group of otherwise unidentified generals. One would have expected Hyrcanus to have inherited his mother's patronage of the Pharisees, and Aristobulus therefore to have taken up his father's Sadducees, yet these religious groups play next to no role in Josephus' accounts of the civil war. The princes needed the support of generals and of others who could deliver military manpower, not of Torah scholars.

In 66 B.C.E., the Roman general Gnaeus Pompeius Magnus (Pompey) invaded Asia Minor, defeated Mithridates VI, the Asian king who had expelled the Romans from the district, and accepted the surrender of Mithridates' son-in-law, the aforementioned Armenian king, Tigranes. In 65, a Roman detachment arrived in Syria, and the warring brothers at once began to compete for the favor of the new regional superpower (meanwhile, a contingent of Judaean aristocrats tried to persuade the Romans to remove the Hasmoneans altogether). At first Pompey's lieutenant in Syria preferred Aristobulus, but Pompey himself eventually backed Hyrcanus and in 63 marched into Jerusalem and captured Aristobulus. To the

The so-called Tomb of Zechariah, a Hellenistic monument cut out of the living rock at the foot of the Mount of Olives.

horror of many Jews, Pompey then entered the Holy of Holies, that is, the innermost chamber of the Jerusalem Temple, where only the high priest was permitted, only on the Day of Atonement. Yet, unlike most previous invaders, he refrained from plundering the Temple. Pompey now named Hyrcanus high priest, but not king, removed the Greek cities conquered by Alexander Yannai from Jewish rule and restored their Greek constitutions.

The arrival of the Romans in Palestine in 63 B.C.E. is often treated by scholars as a watershed in Jewish history. But the fact is that for the first 140 years of Roman rule, little essentially changed. The Romans were rather more interventionist than their Hellenistic predecessors had been, but still at first preferred to rule through local agents. The Romans made many changes small and large in the administrative organization of Jewish Palestine, and meddled tirelessly in the affairs of the Jewish ruling classes, but allowed the Jews to remain a more or less autonomous nation centered on the Jerusalem Temple and governed by the laws of the Torah. This changed only in the later first century C.E.

In any case, the short-term effect of the Roman conquest was to intensify the Jewish civil war, for the Roman Republic itself collapsed at once into factional warfare, which, among other things, allowed each of the Jewish parties to have the support of one of the competing Roman senatorial factions. On the whole, the Hyrcanian party enjoyed the upper hand, largely because of the talent of Hyrcanus' leading partisan, Antipater, at the all-important skill of making friends with whichever Roman senatorial warlord was more powerful at the moment. However, after the assassination of Julius Caesar in 44, and of Antipater in 42 (by a fellow partisan of Hyrcanus), and the subsequent rise of hostilities within the Caesarian faction between Marc Antony and Octavian, the now-aged Hyrcanus lost everything. In 40, the Parthians took advantage of the chaos in the Roman world by attacking and conquering Syria and Palestine. Antipater's sons, Herod (73–4 B.C.E.) and Phasael (d. 40 B.C.E.), tried but failed to win the Parthians' favor. The Parthians named Antigonus (ruled 40–37 B.C.E.), son of Aristobulus, king, and dragged Hyrcanus off to Mesopotamia, after his nephew had sliced off his ear, thereby rendering him unfit to serve as high priest ever again. The old man was treated with great honor by the large Jewish community of Mesopotamia. Phasael meanwhile committed suicide in the course of battle, and Herod escaped to Rome.

There the senate declared Herod king, without specifying a constituency or a territory, and assigned him the task of reconquering Palestine from the Parthians. Herod did in fact gradually conquer the Palestinian hinterland—the Jewish districts of Galilee, Samaria, Judaea and his native Idumaea—with the help of a detachment of Roman troops and Jewish troops whom he succeeded in raising himself. By unspoken agreement with his overlords, he left the Greek cities of the coast and the Transjordan in peace. Jerusalem was the last place to fall to Herod, and when it did, in 37 B.C.E., Herod's Jewish troops committed a great slaughter of their co-religionists besieged in the city, which Herod restrained only with difficulty. This event, at first glance surprising, is not difficult to understand if we assume that the troops were non-Judaean Jews, like Herod himself. Among such people, resentment against the Judaeans may never have been far from the surface. King Antigonus was captured and sent off to Antony for execution, and Herod now reigned as king of the Jews.

THE HASMONEAN DYNASTY EVALUATED: THE EXPANSION

Progress

As we have seen, in the last thirty years of the second century B.C.E., the boundaries of Jewish Palestine were massively extended: in 130 B.C.E. they contained only the tiny district of Judaea, but by 100, the entirety of the Palestinian hinterland, from the high hills of Upper Galilee in the north, to the edge of the Negev desert in the south, and from the Jordan River, or even slightly beyond it, in the east, to the edge of the coastal plain in the west, was ruled by the Hasmoneans. The people who dwelled within these boundaries, who had apart from the Judaeans previously been a mixed multitude of Idumaeans, Samarian Israelites, and in Galilee probably a mixture or patchwork of Arabs, Greeks and Syrian pagans, some of them of remote Israelite descent, now all became in some sense Jewish.

Little is known about either the causes or the progress of this momentous set of events. The speed and ease with which the conquests of the Palestinian interior (but not the Greek cities) occurred, the fact that the newly conquered districts never rebelled and the shakiness of the Hasmonean kingdom at the time of the conquests, under John Hyrcanus I and Aristobulus I, have suggested to many scholars that the conquests were not quite what they seem from Josephus' sketchy accounts. Some have argued that the conquests may be more profitably viewed as a series of alliances formed by the Hasmoneans with the leaders of the non-Greek districts surrounding Judaea aimed primarily against the local Greek cities.

This is an attractive hypothesis and there is likely to be some truth to it, but it fails to explain why Josephus speaks so unambiguously of conquest. In all likelihood the expansion depended on a combination of coercion and persuasion, and resulted for the annexed nations in a status that combined subjection and alliance—but was in any case distinct from the fate of the conquered Greek cities. In return for adopting Judaism, probably more gradually and incompletely than Josephus implies, the Idumaeans and the rest received not only the Hasmoneans' protection but also a chance to share in the spoils of further conquests. The annexed districts seem to have retained a sort of limited autonomy, under the rule of native governors who may have enjoyed the status of "friendship" with the Judaean king. In a Hellenistic context, friendship is a semiformal state of reciprocal obligation, not necessarily between equals. Thus, the Idumaeans became Jewish but remained simultaneously Idumaeans. The Judaism of the annexed districts must indeed have been gradually adopted and was perhaps not at first very deep. Surely it involved loyalty to the Jerusalem Temple and submission to the legal authority of the high priest. Its main initial effect, though, must have been to change the character of the public life in the annexed districts. John Hyrcanus I shut down not only the Israelite temple on Mount Gerizim but also the pagan temples of Idumaea. Perhaps town markets were closed on the Sabbath. But otherwise, life, even religious life, in the annexed districts at first went on pretty much as before. Even if the Hasmoneans had wished to eradicate all traces of the pre-Jewish religions of the districts, they could not have done so; the state simply had no way to police the day-to-day activities of hundreds of thousands of people. Probably the Judaization of the districts, which was in the long term successful, in that Idumaea and Galilee remained Jewish even after the end of Hasmonean rule and were thoroughly incorporated in the Jewish nation, was helped by the profound cultural and religious ties that existed in any case among the non-Greek peoples of Palestine. Still, there was resistance. The Idumaeans who fled to Egypt in the late second century B.C.E. zealously cultivated there, over the course of centuries, the worship of their ancestral god Qos; and in the late first century B.C.E., an Idumaean associate of King Herod tried to restore the worship of Qos in his native district. It may, furthermore, be no coincidence that Christianity, which was from the start ambivalent about the central institutions of Judaism, originated in Galilee, another of the annexed districts.

Causes

It is unclear why the Hasmoneans undertook their expansion. An obvious answer should not be overlooked—they expanded because they could. Historically most states have viewed acquisition of territory and people with favor, and there is no reason for the Hasmoneans not to have done the same. Though they were weak, they may still have been stronger than poorly centralized districts like Idumaea and Galilee, and surely had a more experienced army. Conquest tended to generate conquest, because it was sensible to pacify conquered peoples by giving them a share in future plunder—one of the chief sources of new wealth in the premodern state. As to the Hasmoneans' policy of Judaizing the conquered nations, we have already seen that the notion that outsiders could join the Jewish nation was several centuries old by the time John Hyrcanus pushed it to its logical limits. So, although there was no precedent for mass conversion, it was at least based on firmly established conceptual ground, and the idea of conversion seems to have exerted special fascination in circles close to the Hasmoneans. In imposing Judaism on their subjects, the Hasmoneans may have been motivated by the biblical idea that the Land of Israel should be "unpolluted" by idolatry. Or they may have been inspired by the example of their allies and friends the Romans, who had for centuries been successfully expanding their territory by combining exceptionally violent military activity with judicious grants of Roman citizenship to some of the people they conquered.

Consequences

It is obvious that the Hasmonean expansion exerted a profound effect on every aspect of Jewish, and eastern Mediterranean, history. One need only imagine the influence on the finances of the Jerusalem Temple and the Judaean priesthood of the vast expansion of their tax base, and the unsettling effect on the Judaean economy of the influx of so much new wealth into the district. Palestinian Jewish society became as a result of the conquests exponentially more complex, much richer and much more turbulent than it had ever been.

It is worth noting the most blatant consequences of the expansion: if Idumaea had not been Judaized, there could never have been a Herod, and if Galilee had not been Judaized, there could never have been a Jesus, though it should also be noted that scholars have struggled to try to isolate the debt of Jesus and the earliest Christianity to their Galilean environment with little success. Otherwise, the effects of the expansion may be very briefly discussed by category.

Demography. The size of the population of ancient Palestine cannot be determined, but it is plausible to suggest the figure of 500,000 for the population of the Palestinian interior. This would imply a population of 100,000–200,000 for the district of Judaea, and so approximately a two- to five-fold increase in the Jewish population of Palestine in the wake of the expansion, bearing in mind, though, that an unknown proportion of the inhabitants of the annexed districts fled.

Economy. The Hasmonean state was enriched by its constant warfare and plunder, especially of the wealthy Greek cities of the coast and the desert fringe, under Alexander Yannai. Much of this wealth went into the pockets first of all of the kings, second, into the Temple treasury, and third, to the priests, who were entitled to receive taxes in kind from all Israelites living in the Land of Israel. But the general population profited, too, for it was they, especially perhaps the residents of the annexed districts, who formed the rank and file of the Hasmonean armies, and got to keep part of what they plundered. We should like to have numbers, but as always the ancient sources provide none.

Politics. Little is known for certain about how the Hasmoneans administered their state, but it does seem likely that they ruled Judaea through the established national institutions, and the annexed districts through "friendly" native governors. The expansion strengthened the representatives of the Judaean institutions—the priests and scholars of the Torah—in some respects, for they now had at least some limited sort of jurisdiction over a vastly increased population. But the expansion weakened them in other ways, for they now had to compete for royal favor with non-Judaean generals and friends of the kings. We have already seen how the conditions of the lengthy Hasmonean civil war tended to favor the advancement of the non-Judaean generals and friends, and marginalize the Judaean priests and Torah experts.

Religion. The mass conversions ought to have been controversial among Judaeans, yet there is surprisingly little evidence that they were. We do know that some Judaeans were contemptuous of the annexed nations, but there is no indication that they were not regarded as Jews. What their Judaism consisted of is a different question, which has already been briefly discussed. It may also be suggested that they introduced some of their own practices into standard Judaism. For example, archaeologists have traced the spread of the practice of burial in *kokhim*—niches hewn out of the walls of caves—from Marisa, the main city of Idumaea, in the third and second centuries B.C.E., to Judaea, in the first century B.C.E., to all of Jewish Palestine, in the first century C.E. and following.

THE HASMONEAN DYNASTY EVALUATED: THE SECTS

Josephus, Rabbinic literature and to some extent the New Testament all seem to agree that later Second Temple–period Judaism was divided into three main sects: Pharisees, Sadducees and Essenes. If by sect we mean a small, self-enclosed religious organization that regards itself as in some measure a "pure" form of the larger society, then the ancient sources may be doubly misleading. In the first place, the Pharisees and Sadducees may not have constituted sects at every period of their existence; in the second place, there were clearly many more than three Jewish sects in the first centuries B.C.E. and C.E. Most likely such groups proliferated because in the centuries since Ezra and Nehemiah, the Jews had internalized the importance of their central institutions, the Temple and the Torah, to a remarkable degree, but their rulers were on the whole too weak or too unconcerned to suppress the inevitable disagreements about Temple practice and Torah interpretation that arose among the priests and the scribes.

The three main groups are first mentioned in connection with the early period of Hasmonean rule. Of the three, the Essenes constituted the most properly "sectarian" group. They lived in self-enclosed communities, held property communally and were very strict in their interpretation of the laws of the Torah, especially the laws of purity. Their contact with nonsectarians, who were regarded as impure, was therefore severely limited, though they depended on a steady flow of (Jewish) converts to keep their sect alive, because for the most part the Essenes, who were males, did not marry. Their devotion to purity, among other factors, led them to reject the legitimacy of the Hasmonean-run Temple, which they regarded as impure, as well. If, as is likely, the organization responsible for the ancient library discovered at Qumran, in the Judaean Desert, in 1947, better known as the Dead Sea Scrolls, was a subgroup of Essenes, then we know much more about them.

By their own account, they had an ongoing quarrel with the Jerusalem authorities, and in particular reviled the memory of an early persecutor of their sect whom they called the Wicked Priest. This is probably Jonathan or Simon the Hasmonean, or perhaps a composite of the two. The sect revered the memory of the high-priestly Zadokite family (the descendants of Zadok, David's priest)—indeed, it may have retained Zadokite leadership for some time. But the Essenes were not merely conservative continuators of pre-Maccabean priestly tradition; on the contrary, they claimed to be in possession of a new revelation, which

Qumran, overlooking the west shore of the Dead Sea. According to the Roman writer Pliny the Elder, it was in this vicinity, "between Jericho and En-Gedi," that the Essenes lived. Other sources (Philo and Josephus) state that they were dispersed throughout the country.

informed them alone of the correct interpretation of the laws of the Torah (to the study of which they were very much devoted), and especially of the correct times for the celebration of the festivals, of which the mainstream authorities were ignorant. These times were based on a solar calendar of 364 days, which was first described in 1 Enoch, a book the sect regarded as sacred. Other Jews used a different liturgical calendar, perhaps something like the occasionally adjusted lunar calendar described much later in the Mishnah, though we cannot be sure. The sectarians were also convinced that the End of Days was coming, and that it would be ushered in by a war between the Sons of Light (the members of the sect) and the Sons of Darkness (everyone else), resulting in the full restoration of the former. It is of great interest that despite the radically countercultural character of the sect and its scarcely concealed hostility to the Judaean establishment, the kings for the most part left them alone. Their brief persecution by the Wicked Priest was a passing episode, never repeated.

Pharisees and Sadducees

Initially, the Pharisees and Sadducees were different sorts of organizations from the Essenes, though by the later first century B.C.E. they were coming to approximate them. The name of the Sadducees (Zadokim in Hebrew) implies a connection with the pre-Maccabean high priesthood of Jerusalem, the Zadokites, a connection the Sadducees therefore shared with the Essenes. A Dead Sea Scroll published in 1994, entitled *Miqsat Ma'asei Torah* (Some cases of the Torah), demonstrated that the Sadducees and the Essenes also shared some details of legal interpretation. But the Sadducees seem to have originated among those supporters of the Zadokites who were willing to come to terms with the new rulers: they recognized the legitimacy of the Hasmonean high priests and the purity of their Temple, and within a generation of the Maccabean Revolt had managed to secure the patronage of John Hyrcanus I. They thereby seem to have acquired the dominant role in making decisions about the details of Temple procedure, and in administering the laws of the Torah. The little that is known about them otherwise is derived from the works of Josephus, who knew the Sadducees not in their Hasmonean glory days but only in the middle and later first century C.E., when they had become a small, snobbish, not terribly influential sect, whose membership was apparently restricted to a few high priests and some of their friends and relatives. Josephus disliked and resented them, and had little to say about them, none of it good.

Before John Hyrcanus I patronized the Sadducees, he is said to have patronized the Pharisees. This was a group of unknown background—though, like all the main sectarian organizations, clearly drawn mostly from the educated Judaean elites. Their name seems to be derived from the Aramaic or Hebrew word for *separation*, but separation from what is unclear. The Pharisees, like the Sadducees and Essenes, were known primarily as students of the Torah, and their interpretative skills were particularly renowned, at least in the first century C.E. Unlike the Sadducees, though, who allegedly derived all their legal lore from exegesis of the text of the Torah, and the Essenes, who claimed to possess a new and supplementary revelation, the Pharisees claimed to derive their legislation in part from an apparently oral body of "ancestral traditions." In fact all the sects, as professional legal authorities (or ex-authorities, in the case of the Essenes), had, as we have seen, to find some way to bridge the gap between the text of the Torah and actual legal practice, the Sadducees' exegesis, the Pharisees' "ancestral traditions" and even to some extent the Essenes' new revelation are all primarily slightly different mechanisms for doing so. In any case, by the first century C.E. the Pharisees were more interested than the Sadducees in maintaining friendly relations with the general Jewish population, but when they were in power in the early first century B.C.E., they had treated the people with marked brutality (they conducted a purge of Alexander Yannai's supporters). Like the Sadducees, they, too, turned in on themselves to some extent in the first century C.E., regardless of their friendliness to the peasantry, turning from an influential scribal/priestly organization into something more closely resembling an exclusivist sect.

Herod (Reigned 37–4 B.C.E.)

King Herod has generally resisted sympathetic treatment. The most detailed ancient accounts of his reign, in Josephus' *Jewish War*, book 1, and *Jewish Antiquities*, books 14–17, though by no means uniformly hostile to the king, portray a man who advanced by flattering the powerful and tormenting the weak, who brought about the deaths of one of his wives, several of his sons and many of his courtiers, who descended into paranoia as he aged (though it has to be admitted that everyone *was* plotting against him) and whose great building projects were the work of a megalomaniac, not a benefactor. Later Jewish and Christian traditions added some refinements to the picture: in rabbinic literature, Herod is portrayed as a repulsively servile figure, and in Christian literature as a latter-day pharaoh, a murderer of babies.

Surely Herod deserved his reputation for ruthlessness, cruelty and paranoia, though we may very much doubt whether he was any worse than such predecessors as Aristobulus I or Alexander Yannai, or such contemporaries and friends as Marc Antony or Augustus Caesar. What is peculiar about the standard treatments of Herod is how historians have allowed moral evaluation to color political and social analysis in a way it tends not to in accounts of the Hasmoneans or of Augustus (with some exceptions in the latter case, like Ronald Syme's celebrated book, *The Roman Revolution*, published in 1939, in which the emperor is portrayed as a fascist generalissimo). Presumably the traditional Christian and Jewish antipathy to the king constitute a partial explanation for this. But modern accounts go beyond the traditional ones in making Herod into a quisling, a collaborator with the Romans who identified fully with his bosses and harbored a deep hostility to his own people.

But there is a different way of viewing Herod, which may not make him seem any nicer a person, but which places more emphasis on the political realities that he was constrained to work with, and is more willing to see him in terms of the traditions of ancient Jewish political leadership. Indeed, in important ways, it was Herod who completed what the Hasmoneans had started, by contributing to the unification of all the Jews of Palestine, Judaeans and non-Judaeans, and by tightening the relations between the Jews of Palestine and those of the Diaspora.

Herod was a product of the age of the civil wars, both Hasmonean and Roman, an age that offered great opportunities to the ruthlessly ambitious. From his grandfather and father he inherited a complex of friendships with Hasmoneans, Nabataean kings and courtiers and important Roman personages. He exploited this inheritance brilliantly and extended it, when as a young commander and administrator in Galilee, he earned the friendship of various local Jewish and pagan grandees and deepened and broadened his relations with leading Romans, most significantly in the later forties with Marc Antony, leader of the Caesarian faction for a time after the dictator's assassination in 44 B.C.E. It was thanks to his friendship with Antony that when the Parthians conquered Palestine in 40 B.C.E., the Roman senate granted Herod and not a Hasmonean the royal title and the job of providing local military support to the Roman legions in their attempt to reconquer southern Syria.

Herod himself helped conquer Jewish Palestine and was later given extensive gifts of non-Jewish territory—the coastal Greek cities, the Golan Heights and other rural territories in southern Syria—by Antony and subsequently the emperor Augustus. But he was considered and considered himself primarily king of the Jews; he seems to have administered the pagan territories on behalf of the emperor and senate and to have received a portion of the revenues from them. But Herod was not Jewish in precisely the same sense as the Hasmoneans had been. He was first of all not of priestly descent, so he could not serve simultaneously as king and high priest. He was, furthermore, not Judaean but a Judaized Idumaean, and many of his domestic policies reflected the concerns of the non-Judaean Jews and their sometimes ambivalent relations to the central Judaean institutions as they had been administered by the Hasmoneans. One of the main tendencies of his reforms seems to have been, in fact, to turn *Judaean* institutions into *Jewish* ones by enhancing their attractiveness to non-Judaean Palestinian Jews and Jews of the Diaspora.

Herod's Reforms

Given his inability to serve as high priest himself, Herod had to reform the high priesthood. His reforms have several interesting characteristics. Under Herod, and after his time until the destruction of the Temple in 70 C.E., the high priesthood was no longer held for life and passed from father to son. Rather, the incumbents held the position for brief terms of irregular length, and the king retained exclusive right of appointment. Clearly Herod was interested in keeping tight control over a position that could easily have turned into a focus of political opposition. After Herod's death, the high priesthood became again de facto dynastic, because Herod's descendants and Roman successors preferred to appoint to the post descendants of Herod's high priests. But the only distinctive characteristic that Herod's appointees shared, as far as we can tell, is that five of the seven who served in the course of the thirty-three years of Herod's reign were not Judaean: one was brought from Babylonia, one resided in Galilee and several came from Egypt. Of the Judaeans, one was Herod's young brother-in-law, the Hasmonean prince Aristobulus (sometimes assigned the dynastic number III) (d. 35 B.C.E.), of whom the king was profoundly jealous, and who drowned under suspicious circumstances, to say the least, after a very brief term of office.

Herod failed to assign an important role to the old religious organizations of the Pharisees and Sadducees. We have already seen that after the death of Salome Alexandra in 67 B.C.E., the organizations, which had played an important administrative role previously, were pushed to the margins by the conditions prevailing in the civil wars; to repeat, the heirs of Alexandra were too busy cultivating generals and raising troops to worry much about Torah scholars. Herod ended the civil war but did not restore the sects. The fact that they had been elite *Judaean* organizations may explain Herod's interest in depriving them of any significant role in his state. From now on they would be small organizations competing for the patronage of the royal women and high priests, and vying with one another for a voice in Temple affairs.

Herod exploited his connections at Rome on behalf of the Jews of the Diaspora. These Jewish communities were permitted by Roman law and convention to conduct their lives according to Jewish law, even when it came into conflict with the laws of the cities where they resided—for example, Jews could not be forced to come to court on the Sabbath. However, local authorities did not always recognize the Jews' rights, and Herod made a practice of intervening with imperial officials on behalf of these Jewish communities. His generous gifts to Greek cities and institutions such as the Olympic games may have been intended primarily to secure Greek cities' goodwill to their Jewish residents. Herod's recruitment of high priests from the Diaspora also indicates his desire to cultivate the support of the Diaspora communities.

Josephus was perhaps right to think that Herod's public construction projects were undertaken for his own glory, but this was surely not their only motivation. Herod built and refurbished fortresses across the country, restored and fortified cities and built a massive shrine at the Cave of the Machpelah in the old Idumaean town of Hebron. The Jews regarded this site as the tomb of the biblical Patriarchs and Matriarchs, and the Idumaeans, also descendants of Abraham and Sarah and Isaac and Rebecca, may have done the same, even before they became Jewish. But Herod's building projects had twin, closely related, centerpieces. He completely rebuilt a tiny, declining old Greco-Phoenician city called Strato's Tower (about halfway between Tel Aviv and Haifa in Israel) as a grand port city, named Caesarea in commemoration of Herod's friendship with Augustus Caesar. Archaeologists discovered in the 1980s and 1990s that Caesarea's harbor, one of the largest in the eastern Mediterranean, was built according to the most up-to-date principles of Roman engineering. The city at once became the leading port of the southern part of the east coast of the Mediterranean, easily crowding out such competitors as Gaza, Ascalon and Joppa, and the main point of entry for the burgeoning Jewish pilgrim traffic from the Diaspora.

The other twin star of Herod's construction was Jerusalem, which was rebuilt from top to bottom. Although the amount of money flowing into the Temple treasury had increased tremendously under the Hasmoneans, they undertook almost

Herod's Temple in Jerusalem (modern reconstruction). The shrine was constructed on a massive scale and sumptuously decorated.

no public construction in the city. The residential quarters grew, so that the city walls needed to be extended, and a palace was built, but the Temple remained the tiny structure built under Zerubbabel in the late sixth century, incapable of containing a vastly increased Jewish population. Herod rebuilt all the public areas of the city on a much grander scale than they had ever been before, but the main feature of his construction was the new Temple, one of the largest structures in the Roman Empire, with a courtyard that could accommodate vast numbers of pilgrims. It was Herod's Jerusalem that the Roman writer Pliny the Elder could describe as "by far the most famous city of the East," and that a talmudic storyteller could call the recipient of nine of the ten measures of beauty that God allotted to the world.

Herod's construction had several important effects. It created many thousands of jobs and would continue to do so for several decades after his death. The Temple was not completed until 62 C.E., only eight years before its destruction, and its completion is said by Josephus to have put 18,000 laborers out of work. Herod's construction projects may thus be seen as the functional equivalent of the Hasmoneans' conquests, now ruled out by the Roman peace, which had also provided incomes for thousands of Jews.

The construction also changed the character of Jerusalem and of Jewish Palestine as a whole. Jerusalem was no longer a remote hill-country town, of interest mainly to Judaean peasants and to the occasional foreign general looking to steal some silver from the treasury of its Temple. It was now the metropolis of all the world's Jews, whether they were Judaean, or from the annexed districts of Palestine, or from the Roman or Parthian Diasporas. Jerusalem had perhaps long been so in a symbolic or sentimental way, but now it was so in reality as well. It is only in Herod's reign and later that one hears of the throngs of Jews from all over the world gathered in the city for the pilgrimage festivals of Passover, Shavuot (the Feast of Weeks) or Sukkot (the Feast of Booths) and of the disturbances that sometimes broke out as a result.

In sum, Herod's policies built on those of the Hasmoneans and turned Jewish Palestine into a single state, a state furthermore closely tied to the Jewish communities of the Diaspora. This achievement, which was of enduring significance, by no means contradicts the probable baseness of his motivations or the brutality of his character, but surely it is as deserving of attention as his sordid family life, which is the main concern of the ancient sources and to which we now briefly turn.

The Herodian Family and Succession

Herod had ten wives, most of whom he was married to concurrently: though Greeks and Romans did not practice polygamy, it was not unknown, if not precisely commonplace, among Syrians, Jews, Arabs and some others. Like most aristocratic marriages in most societies through the ages, Herod's marriages were alliances rather than love matches—thus he was careful to marry a daughter of the Jerusalem priestly elites, a noble Samaritan woman and so on (most of the wives are just names to us). His most important marriage was to the Hasmonean heiress Mariamme (d. 29 B.C.E.), daughter of Alexander, son of Aristobulus II, and of Alexandra, daughter of Hyrcanus II. Mariamme was thus not only Herod's most valuable ally but also his most dangerous enemy, and in the first years of his reign Herod killed not only her but also her redoubtable mother, who was worryingly friendly with Queen Cleopatra VI of Egypt, her younger brother the high priest Aristobulus III and eventually even her aged and harmless grandfather, Hyrcanus II, who had made the mistake of returning from Parthia after Herod's accession. By 28 B.C.E., the only surviving Hasmoneans in Herod's kingdom were his own young sons by Mariamme, Alexander (c. 35–7 B.C.E.) and Aristobulus (c. 35–7 B.C.E.).

Josephus describes Herod's slaughter of the Hasmoneans in melodramatic terms: Herod was in love with his wife, but the couple were driven into suspicion and hatred of each other by Mariamme's scheming mother and other hostile and jealous parties, and the execution of Mariamme was the result of a series of tragic misunderstandings. Josephus drew his account of Herod's family life entirely from the works of Herod's court historian, the Greek orator and Aristotelian philosopher Nicolaus of Damascus. Nicolaus could scarcely deny Herod's brutality to his family, which was proverbial as far away as Rome, where the emperor

Augustus is supposed to have remarked that it was safer to be Herod's pig than his son, so Nicolaus tried to turn it into soap opera.

The middle period of Herod's reign was largely occupied with politics. His Hasmonean sons had been sent to Rome, where they were being raised in the emperor's household. This arrangement was customary for the sons of the so-called client kings—that is, the rulers of semiautonomous districts, mostly in Asia Minor and Syria, within the Roman Empire. The princes thus served as hostages—their fathers' loyalty to Rome was not always beyond doubt—and also grew up as members of the Roman ruling class. Soon after Alexander and Aristobulus returned to Jerusalem, about 18 B.C.E., they were married off. Alexander, the elder and the intended heir to the throne, was married to Glaphyra, daughter of Archelaus, an important client king who ruled Cappadocia, in eastern Turkey; Aristobulus was married to his own first cousin, Berenice. (Herod insisted that pagan men who married into his family be circumcised and observe Jewish law; there may not yet have been a conversion ritual for pagan women. It may be that it was taken for granted that they would adopt their husbands' lifestyle and that their children would be Jewish. This contrasts sharply with later Jewish law. However, the descendants of Alexander and Glaphyra seem not have regarded themselves as Jewish.)

The succession crisis began at once. Herod had an older son called Antipater (d. 5 B.C.E.) by his first wife, a Judaean or Idumaean commoner called Doris (d. 5 B.C.E.), who had no intention of letting his younger half brothers ascend the throne. The plotting and counterplotting lasted over a decade, until shortly before Herod's death, and ended with the execution of all three involved parties, Antipater, Alexander and Aristobulus. The irony was that Herod in any case had little say about who would succeed him, or what would become of his kingdom after his death. In the final analysis, his kingdom was a gift of the Roman senate and emperor, and it was Augustus who would make ultimate decisions about succession.

Herod's final years were catastrophic, and are mostly responsible for the traditional image of the king. By the time of his death, important segments of the population were at the point of revolt. One disturbance, which was minor enough in itself, is of special interest. Herod had a golden eagle set up over the main gate of the Jerusalem Temple. This is often interpreted as an expression of Herod's allegiance to Rome, symbolized by the eagle, and unconcern for the religious sensibilities of the Jews, implied by the apparent violation of the Second Commandment. But matters are not so simple. As we have already seen, the use of images could in some cases be reconciled with the Second Commandment, and surely the priests had done so in this case, in a way that satisfied most Jews. Furthermore, the eagle was a complex and capacious symbol, as susceptible of a Jewish (see Exodus 18) as of a Roman interpretation. The eagle, furthermore, had a special role in the traditional religion of the Idumaeans. Two Judaean Torah scholars, however, did regard it as unacceptable, and their students took the initiative of chopping it down. Herod was then on his deathbed but responded with outrage. Josephus makes it clear that Herod was upset not because he regarded the young men's act as an insult to Rome or to himself but because he regarded

Masada, an imposing natural fortress dominating the Dead Sea and part of the Judaean Desert. Herod fortified this rocky outcrop and built an impressive palace here, with an ingenious water supply. In 66 C.E., during the revolt against Rome, it was captured by Zealots, and it remained in their hands, despite a Roman siege, until 73. Among the many remarkable archaeological discoveries made here are manuscript fragments, one of the earliest synagogues found in Israel and a heap of skeletons of men, women and children, thought to be those of the Zealot defenders.

it as an act of sacrilege. The golden eagle may thus have constituted an attempt by Herod to introduce into the Jerusalem Temple some of the religious imagery of the Judaized nations, in a way that offended some *Judaeans* but actually pleased many Jews.

Herod died in 4 B.C.E., and a series of small-scale uprisings broke out immediately. Augustus decided to divide Herod's Jewish state into several pieces and distribute them among Herod's lesser sons, the only ones who survived. Archelaus (d. c. 16 C.E.) was assigned Samaria, Judaea and Idumaea, and Herod Antipas (20 B.C.E.–39 C.E.) Galilee. The pagan territories of southern Syria were assigned to Herod Philip (d. 34 C.E.). Archelaus was vicious and incompetent. In 6 C.E., the leading Jews and Samaritans asked Augustus to remove him, and he did so. Antipas ruled peacefully for forty-two years, a successful and competent ruler, notwithstanding his reputation among the early Christians, and Philip ruled until 34 C.E. Though Herod's Jewish state did not survive his death as a political unit, as a religious, cultural and social entity it fell only in 70 C.E.

THE FIRST CENTURY

The Roman historian Tacitus devoted three words to the history of Palestine during the long reign of the emperor Tiberius (14–37 C.E.): *Sub Tiberio quies* (under Tiberius, calm). But matters looked very different to the provincials themselves. Josephus wrote of incompetent and greedy Roman administrators, rioting, brigandage, growing revolutionary organizations and no fewer than six messiahs, including Jesus of Nazareth, all of whom the Roman government hunted down and executed. The Jewish historian regarded these events as marking the beginning of the unraveling of Roman-Jewish relations, a process that culminated in the destruction of the Temple and city of Jerusalem in 70 C.E.

But there is something to be said to Tacitus' perspective. Inept administration, brigandage and rioting were not uncommon, especially in newer Roman provinces, and usually did not lead to revolt. But in Jewish Palestine, order really did collapse. There was a respite under Agrippa I (10 B.C.E.–44 C.E.; ruled in northern Palestine from 38, and in Judaea from 41). Agrippa was son of Aristobulus, son of Herod and Mariamme, and so both a Herodian and a Hasmonean, and well liked by his Jewish subjects. The decades that followed his death, though, were tumultuous even by Roman provincial standards. What was distinctive about the situation in Palestine was that significant parts of the Jewish aristocracy participated in the tumult, not just the poor and dispossessed, as elsewhere.

In Judaea, this aristocracy consisted mainly of the descendants of Herod's appointees to the high priesthood, who were known as high priests whether or not they actually held the post (the high priesthood proper was filled by appointment, as under Herod, and held for brief terms; in most periods, Herod's royal descendants had the right to appoint the high priests). Also important were minor descendants and relatives of Herod. Herod's royal descendants—for example, Herod Antipas, Agrippa I and his children Agrippa II (27/28–c. 98 C.E.) and Berenice (28?–after 81 C.E.)—in addition to appointing the high priests and overseeing the Temple treasury, all maintained houses in Jersualem, though only Agrippa I actually ruled Judaea. On the other hand, the old religious organizations of the Pharisees and Sadducees now functioned mainly as sects, and though they retained some influence among the temple staff and bureaucrats ("the scribes" of the New Testament and rabbinic literature) and were numerous in Jerusalem, they were of little importance elsewhere in the country. Furthermore, some of the more stable revolutionary organizations, like the Sicarii (Latin for "assassins"), and messianic groups, like the Christians, assumed in the course of the first century a sectarian character.

By the fifties and sixties, the Roman governors were without exception corrupt and oppressive. Some of them, unable to suppress the brigand and revolutionary groups, hired them as private extortionists and assassins. The high priests and minor Herodians had their own private armies of slaves and dependants, whom they exploited as *their* extortionists and assassins—oppressing their social inferiors and fighting each other, their family relationship and shared privilege having generated not cohesion but contention and jealousy. The royal Herodians, for their part, tried to play their traditional role as intermediaries between the Jews and Rome, but were increasingly losing their grip.

Early in 66, disturbances erupted throughout the country. For the most part, these were symptoms not of hostility to Roman rule but of its collapse. In the cities in and near Palestine, rioting between Jews and "Greeks," as pagans were called regardless of their ethnicity or language, resulted in a series of massacres, in most places of the Jews, but in Tiberias of the Greeks. There were also battles between cities, and between cities and the peasants of the surrounding countryside. In Jerusalem, meanwhile, the Roman governor, Florus, provoked an uprising by plundering the Temple treasury, and tried to quell the rising by force, but had to flee the city. Agrippa II attempted to restore the peace, but he, too, was forced to flee. In early summer 66, Cestius Gallus, the governor of neighboring Syria, arrived with a force of legionary troops but unexpectedly withdrew before even trying to gain control of the city, thereby granting a decisive victory to the revolutionary party in Jerusalem.

The leaders of this party were mainly wealthy young men, especially high priests. They now attempted to coordinate the scattered uprisings in the Palestine countryside, sending out agents to wrest control from the various brigand chiefs and country landlord/adventurers around whom the local risings had coalesced. But the Jerusalemites were largely unsuccessful. When the emperor Nero dispatched a large army to Palestine under the command of the eminent Roman senator Vespasian and his son Titus, in 67, the revolt outside Judaea quickly collapsed, and the main local rebel leaders, John of Gischala, in Galilee, and Simon bar Giora, in Idumaea and Peraea, fled to Jerusalem with groups of armed followers. There they seized control of the revolt and proceeded to fight each other.

Vespasian, meanwhile, had become embroiled in the Roman civil war that erupted after the assassination of Nero in 68, and in the summer of 69 had himself declared emperor by his troops and marched on Rome to seize the throne, leaving the quelling of the revolt to Titus. In spring 70, with the Judaean countryside subdued, Titus laid siege to Jerusalem. The city, packed with refugees, soon began to starve. On 17 Panemos (Tammuz=June/July), the priests ran out of lambs and the Temple cult came to a halt. Three weeks later, on 10 Loos (Ab=July/August), the Roman troops set the Temple on fire, according to Josephus' account, against Titus' wishes. There is no doubt, though, that the Roman troops committed a massive slaughter. Josephus states that 1,100,000 Jews were killed. This is surely incorrect: the entire population of Palestine, Jewish and pagan, is unlikely to have exceeded 1 million. Nevertheless, Josephus was present at the siege, in the Roman camp (he defected in 67); though he may have guessed incorrectly, he was certainly right in thinking that the death toll was very large. He also claimed that 97,000 Jews were enslaved—a more plausible number that could have been based on records: the Roman army is more likely to have counted prisoners than corpses.

The following month, the army razed what was left of Jerusalem. Vespasian now officially transformed Palestine into a Roman province, named Judaea, and in the process stripped the Jews of the autonomy they had continued to enjoy in a limited way even after the death of Herod. The self-governing Jewish state, brought into formal existence by the Persian kings in the sixth century B.C.E., now ceased to exist.

2

THE MAKING OF THE DIASPORA

Oded Irshai

Seventy C.E. *is one of the fateful dates in Jewish history: the Jerusalem Temple, the focus of the Jewish world, and its spiritual center, was burned down by Roman soldiers. The city was left in ruins, and the treasures of the Temple were paraded in triumph in Rome. The pretext for the Roman invasion was a revolt launched in 66* C.E. *by Jewish nationalists impatient with Roman rule. Resentment had been smoldering for decades, an explosive mixture of religious sensibility and national pride heightened by anger at the burdens of taxation and the insult of foreign occupation. That the rebels managed to keep the might of Rome at bay for four years seems almost incredible; in fact isolated pockets of resistance held out for another three years, the last Zealot stronghold to fall being Herod's fortress palace of Masada, overlooking the Dead Sea. Sixty years later, the embers of Judaean revolt flared up again under the revolutionary leader Bar Kosiba (d. 135), commonly known as Bar Kochba. This uprising, which lasted from 132 to 135, was crushed by the Romans, and the political aspirations of the Jews seemed to be definitively ended.*

What enabled the Jewish people to survive these two national catastrophes was in great measure the existence of the Diaspora, a network of communities extending over large parts of the Roman and Persian empires. This chapter tells the story of the Diaspora from its beginnings to the time when these great empires were taken over by two new religions, Christianity and Islam. But it must be emphasized that important though the Diaspora was for the survival of Judaism, the Land of Israel was by no means emptied of Jewish life during this period. Indeed, as we shall see, this was where

Opposite: A man holding up an open scroll: mural painting from the synagogue of Dura-Europos on the Euphrates. This lavishly decorated synagogue (dedicated 244/245 C.E.) is among the most impressive remains of Diaspora Judaism. This picture is part of a group surmounting the Torah shrine, and probably represents the public reading of the Torah, one of the principal activities that took place in the synagogue.

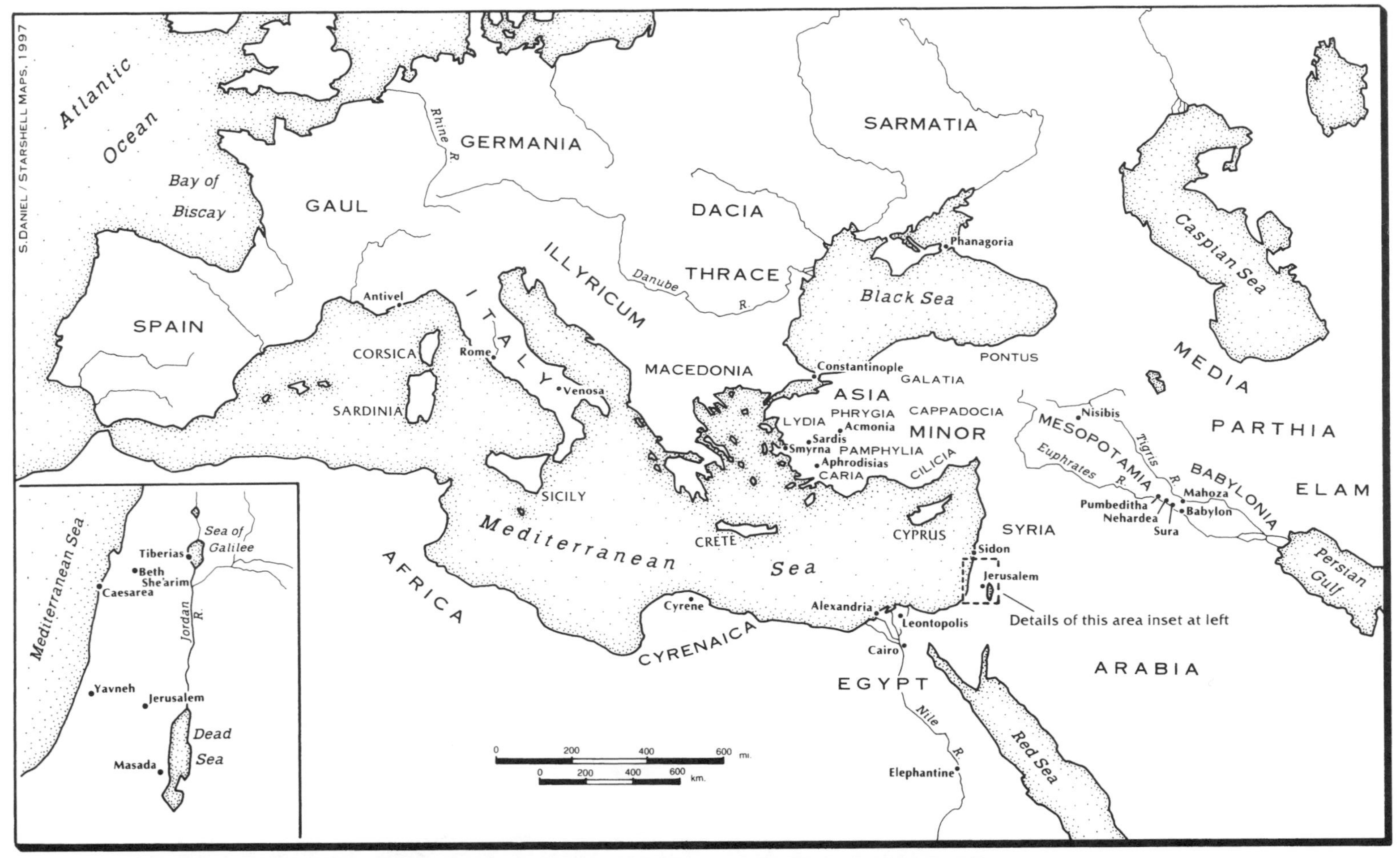

The Growth of the Diaspora in the Early Middle Ages

major developments in Jewish religious culture took place, ones that were to enrich the life of the Diaspora. A continuing tension between the Land of Israel and the Diaspora is a marked feature of our story.

IMAGES OF THE DIASPORA: (586 B.C.E. TO C. 650 C.E.)

The term *Diaspora*, commonly used today to designate the Jews living outside Israel, comes from a Greek word meaning "dispersion." It stands in sharp contrast to the biblical term *galut*, "exile." Though both indicate a relationship to a center, they denote two very different outlooks, representing different historical situations. Whereas *galut* reflects the earlier biblical notion of punishment by banishment, *diaspora* is closer in tone and content to the Greek idea of colonization. (Even before the conquests of Alexander the Great, the Greek cities had been sending out willing citizens to colonize territories in the Mediterranean area.) Thus, contradictory notions of exile and diaspora are scattered throughout the rabbinical sources, reflecting a variety of attitudes as well as differing historical contexts.

The idea of exile is ingrained in biblical thought. The Land of Israel was always considered a gift bestowed by God on the people of Israel, hence the importance of the idea of the Promised Land. However, the people of Israel deemed this inheritance a privilege that they had to be worthy of, and believed that should they fail in this charge, the land would be taken away from them. Much of biblical historiography revolves around this belief. The danger of exile, to which Israel became exposed following the rise of the Assyrian Empire in the eighth century B.C.E., brought about a mood of self-examination and led to the recognition that the prerequisite for maintaining the land was the fulfillment of God's commandments.

Thus the exile of the people of Israel was seen as a punishment for sins such as idolatry, violation of the Sabbath and injustice according to the precepts of the Biblical Priestly Code. One of the most outstanding sins for which the Israelites suffered exile was the violation of the cycle of sabbatical year. The essence of this law was the requirement to leave land fallow every seventh year, and to free all Hebrew slaves, remit all debts and restore lands to their original owners every fiftieth year. The grave repercussions of transgressing these commandments are stated in the Book of Leviticus (26:34): "Then shall the land make up for its Sabbaths; for all the time that it lies desolate and you are in the land of your enemies the land shall rest and make up for its Sabbaths." This was later reiterated in 2 Chronicles 36:19–21: "And they [the Babylonians] burnt the house of God . . . to fulfill the word of the Lord by the mouth of Jeremiah: Until the land has made up for its Sabbaths; for all the time that it lay desolate it rested to complete seventy years."

The seventy years' exile prophesied by Jeremiah (25:9–12), however, came to be seen as more than punishment. Exile served in the eyes of later prophets like Zechariah (1:12; 4:9) and in the eyes of the Chronicler as the keynote of a "realized eschatology" of redemption and restoration of the Temple and the Land, indeed the inauguration of a new era. Exile was thus established as a central concept in Jewish thought at the very start of the Second Temple era (515–70 B.C.E.).

The story of the early exiles was explained in the previous chapter. The Bible records two exiles to the east (in 721 and 586 B.C.E.). The earlier was that of the northern Kingdom of Israel or Samaria, known as the exile of the ten tribes. The later was that of the southern Kingdom of Judah. The fate of the ten tribes was and still is a great enigma, and during the Middle Ages it served as the basis for a powerful and enduring myth in Jewish as well as in Christian circles (the myth of Prester John). Thus the historical tradition concerning the exiled Jews was reduced to the exile of 586 B.C.E.: the tribe of Judah and the neighboring tribe of Benjamin (in addition to the landless tribe of the Levites, who served a particular function in the people's religious life).

At the same time as the Babylonians were carrying off the populations of Judah and Benjamin, other exiles were fleeing to Egypt, according to the account found in Jeremiah. The importance of the emergence of the Babylonian and Egyptian Diasporas (with whose roots we shall deal later on) exceeds the bare fact that these were the first examples of Jews living in exile. The Babylonian and Egyptian Diasporas emerged as the largest and most influential centers of Judaism in the period under discussion, and were instrumental in the formation of Jewish institutions and culture, especially after the destruction of the historical center in Israel.

We can study the history of these two centers in the immense papyrological documentation on many aspects of daily life in Egypt covering the period between the third century B.C.E. and the fifth century C.E., and also in the voluminous halakhic (legal) texts, such as the Babylonian Talmud and later responsa literature consisting of rabbinic replies to questions from the public. The discovery of the Cairo Genizah manuscripts in 1896 has provided historians with the largest and most elaborate documentation of the lives of the Jews under Muslim rule from the tenth century onward. Inevitably much of our discussion will focus on the history of those two centers.

Babylonian Beginnings

The Babylonian Exile, followed by the Persian conquest in 538 B.C.E. and annexation of Mesopotamia, was an entirely new experience for the Judaean deportees. They came into contact with the natives and with members of other nations: Cilicians, Elamites and others. The period of Persian rule was notable for a sharp increase in intermarriage and the syncretization of cultures and religious beliefs. The Jews, like other groups, were scattered throughout the country and integrated into the local economy, owned their own land, served in the administration, took Babylonian names and spoke Aramaic, the language used throughout the Persian territories.

Modern research on the Diaspora has placed strong emphasis on choice of names, regarding their study as an important tool in the assessment of cultural assimilation. Among the exiles, we encounter a fair number of names based on local deities, such as the Babylonian god Bel and the Persian Mithras, and in Egypt deities such as Isis. In this context it is interesting to note a later rabbinical tradition, originating in a time of strong Greek influence, praising the Israelites who returned from Egypt for retaining their Jewish names (Leviticus Rabbah 32:5).

Though it is difficult to penetrate the internal life of the Jews during their first few centuries in Babylon, we have some hints pertaining to their communal institutions. It seems that they were governed and judged by a body of elders (*zeqenim*). Foreign residents of Babylonian cities had the right to their own communal organization. Although the exiles appear to have immersed themselves comfortably in their new environment, biblical traditions disclose their fervent expectation of the downfall of Babylon and their return to Zion (Isaiah 61:3; Jeremiah 28:9). At the heart of this expectation lay a spiritual dilemma. The notion of a territorial god, whose power was confined to his own land, was prevalent during that period. Thus the banished Israelites were no longer under the jurisdiction of their god, who was scorned for forsaking his children and not being able to save his city from destruction. Were they to change their religious allegiance and worship local deities for protection? The fierce campaign against the foreign gods of wood and stone waged by the prophets Isaiah, Jeremiah and Ezekiel may be evidence of apostasy among the exiles. There was, however, another option. Divine protection could be secured by transferring the deity from his home country to the foreign land. Mesopotamian traditions reveal that this was done with other deities, and the prophet Ezekiel (11:16) hints at that as well with the God of Israel.

An incantation bowl. Many hundreds of such bowls have been found in Babylonia and Mesopotamia, buried upside down in the foundations of buildings, to protect them against demons and other evil influences. They give us a fascinating insight into practical Jewish magic in the talmudic period.

The Babylonian Diaspora became prototypical of Diaspora communities. The society of the exiles managed in a relatively short period to integrate itself into the local society and create within itself some sort of attachment to the new environment (Jeremiah 29:5–7). This was consistent with Jeremiah's advice to the exiles (29:5–7): "To all the exiles whom I have carried off from Jerusalem to Babylon: Build houses and live in them, plant gardens and eat their produce; marry wives and beget sons and daughters . . ." Alongside this attachment, there was ambivalence toward the historical center in Judaea; the exiles nourished their expectation of a return to Zion, but when given the opportunity many preferred to stay in the new land they had grown accustomed to living in. Finally, the Jews in the Diaspora were able to create for themselves cultural and religious institutions to compensate for their separation from their original center of worship. Despite their scorn for the local deities, they may in some cases have adopted some sort of allegiance to them; in other instances, admittedly very few, they transferred their God to their new dwelling place by creating a cultic center with a temple resembling the one in Judaea. We have a hint of this in Babylon, and clear evidence of temple worship among the exiles in Egypt.

Egypt

The temple at Elephantine was unearthed in the early part of this century, with papyrus documents (see page 9) pertaining to the life and institutions of this remotest of communities. Our earliest evidence concerning the cult in this temple dates to the years just following its destruction. Among the papyri is a letter sent in 408 B.C.E. from Yedonia, the chief priest and leader of the Elephantine community, to Bigvai, the Persian viceroy in Judaea, requesting him to order the rebuilding of the temple, destroyed three years previously owing to the machinations of the Egyptian authorities in collaboration with the local Persian governor. In his letter, Yedonia states that "Already in the days of the kings of Egypt our fathers had built that temple in the fortress of Yeb, and when Cambyses came into Egypt he found that temple built, and the temples of the Gods of Egypt all of them they overthrew, but no one did any harm to that temple."

This unique document demonstrates how a Diaspora community, though still dependent on the authorities in the Judaean center, managed to create for itself a comprehensive communal and religious institution to guide and lead its members. Other documents refer to the Elephantine Jews' awareness of the celebration of the Sabbath and the Feast of Passover and that of the Unleavened Bread. This awareness can be gleaned, too, from the recurrence of the names Shabbethai and Haggai (derived from the noun *hag*, meaning "festival") in local documents. Both the Sabbath and the festival of Passover were closely associated with the covenant between God and Israel, and their observance indicates affiliation to the Israelite community. The Elephantine Jews intermarried with local Egyptians who assimilated into the Jewish community. The Elephantine community left few traces, but its example of a social and cultic organization was to be followed during the Ptolemaic period, in the early stages of the formation of the Hellenistic Jewish community.

Not much is known about the development of the Jewish community in Egypt following the demise of the Elephantine settlement early in the fourth century. After Alexander the Great's conquest of the east, the Ptolemies ruled over the region that included Egypt and Palestine. An early Jewish tradition from Egypt attributes the establishment of a large local Jewish community in the early Ptolemaic period to Ptolemy I Soter (305–282 B.C.E.), who allegedly settled 100,000 Jews from Judaea in Egypt, 30,000 of them in military garrisons in different districts (Letter of Aristeas, 12–13). From that period (late fourth century B.C.E.), we have evidence of some of the earliest encounters reflecting the Greeks' genuine interest in the Jewish people. It was either Ptolemy I or his successor, Ptolemy II Philadelphos (282–246 B.C.E.), who initiated a translation of the Torah into Greek. According to a later Jewish tradition, Demetrius of Phaleron, the royal librarian, associated with the foundation of the famous library of Alexandria, suggested making the translation of the Torah (Pentateuch). Accordingly, the king dispatched two envoys to Eleazar, the High Priest in Jerusalem, to request assistance. Eleazar sent seventy-two elders, six from each tribe of Israel, to Alexandria, together with a trustworthy copy of the Torah. The elders managed to perform their task within seventy-two days. The Greek version was then read and approved by the Alexandrian Jews and the king. In the first century C.E., Philo of Alexandria added to this legend the location where the translators performed their work in complete seclusion, the island of Pharos off the shore of Alexandria. Philo emphasizes the miraculous elements of this literary enterprise: "Sitting here in seclusion with none present save the elements of nature, earth, water, air, the genesis of which was to be the first theme of their sacred revelation, for the laws begin with the story of the world's creation, they became as it were possessed and, under inspiration, wrote, not each several scribe something different, but the same word for word, as though dictated to each by an invisible prompter." He concludes with the following statement: "Therefore, even to the present day, there is held every year a feast and general assembly in the island of Pharos, whither not only Jews but multitudes of others cross the water, both to do honour to the place in which the light of that version first shone out, and also to thank God for the good gift so old yet ever young" (*Life of Moses*, 2, 37, 41). By Philo's time, the legend was well established and presumably the original circumstances of the enterprise were forgotten. It has been suggested that the translation into Greek was meant in the first place to respond to the demand of the local Jews for a sacred text for liturgical purposes. For two generations or more after the initial foundation of the Jewish community in Alexandria, knowledge of the Hebrew language among its members was in decline. It was the custom to read in public every Sabbath a portion of the law; there was considerable uncertainty, however, if the congregants were able to follow the reading in Hebrew. Whether it was the Jews or Demetrius of Phaleron who initiated the translation, it is quite plausible to assume that a copy did make its way to the famous Alexandrian library. This translation, commonly known as the Septuagint, meaning "seventy," (an allusion to the number of translators, who in one version of the legend numbered seventy rather than seventy-two). The most significant aspect of the legend lay in Philo's claim, supported by an early rabbinical tradition, that the translation of the Torah was carried out under divine guidance. Philo himself hoped that the entire "human race might be profited [by it] and [through it] led to a better life." He entertained the notion that the Torah might cause each nation to "abandon its peculiar customs, [and] turn to honoring our laws alone" (*Life of Moses*, 2, 36, 44). Although Philo was referring here to the original translation of the Pentateuch alone, by his day other parts of the Bible also had been rendered into Greek. From the second century C.E. onward, Christian writers began to ascribe the translation of the whole body of the sacred texts to the original divinely inspired elders. The Septuagint was to became one of the most important tools of Christian exegesis and polemics (much of it directed against the Jews).

The Ptolemaic period also witnessed the earliest significant production of Jewish prose literature about the past. Modeled on Greek compositions, and based on the conviction that history was of great importance in Greek culture, the works were intended to Hellenize what seemed to be a barbarous history. These works, which thus had a discernible apologetic tendency, were compiled for a Jewish as well as a gentile readership. The modest beginnings of this historical literature include the dialogue of questions and answers on the chronology of the ancient Israelites written by Demetrius the Chronographer, who flourished in the days of Ptolemy IV Philopator (222–205 B.C.E.). Some of the basic chronographical precepts laid down by Demetrius were accepted and adopted in later more elaborate chronographical systems. Thus Abraham's election by God was regarded as the opening of a new era, and the date Moses received the Law was held to predate the events in Troy. The Greek Jewish literature expanded rapidly over the centuries. The important names came from Alexandria; the most famous among them was Philo, whose extensive philosophical readings of the Pentateuch have been preserved.

The choice of names, as attested in the papyri and inscriptions, demonstrates the presence of conflicting cultural tendencies. On the one hand we find a substantial number of Greek names (some of which were peculiar to the Jewish community), alongside local Egyptian names common among the rural folk. There is an abundance of Aramaic names, however, in the early period, and of Hebrew names, especially during the later Roman and Byzantine periods. The most surprising discovery is the frequent occurrence of the name Sambathion or Shabbetai (derived from the term Sabbath). A close study has shown that this name was not used solely by Jews. It became common among groups of gentile observers of the Sabbath, who in certain cases organized themselves as a religious association known as Sambathions.

The struggle for civil rights should be placed at the center of the story of Egyptian Jewry in antiquity. In a world where Jews were not easily recognizable in dress, speech, occupations or leisure pursuits, full civic rights meant full integration in local society. But if we are to go by the behavior of the Greek citizens and authorities of Alexandria during the late thirties of the first century C.E., this coveted social and civic status was far from secure. During the days of the Ptolemies, the Jews in Egypt enjoyed a certain civic status. This was the case particularly in newly founded cities like Alexandria, where the Jews were regarded as "colonists" in the same sense as the Greeks who settled foreign territories following the Macedonian conquest. This special status separated them from the native population. The distinctly sympathetic attitude of the Ptolemaic monarchy toward the Jews of Egypt manifested itself in many ways, but most prominently in their attentiveness to Jewish culture and literature, and in their protection of Jewish religious practices. In the same vein, the somewhat surprising approval of the project of erecting a Jewish temple in Leontopolis was granted by Ptolemy VI Philometor and his wife, Cleopatra II, only on the grounds that it was "in accordance with the Law" (Josephus, *Antiquities*, 13, 71). The acceptance of the Jews by Greek society did not lead to assimilation and weakening of their own identity; it did lead, however, to growing criticism of the most vehement type, in fact to the birth of a new literary genre of anti-Jewish literature. This in turn brought about the production of Jewish apologetic writings in response.

Contributing to the hatred of the Jews were the fundamental contradictions posed by their unique position in the Diaspora. On the one hand, they separated themselves from the pagan society, living as independently organized foreigners looking after their own religious affairs and keeping themselves entirely aloof from pagan worship. On the other hand, they took an active part in civic life, sharing rights and duties, in some places possessing the rights of full citizenship. The resentment felt toward them did not have political causes alone; lurking in the background was a cultural rift between Greeks and Jews. In the Boule [Council] Papyrus, written about 20 B.C.E., the anonymous writer urges the council to "take care that the pure(?) citizen body of Alexandria is not corrupted by men who are uncultured and uneducated," and although the Jews are not explicitly mentioned there is little doubt that the writer had them in mind. The Roman conquest of Egypt in 30 B.C.E. aggravated the paradoxical situation of the Jews. The Romans granted full civic rights only to the Hellenes (Greek citizens). Others, including the Jews, were regarded as second-class subjects. There was no real place for a third group between the Greeks and the Egyptian natives. The Jews therefore lost their long-held civic rights. In 38 C.E., under the emperor Gaius Caligula, the tension between the Jews and Greeks in Alexandria erupted into riots. The Roman governor, Flaccus, declared that the Jews were foreigners. Following Caligula's assassination in 41 C.E., his successor, Claudius, tried to pacify the situation. According to Josephus the emperor reaffirmed the privileges of the Jews (*Antiquities*, 19, 281–285). However, in a letter preserved by chance on papyrus, Claudius voices contrary sentiments. Although he admonishes the Alexandrians for renewing the conflict and warns against the continued violence and enmity, he clearly sees the Jews as no more than longstanding inhabitants of the city and orders them "not to aim at more than they have previously had." The Ptolemaic golden age was never to return. For the Jews of Egypt, the riots of 38–41 C.E. inaugurated an extended period of tension with their neighbors. Events came to a head in the time of the emperor Trajan, when riots broke out between Jews and Greeks in Alexandria in 115 C.E. and spread a year later all over Egypt and neighboring Cyrenaica. The events were described much later by Eusebius of Caesarea, the father of Church history, in his *Ecclesiastical History*, in the following manner:

> In the course of the eighteenth year of the Emperor [Trajan] a rebellion of the Jews again broke out and destroyed a great multitude of them. For both in Alexandria and in the rest of Egypt and especially in Cyrene, as though they had been seized by some terrible spirit of rebellion, they rushed into sedition against their Greek fellow citizens, and increasing the scope of the rebellion in the following year started a great war. . . . [After initial success of the Jews] the Emperor sent against them Marcius Turbo with land and sea forces including cavalry. He waged war vigorously against them in many battles for a considerable time and killed many thousands of Jews not only those of Cyrene but also those of Egypt.

The crushing of this widespread Jewish sedition marked the demise of that flourishing Jewish center for centuries to come. Egyptian Jewry was to resume its leading role in the Diaspora only around the second half of the ninth century. But though, as we learn from our scanty sources from the late Roman and early Byzantine periods, Jews continued to live in the rural areas of Egypt as they did in Alexandria, their central organization as well as their longstanding image as a flourishing cultural and political Diaspora center were definitely shattered. Though a bloodbath of immense proportions did indeed occur, it is difficult to accept as a fact the total demise of that Jewish community. The question thus remains: What happened to Egyptian Jewry after 117 C.E.? The early history of Christianity in Egypt might offer a clue. Christianity in Egypt during the first two centuries had strong Jewish affiliations, and the fact that there are so few traces of Christianity from that period reflects that in the eyes of the local Greeks

Christianity was just another brand of Judaism, hence the weak missionary activity of the Christians. It may be plausibly assumed that following the horrific outcome of the riots in Trajan's days Jews in great numbers joined the ranks of the emerging Christian community.

Asia Minor

Asia Minor occupies a very important place in our understanding of the Diaspora in the Greek and Roman period, because of the large amount of surviving evidence, both archaeological and literary. The origins of the Jewish settlement here are shrouded in mist. The earliest clear evidence refers to King Antiochus the Great (223–187 B.C.E.), who is said to have settled 2,000 Jewish families from Mesopotamia and Babylon in Phrygia and Lydia (Josephus, *Antiquities*, 12, 147–153). From then on until well into the period of the later Roman Empire, although the Jews were not granted full rights they played an active part in civic life. In exchange for contributing to the finances of the cities, they were granted exemption from participating in the pagan rites. The Jews of Asia Minor assimilated into the local cultural milieu, and it seems that on the whole they were accepted by the local gentile society. It is important to stress the sometimes-neglected fact that their presence was not accompanied by large-scale outbursts of violence like those recorded in Alexandria during the first and early second centuries C.E. They did not take part in any of the Jewish riots and uprisings against Roman rule reported elsewhere at that period. Literary as well as epigraphic evidence presents a history of Jewish coexistence with other minorities over an extended period, characterized, however, by complex interactions and extreme contrasts. For although the communities of Asia Minor (and of Greece) stood at the center of opposition and hostility toward the early Christian mission founded by Paul in the mid-first century C.E., those communities were also the first to succumb to this missionary movement.

The history of the Jews of Sardis serves as an example of the complex connections Jews forged with their neighbors in Asia Minor. As early as the first century B.C.E., the local Jews were granted relative autonomy, authorized to bring their disputes before their own court and permitted to practice their religious customs unhindered. Jews were, it seems, very much part of the social fabric, which is borne out by the fact that the local synagogue (a vast and elaborate construction discovered in 1962) was situated in the heart of the town's Roman forum. In fact the basilica-style synagogue, which was in use from the second century C.E. until the early seventh (being remodeled during the fourth century), was originally constructed as part of a large public bath and gymnasium complex.

There are other indications of Jewish influence on the surrounding populace. Inscriptions discovered in Asia Minor (particularly in the city of Aphrodisias in Caria) reveal the existence of a large group of gentile sympathizers named the "Godfearers" attached to the Jewish community. Whether we regard them as a kind of a middle group between Jews and gentiles, or Christians with some distinct leanings toward Jewish beliefs and practices, or, as has recently been claimed, people who merely sought social patronage by the Jewish communities, their existence bears witness to the strong influence of the Jews in that region, and perhaps in other parts of the Diaspora.

Jewish-Christian relations were an important ingredient of the cultural and social atmosphere in Asia Minor. Jewish presence coupled with apostolic tradition consolidated a local practice of celebrating Easter on the same day that the Jews, according to their own calendar, customarily celebrated Passover. This stood in sharp contrast to the custom in other Christian centers. The legitimacy of such a tradition and especially its dependence on the Jewish calendar calculations were to become a perennial issue within Christian circles, debated time and again in Church councils.

The menorah or seven-branched lampstand is one of the commonest Jewish symbols in late antiquity, both in Israel and in the Diaspora. We can only guess at what it symbolized; probably it evoked a variety of religious allusions beyond a simple assertion of Jewish identity: the hope of the rebuilding of the temple (Zechariah 4), the Torah as the light of the world. This Byzantine gold votive medallion, thought to date from the eighth century C.E., is inscribed in Greek: "For the vow of Jacob the leader [of the synagogue?], the pearl-dealer."

Christians often complained that the Jews tried to undermine their missionary activity. In the mid-third century, the famous Christian martyr Pionius cried out in anger to the crowds of Smyrna attending his trial, "I understand that the Jews have been inviting some of you to their synagogues. Beware lest you fall into a greater, more deliberate sin . . . Do not become with them rulers of Sodom and people of Gomorra whose hands are tainted with blood. We did not slay our prophets nor did we betray Christ and crucify him."

If we are to accept at face value the descriptions and traditions in the Acts of the Christian Martyrs, the Jews of Asia Minor served as active agitators in the persecution of Christians.

Nor were the Christian communities themselves immune from internal Judaizing tendencies. In his epistle to the Philadelphians, the second-century bishop Ignatius warned against the division and strife caused by the two factions within the local Christian community, the circumcised Jewish Christians and the gentile Christians.

The Jews of Asia Minor on the whole present a pluralistic way of life with much willingness to share their culture with the native population. Here and in other parts of the Roman Empire there existed a pluralistic society containing subgroups with differing religious tendencies. Recent writers have labeled it as essentially a "society of choice," in which people altered their views and sympathies freely.

Italy

Jews settled in Rome most probably during the second century B.C.E. Nothing is known of their origins. As early as 139 B.C.E., they were temporarily expelled from the city, apparently for proselytizing activities, a clear proof of antagonism created by their strong influence. In the mid-first century B.C.E., Julius Caesar granted the Jews of Rome permission to create their own private associations or *collegia* (essentially synagogues organized as social institutions), at the same time denying others the same privilege. No wonder that the Jews particularly mourned his assassination in 44 B.C.E. His legacy was maintained during most of the period of the Julio-Claudian dynasty, which lasted until 68 C.E. In the course of that period, we witness the formation of different "synagogue communities" in Rome carrying titles like "Augustesians," most probably after Augustus, or "Agripesians" after Marcus Agrippa. Most of our knowledge about these synagogue

Another menorah, this time on a fourth-century C.E. sarcophagus discovered in the Jewish catacomb of the Vigna Randanini in Rome. The Jewish symbol coexists strikingly here with motifs representative of pagan art, such as personifications of the seasons and the three putti treading grapes. The menorah occupies the space normally used for a portrait of the deceased.

communities emanates from inscriptions discovered in the Roman catacombs; they operated as separate and autonomous entities. Like the Jews in Asia Minor, the Jews in Rome lacked any form of central authority.

Augustus and his lifelong friend Marcus Agrippa merited the honor bestowed on them by the Jews for laying the foundations of a modus vivendi between the Jews and the Roman authorities in the entire empire. For instance, Augustus had allowed the Jews to send their annual tax to the Temple in Jerusalem. Their growing power and numbers and their close ties with the court enabled the Jews of Rome to gather 8,000 of their people in a demonstration following Herod's death, to protest against the handing over of the Judaean kingdom to his sons, who were regarded as foreign kings. Just as in Asia Minor, the Jews of Rome were active proponents of Judaism; Horace writes that they tried to "compel others to their throng" (*Sermones*, 1, 142–143). Among their achievements was their ability to influence members of the senatorial circle, some of them close relatives of the emperors themselves. These activities and the public disturbances caused by the appearance of the Christians on the local scene (starting from the early days of the emperor Claudius) brought about tension that resulted in yet another limited expulsion of Jews from Rome and created a wave of attacks on the Jews in the gentile literature of the period. However, neither this nor the traumatic event of the destruction of the Jerusalem Temple (resulting in the transfer of a great number of captives to Rome) hindered the steady development of the Jewish community. Between the second and the fourth centuries, new synagogues were established mainly beyond the Tiber and in the nearby port of Ostia.

The presence of a fairly large Jewish community in Rome (estimated in Tiberius' days to have numbered between 30,000 and 50,000) placed it in a unique position, especially as regards the contacts between the Roman authorities and the Jewish leadership in Palestine both before and after the destruction of the Jerusalem Temple. The local Jews witnessed a succession of visits of official or semiofficial delegations. These embassies were not surprising when Judaea was under the yoke of Jewish client kings such as Herod the Great and his successors, and perhaps even less so when the region was governed by Roman officials. After the fall of the Temple, however, Rome began to receive emissaries sent by the central rabbinical leadership in Palestine. Second-century rabbinical sources describe these embassies as comprising some of the most eminent rabbinical authorities of the time, such as Gamaliel and Akiba. The repeated visits of these sages to Rome might have facilitated the creation of a local center of learning. Though we possess very little knowledge concerning the local sages, in the absence of evidence from other Jewish Diaspora centers this personal contact with Palestinian rabbis appears to have been a unique phenomenon in the western Diaspora.

Gentile Romans who adopted Jewish customs and beliefs are described with disdain in a passage in one of Juvenal's satires: "Some, having a father who reveres the Sabbath, worship nothing but the clouds and the spirit of the sky, and see no difference between eating swine's flesh, from which their father abstained, and that of man. Soon they even take to circumcision. Flouting the laws of Rome, they learn and practise and revere the Jewish law, handed down by Moses in a secret scroll, forbidden to show the way to anyone not observing the same rites."

Juvenal's satire came at the period when Jewish influence on gentiles had reached its peak. During the two decades following the destruction of the Temple, members of the Roman aristocracy began to take active interest in Judaism. In the year 95 C.E., the emperor Domitian slew, along with many others, the consul Flavius Clemens, who was his own cousin, and his wife, Flavia Domitilla, on the charge of "atheism"—drifting into Jewish ways.

GROWTH OF THE DIASPORA: MIGRATION OR CONVERSION?

What were the means by which Jewish communities arose nearly all over the antique world? For this was the case, according to the writer of the Acts of the Apostles, who described in these terms the origins of those who came on pilgrimage to Jerusalem during the first century: "Parthians and Medes and Elamites and the dwellers in Mesopotamia and in Judaea and in Cappadocia, in Pontus and Asia, Crete and Pamphylia, in Egypt and in the parts of Libya about Cyrene and strangers of Rome, Jews and proselytes, Cretans and Arabians . . ." (Acts 2:5–11). The same impression was conveyed by the Roman historian and geographer Strabo, who lived in the time of the Roman emperor Augustus: "This people has made its way into every city, and it is not easy to find any place in the habitable world which has not received this nation and in which it has not made its power felt" (quoted by Josephus, *Antiquities,* 14, 115). Strabo's statement is corroborated by other Greek and Roman writers, who also remarked on the supposed populousness of the Jews.

Strabo offered the following explanation: "And so this nation has flourished in Egypt because the Jews were originally Egyptians and because those who left that country made their homes near by, and they migrated to Cyrene because this country bordered . . . Egypt, as did Judaea." (Strabo, quoted by Josephus, *Antiquities*, 14, 118). Indeed, it is widely accepted that big waves of migration in different periods could account for the wide dissemination of Jewish settlements all over the Greco-Roman world and even beyond its boundaries in the Persian Empire.

Jews migrated for different reasons. The overpopulation of Judaea in the early Seleucid period brought about a wave of migration to other parts of Israel and Egypt in the hope of finding greater economic prosperity. The Babylonian and Egyptian communities sent offshoots to Asia Minor and Cyrenaica respectively. Waves of forced migration were caused by religious persecutions preceding the Hasmonean Revolt in Judaea (167–164 B.C.E.), later internal strife and civil wars, as well as the transfer of large numbers of captives and slaves taken in the course of crushing rebellions against the Greek or Roman authorities, in Israel or in other countries. As we saw earlier, Ptolemy I is said to have transported 100,000 Jews from Judaea to Egypt. Philo attributed the formation of a Jewish community in Rome to the release of many Jewish captives brought there at an early date (*Embassy to Gaius*, 155). Indeed, migration and colonization were the headings under which Philo himself chose to describe the phenomenon of the Jewish dispersion. Using these terms in their Greek context, he ventured to demonstrate to his auditors the bond between the center (Jerusalem) and the communities in the Diaspora. "For so populous are the Jews that no country can hold them, and therefore they settle in very many . . . countries in Europe and Asia, both in the islands and on the mainland. And while they hold the Holy City where stands the sacred Temple of the most high God to be their mother city, yet those [lands] which are theirs by inheritance from their fathers, grandfathers and ancestors even further back are in each case accounted by them to be their fatherland: to some of these they came as immigrants, at the time of their foundation, with the blessing of the founders."

Migration hardly accounts for the numbers of Jews in the Diaspora attested to in the sources. Migration and natural growth cannot alone account for Philo's testimony (even if exaggerated) that in his time there were a million Jews in Egypt alone, and that in Alexandria two out of five quarters of the city were densely populated with Jews (*Against Flaccus*, 43, 55). These statements, placed against an estimated population of Alexandria of about 300,000 free citizens, do call for some explanation. In order to explain these and other testimonies concerning the size of the Jewish population in the Diaspora, it has been suggested that the Jews were engaged from an early period in an active proselytizing mission among the gentiles. The evidence for this widely accepted theory seems at first glance to be quite extensive.

Two of the most famous early rabbinical figures, Shemaya and Abtalion (second half of the first century B.C.E.) were said to have been descendants of

History of Matzoh, The Story of the Jews (Part I—Before the Diaspora), by Larry Rivers (1982). "This is the bread of affliction, as eaten by our ancestors in the land of Egypt." The meaning of Jewish history is fittingly encapsulated in concrete symbols such as the flat, dry wafer eaten instead of bread at Passover. The plainness of the matzoh contrasts with the richness of the history that it evokes. It conjures up poverty and affliction, migration, and above all a continuous history that can be traced back to very remote antiquity.

“My father was an Aramaean nomad.” The story of the Jews begins with wandering, and a way of life not dissimilar to that of Bedouin Arabs today *(top)*. After the Egyptian sojourn, the story moves on to the Land of Israel, and specifically to the city of Jerusalem, set among the hilly landscape of Judah *(bottom)*, from which the Jews take their name. It was here that King Solomon built the Temple to the one God, of which the tiny ivory pomegranate *(inset)* is a unique relic. Dated to the mid-eighth century B.C.E., it is inscribed, “Belonging to the Temple of the Lord, holy to the priests.” It may have originally topped a scepter carried by the priests.

LAURA LUSHINGTON/SONIA HALLIDAY PHOTOGRAPHS

WERNER BRAUN

(INSET) ISRAEL MUSEUM

JEWISH MUSEUM/ART RESOURCE

JEWISH MUSEUM/ART RESOURCE

The earliest history of the people is narrated in the Torah (the five books of Moses). The sequel is embroidered in the Prophetic Books and so-called Writings. Elijah, one of the greatest of the prophets, is remembered for his miracles *(top)*: here the sacrifice to the God of Israel is consumed by fire from heaven, proving his superiority over the pagan god Baal. The Book of Esther, from the Writings, tells how the Jews of the Persian Empire were rescued from a plot to annihilate them. Here the villainous vizier Haman parades the Jew Mordecai through the streets of the capital, dressed in royal apparel and mounted on the king's own horse. Both these paintings come from the richly decorated synagogue of Dura-Europos in present-day Syria.

CHRIS HELLIER/AAA

Of the numerous ancient synagogues excavated by archaeologists in recent times, few are as spectacular as that of Sardis in western Asia Minor. The large synagogue with its colonnaded forecourt was prominently situated in the center of the city, in a complex that included a bathhouse and gymnasium. Clearly the Jews of Sardis were confident of their place in their city and well integrated into its life.

ISRAEL ANTIQUITIES AUTHORITY

The great synagogue of Alexandria (represented in the top left of a mosaic found at Beth Shean in Israel) is completely lost. In its day it was regarded as one of the marvels of the Jewish world: "Whoever has never seen the double stoa of Alexandria in Egypt has never beheld the glory of Israel," said an ancient rabbi, Judah bar Ilai. In Israel, and especially in Galilee, the landscape was dotted with synagogues. Of the synagogue of Kefar Baram *(below)* in Upper Galilee, a fourteenth-century Jewish pilgrim wrote: "The synagogue of Rabbi Simeon bar Yohai is a most splendid structure, built of large, well-carved stones and huge columns. Never have I seen a more magnificent building!"

R. SHERIDAN/AAA

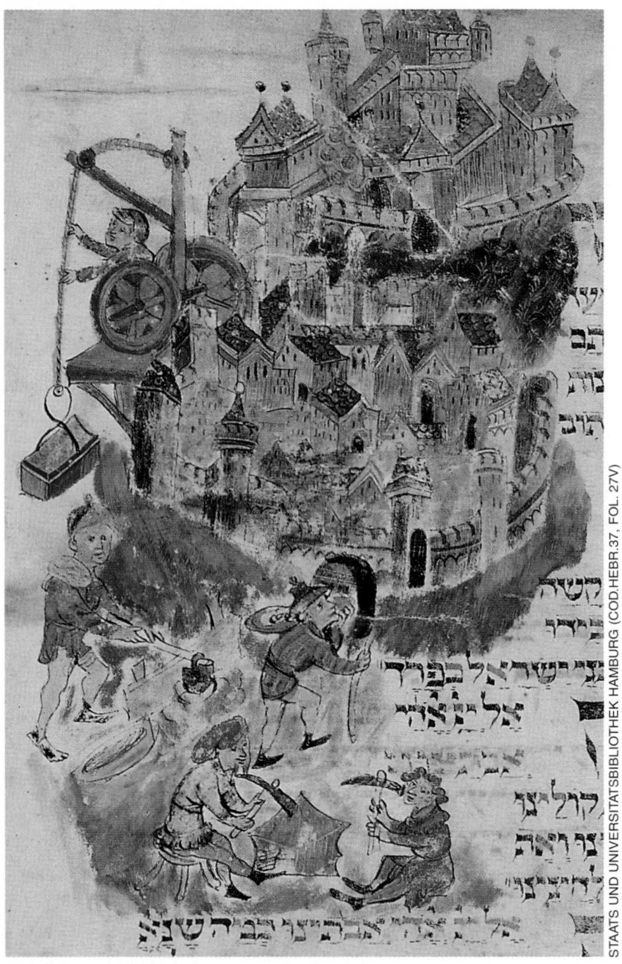

STAATS UND UNIVERSITATSBIBLIOTHEK HAMBURG (COD.HEBR.37, FOL. 27V)

BRITISH LIBRARY (ADD. 27210. FOL 15R)

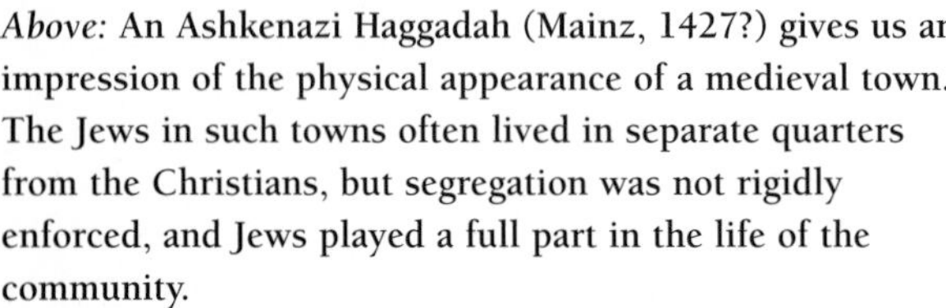

Above: An Ashkenazi Haggadah (Mainz, 1427?) gives us an impression of the physical appearance of a medieval town. The Jews in such towns often lived in separate quarters from the Christians, but segregation was not rigidly enforced, and Jews played a full part in the life of the community.

Above right: Manuscript illustrations afford us many a vivid glimpse of Jewish life in medieval Europe. A picture from the Golden Haggadah, painted in Barcelona in the early fourteenth century, shows the distribution of food to the needy at Passover. To be charitable is one of the highest duties of a Jew: it is known in Hebrew as *tzedakah*, "righteousness."

Right: Süsskind of Trimberg was a successful minnesinger (itinerant poet) in the thirteenth century. He sang of the virtue of woman and the nobility of man.

UNIVERSITATSBIBLIOTHEK HEIDELBERG

BIBLIOTHEQUE NATIONALE DE FRANCE (ITALIEN 973, FOL. 21V)

Guglielmo da Pesaro, a teacher of dancing and the author of one of the earliest extant treatises on the art of dancing, was one of a number of Jews who enjoyed the patronage of Lorenzo the Magnificent in fifteenth-century Florence. He later served the courts of Naples and Ferrara, and apparently ended his life as a Christian.

BRITISH LIBRARY

The Jews played an essential role in medieval society as bankers. It was often they who furnished the capital for major building works and other undertakings, and who administered the transfer of money from one place to another.

ERICH LESSING/ART RESOURCE

Of all the charges leveled at the Jews by Christians in the Middle Ages, the one that seems most unreasonable to us is that of "desecrating the Host" (see page 120). In this painting by Paolo Uccello (titled *The Desecration of the Host*), one of a series made for an altarpiece in 1465–69, a Jew who has bought a consecrated Host from a Christian woman tries to burn it in the presence of his family, but the wafer, identified in medieval Christian doctrine with the body of Christ, begins to bleed, while a Christian mob breaks down the door of his home. In the following scene, the whole family is burned at the stake.

proselytes from Babylon (Babylonian Talmud, Yoma 72 b). Forced mass conversions of gentiles were carried out by Hasmonean kings in the last decades of the second century B.C.E. among the Idumaeans in southern Palestine and the Ituraeans in the north (Josephus, *Antiquities,* 13, 257–58, 319). We also have the story of the conversion of the royal family of Adiabene, a small kingdom situated east of the Tigris in the ancient region of Assyria (Josephus, *Antiquities,* 20, 17–42). Other attempts to convert gentiles on a large scale resulted according to some traditions in the expulsion of the Jews. The Roman writer Valerius Maximus (beginning of the first century B.C.E.) explains that the expulsion of the Jews from Rome in the year 139 B.C.E. was carried out "because they attempted to transmit their sacred rites to the Romans." These instances and others have been adduced as proof that there was a large Jewish mission among the gentiles and that it was successful. The striking remark in the Gospel of Matthew 23:15: "Woe to you, scribes and Pharisees, that you cross land and sea to make one proselyte" seems to bear out this conclusion.

However, a contrary view holds that there was no missionary effort among the Jews at all. Accordingly, the instances alluded to above would be isolated cases that could be expounded in a different context or attributed to special circumstances. In addition, until the first century C.E., it was not entirely clear what conversion to Judaism meant or required from the aspiring convert. Was it enough to commit oneself to the practice of Jewish laws and exclusive devotion to the Jewish God? We also do not know if as early as the Hellenistic and early Roman periods a clear boundary existed between proselytes and Judaized sympathizers, such as the Egyptian Sambathions mentioned earlier and the Godfearers who established some social links with the local Jewish communities. It is now impossible to tell whether observers such as Philo were counting these groups among the Jews of the Roman world. In the context of our survey, one could ask whether the figures quoted above included those marginal groups. Therefore, it is difficult to give a clear answer to our initial question as to the reasons for the increase in the numbers of the Jews, particularly in the Diaspora.

COMMUNAL ORGANIZATION

The central institution in the life of the Jews in late antiquity was the synagogue, particularly in the Diaspora, where it served as a social and institutional vehicle by which the Jews disseminated their influence on the other ethnic and religious groups surrounding them.

The synagogue, apart from being a distinct architectural construction and the main gathering place of the congregants for liturgical and other purposes, was a social concept too. It was the embodiment of internal communal authority and the central institution through which the members of the congregation identified themselves as a religious association, by thus separating themselves from other religious groups. The local synagogue in most of the Diaspora regions served as an autonomous governing body, though it was never defined in legal terms.

Synagogues in Palestine and indeed in most of the Greco-Roman world, unlike those in Babylonia, served not only as houses of worship but as communal centers for social gatherings, public sermons and learning. It ought to be stressed that many of the Diaspora communities lacked central governing bodies; such bodies did exist, however, to some extent in Egypt and in a more prominent way in Babylon, which explains the vitality and duration of these Jewish settlements, and especially Babylon. The lack of such an organization and the particularization of the communities in Asia Minor, Rome and other regions (though they kept close ties with the Palestinian center) might account for the fact that the Jews in those areas did not take part in the series of uprisings against Rome.

Within the prevalent communal system, the key post was that of *archisynagogos* (head of the synagogue), a title that figures prominently in literary sources and inscriptions. He was assisted by other notables such as the *archon* ("ruler") or the *presbyter* ("elder"). The archisynagogos was a lay person and exercised no spiritual or liturgical functions. In many cases the archisynagogoi were honored as leading benefactors of the community; in some cases, as recorded in inscriptions, the title was hereditary. It is quite safe to assert that the archisynagogos was the distant forerunner of the lay leaders of the Jewish medieval communities better known from the responsa literature as the *parnasim* ("governors"). The archisynagogoi were well known to outsiders too, and in pagan and Christian eyes they represented the Jewish community in the Diaspora.

Those dignitaries retained their power and importance throughout the early Byzantine period, as can be gleaned from the imperial legislation recorded in the Theodosian Code. One of the most important functions of the archisynagogoi was presumably to cultivate ties with the Jewish Patriarch or Nasi in Israel, who was involved to a certain extent in the appointment of this Diaspora official.

The Consolidation of Synagogal Worship

The fall of Jerusalem in 70 C.E. cannot be regarded as the date when the Diaspora was born; however, it was the date at which it reached maturity. The worldview of the Jews and most certainly of those within the Greco-Roman orbit was entirely altered by that event. For during the centuries leading to the destruction of Jerusalem, Jewish writers had adopted the biblical idea of the centrality of Jerusalem and transformed it into a Greek-inspired concept of mythical geography, placing Jerusalem at the very center of the inhabited world—indeed describing it as the "Navel of the earth."

It was Philo, the proud representative of the Jewish community in Alexandria, who added to this rather amorphous concept a realistic touch. We have already seen how, describing the feelings Diaspora Jews had toward Jerusalem, Philo employed the well-known idea of the metropolis and its colonies. In *Special Laws* I, 68, he emphasized the importance of pilgrimage to the one and only place chosen by God for worship: "for he [God] judged that since God is one there should be also only one temple. Further he does not consent to those who wish to perform the rites in their houses, but bids them rise up from the ends of earth and come to this temple. In this way he also applies the severest test to their dispositions."

The early rabbis articulated this sense of holiness regarding the Land of Israel and Jerusalem by formulating a list of ten ascending degrees of holiness, at the top of which they placed the Temple's Holy of Holies into which "only the High Priest [once a year only] on the Day of Atonement . . . may enter" (Mishnah, Kelim 1, 9). Nine out of the ten degrees of holiness were allotted to Jerusalem and the Temple. The laws of cultic purity headed society's agenda, in the eyes of the rabbis who were the inheritors of the teachings of the Second Temple–period Pharisees. Jerusalem's fall thus created not only a tremendous sense of national catastrophe but a huge void in religious sentiment and practice too, not to mention the fact that the entire order of priesthood lost practically overnight much of its social esteem and centrality. The early Christians who opposed the rabbis triumphed in what they deemed a heavenly sign. In consequence, Christianity put even greater stress on its universal mission, retaining in its message little of Jerusalem's centrality.

In the wake of the spiritual and cultic vacuum brought about by the devastation of the Temple, the Palestinian rabbis sought to divert the course of the Jewish religious ethos, offering new directions, such as the popular study of the Torah and consolidation and institutionalization of synagogue worship. This shift concerned the Palestinian synagogues more than those in the Diaspora, in which prayers were already recited and the scriptures were expounded in public, as recorded by Philo: "They have houses of prayer and meet together in them, particularly on the sacred Sabbaths when they receive as a body training in their ancestral philosophy" (*Embassy to Gaius*, 156). However, during the period from 70 C.E. down to the seventh century and even later, substantial changes took place in synagogue worship.

The frescoes of Dura-Europos show how biblical paintings in synagogues complemented the public reading of the sacred text. Here, Pharaoh's daughter rescues the infant Moses from the Nile (Exodus 2:5). Later, perhaps under the influence of Christian and Muslim iconoclasm, Jews abandoned the use of such paintings in synagogues.

The Aramaic Targums—the verse-by-verse translations of the Torah into the Aramaic language—became more standardized, accompanying the weekly reading from the original Hebrew text of the scripture. Some of the Targums embodied allusions to the current rabbinical scriptural exegesis, enabling Jews who knew no Hebrew not only to follow the scriptures but also to obtain an interpretative reading of them. The Greek-language Septuagint fell out of favor among the rabbis, perhaps because, backed by its reputation of being a divinely inspired text, it had come to serve Christian missionary and polemical goals. As a result, during the early decades of the second century the rabbis sponsored a new Greek translation of the Bible, much closer to the Hebrew than the Septuagint translation. The end result, which was presented to the rabbis by a proselyte named Aquila, was received by them with much praise. However, both Greek translations continued to form an integral part of the public rite in the synagogues of the Roman (western) Diaspora, in which Greek remained the predominant language.

The scriptural translations were accompanied by yet another device of popular teaching, the public sermon. Some of these sermons were quarried together with other homilies and portions of biblical exegesis to form the great body of midrashic literature, which came to constitute a kind of running commentary on the scriptural readings. The sermons, together with the Aramaic Targums and the Greek translations, became an important vehicle in the popular dissemination of the Torah and its interpretation.

During the middle of the sixth century, in a period of mounting tension between Christians and Jews, the Byzantine emperor Justinian I intervened in an internal Jewish dispute concerning the use of languages in synagogue worship, and decreed the following:

> It was right and proper that the Hebrews, when listening to the Holy Books, should not adhere to the literal writings but look for the prophecies contained in them, through which they announce the Great God and the Savior of the human race Jesus Christ. . . . We decree, therefore, that it shall be permitted to those Hebrews who want it to read the Holy Books in their synagogues and, in general, in any place where there are Hebrews, in the Greek language before those assembled and comprehending, or possibly in our ancestral language (we speak of the Italian language), or simply in all the other languages. . . . We also order that there shall be no license to the commentators they have, who employ the Hebrew language to falsify it at their will, covering their own malignity by the ignorance of the many. Furthermore, those who read in Greek shall use the Septuagint tradition, which is more accurate than all the others. . . . Let all use mainly this translation; but in order that we shall not appear to prohibit them all other translations, we give permission to use also Akilas's [Aquila's] translation. . . . What they call Deuterosis [Mishnah], on the other hand, we prohibit entirely, for it is not included among the Holy Books . . . nor shall those who are called among them Archipherekitae [possibly those who delivered the public sermons] or possibly Presbyters or Didascaloi [teachers] have the license to hinder them from this by any deceits or excommunications.

What prompted Justinian to intervene in the synagogal service is unknown. Emerging unequivocally from this episode is the recognition by the imperial authorities, as well as by Jews, of the synagogue as a c institution in Jewish communal life. Indeed, synagog services were becoming increasingly recognized as th alternative to the Temple worship and cult.

A carved basalt seat from the synagogue of Chorazin in Galilee. The Aramaic inscription reads: "May Judah son of Ishmael who built this stoa and its staircase be remembered for good. As his reward may he have a share with the righteous."

During the early centuries of the Common Era, synagogal prayer underwent major developments. It is generally supposed that the formation of a fixed liturgy based on the format used in the Temple was begun by the rabbis of the Yavneh academy (founded shortly after the destruction of the Temple), and a grea achievement it was indeed. To this standard prayer fo mat, later generations (starting from the fourth to fift centuries) affixed a body of liturgical poetry original representing some sort of resistance toward standardiz forms of prayer but at the same time reflecting a strong devotional impetus that fixed prayer might have lacked. Apart from being a form of worship, early classical liturgical poetry contained in an artistic form rabbinical teachings and biblical exegesis and thus played an important role in the spreading of this body of learning. Its outstanding lexical richness and its ornate literary style disclose not only the unique qualities of the Hebrew language used at the time but also some borrowing from Greek and its literary conventions. Clearly the Greek language continued to play a role in the synagogues, because we find that during this period some Christians attended services. John Chrysostom, the bishop of Antioch, in a series of sermons delivered in the years 386–387 C.E., rebuked members of his community for attending the synagogues and observing Jewish festivals.

Jewish liturgical poetry continued to evolve and change in Palestine in the coming centuries and thus brought about the formation of a Palestinian Rite. From the tenth century, we witness the birth of new centers of liturgical poetry, the most influential among them being Babylon, where a distinct rite emerged. The standardized liturgy was slowly disseminated in the Diaspora during the early medieval period, making its way from Babylonia to Spain and from the Palestinian center to Egypt and Byzantium and via Italy (at the turn of the tenth century) to the early German Jewish communities in the Rhine Valley. Both liturgical trends shaped the later synagogal service; in fact, their influence is still felt today.

THE REDACTION AND CANONIZATION OF THE MISHNAH

In the aftermath of the fall of Jerusalem, the prevailing atmosphere among some Jewish circles in Judaea was of great grief—indeed, voices of extreme despair were calling for the self-annihilation of the Jewish people. Leading authorities among the rabbis headed by Yohanan ben Zakkai convened in Yavneh, a city in the Judaean plain, and began a process of spiritual as well as political restoration.

Under these grim circumstances arose the need to assemble, sort and codify the vast body of oral knowledge and tradition of the Torah known as Halakhah. The urge to do so was vividly portrayed by the rabbis themselves:

> When the sages came together in the vineyard of Yavneh, they said, "The time is coming at which a person will go looking for a teaching of Torah and will not find it, a teaching of Scribes and will not find it. Since it is said: 'Behold, the days are coming says the Lord God when I will send a famine on the land not a famine of bread, not a thirst for water but of hearing of the words of the Lord . . . but they shall not find it' " [Amos 8:11–12]. The word of the Lord refers to Prophecy. The word of the Lord refers to [the knowledge of] the End.
>
> Not one word of the Torah is the same as another word of the Torah. They said: Let us begin from [the rulings] of Hillel and Shammai [founders of the two early rabbinic schools] (Tosefta, Eduyot 1, 1).

Though the rabbis hinted at a need for consoling prophecy and apocalyptic visions, a need articulated and fulfilled in the apocalyptic literature of the period (such as the Fourth Book of Ezra, the Syriac Apocalypse of Baruch and the Christian Book of Revelations), they themselves opted for the consolidation of the Halakhah. This was the initial step on the long road that would lead to the redaction of the Mishnah by Rabbi Judah the Patriarch (Nasi) about 200 C.E.

One of the main goals of these scholars was to collect and codify the disparate body of halakhic rulings that had slowly evolved during the greater part of the Second Temple period. The method by which these rulings were arrived at is still enigmatic. Central to this method, however, was the interpretative process called *derashah*, by which the scriptures were painstakingly studied and inquired into in order to extract from them or to assess in their light various points of law. Exposition of scripture through derashah allowed for flexibility and originality in legal rulings; nevertheless, in the codification of the Halakhah, authentic oral tradition was regarded as more authoritative than innovative interpretations based on the exposition of scripture. Within this great cluster of oral traditions were many sectarian traditions too. There were significant practical differences between the Sadducees and Essenes on the one hand and the Pharisees on the other. The two former sects seemed to have dissolved during or as a result of the Great Revolt of 67–73 C.E. The latter, however, or at any rate their spiritual heirs, the rabbis, managed to sustain their power and transmit their halakhic traditions, and eventually to assemble them in the Mishnah.

The sources of the Mishnah were quite diverse. For instance, rulings concerning Temple worship, purity and priestly lineage that naturally originated in priestly circles were preserved predominantly by the priests. Along with descriptions of Temple ceremonies and processions, these formed some of the oldest layers of the Mishnah. Other rulings originated in testimonies concerning cases brought before the courts of law. The courtroom deliberations were omitted. At times the Mishnah contented itself with a brief outline of the case; at other times even these basic details were omitted and only the plain ruling was stated.

The transmission of the different traditions, from one rabbi to another or among organized groups of disciples, was a process as diverse as the sources from which the traditions arose. During the period of the Yavneh academy and in the following two generations, this gave rise to an array of expositions, interpretations and reasonings representing differing schools of halakhic thought and scriptural exegesis. At the same time during the greater part of the second century, the halakhic rulings were being assembled and arranged according to themes and categories. These various collections were finally redacted and codified by Rabbi Judah the Patriarch. The great merit of his work lies in the fact that he incorporated the available rulings, selected and combined various sources, laid down authoritative principles and decisions. In so doing he made the final redacted version of the Mishnah representative of the diverse circulating collections of teachings and ensured its universal acceptance.

Rabbi Judah's great project coincided with the initial efforts to canonize the New Testament in the second half of the second century C.E. Both enterprises served to enhance a powerful sense of unity in each camp.

The compilation of the Mishnah marked the peak of the Palestinian center's spiritual and political ascendancy; it also coincided with the initial signs of the parting of the ways with the Babylonian center. Mounting economic difficulties as a result of the Bar Kochba Revolt, which ended in 135 C.E., coupled with Roman religious persecution, had brought about not only a great decline in the Judaean Jewish population and a large migration to the Galilee, but a growing wave of migration to the Diaspora. This grave situation called for action. Palestinian sages embarked on a fierce campaign to promote the image of the Holy Land and to emphasize the importance of living there. The following current texts testify to the severity of the situation:

> A person should live in the Land of Israel, even in a town in which the majority of residents are gentiles, and not abroad, even in a town in which all of the residents are Israelites (Tosefta, Abodah Zarah, 4, 3).

> At another time Rabbi Eleazar son of Shammua and Rabbi Johanan the Sandal-maker were going to Nisibis [in northern Mesopotamia] to study Torah under Rabbi Judah son of Betherah. When they reached Sidon [on the Mediterranean coast just outside Palestine], they remembered the Land of Israel, raised their eyes and wept, and rent their garments. . . . Thereupon they returned to the Land of Israel.

A custom that became more and more fashionable during the third century was the burial of Diaspora Jews in the Land of Israel. This custom and the expansion of the famous necropolis of Beth She'arim (in western Galilee) suggest that Israel remained the most desired and cherished land of the Jews. In fact, some local sages endorsed this custom and revered it. However, there were others who described it as outrageous and greeted the coffins of the dead coming from abroad with insults.

Though it might seem from our description that the image of the Land was somewhat deteriorating during the second to fourth centuries, throughout the period in question immigration to Palestine continued among the Diaspora Jewry. Jews from Babylon, Cappadocia, Tyre, Sidon and from other Greek-speaking regions emigrated and settled in distinct communities in the most important centers of learning and commerce in Israel—Caesarea, Tiberias and Sepphoris. They

Sarcophagus from the catacombs of Beth She'arim in western Galilee. Prominent Jews were buried here, some in grandiose marble coffins adorned with scenes from Greek mythology. Others were encased in more modest limestone sarcophagi like this, bearing more "neutral" designs.

might have been few in number but their presence was felt. In light of what we have said, the presence of Babylonian Jews in Palestine is most revealing. The Land of Israel remained a center of learning, and Babylonian students went to study in the local academies (yeshivot).

THE PALESTINIAN CENTER AND THE DIASPORA: THE STRUGGLE TO MAINTAIN SUPREMACY

The subordination of the Diaspora Jews to the Palestinian center was deeply rooted in biblical law and practice (Deuteronomy 17:8–13 [Law Courts]; ibid. 16: 16 [Pilgrimage]). During the Second Temple period, this subordination was enhanced by pilgrimage from all over the Diaspora and by the collection of money for the Temple in Jerusalem. Suffice it here to quote Josephus' testimony: "The Jews [of Babylonia] . . . trusting the natural strength of these places [that is, Nehardea and Nisibis] used to deposit there the two drachm coins [equivalent of the half shekel (Exodus 30:13)] which it is the national custom for all to contribute to the cause of God, as well as any other dedicatory offerings. . . . From there these offerings were sent to Jerusalem at the appropriate time. Many tens of thousands of Jews shared in this convoy of these monies." (Josephus, *Antiquities*, 18, 312–13). In another context, he attests to the fact that everywhere that priests have settled whenever they marry someone, they consult the register placed in the law courts of Jerusalem to check the lineage of their spouse (Josephus, *Against Apion*, i, 7).

After the destruction of Jerusalem and its Temple, two factors contributed to the continuing Palestinian supremacy over and influence on Diaspora Jewry: the indisputable preeminence of its academies as centers of learning, and the office of the patriarchate—described recently as a "a lay monarchy." The function of these powerful institutions within the context of the Diaspora-center relations is of prime importance.

In order to maintain their close ties with the Diaspora after 70 C.E., the Palestinian sages had to assert the dominance of the center's teachings and judicial authority.

In no other matter was Palestinian primacy and supremacy as conspicuous as in calendar calculation and intercalation. The Jewish calendar, which was (and still is) based on the cycles of the moon (with some required adjustments to bring it in line with the solar year), was determined and announced by the Sanhedrin in Jerusalem on the basis of witness testimonies concerning the size and position of the moon. The results were then communicated to the Diaspora Jews. Thus, the Diaspora Jews were totally dependent on calendar issues being decided and decreed in the Palestinian center. An epistle sent by Rabbi Gamaliel the Elder (who lived in the period preceding the destruction of Jerusalem) and preserved in the Babylonian Talmud reads as follows:

> It once happened that Rabban Gamaliel was sitting on a step on the Temple Mount, and the Scribe Johanan stood before him while three cut sheets were lying before him. "Take one sheet," he said, "and write an epistle to our brethren in the Upper Galilee and to those in Lower Galilee. . . . Take another sheet and write to our brethren of the South. . . . And take the third and write to our brethren the exiles in Babylon and to those in Media, and to all the other exiled [sons] of Israel saying: 'May your peace be great for ever. We beg to inform you that the doves are still tender and the lambs still too young and that the crops are not yet ripe. It seems to me and to my colleagues to add thirty days to this year' [so that the items mentioned will be more suitable as offerings in the Temple]."

Issues pertaining to the calendar, it was understood, were the prerogative of rabbinical authority. It was even said that God acceded to their authority. Within this framework a hierarchy was established whereby the Diaspora Jews acceded to Palestinian sages headed by the patriarch, who was the supreme authority on this matter. However, following the fall of Jerusalem and the Bar Kochba Revolt, the first signs of political dissent appeared. Prominent among them were Babylonian attempts to usurp the authority of intercalation. The attempt was carried out by a former Palestinian sage, Hananiah (c. 135). The opposing Palestinian sages declared that the existing hierarchy is scripturally imposed through the famous words of the prophet Isaiah: "For out of Zion shall come forth Torah" (2:3). On the basis of this phrase, Hananiah's actions, according to the story, were regarded as heretical and he was liable to suffer banishment. Even the Christian world understood the unique position of the Palestinian sages. Tradition has it that when in the sixth century a Christian convention gathered in Alexandria to discuss matters concerning the computation of the Christian calendar, a certain Jew named Phinehas from Tiberias was present.

Calendar computation and intercalation continued to stand at the center of tension between Palestine and Babylon. Thus, in the year 921 C.E. a major controversy concerning calendar computation broke out between the leaders of the two centers. Although as late as 835 the Babylonian leaders had reaffirmed the supremacy of the Palestinians in matters concerning the calendar, by 921 the Babylonian ascendancy in this matter was so established that most of the Jewish communities preferred to follow them.

Apart from their insistence on deciding matters relating to the calendar, Palestinian sages tried from the start to ingrain the idea of Diaspora subservience to the Torah center in Palestine. Thus when Thaddeus (a local leader of the Jews of Rome) accustomed the Roman Jews to eat "helmeted" goats on the night of Passover, the sages sent a message to him: "If you were not Thaddeus, we would have excommunicated you, because you make Israel eat sacred flesh without the Temple" (for the Passover lamb was eaten that way only in the Jerusalem Temple) (Babylonian Talmud, Pesahim, 53a). Another way for Palestinian sages to assert their authority was to supervise the internal affairs of the Diaspora communities. Sages from Yavneh traveled wide, on their own or in delegations. They journeyed to Alexandria, Rome, Cilicia, Cappadocia, Galatia and North Africa, and whenever they were not on official visits to the Roman authorities, they taught and instructed the local communities. The dictum found in a later source that "there is no ordination outside the Land [of Israel]" (Palestinian Talmud, Bikkurim, 3, 65d) may even indicate that they established local judiciaries as recognized offshoots of the Palestinian center.

The Palestinian Academies and the Palestinian Talmud

Above all, it was the literary output of the Palestinian academies that accorded them great prestige and assured them a constant flow of students, many of them from the Diaspora. The peak of their activity was during the third and fourth centuries, when they flourished mainly in three different centers, in Tiberias, in Caesarea (which had become the Palestinian metropolis) and in Lydda (Diospolis). This is not to discount smaller centers of learning scattered in the Galilee. The main literary production coming out of the Palestinian academies was the Palestinian Talmud (also known as the *Yerushalmi*, the Jerusalem Talmud). Both the Babylonian Talmud and the Palestinian Talmud were the fruits of extensive deliberations on and intensive studies of the Mishnah. The sages included in their discussions clusters of teachings that Rabbi Judah the Patriarch rejected from the Mishnah, texts that received the appropriate epithet Toseftot (Additions) or Beraitot (Externals). As expected, the Jerusalem Talmud paid special attention to the first order of the Mishnah, which deals with agricultural laws, for these laws still applied in Palestine.

The Palestinian Talmud is characterized by its language, Western (Palestinian) Aramaic containing a substantial number of Greek and Latin loan-words, and even more by its concise discussions and its somewhat terse style—a complete opposite to the discursive style of the Babylonian Talmud. Whereas the Babylonian Talmud regarded the statements and wording of the Mishnah as final

Archaeological exploration of synagogues in Galilee and elsewhere has brought to light a number of surprising features. Several have mosaic floors, revealing the influence of pagan religion and art. Here, in a finely executed mosaic pavement from a synagogue at the hot springs outside Tiberias (fourth century C.E.), the signs of the zodiac surround the sun god, Helios, in his four-horse chariot.

and went to great lengths to substantiate and defend them, the Palestinian Talmud makes little effort to clarify the Mishnah. Very little is known of the process by which the Palestinian Talmud was compiled and redacted. It seems to have been given its final form during the second half of the fourth century C.E., more than a century before the redaction of the Babylonian Talmud. Its redaction, it seems, came about as a result of the deterioration in the political and religious conditions of the Jews in Palestine during that period, which in turn caused decline in the academies' activities as early as the first half of the fifth century. From then on, though the study of the Torah did not cease, the halakhic works produced in Palestine were by far inferior to the Babylonian Talmud and the later gaonic responsa literature. Although the Palestinian Talmud's authority and with it the entire body of Palestinian halakhic teachings continued to prevail during the early part of the Middle Ages, not only locally but in the regions that were previously under the Roman and Byzantine influence too, the decline of the Palestinian yeshivot impaired the center's reputation. However, the final battle for the supremacy between the two centers was still to take place.

The Palestinian Patriarchate: Lay Leadership with a Royal Pedigree

Another way of exerting power over the Diaspora communities was through the office of the patriarchate. The origins of the patriarchate and the period of its inception are still very much debated. But although these factors are shrouded in mist, the principles forming the political posture of the office as well as its mode of operation are clearer.

Recently it has been suggested that the patriarchate signified the major shift in leadership from priestly dominance to a lay-controlled system, a shift that occurred in the aftermath of the Great Revolt. In that context, one ought to view the ascendancy of the Yavneh academy and later centers of learning as reflecting the initial stages of this development. Nevertheless, although the priests lost their center and source of power, they still had their highly reputed priestly lineage to sustain their claim for a central role in the leadership, and to contest claims brought by others.

The earliest historically sound traditions about the patriarchate are from the late second century C.E. At this stage during the days of Rabbi Judah the Patriarch, we encounter for the first time the patriarch's claim for power and leadership as based on royal descent from the House of David. Judah the Patriarch was a descendant of Gamaliel, whose dynasty was traced to Hillel the Elder, who came from Babylon about a century before the destruction of Jerusalem. Members of the family were, according to rabbinical sources and the New Testament, leading figures in first-century Jerusalem. According to the Palestinian Talmud, Rabbi Levi said: "They found a genealogical scroll in Jerusalem, and written in it was 'Hillel is from [those] of David' " (Taaniot 4, 2, 68a). The deep connotations of this statement were the confirmation of the messianic dimension of the patriarchate, a dimension not lost on Rabbi Judah. The underlying scriptural legitimacy of the claim for Davidic lineage, a claim presented in many anecdotes and discussions involving Rabbi Judah the Patriarch and his descendants, was the verse in Genesis 49:10: "A scepter shall not depart from Judah, nor a lawgiver from between his feet, until Shiloh shall come," a verse the patriarchs claimed was referring to them. But it was this very same text that attracted the attention of the Church fathers too. This blessing spoken by Jacob was expounded as referring to Jesus' royal descent and messianic ministry. It is not surprising, therefore, that the Church fathers went to great lengths to discredit the patriarchal claims for a Davidic pedigree. Fortunately for us, their writings serve as an important source of knowledge of the actions and influence of the patriarch, especially in the Diaspora communities.

The famous third-century Church father Origen of Caesarea wrote: "Now, for instance, that the Romans have the ruling power and the Jews pay the two drachmas tax to them, we who have experienced it know how great is the power wielded by the ethnarch, with the emperor's consent, indeed he differs in no way from a king of the nation." Though it might seem a gross exaggeration on Origen's part, rabbinical sources as well as later imperial legislation, Church fathers' polemics and gentile writings do attest to this as a most powerful office.

The patriarchs exercised their control and coercive powers over the Diaspora communities in different ways. Their prerogatives were quite extensive, including deposition and appointment of local officials (leaders as well as judges), imposition of halakhic rulings and collection of taxes. An imperial law from 399 C.E. cited in the Theodosian Code sent by the emperor Honorius to Italy and North Africa prohibiting the collection of taxes gives the following description: "the Archisynagogues, the presbyters of the Jews and those they call Apostles who are sent by the patriarch on a certain date to demand gold and silver, exact and receive a sum from each synagogue and deliver it to him."

Although five years later the emperor annulled his prohibition, it took the Roman authorities approximately another two decades to abrogate the office of the Palestinian patriarch. The exact circumstances and reasons for taking this action are not entirely clear, though it seems that Gamaliel VI (the last patriarch) fell out of favor with the imperial authorities. The end of the Palestinian patriarchate left a big vacuum, and it is difficult to know who were the members of the "two judicial councils" (Sanhedrins)—mentioned in an imperial law from 429—as governing the affairs of the Jews in the two Palestinian provinces. In sixth-century Christian sources, we find an allusion to "the Priests of Tiberias." What was meant by this is difficult to assess. Were the Palestinian priestly circles able to resume their power and influence?

The end of the Palestinian patriarchate not only signified the end of an era, but it also left the Diaspora communities without their last and most important link and symbol of unity with the Palestinian center. With the ensuing decline of the Palestinian academies, the spiritual hold that Israel had over the Diaspora was weakening, and the road for Babylonian usurpation of power and influence over the Diaspora was open.

THE EMERGENCE OF BABYLONIAN HEGEMONY

By the early first century C.E., Babylon was most probably the largest and most prosperous Jewish center outside the Land of Israel. An uprising in Mesopotamia in the wake of a Roman advance in the year 116 proved to be very costly for the Jews; however, Parthian territory remained intact, and the Babylonian Jews were not to suffer under the Roman yoke. When the last king of the Parthians died in 227 C.E., on the dawn of the Sassanian Persian Empire (226–651), a leading Babylonian sage lamented the past and expressed his anxiety at the advent of the new era. It should be stated, though, that the recent past of Babylonian Jewry had not been all that tranquil. The first-century episode with the two Jewish bandit brothers Asinaeus and Anilaeus, natives of Nehardea who terrorized the people in their region and in the end brought about a great massacre of their brethren (Josephus, *Antiquities*, 18, 310–79), must have cast some shadow on the relations between the Jews and their neighbors.

Unlike the Parthians before them, the Sassanians exercised a much more centralized system of government, coupled with the revival of the ancient Persian Zoroastrian (Mazdaean) religion and the establishment of a most powerful priestly hierarchy. The latter proved later to be a source of hatred toward the Jews.

However, apart from some isolated cases of religious zealotry resulting in persecution of the Jews, the Zoroastrian authorities left the Jews in peace, showing no tendency to convert them. The situation under the secular Sassanian rulers was very much the same. They, too, enabled the Babylonian Jews to live in relative tranquillity. The Sassanian kings, notably Shapur I, Shapur II and the mother of the latter, Ifra Hurmiz, even demonstrated respect for their Jewish subjects and cultivated good relations with Jewish dignitaries. But again during the long period of the Sassanian rule we do hear of a few cases of political persecution resulting in large-scale killings of Jews. With hardly any persecutions, though with some tension with other minority groups such as the Christians, the Jews generally speaking could and did lead a relatively peaceful existence. Thus the conditions under which Babylonian Jewry flourished were much more favorable than those of the Jews living under Roman rule.

Under such circumstances of continuous stability and prosperity, beginning in the early days of its exile from Judaea in 594 B.C.E. (though our knowledge of that period up until the Sassanian era is extremely meager), Babylonian Jews developed a striking sense of self-assuredness and "local patriotism." Armed with such feelings and convictions, the Babylonian Jews began to assert their position in different ways. Thus, their struggle with the Palestinian center cannot be described in terms of a sudden outburst of tension but as an evolutionary process, which we shall now try to sketch. In the eyes of the Babylonians themselves, events in the third century were a watershed in their relationship with the Palestinian center. The most prominent among them was the arrival of Rav (a leading disciple of Rabbi Judah the Patriarch) in Babylon in the year 219 C.E. This is one of the most outstanding events recorded in the famous eleventh-century *Epistle of Rav Sherira Gaon*, which contains a detailed history of the compilation of the Mishnah and Talmud. Why the Babylonian Jews emphasized the importance of that event becomes apparent when we read the following statement uttered by an anonymous third-century sage: "We have made ourselves in Babylon the equivalent of Israel [in legal matters] from the arrival of Rav in Babylonia" (Babylonian Talmud, Gittin, 6a). With Rav also arrived the redacted code of the Mishnah. It was an epoch-making event, which might have been regarded in the local collective consciousness as secondary only to the giving of the Ten Commandments. In retrospect, this event marked the emergence of the "Torah of Babylon."

The Jews of Babylon cultivated their historical consciousness, cherished their past and utilized it to promote their supremacy. Hence their claim for possessing the purest lineage, as in the following statement: "Rab Judah said in Samuel's name [both third-century sages] . . . All countries are as dough [i.e., mixture] in comparison to Palestine and Palestine is as dough ıelative to Babylon" (Babylonian Talmud, Kiddushin [on marital laws], 69b).

Their ancestral history was used to create an elaborate local biblical ("sacred") geography at times in contrast to the actual biblical statements, as in the case of the three biblical giants Ahiman, Sheshai and Talmai. Although Numbers 13:22 locates them near Hebron, Babylonian sages attributed to them the building of three islands in the Euphrates (Babylonian Talmud, Yoma [a tractate on the Day of Atonement], 10a). Babylonian Jews were well aware of the fact that Babylon was the cradle of the Jewish people: they asserted that the people of Israel had been exiled to Babylonia because the house of Abraham came from there (Babylonian Talmud, Pesahim [on Passover], 87b).

Beyond the realms of mythic history, the Babylonian Jews' claim for supremacy was based on traditions regarding their more recent past, the early days of their exile. A fourth-century tradition relates the following: "They were exiled to Babylonia and the Shekhinah [i.e., the divine presence] was with them . . . Where in Babylonia? Abaye said: In the synagogue of Huzal and in the synagogue of Saf ve-Yatib in Nehardea." (Babylonian Talmud, Megillah, 29a). Put together with two other traditions—a later one claiming that ashes from the burned First Temple were placed underneath certain synagogues in Babylon, and an earlier tradition asserting that the Ark from the First Temple was transferred to Babylon (contrary to a mishnaic tradition that it was concealed in a secret place underneath the floor of the Jerusalem Temple)—we have some of the most essential ingredients in the mounting contest for hegemony between the two centers. The impact of such traditions cropping up following the fall of Jerusalem in 70 C.E. should not be underestimated. The Babylonians, according to their own claims and traditions, emerged as the sole keepers of the most authentic relics of the glorious biblical past.

The significance of these traditions was naturally not lost on the Babylonian sages. However, in practice they were slower in implementing what they considered was right to teach and preach about. In numerous instances the Babylonian Talmud continued to maintain the precedence of Israel in halakhic matters. The special status of the Palestinian center was never adduced as emanating from the

The Temple as portrayed in a wall painting from the Dura-Europos synagogue. It is an idealized representation, combining elements from the tabernacle of the Exodus story, the historical Jerusalem Temple (compare the picture on page 46) and the fully restored Temple of Messianic times. Aaron, the original high priest, dressed in the costume of his Persian counterpart, presides over the reinstituted animal sacrifices, temporarily interrupted by the Roman conquest. Note the central presence of the menorah, and the synagogal Ark of the Torah occupying the place of the Ark of the Covenant.

superior knowledge possessed by its sages, but rather from its age-old prestige and holiness. Thus, while still adhering to the principle of subservience to the Land of Israel, and while Babylonian students flocked to study in Palestinian academies, the Babylonians established a strong, independent community, capable of handling its entire affairs. The yeshivot of Babylon and the office of the ethnarch, the head of the community, were the means that enabled Babylonian Jewry to establish its independent position, assert its supremacy and in the long run to secure its hegemony. As was done in Palestine, the Babylonians cultivated the position and importance of the two leading symbols of power within society—its political as well as its intellectual leaderships.

The most famous representative of the autonomous Jewish community in Babylonia was certainly the exilarch. Our earliest testimonies concerning this office come from the days of Rabbi Judah the Patriarch, the early third century, though it is reasonable to assume that exilarchs operated in Babylon slightly earlier than that.

The exilarchs' claim to leadership and eventually to fame was their contention that they, too—just like their equivalents in Palestine—were descendants of the royal House of David. Later traditions from the gaonic period (eighth to ninth centuries) present genealogical lists in which the exilarchs' pedigree is traced back to the last king of Judah. It goes without saying that these lists were legendary in nature, though some of the names, notably those from the third to the sixth centuries, might have been derived from archival material. In any case, the lists represent an effort to grant the office of the exilarch an aura of archaism and enhance its legitimacy. The power of the exilarchs, like that of their counterparts the Palestinian patriarchs, was acknowledged by the Sassanian rulers who, at least in some cases, kept close ties with the exilarchs. This enabled them to coerce people, at times through force, to comply with their or their court's decisions. There was, however, a fundamental difference between the office of the two leaders. It lay in the basic principle guiding the activity of both, as in the following famous statement from the Babylonian Talmud, Sanhedrin, 5a: "Genesis 49:10 . . . it has been taught: 'A scepter shall not depart from Judah': this refers to the Exilarchs of Babylon who rule over Israel with scepters; 'nor a staff': this refers to the descendants of Hillel [in Palestine] who teach the Torah in public." According to this anonymous tradition, the line to be drawn between the two dignitaries was as follows: the patriarch tended to be a spiritual or religious figure and the exilarch a secular administrative leader. One fact clearly emerges: regarding the historical roots of their leadership, both leaders were on a par. As to the realities this statement was meant to reflect, they seem less clear cut. Indeed, the exilarchs were not involved, it seems, in the appointment of judges, a prerogative the patriarchs held on to even in the face of mounting criticism, especially during the second half of the third century when their appointees were regarded to be unqualified. But on the other hand, the exilarchs approved the appointment of judges and gave financial guarantees in case of mistaken judgments on their part.

In the sphere of communal affairs, the exilarchs exercised a more centralized rule. For instance, they appointed market inspectors who examined prices (according to a different tradition, their task was to examine measures), an appointment that in the Roman sphere was entirely in the hands of the local town councils.

The relations between the Babylonian sages and the exilarchs were on the whole correct, though some of the sages disliked the exilarchs' regal pomp and others criticized their servants or other entourage members. The general public, however, as much as we are able to judge from the few allusions in the Babylonian Talmud, admired the exilarchs.

If the exilarchs signified in the eyes of the Babylonian Jews some sort of royalty and a source of pride, the institution that contributed most at first to their independence of the Palestinian center and later to their hegemony was the Babylonian academies.

There were three main centers of learning in Babylonia: Nehardea (which was destroyed in 259 C.E.), Sura and Pumbedita. Following the Muslim conquest in 642 C.E., the latter two moved to Baghdad, retaining their old names.

The Palestinian academies were first and foremost courts of law and as legislative councils modeled on the Jerusalem high court, the Sanhedrin, but the Babylonian yeshivot were organized as centers for learning. Although we possess only scanty descriptions of the Babylonian yeshivot during the talmudic period (their internal arrangement or their curriculum), the tenth-century Rabbi Nathan the Babylonian comes again to our aid with his elaborate description of the yeshivot in Baghdad, which, as traditional institutions, probably faithfully conformed to the physical details of earlier examples.

The number of scholars in each yeshivah was limited to seventy, reflecting the number of members of the Sanhedrin. At least during the gaonic period, more students were attached to the academies. The order of sitting, according to the

The prophet Samuel anointing David (1 Samuel 16:13). This wall painting flanks the Torah shrine in the synagogue of Dura-Europos, the position stressing its importance. David is distinguished from his brothers by a purple toga, presumably an indication of his own future kingship, but also a hint of the messianic ruler who will be descended from him.

tenth-century document mentioned on the previous page was as follows (rendered freely from Nathan's description): "The Rosh [literally, head] of the academy sits, facing him are ten people; they are called the 'First Row' . . . seven of them are called 'Rosh Kallah' [leader of the row]. Each of them supervises ten members of the Yeshivah [the term used in the original was *Sanhedrin*]."

Nathan goes on to describe in detail the method of reciting lessons and the examinations set in the academy, alongside the discipline, manners and respect demonstrated by the students toward their colleagues and toward the head of the academy. The Babylonian academies, at least during the talmudic period, were known to admit scholars on their own merit. This was to change later on, when principles of hereditary power and dynastic order used by the exilarchs were put into practice in the academies too. This was not the case during the formative age, the age in which the academies produced, compiled and redacted the biggest intellectual and religious enterprise of that era, namely, the Babylonian Talmud.

The Babylonian Talmud

The Babylonian Talmud consists of 5,894 folio pages (2.5 million words), of which two-thirds are Aggadah (scriptural exegesis, anecdotes, homilies, legends and so on) and only one-third Halakhah. This immense output was the product of endless discussions in the yeshivot as well as public preaching in the local synagogues. As in the case of the Palestinian Talmud, the study of the Mishnah was central. The redacted version of the Mishnah brought by Rav from Israel was subjected to close scrutiny, and in the process differences in the versions of the text were explained as differences of opinion and ruling; this, as has been suggested, explains the freedom of the Babylonian Talmud's textual criticism of the Mishnah. The great merit of this Talmud lies in its reflection of intellectual sharpness, creative thinking and inventive argument. The emphasis on the study and analysis of the Mishnah originated in the notion that nothing is superfluous in that text—every word counts, each verse has its reasoning and each ruling its logic. Ongoing deep analysis of text and subject matter resulted in the most interesting activity of the Babylonian sages—the formulation of general principles of Halakhah, as well as the study of the methods of their application. The formulated principles became important vehicles in the decision making in the Talmud itself. Thus, on the basis of some scattered hints in the Talmud, it has been recently suggested that the academies were not only a center for theoretical studies but that they acted at least in some cases as law courts too. Finally, the unique style of the Talmud must be acknowledged, for it reflects the imaginative quality of discourse and discussion typical of the Babylonian academies, and shows little attempt on the part of the redactors to present the text in a more systematic and concise form. Another unique institution of Babylonian Jewry was the "Kallah Season," when the academies were open to the general public. Encouraged by the sages every year at a designated time, the masses flocked to the yeshivot to study Torah. The Kallah Months popularized the study of the Torah and strengthened the ties with the public: the people attending began to seek the aid of the sages on a regular basis. Responsa literature represents a further development of this phenomenon.

During the period following the redaction of the Babylonian Talmud, academies expanded and their heads, known as the geonim, became the supreme leaders of Babylonian Jewry. Following the Muslim conquest of the Near East, North Africa and Spain (extending from the 630s to 711 C.E.), many parts of the Jewish Diaspora came under the influence of the thriving Babylonian center. The Palestinian center did maintain some influence (in southern Italy and Egypt), but only as a shadow of its past. A venomous piece of anti-Palestinian propaganda from the early days of the ninth century demonstrates the prevailing atmosphere. The fragmentary text, discovered in the Cairo Genizah, was an epistle sent by a sage named Pirkoi, the son of Baboi, from Babylon to the Jews in North Africa. After acknowledging that new centers of learning had been established in Spain and North Africa, Pirkoi complains about the pupils of the Babylonian academies who then learned the customs prevalent in Israel and arrived in North Africa and followed those ignorant customs and habits. Pirkoi abhors the Palestinian customs and defines them as "customs of apostasy," a consequence of the state of apostasy Israel was in due to Christian rule. Pirkoi advocated the supremacy of the Babylonian Talmud and asserted that the only sources of authentic Oral Law were the Babylonian academies, and thus it was fitting that only from them should Torah go forth to all countries. Four centuries later, the great Jewish philosopher and halakhic authority Maimonides wrote, "Whatever is already mentioned in the Babylonian Talmud is binding on all Israel."

The Babylonian academies cultivated their ties with the communities of the Diaspora. An elaborate mechanism of correspondence was developed, through which the academies aided and guided the communities on legal, scriptural and secular communal matters. In return for their services, the yeshivot demanded fees and allegiance. Gradually the bond between the congregations and the centers of learning became based on the obligation of the former to contribute to the upkeep of the latter. The Babylonian system at last supplanted the old Palestinian custom. What ultimately seems to have secured Babylonian ascendancy was the creation of an independent center of learning and teaching with its own extensive literary output that was disseminated all over the Diaspora.

3

A Rejected People

Ora Limor

The Church, so as to establish its own identity, had to emancipate itself from the Jewish matrix. The result was a rhetorical denigration of Judaism that endured for centuries. After the conversion of the Roman Empire to Christianity at the beginning of the fourth century, the Jews of Europe became subject, directly or indirectly, to the power of the Church. Sometimes Christian rulers exercised tolerance and restraint; sometimes they gave way to pressure to persecute the Jews. In extreme cases, there were violent attacks on Jewish life and property. The story of the Jews under Christian rule is complex and many-faceted. The negative side is all too obvious; the positive must not be understated. The two religions influenced each other in many ways, and there were periods of coexistence and even active cooperation. Nor should we forget that some of the most enduring monuments of Jewish culture were produced in these unpromising conditions.

Opposite: **The Church and the Synagogue, Strasbourg Cathedral (completed 1230). A conventional representation of the victory of the Church, which can be found on several cathedrals in France and England, and on many medieval manuscripts. The Church is crowned and triumphant; the Synagogue is downcast and blindfolded, holding a broken lance.**

But the Jews who killed him and refused to believe in him, to believe that he had to die and rise again, suffered a more wretched devastation at the hands of the Romans and were utterly uprooted from their kingdom, where they had already been under the domination of foreigners. They were dispersed all over the world—for indeed there is no part of the earth where they are not to be found—and thus by the evidence of their own scripture they bear witness for us that we have not fabricated the prophecies about Christ. . . . We recognize that it is in order to give this testimony, which, in spite

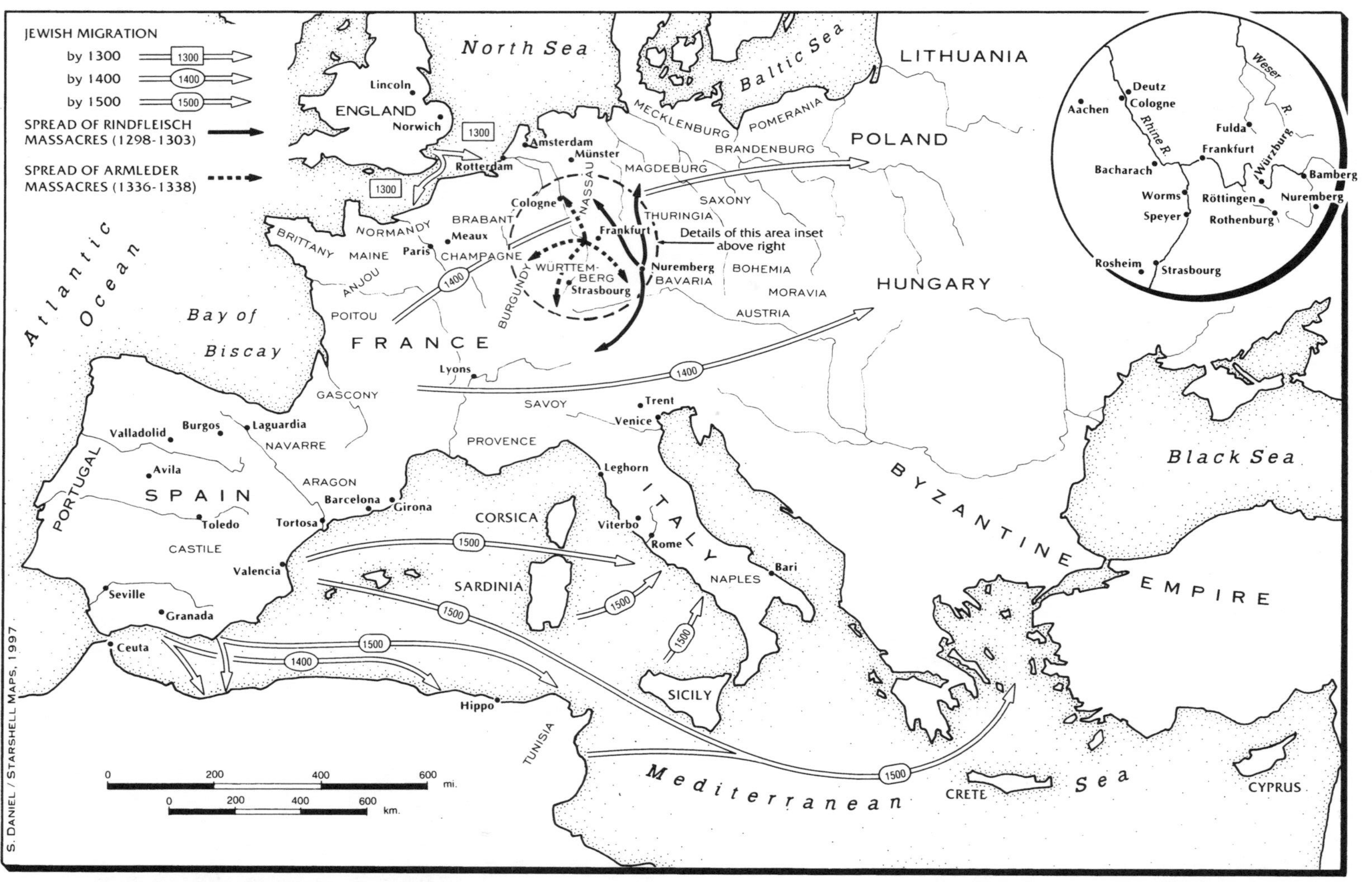

The Medieval World

> of themselves, they supply for our benefit by their possession and preservation of those books, that they themselves are dispersed among all nations, in whatever direction the Christian Church spreads. . . . This is the reason for His forbearing to slay them—that is, for not putting an end to their existence as Jews, although they have been conquered and oppressed by the Romans; it is for fear that they should not forget the Law of God and thus fail to bear convincing witness.
>
> —AUGUSTINE OF HIPPO, *THE CITY OF GOD*

Augustine (354–430), the greatest thinker of Christian antiquity, who shaped Christian thought on many doctrinal problems, also formed Christian theology on Jews and Judaism. He wrote in late antiquity, when the Roman Empire had already become Christian and Christianity had clearly triumphed throughout the civilized world. Nevertheless, Christianity still had to contend with various competing religions, both in the Roman world and elsewhere. Yet neither Augustine nor any other Christian thinker found it necessary to formulate an attitude of tolerance toward other religions or sects—with the sole exception of Judaism. Ultimately, after the pagans had been converted and the Catholic Church had wiped out its competitors, the Jews were the only religious minority tolerated in the Christian world. The above quotation from Augustine's *City of God* might be interpreted as an acknowledgment that the Christian mission to the Jews had failed, a theological justification of that failure—namely, that the failure was simply part of a divine plan, which was to leave the Jews as both reliable witnesses to and demonstration of the truth of the Christian Gospel. Their mere existence testified to the antiquity of Christian Scripture with its prophecies of Christ; their dispersal, a humiliated minority among the Christians, deprived of political independence, testified to the error of their ways. Augustine had thus devised a formula for Jewish existence in the Christian world, based on relative tolerance and degradation—two poles between which a delicate pendulum swung back and forth, depending on the specific political, economic and social circumstances of the time. Christian theology, again following Augustine, even assigned the Jews a role in the plan of divine salvation. At the End of Days, they, too, would recognize Christian truth, and that would be the last stage in the march of history, to be followed by the Kingdom of Heaven on earth.

Until the advent of these sublime events, the Jews could maintain their mistaken faith and the Christians should not forcibly convert them; but Jewish perversity (their nature as defined by Christians) had to be reflected by their social standing, which was necessarily inferior to that of the Christian majority—lest "the children of the free woman should serve the children of the maid-servant." There was a delicate, problematic balance between these two contradictory Augustinian principles, protection versus restriction. As we shall see later, one might say, in general terms, that this balance was weighted from the twelfth century on in favor of constantly graver and more oppressive restrictions and persecution. Nevertheless, it is important to note that from the very start, Church theology reserved a place for the Jews in Christian society. They were seen as a factor in the divine plan, part of human society, and as such they were permitted to exist alongside the Christians. On the other hand, one should also remember that such sweeping terms as *Christianity* and even *Church*, with their implications of monolithic uniformity, are also misleading. Opinions were divided within the Church itself on various theological and legal questions of vital significance—and not only in relation to Judaism. The popes were generally in favor of legality and orderliness, as attested by the various papal bulls on the Jewish question. Contrasting militant positions were not infrequently expressed by popular preachers and local priests, sometimes leading to persecutions and anti-Jewish riots. Jewish-Christian relations were extremely complicated; they varied greatly in nature and complexion from place to place and from time to time, embodying internal contradictions that were inextricably bound up in the basic principles dictated by what we might call "Augustinian tolerance."

Jews and Christians have been living together since the beginnings of Christianity—almost 2,000 years. For a brief span of time, the Christians were a small minority of the Jewish population of Palestine. Later, after the early Christians had begun to preach to the gentile nations, the tables were turned. The new religion was gradually accepted by a majority of the populace in the Roman Empire, and the Jews became a minority. Since the time of Constantine (d. 337), when Christianity became first a permitted faith and then the state religion, it was no longer possible to speak of Judaism and Christianity as equals. Nevertheless, it would be wrong to portray Christianity as the sole active force and the Jews as merely passive. Although a minority—at times a degraded minority—the Jews always retained channels of reaction and response, though the response was sometimes directed exclusively inward.

SISTER FAITHS

Judaism and Christianity are sister faiths. Christian art and exegesis used various kinds of kinship images to describe their relationship. Sometimes they are portrayed as mother and daughter, as two sisters, as two brothers. Jacob and Esau, Rachel and Leah are two prominent examples. Christianity sees itself as Rachel, or as Jacob—that is, the younger child, the favorite; Judaism is cast in the role of Esau, who forfeited his birthright, or of Leah, the neglected sister, whose husband preferred her younger sibling. The Jews, for their part, consider themselves to represent Jacob, while their foes are Esau—that is, Edom, the eternal foe—a sobriquet applied to the Roman Empire and later to its successor, the Church. Thus, each religion saw itself as beloved and chosen, and its counterpart as the rejected sibling. Still, Esau was Jacob's brother, and the very same biblical metaphor was used by each faith to describe their relationship.

The stories, heroes and prophecies of the "Old Testament" are the building blocks of Judeo-Christian culture. The Old Testament in fact represented the first meeting place of the two faiths, for each acknowledged its sanctity; but it was also an arena of conflict, as they contested its meaning. Hence, although the Jewish attitude to Christianity is in reality more complex, and Judaism consistently lays emphasis on the differences rather than the similarities, one may nevertheless

Scenes from the life of St. Anne, Notre Dame Cathedral, Paris (twelfth century). These images, in contrast to those shown on page 86, underline the close relationship between Christianity and Judaism. The grandparents of Jesus are dressed as contemporary Jews. St. Joachim wears the typical pointed Jewish hat, and the priest in the temple is represented as a rabbi in a synagogue. The Rue de la Juiverie (Jewry Street) was located a stone's throw from the front of the cathedral, so the figures may portray actual Jews.

speak, in rather general terms, of a kind of kinship or family resemblance, though the relationship is hardly symmetrical. The bitter theological dispute that raged between Judaism and Christianity for centuries was in a sense a domestic quarrel; little wonder, then, that it was particularly suffused with tension and rivalry.

Judaism and Christianity shared a conception of a historic mission, a belief in a single literary corpus from which all truth flowed and a conviction of divine election. Each was sure that it, and it alone, was the "true Israel." The Jews claimed to be the descendants of the Israelites who received the Torah at Sinai, whereas the Christians argued that the crown of divine election had shifted from "Israel according to the flesh"—the Jews—to "Israel according to the spirit"—the Christians; Israel in the spirit, not genetic Israel, was the "true Israel." As Paul wrote in the Letter to the Romans (9:6), "For not all who are descended from Israel belong to Israel," meaning that for the Christians, Israel and Judaism were by no means identical.

The Christian view of the relationship between Christianity and Judaism is succinctly and meaningfully embodied in the visual portrayals of Ecclesia and Synagoga—the Church and the Synagogue—so common in medieval sculpture and illumination from the ninth century on. The figure of Synagoga stands on the left, that of Ecclesia on the right, and this distinct positioning carries meaning, for right symbolizes what is good and just. Ecclesia and Synagoga are represented as two women, personifications of collective entities and abstract ideas—

Christianity and Judaism. Each has its own characteristic attributes, which, like the figures that they inform, carry on a dialogue. Ecclesia is identified by the cross at the tip of her scepter, while Synagoga bears the two tablets of the Covenant; but the tablets are falling from her hands, thus symbolizing a subdued and dejected Judaism, contrasting with a proud and triumphant Christianity. In some representations they are two queens wearing crowns. But while Ecclesia's crown is firmly on her head, Synagoga's is unsteady, on the point of falling, as if portraying a queen of the past who has lost her power. The most familiar figure of Synagoga shows her blindfolded. While Ecclesia's eyes are wide open, her "sister" is unseeing, with bowed head. The broken scepter, the falling crown, the fallen tablets of the Covenant and the veil over Synagoga's eyes define the figure and, through her, the image of Judaism in the Christian world. Judaism was once the chosen queen, but she has forfeited her kingdom. The law to which she clings is outdated; the blindfold over her eyes shuts out the light of truth and love, as noted by Paul (2 Corinthians 4:4): "In their case the God of this world has blinded the minds of the unbelievers, to keep them from seeing the light of the gospel, of the glory of Christ." Nevertheless, despite the conflict, the two figures communicate, and neither is comprehensible without the other. Ecclesia and Synagoga, then, are two sisters, simultaneously defining the collective entities that they embody, the theological ideas shaping their characteristic features and their mutual relationship.

THE PARTING OF THE WAYS

Not only in symbolic terms are Christianity and Judaism sister religions but also in a historical sense. Early Christianity and Rabbinic Judaism, as it took shape during the period of the Mishnah and the Talmud, grew out of the Judaism of the Second Temple period, each offering its own interpretation of that Judaism's basic articles of faith. Christianity was born of Judaism—but in conflict, a conflict that in time created two separate, hostile religions. There is a good deal of scholarship indicating the similarity between early Christianity and the Judaean Desert sect. In addition, various beliefs of the early Christians are polemical responses to Judaism, which denied that Jesus was the Messiah and insisted that the Law of Moses retained its validity even after Jesus' advent. One can discern the conflict not only in beliefs but also in rituals, liturgical texts and biblical exegesis. But there was also some flow in the opposite direction, from Christianity to Judaism—although this flow was more covert and therefore more difficult to discern. In other words, although early Christian writings, from the New Testament on, are imbued with anti-Jewish polemics, the traces of anti-Christian polemics in the contemporary Jewish literature are more obscure. Perhaps Jewish pride, the Jews' confidence that their path, and theirs alone, was the right one, produced a strategy of systematic, stubborn disregard for the Church's impressive achievements and the theological challenge of the Christian faith. At the same time, a careful, objective reading does uncover traces of anti-Christian polemics, sometimes elusive and covert, in Jewish literature too—talmudic legends that humiliate Jesus and Mary, and liturgical texts that include hopes for vengeance and Jewish redemption.

The theological disagreement about whether the messianic era had already started was also a practical disagreement as to the proper way of life—namely, whether observance of the religious precepts of Judaism, the Law of Moses, was necessary. In the fifteenth chapter of Acts, one reads of a council held at Jerusalem—the First Church Council, which discussed the question of whether gentile converts to Christianity should be required to circumcise themselves and observe the Law. Peter finally decided on a compromise: gentile converts were to be treated leniently, were required only to refrain from idolatry, from licentious behavior and from the consumption of unclean flesh. Thus there began to emerge a major distinction between Jewish Christians, who were circumcised and observed the Law of Moses, and gentile Christians, who were exempt from those duties. The emergent Christian world was soon divided into two modes of worship, as practiced in "the Church from the Circumcision" and "the Church from the Gentiles" respectively.

Once the Christian mission to the Jews had failed, the pagans became the major target of vigorous missionizing efforts. Since the Law of Moses and the need for circumcision had been waived, it was much easier for pagans to convert. The promise of salvation as a reward for faith alone satisfied deep yearnings that were then spreading through the Roman Empire—yearnings for the salvation of the soul. Thus the new religion attracted people from all walks of life in late antiquity. Quite quickly, the Jewish Christians became a small, marginal group that, excluded from both Judaism and Christianity, ultimately disappeared. For a time, one could speak of some missionary competition between Judaism and Christianity, for contemporary Jewry, too, was receptive to proselytes, though Judaizing efforts were aimed mainly at gentile intelligentsia and aristocracy. However, at some time in the fourth century, after the final triumph of Christianity, the Jews lost any missionary impetus—and soon also lost the freedom and ability to promulgate their faith. Throughout the Middle Ages and the early Modern Era, conversion was generally a one-way movement—from Judaism to Christianity, although a few cases of the reverse are known.

In 70 C.E., after the failure of the First Revolt against the Romans, the Jewish Temple lay in ruins; the Jews had lost their political independence. The Jewish presence in Palestine was not obliterated; it continued to exist and in fact flourished, particularly in the Galilee and in parts of Judaea, for many centuries. Neither do the beginnings of the Jewish Diaspora date from that point in time: there had long been large Jewish communities in various Mediterranean cities in Italy, Spain and southern France. Nevertheless, the dramatic cataclysm took on crucial significance. Christians saw it as a punishment for the rejection of Christ, a justification of the Christian cause. Thus Jesus, gazing on Jerusalem in the Gospel according to Luke (19:43–44), utters a self-fulfilling prophecy: "For the days shall come upon you, when your enemies will cast up a bank about you and surround you and hem you in on every side, and dash you to the ground, you and your children within you, and they will not leave one stone upon another in you; because you did not know the time of your visitation." For the Jews, too, the destruction of the Temple symbolized the beginning of Exile and became the foundation for a new Jewish identity, largely different from what had gone before. The same event thus became a focal point for the creation of two opposing religious identities. By the first half of the second century C.E., about two generations later, the rift between Judaism and Christianity was irrevocable.

Centuries of Christian persecution of the Jews could not erase the historic trauma of Judaism's rejection of the Jewish believers in Christ. The New Testament in fact accused the Jews of having approved the crucifixion of Jesus and persecuted his disciples. Stephen, the first Christian martyr, was killed not by pagans, it was claimed, but by Jews. As far as Christian theology was concerned, the Jews were still the persecutors and the Christians the persecuted; this interpretation of the situation persisted even when Judaism had become a small, despised minority in a large, self-confident Christian world.

CHRISTIANITY THE STATE RELIGION

After the emperor Constantine had converted to Christianity and Christianity became a recognized faith and, gradually, the favored religion of the empire, the balance of power between Jews and Christians changed completely. The Edict of Toleration of 313 C.E. guaranteed universal religious freedom, but the triumph of Christianity in the ruling circles specified that Judaism was a minority religion whose believers were subjected to various restrictions. Christian propaganda gradually began to influence imperial laws, and from the fifth century on the authorities' attitude to the Jews steadily worsened.

For example, until the beginning of the fifth century, Roman imperial legislation had dealt with Jews and heretics in separate laws; most laws passed between the beginning of the fifth century and the middle of the sixth, however, lumped them together, exemplifying a decisive shift in the attitude to the Jews: hitherto members of a permitted religion, they now labored under restraints similar to those imposed on heretics and pagans. In Justinian's Code (529–565), the authoritative and ordered statement of Roman law, the Jews were subjected to legal restrictions similar to those affecting heretics, pagans and Samaritans: they were barred from holding public office or testifying against Christians in legal proceedings involving a Christian litigant, except in matters of wills and contracts (heretics could not testify under any circumstances).

Thus, although the Jews' situation was somewhat better than that of heretics and pagans, the similar phrasing and legal treatment of all three groups was not conducive to easy distinction among them. The Jews, like the heretics, were called a "sect," a neutral term that had assumed negative connotations; they were forbidden to convert slaves and to build new synagogues. They gradually became second-class citizens of the empire. This is stated quite explicitly in the commentary to a law of Theodosius II, dated January 31, 438:

> This law orders in particular that no Jew and no Samaritan shall attain any honour of State government or administration, and that on no account shall they receive the

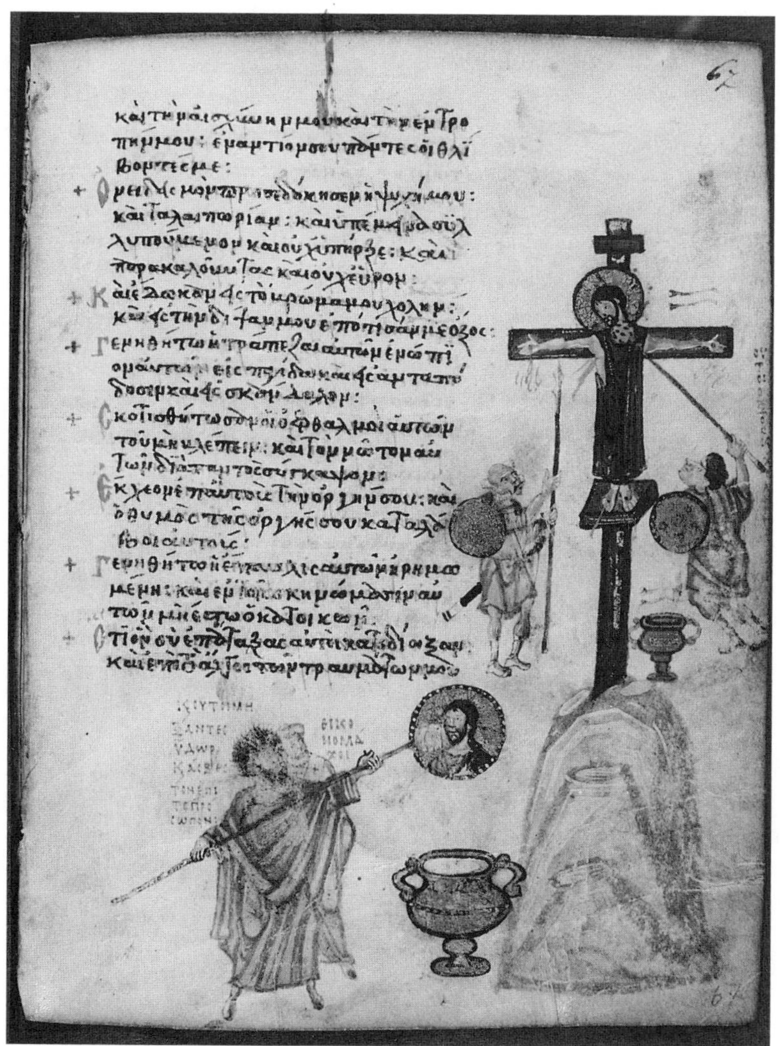

An uncompromisingly hostile image of the Jews, as tormentors of the crucified Christ (from a ninth-century Byzantine psalter). One Jew holds a lance with which he has pierced Christ's side; the other thrusts a sponge dipped in vinegar in his face (an interpretation of Psalm 69:21). The figures in the foreground, echoing the action with the sponge, are iconoclasts whitewashing an icon of Christ. The controversy about icons tore the Church apart at this time, and the iconoclasts were regularly categorized by their enemies as "Judaizers."

office of Protector, nor be prison guards, lest perchance they dare molest Christians, or even priests, under pretext of any office. . . . They shall not dare to construct anew any synagogue. . . . But let them know that this is allowed them, that they should repair the ruins of their synagogues. . . . This, however, is particularly comprehended in this law, that no Jew shall dare transfer to his law a Christian, slave or freeborn, by any persuasion whatsoever or be punished by death and loss of property.

THE JEWS IN THE EARLY MIDDLE AGES

Jewish communities existed for years in both parts of the Roman Empire. After the fall of the empire in the West (end of the fifth century), the Jewish communities were divided between Eastern Jews, that is to say Jews who lived under Roman rule in the eastern part of the empire, known as Byzantium, and Western Jews, who lived in the new Barbarian kingdoms. During the Middle Ages, Jewish communities existed in many cities in Byzantium and their life was different in many respects from Jewish life in the West. In Byzantium the Jews were a permitted and important group among the major communities of the population, taking part in the flourishing economic and commercial activities of urban life. Byzantine society was preoccupied with theology, a fact that led occasionally to anti-Jewish regulations and outbursts. Nevertheless, until the sixth century they enjoyed relative tolerance. The application of Justinian's law marked the beginning of a deterioration in their position. During the rule of subsequent emperors, and especially during Heraclius' rule (610–641), Jews were baptized under coercion and were driven to a very marginal place in society.

In Western Europe, most of the Jewish communities were direct successors to communities that had already existed in the Roman world, mainly in the commercial cities along the Mediterranean coast—in Italy, Spain and the south of France. The Jews of these communities claimed roots far back in antiquity, citing old foundation myths that entitled them to honor and respect; in a certain sense, this was also one way to absolve themselves from any involvement in the Crucifixion.

Jewish-Christian relations in Western Europe during the early Middle Ages were generally quite tranquil. As the Roman Codex was not known in the western kingdoms (unlike Byzantium), its anti-Jewish laws were also unknown there, while the laws of the Germanic kingdoms guaranteed all subjects equal freedom and protection. The Christianization of Europe was a gradual process, and even after all Europeans had embraced Catholic Christianity, one could hardly refer to Europe as Christian.

An exception in this respect was Visigoth Spain. After the Visigoth kings abandoned Arianism (the belief of a Christian sect that Christ was not coequal with God) and accepted the Catholic doctrine of the Holy Trinity in 586, they embarked on a policy of uniting the entire population into one perfect Christian society, accordingly adopting a palpably anti-Jewish line. It is not clear who initiated this anti-Jewish legislation; presumably, kings, bishops and nobles cooperated in the endeavor, for both political and religious motives. Several Christian councils convened under the auspices of the Visigoth monarchs issued anti-Jewish laws whose ultimate goal was to convert the Jews. Economic and social contacts between Jews and Christians were limited, conversion to Judaism was prohibited and Jews were barred from holding public office or possessing Christian slaves. Typical of this period is the literary activity of Isidore, bishop of Seville. Among his numerous works one finds the title *On the Catholic Faith against the Jews*, which includes an anthology of biblical proof-texts, arranged by subject, and purporting to prove that the Christological story was predicted by the Old Testament prophets and to refute the Jewish truth. A kind of inventory from which future disputants picked arguments to prove their points, this book became a firm foundation for Christian polemics against Judaism.

The discomfort due to Jewish presence varied from place to place. In many places Jews enjoyed relative calm. A contributing factor to this situation was the considerable variety of the European populations—Romans lived alongside Germans, and Germans themselves belonged to many different tribes. Within this multiplicity there was also a place for the Jews, who indeed lived and worked in comparative security, to all intents and purposes an integral component of their societies. It was only natural that such proximity between Jews and Christians aroused some concern on the part of the Church, which did its best to curtail interreligious contact and to prevent Jewish rule over Christians. The Church had in fact never relinquished its ambition to convert the Jews. Although it objected to enforced conversion, it never went so far as to define the precise meaning of the word *enforced*. Moreover, Jews were converted during riots and under fear of death. Later, when trying to return to Judaism, they were punished as heretics.

Church leaders also feared the influence of Jewish customs on their Christian neighbors, for, after all, Jews observed the biblical Law, in which Christians, too, believed. They were particularly apprehensive of some Christians' inclinations to observe the Sabbath. Sources from the Carolingian period (751–987) express profound fear for the integrity of Christian society in the face of the Jewish presence. Jews were apparently not averse to proselytizing among Christians and were indeed frequently successful. Little wonder, then, that the Church was worried, and as a result local synods enacted regulations forbidding Jews and Christians to eat or live together.

Evidence of the Church leaders' fears of Jewish influence is provided by literature written against the Jews. Agobard, bishop of Lyons, complained in letters written from 822 to 828 that simple, ignorant Christians were attracted to Judaism. Besides composing a tract named *On the Superstitions of the Jews*, he initiated legislation obliging Jews to attend Christian sermons. Agobard also made attempts to baptize Jewish children without their parents' agreement, but was forced to relent after the emperor Louis the Pious intervened. His tract provides important evidence about the Jews in the ninth century, as few Jewish sources have reached us from this period in Western Europe. Agobard's successor, Amulo, also wrote a work against the Jews in 846, which was addressed to the emperor Charles the Bald and urged him to adopt anti-Jewish legislation. Amulo, perturbed by Jewish proselytizing and by some Christians' fascination with Judaism, included in his book arguments against the Jewish religion and in favor of Christianity. It was probably at Amulo's instigation that a church synod of the cities of Meaux and Paris enacted anti-Jewish regulations in 845 to 846. Jews were forbidden to convert their slaves to Judaism, to serve in public office, to build new synagogues and to appear in public during Easter. It was similarly forbidden for Jews (and Christians) to sell slaves to Muslim countries.

The regulations were harsh; however, Charles the Bald did not ratify them. They were never actually implemented, and it is doubtful whether they had any real effect on Jewish life. This imperial policy is representative of the policies of most monarchs in the early Middle Ages, and much legislation of this kind, though not uncommon, was never put into effect; it attests more to the Church's fears that the Jewish minority might influence the Christian majority than to any steps actually taken to avert such influence.

What lay behind these churchmen's apprehensions? One could hardly imagine that there were indeed extensive Judaizing tendencies among Christians in the early Middle Ages; perhaps works like those just described testify more to inherited complexes than to actual facts. There were nevertheless a few well-known proselytes, of whom the most celebrated was Bodo, deacon of Louis the Pious. Perhaps meetings that Bodo had held with Jews caused him to doubt his own religion and convinced him of the truth of Judaism. Feigning the intention to go on a pilgrimage to Rome, he fled to Muslim Spain, where he converted. A nephew who had accompanied him on the journey followed suit. Bodo was circumcised at Saragossa and renamed Eleazar; he grew a beard and married. We know of his missionary activities from his correspondence with Paulo Alvaro (d. 861), conducted from Cordoba. It is said that he convinced the Muslim authorities to enact a regulation presenting Spanish Christians with the choice: to die or to convert to Islam or Judaism. Persecution of the Christians ceased only after Charles the Bald intervened.

Bodo was not the only famous proselyte. Others were Wecelin, a monk at the court of Duke Conrad in the early eleventh century; Andreas, archbishop of Bari; and Johannes, a Catholic priest of Norman extraction who converted and took the name Obadiah. He, too, was forced to escape to a Muslim land. However, these few examples hardly attest to a widespread phenomenon of conversion. In any case, it is quite clear that whatever movement existed was two-way; it was in fact far easier and more common to convert from Judaism to Christianity. Among the converts to Christianity were well-known figures, such as the son of Rabbi Gershom Meor ha-Golah (960–1028), the greatest spiritual leader of German Jewry in his day. The intense hostility toward Christianity revealed during the pogroms of 1096 in Germany and France is sometimes attributed to the fear of such conversions and the considerable extent of the trend.

Something of the motives that caused Jews to cross the line and become Christians may be deduced from an autobiographical work by one Hermannus, who apostatized in the first half of the eleventh century. Hermannus was born Judah, son of David Halevi, member of a respected family of Jewish merchants in Cologne. As a youth he was sent by his family to recover a debt from the bishop of Münster. The youth stayed with the bishop in his home for twenty weeks, accompanied him on his journeys, visiting churches and attending sermons. He even took part in a religious disputation with Rupert, abbot of the monastery of Deutz. On returning home, he married, but could find no peace for his soul. Finally, he fled to a monastery, was baptized and became the Augustinian monk Hermannus. As we see, then, the barrier between the two faiths was never high enough to prevent penetration from one side to the other. Most plausibly, there were many attractions for the Jewish convert to Christianity—some theological, others social, economic and political.

THE JEWISH MINORITY IN MEDIEVAL EUROPE

The Jewish minority in Europe became a coherent entity about the same time as Europe itself emerged as a well-defined Christian entity—on the cusp of the twelfth century. In other words, once the term *Christian Europe* became meaningful, one could also speak of the Jewish minority in Christian Europe as a distinct religious and cultural body.

Our information about the inner life and spiritual world of the Jews in the early Middle Ages is rather sparse. Only in the tenth and eleventh centuries does a clear pattern begin to materialize, consisting of cohesive Jewish communities that controlled their own affairs through various enactments and maintained orderly relations with the Christian rulers. The main concentrations of Jewish communities and Jewish culture were Ashkenaz (a Hebrew word denoting the German-speaking world, sometimes also including the north of France), and Sepharad (the Iberian Peninsula, sometimes also including the south of France); but there were other concentrations, either in Catholic Europe (England, Italy) or in the Byzantine Empire.

Ashkenaz

It seems probable that Jews first came to Germany from Italy and the south of France, and that the Jewish communities in Germany developed in tandem with the spread of Christianity. They tended to settle in particular in cities and along major trade routes. As a rule, the Holy Roman emperors of the Carolingian dynasty and later, as well as other secular leaders, were favorably disposed toward the Jews and protected them from harm. The Jews were seen as an important constituent of European society because of their economic role as merchants, especially international merchants. In order to attract them to settle in various cities, the local rulers granted them privileges and charters, which essentially provided the legal basis for the existence of Jewish communities in European cities.

The Jews of Rome receive a charter of privileges from the emperor Henry VII in 1312. From a contemporary manuscript. Note the distinctive Jews' hat, and the stereotyped exotic appearance of the leading Jew.

These privileges guaranteed the Jews protected rights of residence, burial grounds, autonomy in regulating their own affairs and even economic benefits. A famous example is the charter of privileges granted in 1084 by Bishop Rudiger of Speyer to the Jews he invited to settle in his city:

> In the name of the Holy and indivisible Trinity, I, Ruderigus . . . bishop of Speyer, upon making the town of Speyer into a city, thought that I would increase the honor of our place one thousand-fold if I also brought Jews to reside therein. And I settled the Jews that were brought outside the community and the residential quarters of the other townspeople. And in order to ensure that they would not be easily harmed by the rioting of the vulgar masses I encircled them with a wall. . . . I granted them permission and privilege to engage in the exchange of gold and silver and to buy and sell as much as they pleased. . . . And in addition I granted them, from the church's estate, a burial place as their possession. . . . And as ruler of the city among the residents, so is the *archisynagogos* among the Jews: he is to judge any dispute and suit that should arise among them or against them. . . . In general, to augment my benevolence I have granted them laws of such benefit to the Jewish people as to be unprecedented in any of the Teutons' cities.

This privilege and others like it paint a picture of relatively tranquil coexistence between the Christian majority and the Jewish minority during the early Middle Ages, right up to the late eleventh century. A similar picture, with further evidence of close economic ties between Jews and Christians, is provided by Jewish sources, such as the responsa literature ("queries and replies"—an exchange of letters in which a Jew consults a rabbi on a halakhic matter). It was only natural that these economic ties produced halakhic problems, since the precepts of Jewish law were not always in accord with the needs of commerce. Thus, medieval Jewish scholars exercised all their ingenuity to exclude Christians from the category of "idolaters"; otherwise, it would have been forbidden to conduct business with them.

The privileges granted the Jews were part of the prevailing system of government: rather than a single, common law for all citizens, "private" laws guaranteed the status of different groups. In this sense, the Jewish community was no different from other corporate bodies in the European cities, such as artisans' and tradesmen's guilds, which also had their own laws and were protected by the rulers. Thus, the Jews enjoyed quite far-reaching legal autonomy. Medieval governments recognized the existence of different legal systems, and Jewish legal autonomy was no exception. However, as a minority within a Christian majority, the Jewish community could not entirely avoid legal contacts with Christian law, though the degree to which Jews appealed to non-Jewish courts varied from place to place—it was a common phenomenon in Spain but much less evident in Germany. The talmudic rule *dina de-malkhuta dina*, that is, "the law of the [host] country is binding," implies recognition of the rulers' legislation and has been accepted by Jews right up to modern times.

Naturally, Jewish jurisdiction was limited to their own internal affairs. Otherwise, they were obliged to attend the Christian courts—creating a situation that created problems for both Jews and Christians. One reflection of these problems is the so-called Jewish Oath, the judicial formula that Jews were required to swear on occasions when they appeared before a Christian tribunal. Those versions of the Jewish Oath that have reached us attest to Christian attempts to neutralize the Christian elements that Jews could not accept, but without affecting the effectiveness of the oath. Some formulations were particularly humiliating; but in view of their length and verbosity, it seems doubtful whether they were ever really used. At any rate, the Jewish Oath exemplifies the efforts made to integrate the Jew into the prevailing process of law and, consequently, into the life of the Christian majority in general.

As evidenced by the privileges granted the Jews, the medieval emperors considered it their duty to maintain peace in their realms and to protect their subjects. In this context Jews were seen as requiring special protection, and imperial law severely punished attempts to molest them. The fact that Jews did not carry arms made them particularly vulnerable and had a deleterious effect on their legal and social status. They became wholly dependent on the monarch's protection and were ultimately defined as being in his servitude—"servants of the royal chamber," a notion that made its first appearance in a privilege of Emperor Frederick II in 1236 and was thenceforth applied to the Jews of Germany throughout the Middle Ages. The Jews' enslavement to the royal chamber—or treasury—delineated them as a group in need of special protection, but it ultimately reduced their status to one of servility. The protection granted them by emperors and other leaders is sometimes interpreted in the context of the overall feudal system, which was an intricate web of relations of dependence and protection among landowners and their vassals. The truth is, however, that the Jews never became an integral part of the feudal world—they couldn't own land or give military service—and their protected status served to set them apart as an inferior entity.

Jews generally tended to settle in their own separate neighborhoods or streets. The desire to keep together is common to all minority groups; it is motivated by security and by economic and cultural needs. Other associations, such as professional corporations, also tended to congregate in their own neighborhoods. As far as the Jews were concerned, this tendency was in sound agreement with the policies of the authorities, which were responsible for the Jews' protection; but the rulers did not force the Jews to live in separate quarters. In this respect the Jewish quarters of the Middle Ages must be distinguished from the ghettos of the early Modern Era, imposed on the Jews as a whole by the Christian authorities.

In the commercial cities of the Rhine Valley and elsewhere, Jews were granted a residential area in the heart of the city, near the market. However, the miniature dimensions of the cities caused constant friction between Jews and Christians, and the segregation was never absolute. From the twelfth century on, the Church became concerned with the proximity of Jewish and Christian residences. Appropriate regulations, designed to keep the two groups well apart, became increasingly common from the thirteenth century, though the Christian authorities still refrained from interfering in the internal life of the Jewish quarter, where the Jews enjoyed maximum autonomy.

The Jews of Western Europe were organized in communities—a characteristic Jewish institution with roots far back in antiquity. The community regulated its members' lives in accordance with Jewish law and maintained public institutions in the areas of governance, education, welfare and religion. Though the different communities were interconnected, each was almost completely independent. They were entitled to impose certain punishments—excommunication (*herem*) and flogging—and their decisions were binding on all members. Communal leaders were generally prominent scholars who were active in both intellectual and socio-political fields.

Within the communities one could find a broad range of spiritual activity, centering on the study of Halakhah (Jewish law) and the interpretation of sacred texts. Biblical exegesis flourished in the north of France in the late eleventh and twelfth centuries. First and foremost in this area was Rashi (the Hebrew acronym of Rabbi Solomon Yizhaki = son of Isaac) (1040–1105), who is considered the greatest medieval commentator on the Talmud, and one of the leading commentators on the Bible, and he was followed by his disciples, who were active mainly in Champagne, Normandy and Paris. The novel element in these exegetes' work was their effort to interpret the Bible according to the literal meaning of the text. Interestingly, their work was not without influence in the Christian world. Biblical commentators from the monastery of St. Victor in Paris also preferred literary interpretation to the more usual allegorical exegesis, which had been common in Christianity since Origen, the second-century scholar who was one of the most learned of early Church Fathers. It would seem that as part of the cultural movement known as "the twelfth-century renaissance," scholars of the two schools maintained some communication, which served more for intellectual needs than for interfaith disputation. A similar tendency may be discerned also in other spheres, such as pietism and asceticism. Thus, scholars have noted affinities between the Ashkenazi pietistic movement (Hasidei Ashkenaz) and Christian Franciscan spirituality.

The Babylonian Talmud, the foundation of Jewish life in Ashkenaz from the eleventh century on, became a focus of vigorous exegetical activity, endeavoring to adjust Halakhah to the specific circumstances of medieval Europe. The acceptance of the Talmud by Ashkenazi Jewry involved a certain amount of tension between its adaptation to the changing historic reality and the desire to preserve Jewish identity at any cost. The Jewish way of life was based on an oral tradition, handed down from father to son, which had created a whole system of binding, hallowed customs and rituals. Halakhic literature—comprising responsa, legal decisions and exegesis—preserves the legal rulings and enactments in the various walks of life promulgated by the rabbis; it is indeed the major characteristic of rabbinical creativity throughout Europe. During the thirteenth and fourteenth centuries, the rabbinate, the main leadership of the community, became institutionalized concurrently with a process of professionalization and monopolization that took place in all social and economic systems of the time.

Sepharad

The Jewish communities of Christian Spain took shape at the time of the Reconquest, especially in the twelfth and thirteenth centuries. They flourished in

In 1422 the Grand Master of the Order of Calatrava commissioned Rabbi Moses Arragel of Guadalajara to translate the Bible from Hebrew into Castilian. Two friars of Toledo were to instruct him in the Christian interpretation of the text. Here, the Franciscan Brother Arias is instructing the rabbi, who wears a distinctive badge on his right shoulder (see page 110).

the kingdoms of Aragon and Castile, maintaining relations of coexistence with the Christian rulers and their Muslim neighbors. These relations are now known as *convivencia*, a term denoting Jews, Muslims and Christians living together in harmony and mutual tolerance. As the Jews had played during the Christian Reconquest a mediating role between the Muslim and the Christian worlds, the Christians were not averse to availing themselves of the Jews' services and accordingly granted them favorable privileges and economic benefits. Some Jews became quite influential among the ruling circles and reached high-ranking positions. These were the "courtiers," who enjoyed advantages similar to those of the Christian nobility.

In Spain, as in Germany and the north of France, the Jews engaged in a variety of cultural activities. But while these activities in Ashkenaz were more homogeneous and did not involve the secular sciences, Spanish Jews were active not only in the study of Halakhah, the Bible and Talmud, but also in more worldly areas, such as philosophy, literature and science. This greater openness was due no doubt to the greater similarity between the culture of the majority (first Muslim and later Christian society) and that of the Jews, and also to the challenge presented by the high intellectual achievements of the host society. The Jews of

The seal of the medieval Jewish community of Seville.

Christian Spain acted as cultural mediators; they were particularly instrumental in bringing the Greco-Arab philosophical and scientific heritage to the knowledge of the Christian world. Jewish philosophers, Moses Maimonides (Moses ben Maimon, known also as Rambam) (1135–1204) in particular, exerted considerable influence on great Christian thinkers such as Thomas Aquinas. Jewish culture in Spain was largely heterogeneous, the most prominent trends being the philosophical, on the one hand, and the mystical—kabbalistic—on the other. The most important Jewish mystical work—*The Book of the Zohar*, a complete body of literature united under one title, containing a collection of several books that include midrashic statements, homilies and discussion on many topics—was written in Spain in the late thirteenth century.

The Jews in Spain lived in their own quarters, known as *callum*. After the Christian Reconquest, they were generally permitted to remain in the neighborhoods they had inhabited under the Muslims. The Jewish quarter was usually in a convenient and central location; in some places the Christian rulers allotted the Jews choice residential areas, sometimes on land belonging to the local cathedral. The Jews of Toledo lived in a great fortress within the city walls and also owned shops and houses in the city's commercial center. By the end of the fourteenth century, there were twenty-three synagogues in the Jewish quarter of Seville—an indication of the community's size and wealth. At first, as in Central Europe, the Jewish quarter was not closed and exclusive. In the fourteenth century, however, with the appearance of the *conversos* (converts), the authorities made it their business to separate Jews from Christians, and in some places moved the Jews to farther outlying neighborhoods, which were more crowded and less hygienic.

Economic Life

The economic aspects of Jewish life in Spain also differed from the situation in Ashkenaz. Jewish society in Spain was heterogeneous in the professional sense, while German and north-French Jews were active mainly in commerce and, later, in moneylending. By the early Middle Ages, the Jews were already engaged in trade, though some also cultivated the land and grew vines, particularly in France and Spain. Rashi's grandson, Rabbi Samuel ben Meir (known as Rashbam) (1085–after 1158), owned flocks of sheep. Gradually, however, as the feudal structure took root, the Jews were almost completely cut off from the land. In any case, as they were not infrequently forced to flee their homes, Jews tended to prefer portable possessions rather than landed property. Consequently, most medieval Jews lived in cities. Some dealt in international trade, being well served in this role by their contacts with Jewish communities in other countries. In the early Middle Ages, with the disintegration of the Roman Empire and the German invasions, a drastic decline took place in commercial activity, leaving the Jews as practically the only traders. They brought various luxury goods from distant countries—furs, silk and spices. A diplomatic mission sent by Charlemagne in 797 to Sultan Harun al-Rashid included a Jew, no doubt in recognition of his contacts in the Orient and his knowledge of languages.

With the rise of cities and the commercial revolution, beginning in the eleventh century, the Jews were slowly ousted from their hegemony over trade and commerce. The cities of Italy assumed primacy in international and regional trade. The Jews were now seen as competing with the Christian merchants and the Italians in particular, and they were no match for them—particularly as they were no longer exempted, as in the past, from the payment of taxes. At the same time, in view of the Church's strict prohibition of usury, the Jews moved into the moneylending profession—so much so that by the twelfth century the term *judaizare* had become synonymous with lending at interest. Thus, the Jews filled a crucial niche in the developing economic system of Europe, as providers of credit; but this role also made them a target of hatred and loathing. Considered oppressors of the poor and the disadvantaged, they were declared usurers. Their interest rates were indeed very high—generally thirty percent but sometimes as much as eighty percent—presumably because of the particularly high risk involved in such loans, as well as the high taxation imposed on the Jews themselves. Despite the vital importance of Jewish credit, social and ecclesiastical censure of the Jews' function was one of the direct causes of the expulsion of Jews from various countries during the thirteenth, fourteenth and fifteenth centuries. The Jews thus became the focus of hostility for the developing European economy and of guilt feelings on the part of the Christians who were benefiting from it.

CRUSADES AND MARTYRDOM, 1096

About the turn of the millennium, the idea of a unified Christian society began to assume more concrete and emotional dimensions. In 1095 Pope Urban II, preaching at a Church council convened in the French town of Clermont, called on Christians to rise and redeem the Church of the Holy Sepulcher at Jerusalem from its bondage under Muslim rule. The surprising response to Urban's appeal, which culminated in the conquest of Jerusalem in 1099, was an expression of Christian solidarity. The Crusaders, believing themselves warriors in God's service, marched eastward, burning with a messianic fervor, to alter the course of history and hasten the end of its present stage, which would be followed by the Kingdom of Heaven on earth. Crusader fury was directed toward anyone who was not a Christian—not only the distant Muslims but also the nearby Jews, whose conversion to Christianity now became an urgent matter. In the summer of 1096, as the Crusader bands in their eastward thrust poured through the flourishing Jewish communities of the cities of France and Germany, they sounded a call to slaughter first and foremost the enemy within, the Jews, the Christ-killers. The Jews of three cities in the Rhine Valley—Mainz, Worms and Cologne—were attacked by the crusading marchers, mainly Frenchmen, aided and abetted by the local townspeople. Jews were faced with the choice of "baptism or death," and the Jewish chronicles that describe the massacres paint terrifying pictures of the ensuing bloodbath. The attacking Crusaders' religious frenzy was met with an equally fervent faith: most of the Jews preferred to die martyrs' deaths rather than accept Christianity, and in order to prevent forcible baptism of their families, particularly infants, they slew them with their own hands and then committed suicide.

Albert of Aachen, who chronicled the First Crusade, describes in amazement the death of the Jews of Mainz: "The Jews, seeing that their Christian enemies were attacking them and their children, and were sparing no age, fell upon one another—brothers, children, wives, mothers, and sisters—and slaughtered one another. Horrible to say, mothers cut the throats of nursing children with knives and stabbed others, preferring them to perish thus by their own hands rather than be killed by the weapons of the uncircumcised."

Hebrew accounts of the massacres include several particularly horrifying chapters; perhaps the most ghastly is the story of "Mistress Rachel, the young woman of Mainz," related by Solomon ben Samson in his chronicle:

> Who has seen anything like this, who has heard anything like that which the saintly and pious woman, Rachel daughter of R. Isaac ben R. Asher, wife of R. Judah, did? She said to her companions: "I have four children. On them as well have no mercy, lest these uncircumcised come and seize them alive and they remain in their pseudo-faith. With them as well you must sanctify the Name of the holy God." One of her companions came and took the knife to slaughter her son. When the mother of the children saw the knife, she shouted loudly and bitterly and smote her face and breast and said: "Where is your steadfast love, O Lord?" Then the woman said to her companions in her bitterness: "Do not slaughter Isaac before his brother Aaron, so that he not see the death of his brother and take flight." The woman took the lad and slaughtered him—he was small and exceedingly comely. The mother spread her sleeve to receive the blood. . . . The lad Aaron, when he saw that his brother had been slaughtered, cried out: "Mother, do not slaughter me!" He went and hid under a bureau. She still had two daughters, Bella and Matrona, comely and beautiful young women, the daughters of R. Judah her husband. The girls took the knife, and sharpened it, so that it not be defective. They stretched forth their neck and she sacrificed them to the Lord God of Hosts. . . . When the saintly one completed sacrificing her three children before the creator, then she raised her voice and called to her son: "Aaron, Aaron, where are you? I shall not have mercy nor pity on you as well." She pulled him by the leg from under the bureau where he was hidden, and she sacrificed him before the sublime and exalted God. She placed them under her two sleeves, two on each side, near her heart. They convulsed near her, until the enemy seized the chamber and found her sitting and mourning them. They said to her: "Show us the money which you have in your sleeves." When they saw the children and saw that they were slaughtered, they smote her and killed her along with them.

In symbolic terms, Rachel "the mother of children" is the classical mother image, as in Jeremiah's prophecy: "A voice is heard in Ramah, lamentation and bitter weeping. Rachel is weeping for her children; she refuses to be comforted for her children, because they are not" (Jeremiah 31:15). Her sacrifice also recalls the archetypal mother image in Christianity, the Virgin Mary, mother of Christ, who stood at the foot of the Cross when her son was crucified. The figure of the Jewish mother, Rachel, was conducting a dialogue with that of Mary, who played a prominent part in the ideology of the Crusades and was, as it were, competing with her. It was as if the Jews were saying that Rachel exceeds Mary in piety, religious fervor and self-sacrifice.

The Jews' willingness to martyr themselves made a great impression in the Christian camp too, but what most strikes the modern reader, apart from the terrible trauma inflicted on the Jews, is the considerable affinity between the Crusaders' religious consciousness and the Jews' martyrological ardor. The Jews, perhaps reacting to the ideology of the Crusades, evolved their own "Crusader mentality": its ideological expression was an avenging messianism, the conviction that the Jew-haters would meet their fate on Judgment Day; its practical manifestation was a fervent martyrology. The Crusaders were ready for any sacrifice on their way to recover Christ's sepulcher, in the certitude that their actions would fully atone for their sins and earn them eternal life. The Jews responded with their own martyrology, based on the notion known in Hebrew as *kiddush ha-shem* (sanctification of the name), which surpassed its Christian counterpart in its extreme nature and in the heroism that it aroused.

Jewish martyrdom. This illuminated Hebrew manuscript from the Rhineland (Mainz, 1427?) depicts familiar scenes from the apocryphal accounts of the persecution of Judaism under Antiochus IV (see page 25). Medieval martyrs were strengthened by the memory of the victims of Seleucid intolerance.

The protracted, intricate network of Jewish-Christian relations repeatedly reveals the considerable affinity—one might almost say kinship—between the two parties' worldviews and religious consciousness, as well as the intense hostility that it engendered. From the very beginning, each religion defined itself in opposition to the rival faith: Judaism became the absolute "other" for Christians, Christianity the ultimate "other" for Jews. The other religion's symbols took on a negative, demoniac significance. The Christians broke into synagogues, burned them down and tore up scrolls of the Law. The Jews, who could not retaliate by burning churches and smashing crosses, uttered imprecations as they died, cursing "the misdirected ones [the Christians] in the name of the dishonored and accursed hanged one, son of harlotry." They died with the declaration "Hear O Israel, the Lord our God is one Lord" on their lips—a kind of battle cry affirming the Jewish creed of a single God and utterly renouncing the Trinity. In 1096, for the first time, two fully coherent faiths confronted one another, each aware of the divisive rivalry between them. With regard to Jewish consciousness, the events of 1096 were a turning point, constantly recalled in later generations and the Jewish reaction held up as a model of religious conduct.

The behavior of the Christian mobs no longer conformed to the principles of Gregory the Great, who had become pope in 590. He had frowned on forcible conversion, and his position was emulated by most later popes. Some bishops in fact tried to save Jews, whether out of compassion, loyalty to the official ideology or in aversion to disorder and riots. Educated Christians explicitly condemned the riots—an indication that the Christian world was not united in its attitude to the cruel massacres or to the religious fervor that produced them.

Just as the Crusades were an important juncture in European history, the events of 1096 were of crucial significance for the relations between Jews and Christians in Europe. Perhaps, indeed, the wounds were soon healed as far as everyday life was concerned, for the Jews of Germany and France recovered quickly, and economic, social and cultural life was restored. In 1104 the emperor Henry IV issued a decree permitting all Jews who had been baptized under duress to return to Judaism, although this violated Church law. The supportive policies of the secular authorities—particularly the imperial court—vis-à-vis the Jewish communities were maintained, and new communities soon sprang up in Germany and elsewhere.

THE WESTERN CHURCH AND THE JEWS

Throughout the Middle Ages, the papacy maintained its traditional tolerant attitude toward the Jews as formulated by Augustine. The practical aspects of this policy were stated in papal bulls and encyclicals addressed to secular rulers or to Catholic clergy, enjoining them to protect the Jews under their jurisdiction. The most famous of these documents is the bull *Sicut Iudeis*, issued in 1120. From the twelfth to the fifteenth centuries, twenty-three popes reissued the bull, and it was even included in the Canon Law under the title *Constitutio pro Iudeis*. It stresses that the fundamental rights of the Jews must be safeguarded:

> This is why, although they prefer to persist in their obstinacy rather than acknowledge the words of the prophets and the eternal secrets of their own scriptures, thus arriving at an understanding of Christianity and salvation, nevertheless, in view of the fact that they have begged for our protection and our aid and in accordance with the clemency which Christian piety imposes, we, following in the footsteps of our predecessors, . . . grant their petition and offer them the shield of our protection.
>
> We decree that no Christian shall use violence to force them into baptism while they are unwilling and refuse . . . for surely none can be believed to possess the true Christian faith if he is known to have come to Christian baptism unwillingly and even against his wishes.
>
> Moreover, without the judgment of the authority of the Land, no Christian shall presume to wound their persons, or kill them, or rob them of their money, or change the good customs which they have thus far enjoyed in their place of habitation. Furthermore, while they celebrate their festivals, no one shall disturb them in any way by means of sticks and stones. . . . We decree that no one shall dare to desecrate or reduce a Jewish cemetery.

The Church's policies regarding the Jews were based on the consistent notion that one could not force a nonbeliever to believe. The medieval papacy, in the edict just cited and elsewhere, recognized that the Jews, despite their lack of proper belief, were entitled as a fundamental right not only to live among Christians but also to receive special protection in view of their sensitive situation, and to maintain their own religious rites.

The frequent republication of the bull *Sicut Iudeis* in the twelfth and thirteenth centuries was probably due to requests from the Jews, who saw it as protecting them from attack and persecution. Almost all thirteenth-century popes reissued the bull soon after assuming office. Innocent III, pope from 1198, appended an introduction to the famous decree, in which he offered a theological justification for protecting the Jews: "Although the Jewish distortion of the faith is deserving of thorough condemnation, nevertheless, because the truth of our own faith is proved through them, they must not be severely oppressed by the faithful. So the prophet says, 'Thou shalt not kill them, lest in time they forget Thy Law'; or, more clearly put: Thou shalt not destroy the Jews completely so that the Christians may not possibly forget Thy Law which, though they themselves fail to understand it, they display in their books for those who do understand."

When the accusation of ritual murder and ritual cannibalism (blood libel) began to spread through Europe, *Sicut Iudeis* became the basis for papal condemnations and warnings; the popes consistently opposed the blood libel and forbade their flock to repeat the accusations—admittedly without much success. The relative failure of such means invites broader assessment: it is doubtful whether this bull and other similar ones could actually protect the Jews. They attest not so much to the conditions in the cities where the Jews lived as to papal policies. They could not halt rioting or prevent expulsions or restore forcibly converted Jews to Judaism. Rather, they should be seen as a theoretical expression of ecclesiastical tolerance. As such, their importance is undeniable, but their practical influence was hardly decisive.

A major landmark in relations between the Church and the Jews was the Fourth Lateran Council, convened in 1215 at the Lateran Palace in Rome, summoned by Pope Innocent III to discuss urgent issues then troubling Christendom. The Jewish question and Christian-Jewish relations were not among the major points on the agenda, which was primarily concerned with the doctrine of transubstantiation, the spread of the Albigensian heresy—the Albigenses, a dualistic sect, maintained that matter is evil and only the human spirit good, and rejected much Christian dogma—in the south of France and methods of combating it, new calls for a crusade and so on. The council was at pains to create greater unity and uniformity in the Christian world and to achieve a sharper definition of the limits of faith. The resolutions adopted included four regulations relating to Jews, which laid down a policy that would affect Jewish life in Europe for generations to come. They imposed restrictions on the interest rates that Jews could charge and forbade them to hold positions in which Christians would be subordinate to them. They also ruled that Jews who had converted willingly to Christianity could not return to Judaism, and, finally, endeavored to reduce contacts between Jews and Christians by requiring Jews to wear special apparel. The requirement of special dress—the most known, and most pervasive, of the council's resolutions regarding the Jews—was to influence Jewish life right into the twentieth century: "(Canon 68) There are provinces in which a difference of costume distinguishes the Jews and the Saracens from the Christians, but there are provinces in which the confusion has reached such proportions that no distinction whatsoever can be made. It has therefore occurred at times, by mistake, that Christians have mixed with Jewish or Saracen women, and Jews or Saracens with Christian women. So as to remove in the future any pretext of error or mistake in connection with this deplorable licentiousness and confusion, we have decreed that in the future [Jewish and Saracen] men and women shall be differentiated at all times and in all Christian lands from other people through their dress."

This provision was applied to different degrees in different countries and regions; its most familiar—and most long-lived—manifestation was the badge worn by Jews on their outer clothes whenever they left their homes. The modern observer cannot but recall the Nazis' regulation requiring Jews in the occupied countries to wear a yellow badge in the shape of a Shield of David, inscribed with the word *Jude*. However, though this modern badge was certainly a remote descendant of the medieval one, it was quite common in the Middle Ages to show various emblems on one's dress, and indeed the Jews were not the only group identified by a special device. Neither should it be forgotten that the Jews, for their part, were interested in maintaining their identity and avoiding Christian company. Of course, for Christians the wearing of a special badge marked one's membership in a certain knightly order or guild; it was voluntary and indicated the bearer's high station or exclusive status. The Jewish badge, by contrast, was compulsory and, though initially designed to set the Jews apart, in the final analysis it marked them as inferior. Little wonder, therefore, that the Jews made every effort to oppose the decree and, risking punishment, refrain from wearing the badge, but they were not always successful.

The Inquisition's attitude to the Jews is of particular interest. The Inquisition was established by the papacy in the thirteenth century in order to combat various heresies within Christendom, so that the Jews were not originally within its terms of reference. Nevertheless, relapsed converts to Christianity, even if converted under duress, were declared heretics and therefore subject to the jurisdiction of the Inquisition. Jews who aided them were also punished. Christian converts to Judaism, too, were considered heretics and accordingly condemned to burn at the stake—the specific punishment meted out to heretics from the thirteenth century on. Jewish communities that rendered them assistance were severely punished—they had to pay large sums of money, so that the communities were completely impoverished. Pope Clement IV, in a bull *Turbato corde* issued in 1267, ordered the Dominicans and Franciscans to investigate reports that Jews were trying to convert Christians. Other popes repeated this order during the thirteenth century. Sexual relations between Jews and Christians were considered heresy, and those involved could expect to be burned at the stake.

Some of the inquisitors tried to extend the Church's jurisdiction in relation to the Jews. They argued that Jews who maligned Christianity should also be punished as heretics, and that the Church was entitled to interfere in Jewish matters when the Jews themselves violated their own law—that is, to define heresy in Jewish terms. Interference of this sort occurred in 1232, during the Maimonidean Controversy (disputes around philosophical and religious themes in Maimonides' writings), and during the Disputation of Paris in 1240 (to follow), where the Talmud was accused of heresy—meaning heresy against the Old Testament. In both cases the intervention resulted in the burning of Jewish books.

Generally, however, the old rule was observed: the Church did not intervene in the Jews' internal affairs as long as they presented no threat to Christianity. In Spain, too, the Inquisition was concerned mainly with *conversos*, that is, converts to Christianity, not with Jews, as we shall see later.

DISPUTATION AND DIALOGUE

Christianity and Judaism were both convinced of their absolute truth. Each of the two religions was certain that it, and it alone, held the key to the divine message, while the other was in grave error. The conflict assumed various forms and found expression in various literary genres, ranging from explicitly polemical tracts, listing arguments in favor of the writer's side and against his opponent, to exegetical works, mainly biblical commentaries, historiography and belles lettres. Artistic media were also brought into play—we have already discussed the figure of Synagoga, a polemical Christian portrayal of Judaism. Synagoga was not always a dejected, defeated figure, as she is, for example, at Strasbourg Cathedral. She was sometimes shown with a serpent bound about her eyes, as though blinded by a satanic agency. Jews might also be represented by biblical "villains," of whom the most prominent is Cain, shown wearing a Jewish hat—a figure of evil second only to that of Judas Iscariot, the archetypal representative of the diabolical, treacherous Jew. Indeed, such artistic argumentation was accessible to a larger, more varied Christian audience than polemical literature, which was aimed primarily at the intellectual clergy. Jewish polemical works were largely a mirror image of the Christian works, both in the characteristics of the genre and its content.

St. Ildefonsus debating with a Jew. St. Ildefonsus became archbishop of Toledo in 657, during a time of severe discrimination against Jews in Spain under the Visigothic rulers.

Besides the polemic literature, there were also physical, face-to-face confrontations of

Jews and Christians. The very nature of the considerable similarity in the two religions' conceptual worlds, as against the sharp disagreement over the interpretation of those concepts, coupled with the fact that Jews and Christians were constantly rubbing shoulders with one another, produced frequent exchanges on matters of faith. Of course, we have little information about such private arguments. Not so the great public disputations, which were carefully planned by the Christian side and possessed far-reaching propaganda significance.

Heinrich Heine (1797–1856), in a famous poem, described the atmosphere of the disputations as follows:

In the Aula at Toledo
Fanfares blare, the drumbeat rolls,
To a spiritual tourney
Crowds of people swarm in shoals.

It's no secular encounter
With steel sabers, hauberks, heaumes—
Here it's words that are the lances
And they're honed on learned tomes.

Here the champions serve no lady,
They're not gallant paladins—
On this tilting ground the knights are
Rabbis versus Capuchins.

Since the earliest days of Christianity, right up to the thirteenth century, Jews and Christians had been disputing the meaning of the text sacred to both—the Old Testament. Each side accused the other of misunderstanding, sometimes of deliberately distorting, the Bible. The Christians argued that the Old Testament narratives were simply prefigurations of the Christological story. Thus, for example, the Binding of Isaac was a prefiguration of the Crucifixion: "Abraham leading his son to sacrifice denotes God the Father. . . . Isaac denotes Christ. Just as Abraham offered up his only son that he loved, so did God the Father give up His only son for our sakes. And just as Isaac carried the wood on which he would later be placed, so did Christ carry the cross upon which he would later be bound."

The words of the prophets, too, were given a Christological interpretation: many prophecies, argued the Christians, had been fulfilled in Jesus; clearly, therefore, he was indeed the Messiah. Thus, for example, Isaiah's prophecy, "Therefore the Lord Himself will give you a sign. Behold, a young woman shall conceive and bear a son, and shall call his name Immanu-el" (Isaiah 7:14). The Vulgate—the accepted Latin version of the Bible—renders the Hebrew word *'almah* (young woman) as *virgo*, virgin, and accordingly the Christians interpret the verse as referring to the Virgin Mary, mother of Jesus, while Immanu-el was Jesus himself. Isaiah 53, the chapter devoted to "the servant of the Lord" who suffered for mankind, was understood by Christians as referring to Jesus, while Genesis 49:10, "The Sceptre shall not depart from Jacob, nor the ruler's staff from between his feet, until he comes to whom it belongs [or: until Shiloh comes]," foretold that the Jews would lose their political independence after the coming of the Messiah, Christ.

Such interpretations, and their implications, were rejected and held in contempt by the Jews, but that could not mitigate the problems aroused by such verses as "Let us make man in our image, after our likeness" (Genesis 1:26), in which the One God spoke in the plural. The Jews' strategy in disputations was to meet the typological, spiritual Christian interpretations with literal, historical, direct explanations of the text. Although they, too, were not unfamiliar with allegorical exegesis, the bitter conflict with Christianity over the meaning of the text forced them to adhere as far as possible to the plain meaning.

The Jewish-Christian dispute revolved around several areas of contention: the Deity (is God one or three? can God be divine and human at one and the same time?); religious law (should the precepts of Mosaic Law be observed as they stand, or were they abrogated by the coming of Jesus, or were they perhaps always intended merely allegorically?); the Messiah (had he already come, as the Christians claimed, or would he come only in the future, as the Jews believed?); the meaning of Jewish history—that is, why had the Jews languished in exile so many years (for their sin of deicide, said the Christians; for reasons known only to God, retorted the Jews). And there were other subjects too. The furor of the dispute did not lessen with the elapsing years. Scholars have repeatedly come back to the question of the degree to which the written polemical tracts reflect arguments that were actually presented at the face-to-face disputations. Many authorities hold that these tracts were written primarily for internal apologetical reasons; the Jews wrote them for their brethren, to provide them with ammunition for their own disputations, and the Christians wrote them for their co-religionists, to provide them with ammunition against the Jews. However, even if one allows the truth of this argument, it is clear that the great quantity of polemical works written during the Middle Ages and the early Modern Era, mainly on the Christian side, is indicative of the fact that the problem refused to go away.

The thirteenth century saw a change in the nature of the disputations. Up to that time the Christians had drawn their proofs for the truth of Christianity from the Old Testament; now, however, the Talmud provided the grounds for the attacks on Judaism and, consequently, for the substantiation of Christianity. This shift in itself implied another difference: as long as they were citing the Bible, the Christians were fighting the Jews, as it were, on familiar ground, for the Bible was available in a Latin translation, its content was known and there was a standard interpretation. When it came to the Talmud, however, the Christian world was dependent mainly on apostates (such as Petrus Alphonsi at the beginning of the twelfth century or Pablo Christiani in the mid-thirteenth century), who were well versed in Hebrew and familiar with the world of the Talmud and the Midrash. Even learned Christians, however knowledgeable in Hebrew and however capable of reading the Bible in the original tongue, could not approach the talmudic literature unaided. One might say that the entry of the Talmud into the arena of the interfaith dispute in the thirteenth century, through the activities of apostates, vigorously encouraged by the Franciscans and Dominicans, was responsible for a sharp change in Christian Europe's attitude to the Jews. Once they had "discovered" the Talmud, European Christians came to realize that the Jews were not what they had thought them to be. No biblical Jews were these, descendants of the Jews described in the Old Testament; they were talmudic Jews, their behavior dictated by laws and regulations set out in the Talmud—a work fraught, so Christians believed, with heresy and blasphemy.

In 1236 Nicolas Donin, an apostate Jew of La Rochelle, France, sought audience with Pope Gregory IX, to whom he presented a series of complaints against the Talmud. He alleged that the Jews preferred the Talmud to the Bible; that the Talmud contained terrible obscenities, and in particular legends with the most offensive anthropomorphisms; that the Talmud permitted Jews to kill Christians; and that it maligned and blasphemed against the Christian sacraments. Donin's efforts resulted in the so-called Disputation of Paris, held in 1240, in which French rabbis defended the Talmud against Donin's accusations. The disputation—more like a trial—was held under the auspices of Louis IX of France, and it culminated in a verdict confirming the "guilt" of the Talmud and condemning it to be burned. Some 10,000 volumes were burned in Paris in 1242. The event launched a new chapter in Christian-Jewish relations. From then, on, Jewish literature—up to that time a purely internal, Jewish affair—became a target for scrutiny and investigation, for intervention and censorship on the part of the ecclesiastical Inquisition. From the mid-thirteenth century to the mid-sixteenth century, the Talmud was constantly under Christian attack, and its volumes were occasionally consigned to fire for their heresies—events that left a lasting impression on the Jewish world.

In the years following the Disputation of Paris, Christian tactics changed. Christian scholars, again aided and abetted by apostates, wished to prove that hidden in the Talmud one could find proofs for the truth of Christianity. The argument ran as follows: the Sages of the Talmud were already aware that Jesus was the Messiah, and this knowledge was concealed in the Talmud "like pearls in a heap of refuse," to quote the *Pugio fidei* written in the thirteenth century by the Spanish Dominican friar Raymundus Martini. The *Pugio fidei* is a monumental work attempting to demonstrate Christian truth on the basis of various genres of Jewish literature: the Talmud, the Midrash, biblical exegesis, philosophical and kabbalistic literature.

This new Christian mode of disputation was first put to a public test, under highly dramatic circumstances, in July 1263 in Barcelona, at the palace of James I, king of Aragon. The Jewish cause was represented by Rabbi Moses ben Nahman (Nahmanides, or Ramban) (1194–c. 1270), head of the talmudic academy of Girona, then one of the greatest leaders of Spanish Jewry. He was confronted by Pablo Christiani, an apostate Jew and now a Dominican friar, who was supported by the heads of the mendicant orders—it was they who had planned and organized the disputation. Nahmanides, a highly respected figure in Spain who also enjoyed the sympathy of the king, was granted freedom of speech during the dispute on condition that he refrain from defaming the Christian sacraments. If the book he wrote after the disputation may be believed, he was able, despite the limitations, to represent the Jewish position with considerable success; he outlined, in particular, the nature and authority of Aggadah (the nonlegal portions of the Oral Law, the postbiblical religious law), and adroitly unmasked his opponent's ignorance. The Disputation of Barcelona took place toward the end of the period characterized, as we have already mentioned, by *convivencia*. However, the cracks in this good-neighborly atmosphere were already apparent. On the third day of the debate, Nahmanides requested permission to quit the disputation, for fear of the Dominicans who were "terrorizing the world." This request—which was refused—reveals something of the atmosphere in Barcelona at the time. Although the Jewish representative could express himself in relative freedom within the palace, there was much agitation outside, where Dominican preachers were inciting the masses in reaction to the Jew's arguments in the debate. Indeed, the disputation focused on the most crucial points of the interfaith controversy: "And thus we agreed to speak first on the subject of the Messiah, whether he has already come as Christians believe, or whether he is yet to come as Jews believe. And after that, we would speak on whether the Messiah was truly divine, or entirely human, born from a man and a woman. And after that we would discuss whether the Jews still possess the true law, or whether the Christians practice it."

The last question, the practical observance of Mosaic Law, was never debated, but the first were discussed at length, with citations from both the Old Testament and later literature. In the two works written after the disputation, Nahmanides' aforementioned account and a brief Latin report bearing the king's seal of approval, each disputant claimed victory for his own camp. Clearly, it was impossible to determine the true victor in any such religious argument. At any rate, Nahmanides' tract, which recounts his detailed answers to Christiani's queries, was written as a kind of handbook for Jewish use in further disputations with Christians, and as such it aroused the wrath of the Dominicans. They complained to the king of Aragon, and when the latter remained unimpressed, took their protest to the pope. About this time Nahmanides, then seventy-three years old, left his home country, Spain, and immigrated to Palestine, where he settled in Acre. Presumably, his chronicle of the disputation had made it dangerous, if not impossible, for him to remain in Spain, apparently because it might sabotage the friars' missionary assault on the Jews and raise the morale of the latter.

The Disputation at Barcelona had been planned by the Dominicans, as part of the friars' missionary assault on Jews and Muslims. Besides censorship of Jewish books and enforced disputations, obligatory sermons were delivered in synagogues, and Jews were required by law to attend. The preachers demonstrated the superiority of the Christian religion to their audiences, causing considerable perplexity among the Jews at a time of deteriorating relations between them and the Christian majority. One preacher whose name is known was Ramon Lull, a colorful figure who had dedicated his life to converting the world—but Muslims in particular—to Christianity. He wrote numerous books to demonstrate the truth of Christianity, even sailing three times to Tunisia to convert the local Muslims. Tradition has it that on his third trip, at the age of about eighty-two, he was stoned by a Muslim mob and died a martyr's death in the boat returning him home. Among his Christianizing efforts directed at Jews was a book of sermons—a handbook for preachers in the synagogue. Lull himself received permission from the king of Aragon to preach in synagogues on Saturdays and Sundays and show Jews the Catholic truth. He is characteristic of the period in his missionary zeal, fruit of a profound belief in the imminent advent of the Kingdom of Heaven; it was this belief that made the conversion of the Jews such an urgent matter.

The friars' activities in general undoubtedly brought about a deterioration in the condition of Western Europe's Jews. Ramon Lull and his fellow preachers did not impose direct harm on the Jews; but a hundred years later such sermons could undermine relations between the Christian majority and the Jewish minority, perhaps even promoting conversion among the Jews. In 1412, Vicente Ferrer, a Dominican friar of Valencia, preached up and down Castile, inspiring many Christians to repent and some Jews to convert and become *conversos*. He roamed the streets of Castilian towns in the company of bands of flagellants, generating an atmosphere of terror and religious ecstasy that prompted many Jews to take flight. Ferrer persuaded the Castilian court to treat the Jews harshly, burdening them with oppressive social and economic measures. A series of humiliating laws was promulgated: Jews were forced to move out of their comfortable neighborhoods to slums on the outskirts of the cities; their freedom of movement was curtailed; they were forbidden to hold administrative office or any position of authority; they were forbidden to practice medicine or trade in pharmaceutical products—in fact, to engage in trade of any kind. These laws were intended to destroy the basis of Jewish existence and thus to force them either to convert to Christianity or to leave the country.

But not all Jews who converted did so out of fear or because of economic pressure. Many made honest attempts to meet the challenge of Christianity; in so doing, they became convinced of its truth. The famous convert Abner of Burgos (c. 1270–c. 1340) was practicing as a physician in Burgos. In 1295 a false prophet appeared in Avila and predicted that the Messiah would come in that year. After this prediction had failed to materialize, Abner decided to become a Christian. He had long been perturbed by the years of Jewish suffering in exile and by the problem of theodicy in general. Unable to find solace in Jewish writings and in philosophy, he turned to Christian sources. After some twenty-five years of soul-searching, at about the age of fifty, he became a Christian; from then on he was known as Alfonso of Valladolid. He wrote various works, in which he explained why he had converted and offered practical suggestions for the conversion of other Jews. Accusing the Jews of hostility to Christianity, he justified their isolation and the frequent attacks on them. Abner of Burgos' works were a great help to Christian polemicists in Spain in the following years.

The feelings of mutual respect and relative openness characteristic of the Disputation of Barcelona were a far cry from the oppressive fear that pervaded the public Disputation of Tortosa 150 years later (1413–1414). On this occasion an apostate named Gerónimo de Santa Fé (formerly Joshua Lorki, a physician), in the presence of Benedict XIII (c. 1328–1423), tried to prove to the Jews—on the basis of Jewish postbiblical literature—that the Messiah foretold in the Old Testament had already come; that Jesus was that Messiah; and that the Sages of the Talmud were well aware of the fact. Consequently, the Jews who had rejected Jesus had done so out of spite: they were not in error but obstinate and perfidious. They were deliberate unbelievers and so were their descendants—the Jews of the present. At the time of the Disputation at Tortosa, the Jews lacked a leader of the caliber of Nahmanides who could defend their cause; moreover, conditions were quite different from what they had been at Barcelona. In the course of the disputation, many Jews converted, some out of conviction, others out of fear.

In all three big public disputations (Paris, Barcelona, Tortosa) and in others less known, apostates were the heroes on the Christian side. Their role became very important when the Talmud was the focus of the debate. Their central role was due undoubtedly to their familiarity with postbiblical Jewish literature, but also in part to their unique position, on the borderline between the two religions. Apostates were also the authors of many anti-Jewish polemical works, written after their conversion, trying to make others follow in their footsteps. Petrus Alphonsi (twelfth century), Hermannus of Cologne, Alfonso of Valladolid, Gerónimo de Santa Fé and Pablo de Santa Maria (fifteenth century) are several famous examples.

The three great disputations were more in the nature of tribunals than debates; the term *disputation* is largely a misnomer. They were not designed to present a balanced, fair confrontation between two rival parties but to deduce Christian truth from Jewish literature—in other words, to batter the opponent with his own weapons. There was only one possible conclusion: the Jews had to accept Christianity. Of course, these were not the only public disputations held during the Middle Ages but the most famous ones. No others were documented in the same way, and we do not know exactly how many took place. The Jews, for their part, had no interest in initiating them, for they could not possibly prevail in a contest in which both referees and spectators were Christian.

Besides the official—public and learned—disputations, which were conducted exclusively by religious leaders such as monks, priests and rabbis, there were also more popular debates among lay members of the Jewish and Christian communities. We know, for example, of two such debates held by Genoese merchants, one in 1179 at Ceuta, Morocco, and another in 1286 in Majorca. Although such popular, private events were poorly documented, our information nevertheless indicates that the frequent commercial encounters of Jews and Christians could often produce exchanges on religious matters. This should not surprise us: in an age of faith, religion was a vital, effervescent force in many people's lives; it was by no means confined to the clergy.

Although the public disputations naturally cast the Jews in the lowly role of defendants, Jewish literature was at liberty to attack Christianity and its protagonists. A particularly prominent attack of this kind was *Sefer Toledot Yeshu* (The life of Jesus), a Jewish pseudo biography of Jesus telling the stories of the Gospels through Jewish eyes. The framework of the story was probably circulating orally and perhaps even in a written version as early as the third or fourth century in the East. Several versions circulated in eastern Jewish communities (in Byzantium and under Islam) and in Western Europe during the Middle Ages.

Toledot Yeshu has been defined as a work of "counterhistory," which misuses the opponent's most authentic sources (the books of the New Testament) in such a way as to distort the other's self-image and identity by attempting to demolish that opponent's collective memory. The Jewish story does not belie the main elements of the Christian story, but it presents a different interpretation, at variance with the story's original spirit and intention. Jesus was not born a normal birth—because he was the fruit of an adulterous union. He performed miracles—because he stole the "holy name" from the Temple; and he was not found in his grave when sought—because the Jews had exhumed him and buried him elsewhere. The Jewish narrative turns the Christian message upside down: whatever the Christians consider proof that Jesus was the Messiah is cited as proof of his heresy—all this in a racy, rather coarse satire, whose sole purpose was to comfort its Jewish readers by completely inverting the Christian story.

Although the public disputations and polemical literature gave form to the argument between the religions, as well as indicating the depth of their mutual enmity, the mere fact of debate presented an opportunity for dialogue. Indeed, as long as one is engaged in debate, one is trying to acquaint oneself with the other side, to communicate and try to determine what sets the rival groups apart—and what they have in common.

"THE FORMATION OF A PERSECUTING SOCIETY"

Beginning in the eleventh and twelfth centuries, Christian Europe embarked on a process of exclusion, marginalization and, finally, persecution of heretics, Jews, lepers and other groups. The consolidation of Christian society and emergence of a well-defined European consciousness were accompanied by social classification and the use of similar rhetoric in relation to various groups of "others," who were seen as enemies, contaminating society itself. These groups were required to wear distinctive dress for the protection of the true believers. After the Fourth Lateran

The devil and the Jews. The legend of Theophilus, one of the most popular of medieval legends, which influenced the later legend of Faust, portrays the Jews as being in league with Satan. This widespread legend reflected and reinforced the hostile stereotype of the Jews among western Christians.

Council and the formulation of the doctrine of Transubstantiation, the heretics and, later, also the Jews were accused of desecrating the Host, as we will see. Moreover, both Jews and heretics were accused of witchcraft and of using human blood for sorcery. Gradually, there emerged a diabolical image of Judaism, which found expression in art, literature and popular belief.

The deterioration in the Jewish condition at this time was due to a combination of socioeconomic and ideological reasons. As cities developed, and with them the Christian merchant guilds, which were closed to any non-Christian, Jews were gradually forced out of local and international trade. They became mainly moneylenders, a profession off limits to Christians because of the Church's persistent objection to lending at interest. In so doing they played a vital—but detested—economic role and became a symbol of negative power, both economic and religious. The transition to a profit-based economy produced guilt feelings in Christians, because of the growing gap between religious imperatives and economic behavior. Christian guilt was projected onto the Jews, who now became the scapegoat of a changing, troubled society.

Rising tensions in the cities gave birth to two new religious orders, the Franciscans and the Dominicans, both founded at the beginning of the thirteenth century, who made it their business to purge Christianity of all heresies. As we have already seen, their struggle involved vigorous missionizing among the Jews, compulsory sermons in synagogues, enforced religious disputations and sometimes incitement for its own sake.

It was no accident that the friars associated Judaism with heresy. Since the earliest centuries of Christianity, despite the legal and theological differentiation between Jews and heretics, both ecclesiastical literature and popular perception not infrequently lumped the two groups together; Jews were suspected of cooperating with heretical sects and even inspiring them. Each party in the early Christological debates tended to accuse the other of Judaizing. Complaints of Jewish influence were leveled against later medieval heresies—the Passagii (a sect in twelfth-century Lombardy that wished to return to Old Testament religiosity), the Albigenses and the Waldenses (a Christian community created by Peter Valdes from Lyons in the twelfth century); such influence has never been verified. At any rate, the comparison of Jews and heretics in the mendicant preachers' sermons generally signaled a deterioration in the situation of the Jews and contributed to their diabolical image.

THE BLOOD LIBEL

The most extreme and succinct expressions of this process of exclusion and marginalization were the blood libels and the accusations of desecration of the Host. At the beginning of the Middle Ages, Jews were usually described in literature as blind, incapable of seeing the light. As the Middle Ages progressed, however, this condescending image of the Jews gradually gave way to a more negative one. From the twelfth century on, Christians began to believe that the Jew was by no means simply blind and in error; he was a willing, stubborn dissident, a servant of the devil, aware of the real truth but preferring to deny and abuse it. Judas Iscariot's betrayal of the Savior was the embodiment of the Jew's sinful, treacherous and repulsive nature. His present descendants had inherited these qualities and resembled him. The Jews poisoned wells, desecrated the Host, murdered Christians for ritual purposes (as they had murdered Jesus) and used human blood in ritual and magic ceremonies. In short, they were not considered human.

The blood libel, which made its first appearance in the twelfth century and has persisted up to modern times, is a common designation for two different accusations: the accusation of ritual murder—the first to appear—according to which the Jews murder Christians for ritual purposes; and ritual cannibalism—that is, the Jews procure Christian blood and use it in their ceremonies, mainly in order to bake unleavened bread (*matzot*) for the Passover festival. In time the two accusations were conflated, and the more "sophisticated" version of the blood libel charged the Jews with murdering Christians, generally infants, in order to use their blood in preparation for Passover. The Jews, it was alleged, murdered a Christian for that purpose once a year, somewhere else each year, and these murders were vital for the Jewish religion. Therefore, even if undiscovered, a ritual murder was surely committed.

The first detailed case of the charge of ritual murder known to us, *The Life and Miracles of St. William of Norwich*, took place in 1144 in the English town of Norwich. The story was told five years later by a monk named Thomas of Monmouth, who came to Norwich, was fascinated by the story, investigated William's death and wrote a hagiographic account of his life and death. This work is the first literary formulation of the ritual-murder myth.

In Thomas' account, William was a boy of twelve, fatherless, apprenticed to a tanner. His work frequently took him to Jewish homes. On Tuesday, the first day of the Passover festival, William disappeared. According to Thomas' story, on Wednesday, the second day of Passover, after leaving the synagogue, the Jewish leaders tortured the child horribly, shaved his head and stabbed him with thorns until he bled. They then fastened him to a cross, as if to ridicule Christ's suffering and avenge the humiliation of the Jews. Finally, to stop the flow of blood from William's many wounds, they poured boiling water over him. Two days later, on Good Friday, two Jews took the body, put it in a sack and went out to the forest on the outskirts of the town, where they hung the body on a tree. Returning to town, they went to the sheriff, who was their supporter, and bribed him with large sums of money to keep their secret.

On the next day, Saturday, the body of the boy was discovered and the news of his death spread. Some three weeks later, at a church council convened in Norwich, the Jews were accused of the murder. When the council had completed its deliberations, the Jews appealed to the bishop (who was by no means convinced of their guilt) and denied the truth of the accusation. No trial was held, but the mood of the public became ugly and the sheriff invited the Jews to take refuge in the local castle.

In the meantime, William's corpse began to work healing miracles. Nevertheless, despite the wonders that had been witnessed and were continuing, many of the townspeople, including the sheriff and the bishop, ignored the stories and refused to believe in the Jews' guilt. Until the arrival of Thomas of Monmouth, the accusation was not proved. Only in 1149, when Thomas conducted an investigation and summoned witnesses, did the various details begin to crystallize into a coherent story. The final touch was provided by the testimony of one Theobald, "who once was a Jew, and afterward a monk":

> He verily told us that in the ancient writings of his fathers it was written that the Jews, without the shedding of human blood, could neither obtain their freedom, nor could they ever return to their fatherland. Hence it was laid down by them in ancient times that every year they must sacrifice a Christian in some part of the world to the Most High God in scorn and contempt of Christ. . . . Wherefore the chief men and Rabbis of the Jews who dwell in Spain assemble together at Narbonne, where the Royal seed [resides], and where they are held in the highest estimation, and they cast lots for all the countries which the Jews inhabit. . . . Now in that year in which we know that William, God's glorious martyr, was slain, it happened that the lot fell upon the Norwich Jews, and all the synagogues in England signified, by letter or by message, their consent that their wickedness should be carried out at Norwich. "I was," said he, "at that time at Cambridge, a Jew among Jews, and the commission of the crime was no secret to me."

We cannot determine the identity of this Theobald, or the circumstances and motives of his libelous testimony. But there is no doubt that this celebrated "testimony" heard by Thomas solved the murder and showed it to be not an ordinary one, but a ritual murder, a sacrifice offered by the Jews once a year. The Jews of Norwich were never prosecuted, but the reports of the miracles performed by William ranged far and wide, as did the allegation of the murders committed by the Jews. From 1144 to 1290, the year the Jews were expelled from England, there were at least fourteen blood libels in various places in England. One of the most famous was the story of little Hugh of Lincoln, who was supposedly murdered by the Jews of that city; it in fact achieved immortality in "The Prioress' Tale," one of Geoffrey Chaucer's celebrated *Canterbury Tales*. The ritual-murder myth crossed the English Channel, and similar stories cropped up in continental Europe too. Although Christian scholars and European leaders consistently took a firm stand against the allegations, their objections were to no avail. Repeated declarations by popes such as Gregory X essentially had no effect, though they indicate that "Augustinian tolerance" was still alive and that scholars and leaders were still trying to convince their flocks that the Jews were human beings, not children of the devil.

The Jews of Norwich were accused of ritual murder but not of magical use of the blood. This second libel first appeared in 1235 at Fulda in Hesse, and from then on it became an integral part of the myth. Some blood libels were particularly notorious, among them the libel of Trent, whose hero, Simon of Trent, was the only blood-libel "victim" to be officially beatified.

Judicial proceedings held in Trent in northern Italy in 1475 found the local Jews guilty of murdering an infant named Simon, barely two and a half years old, on Easter of that year, after torturing him and drawing his blood to use it in their rites. On the assumption that the act was a ritual murder, planned and carried out by all the Jews of Trent, the men of the little community were arrested, together with relatives and guests. They were interrogated, severely tortured and found guilty. The principal "offenders" were burned at the stake in June 1475, the others executed in January of the next year. The women of the community were also interrogated, but as their part in Jewish religion was considered marginal, they were merely placed under house arrest, and in the end three women converted to Christianity.

The protocols of the trial, which was meticulously documented, indicate that the accused were not interrogated about the murder alone. The investigators were particularly curious as to the details of the Jewish blood ceremonies and their symbolic meanings. With the help of the tortured victims, who were willing to tell their questioners anything just to halt the tortures, the Christians built up a detailed account of the ritual cannibalism practiced by the Jews at the Passover seder. The Jews of Trent confirmed the martyrdom story their tormentors wanted to hear; as the tortures intensified, the story became increasingly horrible. The investigators learned that the Jews needed Christian blood to prepare unleavened bread, to express their scorn for Jesus, to remove their own bad odor, and for various other reasons that, so the wretched prisoners hoped, would satisfy the questioners. The final verdict found the Jews of Trent guilty of desecration of the Sacraments, the murder of a child, cannibalism and sorcery.

Various Jewish communities, including the prosperous one in Rome, interceded, and their efforts finally persuaded Pope Sixtus IV to intervene. The pope was worried not only by the conduct of the local authorities at the Trent trial, but also by the rapid growth of the adoration of little Simon, which lacked official sanction and in fact had troubling theological implications. A papal commissary found Trent in the throes of religious ecstasy—a community fervently worshiping its martyr and impervious to any criticism. After the commissary's inquiry was obstructed, he left Trent fearing for his life, without having much helped those of its Jews who were still alive. Even the pope's direct appeals to the local authorities were seen as improper intervention. Although the papal commissary concluded that the "trial" had not been properly conducted and that the confessions extorted by torture were worthless, the ruler of the city was ultimately declared blameless, and in 1588 Simon was beatified by the Church. The saga of his torture and death, based on the testimonies exacted from the Jews and supporting evidence, became popular reading throughout the cities of northern Italy and southern Germany, giving rise to stories, poems and pamphlets. As late as the seventeenth century, literary works were still being written about the infant martyr, whose tomb had become a popular pilgrimage site while the trial was still in progress; the tomb retained its status as a holy place until 1965, when the Church debeatified Simon of Trent.

Another charge commonly leveled against the Jews in Western Europe, particularly in Germany and Austria, was the desecration of the Host. According to these accusations, the Jews would steal or otherwise lay their hands on the Host—the consecrated wafer of the Eucharist—and ritually molest it: they would stab it till it bled; throw it into boiling water, where it turned into an infant; and subject it to other abuses that caused the Host to reveal its miraculous nature. According to the accusers' logic, the Jews, through their very misdeeds, were in fact confirming the Host's supernatural powers; for otherwise, why would they have stolen and "tortured" it? And once the consecrated bread had thus been forced to reveal its true nature, the Jew had finally fulfilled his mission—to confirm and reconfirm, against his will, the Christian truth. In both blood and Host libels, the Jew was replaying his eternal role as the murderer of Christ and ritually reenacting his horrendous deed of the past.

Both accusations were particularly rife in pre-Reformation Germany. Tormented children and miraculous manifestations of the Host were repeatedly portrayed in woodcuts, and the tales were told and retold in booklets that proclaimed the Jews' heinous sins far and wide. With the coming of print, the dissemination of this anti-Jewish propaganda received a major boost, and pamphlets with detailed accounts of the blood or Host libels were distributed or sold to pilgrims visiting the places where the events had occurred, which had become popular holy sites. The veneration of such sites was also of economic significance, which added to and reinforced their religious importance. The propaganda circulated there probably did much to intensify Christian antisemitism during the late Middle Ages in Germany, Austria and the north of Italy.

During the Middle Ages and the Modern Era, there were some 150 blood libels and 100 Host-desecration charges. Modern scholarship has offered various explanations for the phenomenon. Some scholars have traced it to the behavior of the Jews themselves (such as customs of the Purim festival, when Jews mocked Christian symbols and beliefs—the crucified Jesus and the hanged Haman became one in their mind; or the Jews' slaughter of their own children during the First Crusade). Others have ascribed it to elements within the Christian world (guilt feelings over child neglect, the centrality of the sacrificial myth in Christianity). Whatever the case may be, the recurring charges offered a powerful corroboration of the Jew's image as child of the devil and anti-Christ. William of Norwich, Hugh of Lincoln, the "holy child" of La Guardia (see page 129) and Simon of Trent are only a few of the more prominent infants who were local martyrs, their tombs becoming shrines and pilgrimage sites. As we have seen, objections on the part of the ecclesiastical and intellectual leadership of Europe were to no avail against the religious fervor that these rites aroused; indeed, despite the decline in the number of libels since the beginning of the Modern Era, they have persisted well into the twentieth century.

The plots of the various blood and Host libels constitute an extreme manifestation of the portrayal of Jews as the eternal enemy of Christendom. Toward the end of the Middle Ages, another myth made its appearance in Europe—the legend of the "Wandering Jew" or the "Eternal Jew." The story was told that Jesus, on his way to Calvary with the cross upon his shoulders, begged a Jewish cobbler to let him rest for a moment in his shop. The cobbler rebuffed him and told him to go on his way, whereupon Jesus condemned him to wander forever, until his Second Coming. Since then the Jew has not died—so ran the story—but he continues to roam the world, appearing occasionally in different places, and will continue to do so till Judgment Day. Thus, the Jew, who gazed on Jesus with his own eyes, is the most authentic witness to his messiahship, though he himself remains a Jew. He is condemned eternally to bear testimony—testimony indispensable to Christendom—until the day he himself realizes the significance of his message. His evidence is twofold: he recalls the Crucifixion, at which he himself was present; and his eternal peregrinations attest to his error and to the fact that Jesus was the Messiah.

THE BLACK DEATH

The psychological firmament of insecurity, dread and confusion typical of the late Middle Ages in general contributed to a radicalization of the diabolical image of the Jew and gave rise to anti-Jewish disturbances. In 1320 the so-called Crusade of the Pastoureaux savaged Jewish communities of France and Spain. Further attacks occurred a year later in the same area, during the persecution of the lepers. On both occasions the riots were instigated by Christian preachers.

In Germany, political circumstances—a power struggle between Duke Albrecht of Austria and Count Adolf of Nassau—formed a favorable background for anti-Jewish incidents. In 1298, after an alleged desecration of the Host, anti-Jewish riots broke out in several German cities. The mob, headed by a butcher of Röttingen named Rindfleisch, was driven by both economic and religious motives. They first attacked the communities of a few small towns around Röttingen, going on to larger communities—Rothenburg, Würzburg, Bamberg and Nuremberg. The riots were among the worst to hit the Jews of Germany in the Middle Ages, affecting some forty-four communities. Historians believe that the number of Jews killed during the Rindfleisch riots exceeded those slain in 1096, estimating the death toll at about 5,000 or 6,000. Thus, the end of the thirteenth century was a time of terror and catastrophe for the Jews of medieval Germany. For the next five decades, they lived in constant fear of attacks and persecution, first during the Armleder massacres in 1336–38, in which thousands of Jews lost their lives, and then during the Black Death, the dreadful plague that raged throughout Europe in 1348–50, killing almost one-half of the population.

Anti-Jewish violence during the Black Death was unprecedented in its geographical extent, the number of Jews who lost their lives and the grave danger to the continued existence of the Jewish centers of Europe. It was the worst calamity to befall the Jews of Europe until the Holocaust. The massacres began in the south of France, proceeding from there westward to Spain and northward to France and Germany. In dread of the plague, people sought human agents for the disease, and the Jews were accused of poisoning wells—an allegation that made its first appearance in Savoy in the summer of 1348 and spread from there to the German Reich. It was held that the Jews had launched a worldwide conspiracy to destroy Christian Europe. Although the libel was disbelieved by intellectuals, and even the pope denied its truth, the uneducated masses were convinced of its veracity and accordingly "defended" themselves by particularly savage assaults that all but obliterated the Jewish communities of many large cities—Strasbourg, Worms, Würzburg, Frankfurt, Cologne, Nuremberg are only a few representative names. Many Jews were burned at the stake after "trials" in which they were publicly accused and confessions were extracted from them under fearsome tortures.

Although the immediate motive for the attacks was the accusation of well poisoning, modern scholarship has shown that the reasons were more complex. In some places, those responsible for the violence were the leading burghers, who were eager to seize Jewish property and to that end manipulated the popular hatred. In fact, in many localities the authorities made efforts to investigate the allegations and the Jews were saved. It would seem that political, economic, religious and psychological factors combined here to the detriment of the Jews. The economic crisis of the fourteenth century, escalating insecurity and fear of famine, plagues and other natural calamities all instilled in the common people of Europe feelings of xenophobia and endowed all strangers with a diabolical image. The Jew of fourteenth-century Europe was the ultimate "other," the prime source of all society's trials and tribulations.

EXPULSIONS

Socioreligious transformations, coupled with vitriolic anti-Jewish incitement, finally brought about an endeavor to remove the Jews entirely from European society. From 1290 to 1541 the Jews were expelled from most European countries: England, France, Spain, Sicily, Portugal and many German cities and principalities. By the end of the Middle Ages, Jews were left living in the Papal States, northern Italy and a few German principalities.

Jews leaving Spain.

The first country to do away with its Jewish community was England. At first, King Edward I made efforts to "reform" the Jews by placing limits on usury and extending official supervision of Jewish occupations. This policy was in keeping with the overall centralizing tendencies of the English monarchy, which proposed to create a homogeneous society, subordinate solely to the throne and not subservient to different legal systems. Attempts to integrate the Jews into English society failed, and in 1290 the king published an edict banishing them from the kingdom: some 3,000 Jews (by modern estimates) were forced to leave England forever.

In France, too, there was a connection between the expulsion of the Jews and usury. Here, however, the objections to usury were phrased in religious terms and ascribed to the king's desire to preserve the purity of society. In 1306 the Jews were expelled from France by royal decree, but in 1315 they were permitted to return. The new Jewish community, however, was small and weak, and it suffered further expulsions till the coup de grâce was delivered in 1394–95. Both in England and in France the expulsion accorded with the monarchy's centralizing policies and was part of the transition to new patterns of government.

The lack of centralized government in Germany precluded an overall expulsion of German Jews. Jews were occasionally banished from individual cities or principalities, but Jewish presence in Germany as a whole never ceased. After the Protestant Reformation, however, authorities in Germany also aggravated their persecution of the Jews, who were forced out of their residences and professions. Presumably, the disintegration of the relatively stable structure of medieval society caused a considerable decline in the Jewish condition and, in some places, entirely obliterated their presence.

The Problem of the *Conversos* and the Expulsion from Spain

Christianity had always been a missionizing faith—and its efforts were constantly aimed, from its earliest days, at the Jews. Despite the Church's theoretical objection to forcible conversion, pressure to convert sometimes took on violent proportions. As a result, groups of crypto-Jews (in Hebrew *anusim*)—Jews who had converted under duress and were living double lives, outwardly Christian and inwardly Jewish—came into existence at various times in medieval Europe. As far as the Church was concerned, a convert to Christianity, even one who had converted unwillingly, could not return to Judaism: for the Church, baptism was irrevocable, no less than circumcision.

The designation *crypto-Jews* is associated most readily with the so-called *conversos* of Spain and Portugal—a mass phenomenon that began during the persecutions of 1391 and came to a head in the expulsion of the Jews from those countries. The events of the summer of 1391 created a profound rift in Spanish Jewry, formerly the most well-established and flourishing Jewish community in Christian Europe. Anti-Jewish disturbances broke out among the lower urban classes, incited by the minor clergy and unchecked by a now-weak Castilian monarchy, which had previously defended the Jews. During the riots many Jews chose baptism rather than death at the hands of the mob. When calm was restored, the extent of the blow suffered by Spanish Jewry was revealed: many communities, such as that of Barcelona, had been completely wiped out, and others were greatly diminished.

From that time on, one could speak of two Jewish communities: the severely reduced "official" Jewish community, and a large community of *conversos*—it is difficult to evaluate their numbers. Historians' estimates of the number of Jews who converted during the 1391 disorders vary from a few tens of thousands to 200,000. One should remember, moreover, that the term *conversos* is a general one, designating all those who converted: Jews who had apostatized of their own free will and identified with their new faith, others who had become Christians only outwardly and maintained ties of some sort with Judaism and still others who had been converted by force and now sought ways to live in peace both with themselves and with their new environment. We have already described the role played by converts in Christian missionary and polemical activities, and it is not surprising that some of them strove to persuade other Jews to follow in their footsteps. Among the more famous *conversos* were some members of the Jewish intellectual and economic aristocracy, such as Solomon ha-Levi (1350–1435), rabbi of Burgos, who converted even before the riots, was renamed Pablo de Santa Maria and rose to become bishop of Burgos. His friend Joshua Lorki, the physician, from Alcaniz, Aragon, who served Pope Benedict XIII, followed suit. As a Christian named Gerónimo de Santa Fé, he became an ardent missionary and, as we have seen, represented Christianity at the Disputation of Tortosa in 1413–14.

The mass conversions caused a rupture within the Jewish communities, literally tearing some of them apart. Internally, it created many difficult problems of divorce, distribution of wealth and inheritance; externally, it aroused the suspicions of the ecclesiastical authorities, who were apprehensive of the continuing ties between some of the *conversos* and their former communities. In an attempt to prevent such ties, all contacts between *conversos* and Jews were forbidden. Thus, the king of Aragon wrote after the disorders: "Wherefore we have commanded and enjoined those present that from this time henceforward no converso, whether man or woman, shall live with a Jew or a Jewess, neither shall he converse with them in one room or in one house, neither shall he live with them (in one house) with a wall separating them. Similarly, he is forbidden to eat and drink with them or to partake of their food, or to pray together with them."

Jews who maintained their faith were now subjected to harsh restrictions, with the encouragement of, among others, the wandering Castilian preacher Vicente Ferrer, already discussed. Such measures, combined with the Disputation at Tortosa and the atmosphere of despair that they created in the Jewish communities, prompted further waves of conversion, probably no less extensive than the first wave; the conversions again included respected and learned Jews, some belonging to the communal leadership, for whom baptism opened up prospects of securing high office in secular or ecclesiastical government. During the fifteenth century, many more Jews joined the ranks of Christianity, and the expulsion decree of 1492 forced many others, unwilling to leave their homes for a life of wandering, to do the same.

The *conversos*, who were also known as "New Christians," were thus Christians of Jewish origin and as such set apart from the "Old Christians," who viewed them with suspicion and hostility and considered them crypto-Jews, still secretly faithful to Judaism. Various regulations concerning the "purity of blood" (*Limpieza de sangre*) were promulgated during the fifteenth century; these regulations (which were, however, implemented in practice only toward the end of the sixteenth century) discriminated against New Christians on racial grounds, intending to block their path to high public office whether at court, in the Church or elsewhere, on the assumption that their conversion was merely outward. From the fifteenth century on, the *conversos* found it difficult to obtain high-ranking positions, in contrast to the situation in the early years of the conversion movement. The "blood-purity" regulations were, of course, a deviation from the Church's own principle, as many opponents were quick to point out.

The *conversos*, also known derisively as *marranos* ("swine"), inherited all the stereotypical epithets attached to the Jews. They generally continued to practice the commonly Jewish professions of moneylending, tax farming, medicine and pharmacy, which highlighted the continuity of their existence as Jews and further blocked their progress toward integration in Christian society.

Besides the social problem due to the mass conversion of Jews, the leaders of the Church and the mendicant orders were troubled, at least from the middle of the fifteenth century, by the suspicion that many of the *conversos* were indeed merely Jews in Christians' clothing. The Franciscan friar Alfonso de Espina, in his work *Fortalitium fidei* (The fortress of faith) (second half of the fifteenth century), which was to become a key book in the struggle against the Jews and the *conversos*, described the New Christians as Judaizers in every respect. They adhered, so he wrote, to their ancestral faith and were poisoning Christian society from within. Espina's book provided inspiration for harsher anti-*converso* policies, which were practiced by the Spanish rulers for some twenty years before the expulsion.

In 1469, Isabella, sister of the king of Castile, married Ferdinand, heir to the throne of Aragon, and in 1474 she was crowned queen of Castile. In 1478 the two monarchs, who became known as the "Catholic Monarchs," received permission from Pope Sixtus IV to establish a royal inquisition in their realm. The Inquisition began operations in Seville in 1481, headed by Dominican friars. Like the papal Inquisition, it was an ecclesiastic institution designed to combat heresies, but as it was subordinate to the Spanish monarchy it quickly became a tool for royal surveillance of Spanish society. In the first years of its existence, the Spanish Inquisition concerned itself mainly with the *conversos*; it has been suggested that although its official motives were religious, the real intention was to destroy the *conversos* as a group in order to please the urban elite, hoping that the latter would then support the centralizing policies of the Catholic Monarchs. Other historians, however, believe that the Inquisition was intended to solve a religious problem; and that is what it did, despite the concomitant economic harm to the kingdom. The significance of the inquiries instituted by the Inquisition is also disputed. Some consider the *conversos* condemned by the Inquisition as victims of racial persecution, though most were sincere believers; others believe that they were crypto-Jews, secretly observing Mosaic Law. The overall picture is undoubtedly more complex, and the *conversos*' attitude to their ancestral heritage was by no means uniform. Despite inquisitorial intimidation and the hostile attitude to the *conversos*, some of them were still able to ascend the ranks of the secular or ecclesiastical hierarchy; others, however, were interrogated in the dungeons of the Inquisition in order to test their allegiance to the Catholic Church and save their deviant souls by any means—some of particular cruelty. During the 1480s, inquisitorial tribunals were established in various cities of Castile and Aragon. The proceedings reached a peak of horror in the autos-da-fé held in city squares, ceremonies in which the victims were publicly burned at the stake after being humiliated in a variety of ways.

It was Christian fears of the persistent ties of *conversos* with Jews that finally inspired the expulsion of Jews from Spain. In order to prevent contact, the Jews were transferred to special, remote neighborhoods. The blood libel of the "Holy Child of La Guardia," propagated in trials lasting almost one year (December 1490 to November 1491) in several Castilian cities, accused a group of *conversos* and Jews of horrible acts of profanation of the Host, black magic and ritual cannibalism. All the accused were burned at the stake, and the whole affair shook Christian public opinion in Spain, preparing the ground for the expulsion of the Jews in the year to come. The expulsion decree was signed at Granada on March 31, 1492. That city, the last Muslim stronghold in the Iberian Peninsula, had surrendered to the Christians three months before. The forced conversion of those Muslims still remaining in Spain (at the beginning of the sixteenth century) and the expulsion of all Spanish Jews were designed to create a united kingdom of Spain, subscribing to a single faith. In this respect, the dramatic events of 1492—the conquest of Granada, the discovery of America and the expulsion of the Jews—were all harbingers of the Modern Era in Spain: on the one hand, the discovery of the New World; on the other, the attempt, using the Inquisition, to create a centralized, homogeneous state governed by one law—religious law.

The expulsion decree emphasized the grave harm incurred by the Christians (meaning, of course, the New Christians) because of the Jews, who constantly tried to lead them astray from the Catholic path:

> But we are informed . . . of the great harm suffered by Christians from the contact, intercourse and communication which they have with the Jews, who always attempt in various ways to seduce faithful Christians from our Holy Catholic Faith, to separate them from it, to attract them and corrupt them in their harmful faith and beliefs, as they instruct the Christians in the ceremonials and in the customs of their religion, as they convene meetings at which they read to them and teach them and their children, as they give them books in which they utter their prayers and announce the fast days on which one should fast, as they assemble together with them to read to them and review with them the stories of their Law, and as they inform them of the festivals before the appointed time, as they inform them what they are to hear and to do, as they give them and bring them from their homes unleavened bread and meat slaughtered according to their rite, as they warn them of what to guard against in food and other things for the observance of the faith, and as they convince them with all their might to fulfill and observe the Mosaic Law, and as they give them to understand that there is no other faith or other truth save their own.

If the largest danger due to Jewish presence in Spain was the possible reversion of the *conversos* to Judaism, it was this threat that ultimately brought about the expulsion. The Catholic Monarchs and the leaders of the Inquisition, headed by Tomás de Torquemada, who were responsible for the expulsion decree, must have hoped that many Jews would prefer to stay in Spain but would therefore convert to Catholicism. The hardship involved in leaving one's home country, and the economic loss incurred thereby, certainly caused many Jews to become Christians and remain in Spain; the converts included some of the most prominent members of the Jewish community. Those who elected to adhere to their faith left Spain, most of them for neighboring Portugal, where they received permission to live for eight months until boats could be found to take them elsewhere. Many Jews who did not manage to leave in time were sold into slavery. Under the influence of the Catholic Monarchs, a decree of expulsion was promulgated against the Jews of Portugal too, but the king of Portugal, reluctant to give up the economic advantages of Jewish presence, issued an order to baptize them by force, and all the Jews of Portugal became *conversos*.

In 1536 the Inquisition was established in Portugal as well; it turned out to be even harsher and more inflexible than the Spanish Inquisition. As in Spain, the hatred of the *conversos* was a mixture of religious fanaticism and social envy. Paradoxically, it was the vigorous activity of the Spanish and Portuguese Inquisition that perpetuated the problem of crypto-Judaism. Had it not been for the inquiries and investigations, the problem of the New Christians' identity might not have assumed such significance, but the Inquisition persisted. The problem was further aggravated by anti-Jewish books and sermons that, through their very attacks on Judaism, kept it constantly in the public eye and, in particular, the eye of the *conversos* themselves. Indeed, the phenomenon of crypto-Judaism continued for centuries in Spain and Portugal.

Lacking Jewish books or direct contact with Jewish communities, those of the *conversos* who still wanted to maintain ties with their Jewish heritage had to resort to clandestine measures. Religious customs and observances were handed down orally from generation to generation, frequently only through the women of the family; in the process, distortions crept in. Over the years, they created a religious world of their own, with special customs and a different liturgical calendar, largely influenced by the conceptual world of Christianity.

Most of the New Christians assimilated into the Christian communities of Spain and Portugal. In the seventeenth century, however, many *conversos* left Spain, settled in other parts of Europe and reverted to Judaism, establishing *converso* communities in several European towns such as Venice, Leghorn, Hamburg and, in particular, Amsterdam. The Amsterdam community redefined its Judaism on the basis of its acquaintance with Christianity. However, the way back was not easy. Long existence as crypto-Jews instilled doubts in the *conversos*' minds in regard to not only normative Christianity, but also normative Judaism. The most celebrated representatives of these doubters were the philosophers Baruch Spinoza (1632–1677) and Uriel da Costa (1585–1640). Crypto-Judaism, as it turns out, was liable to lead to skepticism, to rationalistic criticism of religious imperatives in general and even to nihilism.

As to the Jews who fled Spain, many of them went east, finding refuge in the Ottoman Empire. They established large communities there—in Turkey, Greece, Yugoslavia and other countries of the empire. Clinging to their Spanish heritage, spurred on by a feeling of cultural superiority, they maintained and conserved their previous customs, continuing to speak the language they had brought with them from Spain, Judeo-Spanish, which came to be known as Ladino (derived from the word for *Latin*) and is still spoken today. This language preserves a stratum of medieval Spanish, a kind of frozen likeness of the tongue spoken at the time of the expulsion. The story of Spanish Jewry in the Ottoman Empire will be told in full in the next chapter.

EASTWARD BOUND

By the end of the fifteenth century, the Jews were being gradually pushed out of their homes in Western and Central Europe. The expulsion from Spain in 1492 and the frequent expulsions from German and Austrian cities and towns transformed Jewish demography, with the result that the Jewish population of the late Middle Ages was concentrated in the lands of the Ottoman Empire, Poland and the neighboring countries in Eastern Europe.

Most of the expelled Ashkenazi Jews went east, to Poland. Many journeyed in that direction voluntarily, emigrating rather than fleeing, as part of the waves of emigration from Central Europe in general. All the émigrés, Jews and Christians alike, were attracted to Poland because of the economic prospects it offered and the advantageous conditions its rulers promised the newcomers. The beginnings of organized Jewish settlement in Poland (in communities) are generally dated to the thirteenth or the late twelfth century. The Jews made their homes mainly in the new cities then springing up all over Poland. The settlement of Jews in urban communities and their professional profile, mainly as merchants and artisans, were factors of major economic and social importance in a country whose population was primarily rural. Accordingly, the Jews received favorable charters enumerating their privileges and obligations in detail, documents that were to form the legal basis for their existence in Poland.

As they went east, the Jews of Ashkenaz maintained their cultural and religious ties with their German homeland. With them they brought the patterns of behavior that had evolved in Germany, and they corresponded with rabbinical authorities in Germany and Bohemia to obtain guidance in Jewish law. The synagogues established by the Jews of Poland in the first centuries of their existence were basically similar to the synagogues they had left behind, and only later, beginning in the sixteenth century, did a specifically Polish synagogue architecture develop. Even more: the German Jewish émigrés to Poland brought their language with them too—Jewish German, and this tongue, cut off from its German environment, ultimately took on its own features and became an independent language—Yiddish.

The Jewish population of Poland grew steadily, until the Jewish community there became the largest in Europe and an independent cultural center. Estimated at about 10,000 in 1500, the number of Polish Jews had increased to about 750,000 by the second half of the eighteenth century. This demographic force and the favorable legal rights granted the Jews were the foundation for a magnificent community that assumed primacy among Western Jewry.

THE RENAISSANCE AND CHRISTIAN HEBRAISM

The cultural movement known as the Renaissance, which emerged in the fourteenth century, first in Italy and subsequently elsewhere, centered on the heritage of the classical world. The humanist goal was to revivify Christian culture through a return to classical values, which were considered a model worthy of emulation. In this context, the culture of Renaissance Jewry provides us with an interesting case study, as it illustrates the two conflicting trends of integration and segregation characteristic of the Jews of Europe: while Italian Jews were an integral part of the humanist revolution, they nevertheless retained their distinct religious identity.

Since the thirteenth century, Jews emigrating from other European countries had swelled the ranks of Italian Jewry; they came from France, Germany and, in the late fifteenth century, after the Expulsion, Spain. It was therefore a variegated and multifaceted community. In many respects, Italian Jews had a larger part in the culture of the host society than most other communities, and many of them

A Jewish doctor.

were indeed "Renaissance men." They espoused humanistic ideas as a basis for their cultural self-definition, dealt with written text according to new "modern" criteria and tried to widen the scope of their knowledge. Besides its renewed interest in classical models, Jewish humanism put its imprint on patterns of rabbinical learning. Nonetheless, it would be wrong to paint the picture of Jewish history at this time in exclusively rosy colors. Alongside the shared culture, there was also religious tension, and even the Jews of Italy were not immune to occasional outbursts of violence. Put differently, the Italian Jews were indeed Renaissance men, but they were still a marginal minority within society at large.

Mirroring the cultural partnership of Jewish scholars in the general ideals of the Renaissance was an intense interest in Jewish culture on the part of Christians. Humanism, eager to expand knowledge and seeking ancient sources for Christian truth, now evinced a new involvement in Jewish tradition and the Hebrew language. The humanist scholars we now refer to as Hebraists evolved a theory according to which the Jews had preserved ancient, authentic traditions of paramount importance to the Christian world and to Christian culture. Accordingly, they studied not only classical tongues but also Hebrew. Erasmus of Rotterdam (though he himself knew no Hebrew) considered a knowledge of all three languages—Greek, Latin and Hebrew—a prerequisite for a correct approach to the Holy Scriptures. Some Hebraists could boast of prodigious achievements in the study of Hebrew and Judaism. Cardinal Egidio da Viterbo, who studied under the Jewish scholar Elia Levita (c. 1468–1549), established a printing press and purchased a large Hebrew library. The well-known fifteenth-century German Hebraist Johannes Reuchlin made an important contribution to the modern philology of Semitic languages. Well versed in Hebrew and Aramaic, he was one of the first Christians to write a Hebrew grammar as an aid to Christian scholars. His interest in Hebrew and in Jewish culture even brought him into conflict with the authorities. In 1509 a converted Jew named Johannes Pfefferkorn (1469–after 1521) tried to persuade the emperor Maximilian to condemn the Talmud and other Jewish books, which, he claimed, contained anti-Christian material. Reuchlin declared himself firmly opposed, arguing that although the Talmud contained some "weeds," it also offered much of benefit to Christianity. A fierce dispute, to last for several years, raged between Pfefferkorn and Reuchlin concerning attitudes to the Talmud. As a rule, the heads of the Catholic establishment tended to support Pfefferkorn, while the humanist scholars, who championed the study of Hebrew and Jewish literature, generally supported Reuchlin. The dispute over the Talmud thus became a tool for attacks on the Church. Opponents of the Talmud were branded as corrupt and ignorant, and its supporters were portrayed as educated humanists. One should remember, however, that support for the Talmud did not necessarily mean a favorable attitude to the Jews themselves; Reuchlin himself was not sympathetic to Jews but to their literature.

Thus, about the turn of the fifteenth century, Christian scholars were assiduously studying postbiblical Hebrew literature in a quest for the Christian truth hidden therein. Such efforts in themselves were nothing new—we have already mentioned the achievements of the thirteenth-century Spanish Dominican friar Raymundus Martini. Previously, however, these phenomena were few and far between, whereas now the interest in Hebrew literature was widespread, an integral part of Renaissance humanism. One outcome of its influence was the introduction of Hebrew studies in European universities; Hebrew language and culture had become a respectable topic for study, not necessarily associated with a polemical context.

One subject that fascinated Christian humanists—particularly the Neoplatonists among them—was Kabbalah, the mystical lore of Judaism. Count Giovanni Pico della Mirandola dedicated himself to the study of Kabbalah, which he considered an authentic expression of divine truth that had been preserved by the Jews. He studied under various Jewish and apostate teachers, including Johanan Alemanno (c. 1435–after 1504), one of the greatest Italian Jewish kabbalists. Pico believed that Jewish mysticism gave Christian dogma its proper meaning. In his *Oration on the Dignity of Man*, he wrote: "I procured these books [kabbalistic texts] at a not inconsiderable cost, and after reading all of them diligently and with untiring labor, I found in them, as God is my witness, not just the principles of the Jewish religion but the principles of the Christian faith. I found therein the secret of the Trinity, the fulfillment of God's word, the divinity of Christ."

THE REFORMATION AND THE JEWS

The religious crisis that shook the Catholic world in the sixteenth century had its effect on Christian-Jewish relations. Martin Luther, architect of the Reformation, frequently referred to the Jews in his early commentaries on Scripture. He also endeavored to learn Hebrew and admired its conciseness and precision. In theological terms, his position regarding the Jews was no different from that of the Catholics. The divine promise to Abraham, he wrote, was made before the Patriarch was circumcised; consequently, one did not have to be a Jew and to observe Mosaic Law in order to achieve divine grace. Luther considered the Jews rebels against Christianity, but nevertheless reiterated that Synagoga was Ecclesia's sister, a rejected sibling who might possibly be brought back into the family. However, although there was nothing essentially new in Luther's view of the Jews, during the early stages of the Reformation he entertained hopes that the Jews would find it easier to convert to his new brand of Christianity. Presumably, he would have considered such mass conversion as incontrovertible public proof of Christian truth in its Protestant version, for conversion of the Jews was seen as a prerequisite for the advent of the Kingdom of Heaven. The messianic expectations typical of the Reformation period in fact raised Christians' hopes that the Jews would convert en masse.

In his pamphlet *Dass Jesus Christus ein geborener Jude sei* (That Jesus Christ was born a Jew, 1523), Luther explicitly declared that he would inspire the Jews to believe in Jesus, attributing their previous recalcitrance to the Christians' disgraceful behavior:

> Indeed, they treated the Jews as dogs and not as humans, and all their discourse with them was to rebuke them and rob them of their property. And when they baptized them they did not instruct them in the lore of Christianity or in the Christian way of life, but enslaved them to the papacy and to the clergy. . . . I hope that they will treat the Jews well, and if they lead them calmly through Scripture, many of them will become honest Christians and return to their ancestors, to the faith of the prophets and the Patriarchs. . . . If the Apostles, who were also Jews, had approached us, the gentiles, as we, the gentiles, approach the Jews, not one gentile would have become a Christian. Since they approached us, the gentiles, as brothers, we too should treat the Jews as brothers, so that we should be able to convert some of them to Christianity. . . . And though we sing ourselves songs of praise, we are nevertheless gentiles, whereas the Jews are descendants of Christ. We are outsiders and relatives by marriage, whereas they are blood relations, kin and brothers to the Lord. . . . This, therefore, is my request and my counsel, that they be treated kindly and instructed in Scripture, until some of them come over to our side.

Luther entreated the Christians to stop spreading falsehoods about the Jews (referring to the blood libel), to allow them to work and engage in trade rather than in usury and to receive them kindly. Writing in German, as his words were aimed at a Christian readership, he may have hoped that they would also be read by Jews, who would be convinced by his favorable attitude.

The next few years saw Luther's struggle against the Church establishment crowned with tremendous success. The Protestants consolidated their position in Germany, and reforming movements flourished in France, the Low Countries, Switzerland and England. However, the greater his successes among Christians, the greater was his frustration at the Jews' attitude. Refusing to convert, they showed no particular preference for Protestantism over Catholicism. This situation, coupled with the accusations of his Catholic enemies that he supported the Jews and was in reality a crypto-Jew, ultimately made Luther wash his hands of the Jews. In 1537 he rejected an appeal by Joseph of Rosheim (c. 1478–1554), a well-known representative and de facto leader of German Jewry, that he intervene with the elector of Saxony to avert an expulsion decree against the Jews, which even forbade the Jews to pass through Saxony. Once Luther realized that his hopes for mass conversion of the Jews were doomed to failure, his disappointment quickly became unbridled rage. His last writings on the Jewish question, *Vom Shem Hamphoras* (On the ineffable name) and *Von dem Juden und iren Lügen* (On the Jews and their lies), both published in 1543, are coarse and vituperative in the extreme. Luther refers to the Jews in the most abusive and humiliating terms, arguing that it would be easier to convert the devil to Christianity than the Jews: "They are children of Satan, condemned to perdition." In the second of the above-named pamphlets, he expressed concern at the danger of Jews seducing Christians to join their ranks. To counter this threat, he offered "practical advice" that was designed exclusively to eliminate Jewish presence in Germany: their synagogues should be burned down, their homes destroyed, their prayer books and volumes of the Talmud confiscated, their rabbis forbidden to teach, the privileges granted them abolished. They should no longer be permitted to engage in money-

An illustration from Martin Luther's translation of the Bible into German (Wittenberg, 1524). Luther drew on Jewish scholarship in making his enormously influential translation. The picture of the walls of Jericho collapsing depicts a contemporary German town.

lending, but forced to do hard manual labor; and if all that were to no avail, "we must then banish them like mad dogs, lest God's wrath be vented upon us too because of the repulsive blasphemies and all the abominations of which we might be accused."

Thus, Luther's attitude to the Jews shifted from one extreme to another. Some of his supporters were critical of his violent attacks on the Jews, among them Philip Melanchthon. Nevertheless, his anti-Jewish position was typical of most Protestant sects. Some still hoped to convert the Jews and, when rebuffed, treated them with hostility exceeding even that of the Catholic Church. Others accused one another of Judaizing—a popular polemical epithet without foundation.

Some Jews, for their part, perceived the Christian reform movements as attempts to return to Judaism. This was their attitude to the Hussites of Bohemia in the fifteenth century, and this was how some Jews saw the Reformation. Some circles among the Jews expelled from Spain interpreted Luther's activities in a messianic vein, considering them as preparatory to the reversion of Christianity to Judaism. On this understanding, Luther had rebelled not only against the pope but against Christianity itself. More sophisticated Jews also saw the Reformation as an extraordinary event, offering hope for a halt to their sufferings, a promise of greater religious tolerance. Luther appealed to the Old Testament as a source of religious authority; many Reformation leaders evinced interest in Hebrew as the Bible's original, pure language and maintained contacts with Jews who could teach it to them. In addition, the Reformation rejected the elaborate Catholic ritual, with the grandeur of its churches and its veneration of statues and icons. It abolished monastic orders, reduced the number of sacraments and thereby curtailed the power of the symbols of the Christian religion, reverting in some degree to the liturgical style and worship of Judaism.

Luther's about-face regarding the Jews quickly apprised them of their error, shattering their hopes that he would intervene with the authorities. Joseph of Rosheim reacted angrily to Luther's imprecations in *On the Jews and Their Lies*. The Jewish leadership now understood that the conservative Catholic tradition promised the Jews at least some measure of decent subsistence within a recognized legal framework. Lutheranism, on the other hand, as a revolutionary movement, had created a new force, violent and cruel, well-nigh uncontrollable. The difference between the revolutionary Protestant principles and Jewish tradition soon became clear: the Protestant emphasis on *sola fide*—through faith alone—contravened the basic tenets of Judaism, with their insistence on the observance of the religious precepts, the importance of the Oral Law alongside the Written Law and the requirement of prayer in Hebrew but not in the vernacular. In all these respects Judaism was closer to Catholicism than to the Protestant faith. Accordingly, the hopes entertained by both sides quickly gave way to disillusionment, all the more so as the Protestants evolved a religious fervor perhaps more dangerous to the Jews than that of the conservative Catholic religion.

THE COUNTER-REFORMATION

The Protestant revolution was balanced in the parts of Europe that remained Catholic by a parallel upheaval—the Catholic reformation or Counter-Reformation. This was a movement that brought about a fundamental review of Catholicism, among other things devoting attention to the Jewish question and to the problem of the Church's relations with those Jews who lived under its sway.

In July 1555, Pope Paul IV promulgated his bull *Cum nimis absurdum* in which, on the one hand, he set out the rationale for the continued presence of Jews in Europe and, on the other, listed a series of harshly restrictive limits on that presence:

> [It has lately come to our notice] that these Jews, in our dear city and in some other cities, holdings and territories of the Holy Roman Church, have erupted into insolence: they presume not only to dwell side by side with Christians and near their

> churches, with no distinct habit to separate them, but even to erect homes in the more noble sections and streets of the cities, holdings and territories where they dwell, and to buy and possess fixed property, and to have nurses, housemaids, and other hired Christian servants, and to perpetrate many other things in ignominy and contempt of the Christian name. . . . As long as they persist in their errors, they should recognize through experience that they have been made slaves while Christians have been made free through Jesus Christ, God and Our Lord, and that it is iniquitous that the children of the free woman should serve the children of the maid-servant.

Accordingly, the decree issued strict instructions for the future treatment of the Jews. They would all be required from that time on to live in separate areas and were forbidden to possess landed property; their commercial dealings with Christians were restricted; they were allowed to have one synagogue in each city and ordered to demolish all others; they were required to wear an identifying mark in full view; they were forbidden to employ Christian nursemaids, wet nurses or servants; and friendship between Jews and Christians was absolutely prohibited.

Although the preamble to the papal bull more or less repeats the old formulas, one discerns a perception of the Jewish question different from what had been normal in the Middle Ages. There was a greater rigidity, a more marked missionizing intent. In the final analysis, the Holy See was willing to tolerate the continued Jewish presence, but only so that it should be possible to instruct Jews in the Christian truth and, ultimately, to baptize them into the true faith. The bull was combined with further anti-Jewish measures, such as expulsions (some only temporary) and the burning of Jewish books. Even before the publication of the bull, in 1553, volumes of the Talmud confiscated from the Jews of Rome were publicly burned by order of the Inquisition, and similar events took place in other cities of the Catholic world. In time, papal Jewry policy shifted, and the burnings were replaced by Christian supervision and censorship of Jewish books. The ecclesiastical policy of segregation led to the introduction of designated Jewish quarters. The first such neighborhood was set apart in Venice in 1516, and its name—Ghetto—became the generic term for all subsequent Jewish neighborhoods, most of which were established in the second half of the sixteenth century. Jews were also required to attend sermons by Christian preachers, and special institutions were formed to accommodate Jewish converts—of which there were apparently a good many—and educate them.

Despite the oppressive policy, the new measures helped to define the Jews' place in the Christian world. With the Jews secluded in their own residential quarters, the expulsions ceased. While expulsions had been, as it were, a declaration that the Jews had no place in Christian society, closing them off in ghettos had the opposite effect of granting them a well-defined niche in society. Although the book burnings characteristic of the Church's previous policy reflected a desire to destroy Jewish culture in its entirety, censorship of Jewish books (some words and sentences were omitted) was in a sense a recognition that Jewish culture had a legitimate right to exist, and even that Jews—and Christians, too—were permitted to read Jewish literature.

We may assume that the inflexible Jewish policies of the Church at this time were produced by confusion, by the need to review the principle that had guided the Church hitherto—particularly against the backdrop provided by the Reformation and the Catholic-Protestant clashes. Thus, while the Protestants taught that man would be redeemed by his faith alone, the Catholic Church laid emphasis on the importance of certain practices—the Sacraments; but that same church had always taunted the Jews with the argument that practical observance had been abolished by the coming of Jesus and was no longer necessary. The Protestants, moreover, believed in an extreme version of the doctrine of predestination, teaching that man's free will was of no consequence, divine grace being dependent on God's will alone. The Jews, however, held that "everything is foreseen, yet freedom of choice is given"—that is, despite divine foreknowledge, man is nevertheless given the opportunity to choose between good and evil. Thus the Catholics once again found themselves maneuvering between these two extremes. Luther maintained that truth could be found in Scripture alone, negating the obligatory nature of generations of ecclesiastic exegesis. The Catholic Church, for its part, ascribed decisive importance to the works of the Church Fathers; on the Jewish front, however, it rejected the Oral Law and portrayed the Talmud as the devil's work. As it turns out, the Reformation not only forced a redefinition of Catholicism but it also necessitated a reconsideration of the points at issue between Christians and Jews. Against this background one can understand the Church's harsh anti-Jewish policy and vigorous missionizing efforts: it was genuinely apprehensive of Jewish influence. This policy was to remain in force, for the most part, until the nineteenth century.

4

"My Heart Is in the East..."

Jane S. Gerber

"My heart is in the East, and I am at the edge of the West." With these words the poet Judah Halevi sums up the perennial yearning of the Jews for their lost homeland. Judah Halevi eventually found the dislocation intolerable, and he set out on the long journey from Spain to the Middle East. The poet's biography points also to another dislocation: Spain in his day was divided between Christian and Muslim rule, and he had experience of both. In his poetry he portrays the lot of the Jews in both sections as one of captivity and oppression. For the most part, however, life under Muslim rule was more secure and comfortable for the Jewish minority than it was under the rule of Christianity, even if Muslim law accorded Jews a second-class status (a status they shared with Christians) and religious fanaticism occasionally erupted into persecution.

Muslim rule evidently provided the Jews in the Middle Ages with propitious conditions to develop a rich cultural life, both religious and secular. The finest achievements of these times have hardly been equaled before or since.

Opposite: A Moorish-style synagogue in Toledo. The synagogue was rededicated as the church of St. Mary the White (Santa María la Blanca).

Jews and Muslims have coexisted continuously since the rise of Islam in the seventh century in a vast geographic area stretching from Morocco to the borders of China. Even during its period of greatest unity (c. 800–1200) in the Islamic High Middle Ages, the Muslim world never had a single uniform policy toward the treatment of Jews. Jews found greater security and prosperity in the earlier centuries of Islam and suffered from instability and humiliation in the later centuries. At all times, however, tolerance was tempered by disabilities.

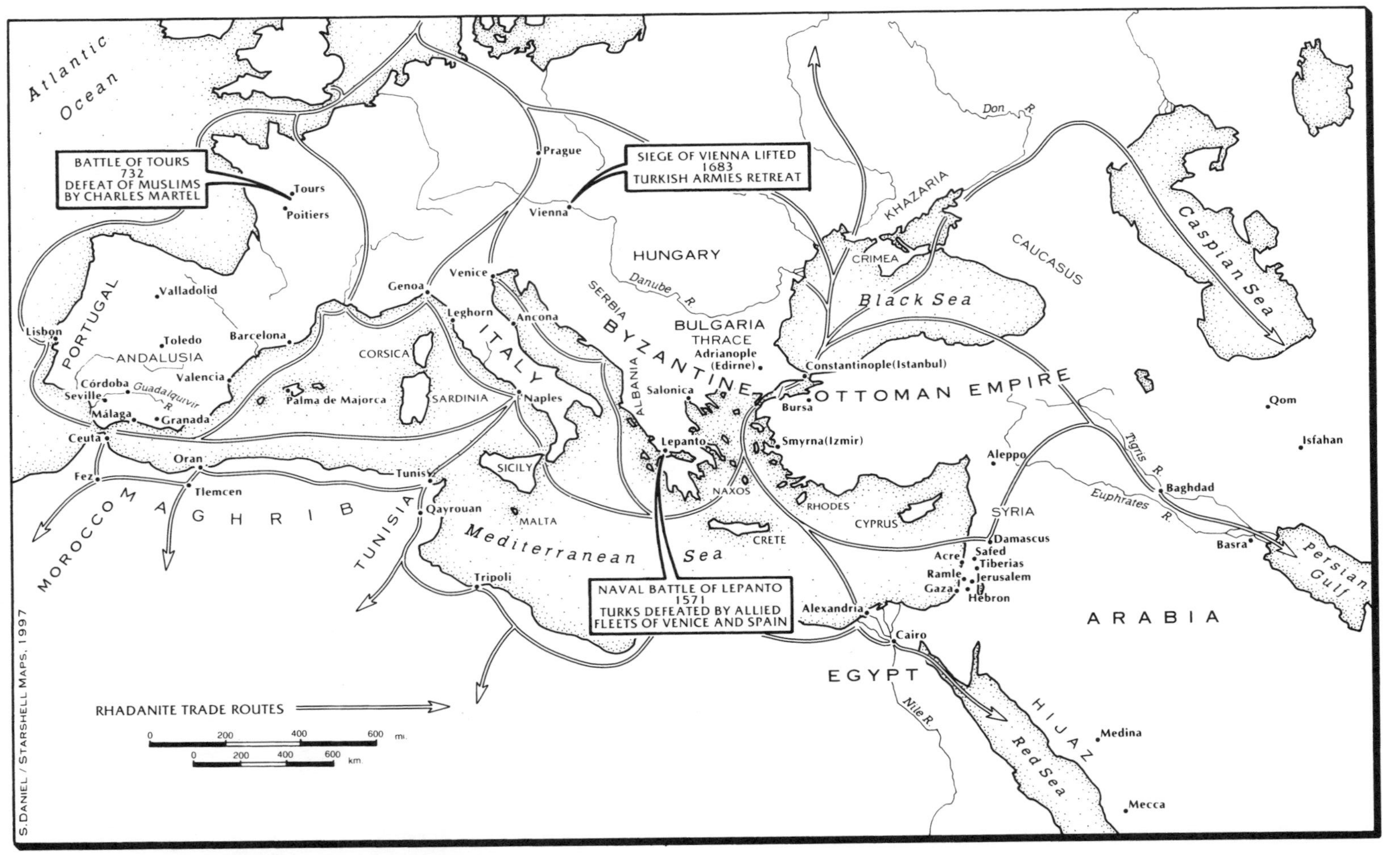

The World of Islam

In the stimulating intellectual environment of medieval Islam, Jews engaged deeply with the surrounding culture, creating a varied and rich civilization of their own. Jewish learning and commerce radiated from the great Muslim imperial centers of Iraq and Spain and the regional economic hubs of North Africa and Egypt. Jewish philosophy, poetry and law were immeasurably enriched by the exciting intellectual challenges of the renaissance in Islamic lands. Although jolted by sectarianism and waves of messianic excitement, the Jews of Islam constituted almost ninety percent of world Jewry until the thirteenth century.

The fruitful symbiosis of Judaism and Islam ceased in the twelfth century, as the fierce fundamentalist Almohades inaugurated persecutions throughout North Africa and Spain. At the same time, conflicts between the Crusaders and various Muslim military regimes choked the once-flourishing Middle Eastern economy. As Muslim military cliques took the reins of power, Jews were progressively forced out of the economy and reduced to a position of subordination. Their traditional intellectual centers in Iraq ceased functioning even before the Mongol devastations of the area.

The steady decline in the security and position of the Jews was interrupted by the advent of the first wave of exiles from Spain to North Africa after 1391. They brought new leadership and energy to Mediterranean lands. After 1492, their impact became overwhelming, as tens of thousands of exiles from Spain poured into the expanding Ottoman Empire, energizing dormant centers of Jewish life and forming entirely new communities. As the Jews of Spain, the most accomplished community of medieval times, moved eastward, they formed a chain of Jewish settlements across the Mediterranean, joined in economic enterprises and scholarship.

By the seventeenth century, however, the forces of creativity and renewal that had enabled Ottoman Jewry to reach new heights were spent. The empire was in a state of decay. The Jews were gripped by exhaustion and disillusionment in the wake of the debacle of the messianic movement of Shabbetai Zvi. Even the brief flowering of mysticism in Safed could not hide the signs of decay everywhere. Although Jews in Muslim lands still constituted one-half of world Jewry in the seventeenth century, the great age of Jewish creativity under Islam was over.

During their millennial sojourn in the world of Islam, enterprising, passionate and God-fearing Jews wrestled with one of the great cultures of world history. In their encounters with Islam, they reshaped Judaism in creative and enduring ways.

ISLAM AND THE JEWS: THE EARLY ENCOUNTERS

Jews already enjoyed a long history of life in the Diaspora when Islam appeared on the historical scene in seventh-century Arabia. They were deeply rooted in both the Roman and Persian empires and widely scattered in urban and rural areas. Their Greek-speaking communities in the Western (Roman) dispersion dotted the Mediterranean littoral from the coast of Spain, across North Africa, and were heavily concentrated in the Fertile Crescent and Asia Minor. After the conversion of

Rome to Christianity in the fourth century, Jewish life steadily declined. Generally worsening economic conditions in the empire, combined with attacks against the Jews and Judaism, reached their height in the sixth and seventh centuries.

The Aramaic-speaking communities of the Eastern (Persian) dispersion, traditionally more at ease than in Christendom, were also in a state of decline as the more pluralistic civilization of the Sassanian Persian Empire (226–651) succumbed to religious intolerance and economic chaos by the sixth century. Most densely settled in the border provinces of the two empires, the Jews were caught in the continuing battles wearing the two powers down. They tended to favor the Persians in their global struggles, especially in light of the active persecution they suffered in Christian domains in the late sixth and early seventh centuries. The proscription of Judaism at the time threatened their very survival. Byzantine retribution for their siding with Persia was fierce. Occurring only a few years prior to the appearance of the first Muslim raiders in the area, these upheavals undermined both empires and set the stage for the facility of the Arab conquests.

Culturally, too, the Jews were fragmented on the eve of the Muslim conquests. The gulf between the Greek-speaking Roman dispersion with its spiritual center in Palestine and the Aramaic-speaking dispersion in Babylonia was reflected in a myriad of divergences in local custom and ritual practice. Even the semiannual pilgrimages for talmudic study at the academies of learning in Iraq, which brought both dispersions together, couldn't mask the deepening rifts between the two segments of world Jewry. Jews had always regarded union under one imperial authority with some degree of trepidation. The presence of two kingdoms was seen as God's way of providing a beleaguered Jewish people with an escape hatch. The new imperial reality of a united Mediterranean, which Islam introduced, could be either a blessing or a curse; it could provide a welcome source of potential stability and a patina of unity to a severely fragmented world, or it could become a source of focused hostility and potential danger.

While seventh-century Jewry languished in Spain and Byzantium, facing persecutory movements at both ends of the Mediterranean, some islands of prosperity existed. The Jews of Arabia were organized tribally, enjoying a great deal of economic power in some of the key oases of the Hijaz, the Arabian Peninsula. Their ancient South Yemenite center of Himyar dominated the spice trade, harboring memories of a valiant warrior king, Dhu Nuwas, a convert to Judaism in 520, whose legendary exploits during the sixth century were still the subject of proud Arabian oral traditions. In the Hijaz, Jews engaged in viticulture and agriculture as well as commerce. Many of the pagan tribes in the region of the oasis of Yathrib (later Medina) owed allegiance and tribute to the prosperous Jewish tribes of the area. The elevated status of the Jews in Arabia was of critical importance as the context in which the Prophet Muhammad and his early followers interacted with the Jewish people and spread their message.

The emergence of the Prophet Muhammad in 610 from the great tribe of Quraish in Mecca seemed to augur well for the Jews. Impressed with biblical traditions and holding the Jews in high regard, Muhammad initially invited them to join his new community of faith. Much of what they heard from the mouth of the Arabian prophet—compulsory fasts and almsgiving, direction of prayer to

Jerusalem, lofty principles of justice and the absolute indivisibility and invisibility of God—were concepts quite familiar to them. Indeed, they had introduced and spread many of these notions among the pagan tribes of Arabia. But the Jews refused to concede that Muhammad was the seal and the last of the prophets sent by God, as he claimed. According to Jewish tradition, prophecy had ceased centuries prior to Muhammad. Even Muhammad's versions of biblical accounts appeared garbled and corrupted.

The majestic golden-domed Mosque of Omar (Dome of the Rock) dominates the Old City of Jerusalem, a reminder of the close attachment of Muslims to the Jewish Holy City. Originally Muhammad and his followers faced Jerusalem, like the Jews, when they prayed, and Muslims believe that he ascended to heaven from this spot. The mosque was constructed on the site of Solomon's Temple, and completed in 691 C.E.

Soon the passionate new religion of Islam began to define itself in opposition to its two monotheistic predecessors. To rebut those who believed in the divinity of Jesus, for example, Muhammad's message soon incorporated into his Scriptures, known as the Quran, the view of God as "unique, alone, He does not beget and is not begotten, none is equal to him." Jews, on the other hand, were castigated for their refusal to join Islam and subjected to harsh terms of tribute. At the same time, however, both Judaism and Christianity were recognized as kindred, if inferior, faiths based on revelations. The continuing existence of these separate monotheistic faiths was (and is) justified in a single verse in the Quran: "Say, O believers! I shall not worship what you worship. You do not worship what I worship. I am not a worshipper of what you have worshipped and you are not worshippers of what I have worshipped. To you, your religion. To me, my religion" (Sura 109).

As Muhammad progressed in hammering out his new faith in the fledgling Muslim community of Medina (where he fled in 622), he began to engage in increasingly heated polemics against the Jews. When the Jews rejected Muhammad outright, he excoriated them in vivid terms. Echoes of these bitter exchanges can still be heard in the Quran. The Jews were vilified as corrupters and perverters of Scripture (Sura 4:44) and cursed by Allah for their "disbelief." Their lot was described as one of "humiliation and wretchedness" since "they are visited with wrath from Allah" (Sura 2:61).

Polemics soon gave way to military campaigns that brought terrible consequences to Arabian Jews. Where politically expedient and militarily feasible, Muhammad did not hesitate to subjugate or expel some Jewish tribes from Arabia or to decapitate all male members of other Jewish tribes. Those "infidels" who survived were required to submit to Muslim authority and to pay tribute. This arrangement was sanctioned in a quranic injunction: "Fight against those to whom the Scriptures were given, who believe not in Allah nor in the Last Day, who forbid not what Allah and His apostle have forbidden, and follow not the true faith, until they pay the tribute out of hand, and are humbled" (Sura 9:29).

Muhammad officially accorded a low level of toleration to Jews, as to Christians, but the relative tolerance or intolerance of Islam was to fluctuate widely over the centuries. The Prophet recognized the validity of Judaism and Christianity because both possessed written revelations, but classical Islamic legal theory holds that the possessors of Scripture should be opposed until they surrender. Thereafter, the imposition of payment of tribute in the form of discriminatory taxes was only one of several obligatory signs of humiliation that they would bear. In return for their adherence to special discriminatory regulations, however, they would be offered protection (hence the term *ahl ad-Dhimma* or *dhimmis*, "protected people," applied to them). In other words, subjugated Jews and Christians would be permitted to reside in the House of Islam with certain limitations placed on them.

The importance of the precedents of the Prophet in defining the status of the Jews cannot be overestimated. For pious Muslims everywhere until today, the utterances of Muhammad, the examples of his adjudication and the sayings attributed to him (*sunna*) form a seamless fabric intended to serve as an immutable guide to all believers. They are invoked in times of crisis, sometimes manipulated for political or dynastic purposes, but offer a compelling guideline for daily human exchanges between groups.

Muslim civilization, from the outset and by its own perceptions, was defined by religion. Most areas of life fell under the purview of religion. The world was imagined as being divided in two camps. The world of Islam, *Dar al-Islam*, the House of Islam, was the civilized world in which Muslim law and, theoretically, order under a Muslim government prevailed. The rest of the world was known as *Dar el-Harb*, the House of War, the region inhabited by infidels who had yet to accept the Muslim faith and submit to Muslim rule. Within the House of Islam, the Muslims preserved a niche for the so-called protected people or "people of the Book," *ahl al-Kitab*—the Jews and Christians whose scriptures and monotheism entitled them to some place in the world of Islam. The *dhimma* was conceived as a pact or contract between the Muslim ruler and the non-Muslim monotheistic subjects. The terms of that contract were left for the jurists to define.

The ambiguous nature of early Islamic tolerance toward Jews is elaborated in one of the earliest Muslim legal handbooks, Abu Yusuf's eighth-century classic *Kitab al-Kharaj* (Book of taxes). This scholar's unique approach joins symbols and practices of tolerance with visible signs of humiliation to be borne by Jews and Christians. Distinguishing signs included special clothing regulations or "marks of recognition," which served to provide tangible proof of the bearer's inferiority. Distinctive colors of clothing, haircut and headgear were assigned to Jews and Christians. They were prohibited from riding horses or camels (considered noble steeds and hence reserved for Muslims) and from walking in certain areas. Their houses of worship and residences had to be lower than those of Muslims as a sign of respect. No new houses of worship were to be constructed. Their worship had to be inconspicuous and inoffensive. In other words, the basis of the *dhimmi* contract known as the Pact of 'Umar was the supremacy of Islam and the subordination of non-Muslims, symbolized by certain social restrictions and by the payment of special taxes from which Muslims were exempted.

Sometimes the distinctions borne by Jews and Christians under Islam reached absurd proportions, such as the decrees that Jews were to wear large bells to announce their presence or humiliating neckpieces so that even in the public baths there would be no mistaking their identity. Each shoe of a pair had to be of two different materials so that Jews would be readily recognizable and ludicrous. The fact that clothing restrictions were repeatedly legislated is proof that they were generally not enforced.

The strictness of anti-*dhimmi* legislation varied. In late-medieval Iran, for instance, Jews were prohibited from going outdoors in the rain because they were considered to be pollutants. In Yemen, Jews were forced by law to clean the public latrines and to relinquish orphaned children to be raised as Muslims. Theoretically, no new churches or synagogues were to be built anywhere; existing ones could be inconspicuously repaired. In other words, Jews were to be tolerated, but as second-class subjects in a world where signs of superiority of the dominant faith would be palpable and pervasive.

Muslim superiority became institutionalized by the late eighth century, while implementation of its various details remained subject to local leaders and regional variations. How much of this legislation was theoretical and how much was actually applied depended on such factors as the security and outlook of the individual ruler, the atmosphere of religious fervor in a particular regime and whether the government was sectarian or fundamentalist. By and large, the early Muslim centuries were ones of greater tolerance toward non-Muslims; the later centuries were marked by growing intolerance and humiliation. *Dhimmis* usually fared better under Sunni Muslims than under Shiites.

Dhimmis were not allowed to forget their inferior status, however. In most cases, Jews were excluded from public office, based on quranic precedents. All litigation between Muslims and *dhimmis* was under the jurisdiction of Muslim law, which didn't recognize the validity of the oath of a *dhimmi* versus a Muslim's. The blood of a *dhimmi* was valued at one-half that of a Muslim. *Dhimmis* were not permitted to marry Muslim women, under pain of death, though Muslim men were free to marry Jewish or Christian women (who would be required to convert to Islam). In addition, Christians and Jews were subjected to a special discriminatory poll tax (*jizya*) and discriminatory land taxes (*kharaj*). Non-Muslim tributaries were expected to hand over a percentage of the produce of their soil to the Muslim community. As the taxable area of land decreased owing to conversions to Islam in the early centuries of Islam, the fiscal burdens on the non-Muslims increased proportionately. Special fines and tributes were often levied on non-Muslims as a matter of course. With the passage of time, the extortionary policies of local Muslim rulers played a decisive role in the eventual impoverishment of the Jews in Muslim lands.

But Arab pragmatism, combined with the manpower needs of a small conquering minority, called for the utilization of minorities in the initial stages of Muslim expansion. The Islamic holy war (*jihad*) was pursued against pagans, not

Jews. The conquering armies were small, and rich provinces needed to be rebuilt and administered. It made more sense to make use of than to persecute the monotheistic minorities. Still, when the discrepancy between discriminatory theory and liberal practice was too great—that is, when Jews became too powerful or enjoyed too many rights—there was always the danger that Muslim reformers would insist on the restoration of stringent dress codes and other onerous and humiliating restrictions.

On balance, the "protected status" of *dhimmi* offered the Jews of Islam several important concessions that they lacked in contemporary Christian Europe: they could freely practice their religion, they could move about and reside almost everywhere in the world of Islam (with the notable exception of the Arabian Peninsula) and they were permitted to engage in a wide variety of professions, provided that they were not in a position of authority over Muslims. The *dhimmis* were considerably better off than slaves, although obviously much worse off than Muslims. Compared with the essential protections of the Pact of 'Umar, the disabilities involving social status and prestige were relatively minor annoyances, more psychological than practical in their effects. In fact, the blend of religious guarantees and subtle discriminations did not strike the Jews as particularly menacing, and the emerging affluence of the world of Islam soon proved to be a magnet. By the ninth century, Jews found themselves united under a new world power that would guarantee them much autonomy to pursue their lives as they themselves saw fit.

THE MUSLIM CONQUESTS AND THE EMERGENCE OF A NEW MEDITERRANEAN ECONOMIC ORDER

The Muslims moved out of Arabia with religious and military fervor. Palestine, Syria and Egypt were subdued within a decade of Muhammad's death in 632. Soon thereafter, Persia fell. After decades of indecisive battle, North Africa succumbed to the Muslim armies, and by the second decade of the eighth century most of Spain fell to the Muslims without resistance, as warring rival Visigothic princes opened up the gates of their cities to the strangers from North Africa. The Arab armies stood at the gates of France before they were finally repulsed. The eastern capital of the Byzantine Empire, Constantinople, would require another half millennium before it, too, fell to the Ottoman Turks in the fifteenth century. But as the dust of battle from the fierce conquests and local resistance settled, the world of Islam would prove to be, with a few notable exceptions, an asylum for Jews for the next millennium.

After the plunder and devastation of the conquering Muslim armies ceased, Islam was still periodically convulsed by internecine conflicts. But with the initial period of dynamic conquests completed, a virtual free-trade zone was established in the Mediterranean. New cities soon emerged out of the nuclei of Muslim garrisons. Trade quickened and pent-up energies were released. Old routes that had fallen into disuse were repaired and new avenues of trade were established. The emergent unity of the Mediterranean under Islam in a *Pax Islamica* is somewhat reminiscent of its ancient unity under the *Pax Romana* of the first and second centuries. Political boundaries within the Muslim orbit were not barriers to trade, and a new economic unity emerged with the Mediterranean as one great trading zone.

Since freedom of passage and freedom of settlement were open to members of the minority monotheistic faiths, flourishing Jewish settlements soon appeared in the new centers of Muslim worship and trade. The new Islamic cities did not have citizens in the modern sense. Each was an island that contained separate peoples, tribes and communities, with many foreigners coming and going, adding to the complex human mix. Organizationally weak, the Muslim cities nevertheless dominated the surrounding regions. Fez, Qayrouan (medieval Tunis), Fustat (Old Cairo), Ramle (in Palestine) and Baghdad, initially small garrison towns of conquering troops, soon emerged as significant centers of urban and Jewish life. In those towns where petty Muslim courts were established, as in Basra in Iraq or Malaga and Seville in Spain, Jews clustered and found employment among the court circles.

Economic incentives combined with religious disincentives to drive the Jews off the land. Formerly, the Jews had been a primarily rural people. Whole provinces of Iraq were abandoned as Jews flocked to the cities, unable to compete with newly converted Muslim cultivators who were not subject to discriminatory land taxes, poll taxes and the self-imposed religious tithes that made agriculture economically unfeasible for Jews. The memory of Jewish agricultural concentration remained in nomenclature. Ninth-century Arab geographers still called southern Iraq Yahudistan, the land of the Jews. One of the results of the Muslim conquests was the decisive transformation of the Jews into an urban people. As a Moroccan Arabic proverb remarked, "A city without Jews is like bread without salt."

Most major towns were located on the sites of former Roman settlements, revived and redesigned along the patterns of the new civilization. Such public areas as the markets and the mosque were centrally located; communal activities were held in these open spaces, often around a tiled fountain. Otherwise, the streets of the Muslim cities were generally quite narrow and serpentine, with numerous cul-de-sacs. Shops were concentrated in specific districts, according to what they produced or sold. Typically, residences lined winding streets that followed the natural slope of the terrain to allow for drainage through a channel in the middle of an adjacent valley. Main thoroughfares were unnamed, but the small alleys were named for people who lived there. Behind austere undecorated walls, the private homes were multigenerational dwellings that were frequently opulent. Jews tended to conceal their possessions from public scrutiny to avoid envy and to adopt the low-key lifestyle dictated by Muslim religious sensibilities.

Jewish residence often predated the Muslim conquests. As the towns expanded or new towns formed, there was a concomitant growth and expansion of Jewish communities. With new Jewish communities, there followed new synagogues—a clear indication that implementation of the Pact of 'Umar was only sporadic. But no exclusively Jewish neighborhoods existed in the cities and towns of Egypt, North Africa, Spain or the Middle East during the high Middle Ages, even though areas of Jewish residential concentration were common. Generally speaking, Jews preferred to live in walled neighborhoods with gates that could be barred for security; the blocks of houses in such cul-de-sacs were often protected by a guard who would make his rounds at night with dogs and a lantern. Before the Muslim conquests, Jews in towns in North Africa or Spain often lived alongside the city walls or gates. Soon after the conquests, those areas became known as *Bab el-Yahud* (the gate of the Jews), as in the case of Cordoba or the city of Fez in Morocco. Residential segregation was not necessarily discriminatory; it was a time-honored trait typical of Middle Eastern patterns of city dwelling that tribesmen, craftsmen, kinship groups and clans lived together in the pluralistic Near Eastern urban setting. In the heyday of Islam (the tenth and eleventh centuries), Jews, Muslims and Christians lived side by side, often in the same dwellings. Compulsory Jewish residential quarters or ghettos (the *mellah* in Morocco, the *hara* in Tunisia and the separate villages of Jews in Yemen) did not appear until the fifteenth century and thereafter. Living in such ghettos was correctly viewed as a hardship by their Jewish residents.

Trade was fundamental to Islamic life from the outset, in large part because Muhammad had been a merchant from the commercial oasis of Mecca. According to Muslim (but not Jewish) tradition, Abraham's son Ishmael, the forefather of Islam, was a textile merchant. Commerce was always esteemed under Islam, while agriculture was held in very low repute, as were those who engaged in it. Many traditions ascribed to Muhammad praise commerce; few show any respect for agricultural labor. The situation was to worsen over the centuries as agricultural land was parceled out to military officers, most with no knowledge of and even less interest in the long-term prosperity of their landed domains.

The circumstances of the medieval Muslim world were uniquely favorable to large-scale commerce over long distances. For the first time in history, a vast region of the globe was united under a single political and cultural system. The quasi-global economy of Islam eventually stretched from Iberia to the borders of China as men, ideas, goods and armies moved freely between East and West. Mobility was facilitated by early oral Islamic tradition and practice, which regarded travel for the sake of knowledge (*rihla* or *talab el-ilm*) as a venerable and pious activity that might even assure entry into Paradise. According to one source, the Prophet himself said, "Those who go out in search of knowledge will be in the path of God until they return." Or, as the traditional phrase put it, "In mobility there is blessing" (*f'il haraka baraka*). In the Talmud, too, travel for the sake of learning was commended.

Not surprisingly, Arabic travel literature increased during the eighth and ninth centuries, expanding the available knowledge of routes and of the remote areas of the explored world. As Muslims departed Spain to study at the feet of famous scholars in North Africa, Cairo and Persia, Jews, too, traveled far and wide with a remarkable degree of casualness. Regular commuting of Jewish merchants between Spain, Sicily, North Africa, the eastern shores of the Mediterranean and the Indian Ocean occurred from the ninth through the twelfth centuries. Medieval Jewish documents spanning almost 1,000 years, preserved in the treasure trove known as the Cairo Genizah, show how natural it was for Jews to be on the move. It was not unusual to make several journeys from Spain to India during one's lifetime. One Genizah letter from Alexandria concerning the habits of a merchant from Tunisia casually states, "I am astonished that he has not come around Passover as he is accustomed to do." Genizah documents note the frequency with which Jews moved between various parts of the Mediterranean and the Indian Ocean, for the sake of contracting marriages for their offspring or establishing new branches of business. The family was considered the ideal form of business partnership, with ties of blood superseding ties of marriage. Jews preferred to travel by sea, because one didn't desecrate the Sabbath if the journey began before the Sabbath; the requirement of halting or departing from a land caravan for a day could be extremely expensive. Land travel also carried the added menace of desert marauders. Moreover, the Muslims had made the sea routes eminently safer by constructing lighthouses along the shores and introducing new, improved naval vessels; even so, ships in this era stayed close to shore, and in winter, when tides were tricky, traders either stayed at home or took the land routes. A medieval Jewish merchant might well own a house in Qayrouan and another elsewhere, perhaps in Egypt or Palestine or Syria. Thus was fashioned an overarching culture and cosmopolitan community that shared many features, exchanging new tastes and technologies along with goods, services and ideas. Although the rhythm of life in all Jewish communities was determined by the religious calendar, it was also shaped by the comings and goings of their itinerant Jewish merchants. As one of the Genizah correspondents writes, "The synagogue is desolate, for the Maghrebis have left."

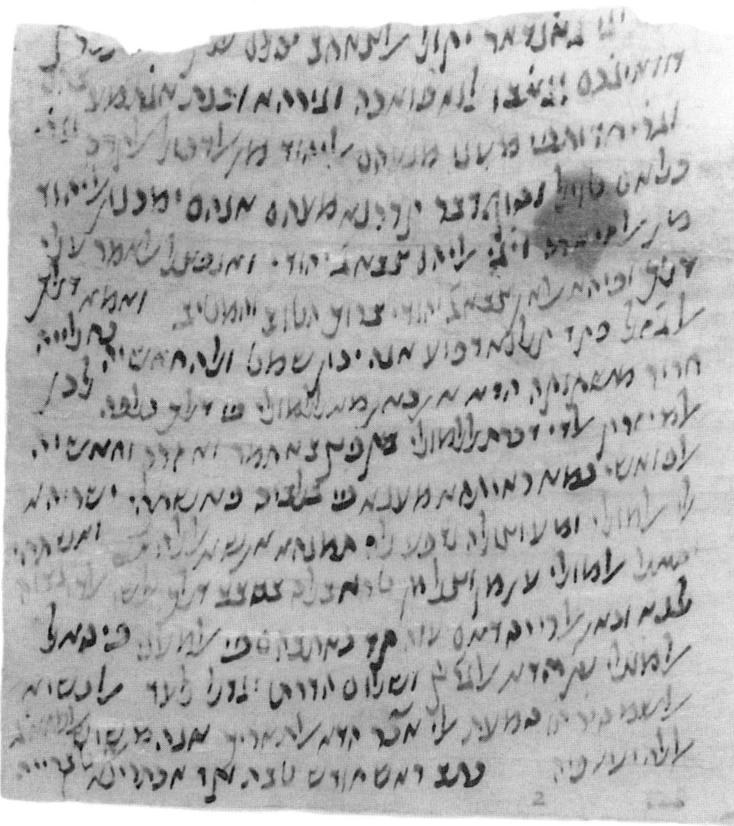

A letter from the Cairo Genizah, dated December 20, 1236. A traveler to Jerusalem writes to a relative back in Egypt who is intending to travel to the city, at that time under Crusader rule for the second time.

Jewish travel and commerce were facilitated by the medieval Muslim notion that law was personal, not territorial, and a person was judged according to the law of his religious community. Jewish law, in any case, was uniformly applied, regardless of the country or province in which it was administered. Muslim law, too, together with the near universality of the Arabic language, provided a single unifying authority. Genizah letters are oblivious to political boundaries, as Jewish merchant families (often in partnership with Muslims) moved back and forth between rival kingdoms. To be sure, there were customs stations everywhere, but both Christian and Muslim powers in the high Middle Ages seemed intent on preserving a free-trade community in the Mediterranean. The philosopher, halakhist and physician Maimonides remarks casually in a responsum in the twelfth century that Jews were regular passengers on boats commuting between Seville and Alexandria.

Serious studies of this era have pointed out that the learned merchant was the standard-bearer of medieval Muslim civilization. The Muslim pilgrim's customary wish was "May your *hajj* be accepted, your sin be forgiven and your merchandise not remain unsold." Jews drew freely from this intellectual and commercial climate as a large and influential commercial class began to arise all over the Middle East in the eighth and ninth centuries. Jewish, Muslim and Christian mercantile families dealt with one another in partnerships, and "formal friendships" characterized business relationships.

Jewish documents from the medieval Muslim world are striking for the enormous variety of goods manufactured and traded by Jews. The Genizah collection includes more than 300 letters to and from the Tunisian merchant-scholar Nahrai ben Nissim, a regular commuter between Tunisia and Egypt in the eleventh century. His transactions over the course of a fifty-year career (1045–96) involved merchandise from Spain, North Africa, Sicily, Egypt, Syria and India. His extremely diversified trade included almost all the staples and luxuries of the commercial world of his day: flax and silk, olive oil and spices, metals and books, jewels and chemicals, food and hides. His detailed surviving accounts reveal a man of exceptional organizational and intellectual abilities who worked in partnership with a variety of experts, but it appears that such versatility in trade was an exception. Usually, leading merchants worked closely with others specializing in one item of commerce. It appears that the Jews were among the first to understand the importance of credit and its utility in long-distance trade.

From a ninth-century Arabic account, *Kitab el-Masalik wa'l Mamalik* (The book of the roads and kingdoms), we learn incidentally of the remarkable commercial activities of a Jewish international trading firm known as the Radhanites, which may have been based in southern France or Spain. Their trade stretched across several continents, with branches in many ports and commercial outposts. Their representatives followed four distinct land and sea routes. One went northward through Europe via Prague, Bulgaria and the land of the Khazars in the Crimea. Two proceeded along the Mediterranean littoral and ended in Iran and Iraq (the trip from Cordoba to Baghdad normally took a year). The fourth went by sea and land all the way to China. Generally speaking, most of the commercial agents of the Radhanites went only part of the route, making trades with colleagues who had accumulated merchandise on an adjacent leg of the whole route. These traders used Hebrew, Arabic, Persian and Greek as well as "the language of Franks, Andalusians and Slavs." Hebrew was understood in educated Jewish circles the world over, giving the merchants a kind of lingua franca not only for trade but also for religious and intellectual discourse.

Although distance seems to have been no obstacle to traders, the Jewish custom of hospitality to strangers certainly assured merchants that they could maneuver in foreign territories. Their innovative use of letters of credit (known as *suftaja*) enabled them to conduct business comfortably over vast distances. This development of early capitalist tools probably originated among the Jewish bankers of Baghdad, such as the Bnei Amram and the Bnei Netira. Curiosity about distant lands seems to have animated both Jews and Arabs. Among the more fascinating trading posts that Jews reached was the Jewish kingdom that emerged in the Crimean area of Khazaria in the eighth century. The conversion of its king to Judaism may have represented a calculated political declaration of neutrality for a kingdom wedged between the borders of warring Byzantium and Islam. But to the Jews, the very existence of the Khazars was uplifting. The ruling house of this Turkic kingdom remained Jewish until the tenth century, serving not only as an important trading post into Central Asia but as a tantalizing symbol of a sovereign Jewish realm. The Jews of Spain, ever sensitive to questions of Jewish powerlessness, were particularly fascinated by the Jewish Kingdom of the Khazars.

The naturalness with which medieval Jews engaged in commerce over long distances, aided by their uniform codes of law and the presence of co-religionists all along the route, should not obscure the considerable perils they confronted. Genizah letters are replete with allusions to shipwrecks and the merchants' sense of gratitude to God for deliverance from danger. In anticipation of the ever-present threat of piracy, banditry and assaults by the crew, merchant ships tended to travel in convoys. Frequently, such phrases as "We arrived safely in Alexandria for God protected us from pirates" appear in Genizah documents. Piracy, which colored all aspects of sea commerce, was an arm of the continuing holy war between Islam and Christendom and was especially active near Byzantine shores and in the eastern Mediterranean in the eleventh century. Again, in the sixteenth century, Jews were caught in the middle of the wars of piracy between an ascendant Europe and the emergent Ottoman superpower. So well known and feared was the pirates' nest off the coast of Libya that merchants would write their families in relief as soon as they passed by safely.

Jews captured by pirates could count on ransom and rescue by fellow Jews in the area when they were brought to the slave market, generally deprived of all possessions including the clothes on their backs. Repeatedly, communities in Egypt were summoned to redeem men and women from the hands of pirates. One fragmentary letter describes how burdened the Egyptian community was with the frequent demands for ransom:

> We turn to you today on behalf of a captive woman who has been brought from Byzantium. We ransomed her for 24 dinars besides the government tax. You sent us 12 dinars; we have paid the remainder and the tax. Soon afterwards sailors brought two other prisoners, one of them a fine young man possessing knowledge of Torah, the other a boy of about ten. When we saw them in the hands of the pirates, and how they beat and frightened them before our own eyes, we had pity on them and guaranteed their ransom. We had hardly settled this, when another ship arrived carrying many prisoners. Among them a physician and his wife. Thus we are again in difficulties and distress. And our strength is overstrained, as the taxes are heavy and the times critical.

The burden of ransoming Jewish captives fell most heavily on the Jews of Alexandria, who pleaded with other Egyptian cities to share their charitable burdens, imposed on them by geography: "Kindly take care of this man and his large family as long as we are busy with collecting money for the poll tax of the poor. We have already paid for ninety of them. We have promised him to finance his return to the Land of Israel when he will come back from your place."

At times of international upheaval, such as during the Crusades, or later during the Chmielnicki massacres of the Jews in Poland in 1648, cries of Jewish distress and the obligation to ransom Jewish captives resonated as far away as the southern reaches of Morocco. The unity of sentiment and shared sense of mutual responsibility animating widely dispersed communities is movingly expressed over and over again. Some of this unity may have stemmed from the constant movement of Jewish populations and the realities of mutual dependence that the Jews understood all too well.

Although the international traders were perhaps the most spirited and high-profile members of the Jewish community under Islam, most Jews earned their livelihood as local merchants, craftsmen or artisans. Judaism has never regarded manual labor as degrading, and the Bible and Talmud praise manual labor. One of the duties of a father was to teach his son a trade. Even scholars were expected to engage in some craft, not to live off the fruits of Torah. The usual form of manufacture was in one's home or a small family workshop. Manufacturing was generally for the local market, with only a few commodities being produced for an international market.

Genizah entries clearly indicate that Jewish women also played economic roles in manufacturing and, to a lesser extent, in commerce. In addition to their work in the household, they were expected to engage in some other kind of work. Marriage contracts often stated whether a wife's earnings belonged to her husband or whether she was allowed to retain them. A husband was expected, by Jewish law, to provide for all her physical needs. Jewish contracts explicitly protected the woman's economic rights in case of widowhood or divorce and provided for her protection in the event that her husband should not return from his travels. Textile production, whether at home or in workshops, was the main area of women's gainful employment. The products of female industry were sold by female brokers. Jewish female merchants circulated freely, bringing textiles, threads, perfumes or flour to Muslim women, just as they later moved freely as vendors in the harem of the palaces in Istanbul. Women doctors appear in Genizah lists, as do teachers. Domestic help and nurses for children were provided by female servant/slaves, whose presence was permitted only with the consent of the wife. Concubines were absolutely forbidden by Jewish law, although customary in Muslim households. Slaves (pagans from Central Asia in the early Middle Ages) were a major commodity of Muslim traders. Domestic service by slaves was a temporary occupation in Jewish homes, since Jewish law required that they be redeemed and converted after a designated period of time. Thereafter, in accordance with Jewish law, they became full members of the household.

Although women did not share any roles with men in the synagogue, the source of all honors and prestige in the community, they are generally referred to in the thousands of Genizah documents with genuine respect and affection. Occasionally women are listed as significant donors to synagogues, a clear sign of their status as independent property owners.

Women played an active role in the education of their children, often acting as tutors for their sons at home. They also played a decisive role in securing formal education for their children, insistently providing for it in their wills.

Occasionally they even served as teachers, though usually not in a formal classroom setting. In one case, we learn of a woman teaching assistant to a male in a classroom setting. She "rushes around" the classroom while the male teacher physically restrains the rambunctious students. It is unclear whether she was an instructor primarily of the so-called female arts of embroidery and needlework in many of the references to women as teachers or whether she taught Torah.

From the available documents, it is quite difficult to ascertain how widespread was Jewish female literacy. Some notable women attained high levels of literacy, particularly in cases where fathers did not have any sons and would devote themselves to their daughters' education. Many women also seem to have learned passively through listening while their brothers recited by rote as they were tutored at home. A poem written by Hai Gaon (939–1038) of the Babylonian city of Pumbedita recommends that parents purchase books and hire tutors for both sons and daughters. In a Genizah dirge, a father laments the death of his learned daughter. In the case of one scholar from Qayrouan, we read that his daughter was considered "a scholar of Torah and a righteous woman." We even have evidence of a female false messiah in medieval Cairo, a clear indication that Jewish women were held in high regard!

Some of the Genizah documents were composed and transcribed by the women themselves, not dictated to men. We possess one example from fourteenth-century Yemen of a Bible codex calligraphed by a woman. In the colophon, the calligrapher, Miriam bat Benayahu Ha-Sofer (the Scribe) apologizes that her work is of such poor quality, explaining that she was suckling a child while working. Perhaps this is not as surprising as it appears, since piety and learning were so closely linked in the value system of the Jewish community. In general, the status of Jewish women was much higher than that of their female Muslim or Christian neighbors. The greater freedom of Jewish women often made them reluctant to move into shared courtyards with Muslims, where there would be pressure to maintain stricter rules of female seclusion. Although the birth of a son was cause for exuberant congratulations in the medieval society reflected in the Cairo Genizah, no letter on the happy tidings of the birth of a daughter exists. The birth of a girl as a first-born child was auspicious, as she averts the evil eye, but it evoked none of the enthusiasm evident in the following letter from medieval Tunisia: "Your letter containing the great news and joyful tidings about the blessed, blissful, and auspicious newborn has arrived. We had here much joy, music, and congratulation gatherings because of this. . . . Yes, my brother, you are to be congratulated, and very much so. May God bestow on me that both you and he will live and may God make him a brother of 'seven and even eight.' May God strengthen your arm through him and establish by him your honored position and fulfill in your case: 'Instead of your fathers there shall be your sons, you will make them princes all over the country.'

In the early centuries of Islam, Jews engaged in virtually every occupation. But poverty was also common. During the High Middle Ages, approximately one-quarter of the community could be categorized as beggars living on the charitable rolls of the community. After the twelfth century, the numbers of dependants increased as Jewish economic opportunities contracted. The reasons for this decline were multiple: as the Muslim world became more feudal, Jews were pushed out of commerce by Muslims. Also, with the passage of time, Muslim guilds grew stronger. As in Europe, they were generally connected to religious orders and were not open to Jewish membership. Additionally, the Italian principalities gaining a foothold in the Near East by the tenth century began to bar Jews and even goods owned by Jews from international commerce. Consequently, an increasingly large percentage of the Jews were dependent on the largesse of the few wealthy members of the community. Inevitably this would lead to tensions over tax apportionment in the community, especially in regard to meeting the unending levies imposed by the Muslims.

The rich documentary evidence of trade in luxury goods should not obscure the fact that most Jews engaged in petty trade and modest crafts. In the early years, Jewish craftsmen were distinguished for their high degree of intricate specialization, especially within the textile and silk trade. From Genizah documents, the historian Shlomo Dov Goitein has identified more than 450 different occupations engaged in by Jews in the world of medieval Islam. Details of Jewish production of luxury goods, fine brocades, elaborate metalwork and delicate jewelry fill the pages of the Cairo Genizah. Some of these specialties, such as gold- and silver-smithery, remained a monopoly of Jews in Muslim lands until recently, the secrets of the trade being transmitted from father to son for generations. Travelers throughout the Mediterranean note the high degree of concentration and artistry of Jews in smithery and jewelry making in the heartland of Islam as well as in its peripheries, such as Morocco and Yemen. Other specialties, like embroidery with threads of gold leaf, were also typically Jewish occupations.

Since talmudic times, Jewish communities have traditionally included professionals such as doctors, scribes and teachers. One of the most important and prestigious occupations to emerge among Jews in Muslim lands was that of the physician. Medicine blossomed under Islam as Jews were exposed to ancient Greek medical texts in translation. The preponderance of Jews in medicine may be explained, in part, by the fact that it was a profession demanding literacy. The Muslims had translated an array of ancient Greek medical works into Arabic. Multilingual Jews referred to medical classics with ease.

The highly esteemed profession of physician was passed on from father to son. Maimonides served as a court physician in twelfth-century Fustat. His son Abraham followed in his footsteps in the same profession. As late as 1409, a descendant, David II ben Joshua, still served as a doctor. Service as doctor at the court often opened the doors to leadership within the Jewish community. An unbroken chain of medical men represented the official leadership of the Jewish community of Egypt. Arabic chronicles reveal that even the most uncouth generals had a healthy respect for literacy, particularly literacy in ancient books, which doctors were required to study. Trusted physicians were often appointed to administrative posts in the government; in this traditional fashion, Hasdai ibn Shaprut (c. 915–c. 970) embarked on his stellar political career in Cordoba and quickly made a mark for himself, particularly in dealing with customs revenues. One position led to another as he gained the caliph's confidence, for the gratitude of 'Abd ar-Rahman III proved to be as large as his colossal architectural ambitions and his need for cash to fulfill them. Before long, the ruler appointed Hasdai head

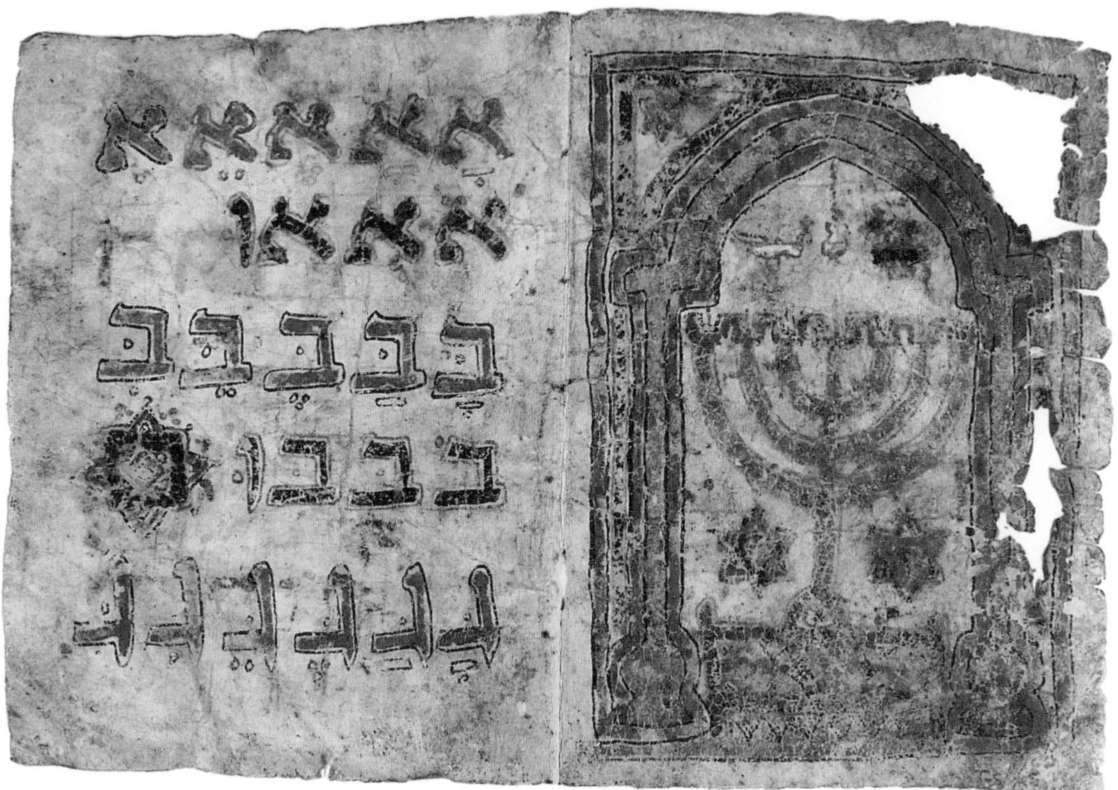

A fragment of a child's primer to teach the Hebrew alphabet, from the Cairo Genizah. Hebrew grammar was the basis of education for Jews in the Middle Ages, and even Arabic was written in Hebrew letters. Note the ubiquitous menorah. The six-pointed stars should not be considered as Jewish symbols at this date, but merely as decorative features.

of the Jewish community, and eventually he was entrusted with delicate diplomatic missions on behalf of the caliphate.

Every century produced its share of famed Jewish doctors who rose to high administrative positions. The first official heads of the Jewish community of Fatimid Egypt in the tenth century were Tunisian doctors who had arrived with the conquerors from the West. The trusted physicians of the Fatimid conquerors soon became administrators and organizers of taxes and customs duties. Eagerly courted by sultans and pashas, Jewish physicians in the later medieval period obtained pensions to serve as permanent "official doctors" in the Turkish court. As illustrated by the career of Moses Hamon (c. 1490–1554) in sixteenth-century Istanbul, royal physicians could be very effective in defending Jewish rights. The Hamon family, originally from Granada, immigrated to Turkey after 1492. Moses' father, Joseph, became physician first to Sultan Bayezid II and later to Selim I. Moses would serve also as official doctor to Suleiman the Magnificent, becoming one of the most powerful Jews in Turkey. In the 1540s, when several communities were hit with a wave of persecution after Armenians charged that Jews were using Christian blood for ritual purposes (the blood libel), Moses Hamon obtained an imperial decree (*ferman*) in 1553 repudiating the blood libel and promising imperial protection against all such accusations in the future. Hamon also emerged as an important patron of Jewish learning and a leading diplomat of his day. In 1588 Moses' son, Joseph, negotiated the renewal of Jewish residential rights in the city of Salonica. Despite these and other illustrious achievements in diplomacy and medicine, Hamon, like other Jewish courtiers in Muslim political circles, ultimately fell from favor, the victim of court intrigues. Nevertheless, the tradition of Jews serving as official physicians in Muslim court circles continued in Turkey for several centuries. In 1618, for example, forty Jewish physicians were appointed to the sultan's court, in addition to foreign Jewish physicians employed there.

What explains the prominence of Jewish physicians in the world of Islam? Classical Jewish sources had placed special emphasis on bodily health. Talmudic sources even enjoin that no Jewish community be established without a resident physician. During the Middle Ages, Jews were keenly attuned to the surrounding Arab culture, a culture that strongly stressed classical Greek learning, specifically in the sciences. Thus the study of medicine was an integral part of Islamic civilization and also of the Jewish curriculum. Although questions of cultural diffusion are extremely difficult to answer, clearly the Arab focus on the sciences and their translations of Greek scientific and philosophical works had the profoundest influence on the Jews. The output of Jews and Christians in the writing of Arabic medical works was out of all proportion to their numbers. The profession of medicine was also closely allied with pharmaceutics. In the wake of the revival of Greek sciences, coupled with the expansion of Muslim trade to India and farther east, Jewish traders in spices and herbs formed part of the bustling economy. Like all minorities, Jews sought to find a niche in the new professions esteemed by the Muslims. Medicine and pharmacy were the most conspicuous of the wide range of new occupations enjoyed by Jews in Muslim lands, alongside commerce and the manufacture of luxury goods, banking, and gold- and silver-smithery.

JEWISH INTELLECTUAL LIFE IN MUSLIM LANDS IN THE EARLY MUSLIM MIDDLE AGES

Within a century after the Muslim conquests, Islam created a revolution among the conquered peoples. It was not only a military conquest but also a religious one. The new Islamic cities founded by the conquerors served as nuclei of Arabization. Alongside the spread of their religion, the Arabs imparted their zeal for the language of their religion, Arabic. By the ninth century, Jews were speaking Arabic, often with an admixture of Hebrew, written primarily in Hebrew characters. Jews tended to be bi- or even trilingual. As they became Arabic speakers, they were exposed to an entirely new philosophical vocabulary and an exciting variety of new concepts. For the first time since antiquity, Jews had access to the Greek classical tradition. Selectively translated for inquisitive caliphs, the Hellenistic legacy deeply challenged the assumptions and mode of thought of Muslims and Jews.

The adoption of the Arabic language enabled the Jews to absorb the dominant surrounding culture in a way that they never would in Europe. Medieval Jews wrote most of their significant works in Arabic in the world of Islam (except their poetry); they did not write in Latin and hence never engaged in a real dialogue with European Christian culture. As we shall see, the cultural symbiosis with Muslim civilization reached its highest form, paradoxically, in Hebrew poetry in

Spain. The dialogue between Judaism and Islam, so intense in the early centuries of Muslim rule, ceased to be meaningful by the later Middle Ages. The renaissance of Jewish cultural life in the later Middle Ages in Ottoman lands was an internal development primarily of rabbinic culture with very little intellectual engagement with the surrounding Turkish culture.

The Middle Ages is often regarded as the age of the geonim. To a great extent, ancient rabbinic culture and talmudic civilization developed into Judaism as we know it today as a result of the collective efforts of a succession of Jewish leaders, known as the geonim, who resided in Baghdad until the eleventh or twelfth centuries. Heirs to the talmudic learning that thrived in Babylonia, the Jewish scholars of medieval Baghdad built on past traditions to meet the challenges of the new civilization.

Soon after the establishment of the Abbasid dynasty, the Arab caliphate that ruled from Baghdad 750–1258, the ancient Babylonian schools of talmudic learning were transferred to the new capital. The scholars in the two academies of Baghdad (which retained the ancient names of the cities of Sura and Pumbedita) contended that they were continuing the traditions of earlier teachers, *tannaim* and *amoraim*. This was indeed the case, as the position of head of the academy, gaon, was not an elective office but rather passed down hereditarily in an elaborate system of succession. The structure of the academy and the scope of its ancient functions were also unaltered.

The gaon was the highest authority on religious law, entitled to expound it in public lectures: he appointed and dismissed local Jewish functionaries such as judges, cantors and ritual slaughterers. Some geonim achieved renown throughout the Jewish world; many geonim, however, were mediocre, since the principle of hereditary succession also enfeebled the institution and disqualified many talents from advancing to the highest levels of office. Often the gaon was quite elderly when he finally reached the position of supreme authority in the academy. Both Sherira Gaon (906–1006) of Pumbedita, and Hai Gaon, among the greatest geonim of medieval times, were in their late nineties when they acted as decisors of Jewish legal questions.

The academies in Baghdad combined several roles; as a seat of learning they received scholars from all over the Diaspora twice yearly. They also served as judicial bodies that ruled on important issues. In addition, their interpretations played a legislative role in keeping Jewish law abreast of the changing conditions in the Muslim world. As a Jewish parliament, they were respected even beyond the borders of Islam among Jews in Christian Europe.

The two academies shared and sometimes competed for the loyalties of the Mediterranean Diaspora. They were also challenged by the continuation of an academy of learning with its own gaon in Palestine. All three academies competed to some extent for support from the same sources: donations set at fixed times of the year, fines earmarked for the academies, private donations contributed by individuals on special occasions of family joy or tragedy and, finally, contributions included with queries brought by itinerant merchants. In the spring and the fall, during the Hebrew months of Adar and Elul, the gaon would deliver public lectures before the assembled scholars who had convened in Baghdad. His pronouncements on rabbinic issues would be considered authoritative. His answers to legal queries would be collected and sent abroad and circulated throughout the Muslim world. Some of the replies, known as *teshuvot* or responsa, were entire books. Their impact was enormous, since few Jewish communities possessed copies of the Talmud in the early Middle Ages and consequently were unsure on many basic issues of Jewish law. Even elementary questions such as the order of prayer needed to be fixed. The answers to queries about the rudiments of prayer by Gaons Amram Bar Sheshna (856–874) and Saadia formed the basis for the Jewish prayer book. The gaonic literature produced during the critical centuries of Muslim unity helped create a unity of Jewish practice, universally respected by far-flung communities, thereby preventing the Jewish people from fragmenting into a series of local and increasingly separate civilizations.

The geonim faced a formidable task. Texts of the Talmud required codification. Explanation for the laws was lacking. Rudimentary knowledge of the Hebrew language made biblical comprehension difficult. No handbooks of law existed to inform people what to do without tedious research or specialized talmudic knowledge. Moreover, in the atmosphere of philosophical inquiry that pervaded Muslim intellectual circles in tenth-century Baghdad and North Africa, Jews began to ask new and more sophisticated questions of their tradition. Thus the work of the geonim was both a continuation of the old and something new. In keeping with the intellectual activities of contemporary Muslim scholars, the geonim engaged in the codification of Jewish law and the elaboration of Jewish traditions in the new spirit of philosophical inquiry of their day. Their reasoned introductions to talmudic tractates also emulated the scholarship in the Muslim schools of law.

Saadia Gaon was undoubtedly the greatest representative of the gaonic tradition who employed some of the tools of Muslim philosophers to produce an enormous legacy. Although he was born in Egypt and hence an outsider in the rabbinical order of succession to the leadership of a yeshivah in Baghdad, he was appointed gaon of Sura in 928. His appointment was probably motivated partially by the need to meet the challenge of sectarians among the Jews and in recognition of his formidable qualifications. He was also known as combative, having composed his first polemical work at the age of twenty-three. During his tumultuous career, he did not shy away from controversy.

Saadia understood that his generation was challenged to the core by theological issues raised by exposure to Greek philosophy in its Arabic garb. He confesses his grief at the confusion and regnant religious skepticism of his co-religionists in the introduction to his major philosophical work, *Sefer ha-Emunot ve-ha'Deot* (The book of beliefs and opinions): "When I considered these evils, my heart grieved for my race the race of mankind, and my soul was moved on account of our people Israel, as I saw in my time many of the believers clinging to unsound doctrines and mistaken beliefs while many of those who deny the faith because of their unbelief and despise the men of truth, although they are themselves in error—I felt that to help them was my duty and guiding them aright an obligation unto me."

A Muslim contemporary of Saadia's remarked in a similar vein of the prevailing intellectual atmosphere in Baghdad of his day, "Muslims, Jews, Christians and Magians—they all are walking in error and darkness. There are only two kinds of people left in the world: the one group is intelligent, but lacking in faith; the other has faith, but is lacking in intelligence."

Saadia's works were intended to fill a definite social function. He addressed himself to a learned audience in an orderly and logical manner. Saadia was a pioneer in many fields of Jewish literature. Among his outstanding works were an Arabic translation of the Bible, a rhyming dictionary that served as a foundation for the poetic revolution that would soon emerge and his *Sefer ha-Emunot ve-ha'Deot*. This treatise was intended to allay the growing doubts among Jewish intellectuals about their own tradition as they confronted the rationalist traditions of Muslim philosophers. It represented the first systematic attempt to present Judaism as a rational body of beliefs, much in the spirit of the Muslim theologians of his day. His philosophical work and his fight on behalf of the rabbinic tradition against the challenge of the Karaite sect, which rejected the authoritative position of the Oral Law or Talmud among the Jewish people, are undoubtedly his enduring contributions to Jewish history. Maimonides summed up Saadia's place in Jewish history in his *Epistle to Yemen*: "Were it not for Saadia the Torah would have almost disappeared from the midst of Israel; for it was he who made manifest what was obscure therein, made strong what had been weakened."

Baghdad was only one of several seats of scholarship that flourished under medieval Islam. Until the Crusaders invaded Palestine in 1099, destroying the Jewish community there, the Palestinian gaon commanded widespread respect and loyalty. Although Palestine had lost its religious prerogatives as the legislative authority in Jewish life before the rise of Islam, it retained the important prerogative of declaring the religious calendar for the entire Diaspora. On occasion a vigorous gaon would try to retrieve some of the other ancient prerogatives of the Holy Land, but they were vigorously resisted by the academies of Baghdad. The city of Qayrouan also played a role in the development of knowledge. Although very little data have survived from medieval Tunisia (Qayrouan was destroyed by Bedouin tribes in the mid-eleventh century), we know that the scholars of Qayrouan were regarded with great respect by the leading geonim of the age. Tunisian merchants played an active role in keeping scholarship alive in this important Jewish commercial center of North Africa. Jewish scholarship was transferred to the Ashkenazi Jewry of Europe via Qayrouan to Italy. Farther west in Morocco, talmudists and linguists found congenial company in the city of Fez. Its leading scholar, Isaac Alfasi (1013–1103), transmitted many of the insights of North African Jewish learning with him when he migrated to Spain. Each center played a distinctive role that contributed to the sum total of Jewish knowledge. Wherever Jews engaged in scholarship in the metropolitan centers of the Islamic world, they shared facets of the cultural ethos of the ruling Muslims, particularly their interest in science, law and philosophy. Jewish acculturation, an ongoing process throughout Jewish history, was a dynamic force during the Islamic Middle Ages. Jews always tended to gravitate to and emulate stimulating cultures around them, adapting and transforming competing ideas to fit them within their own frames of reference.

Undoubtedly the most fruitful encounter of Arab culture and Jewish imagination emerged in Muslim Spain, known as al-Andalus. During the tenth and eleventh centuries, several dazzling centers of Muslim civilization arose in the courts of the petty Spanish kingdoms, vying with one another as patrons of the arts. The Ummayad prince 'Abd ar-Rahman I chose Cordoba as the capital of his new Islamic Kingdom in the eighth century, after his escape from Syria, because of its central location and the fertility of the surrounding countryside. Seeking to rival Baghdad in splendor and learning, its successive Ummayad rulers imported artists and artisans from the East. Slowly they introduced much of the ceremonial trappings of their rival Abbasids as well as their irrigation techniques and favorite foods. By the 900s Cordoba reached its zenith, becoming home to at least 100,000 inhabitants of various nationalities and ethnic groups. It boasted 700 mosques and perhaps as many as 3,000 public baths within the city limits, paved and illuminated streets, indoor plumbing in the homes of the rich and countless villas dotting the shores of the river Guadalquivir. A visitor described this tenth-century urban center as "the majesty and adornment of the world, the wondrous capital . . . radiating in affluence of all earthly blessings."

Cordoba's sparkling cultural life at the height of the Ummayad caliphate was enriched by seventy libraries, with the caliph's library alone reportedly stocking 400,000 volumes. Recognized as a center of medicine and technology, the city also boasted numerous observatories. Cordoba's great mosque was an architectural gem that rivaled in size and beauty the most famous religious monuments in the Islamic heartland. Its ornamentation included quranic quotes in elaborate ornamental script, vegetal motifs sculpted in the capitals of endless rows of columns and intricate abstract leaf-scroll patterns derived from Arabic calligraphy. Not only did this mosque set the pattern for Islamic art in Spain, but it also served as a source of inspiration and imitation for synagogue architecture, as evidenced by the two remaining medieval synagogues in present-day Toledo.

The description of this cornucopia of riches recorded by the court physician and statesman Hasdai ibn Shaprut reflects the keen eye of a man immersed in the splendors of his world:

> The land is rich, abounding in rivers, springs, and aqueducts; a land of corn, oil, and wine, of fruits and all manner of delicacies; it has pleasure-gardens and orchards, fruitful trees of every kind, including the leaves of the trees upon which the silkworm feeds. . . . There are also found among us mountains . . . with veins of sulphur, porphyry, marble and crystal. Merchants congregate in it and traffickers from the ends of the earth . . . bringing spices, precious stones, splendid wares for kings and princes and all the desirable things of Egypt. Our king has collected very large treasures of silver, gold, precious things, and valuables such as no king has ever collected. His yearly revenue is about 100,000 gold pieces, the greater part of which is derived from the merchants who come hither from various countries and islands.

As in the East, Sephardi Jews shared the cultural orientation and political ethos of the ruling Muslims. Their humanistic education went even further, however, to include a remarkable variety of subjects from astronomy to astrology,

DET KONGELIGE BIBLIOTEK, COPENHAGEN

ART RESOURCE

Moses Maimonides (see page 169) is considered the greatest Jewish thinker of the Middle Ages. He was born in the Andalusian city of Cordoba, birthplace of two other famous philosophers, the Roman Seneca and the Muslim Averroes, who was Maimonides' contemporary. Maimonides' statue *(top)* now dominates a square in the Jewish quarter of Cordoba that bears his name. The page from an illuminated manuscript *(left)* of Maimonides' great philosophical work, the *Moreh Nebukhim* (The guide for the perplexed), depicts the Greek philosopher Aristotle, who was one of the main sources of his thought. It was the great achievement of Maimonides to present a perfect fusion of biblical and Aristotelian ideas.

THE JEWISH NATIONAL AND UNIVERSITY LIBRARY

Aspects of Jewish art in Muslim lands: in the absence of representational art, the emphasis was on calligraphy and abstract design. The Burgos Bible (dated 1260) is one of the oldest surviving illuminated Hebrew manuscripts from Spain. These "carpet pages" *(top)* precede the Writings. *Right:* Carved wooden doors and a Hebrew inscription (thirteenth century) from the Holy Ark of the Ben Ezra synagogue in Old Cairo. (This is the synagogue from which the famous Genizah manuscripts were recovered.)

DAVID HARRIS/ISRAEL MUSEUM

COURTESY JTS

Above: The Paradesi Synagogue of the "White Jews" in Cochin (south India), dating originally from 1568.

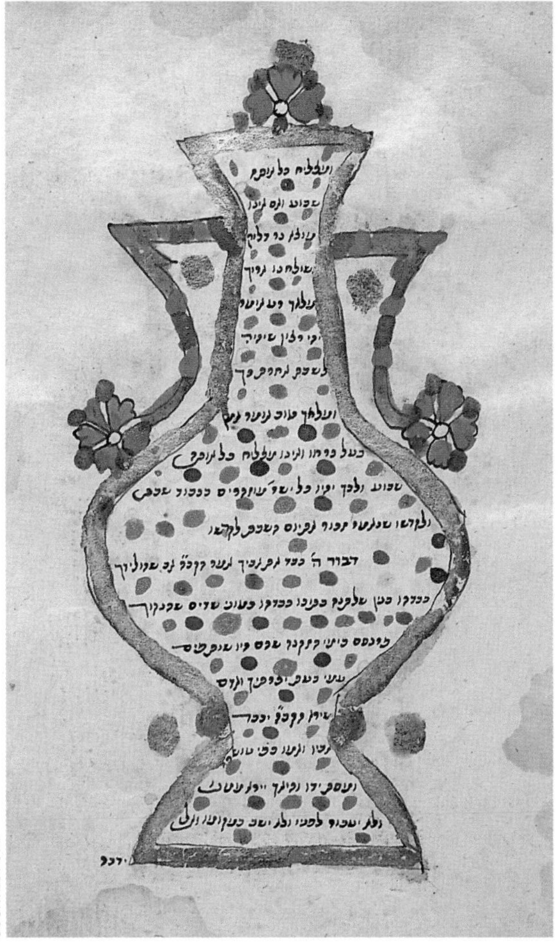

COURTESY JTS

Left: Decorative features are to the fore, also in this page from a manuscript copied in Baghdad(?) in 1696–97.

ERICH LESSING/ART RESOURCE

Jewish Wedding in Morocco, by Eugène Delacroix (1841). Delacroix visited North Africa in 1832, and returned to France with a large number of sketches of Jewish and Arab life that furnished him with material for oil paintings like this one. Delacroix was attracted to the colorful and exotic vibrancy of the people he encountered in the Maghreb, with whom his Jewish interpreter, Abraham Ben Chimol, served as a useful link.

The Nathanson family of Copenhagen, by C. W. Eckersberg (1818). Mendel Levin Nathanson was a stalwart campaigner for emancipation of the Jews of Denmark (achieved 1814) and for religious reforms. All his children eventually became Christians, with his blessing. This portrait of a well-to-do and assimilated family presents a striking contrast with the picture opposite, illustrating the great diversity of Jewish lifestyles in different places and social strata.

Political emancipation meant the acquisition of citizen rights and duties, including military service. Jewish soldiers fought in the armies of the European nations, like these German troops encamped before Metz in Lorraine during the Franco-Prussian War, in a romantic representation of massed Jewish soldiers praying in the open air on the Day of Atonement, 1870. The optimistic motto at the top is taken from the biblical prophet Malachi (2:10): "Have we not all one father? Has not one God created us?"

DAVID HARRIS/ISRAEL MUSEUM/FEUCHTWANGER COLLECTION, PURCHASED AND DONATED BY THE ISRAEL MUSEUM BY BARUCH AND RUTH RAPPAPORT OF GENEVA

The admission of Baron Lionel de Rothschild as a member of the British Parliament without having to take a Christian oath in 1858 was a significant step in the extension of full civil rights to the Jews of Britain. The baron was a leading financier, who in 1847 had brokered the £8 million Irish Famine Loan; it was he, too, who in 1875 advanced £4 million to Disraeli for the purchase of a large share in the Suez Canal by Britain.

PRIVATE COLLECTION

RUSSIAN MUSEUM OF ETHNOGRAPHY

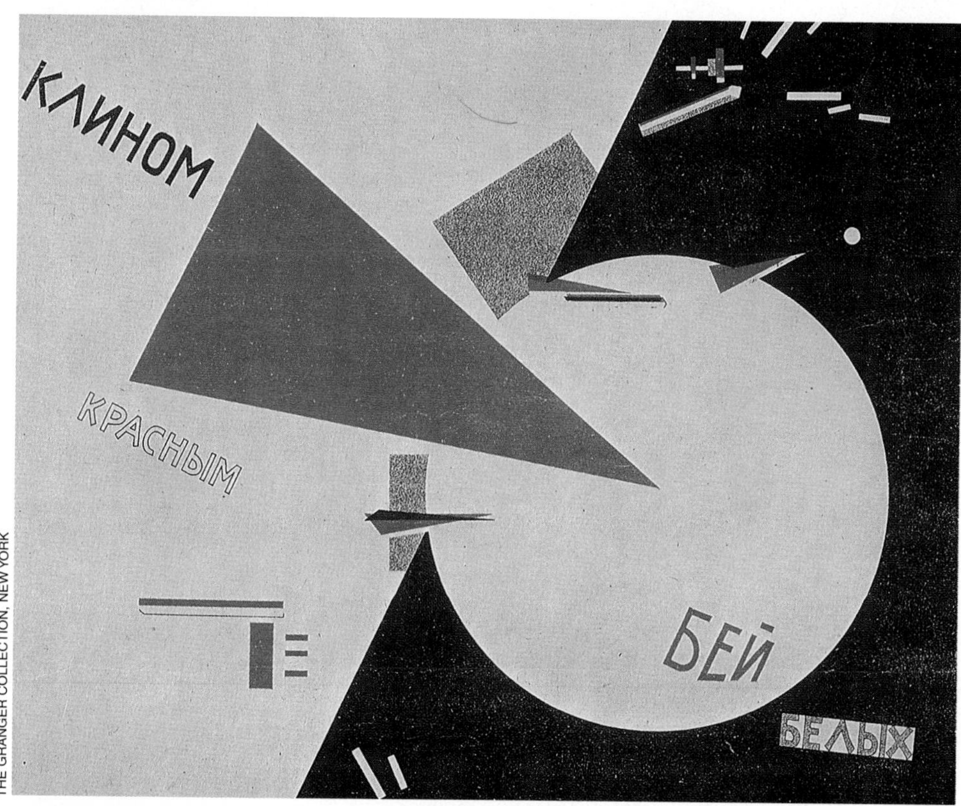

THE GRANGER COLLECTION, NEW YORK

Two contrasting representations of contemporary Russian political reality by Jewish artists. Using the well-known biblical encounter between David and Goliath, in which the shepherd boy slays the giant warrior with a pebble, a folk artist about the end of the nineteenth century depicts, in a *lubok* (folk print), the powerless Jewish community confronting the awesome might of the tsarist government. El Lissitzky (1890–1941) was fond of the unsophisticated "spiritual quality" of Jewish folk art such as the *lubok*, but in 1920 Jewish communal affairs in Russia were put in the hands of the Yevsektsia, the Jewish section of the Communist Party, which aimed to Bolshevize the Jewish masses and eradicate nationalist aspirations. Lissitzky and Jewish artists like him turned to abstract, geometric art, which was considered more universal. His poster (c. 1920) *Drive Red Wedges into White Troops!* dates from this period.

Mass migration transformed the face of the Jewish world in the years between 1881 and 1914. More than 2 million Jews left the continent of Europe in this period (ten times as many as had left in the previous forty years); eighty-five percent of them settled in the United States of America, where they became one of the largest immigrant groups. In the postcard print *(below)*, immigrants who have prospered in America hold out welcoming arms across the Atlantic to visibly indigent Jews from Europe. Poverty was only one motive in this movement; the Russian pogroms and the rise of antisemitism were also significant factors. The banner reads: "Shelter us in the shadow of your wings" (a liturgical phrase based on Psalm 17:8). The steamship reminds us of the crucial part played in this mass movement by technical advances in transport. The patriotic Torah mantle *(top)* inscribed in Hebrew "The banner that protects Judah" was made in 1914 by Minna Fine of Baltimore. Minna and her husband, Israel, had come to Baltimore from Lithuania in 1891.

SMITHSONIAN INSTITUTION/GIFT OF ISRAEL FINE/9213003

JEWISH HISTORICAL MUSEUM, AMSTERDAM

geometry to optics, calligraphy to rhetoric, music and metrics. A special emphasis on the arts and foreign tongues mirrored the prevailing Arab cultural tastes in the courts that judged a man by his literary skills as well as his social graces. One of the hallmarks of the Sephardi tradition was the special melding of rigorous Judaic study alongside this rich secular curriculum. Blending the two separate academic traditions, while bearing himself with sophistication and speaking with dignified eloquence, the Spanish Jew introduced a revolutionary synthesis of Jewish traditions and Arab culture. Sephardi exceptionalism consisted precisely in this synthesis of Arab and Jewish cultures with its emphasis on the arts and a great deal of *joie de vivre*.

A father's admonition to his son from medieval Spain expresses quite well the emphasis the educated Jew placed on mastery of the two worlds of knowledge, the Jewish and what they called "the Greek," or more accurately the Arab humanistic, with its emphasis on eloquence of expression:

> My son, listen to my precepts, neglect none of my injunctions. Set my admonitions before thine eyes, thus shalt thou prosper and prolong thy days in pleasantness. . . . Seven years and more have passed since thou didst begin to learn Arabic writing but, despite my entreaties, thou hast refused to obey. Yet thou art well aware how our foremost men only attained high distinction through their proficiency in Arabic writing. . . . Therefore my son! Stay not thy hand when I left thee, but devote yourself to the study of Torah and to the science of medicine. . . . As the Arabian philosopher holds, there are two sciences, ethics and physics. Strive to excel in both! . . .
>
> Be punctilious in regard to grammatical accuracy. . . . A man's mistakes in writing bring him into disrepute. . . .
>
> See to it that thy penmanship and handwriting are as beautiful as thy style. Keep thy pen in fine working order, use ink of good color. Make thy script as perfect as possible. . . . Examine thy Hebrew books at every new moon, the Arabic volumes once in two months.

This illuminated manuscript, of a king consulting astronomers, illustrates the adoption by Jews of Persian artistic modes in seventeenth-century Iran, which includes the library of translations of ancient Persian classics into the Judeo-Persian language.

Perhaps no better illustration of the new cultural synthesis can be found than in the medium of Hebrew poetry that flourished between 950 and 1150. Arab society has a special attachment to its language; Arabs believed (and still believe) that the excellence of the Arabic of the

Quran was proof of the perfection of Islam itself. Poetry was especially esteemed in Arabic. Excellence in the use of Arabic was not only a prerequisite for public service, but refinement in diction and expression, to the point of affectation, was also considered essential to political advancement in the court. Arab society delighted in eloquent turns of phrase, ornamental details and the use of arcane words.

No doubt understanding the implications of verbal virtuosity for political success, the Jews of Muslim Spain quickly adapted their curriculum to reflect some of the subtleties of Arab tastes. Not surprisingly, since the claims about the superiority of the Arabic language were never divorced from claims about the superiority of Islam, Jews began to explore the special qualities of Hebrew, engaging in the same verbal pyrotechnics as their Arab models. Jews felt inspired to prove to themselves even more than to the Arabs that Hebrew was as supple and marvelous a divine tool as was Arabic. Inventiveness and cleverness in Hebrew gained popularity. Verbal jousts and competitions in Hebrew recall were accompanied by the imitation of rhymes, motifs and themes of courtly Arab society. The emergent Jewish literature was a product of a new Jewish social class of courtiers and professional poets. Poetry would accompany leisurely meals at parties. The poem, recited by the poet, sometimes spontaneously, would be read or sung to the accompaniment of a lute, while a charming male or female youth served goblets of wine throughout the evening's entertainment. Poems would be circulated in beautiful calligraphy on perfumed paper. Sometimes the sensual atmosphere of the salon would itself become the main subject of a poem. Professional dancers and musicians were in attendance, while scintillating conversations focused on politics or literature. These elegant salons brought together communal leaders, religious thinkers and other members of the most prominent social class. The patronage of poets and their flattery of their patrons were recognized social institutions.

In this atmosphere, where Arabs embellished and explored geometric designs in calligraphy, the Hebrew script also became an art form. The carpet pages of manuscripts celebrate the artistic qualities of the Hebrew alphabet. Hebrew illuminated manuscripts were a by-product of the new artistic appreciation, especially in Spain, as later in Iran. When paper was introduced into the Islamic world in the eighth century by Chinese merchants, books became more affordable and readily available. The manufacture of paper reached Spain by the tenth century. The appearance in Spain of Jewish classics helped the local community assert its religious and cultural independence from the academies in the East. It was no longer necessary to wait six months or longer for an answer to a query from the gaon of Baghdad. One could acquire the text of the Talmud and train scholars locally. Book collections became a sign of conspicuous consumption in Muslim lands. Property lists from the Cairo Genizah reveal that large book collections, often Arabic translations of Greek classics, were common possessions in the households of scholarly Jewish merchants.

The poetic revolution that symbolizes the era that was to become known as the Golden Age of Spain began inconspicuously in the tenth-century reign of 'Abd ar-Rahman III, when the caliphate of Cordoba was established. Among the servants at the court, Hasdai ibn Shaprut imbibed the mores of his Arab contemporaries and began to patronize Jewish poets. He invited Jewish talent from North Africa and Iraq to join the coterie of literati who adorned his private "court" in Cordoba. He also sponsored a talmudic scholar from abroad, Moses ben Hanoch (d. 965), to open a talmudic academy in Cordoba. Experiments in Hebrew prosody had been circulating in North Africa since the late ninth century. By Hasdai's day, a breakthrough in Hebrew poetry occurred as a result of the professional rivalry between two gifted poets in his service, Dunash ben Labrat (c. 920–c. 990) and Menahem ibn Saruq (c. 910–c. 970). In their venomous exchanges, Dunash daringly introduced Arabic rhymes and meter into Hebrew, thereby inventing tools that could be used for a poetic revolution. This process was facilitated by the close affinities between the Hebrew and Arabic languages.

The prosodic innovations introduced into Hebrew poetry in tenth-century Cordoba were more radical than might at first appear, for the Arab forms were associated with popular street tunes, love songs and drinking songs, while Hebrew poetry had been almost exclusively religious poetry that followed accepted conventions and was earmarked for designated places in the liturgy. But the Jewish poets of Spain were as daring as they were innovative. Jews had been writing poetry for a millennium for communal purposes. Now, for the first time, the poets were able to create in two modes, the secular and the profane, refashioning the Islamic motifs and conventions to produce something entirely new.

Poetry would become the finest expression of the two centuries of Golden Age culture. Hebrew poets connected to patrons and courts flourished in the many cities and petty kingdoms of Spain. Moses ibn Ezra (c. 1055–after 1135), Solomon ibn Gabirol (1020–1057), Samuel ibn Nagrela (993–1056) and Judah Halevi (1075–1141) are among the most famous of literally hundreds of poets to practice their craft. And Andalusia was not alone in encouraging this flowering of poetry—Sicily, Cairo, Qayrouan and Egypt followed the Iberian cues with their own circles of Hebrew poets. The popularity, not to say omnipresence, of poetry in the daily life of the middle-class Jews is almost staggering.

The poetic revolution in form was paralleled by a revolution in content, for the new poetry was intended for new purposes: entertainment, amusement and self-expression, as well as for displaying virtuosity. Wine was a favorite topic for improvisation among Arabs, despite Islamic prohibitions against the consumption of alcohol. So, too, the Jews picked up the theme and embellished it, expanding on the bouquet, color and bubbles of the wine, or even on the beauties of the crystal goblet in which it was served. Some poets, like Ibn Nagrela, composed entire collections of wine poetry. But almost any object might become the focus of a poem. The poet Yehudah al-Harizi (c. 1170–after 1235), for example, enumerated the exploits of a flea in rhyme, and Halevi could not resist composing an ode on discovering the first gray hair on his head.

The forceful turns of phrase that were created by the unexpected combination of lofty and inconsequential themes can be seen in the reflections of Abraham ibn Ezra (1089–1164) on an old, tattered cloak:

The Alhambra Palace in Granada, one of the wonders of Moorish architecture. The Jewish vizier Yehoseph, son of the courtier vizier and poet Samuel ibn Nagrela, had a hand in its construction, and the palace is described in a beautiful Hebrew poem written in his honor by Solomon ibn Gabirol:

Before him kings and ministers give way,
By him kings rule and ministers hold sway:
They have appointed him their overlord,
They are like cattle when the lion has roared . . .

I have a cloak that is like a sieve to sift
wheat or barley. I spread it out like a
tent in the dark of night, and the stars
shine through it: through it I see the moon and the
Pleiades, and Orion,
flashing his light. I am afraid of counting
all its holes, which are shaped like the
teeth of a saw. No thread can hope to mend
its gaps with warp and woof. If a
fly landed on it with its full weight, it
would quickly regret its foolishness.
O God, give me a robe of glory in
exchange—This would be properly
tailored!

Yet for all the lightheartedness and frivolity of some poetry, melancholy meditations on the ephemeral nature of life were never far removed from the imagination of the typical court poet, sometimes even breaking through in moments of carousing. Rather than concluding that one must seize the moment, however, thoughts of the imminence of death provoked profound religious expressions of God's eternity. A flood of refreshingly new devotional poetry flowed from the pens of the Spanish poets. Although liturgical poetry was intended to fill specific spots in the religious calendar, the new religious poetry was transformed by the inclusion of the poet's personal religious feelings and philosophical ruminations. Ibn Gabirol enriched the standard poetic praise of the marvels of the universe as proof of the wonders of the Creator with descriptions drawn from findings in astronomy. Similarly, Isaac ben Ghiyyat (1038–1089) used scientific data in his religious poetry for Yom Kippur, another example of a medieval thinker interweaving nature with the divine in order to extol the majesty of God. Gabirol's musings on the kingship of God in his *Keter Malkhut* enlarged the religious self-expression of the Jewish people through their permanent inclusion in the High Holidays prayer book. At the same time, every stanza of this extended poem closes with a biblical quotation, to the undoubted delight of his discerning audience.

Far from being rare, the poet's remarkable facility for moving between the secular and the religious was typical of the Golden Age. Secular love themes were adapted to describe the love between God and Israel as the motif of thwarted love became a favorite for liturgical poets, who felt that it mirrored the plight of the Jewish people. Also, the biblical motif of God's desert romance with his people was not far removed from the romantic desert ballads that were standard fare in pre-Islamic poetry.

Neither was the intrinsic appeal of natural beauty ignored by the Hebrew poets of Spain. Sometimes these were wedded to biblical allusions. But surely the most novel of all medieval Jewish poems were those of Samuel ibn Nagrela about his experiences as grand vizier of Granada and leader of Muslim troops. Anything but conventional, Ibn Nagrela was convinced that he was the noble descendant of ancient Israelite kings. His long and luridly descriptive poem of the Battle of Alfuente of August 1038 is a remarkable blend of individual hubris, biblical allusion and Arab battle exploits. Samuel's prominent position was unusual. No Jew had ever led Muslim armies, let alone written poetry about the experience. More daring still, Ibn Nagrela engaged in religious polemics with the leading Muslim scholar of his day, Ibn Hazm. Perhaps it was these religious indiscretions, plus the extravagance of his son Joseph, so contrary to the subordinate role assigned to a Jew in Islam, that sparked a pogrom in Granada in 1066.

Traditional Jewish themes of exile and redemption were central to the new poetry. Courtiers as comfortable as Hasdai ibn Shaprut could declare sincerely that they would gladly give up all the riches of Spain if they could be redeemed in the Land of Israel. Often the poet reveals the Jewish insecurity at being caught in the Spanish Reconquest between the forces of Islam and Christendom. Rather than despair, the poets reiterated the ancient Jewish messianic hopes of redemption, confident that God was still attached to his people and their traditional land. Perhaps the most famous of these odes was composed by Judah Halevi before his departure from Spain for Palestine in 1141:

> My heart is in the East and I am at the edge of the West. Then how can I taste what I eat, how can I enjoy it? How can I fulfill my vows and pledges while Zion is in the domain of Edom and I am in the bonds of Arabia? It would be easy for me to leave behind all the goods of Spain: it would be glorious to see the dust of the ruined shrine.

The poetry of the convivial Golden Age was embedded in a materialistic way of life that allowed for the coexistence of religious and worldly impulses. Although this tension lay at the heart of this literature, it is not at all clear how well the Sephardi intellectuals balanced these seemingly irreconcilable poles of religion and worldliness in their daily and religious lives. We do have some hints of their private misgivings about personal indiscretions inserted in their poetry. In retrospective passages, Halevi laments his misspent youth. In some works, Moses ibn Ezra championed a life of pleasure and abandon, but he also composed complex penitential dirges. Even as Ibn Gabirol participated lustily in the court intrigues of his day, he expressed loathing for the superficialities he encountered there. But how lax were the poets, really, when all is said and done? We don't know. There also existed rabbinic dispensation for some breaches of Jewish conduct connected with courts and representation by Jews at the courts. One of the greatest medieval Jewish leaders, Hai Gaon of Baghdad, seems to condone the frivolity of wine fests in the following responsum:

> As to your question as to one in our time who drinks [wine] to the accompaniment of music, especially among non-Jews: he is culpable and to be excommunicated, unless he is a courtier and works for the protection of the Jews and trusts himself not to lapse into licentiousness, and unless it is known that at the time [of drinking and listening to music] he is concentrating on the destruction of the Temple, and he is forcing his heart to be sad and not enjoying himself. And when he listens [to the music] only out of deference to the king in order to benefit Israel. For the last hundred years and more there have been in Iraq men in the king's service whom the rabbis permitted such things.

Medieval Andalusia marked the high point of Jewish assimilation of Muslim cultural trends, but there were dangers inherent in the process. Some Jews were frankly confused by the clashes in values. Assimilation sometimes took the form of intellectual floundering and social breakdown, and voluntary conversions from Judaism were not uncommon. Sometimes they were rationalized as occurring after immersion in the study of Arab history or exposure to the Quran. But even those Jewish intellectuals who did not convert found the novel philosophical arguments and rational discussions that they heard in the exclusive salons of Islamic society to be challenging and confusing. Judah Halevi tried to meet the challenge that medieval philosophy posed to Judaism in his famous work the

Kuzari, by repudiating philosophy and extolling the superiority of Judaism, the Hebrew language and the unique qualities of the Land of Israel. It would take the greatest leaders in the East and West, Saadia Gaon in tenth-century Baghdad and Moses Maimonides in twelfth-century Egypt, to meet the intellectual challenges of Islamic thought head-on by incorporating philosophical traditions of the Greeks and Arabs into a systematic reworking of Judaism.

MOSES MAIMONIDES AND HIS TIMES

Moses Maimonides was the greatest medieval Jewish thinker. Living at the end of the Golden Age of Spain, a time of renewed persecution and uncertainty for the Jews, Maimonides gained wide recognition and influence as a jurist and philosopher, community leader and physician. His prodigious legal writings mark a high point in the history of Jewish legal thought. His enormous intellectual output was remarkable in its own right. When viewed in the context of his voluminous correspondence, his active communal leadership and his demanding service as physician to the Muslim court, his achievements are astonishing.

Because he was such a prominent public figure and prolific correspondent, we know a great deal about his life. He was born in Cordoba in 1135, son of Maimon, a judge in the local rabbinical court. Maimonides' father was descended from a long line of judges and had studied with the greatest legal scholar of Spain, Rabbi Joseph ibn Megash (1077–1141). In keeping with the accepted practice among the educated Jewish families of his day, the father served as tutor to his son, introducing him to a broad curriculum of sciences and law, philosophy and languages. As was customary, he also gave his son proper medical training.

In 1147 the fanatical fundamentalist Almohade dynasty swept into Spain from Morocco. They were consumed by a puritanical spirit and railed against the lax mores of the Muslim kingdoms in Spain: they also called for the conversion of all Christians and Jews to Islam. The Maimon family, like tens of thousands of other Jews in Spain, began to wander in flight.

Most Jewish refugees from the Almohades fled northward to Christian Spain, but the Maimons stayed in Muslim Spain, witnessing the devastation all around them. During these early years of uprooting, the youthful Maimonides managed to write two books, an introduction to the terminology of logic and a work on the rules of the calendar. The former revealed how basic Aristotle was to his training and temperament; the latter was illustrative of his lifelong interest in science. Like all of his writings except his great Hebrew work, the *Mishneh Torah*, these books were composed in Arabic.

In 1159 or 1160 the family settled in Fez, a choice of asylum that continues to puzzle historians because Morocco was the heartland of the Almohades. Thousands of Jews in Morocco had been forced to convert at the height of the Almohade persecutions, many continuing to practice a crypto-Judaism while paying lip service to Islam. It is not clear whether the Maimon family lived as crypto-Jews during these years in North Africa or arrived there during one of the sporadic lulls in the persecutions. In light of the widespread crypto-Judaism, Jews turned to their leaders for advice. Some Jewish leaders counseled the masses to stand firm against forced conversion, even if it meant martyrdom. In his *Epistle on Martyrdom*, however, Maimonides took a more humane view, arguing that some precepts of Judaism must always be obeyed (for example, the prohibition against murder), though others could be violated if necessary. Maimonides counseled temporary conversion, averring that Islam was not idolatrous in any event and therefore did not demand of a convert the awesome transgression of committing idolatrous practices. He added, however, that one should leave the land of persecution as soon as possible, and that in the meantime, private adherence to Judaism should be strictly followed.

In 1165 the Maimons abruptly left North Africa, perhaps as a result of being reported for crypto-Judaism to the authorities. After a brief sojourn in Palestine, they settled in Egypt. When their father died, Moses and his brother David pooled their inheritance to start a gem business. David managed the firm and handled the day-to-day business while Moses pursued his scholarship. As one plied the Indian Ocean, the other composed his major works in Fustat. Several letters between the two that somehow found their way into the Genizah illuminate the deep affection they bore for each other.

In 1173 David drowned in the Indian Ocean, and Moses Maimonides was forced to take up medicine to earn a living. Soon, his fame as a doctor brought him to the attention of the ruler Saladin and his vizier, al-Afdal. His medical writings and overall approach to moderation for good health won him a wide following of patients, including the dissolute courtiers in Cairo. Service to the court and the harem, which would have been considered a distinct honor by most people, was to Maimonides a painful distraction from his *real work*—the composition of the *Mishneh Torah*. By the 1180s he had probably also become head of the Jewish community of Egypt (*rais el-yahud* or *nagid*). His arduous routine can be glimpsed from a famous letter that was preserved by his student and translator:

> I dwell in Misr [Fustat] and the Sultan resides in Cairo; these two places are two Sabbath days' journey distant from each other. My duties to the Sultan are very heavy. I am obliged to visit him every day, early in the morning; and when he or any of his children, or any of the inmates of his harem, are indisposed, I dare not quit Cairo, but must stay during the greater part of the day in the Palace. It also frequently happens that one or two of the royal officers fall sick, and I must attend to his healing. Hence, as a rule, I repair to Cairo very early in the day and even if nothing unusual happens I do not return to Fustat until the afternoon. Then I am almost dying of hunger. . . . I find the antechambers filled with people, judges and bailiffs, friends and foes—a mixed multitude who await the time of my return.
>
> I dismount from my animal, wash my hands, go forth to my patients, and entreat them to bear with me while I partake of some light refreshment, the only meal I take in the twenty-four hours. Then I go forth to my patients, write prescriptions and directions for their several ailments. Patients go in and out until nightfall, and sometimes even, I assure you, until two hours and more during the night. I converse and prescribe for them while lying down from sheer fatigue; and when night falls, I am so exhausted that I can hardly speak.

> In consequence of this, no Israelite can have any private interview with me, except on the Sabbath. On that day, the whole congregation, or at least, the majority of the members, come unto me after the morning service, when I instruct them as to their proceedings during the whole week; we study a little until noon, when they depart. Some of them return, and read with me after the afternoon service until the evening prayers. In this manner, I spend that day.

In 1165 the Jews of Yemen were subjected to persecution and forced conversion. As often happened at such times, a false messiah arose, promising redemption if the Jews converted. When the despairing Yemenite community turned to Maimonides for advice, he was faced with a twofold task. On the one hand, he had to strengthen the community's belief in Judaism in the face of the taunts of their neighbors that Islam had triumphed. On the other, it was necessary to neutralize the pretensions of the false messiah while retaining the people's faith that future redemption would surely occur. At the same time, Maimonides had to find some reasonable explanation for the sufferings of the stalwart community of Yemenite Jews. This critical advice had to be openly circulated, despite the dangers it might pose to its author.

His *Epistle to Yemen*, composed in 1172, masterfully upholds the faith of the despairing community, tactfully rejects the triumphalist assertions of Islam and at the same time offers the Jews hope that a messianic redemption is not far off. Maimonides even dared to offer a projected date of the redemption, 1210, sufficiently distant to cool the messianic fever around him. For his several important treatises, Maimonides was affectionately remembered in Jewish history not only as a legal giant but also as a consoling and forceful leader.

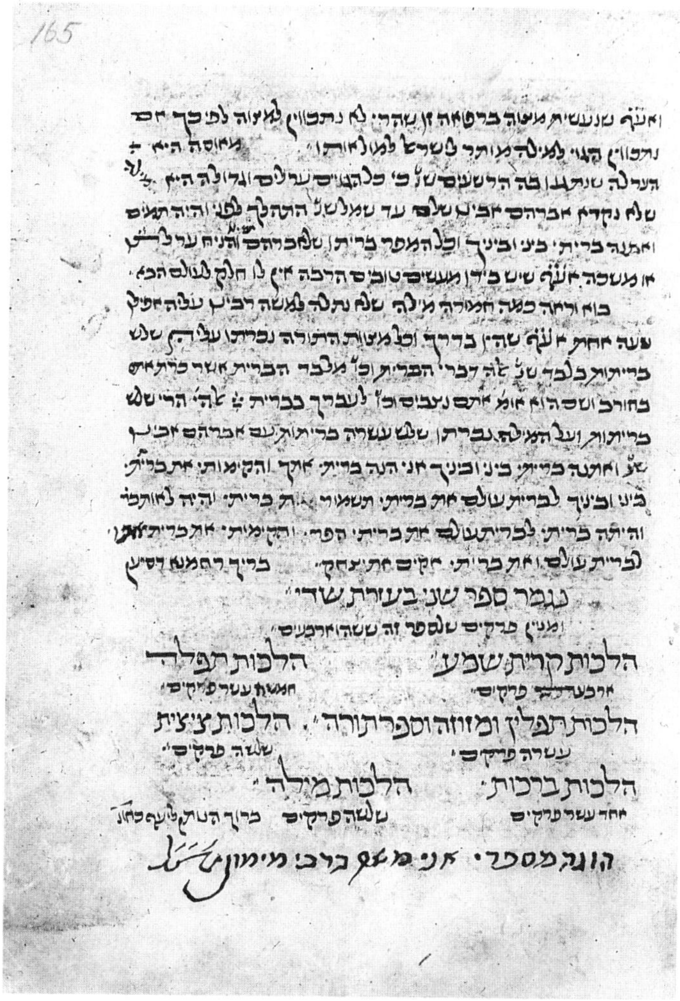

Maimonides' *Mishneh Torah*, one of the most authoritative codifications of Halakhah (Jewish law). Notice Maimonides' signature at the bottom of the page.

Yet neither his stellar medical career nor his works of public leadership best exemplified his forcefulness and brilliance; his most enduring influence derives from his encyclopedic output in the field of Jewish law. Maimonides' great legal study is the fourteen-volume *Mishneh Torah* completed in 1178. Writing in a clear Hebrew, Maimonides systematically organizes all of Jewish law by topic, illustrating the logical connections between subjects covered in the Talmud and offering frequently daring and original explanations that included philosophical discussions of legal issues. The work was novel for its melding of the Jewish legal tradition with broader philosophical currents. Although the work was hailed for its clarity and organization, it was also attacked because it stated what the law was in any given situation, rather than conveying multiple points of view on the law, which is the quintessence of talmudic discourse.

But it was Maimonides' last major work, the *Moreh Nebukhim* (The guide for the perplexed), that is his richest symbiosis of the classical philosophical and ancient Jewish traditions. It was also his most controversial work. Completed in 1190, it was intended for a select group of his students who were schooled in classical studies (that is, the Arab curriculum of science, philosophy, logic and metaphysics) and were unable to combine this body of knowledge with the Torah. In a most sophisticated manner, Maimonides set out in his guide to prove that Aristotelianism and Judaism could complement each other and that the fundamental beliefs of Judaism (which he spells out) are rational. His attempts to make peace between Judaism and philosophy, partially by showing that biblical material could be understood allegorically and that Aristotelianism could provide proof of the existence of God, would soon come under severe attack. As Jewish life in Muslim lands declined, the scientific and philosophical tradition that Muslims and Jews had shared fell into disrepute. Yet at his death in 1204, Maimonides was recognized as a rare genius in his age, the last and most influential in a line of Sephardi grandees who had fashioned a rich culture out of strands in the broader culture without sacrificing their traditional values.

THE JEWISH COMMUNITY AND ITS DISSENTERS

Jews were not citizens of a country in the modern sense. They were protected subjects of various Muslim princes and were empowered to rule themselves. Hundreds of autonomous Jewish communities dotted the vast Muslim realm, held together by common history and traditions, legal recognition of their minority religious status and official recognition of certain overarching leaders. They owed loyalty to the heads of their communities and to their central religious authorities in Iraq (the geonim). At the same time, a caliph or government official would also deal with a secular representative of the Jews who was selected by his coreligionists pending government approval. On the local level, appointive officers also represented the Jews before the authorities.

Jewish self-government had a long history of development before the Muslims appeared on the historical scene. The Jewish community in every locality was responsible for providing all the services necessary to keep religious life running smoothly. Thus there was ample opportunity for leadership in the myriad of institutions found wherever Jews resided. Each community was responsible for the provision of a court of law, the cemetery, the ritual bath, the public oven, the ritual slaughterer and ritual circumciser. The community was expected to provide education for those boys whose families could not afford private tutors. It also possessed an array of charitable chests, many of which went back to Greco-Roman times. These chests made provision for a wide variety of social services that a Jewish community was expected, by Jewish law, to provide, especially to its poor, widowed and orphaned.

The two academies of Iraq functioned for hundreds of years as the leading legislative and judicial institutions of the Jews but never without opposition or competition. The Jewish world was led by the geonim but never exclusively by them. The academy of learning in Palestine and its gaon commanded the loyalties and support of the Jewish Diaspora. Areas of authority between Babylonian and Palestinian geonim were sometimes blurred. In times of hardship, competition for limited Jewish contributions could be keen, especially when a dynamic Palestinian gaon faced no resistance from a weak leader in Iraq. Many overlapping authorities could claim allegiance from the Jews, especially in an age when Muslim sovereignty was itself divided and contested. The relationship between the central academies of learning in Baghdad and the individual Jewish communities attached to them was both spiritual and financial. It has been suggested that some of the differences between Ashkenazi and Sephardi Jewry that emerged in medieval times stemmed directly from the greater reliance of the Jews of Europe on Palestinian precedent as represented by the gaon in Palestine, as against reliance on the teachings of the geonim of Baghdad prevailing in the Jewish dispersion in the world of Islam.

The procedure enabling the academies to survive for so many centuries was the following: local Jewries sent contributions from all corners of the Diaspora to Baghdad. Set divisions of contributions were worked out from different regions of Jewish settlement. In addition, many communities, such as Cairo, had both Palestinian- and Babylonian-style synagogues in their midst. The name of the gaon of the academy to which they were attached was invoked in the local synagogue. This prayer for the scholars of Israel is still repeated in Jewish prayer books. Geonim bestowed honorific titles on fund-raisers or particularly munificent donors to their institutions. Although there appears to have been some tacit agreement on how Diaspora support was to be divided, sometimes Jewish communities transferred their allegiance (and monetary support) if a gaon was especially dynamic; generally the ties linking a particular congregation to one of the academies in Iraq lasted several generations. Communal officials of far-flung synagogues often owed their position and prestige to their appointments from Baghdad. The Iraqi academies insisted on their exclusivity; it was considered inappropriate to send the same query to both academies for a legal opinion. Public appeals for the upkeep of the two yeshivot, however, would often be held in the same synagogue. Although the maintenance of both centers of learning was considered a religious obligation, in actual practice the prestige of the individual institution (and its financial soundness) depended on the reputation of its ruling gaon. Rivalries plagued the two institutions throughout the hundreds of years that they functioned. Many of the rivalries appear petty in retrospect, but the medieval Muslim world was rife with them, and institutional multiplication and competition for support is standard in the Jewish community.

Alongside the office of gaon was the office known as the *Rosh ha-Golah* (Head of the exile) or exilarch. This ancient office predated the advent of Islam to Iraq; its existence was confirmed by the Arabs at the time of the conquest of the Persian Empire in the 640s. The exilarch possessed powers of appointment of judges, collection of taxes and jurisdiction in matters of Jewish inheritance and divorce.

Since these powers overlapped those of the geonim, the potential for conflict always existed here too. Geonim were expected to countersign decisions of exilarchs in a pro forma way. One of the great controversies of medieval Jewish life that has come down to us is a lively dispute between Saadia and the exilarch of his day, when Saadia refused to countersign an inheritance settlement. Bitter accusations and excommunications were exchanged between the two leading figures in the Jewish world. Intervention of the bankers of Baghdad and recourse to Muslim authorities could not resolve the sordid quarrel. Such controversies naturally weakened the integrity of both institutions. Gradually, the power of the exilarch declined. By the eleventh century, it was a more or less honorific title, but in its heyday, the office of exilarch commanded much respect and even awe. He would confirm the appointment of the geonim and would represent the Jews in the caliphal palace. The main source of the exilarch's strength (aside from the considerable financial leverage that he possessed) lay in his claim that he was descended from the royal house of King David. This claim, especially for Muslims who had high regard for illustrious genealogies, was a source of unusual charisma. We possess a rare glimpse of the installation of an exilarch and his quasi-royal power from tenth-century Baghdad:

> When there was a communal consensus on the appointment, the Heads of the Yeshivot, together with their students, all the leaders of the congregations, and the elders would gather in some prominent individual's house in Baghdad. He would be one of the greatest of that generation, such as Netira (the court banker). . . . The community would gather in the main synagogue on Thursday. The exilarch would be installed by the laying of the hands. The shofar was sounded . . . and when everyone heard it, each of them would send a gift—each according to his means. All the leaders of the congregation and the wealthy would send fine clothes, jewelry, and gold and silver vessels. . . . The exilarch, for his part, would take great pains in preparing a feast for Thursday and Friday which included all kinds of food and drink, and all sorts of confections.
>
> When he arose on Saturday to go to the synagogue, many of the prominent members of the community would accompany him there. At the synagogue a wooden dais had already been specially prepared for him. It was seven cubits in length and three in width. It was entirely covered with fine fabrics of blue, purple and crimson silk. . . . Meanwhile, the exilarch himself was hidden from sight together with the heads of the Yeshivot. . . . When everyone was seated, the Exilarch would emerge from the place where he was hidden, and when the people saw him, they would all rise to their feet and remain standing until he was seated alone on the dais that had been set up for him. Next, the Head of the Sura Yeshiva would come out and take a seat after bowing to the Exilarch, who would return the bow. After him, the Head of the Pumbeditha Yeshiva emerges, bows and sits on the Exilarch's left. Throughout all this the people remain standing. . . . An empty space remained between each of the Geonim and the Exilarch. Over his head spread a canopy of precious fabric which was suspended by a cord of fine linen and purple.

The description bears all the earmarks of a coronation ceremony. The ritual pomp that concluded the service was followed by seven days of lavish dining and entertainment of the scholars at the home of the exilarch. Whenever he went outside, the exilarch circulated in a processional that was likened to the caliph's entourage. When he represented the Jewish community in the caliph's palace, he would be accorded extravagant ceremonial respect by the servants of the caliph. His office was a fragmentary reminder of the awesome power once held by Jewish royalty in their ancient independent kingdom.

If the exilarch represented the Jewish community of Iraq and, theoretically, all the Jews of the Muslim realm, practical realities were quite different. Local autonomy and regional powers prevailed: it took several months for the caliph's command to reach the province of Spain from Damascus, or later, Baghdad, a distance of some 3,000 miles. Moreover, the Fatimids, tenth- and eleventh-century Shiite rulers of Egypt and Palestine, did not look kindly on the Jews' seeking redress and representation in the rival capital in Baghdad. Territorial heads of the Jewish community, known by the biblical Hebrew title of nagid or prince, sprang up throughout the Muslim world during the tenth century. The title first appeared in North Africa and was commonly used thereafter in Spain, Morocco, Tunisia, Egypt and Yemen. Some negidim had wide powers in the Jewish community, appointing judges, administering justice and serving as guardians or trustees of estates. Scholars ate at their table. They were generally appointed for life. They represented their local communities at the courts of the Arab governors; their coercive powers were derived only through their influence within the Muslim government. Their role as protector of the Jewish community against government injustices was double-edged: the nagid was also responsible for seeing that Muslim discriminatory laws against the Jews were obeyed. Negidim frequently played an important role as peacemakers within the Jewish community. The most famous nagid was the eleventh-century Spanish Jewish poet, halakhist and military leader Samuel ibn Nagrela, also known as Shmuel ha-Nagid. The descendants of Moses Maimonides served as negidim in Egypt for at least two centuries after his death.

Exilarchs and geonim from the eighth century onward cooperated in establishing the Babylonian precedent as the binding or normative law and practice throughout the Jewish world. They succeeded in creating a modicum of uniformity even when local customs continued to prevail in the widely dispersed Jewish nation. Titles and trappings of power notwithstanding, the Jews of Muslim lands, and especially their geonim, had some difficulty holding the whole Jewish enterprise together. Geographic dispersion and long-distance communication, personal rivalries and competing seats of authority, and regional versus central controls were accentuated by the periodic political struggles within the Muslim world. The sectarian conflict within Islam during the early centuries of rule, especially felt in Muslim intellectual circles in Iraq, was reflected in Jewish society as well. Militant messianic movements and shadowy messianic figures began to arise in the remote fringes of Iraq and Iran, preaching armed struggle against both Muslim and Jewish authority. Figures such as Abu Isa of Isfahan (c. 745–755) and his disciple Yudghan (756–76) offered their naive rural followers a mixed message of messianic redemption, asceticism and a blend of Jewish and Muslim practices. Their revolts were hastily suppressed by the Jewish establishment in Baghdad with the military assistance of the Muslim authorities. Many instances of messianic pretenders continued to plague Jews in Muslim lands, from Morocco to Yemen, from Palestine to Afghanistan. Most messianic pretenders played on the deep Jewish yearning to end their exile. They found receptive audiences in provinces racked by Muslim rebellions, which were frequently cloaked in the form of religious dissidence. The example proved to be contagious.

The continuing humiliations at the hands of the Muslims seemed to have a cumulative effect. By the tenth century, expressions of despair and impatience could be felt at both ends of the Mediterranean. Even normative rabbinic leaders expressed impatience at the continuing Jewish suffering in exile. Hai Gaon, one of the greatest medieval geonim, reflected this impatience in the following description of God:

> He has been like an enemy to his children.
> When they died, he did not bury them.
> Seeing their corpses strewn on the ground,
> He did not order to collect their bones,
> Nor did he care to cover them with earth.

Even amid his life of ease in the opulent court of Abd ar-Rahman III in Cordoba, Hasdai ibn Shaprut beseeched the king of the Khazars for any glimmer of knowledge on the date of God's redemption of the Jews and their return to the Land of Israel. Hasdai sincerely expressed his preference for such an eventuality over his life of comfort and abandon in the court of Cordoba. Solomon ibn Gabirol plaintively concludes a poem with the biblical cry "Why do you forget us without end?" (Lamentations 5:20) while Abraham ibn Ezra, enduring the Almohade persecutions, went even further in his despair at God's silence in the face of Jewish suffering, exclaiming, "If you wish to redeem me, redeem!/ If not—let me know!" Judah Halevi, famed for his poems of yearning for Zion, plaintively asks, "Will the Lord reject me forever? Is there no end to my waiting?"

More serious than the ephemeral messianic movements, however, was the ideological threat to the hegemony of the rabbis and the integrity of the rabbinic tradition in the movement known as Karaism. Karaism began with a religious reformer, Anan ben David, in eighth-century Iraq. Anan was a learned man who had been bypassed for a position of Jewish leadership and raised serious questions about the validity of the rabbinic tradition and its leaders. Eschewing the Oral Law as man-made and not divine, Anan recommended that Jews seek enlightenment and guidance directly in the Bible rather than in the rulings of the rabbis. Did not the Bible enjoin "Do not add to it" (Deuteronomy 4:2, 13:1) in direct contradiction to the countless rulings and elaborations that had grown up around the creators of Oral Law from the ancient scribes down to his contemporary geonim?

Perhaps taking their cues from Shiite propagandists, Karaites counseled extreme asceticism. They questioned Jewish festivities, even the joy of Sabbath, at the time that the people languished in exile. Anan considered rabbinic Judaism to be contrary to the spirit of national mourning that should prevail. Karaites soon introduced the habit of elaborate fasting, forbade the consumption of some permissible meat, enforced a prohibition against lighting candles on the Sabbath and called for the return en masse to Jerusalem. They questioned the rabbinic method of fixing the Jewish calendar, thereby throwing Jewish religious unity into disarray. Their stricter dietary regulations based on literal readings of the Bible and their extension of the degrees of prohibited marriages placed the viability of the Jewish people in peril.

Before long, the Karaites produced their own line of scholars who served as recognized authorities. Benjamin al-Nahawendi and Daniel al-Qumisi in ninth-century Persia added fresh ideas to the spreading movement. Al-Qumisi called on the Karaites to establish a community of mourners in Jerusalem. Another Karaite scholar, al-Qirqisani, was extremely outspoken in his advocacy of the right and duty of the Jewish scholar to arrive at independent judgment based on reasoning. Karaites rapidly gained converts with their passionate rhetoric and compelling anti-establishment message.

As their call for a return of mourners to Zion spread, a significant Karaite settlement emerged in tenth- and eleventh-century Palestine. Their solemnity is reported by one tenth-century observer: "The Karaites have assembled in Jerusalem righteous and pious men and have set up alternating watches for continuous prayers of supplication. They seclude themselves from the desires of this world, having renounced eating meat and drinking wine. They read the Torah and interpret it, acting as both teachers and students. They have abandoned their businesses and forgotten their families; they have forsaken their native land, left their palaces and live in huts made of reed. They left the cities to go up to the mountains, they doffed their fine garments and don sack cloth."

Before long, the Karaites were composing their own legal handbooks and producing rich merchants and craftsmen, in contradiction to their own stated ideology of asceticism and independent legal reasoning. Egypt in particular housed a powerful Karaite community. The movement was quelled in Spain and Iraq, but only with the powerful alliance of the Jewish establishment and the Muslim authorities.

Although the Karaite challenge was ultimately contained, their approach left an enduring mark on Judaism. They stimulated a powerful reawakening in the Jewish community among the rabbis. Their challenge forced the rabbinical authorities to clarify their own positions and to wage a militant fight for supremacy over the souls of the Jewish people. Their emphasis on the Bible as the source of all law encouraged the expansion of biblical studies and the development of the study of the Hebrew language. Their fervent plea for a return to the Land of Israel accelerated Jewish settlement in a province of Islam that had received only minimal Muslim interest before the advent of the Crusades. After the Crusader onslaught on Palestine in 1099, Jewish life in the Holy Land virtually ceased for several centuries. The center of Karaite literary activity moved to the Byzantine Empire and from there to the Crimea and medieval Poland and Lithuania. The fact that the Karaites never seceded from the Jewish community is somewhat a mystery. They remained a faction of diminishing importance down to the twentieth century. Their ultimate failure to capture the hearts of the majority of the Jewish people can be attributed to several causes. Their asceticism ran

A "carpet page" from a tenth-century Karaite Bible.

counter to the optimism of traditional Judaism. Nor was it possible to live solely by the Bible without practical exegesis that could update ancient and sometimes arcane rulings. The Karaites themselves were soon forced to develop a corpus of scholarship not unlike that of the rabbis. Additionally, the rabbinical opposition could count on the sympathetic support of the Muslim authorities who knew all too well the contagious danger of sectarianism.

JEWISH LIFE IN MUSLIM LANDS IN THE LATE MIDDLE AGES: FROM DECLINE TO SEPHARDI RENEWAL

From the twelfth through the fifteenth centuries, most Jews confronted increasingly difficult circumstances under Islam. The nature of Muslim rule was changing dramatically everywhere. Military despotisms and rebellious troops disrupted urban life, and travel became increasingly hazardous for Jews, with the breakdown of central authority and public order. All people suffered in North Africa as Bedouin tribes reduced cities to rubble and interfered with all internal communications. As the feudal military order of the Mamelukes consolidated its hold in thirteenth-century Egypt and Palestine, Jews were pushed out of many of their traditional crafts. The Muslim guilds became exclusivist, and a Muslim group known as the Karimi merchants barred Jews from their former routes of trade in the Indian Ocean. At the same time, the Italian city-states of Pisa, Amalfi and Genoa gained trading footholds in the Levant and pressed their trading advantage in the Mediterranean Sea by crowding out the Jews. To be sure, all groups suffered from the devastations of the Mongol invasions that toppled the Abbasids in 1258. But the Jews were special targets of persecution as the Crusaders ensconced themselves in Syria and Palestine. As their communities languished, Jews began to seek new refuges outside the world of Islam.

We lack a continuous account of the bitter centuries following the Almohade persecutions in North Africa. There is a large gap in our sources, indicative perhaps of the fact that Jewish life was forced underground for several generations. By the thirteenth century, the cities of Fez in Morocco and Tlemcen in Algeria once again hosted lively communities allied in commerce and learning with Muslim and Christian Spain and the island of Majorca. The Maghreb—northwest Africa—was again the site of Jewish courtiers and merchants whose commerce in gold, feathers, spices and exotic animals reached southward into the Sahara. Berber dynasties, always at war with one tribal group or another, called on the Jews to serve in delicate diplomatic capacities. Royal favor, in turn, enabled the Jews to rebuild their communities and to reestablish their network of educational institutions. Eventually, the relatively good fortune of the Jews in the Maghreb provided the impetus for renewed immigration to the area.

In June 1391, a year-long orgy of violence against Jews broke out in Seville. The bulk of Spain, then under Christian rule, was soon engulfed in one wave of pogroms after another. A contemporary chronicler remarks succinctly that the rioters, after setting fire to the gates of the Jewish quarter "killed many of its people, but most changed their religion . . . and many died to sanctify the Lord's name and many violated the holy covenant [by converting to Christianity]." The religious fervor propelling the rioters was unmistakable; converts were spared without exception. The rioters marched into the Jewish neighborhoods as if embarked on a crusade, and the disorders ceased after the Jews converted and their synagogues were transformed into churches. The mobs were also motivated by economic envy at the affluence of medieval Spanish Jewry, looting, pillaging and destroying records of loans owed to Jews. Wherever the rioters came in Iberia and the Balearic Islands, Jews were given the same choice: conversion or death. In the obliteration of the Barcelona community, which would not be reestablished until modern times, even its renowned rabbi, Isaac ben Sheshet Perfet (1326–1408), may have been among the converts.

Estimates of the total destruction of 1391 differ widely, but it is generally believed that perhaps 100,000 Jews converted, another 100,000 were murdered and yet another 100,000 survived by going into hiding or fleeing from Christian Spain to the world of Islam. The survivors had to deal with some of the most difficult questions of reconstruction: how to relate to the growing number of converts who were, after all, their own relatives? How should the émigrés adapt to the slower-moving, less sophisticated ambiance of North Africa and its indigenous communities? Since their savings and means of livelihood were gone, what could they do to recoup their strength and former community luster under the restrictions of Islam? The challenge of integrating the refugees of 1391 was not easy. Friction was inevitable, but tragedy tended to stimulate the Jews to new formulations and reorganizations.

The refugees of 1391 included several famous rabbis of Spain and Majorca. Barcelona's scholarly leader Sheshet Perfet reached Algeria after a period of wandering in Tunisia. Armed with an extensive library salvaged from the upheaval, he was duly acknowledged as the leader of the Algerian community, despite his prior conversion under duress. Besides, much of the refugee community had also experienced forced conversion. Entire circles of scholars and their students, such as Zemah Duran and his son Simeon ben Zemah Duran (1361–1444) also reached North Africa. With the advent of the Sephardi refugees of 1391, a new era in Jewish life began in the Maghreb.

The tribulations of the refugees before finally gaining asylum in Algeria are mirrored in contemporary accounts: "One day a ship arrived here from Majorca with forty-five forced *conversos* from Majorca, Valencia and Barcelona. The governor wanted to admit them to the city for reasons of self-interest, for he would collect from them one doubloon per head, an arrangement prompted by a certain person. They were originally admitted free of charge, and the *qadi* rebuked some Arabs who came and asked not to let them land."

Despite the initial difficulties, the refugees succeeded in establishing émigré communities, providing the foundations for a new community that would increase enormously after 1492. North Africa was the first site of refuge, but by no means the only one. The Spanish victims of the 1391 persecutions settled wherever they could reach—Albania, Crete, the Venetian islands in the Dodecanese, Egypt, Aleppo, Jerusalem, Italy. Their arrival was not a one-time event. Throughout the fifteenth century, Sephardi refugees continued to trickle into the exile communities as conditions on the Iberian Peninsula worsened for the Jews. They carried with them their customs and precedents based on Jewish communal legislation of Toledo or Valladolid. Their tenacious loyalty to disparate Iberian customs and their insistence on the superiority of their ways provoked friction with indigenous Jewish communities everywhere. Although Jewish customs have always differed from place to place, it is accepted procedure that local customs should prevail, provided that they don't run counter to Jewish law. The Sephardim angered the indigenous Jews by their certitude that their more lenient *kashrut* was correct, their marriage customs more authentic and advanced. Additionally, the many conversions in the midst of the newcomers raised a host of vexing halakhic and social problems that even considerable goodwill would not have been able to easily solve. Soon, an important corpus of rabbinic responsa, much of it by the leaders from the Duran family, revitalized rabbinic learning in Algeria. The immigrants soon rose to positions of prominence in their adopted countries, resuming the accustomed roles of courtiers, translators, financiers and diplomats that they had played in Spain, this time in the service of the North African Muslim kings and princes. The very prominence of the newcomers and the rapidity with which they achieved it could not help adding to the chagrin of the native communities.

A stream of émigrés from Spain also reached the eastern Mediterranean in the early fifteenth century to renew Jewish settlement in Palestine. Barred from Christian vessels, entire families banded together and rented ships destined for Palestine, convinced that the recent persecutions marked the beginning of the messianic era. This expectation heightened among the Sephardim with the fall of Constantinople to the Turks in 1453. Soon, the Sephardi population in Jerusalem rose sharply, and by the middle of the century the only language shared by the heterogeneous group of Jews there, hailing from every corner of Europe and the world of Islam, was Hebrew. Travelers to the Holy Land noted the ubiquity as well of Spanish.

Soon after the fall of Constantinople to the Ottoman Turks, Isaac Zarfati, an Ashkenazi Jew, urged his co-religionists to forsake the insecurity of Europe for the new possibilities that the Turkish Muslim conquests augured for Jews in the East:

> Brothers and teachers, friends and acquaintances! I, Isaac Zarfati, though I spring from a French stock, yet I was born in Germany, and sat there at the feet of my esteemed teachers. I proclaim to you that Turkey is a land wherein nothing is lacking, and where, if you will, all shall yet be well with you. The way to the Holy Land lies open to you through Turkey. Is it not better for you to live under Moslems than under Christians? Here every man may dwell at peace under his own vine and fig-tree. Here you are allowed to wear the most precious garments. In Christendom, on the contrary, ye dare not even venture to clothe your children in red or in blue, according to your taste, without exposing them to the insult of being beaten black and blue. . . . All your days are full of sorrow, even the Sabbaths and the appointed times for feasting. . . . They bring false accusations against you. . . . They continually lay double punishment upon you. . . . They prohibit teaching in your schools; they break in upon you during your hours of prayer. . . . And now, seeing all these things, O Israel, wherefore sleepest thou? Arise! and leave this accursed land for ever.

The conquest and the enthusiastic invitation were well timed. In a few decades, the greatest catastrophe of the Middle Ages, the expulsion from Spain, befell the Jews.

THE EVENTS OF 1492 AND THE RENEWAL OF JEWISH LIFE IN OTTOMAN LANDS

The expulsion of the Jews from Spain in 1492 was repeated in Portugal, Sicily, the Kingdom of Naples, the Papal States, the Dalmatian coast and several other Italian states throughout the sixteenth century. Jews were driven out of one city and province after another, briefly finding refuge, only to be pushed out yet again. Each time they gradually moved farther eastward and southward: the Muslim world once again became host to hundreds of new or revitalized Jewish settlements. As they wended their way east, they tended naturally to be melancholy, for the world that they knew had collapsed. The greatest Jewish community of Europe, that of Spain, had been annihilated. Their remnants in Portugal had been forcibly converted in

1497. Even this conversion gave them no peace. In 1506 a massacre of thousands of secret Jews in Lisbon forced the king to open the barred doors of Portugal to the survivors, flooding the Mediterranean again with refugees. Traditional Jewish acceptance of suffering alternated with expressions of fury at an unseeing and uncaring deity. Elegies written after the expulsions defiantly question the ways of the divine: "Alas, our Father, is this the recompense we have sought?" "Is this the way a father treats his children?" Rabbi Solomon Alkabetz (c. 1505–1584), the great Sephardi poet of Safed in Palestine, declared that the Jews had already suffered too much, calling on God to take notice and save them.

The path out of Spain was strewn with casualties. The Spanish monarchs had provided only four months for the magnificent community to wind up its affairs and depart. Unlike the circumstances of the later expulsion of the Muslims in the seventeenth century, the monarchs Ferdinand and Isabella made no arrangements in 1492 to transport the Jews elsewhere. Boats from Italy and North Africa began to crowd into the Spanish ports as the departure date of July 31 approached. All too many captains, unfortunately, whether Genoese, Ragusan, Venetian or Arab, were venal enough to try to sell their passengers and seize their belongings. In addition, the nearest ports of Algeria and Tunisia were inaccessible, blocked by the occupying Portuguese power wanting nothing to do with Jewish refugees in North Africa. The fortunate few who reached the coast of Morocco were despoiled along the route inland before they finally succeeded in reaching the inland kingdom of Fez. The grief-stricken chronicles of 1492 reflect details recounted by eyewitnesses of the tragic succession of events:

> Those communities that lived near the sea boarded boats from Biscay, Catalonia and Castile, some large and some small, for when news of the decree was announced, these boats came from as far away as Genoa and Venice. Some set sail for Muslim lands, such as Oran, Alcasar, and Bougie, which are far from the coast of Cartagena. Thousands and thousands of people came to the port of Oran. The inhabitants of the country, on seeing the great number of ships, complained and said: Lo, they are making the country narrow for us; and they are coming as enemies to destroy us and to take us as slaves and as bondswomen. . . . Assemble yourselves and let us go to the fortified cities and fight for ourselves and our children. And so they did; they shot at the ships with cannon and other instruments and destroyed part of the Jews. But in the end, when they heard of the expulsion, the king received them kindly, for an intercessor stood up for them in the person of R. Abraham. . . . Once the Jews finally settled on dry land, they sought for themselves places to settle, but the city was too small to absorb them. The king then built them wooden houses outside the city.

Another chronicler, the sixteenth-century Portuguese Jewish historian and poet Samuel Usque, recalls how the refugees were left ashore on deserted islands, "babies begging for water, mothers raised their eyes to heaven, while others, reduced to abandonment and despair, dug their own graves." But the catastrophe was not only man-made. Shortly after 12,000 Jews landed safely in the Algerian town of Tlemcen, a plague broke out. Almost 3,000 Jews died and thousands made their way back to Spain and converted, despairing at the combined fury of man and God. Introductions of books composed by Jews in the Maghreb after

1492 are replete with harrowing details of treachery. According to Judah ben Jacob Hayyat (c. 1450–c. 1510), one refugee intellectual who escaped to Morocco:

> One Ishmaelite from Spain, from the same locality as I, arrived there [Morocco] and told slanderous stories about me, and people believed him as if there had been three witnesses. They smote me, they wounded me . . . and threw me into a deep pit with snakes and scorpions in it. They presently sentenced me to be stoned to death, but promised that if I changed my religion [to Islam] they would make me captain over them. . . . But the God in whom I trust frustrated their design. When I had been there for almost forty days in darkness and in gloom, with scanty bread and water by measure, my belly cleaving to the ground, in hunger and in thirst and in nakedness and in want of all things, God stirred up the spirit of the Jews in Chechaouen, and they came thither to redeem me.

Given the instability throughout the Mediterranean, many Jews resigned themselves to making the best of their harsh refuges, forming scores of communities in Morocco, Tunisia and Algeria. But local conditions in North Africa were so unstable and the new threat of Spanish or Portuguese occupation there so frightening that many Jews moved on to Egypt and the Ottoman Empire. The sixteenth century was a time of massive Jewish migration, only the minority able to find a place "to rest their weary feet." The indigenous Jewish communities in all the Muslim kingdoms were soon flooded with Spanish exiles and Sephardi customs, and the Castilian language crept into all facets of Jewish life. Within a generation or two, it is increasingly difficult to distinguish between Sephardi Jews and the native Jews in the Muslim world. Even when Spanish Jews tenaciously preserved their genealogies and distinctive practices, a blending of the old and new began. Wherever they arrived in North Africa, Sephardim would assume the helm of leadership in their adopted community, absorbing the native Jewries into them. Their knowledge of conditions in Europe and of European languages made them attractive partners and diplomats for local Muslim rulers conducting their private diplomacy with Spain, Portugal and Holland. Thus a new Sephardi nexus began to develop, linking the dispersed Sephardi refugees in North Africa with their co-religionists (often relatives) in the emergent mercantile posts of

A protective amulet from Oran, Algeria. Amulets formed an integral part of the popular religion of Sephardic Jews in North Africa and the Balkans.

Western Europe and the New World. For a while, the Spanish exiles in Muslim lands provided a unique link between the world of Islam and the world of European diplomacy and commerce. Nowhere was this more apparent than in the heart of the Ottoman Empire.

The Ottoman Turks began their expansion into Asia Minor in medieval times as one of many rival Turkish warring tribal groups. Initially establishing a bridgehead in Anatolia about 1300, they expanded relentlessly from there throughout southeastern Europe all the way to the Danube. They had by-passed Constantinople, but under Mehmet II finally captured that Byzantine capital in 1453, continuing their campaign under Selim I with the conquest of Egypt, Syria and Palestine in 1516–17. The last of the conquering sultans, Suleiman the Magnificent, captured Hungary in 1526. In the east, he temporarily took Iran and most of the Caucasus in 1535, while also extending Ottoman control over all of North Africa except Morocco. Almost half the Jews then living found themselves under the rule of the Ottoman Empire by the end of the sixteenth century.

The dynamic Ottoman sultans of the fifteenth and sixteenth centuries realized the potential assets the skilled and talented Sephardi exiles brought to their shores. Many of the refugees had studied in the advanced universities of Portugal or Italy before finding refuge in Turkey. Others imported with them techniques of production that they had acquired in Europe, such as the production of superior-quality wool comparable to the long-haired Spanish merino wool. The émigrés quickly established vital textile production centers in Turkey and Palestine as they worked in all facets of textile manufacture, including spinning, weaving and dyeing, both in factories and home workshops. The main streets of Salonica, as well as the Jewish quarters of Istanbul, were lined with shops dealing in textile goods. Guilds of Jewish textile workers organized their own welfare and social institutions, like the later Jewish textile workers in Eastern Europe, introducing special legislation to control conditions of work and quality of production. Agents of Salonica textile merchants fanned out into the Balkans and Italy on behalf of their employers in Salonica. So appreciated was Jewish textile manufacturing by Ottoman authorities that the Jews were forced to pay the discriminatory poll tax (*jizya*) in Salonica with bolts of woolen cloth for making the uniforms of the dreaded Janissary military corps.

A Jewish cloth-seller from Istanbul.

Sephardi artisans and craftsmen were a welcome labor force, renowned for their skills as manufacturers of advanced munitions so vital for an empire at the peak of its expansion. The Jews were regarded as a welcome and valuable supplement to the existing warrior and agrarian classes, for they were a people capable of taking risks, knowledgeable about prices and economic conditions in far-off places and eager to retain or renew their contacts with their dispersed relatives all over Europe. Moreover, after the suffering they had endured in Christendom, their loyalty to the

Ottoman Turks could scarcely be doubted. Bayezid II is reported to have ordered his provincial governors to assist the wandering Jews by opening their borders, allegedly remarking, "You call Ferdinand a wise king, he who impoverishes his country [through expelling the Jews] and enriches our own!" In 1551 a European visitor to Turkey described the Sephardim there as "not long since banished and driven from Spain and Portugal, who, to the great detriment and damage of Christendom, have taught the Turk several inventions, artifices and machines of war, such as how to make artillery, arquebuses, gunpowder, cannonballs, and other weapons." One European observer rued that the Jews had not all been destroyed with the expulsion from Spain, so formidable was their military know-how.

The imperial Ottoman policy not only welcomed Jews but also sought to increase their numbers in specific areas by forcibly moving people around in compulsory population transfers. Jews were transferred from Thrace, Anatolia and Rumelia to Istanbul. Others were forced to settle in Salonica and in Cyprus. When the island of Rhodes was conquered in 1523, Suleiman the Magnificent ordered 150 wealthy Jewish families moved there from Salonica. When the Turkish forces vanquished Cyprus in 1570, the sultan intended to build up its local textile industry through the forced transfer of 1,000 Jewish artisans and merchants of Safed. In this instance, Jewish delegations warded off the implementation of the decree, even though the sultan promised that the coerced migrants would be granted tax exemptions for twenty years, as well as free housing. This harsh system of forced relocation, known as *sürgün*, was deplored by contemporaries for the cruelty and hardship that it inflicted. In the long run, however, the combined imperial policies of conquest and deportation dispersed the Jews in the leading new commercial centers of the empire.

Greek- and Arabic-speaking Jews, residents of the eastern Mediterranean for centuries, were soon overwhelmed by the sheer volume of Spanish exiles. Old communities, such as Cairo, Jerusalem and Aleppo, were revitalized by the newcomers, and new communities sprang up everywhere. Above them all, Salonica and Istanbul towered as representative of this new era in Jewish civilization. Salonica, especially, soon to be known as the "Jerusalem of the Balkans," dwarfed all other Ottoman cities in terms of its Sephardi population, number and variety of congregations, diversity of talent and abundance of rabbinic leaders. A European visitor to Salonica in 1533 estimated that there were 20,000 Jewish males in the city, constituting a majority of the population, outnumbering the combined total of Greeks and Turks living there. Visitors noted with surprise that the entire commerce of the city, including its famed port, ground to a halt on the Sabbath. Turkish census figures for Istanbul note that Jewish households totaled 8,070 (56,490 people) in 1535. In 1638 the Turkish traveler Evliya Çelebi visited the capital and reported that the 11,000 Jewish families (77,000 people) numbered twice the local Greek population.

Ottoman Jewry was probably the most heterogeneous in Jewish history. Census figures alone cannot convey the diverse cultural richness and cosmopolitanism of the Ottoman Jewish communities. Alongside the indigenous Greek-speaking Jews, known as Romaniotes, the names of the congregations of Istanbul and Salonica reflect the streams of immigration from Hungary, Germany, France, Provence and Bohemia who preceded the larger influx of the sixteenth century. Each attempted to retain its language, customs and separate ritual. The population mix became even more complex after 1492, when the Spanish, with their fierce devotion to their language and customs, arrived in boatload after boatload. It was not long before Ladino, the Castilian spoken by the generation of the expulsion, written in Hebrew characters, would triumph over Greek, Italian, Provençal and Yiddish as the lingua franca of the Jews.

Each Ottoman town was autonomous, and each community retained its autonomous structure and separate customs within each congregation. This setup conformed to the Ottoman principles of rule quite well. Ottomans were basically interested in the maintenance of public order and the prompt remittance of taxes on the part of the *dhimmi*. They left internal Jewish affairs to the Jews to resolve. A sixteenth-century rabbi of Salonica, Joseph ibn Leb, captures this community structure in his description: "In Salonica, every [Jewish] man speaks his own native tongue. When the exiles arrived, each vernacular group founded an independent congregation, there being mobility from congregation to congregation. Each congregation maintains its poor; each congregation is entirely separate in the Crown register. Thus each congregation appears to be an independent city." In Istanbul, the various congregations followed the will of the majority in a Jewish representative delegate body. In Salonica, each congregation had almost total freedom. Among the first publications produced on the printing presses of Istanbul was a polyglot Bible in Judeo-Greek, Ladino and Hebrew, a treasure from 1547 housed today in the Rare Book Room of the Jewish Theological Seminary of America in New York.

A sample of the names of the congregations of Salonica speaks for the diversity of the community: Lisbon, Evora, Catalonia, Gerush Sepharad, Sicily, Apulia, Calabria, Otranto, the Maghreb, Provence, Saragossa, Corfu, Huesca, Toledo, Aragon, Andalusia and Cordoba. The continuing stream of immigrants to the empire sparked congregational splits. Many of the newcomers tended to retain ties with the Iberian Peninsula for a time, underscoring the conflicting feelings that people had about those converts who had chosen to remain in Iberia rather than leave in the first wave of 1492. Despite such internal dissent, the community as a whole joined rank when it came to assisting secret Jews or Jews in distress elsewhere. When, for instance, Venice decided to expel its population of former crypto-Jews in 1550, Salonica's leaders immediately invited the homeless families to live with them on a trial basis, assuring them that they could stay tax-free until they reestablished themselves.

Over the course of time, inevitably, the initial divisions disappeared. The great yeshivah of Salonica, established in 1520, was a leveler. Only the immigrant generation was as tenacious, in any event, in adhering to its ancestral customs. In addition to the passage of time, another important factor in muting the differences and tensions among the many communities was the introduction of a widely accepted code of law, the *Shulhan Arukh* (Spread table), created by a Sephardi scholar, Rabbi Joseph Caro (1488–1575).

Joseph Caro was born in Spain, transported by his family to Portugal after the

1492 expulsion and taken to the Balkans after the Portuguese conversions of 1497. In the 1520s, in response to the upheavals of his generation, Caro began to write a massive compilation of Jewish law called *Bet Yosef* (The house of Joseph). In summarizing Spanish and other practices, Caro sought to offer the

In sixteenth-century Istanbul, Sephardi immigrants lived side by side with native Byzantine Jews. In this edition of the Torah, printed in 1547 by the Italian printer Eliezer Soncino, the Hebrew text (in larger characters) is flanked by translations into Spanish (*right*) and Greek (*left*), all in Hebrew characters. At the top is the Aramaic Targum and at the foot Rashi's commentary.

authoritative decisions of earlier great Sephardi codifiers on every conceivable issue of practical importance. After completing this magnum opus, Caro wrote a handy digest of the binding rabbinic rulings, known as the *Shulhan Arukh*. It became instantly popular after its appearance in 1564, spreading rapidly throughout the Jewish world because of the advent of printing and offering an accessible and functional code based on extant Sephardi practice. In this way, Caro solved some of the confusion that Ottoman heterogeneity and the repeated upheavals of the sixteenth century had wrought.

The Ottoman Empire soon became the schoolhouse for dozens of scholars. With so many congregations, it was not difficult to employ the multitude of Sephardi scholars who had made Istanbul and especially Salonica their home. The great issue of the sixteenth century that absorbed scholars such as Levi ibn Habib (1483–1545) and Samuel de Medina (1506–1589) was the burning question of the integrity of local custom and the problems of marriage and divorce raised by the newcomers who had been forced converts in Iberia. This was reminiscent of the earlier generation of émigré scholars in post-1391 North Africa, except now the scale of the problems was even greater. Social tensions were evident as well, as Ashkenazim from Northern Europe and Sephardim from Spain were thrown together for the first time. The Ashkenazim were astonished at the worldliness of the Sephardim, who in turn were openly disdainful of their less sophisticated co-religionists. Sephardi pride in their noble lineage was as irksome as their imperious demeanor. As previously tranquil communities became embroiled in controversies that sometimes endured for decades, the scholars tried to establish some modicum of peace.

Eventually, the Sephardim in Turkey won the upper hand because of their superior numbers, erudition, self-confidence and active leadership corps. Their customs became prevailing practice, obliterating most of the centuries-old traditions of the North African, Greek and Middle Eastern Jews. Only a small remnant of Romaniotes managed to hold on to their ancestral Greek language and Judeo-Greek ritual. In many parts of the empire, Arabic remained the favored language of the residents, even where Sephardi customs prevailed; the Sephardim in Egypt, Syria and parts of North Africa gradually relinquished Ladino for Arabic. In Asia Minor, Anatolia and the Balkans, almost all the Jews, even those who had no Sephardi ancestry, became Ladino speakers.

Perhaps the greatest innovation that Sephardim brought to the world of Islam in their cultural baggage was the innovation of Hebrew printing. Soon after movable type was introduced in Europe in 1470, the open-minded Jews of Iberia introduced printing in Hebrew in Spain and Portugal. At the time of the expulsion, Jews were prohibited from transporting any valuables out of Spain. But the ruthless monarchs and their officials had no idea what Hebrew printing was. Thus exiles left with their typeface, immediately establishing presses in Morocco, Italy and Turkey. Two refugee brothers, David and Samuel ibn Nahmias, set up a printing establishment in Istanbul immediately after their arrival in 1493. By 1510 a Hebrew press was functioning in Salonica. Later, presses began to flourish in Izmir (1646), Edirne (1554), Safed and Egypt. The famed Soncino printing house of Italy relocated to Istanbul and Salonica as the censorship policy of the

Counter-Reformation made Italy an inhospitable place to print in Hebrew. The conservative Turkish Muslim authorities were wary of the invention of printing; the sultan Bayezid II was aware of its subversive potential and issued a decree forbidding printing among his Muslim subjects. But the Jews were granted permission to print, provided that they used Hebrew or Latin but not Arabic characters. For a long time, the only printing to originate in the vast empire was among the Jews. An Armenian press was established in Istanbul in 1567, and in 1627 a Greek press was imported by a native of Cephalonia who had studied at Oxford. It was not until the eighteenth century that printing in Arabic characters was authorized by Muslim officials in the Middle East, and even then, no religious books were to be included. The imperial decree authorizing printing in the Turkish language in Arabic characters was issued on July 5, 1727, "in the high God-guarded city of Constantinople." Presses and types were obtained from Jews and Christians in the city, and the first typesetters and founders were drawn from the Jewish population.

A renaissance of printing and literacy emerged for the Jews in sixteenth-century Turkey. Because the early printings included editions of many rare manuscripts written by the last generation of scholars in Spain, these were preserved from inevitable oblivion. More important, however, a voluminous literature of rabbinic responsa flowed from the presses of Salonica and Istanbul, testifying to the enormous productivity and vitality of the rabbis of the first generation of resettlement. The relative affluence of a small Sephardi elite provided support for scholarship among wider circles. Wealthy families amassed books and created libraries that were open to students. The Alatun family, for instance, in Salonica, created a special college, supporting its activities and students and endowing it with books. Wealthy philanthropists funded yeshivot, which in turn gave employment to the many unemployed refugee scholars. Through the dissemination of Sephardi works in print, the cultural ideals of the Iberian elite survived the transition to the more placid Levant. The great yeshivah of Salonica attracted students from elementary through the most advanced level of education from all over the empire, and even from Ashkenazi centers of Eastern Europe. As a result of these activities, there was a remarkable efflorescence, albeit brief, in the field of religious law. Halakhah was a natural field of study, particularly in light of the multiplicity of legal issues that arose as people of such diverse backgrounds were thrown together in dense areas of settlement, accompanied by so many students and rabbis. Until the end of the sixteenth century, this halakhic scholarship continued to blend traditional Jewish learning with philosophical and scientific discussions.

The first generation of rabbis in the Ottoman Empire included Jacob ben David ibn Yahya (1475–1542), Joseph Taitazak (1487–1545?), David ibn Abi Zimra (1479–1573), Jacob Berav (1475–1546) and Levi ibn Habib. Probably the greatest legal authority of the first generation after the expulsion was Samuel de Medina of Salonica, who has left hundreds of rabbinical responsa. In their day, they were all well known to wide circles of Jews in Palestine, Egypt, Turkey and Crete.

The output of Ottoman Jewry also included new works of science and poetry, which had been so characteristic of the exceptional scholarship of Spain. The press in Safed was the chief disseminator of the new kabbalistic writing emerging among the large circle of mystics in sixteenth-century Palestine. In addition to preserving texts from their Iberian past and disseminating new currents of thought such as the Kabbalah of Safed, the Ottoman presses also sustained links to the living Hispanic culture. It is noteworthy that the contemporary best-seller of sixteenth-century Spain, the classic work *La Celestina* by the *converso* author Fernando de Rojas (d. 1541), was published in Salonica in Hebrew translation. The exiles kept abreast of Iberian trends for centuries. Even after all ties with Iberia were finally broken, the Ladino presses remained an active cultural force in Turkey, culminating in the Ladino encyclopedia of biblical and folk tales known as the *Me'am Lo'ez*. This classic multivolume work filled an important void for the masses, most of whom were not learned in Hebrew but could handle a popular work in Judeo-Spanish. It is a striking feature of Jewish intellectual life in the Ottoman Empire that very little exchange with the surrounding Turkish society seems to have developed. In contrast to the earlier engagement in Muslim thought in Cordoba or Baghdad, few traces of Turkish culture can be found among Ottoman Jewry. The only exception is in the field of music, where Jews adopted and adapted Turkish musical traditions for their own needs. It is not entirely clear why Turkish culture was of so little interest to the Jews. Was it that the Iberian heritage was all-consuming as a result of the enormity of the trauma of the expulsion? Or was Turkish culture inaccessible because it was embedded in a military and administrative elite that was almost impenetrable to the Jews? It is hard to say. One thing is clear—few rabbis knew Turkish, even when Ottoman culture was at its height in the sixteenth century. By contrast, contemporary Persian Jews underwent a renaissance of their own in the Golden Age of Safavid Iran in the new Iranian capital of Isfahan.

The traditional pattern of Jewish leadership in Muslim lands—the courtier rabbi and merchant scholar—continued in the Ottoman Empire. A new twist was added. Diplomats who had been either forced to convert in Iberia or who had been raised as secret Jews by forcibly converted parents assumed a leading role in Ottoman statecraft. To the delight of their Muslim employers, they frequently harbored a deep and abiding resentment toward Spain, one of the chief enemies of the Ottoman Empire. At the same time, they had an intimate knowledge of European languages and economic conditions and could accomplish delicate diplomatic feats out of the public eye. For a Moroccan monarch, for example, to deal with Christian Europe openly would have inflamed religious passions among the masses and the Muslim clergy. In any case, Muslim diplomats were loath to personally travel to Europe and to endure the indignities of engaging in the rituals and politesse with "infidels" that diplomacy required. Better to leave these disagreeable tasks to Armenians, Greeks or Jews. Perhaps none was more suited to this role than Doña Gracia Mendes (1510–1566) and her partner and nephew Don Joseph Nasi (1524–1579).

Doña Gracia Mendes was born Beatrice de Luna in Portugal, a child of the first generation of forced Portuguese *conversos,* among whom the memories of persecution were fresh. Only four years prior to her birth, the massacre of more than 1,000 *conversos* in Lisbon had prompted the king of Portugal to ease some of the draconian measures against the converts (most of whom were secretly practicing Judaism), permitting them to move around more freely to engage in commerce. Doña Gracia married a fellow convert who was active as a banker and gem trader in Europe. In 1536 the Inquisition was introduced in Portugal and many *conversos* began to fear for their lives. The practice of Judaism by *conversos* was considered heresy, punishable by burning at the stake, in the eyes of the Inquisition. When Doña Gracia's husband died in 1537, she fled Portugal and began to wander across Europe, continuing her husband's banking and commercial relations with France and Antwerp. She kept dodging the clutches of the Inquisition, eventually openly returning to Judaism in Italy. But safety continued to elude her, even as her fortunes grew. In 1553, with the help of the Ottoman Jewish courtier physician Moses Hamon and Sultan Suleiman, Doña Gracia made her way to the Ottoman capital. Her majestic entrance into the city was recorded by contemporaries.

Doña Gracia's multifaceted achievements in Istanbul became legendary. She built schools and synagogues, rescued and redeemed secret Jews threatened by the Inquisition in Western Europe, endowed hospitals and book printings, all the while trading on a grand scale with Europe. The Ottoman Empire was soon dotted with synagogues named La Seniora or ha-Giveret in honor of her largesse.

Despite all these activities, however, history remembers Doña Gracia principally for her extraordinary diplomatic efforts in defense of secret Jews in Europe. When twenty-four Sephardi merchants were burned in the Italian city of Ancona, after having been promised that they could settle in the city and would not be punished for having shed their Christian masks, Doña Gracia responded in 1555 by organizing a boycott of the port of Ancona by all merchants of Turkey. She received the assistance of Suleiman the Magnificent, who personally protested to the pope, to no avail. Although her boycott failed and she was unable to achieve her political goals, her spirited defense and strong-arm tactics to persuade the rabbis of Turkey to rally to her cause left a vivid impression on contemporaries.

After her death in 1566, her nephew Don Joseph Nasi continued her business and diplomatic roles. A favorite of Sultan Selim II, Joseph Nasi at once carried on the expansion of her commercial empire and also acted as the Ottoman Empire's unofficial foreign minister. He negotiated a treaty with Poland and arranged for Ottoman assistance of a revolt in the Netherlands against the Spanish Habsburgs. For his well-timed advice that led to the Ottoman conquest of Cyprus, he was rewarded with a dukedom on the island of Naxos and concessions to develop the city of Tiberias in Palestine. Calling on the Jews of Italy to return to this ancient site in the Land of Israel, Don Joseph Nasi rebuilt the walls of Tiberias and started a silk industry there. After the Turkish defeat at the hands of the Spaniards and Venetians at the great naval battle of Lepanto in 1571, Joseph Nasi's influence declined. Following his death in 1579, his wife, Reyna, continued his philanthropic activities from their palatial Istanbul residence. But the height of Jewish influence in commerce and diplomacy was passing. By the end of the century, Greeks had replaced the Jews as the main advisers to the Turks. The Golden Age of Turkish Jewry was over.

INTELLECTUAL CURRENTS IN THE OTTOMAN EMPIRE: MESSIANISM AND MYSTICISM IN AN AGE OF DESPAIR

The image of restless vitality that the economic and communal history of the Jews in the Ottoman Empire presents was only one face of the Jewish people. Behind all the renewal and rebuilding, sixteenth-century Jewry was conflicted and tormented—torn by doubts about themselves, by questions why so many had converted in Spain and why God had subjected them to such enormous suffering. Although many people could be consoled by the traditional Jewish belief that God was punishing the Jews for their sins and that a just God acted out his will in history although his ways were inscrutable, others were not convinced. Some teachers argued that Jews had brought their disaster on themselves by flirting with Greek rationalism and Arab philosophy in Spain. At the same time, it was argued, expulsion was a sign of God's concern for his children, a summons for them to mend their ways, not a sign that he had rejected them. Such arguments could be heard across the Mediterranean from teachers as widely dispersed as Rabbi Abraham Gabison in Algeria and Rabbi Moses Almosnino (c. 1516–1580) in Salonica.

A generation of historians arose, the first generation of Jews to write history since biblical times, concerned with recording the incredible events that had unfolded before them. Joseph ha-Cohen, Samuel Usque and Solomon ibn Verga sought to record and decipher the meaning of the cataclysmic expulsions and torments that had befallen the Jews. From their perspective in Muslim lands, the events continuing to rock Europe, especially the mighty Ottoman conquests that threatened to shake the very foundations of Christendom, were surely part of a larger schema. Throughout Europe, messianic stirrings once again animated the Jews. Paradoxically, these stirrings took hold and accelerated just as the Sephardim were setting down roots in new places—the Atlas Mountains in Morocco, the Saharan reaches of Algeria, the steppes of Central Asia, the Portuguese possessions in the Far East beyond the reach of the Inquisition. Just beneath the surface of the network of new communities, with their practical edicts to facilitate commerce and reestablish orderly communities, were submerged the tensions between waiting for redemption and building in the present, hope and despair that were ready to ignite if circumstances permitted.

It is perhaps not surprising that some Jews turned to radical formulas in the prevailing gloom. Seemingly small incidents, like the bizarre career of David Reubeni (c. 1500–1535), reveal how volatile the situation of the Jews was. Reubeni appeared in Italy and Portugal in the 1520s, proclaiming himself to be a commander-in-chief from the lost Israelite tribes of Reuben, Gad and Menasseh, sent to announce the imminent redemption of the Jews. His odd call had a profound impact, particularly among the struggling *conversos* in Portugal. Among them was a secret Jewish courtier, Diego Perez (1500–1532), who went so far as to have himself circumcised and changed his name to Solomon Molcho. Molcho fled to Salonica and proceeded to immerse himself in mystical studies. Then he followed Reubeni to Italy hoping to persuade the pope to begin a crusade to liberate the Holy Land from the Ottomans with *converso* troops. Ultimately, Molcho was burned at the stake by the Inquisition in Italy in 1532. Reubeni also met a violent death soon afterward. But Ottoman Jewry continued to be agitated. Like Molcho, many Jews turned to the study of mysticism, reading into the classical Sephardi mystical text, the *Zohar*, in order to comprehend contemporary events.

One outstanding characteristic of the intellectual rabbinical leaders of the Ottoman Empire was their ability to combine mystical and halakhic studies with apparent equanimity, reserving their mystical studies for private study groups. For many decades, mysticism was one segment of a broader mix of study texts. The great halakhic authority of the sixteenth century, Rabbi Joseph Caro, was at one and the same time a great codifier of law and rationalist and a mystic who had private experiences of divine communication. But in one corner of the Ottoman Empire, in Palestine, mystical contemplation and creativity prevailed almost exclusively.

During the sixteenth century, scholars from all over the Mediterranean gathered in the small town of Safed in the Galilee and in the city of Jerusalem and delved into mystical lore. Between 1500 and 1600 the Jewish population of Safed grew to more than 10,000, and the town contained as many as twenty-one synagogues and eighteen talmudic academies. Many different forms of mysticism were practiced in this picturesque but obscure provincial town. Here the Kabbalah (the technical name for the Jewish mystical movement) flourished under the leadership of Joseph Caro, Solomon Alkabetz, Isaac Luria (1534–1572) and Hayyim Vital (1534–1620). Fasting frequently and engaging in mystical meditations, they would take long walks to the tombs of ancient teachers buried in the Galilee and hold special vigils of an ascetic nature. Led by Luria, Jewish mysticism assumed a new structure in Safed and was infused with messianic meaning. The Sabbath acquired new rituals and melodies. One of the enduring legacies of the movement was the religious hymn *"Lekha Dodi"* (Come, my beloved), now sung in every synagogue on Friday night to greet the Sabbath. It was composed by Solomon Alkabetz to depict the loving relationship between God and Israel, with the Sabbath representing Israel's divine bride. The words tremble with messianic expectation. The Safed poet Israel Najjara (1555–1628) also sang of messianic expectations that were imminent. The mystics wept over the destruction of Jerusalem, introducing midnight vigils and public mourning rituals.

The greatest leader of the mystical movement of Safed was Isaac Luria. Luria was born in Jerusalem of an Ashkenazi father and a Sephardi mother. He grew up in Egypt, where he unsuccessfully tried to engage in business and then shunned society to study the *Zohar*. In 1569 he settled in Safed and introduced an entirely new structure of Jewish mysticism, which later became known as Lurianic Kabbalah. In Luria's view, the suffering of the Jews was not a punishment from God at all. Rather, it mirrored the divine state of exile. Jews were in a unique position to assist God in restoring wholeness to the world if they would only understand events properly and act accordingly. Luria assured his students that the process of restoring divine wholeness, the uplifting of the divine sparks that had been scattered, was imminent, and Jews, as partners with God, were playing a vital, indeed critical, role. The basic motif of the Lurianic Kabbalah was the notion of exile, with God himself experiencing the pains of exile with his people. Luria's comforting message, although intended for his select circle of disciples, began to spread to Izmir and Salonica as the printing press of Safed disseminated his ideas or versions of his ideas elaborated by his students.

The Jews of Turkey were ripe for a messianic explosion. The entire generation after the expulsion, from its leaders like Isaac Abravanel (1437–1508) on down to the man and woman in the street, awaited miraculous events. The strange story of David Reubeni and Solomon Molcho had been merely a hint of what could occur. The spread of Luria's ideas to the masses popularized an active mysticism. Jews tended to read the signs of their time in uniquely messianic terms. The expulsion from Spain, viewed in the context of the rise of Ottoman might and the crumbling of Christian Europe, the earthshaking challenge to the papacy of the Reformation and Counter-Reformation, coupled with the continuing witch-hunts of the Inquisition, which kept ferreting out secret Jews for the flames, were explained as constituting part of a larger plan. The Lurianic Kabbalah was making considerable progress in capturing the imagination of wide circles in Turkey. The messianic atmosphere was heightened by events from outside impinging on Turkish Jewry. Between 1648 and 1655, tens of thousands of Jews from Poland streamed into the Ottoman Empire, refugees from the Chmielnicki massacres. All these factors seemed to augur that the End of Days was at hand. It was at this critical juncture that Shabbetai Zvi (1626–1676) began his fantastic career.

Shabbetai Zvi was born in Izmir into a comfortable family attached in business to English and Dutch merchants. He received a traditional Jewish education from leading rabbis in the city and was exposed to Kabbalah from his youth. He seems to have shown signs of eccentricity and depression as a teenager, engaging in ascetic practices and violent mood swings. His father pushed him out of the house, dispatching him from Izmir. He continued to engage in mystical studies. In his elated moments, he thought that he was the Messiah. The catastrophic events of 1648 in Poland had a deep impact on this sensitive youth. Refugees were streaming into Turkey by the thousands. Shabbetai Zvi began to deliberately and publicly violate Jewish law, and as a result he was thrown out of the Portuguese synagogue of Izmir, to which he had returned, and forced to leave the city anew in the early 1650s. He began to wander, all the while in contact with mystical circles in Salonica, Egypt and elsewhere. During these years of wandering, he composed a heretical benediction to God "who permits the forbidden," moving on to Cairo and eventually to Gaza. In Gaza, Shabbetai Zvi had a fortuitous meeting with Nathan of Gaza (1643–1680), a charismatic mystic and healer, who declared the young man to be the Messiah. This pronouncement in 1665 electrified Shabbetai Zvi, confirming what he already believed to be the case and setting in motion a fateful chain of events. He soon received enthusiastic endorsement of his messianic mission from the rabbis of Jerusalem. Nathan began to spread the news of Shabbetai Zvi's innovative practices far and wide, demanding faith in him as the Messiah. He promised that Shabbetai Zvi would soon overthrow the Ottoman sultan, reconstitute the lost tribes of Israel in the Promised Land and bring about the final uplifting of the divine sparks that had been entrapped (according to Lurianic Kabbalah).

Shabbetai Zvi enthroned in splendor. Frontispiece of a Sabbatean prayer book, Amsterdam, 1666.

Shabbetai Zvi returned in triumph to Izmir, appearing publicly in the synagogue wearing royal garb, after leaving a trail of frenzied believers in his wake in Syria. But some Jews began to have doubts, and the community split between believers and nonbelievers in Shabbetai Zvi. To counter the disbelievers, he announced that he was God's anointed, and pandemonium ensued. Worried about the impact of his preachings, some Jewish leaders in Istanbul alerted the Ottoman authorities to his activities. He was finally arrested in February 1666 by order of the grand vizier, Ahmed Koprulu, but permitted to continue granting audience in his confinement in Istanbul and Gallipoli. Hymns were composed in his honor, new festivals were celebrated in prison and pilgrims proceeded to pay homage to him in his confinement. Agitation about his mission continued to grow, spreading from the Ottoman Empire to Europe. Merchants and scholars as far away as Amsterdam awaited the latest pronouncements of the "Messiah" and his "prophet" Nathan. The authorities finally decided to put an end to the disorders, seeing the disruption of the local economy due to the agitation of the Jews. In September 1666, Shabbetai Zvi was offered the choice of conversion to Islam or death. He chose conversion. But while he was a Muslim overtly, he continued to claim his messiahship and engage in his unique practices with his followers for the next decade. He finally died in exile in Albania.

The debacle of Shabbetai Zvi's career and the finality of his death should have spelled the end of the movement. But even after his death, Nathan of Gaza continued to preach, fitting the apostasy and death of Shabbetai Zvi into a messianic context that had some Christological overtones. Although disappointment and disillusionment in the Jewish world were widespread, and many people, including rabbinical authorities, repented of their excesses and returned to normative practices, many others refused to acknowledge that they had been duped. Rationalizations about Shabbetai Zvi's conversion soon began, and Sabbetean practices continued covertly. Belief in Shabbetai Zvi became a burning issue in the Jewish community, especially in Turkey, with some rabbis secretly continuing to believe in his mission for decades. As new information surfaces, it is apparent that many followers actively continued their pro-Sabbetean beliefs through the eighteenth century. The paradox of a Messiah who takes on a religion that he doesn't believe in was not lost on former *conversos* scattered throughout Europe and Muslim lands. Shabbetai Zvi's conversion was a poignant reflection of their own haunted past.

Small circles of believers in the messiahship of Shabbetai Zvi survived, especially in Salonica. Soon after his death, a group of followers apostasized to Islam in 1683, led by the family of Shabbetai Zvi's wife, Sarah. They formed a sect of Judeo-Muslims known as the Dönmeh, who continue to practice their own form of religion in Turkey today. The fear of renewed messianic outbursts did not cease; references to Shabbetai Zvi were expunged from sources. Turkish rabbinical authorities became increasingly suspicious of innovation. The explosion of further messianic hopes had to be carefully contained and returned to its legitimate place in daily prayers.

With the failure of the Sabbetean movement and the conservative rabbinical response in its aftermath, the Jews of Muslim lands entered a new phase. The Ottoman Empire had already begun its gradual process of decay with the death of Suleiman the Magnificent in 1566. His death on the battlefield was concealed by the grand vizier as the sultan's embalmed body was carried in a litter for three weeks, until a new sultan, Selim II, was safely enthroned. The death of the vigorous sultan succeeded by the feeble heir, known in history as Selim the Sot, was symbolic of a deeper process that was unfolding. Europe was unaware of the pervasive deterioration of all layers of Ottoman society, until in 1683 the Ottomans failed for a second time to take Vienna. Soon thereafter, the choicest Ottoman conquests in Europe, including Hungary and Serbia, were relinquished. Now, instead of the strength and menacing presence of an expansive Ottoman Empire, its weakness would pose unending problems for Europe. Thus both the Muslim world, for its own reasons, and the Jews of Islam, as a direct result of the Ottoman decay, began to sink into a state of stagnation. By the seventeenth century, travelers to the world of Islam brought unanimous accounts of Jewish travail back to Europe. The situation of the Jews was indeed a sorry one. With the empire in a shambles, the roads impassable, the sultans incompetent and the economy stagnating, the minorities of the Middle East had only one recourse for protection. The Jews of Muslim lands began to look to Europe for succor. It was in Europe among the Ashkenazi masses that the future of Jewish history was now unfolding.

The Jews remained a minority of diminishing numbers and importance in the world of Islam. Their horizons had narrowed and their tenure was much less secure. The early tolerant phase of Islam had given way to the more intolerant and humiliating one. And as the Christian minorities of the Ottoman Empire awakened to their own national identities, the Jews would be confronted with the force of Christian anti-Judaism in their midst, combined with the force of increasing Muslim intolerance toward all non-Muslims. The combination of the two would spell new challenges to this ancient people. Their only recourse was to look to an ascendant European Jewry for protection and enlightenment. The Golden Ages of Jewish life in Muslim lands were permanently over.

5

Into the Modern World

David Sorkin

Opposite: *Lavater and Lessing Visit Moses Mendelssohn*, by Moritz Oppenheim, 1856 (see page 222).

The emergence of a new epoch, like the fall of an empire, is by nature protracted and disorderly. So it was with the Jews' integration into the modern world.

The first epoch of Jewish history, characterized by the struggle for sovereignty in the Land of Israel, and by a sacrificial cult centered on the Temple in Jerusalem, came to a gradual end in the period 70–135 B.C.E.

In the second epoch, Jews lived as a minority on the sufferance and under the rule of others, maintaining a certain autonomy through their own religious institutions. The roots of this arrangement go right back to the Babylonian Exile in the sixth century B.C. *The epoch of the autonomous community closed by gradual stages during the period from the end of the Thirty Years' War in 1648 to the end of the First World War in 1918.*

This was a period of profound political, economic and social change for the whole of Europe and ultimately for the entire world. For the Jews of Europe, it was the period during which they became integrated into the societies in which they had previously lived as denigrated minorities.

This integration, which took very different forms in different countries, occurred in the context of fundamental political reforms in these countries themselves. The Jews, along with other previously powerless groups, were emancipated, and achieved equal rights with their fellow citizens.

During this same period, however, another model of emancipation was emerging: not integration into the nation-state, but the creation of a separate, Jewish, national entity.

Jewish Settlement in the Old World: 19th Century

S. DANIEL / STARSHELL MAPS, 1997

HARBINGERS

Beginning with Abraham, migration has loomed large in the history of the Jews, often closing one age and opening another. It is therefore hardly surprising that integration into the modern world began with a migration. Throughout the Middle Ages, the Jews moved eastward. The persecutions during the Crusades, the expulsions from England in 1290 and France in 1394 and then from the Germanies in the pre-Reformation era (Linz, 1421; Cologne, 1424; Bavaria, 1442 and 1450; Moravia, 1454) and during the Reformation (Saxony, 1537; Thuringia, 1540s; Brandenburg, 1572) sent Ashkenazi Jews into Eastern Europe and especially into the Polish-Lithuanian Kingdom. The majority of Sephardi Jews who fled the Iberian Peninsula between 1391 and 1492 went east to the territories of the Ottoman Empire and to North Africa. The result was that in 1648 the greatest proportion of the world's 1 million Jews lived in the East: seventy percent of Europe's populace was largely concentrated in Eastern Europe, whereas another thirteen percent lived in the Ottoman Empire and the remaining seventeen percent in North Africa. The seventeenth century saw this eastward traffic reversed.

The Peace of Westphalia in 1648, after the Thirty Years' War, marked a watershed in European history. Not only did it end the century of warfare following the Reformation, but in acknowledging Europe's religious stalemate and recognizing the three dominant branches of Christianity (Catholicism, Calvinism and Lutheranism), it ushered in an age of growing religious tolerance—though not without significant lapses. Economic and political considerations, mercantilism and *raison d'état* began to overshadow matters of faith. Rulers eager to consolidate dynastic and state power by building standing armies and bureaucracies and rebuilding shattered economies welcomed enterprising religious minorities. Holland became the prime example of a religiously plural society made prosperous by commerce. The German principality of Brandenburg extended tolerance to dissenting Protestants in 1664 and became a refuge for Huguenots after France revoked the Edict of Nantes in 1685. The Act of Toleration in 1689 made England a model by granting Catholics and dissenting Protestants basic rights (although they were excluded from political life).

Under the aegis of such policies, Jews began to move westward from the 1570s, resettling Western and Central Europe. New patterns of Jewish life thus emerged. Although the autonomous community was often re-created during the initial period of resettlement, it slowly but surely ceased to be the prime structure. In some instances the autonomous community was slowly dismantled; in others the Jews lived under new legal arrangements of partial or full equality. The new communities that developed were associated with two social types: the Court Jew and the port Jew.

Court Jews, or Jews who served rulers as financial advisers and manufacturers, bankers and purveyors to armies and even as diplomats, were common throughout Europe but most numerous in Central Europe. In the 300 or more polities of the Holy Roman Empire, it was a common saying in the late seventeenth and eighteenth centuries that "every court has its Jew." Thus the Holy Roman emperor Leopold appointed the financier Samson Wertheimer (1658–1724) Imperial Court Factor in 1703, in recognition of the fact that "he and his son are constantly busy serving us and the public."

A ruler's invitation to a Court Jew often led to the growth of a new Jewish community: the man would bring with him not only his family and servants but also his business employees and religious retainers. It was common for him subsequently to obtain permission either for others to join him or to consolidate the status of Jews already present in the region. Moses Wulff (d. 1729) arrived in

The four sons, from a manuscript Passover Haggadah by Joseph bar David Leipnick of Moravia, Altona, 1740. In the eighteenth century, there was a revival in the art of illuminating Jewish manuscripts, for the use of wealthy Court Jews.

Dessau in 1685 as the Court Jew of Prince Johann Georg I. He reorganized the currency, established postal and transportation services, funded the army and managed the prince's estates and the collection of fees. When he arrived, some twenty-five Jewish families had recently settled in the area. His presence enhanced their position; they were permitted to build a synagogue in 1687. In the next 100 years, the community would grow to number almost 1,000 souls.

In aiding their rulers' efforts to fortify central power by establishing state bureaucracies, the Court Jews also inadvertently undermined the basis of Jewish autonomy. The centralizing state was intent on bringing its subjects under immediate supervision, so it attempted to level the intermediate corporations or estate organizations—for example, guilds—characteristic of feudal life. The autonomous community represented just such an intermediate corporation, and thus the state could hardly brook its reestablishment. In 1671 Friedrich Wilhelm of Brandenburg, who crowned himself king of Prussia in 1701, declared "that the Jews and their commerce seem not detrimental to us and to the country but rather beneficial," and admitted fifty wealthy Jewish families recently expelled from Vienna. The resulting community in Berlin began as a typical autonomous one, but the state persistently acted to diminish its authority. In 1698 the state first asserted its right to regulate the election of community leaders, and then, after investing those leaders with greater authority over the administration of welfare and taxation, required their close supervision. In the Jewry law of 1750, which the French politician Mirabeau deemed "worthy of a cannibal," the state fixed the exact number of community officials; prescribed permitted and prohibited occupations (even stipulating the very goods the Jews could trade); transferred legal decisions affecting property from the *bet din*, the local rabbinic court of law that adjudicated on internal affairs of the community, to the Prussian courts (which would rule on the basis of Jewish law in consultation with the appropriate Jewish authorities); and placed all the Jews' affairs under the direct supervision of the bureaucracy, in the War and Domains Office. In Dessau the state abrogated the Jews' juridical autonomy in 1774.

These new communities displayed elements of both continuity and discontinuity with the past, as did the people themselves. The Court Jews lived simultaneously in two worlds, one foot in the larger society of the court, one in the Jewish community. Some Court Jews were fully pious, living a life little different from that of their medieval forebears. Moses Wulff, for example, who was a descendant of the famous rabbi and influential scholar Moses Isserles (c. 1525–1575), lived an exemplary Jewish life, using the fortune he amassed as a Court Jew to fund a study house and a Hebrew press. Samson Wertheimer retained his beard and was reported to have dressed "like a Pole." In contrast, Joseph Oppenheimer (1699–1739), known also as Jüd Süss, who served as finance minister to the duke of Württemberg, ceased to observe the dietary laws and attend synagogue, even on the Day of Atonement, lived opulently and participated in the loose sexual life of the court. Nonetheless, Oppenheimer continued to define himself as a Jew, using his position as a Court Jew to gain the Jews readmission to Württemberg (they had been expelled in 1521). When the duke of Württemberg suddenly died and Oppenheimer was arrested and illegally held responsible for his employer's policies, he refused baptism, insisted on kosher food and was martyred on the gallows.

The resettlement of the Jews in Central Europe marked a major demographic change but not necessarily a fundamental alteration in the attitude of the larger society toward the Jews and Judaism. Although the interests of the state and the impetus to formulate mercantilist policy were paramount, and secular and religious strains of philosemitism proffered a favorable image of the Jew, old prejudices died hard. The Central European states attempting to graft mercantilist policies on to essentially agrarian societies prized economic expertise but condemned some of their most able practitioners. The state favored commerce, yet the medieval notion of the "money Jew" still largely held.

The result was that the Court Jews and the communities that developed around them lived with overt tensions. Wealthy Jews whose usefulness was incontrovertible were welcomed, but they were subjected to restrictive legislation and closely supervised. The mass of poor Jews, many of whom lacked fixed residence or occupation and who perhaps constituted half of all the Jews in Central Europe in the eighteenth century, were rigorously and systematically denied admission by the state. Widespread poverty might well have been the result of mercantilism itself, which benefited the few prosperous Jews and imposed hardship on the rest. Moreover, the children of wealthy Jews were subjected to the same discrimination as the poor: if they had no means or ability to be useful, they were denied the right of residence.

Naturally, these ambiguities adversely affected the lives of individual Jews. The Court Jews and their peers, for example, were necessarily intimately involved with the life of society but were prevented by their inferior legal status from participating fully in it.

Extensive evidence of the acculturation of Jews into surrounding societies existed long before the lifting of legal restrictions based on religious differences across Europe after the French Revolution, the event commonly known as emancipation. Jews had learned vernacular languages and taken part in cultural events (the rabbis in Hamburg, Altona and Wandsbek, for instance, lifted the ban on theater and opera attendance in 1725). There were also myriad complaints from rabbis of lax observance and indifference on religious matters. Jews also seemed to be abandoning the Jewish courts by bringing civil suits to gentile courts, a practice that, as we saw in the case of Prussia, the state authorities encouraged. Yet at the same time that Jews were being integrated in many ways, they also continued to suffer demeaning and restrictive legislation.

The Haskalah (c. 1720–1880), or Jewish version of the Enlightenment, beginning in Berlin, emerged as an apparent resolution of this contradiction or at least as a means to alleviate its impact. The early Haskalah was an effort to revive those internal Jewish intellectual traditions that would make possible a reengagement with European culture. In the period following the Reformation, a version of Judaism had developed that rested primarily on the study of Talmud and Kabbalah to the exclusion of biblical exegesis, philosophy in Hebrew and attention to Hebrew language and grammar. The Haskalah, which was created by autodidacts, medical students (from 1670 Jewish students were admitted to the medical faculties of such German universities as Halle and Frankfurt-on-Oder) and sympathetic rabbis, aimed to revise the narrow curriculum of contemporary Judaism by reviving the traditions of biblical exegesis and philosophy in Hebrew. Moses Mendelssohn (1729–1786), the most eminent of the autodidacts and a descendant of Moses Wulff, devoted his first Hebrew writings to renewing the tradition of Hebrew philosophy by introducing the ideas of the philosopher Christian von Wolff, considered the spokesman of the Enlightenment in German-speaking Europe. Mendelssohn offered an updated version of the medieval tradition of literalist biblical exegesis in a commentary on Ecclesiastes in 1770 and in his famous German translation of the Pentateuch of 1779–83 (the translation was printed in Hebrew characters), which was accompanied by a commentary and a general introduction in Hebrew.

The Haskalah began, then, as an intellectual effort to renew Judaism. In the 1770s and 1780s, the elite sponsored the exponents of Haskalah in the hope that the movement might either gain them an improved legal status or access to the larger cultural and intellectual world. The elite offered support by giving the Maskilim (those engaged in the Haskalah) positions tutoring their children or as clerks in their businesses, but also enabled them to publicize their ideas by establishing the first modern journal in Hebrew, *The Assembler* (1784–97), as well as a Hebrew press.

The emergence of the Haskalah was characteristic of Jews in a declining autonomous community. It was an attempt to find an ideological solution to overt tensions in a society permeated with Enlightenment ideology. The port Jews, in contrast, since they lived neither in autonomous communities nor in remnants of them, did not develop an equivalent of the Haskalah. They instead found a more direct path than ideology to integration.

The port Jews comprised two groups. Either they were Sephardim from the Iberian Peninsula, refugees who had lived outside Judaism as *conversos* and were thus accustomed to being integrated into the larger society, or they were Italian Jews who had a more flexible understanding of Judaism, which permitted an unbroken connection to European culture.

The *conversos* left the Iberian peninsula throughout the sixteenth and seventeenth centuries. Although they were admitted under a variety of disguises, the authorities often knew or suspected the truth but preferred to turn a blind eye. The port Jews thus gained admission for the same utilitarian reasons as did the Court Jews: the wealth they could generate convinced rulers to act on *raison d'état* rather than on religious considerations.

The Sephardim moved to the Mediterranean ports of Venice and Leghorn, to the Atlantic ports of Bordeaux and London, Amsterdam and Hamburg, as well as to the New World ports of Jamaica and Surinam, Recife and New Amsterdam. Moreover, many of those who remained in Spain and Portugal were active in business as well. The result was a Sephardi trade network that connected the old Mediterranean routes with the new Atlantic economy. In an age without a developed banking system, these merchants had the great advantage of being able to do business with, and to draw bills of exchange on, relatives, friends or business associates whom they could trust or, if the need arose, could bring to justice using

Port Jews at worship: the synagogue of the Portuguese Jews in Amsterdam, by Bernard Picart (1663–1733).

the Jewish courts. They traded in sugar cane, silk, tobacco and diamonds, importing raw goods from the Dutch and Portuguese colonies and distributing the finished products throughout Europe.

The Gradis family of Bordeaux illustrates the commercial success of the port Jews. Diego Gradis arrived in Bordeaux from Portugal sometime in the 1660s and became active in the textile trade as well as in exchange and banking, making use of his Sephardi contacts in the Iberian Peninsula and in other Atlantic port cities. In the second decade of the eighteenth century, his sons ventured into the new colonial trade and made their fortunes. David Gradis (1665–1751) purchased ships and traded with French possessions in the Caribbean. At his death, he had achieved considerable success, living in comfortable quarters in town. His son

Abraham (c. 1695–1780) extended the trade to Canada, where he also provided the French with supplies in their colonial war with the British. He treated the firm Gradis et fils as if it represented surrogate nobility, and lived "nobly," maintaining a splendid city residence as well as a country estate with exotic gardens.

Diego Gradis had arrived in Bordeaux as a new Christian who enjoyed the privileges extended to the members of such merchant corporations (*marchands portugais*). Until late in the seventeenth century, he and other *converso* émigrés maintained this fiction by baptizing their children, marrying in churches and burying family members in Christian cemeteries. Thereafter, they emerged publicly as Jews. They ceased baptizing their children in the 1690s, and after the turn of the century registered their marriages but did not hold them in church. In 1723 these Sephardi Jews were officially recognized and the privileges they had enjoyed as "New Christians" were confirmed for them as publicly professing Jews. The Sephardi Jews of Bordeaux retained their original status as a merchant corporation within society; they were never an autonomous community.

Port Jews elsewhere attained a new legal status as well. The Jews of London were from the start a voluntary community rather than an autonomous separate one. *Conversos* who had settled in London in the 1520s and 1530s and again in the 1580s and 1590s had been dispersed not long after their Jewish identity had become known. In the mid-seventeenth century, a new group arrived and was allowed to stay. The Puritans were willing to tolerate them for political as well as millenarian religious reasons (some Puritans thought the presence of Jews in England would spark the Second Coming). Cromwell convened a conference in Whitehall in December 1655 to deal with the Jews' status, which he dissolved before it had made a recommendation. The Jews were thus allowed to remain without a formal decree being issued or a Jewry law being promulgated. Having organized themselves into a voluntary community, they in 1656–57 acquired a plot for a cemetery and a house for public worship. In 1697 the London Stock Exchange designated 12 of its 124 seats for Jews.

The port Jews in other countries were also the first to receive legal declarations of new status. The United Provinces (Holland) had been a major destination for *conversos*, who settled in Antwerp in the 1570s and then in Amsterdam from 1595. From the beginning of the seventeenth century, Jews were considered residents of Holland and could become burghers of Amsterdam. In the mid-seventeenth century, Spain challenged that status (over the question whether Jews domiciled in Holland had the right of other residents to engage in trade and live in Spain and Portugal). In response, the Estates General of the Republic of the United Provinces declared on July 13, 1657, that the "Jewish nation are truly subjects and residents of the United Netherlands."

Jews in the British colonies enjoyed a similar new status. In the interests of populating the colonies, Parliament passed the Plantation Act on March 19, 1740, which recognized as a "natural born subject of this kingdom" anyone who had lived in the colonies for seven years. The act permitted Jews taking the oath of naturalization to omit the words "on the true faith of a Christian."

The political advantages the *conversos* experienced should not blind us to their vicissitudes. Alert to threats like the Inquisition and traumatized by emigration, they suffered the anguish of having to feign belonging to a faith they did not profess while not practicing their own. They were racked by guilt and uncertainty, and begged the Lord for compassion and mercy. Once they emerged again as Jews, their deep feelings found expression. The *converso* poet João Pinto Delgado (1580?–1653), who fled Portugal for Rouen and subsequently moved to Antwerp and then Amsterdam, captured such emotions in the closing lines of his poem "In Praise of the Lord":

> When the humble man whose face was covered
> by the affronting veil, in that moment
> receives a goodly portion of rare glory;
>
> An ancient pact which for the loving lover
> was the recompense for his faithful zeal,
> for his saintly fear and for his constant faith.
>
> If you promised us a heaven of metal,
> for our sin's sake, forget all our forgetting
> and let your mercy cast aside all our fearing.
>
> The heart that has been the most cut off from you
> gather to yourself, so that it may remain
> purer than gold drawn from the crucible:
> O happy he who can such a blessing gain!

The former *conversos*, reestablished in their Jewish identity, had to undergo a process of reeducation. In the Iberian Peninsula, they had been deprived of the sources of their faith; neither libraries nor teachers were available. Although much could be gleaned by reading Christian polemics against the grain, direct encounter with the key texts of Judaism was usually impossible. As the *conversos* reached safe ports, they produced a vernacular literature (Spanish and Portuguese) of translations, compilations and analytical treatises to reeducate themselves and future immigrants.

Because their Judaism was fully compatible with secular culture, the former *conversos* did not fully jettison the experience of belonging to the larger society. The famous Etz Haim Yeshivah in Amsterdam, for example, integrated secular subjects such as vernacular language, arithmetic and geography into a curriculum of Jewish subjects that included the independent study of the Bible and Hebrew language alongside study of the Talmud. The yeshivah was the envy of Ashkenazi visitors not only because of the curriculum's breadth but also because a system of grading was used: in contrast to the practice in Jewish schools of Eastern Europe, students were divided by age and ability and progressed each year to a new level of study.

Some former *conversos* also manifested their past experience of living outside the authority of Jewish law by being lax or altogether neglectful of observance but retaining their Jewish identity in their loyalty to the community. This pattern is evident in the Gradis family. David Gradis, the ship owner, belonged to the first generation allowed to profess Judaism openly. He served as a syndic (*gabbai*), a collector of dues and charitable contributions, for the community, purchased the land for a cemetery, encouraged other *conversos* to return to Judaism and disowned a niece who converted to Christianity. The extent of his observance remains an open question. In the next generation, by contrast, Abraham did not keep the dietary laws, selectively observed the holidays and in general questioned the authority of the Oral Law. Nevertheless, he remained active in the Jewish community, always being ready to contribute funds and to intercede with the authorities. He also acted as a reforming philanthropist, helping to shape a new curriculum for the Jewish school that included vocational subjects (French, arithmetic) as well as study of the plain meaning of the Bible according to grammar rather than the rabbinic tradition of interpretation (Midrash).

One can see similar behavior in London. Wealthy Sephardi merchants lived like Christian gentlemen, maintaining country estates as well as town residences, and supporting in the appropriate style mistresses as well as wives. Although these grandees often lived at a distance from the synagogue in town or out of reach of one in the country, they still continued to identify as Jews and to support the community with their wealth and influence.

The *converso* experience could also lead altogether beyond belief in revealed religion. At one end of the spectrum of *converso* identity was the skepticism of someone like Uriel da Costa, who after returning to Judaism was twice excommunicated, the first time for questioning whether the idea of the immortality of the soul was derived from the Bible and the second time for doubting whether the Mosaic Law had divine sanction and wondering if all religions were human inventions. The philosopher Baruch Spinoza, who was also excommunicated by the Jewish community of Amsterdam, in 1656, questioned the authority of the Bible and offered a rationalist ethics entirely free of revealed religion. Although he was clearly a theist, he became the symbol of atheism, and his books were long banned from publication in many countries.

The second variation of the port Jew was manifested in the flexible Italian tradition. In Trieste, which was the free port of the Habsburg Empire, the Jews had long accepted the premise that secular and sacred studies were complementary. This notion of acculturation was embodied in the Italian tradition of the rabbi-poet-doctor. The Jewish community of Trieste was thus able to participate in the Enlightenment that emanated from both Vienna and Italy, yet it neither needed nor produced a Haskalah.

Although port Jews and Court Jews were two distinct types, there was considerable overlap. Port Jews also served sovereigns as bankers and purveyors. A consortium of Dutch Sephardim, for instance, provisioned the armies of the Prince of Orange in Holland, and later, when he became King William III of England in 1689, floated enormous loans to support his army and claims to the throne. The port Jews nevertheless remained distinguishable from the Court Jews in legal status and in the commercial societies where they lived.

The experience of the port Jews and Court Jews exhibited the diversity of Jewish life that arose as a result of westward migration. That way of life was bursting, or had already burst, the boundaries of the autonomous community; it thereby prepared the way for the more far-reaching changes to come.

THE FIRST TRANSFORMATION

Emancipation was the great enabling event of the long nineteenth century, the period from 1789 to 1917. To say that is not to accept the view of those incurably partisan contemporaries who either celebrated emancipation as redemption from exile and an end to exclusion or castigated it as conversion through assimilation. That emancipation so exercised contemporaries is, of course, testimony to its symbolic importance. Yet emancipation's impact was also substantive, the sine qua non for the transformation of the Jews in Western and Central Europe. It acted in concert with other factors, such as embourgeoisement and secularization, to affect virtually every area of Jewish life. For Court Jews and Jews in former autonomous communities, emancipation offered the essential freedom that initiated or accelerated their transformation. For port Jews, emancipation confirmed or extended the freedom that allowed their transformation to continue.

An adjustment of the Jews' political status was on the agenda of *ancien régime*, or pre-revolutionary, governments in the closing decades of the eighteenth century. In Prussia, Christian Wilhelm Dohm, a state archivist and political journalist, set the terms of debate in a 1781 tract in favor of emancipation, *On the Civic Amelioration of the Jews*. Arguing that "the Jew is more man than Jew," Dohm attributed the differences between Jews and Christians to the oppression the Jews had suffered: "When the oppression [the Jew] experienced for centuries has made him morally corrupt, then a more equitable treatment will again restore him." Dohm urged that the Jews be given immediate equality and in return be encouraged to shift their occupations and to reform their education. In the Habsburg Empire, Joseph II issued an edict in 1782 granting the Jews religious tolerance, which was also designed to "make the Jewish nation useful and serviceable to the State" by giving access to the schools and all occupations. In France, Louis XVI, after extending limited religious tolerance to Protestants in 1787, charged Malesherbes, the civil servant who had presided over that effort, to do the same for the Jews: "You have made yourself a Protestant; now I shall make you a Jew; occupy yourself with their future."

Would the *ancien régime* governments have emancipated the Jews? How long would it have taken? These questions can never be answered. Instead, emancipation was rushed howling into the world by the French Revolution, which also irrevocably divided the political firmament. With the revolution as instigator, emancipation was linked to liberalism and automatically rejected by liberalism's opponents. Yet opponents were not the only liability of a revolutionary birth: emancipation's advocates were deeply ambivalent. The proponents of emancipation conceived of it as a contract to give rights in exchange for the regeneration—the remaking of Judaism and the Jews—that would make the Jews worthy of citizenship. That notion of regeneration was ubiquitous, although it could take the form of a legislated requirement or an implicit demand.

Despite the fact that emancipation was generally linked to liberalism and regarded as a contract, the actual process varied in scope and duration from country to country. The emancipation process varied in scope according to the Jews' prior legal status: in some cases all rights were at issue, in others only a limited range of rights. Emancipation varied in duration because it presupposed a civil society based on the rights of the individual and on equality. The longer it took to create such a society, the longer was the process of emancipation.

In France, emancipation had the character of the revolutionary process to which it belonged, being comprehensive in scope but limited in duration. The issue came to the National Assembly in 1789 because it was unclear whether the Declaration of the Rights of Man and Citizen applied to Protestants and Jews. After admitting Protestants to citizenship through the civic oath, the assembly debated the question of the Jews in December 1789. In these debates, the Girondist count Clermont-Tonnerre made his famous statement sounding the death knell of the autonomous community: "The Jews should be denied everything as a nation, but granted everything as individuals." Yet the chief proponent of emancipation, Mirabeau, had the issue shelved. Why?

Of the 40,000 or so Jews in France, about eighty-five percent were Ashkenazim living in Alsace in the northeast. These Jews lived in a declining autonomous community burdened with debt and courts increasingly bereft of authority. As a result of occupational and residential restrictions, the majority of Alsatian Jews engaged in petty trade and credit, which constantly brought them into conflict with the peasants and the guilds. The much smaller community of Sephardi port Jews in the southwest, in Bayonne and Bordeaux, was integrated into the surrounding society, unlike their brethren in Alsace.

After the National Assembly's delegates from Alsace objected that the Jews were aliens unfit for citizenship, Mirabeau ended the debate because he thought the issue would lose him the vote.

Representatives of the Sephardim were thereby convinced that they would fare better independent of the Ashkenazim. After asserting that their legal privileges set them apart from the Ashkenazim, the Sephardim gained complete equality in a decree of January 28, 1790. As Talleyrand pointed out, this community had already complied with the emancipation contract.

The cause of the Ashkenazim was saved by the revolution's radical turn: the Jacobins argued that the logic of the new constitution of September 3, 1791, required equal rights for the Jews. On September 27, 1791, the Ashkenazim gained equal rights without regeneration being mentioned.

In under two years, full rights had been achieved. During the next few years, France's armies carried emancipation beyond her borders to the Netherlands in 1796, northern and central Italy in 1796–98 and to western Germany in 1797.

Emancipation was not final, however. Napoleon reopened the issue as part of his larger reevaluation of the revolutionary legacy. He saw emancipation in Alsace as an act of "unwise generosity." On the basis of complaints about Jewish creditors, he thought Alsatian Jewry had not undergone the desired regeneration. In addition, emancipation had left the Jews' legal status undetermined, so that no recognized religious structure connected the Jews with the state, a matter of concern to a despot like Napoleon. Moreover, the former community in Alsace had been heavily in debt; in the absence of such legal recognition, no one could levy official taxes to pay those debts.

In 1806 Napoleon convened an Assembly of Jewish Notables who were presented with a set of twelve questions designed to ascertain whether Judaism was compatible with France's laws. An ultimatum accompanied the questions: "The wish of His Majesty is that you should be Frenchmen; it remains with you to accept the proffered title, without forgetting that to prove unworthy of it would be renouncing it altogether." The lay and rabbinic leaders offered answers that satisfied both Napoleon and their consciences. The answers did, however, entail a redefinition of Judaism as a religion rather than an all-embracing culture and the rabbi as a spiritual leader, as well as the recognition of the primacy of civil over religious law.

In typically grandiose fashion, Napoleon convened a Grand Sanhedrin—a version of the supreme Jewish court, which had not met for almost 1,500 years—to confirm this ideology of emancipation so that the Jews, as he put it, could "find Jerusalem in France." Napoleon in 1808 rewarded the Jews' loyalty with a recognized legal framework, the Consistory—a religious tribunal or governing body, created on the model introduced for Protestants—to sustain Judaism. Local consistories, part of the system that still exists in France and elsewhere, represent Jews of a region and send delegates to the central body in Paris, which is responsible for the maintenance of the chief rabbinate and the rabbinical seminary.

The Jews of Amsterdam welcome King Louis Bonaparte, the brother of Napoleon (1806). The Ashkenazi synagogue is on the right, the Portuguese synagogue (see page 206) on the left.

Although this system also made possible the payment of Alsatian Jews' debts, Napoleon punished them for failing to regenerate themselves by limiting residence rights and occupations for a period of ten years in the so-called Infamous Decrees of March 17, 1808, a clear violation of their equality.

The effects of the Infamous Decrees were not lasting. Following the restoration of the monarchy in 1814, the Bourbon king Louis XVIII did not renew them, and the state accorded Judaism equality with Christianity in 1831 by assuming responsibility for the salaries of its officials.

In England, emancipation was part of the process of freeing religious minorities of legal disabilities. Emancipation in England was limited in scope and of medium duration, and primarily designated the ability to hold political office. Jews, like dissenting Protestants and Catholics, were excluded from office but were deemed subjects of the Crown if they were native born. By the beginning of the century, Protestant dissenters were granted full rights, as were Catholics in 1829, leaving the Jews as the only minority without rights.

Emancipation bills presented to Parliament from 1830 to 1833 passed in the Commons but failed in the Lords. Having missed their objective with a frontal assault, the leaders of Anglo Jewry tried a step-by-step flanking movement. The first Jew was called to the bar in 1833, and the first elected to the office of sheriff of London in 1835 (with a special bill passed by Parliament). In 1845 Parliament opened the holding of municipal office to Jews.

At this point, all restrictions had been lifted except the ability to sit in Parliament. In 1847 Lionel de Rothschild (1808–1879) was elected to Parliament by the City of London but was unable to take his seat because of the required oath, which included the words "on the true faith of a Christian." This ritual of election and refusal to swear the oath was repeated a number of times, until in 1858 Parliament reached a compromise that allowed each House to determine its own oath. Rothschild was finally able to take his seat.

In the German states, emancipation was part of the liberal-étatist process that eventually created a unified, constitutional polity in 1871. Here emancipation was at its most intense, being comprehensive in scope and protracted in duration. The full range of rights was at issue; the subject was publicly debated for some ninety years; and the emancipation contract requiring regeneration in exchange for rights was written into legislation.

Emancipation first reached the German states either directly with Napoleon's armies or indirectly in response to French activities. French occupation brought emancipation to the Rhineland in 1797–98 as the ghetto walls tumbled in Mainz and Bonn. Napoleon's brother Jérôme emancipated the Jews when he became king of the newly created Kingdom of Westphalia in 1808, and the Jews of Frankfurt-on-Main gained civil equality in 1811. In reaction to the French model, Württemberg in 1807, Baden in 1809 and Prussia in 1812 enacted emancipatory legislation as part of larger constitutional and/or political reforms.

Napoleon's fall and the restoration changed the effect of the French revolutionary heritage on the Germanies. The failure to unify Germany also meant a failure to emancipate the Jews. The 1814–15 Congress of Vienna, convened to reorganize Europe after the Napoleonic Wars, returned the issue of Jewish emancipation to individual governments. The emancipation process now stagnated or was reversed. Prussia restricted its edict of 1812 through administrative practice. The smaller south German states, which were the first to develop limited parliamentary government, repeatedly debated the issue and legislated regeneration and equal duties without granting full equal rights.

The Revolution of 1848 similarly failed to bring about emancipation but did succeed in making it one of liberalism's principles. The Frankfurt National Assembly approved a bill granting equality to the Jews, and the restored Prussian government incorporated it into the constitution of December 1848. With the collapse of the revolutionary movement, the Prussian government undermined that equality through additional legislation.

Emancipation was finally achieved with unification. Discrimination on the basis of religion was declared illegal at the creation of the North German Confederation in 1867, and in July 1869, "all existent restrictions on civil and political rights derived from the difference in religious confession" were repealed. Public and political offices were now opened to Jews. At the establishment of the new German Empire in 1871, these provisions were extended to the territories that did not belong to the North German Confederation, such as Bavaria.

Emancipation either set in motion or accelerated the transformation of the Jewish population of Western and Central Europe into a predominantly urban middle-class group. Freedom of residence led to widespread urbanization throughout Europe. Under the *ancien régime*, Jews could not legally reside in Paris. In 1789 several hundred Jews lived in Paris under police surveillance. By 1880 some 40,000 Jews lived in the capital, more than sixty-five percent of French Jewry. In Alsace there was also a discernible migration from rural areas and villages to small towns and provincial centers. French Jewry urbanized at a faster pace than the general populace: though in 1871 some twenty percent of the people lived in district capitals and large towns, over sixty percent of Jews were city or town dwellers. In the German states, the number of Jews in centers with populations over 20,000 quadrupled between 1816 and 1871. Berlin, where about 3,000 Jews lived in Mendelssohn's day, had 36,000 Jewish citizens in 1870. German Jews also urbanized more quickly than the general populace.

Freedom of residence and occupation led to upward mobility. Jews became economically productive citizens as a result of the commercial and industrial revolutions and not, as envisioned by advocates of emancipation, through artisanry and farming. In fact, the very occupations they were supposed to abandon—itinerant peddling, used-clothes dealing and money handling—had positioned them to take advantage of an expanding economy.

Throughout Western and Central Europe, the Jews improved their positions in commerce, becoming shopkeepers, wholesalers and even manufacturers. In 1861 fifty-eight percent of the Jews in Prussia were employed in commerce and credit; only two percent of the general populace was similarly employed. Tax rolls show that by the time of emancipation in 1870, fully eighty percent of German Jewry was solidly middle class, with some sixty percent in the upper-income bracket. In England, about 8,000 to 10,000 Ashkenazi immigrants arrived in the period from 1750 to 1815 and initially plied the streets as old-clothes traders and fruit hawkers. By 1850 such Jewish peddlers had disappeared, they or their children having achieved middle-class occupations.

The Dreyfus family of Alsace is a striking example of this development. Jacob Dreyfus was a rural peddler and moneylender who moved to Mulhouse in 1835. His son Raphael became a commission agent in the textile trade and in 1862 opened his own cotton mill, eventually becoming one of the wealthier manufacturers in the area known as the Manchester of Alsace. His youngest son, Alfred (1859–1935), would forsake the family business for a career in the army.

Joining the professions played a secondary role in the Jews' upward social mobility; nonetheless, a move into the professions was evident in Paris before 1840, becoming more pronounced after 1870. The southwestern German states of Württemberg, Baden and Hesse admitted Jews to the bar before the Revolution of 1848, and by 1858 Jews accounted for ten percent of the solicitors in Württemberg.

To be sure, such changes did not take place everywhere at the same pace or to the same extent. In Alsace in the first half of the century, the rural economy remained largely intact, and many Jews continued to be involved as they had been prior to emancipation. About mid-century, however, urbanization accelerated, and the Jews, like others, turned to new occupations. Although the rate of development of the province of Posen lagged behind that elsewhere in the German states, even there evidence of improved economic circumstances was unmistakable.

The Rothschild family was the outstanding symbol of such success. In Frankfurt-on-Main, Meyer Amschel Rothschild (1743–1812) had during the Napoleonic period abandoned moneylending and currency exchange for banking. His five sons then extended the firm's reach to five major centers of European commerce—Paris, London, Vienna and Milan, in addition to Frankfurt—in the process creating the wealthiest and most successful private European bank of the nineteenth century. Although the example of the Rothschilds encouraged the association of Jews with capitalism, such fabulous wealth was the exception, the rule being modest middle-class prosperity.

Just as the Jews were entering the middle classes economically, they were also developing a form of middle-class politics. The politics of emancipation had already begun to emerge under the *ancien régime*. Moses Mendelssohn, for example, who had asked Dohm to write his famous tract, rejected the notion that the Jews had to undergo regeneration in exchange for rights, arguing in *Jerusalem, or On Religious Power and Judaism*, 1783, that emancipation should be given unconditionally on the basis of natural rights. In contrast, David Friedlander (1750–1834), Mendelssohn's disciple, who led a campaign to improve the Jews' legal status in Prussia in the late 1780s and early 1790s, based the Jews' claim to rights on their usefulness to the state. In France, Zalkind Hourwitz (1751–1812), who shared the 1788 prize of the Metz Royal Academy for the best essay on the means to make the Jews in France more useful and happy, argued that the Jews deserved equality as men and that governments had to respect their religious differences. In the early days of the revolution, he actively lobbied on behalf of Jewish rights.

A number of important figures continued these efforts in the nineteenth century. Adolphe Crémieux (1796–1880) began an eminent political career with a twenty-year battle to abolish the medieval Jewish Oath, the discriminatory *more judaico*, which required that Jews swear a degrading oath very different from that sworn by others. He succeeded in its abolition in 1846. Gabriel Riesser (1806–1863), a lawyer and the first Jewish judge in Germany (appointed 1859), actively campaigned for equality, arguing that equal rights were recompense for the equal duties that the Jews were already fulfilling. Riesser firmly rejected the notion that the Jews had to regenerate either Judaism or themselves, let alone convert, in exchange for rights.

The Damascus Affair of 1840 served to galvanize such politics. The accusation of blood libel was made when the superior of a Franciscan order in Damascus, and his servant, disappeared. The Jewish quarter was searched, leading Jews were tortured and one died under the ordeal. The incident elicited a public outcry in the West and an immediate response from the Jewish world. French and English Jews lobbied their respective governments, and Crémieux accompanied Sir Moses Montefiore (1784–1885), the recognized leader of Anglo Jewry, on a trip to Damascus. They succeeded in having the remaining Jewish prisoners exonerated and liberated.

The experience of the Damascus Affair convinced Crémieux and other French Jews of the need for an organized pursuit of emancipation politics at home and abroad. As a result, the Alliance Israélite Universelle, whose aims were "to work everywhere for the emancipation and moral progress of the Jews," was founded in Paris in 1860 as the first international Jewish organization.

The close relationship of such emancipation politics to general liberal politics is evident in the successful careers of Crémieux and Riesser and a host of other Jews. Crémieux served in the Chamber of Deputies, twice as minister of justice (1848 and 1870), and in 1875 was elected senator for life. Riesser was elected second vice-president of the German National Assembly in 1848 and a member and later vice-president of the Citizens' Council in Hamburg in 1859, and he also served on the Hamburg High Court. The Revolutions of 1848 in general brought Jews onto the political scene as elected representatives and radical activists. When the Imperial Government collapsed in Vienna, Adolf Fischoff (1816–1893), a young medical student, became president of the Committee of Public Security, the highest governing body during the revolution, and a number of Jews were elected to the Austrian National Assembly.

The transformation of Western and Central European Jewry that emancipation facilitated extended beyond demographics, economics and politics to culture and religion.

REMAKING THE JEWS AND JUDAISM

In the age of emancipation, the Jews of Central and Western Europe created a secular bourgeois Jewish culture whose authority derived not from Jewish law (Halakhah) but from an ideology of emancipation. This culture could include, and for many persons did include, Judaism, yet by and large it was a Judaism reconceived as a religion compatible with middle-class mores and culture. This new Jewish culture, like bourgeois culture in general, developed a vernacular-language public sphere; the press was its representative if not its principal medium, and imaginative fiction and visual art became important elements. Yet the social foundation of this bourgeois culture involved a process of acculturation that took different forms and occurred at a varied pace.

The new relationship to secular culture had its roots in the widespread acculturation that preceded emancipation. Its most powerful symbol was Moses Mendelssohn. Mendelssohn's role as the "Socrates of Berlin," one of the preeminent figures of the German Enlightenment testified to the fruits of acculturation.

Within the declining autonomous communities in Central Europe, the new relationship found theoretical expression in the Haskalah. In his *Words of Peace and Truth* of 1782, written in response to Joseph II's Edict of Tolerance that opened the schools to the Jews, the Berlin Hebrew author Naphtali Herz Wessely (1725–1895) advocated the study of secular subjects (vernacular languages, geography, arithmetic) as independently valuable. He also recommended a reform of the Jewish curriculum to include the Bible and Hebrew language along with the Talmud. The Maskilim and their allies institutionalized this new relationship by founding a number of schools that featured a dual secular and religious curriculum (Breslau, 1791; Dessau, 1799; Seesen, 1801; Frankfurt-on-Main, 1804; Wolfenbüttel, 1807).

The Paris Sanhedrin in 1808 authorized this new relationship to secular culture. By affirming the value of citizenship, recognizing the priority of civil over religious law and reconstituting Jewry as a religious group (in the Consistory), the Sanhedrin presented an ideology of emancipation that also presumed and promoted acculturation.

Religious authority and the new bourgeois Jewish culture were inversely related: the new bourgeois culture grew as religious authority declined. As the example of the Sanhedrin demonstrates, emancipation played a significant role in propelling the process. Emancipation in Holland in 1796 brought the creation of a new synagogue, Adath Jeschurun, which introduced changes in decorum and atmosphere of the service. Emancipation and the establishment of a consistory in the new Kingdom of Westphalia in 1808 resulted in changes in decorum in the service, the establishment of a seminary to train teachers and rabbis and, last but not least, the authorization to consume legumes at Passover because of wartime conditions, which was contrary to Ashkenazi practice. These efforts were short-lived, however. Adath Jeschurun collapsed as an institution with the creation of a unified consistory in Holland in 1808, and the Westphalian experiment ended with the fall of the kingdom in 1813.

It was in the German states, where the emancipation process was at its most intense, that religious authority first faced a direct ideological assault, and it had lasting consequences. The New Israelite Temple Association inaugurated its Temple in Hamburg in October 1818. The prayer book was printed from left to right, rather than right to left; a choir and an organ were introduced; the reading from the Prophets (Haftorah) was dropped from the Sabbath service to leave more time for a sermon in German; and, perhaps of the greatest significance, passages in the liturgy dealing with the return to Zion and restoration of sacrifices were altered or omitted.

Immediate opposition arose to the Hamburg Temple. The city's rabbinical judges condemned its heterodox Judaism and solicited letters of support from rabbis throughout Europe. The resulting publication, *These Are the Words of the Covenant*, served to articulate an emerging Orthodoxy. Moses Schreiber (1763–1839), who was to become a leader of Orthodoxy in Central Europe, attacked the subversion of authority: "These people do not have the right to choose to exclude themselves from the public." He asserted that he would prefer that the Temple members apostasize rather than "remain within the faith of Israel and establish a party of their own."

The controversy in Hamburg began to draw indelible battle lines. One marker of those lines was the emergence of the modern rabbi or "rabbi doctor." A new generation of such university-educated rabbis, whose authority drew as much on their secular education as their mastery of Jewish texts, began to appear in the 1830s. These men were practitioners of the new academic study of Judaism (or *Wissenschaft*)—the application of such secular disciplines as philology, philosophy and history to Jewish texts. The rabbis saw themselves not as judges of Halakhah but as teachers, preachers and pastors.

Rabbi doctors began to gain a foothold in the communities during the 1830s and 1840s. In the 1820s and 1830s, some of the German states in the southwest, for example Baden and Württemberg, began to require that rabbis have a university education in order to be certified. Also in the 1830s, some major urban communities like Breslau fought bitter battles over whether to appoint such rabbis.

These rabbis asserted their authority over the efforts at reform through a series of rabbinical conferences in the 1840s (Brunswick, 1844; Frankfurt, 1845; Breslau, 1846). In Frankfurt (1842) and Berlin (1845), lay groups had formed, claiming the right to determine the direction of reform without consulting the rabbis or the major sources of Judaism. The rabbis attempted to wrest control from these laymen. Starting from an affirmation of the Paris Sanhedrin, these conferences tackled such issues as use of the vernacular in the liturgy and belief in the Messiah. In some cases the participants came from communities untouched by reform, and they first introduced reforms after attending the conferences.

Further divisions resulted from the conferences. The rabbi and scholar Zacharias Frankel (1801–1875) resigned from the Frankfurt Conference, objecting to the use of the vernacular in the liturgy, proclaiming that "the preservation of Judaism is the innermost core of my life and the aim of all my endeavors." Frankel went on to become the leader of "positive-historical Judaism," which attempted to use the new disciplines of academic study to preserve and revitalize traditional practice and belief. He headed the first modern rabbinical seminary, the Jewish Theological Seminary, founded in Breslau in 1854.

The rabbi Samson Raphael Hirsch (1808–1888) had begun to voice a theology of neo-Orthodoxy in his writings during the 1830s. In opposition to the reformers, he envisioned a rigorously observant Judaism fused with secular humanist European culture. With his appointment to head the Adas Yeshurun

Congregation at Frankfurt in 1851, he was given the opportunity to shape a community to embody his ideas, and the city became a center of Orthodox Judaism in Germany.

The religious divisions within German Jewry became fixed with the establishment of competing institutions, a development epitomized by the creation of rabbinical seminaries. Frankel's Breslau seminary, which took a middle ground, had been the first. Two decades later, the Reformers, in 1870, and the Orthodox in 1873, succeeded in founding seminaries of their own in Berlin. Despite their divisions, the three seminaries all subscribed to the ideal of the "rabbi doctor" who was proficient in secular as well as Judaic studies.

The competing factions of German Jews were incontrovertibly divided over religious issues. They were nonetheless united by their common adherence to an ideology of emancipation, the view that the Jews were a religious rather than a national or ethnic group and that as such they had a "mission" to be moral exemplars, maintain the truth of monotheism and hasten the coming of the messianic age. By means of these precepts, all the denominations promoted acculturation.

Elsewhere in Europe, an acculturated Judaism developed with fewer fireworks. In France, certain prominent persons like Olry Terquem (1782–1862), author of the *Lettres Tsarphartiques* (1821–41), and the newspaper editor Samuel Cahen (1796–1862) advocated reforms, but religious change remained in the domain of the highly centralized Consistory, where lay elites exercised as much control as, if not more than, the rabbis. In consequence, such change evolved slowly and left communal unity intact. By mid-century, French synagogues featured confirmation ceremonies and organs, rabbis and cantors who dressed increasingly like their Catholic counterparts and vernacular sermons in which an influential rabbi, Lazare Wogue (1817–1897), could declare, for example, that "we are not a *people*, we are a *religion*." French Judaism had clearly drawn closer to its Catholic environment.

In England, there was greater division than in France, though nothing comparable to that in Germany. Two breakaway synagogues ruptured the unity of this synagogue-based community about mid-century. The West London Synagogue of British Jews, established in 1810, brought together Ashkenazim and Sephardim in a rite whose most radical innovation was the abrogation of the second day of holidays (all festive days had traditionally been doubled, to account for doubt in exactly determining the calendar). The Manchester Reform Association of 1856, many of whose members were of German Jewish origin and acquainted with German Reform, used the West London prayer book but maintained the second day of the holy days.

The Orthodox synagogues, under the leadership of the first chief rabbi of the British Empire, Nathan Adler (1803–1890), who was appointed in 1844, met this challenge by slowly adopting much of the program of Reform. Adler introduced decorum in the synagogue service and deference and authority in communal affairs, all of which were institutionalized with the creation of the United Synagogue in 1870. As chief rabbi, he presided over the religious courts and had a monopoly on rabbinic ordination. In an effort to make himself the Jewish equivalent of the archbishop of Canterbury, he alone had the title rabbi—other rabbis were called reverend, and they all wore vestments resembling those of their Anglican counterparts. A non-Jewish visitor to the recently refurbished Great Synagogue in 1852 wrote in the London *Times* that it "was on the whole resembling a handsome English Protestant Church but for the absence of communion table, pews and pulpit and for the presence of the orchestral platform in the centre. The first thing that struck a Christian (next to hats), he would be surprised to see the respectability of their appearance, all dressed in black, many in evening dress . . ." Adler clearly succeeded in creating an acculturated Judaism in keeping with the standards and decorum of the established Church of England.

Religious changes, though a significant part of the process of acculturation and creation of bourgeois Jewish culture, were only one aspect. Of equal importance, though perhaps less immediately visible, was the impact of such institutions as schools, since literacy in the vernacular was essential to nineteenth-century bourgeois culture. In the course of the nineteenth century, the percentage of Jewish children receiving a secular education or attending state schools rose dramatically.

In the early part of the century in the German states, the schools founded by Maskilim that featured a dual curriculum of secular and religious subjects were attended by no more than about twenty percent of the eligible Jewish children in a town or region, and at least half of these came from the poorest families. These schools also served as models for the numerous elementary schools founded after 1815 in anticipation of, or in response to, legislation for compulsory education. Elementary schools reached their apogee about mid-century: in Prussia in 1847, about half of the eligible Jewish students attended Jewish elementary schools. The proportions declined steadily in the second half of the century (1886: thirty-seven percent; 1901: twenty-nine percent) as the establishment of schools admitting students belonging to various religions (*Simultanschulen*) removed many of the remaining obstacles for attendance at state schools.

In France, education, like religion, was in the hands of the Consistory. Since many Jewish parents seemed reluctant to send their children to state schools, and in some cases faced opposition in the schools (whether from authorities, teachers or fellow students), the attendance figures remained relatively low: in 1810 only about twenty percent of eligible Jewish students attended state schools in Lorraine, whereas in Alsace the figure was closer to ten percent. To address this problem, the Consistory decided to found Jewish primary schools, following the model of the Protestants. The first such primary schools opened in Metz in 1818 and Paris in 1819, with ten more functioning by 1821. The Guizot law of 1833, which promoted elementary education and state support of denominational schools, was a further impetus. But as late as 1833, it was estimated that in the Lower Rhine under ten percent of Jewish children were receiving a modern education; the majority still attended clandestine Jewish schools, the traditional *heder*. By the 1850s, however, there was a dramatic change, as the majority of Jewish children attended either Jewish or state elementary schools. In Paris, for example, so many Jewish children attended the *lycée*, but did not receive instruction in Jewish subjects, that in 1850 a supplementary course in Judaism was introduced under the direction of the grand rabbi, with students from four high schools gathering at the *lycée* Louis-le-Grand four times a week.

Perhaps the most significant evidence of the development of a bourgeois Jewish culture was the emergence of a vernacular-language Jewish press. About the fourth decade of the century, a number of newspapers began publication: the *Allgemeine Zeitung des Judentums* (1837) in Germany, the *Jewish Chronicle* (1840) in England and the *Archives israélites* (1840) and *Univers israélite* (1844) in France. All of these journals promulgated a variant of the ideology of emancipation—that is, they advocated political emancipation and the duties of citizenship as well as the maintenance of Jewish particularity.

In its early years, the *Archives israélites*, edited by Samuel Cahen, served as a forum for the discussion of religious reform; endorsed the founding of separate Jewish schools as a means to sustain knowledge of Judaism and a distinct Jewish identity; reported on the 1845 rabbinical conferences in Germany, decrying the French rabbinate's lack of participation; called for Jews to defend themselves against conversionary efforts by extolling the morality of the Talmud; defended the use of Hebrew rather than the vernacular in the liturgy and proclaimed the virtue of unity within the Jewish community.

A recent historian has succinctly characterized the role of the *Jewish Chronicle* in words that can be applied mutatis mutandis to the other newspapers as well: "By interpreting the world to the Jews in Britain and representing them to the majority society, the *Jewish Chronicle* played a fundamental role in shaping Anglo-Jewish identity. It defined the parameters for debate on communal and other issues; it gave Jews in Britain an awareness of what was happening to Jews in other countries; it offered them a digest of Jewish cultural activity; and it functioned as a forum for the discussion of Judaism."

An important event in exhibiting the efficacy of the press was the Damascus Affair. The newspapers published the latest news of the incident and thereby helped to rally support in what became the first international cause célèbre of the emancipation era. The press encouraged and demonstrated Jewish solidarity under the new conditions of full or partial emancipation. In the words of the *Archives israélites*, "Even if we have become the sons of different homelands, we have not repudiated the religious fraternity that has been bequeathed to us by thirty centuries of glory and suffering."

The press was perhaps the central constituent of a new Jewish public sphere whose development paralleled that of the majority society. Art was another. Imaginative fiction and the visual arts figured significantly in the creation of nineteenth-century bourgeois culture in general and in bourgeois Jewish culture in particular. Much of this art combined nostalgia for a Jewish past that was disappearing with a celebratory portrait of contemporary bourgeois Jewish life. The novels and short stories by Berthold Auerbach (1812–1882) on the Black Forest, Leopold Kompert (1822–1886) on Bohemia and Daniel Stauben on Alsace effectively portrayed rural and small-town life. Stauben wrote in his *Scenes of Jewish Life in Alsace* of 1860, "We have tried our best to portray this contemporary form of ancient Judaism, which is alas on the verge of disappearing. . . . Already, in more than one place, it is being obliterated like everything that ages. Thus, we must hasten to record quickly the most characteristic traits."

The visual arts similarly sought to record the past for a self-satisfied present.

An illustrated volume of paintings by Moritz Oppenheim (1800–1882) "may well have been the most popular Jewish book ever published in Germany." Some of his rural scenes, like *Sabbath Eve* and *Passover*, depicted religious observance in a pre-emancipation setting and also substantiated the dignity and integrity of Judaism. In other works, Oppenheim showed contemporary incidents: Jewish patriotism in his famous *Return of a Jewish Volunteer from the War of Liberation* and the later *Yahrzeit*; and the immortalization of the Haskalah's great hero at a mythic moment—Mendelssohn and his gentile friend Gotthold Ephraim Lessing interrupted at a game of chess by Johann Kasper Lavater, a Zurich preacher responsible for drawing Mendelssohn into a draining theological dispute. Oppenheim's works combined loyalty to and affection for Judaism with German culture and German patriotism.

The acculturation that provided the social background for this new bourgeois Jewish culture took infinite forms that varied from town to country and according to class, profession and gender, and occurred in one generation or extended over a number of generations.

A rapid process was common among the first generation or two of Jewish intellectuals. The German scholar Leopold Zunz (1794–1886), one of the founders of the academic study of Judaism, was a student at Wolfenbüttel, the first traditional

Return of a Jewish Volunteer from the War of Liberation, by Moritz Oppenheim.

heder to be transformed into a school with a dual secular and religious curriculum. He later attended the University of Berlin, where he also served as a preacher at a private synagogue and became an advocate of Reform. The novelist Berthold Auerbach studied at *heder*, a community school that featured a dual curriculum and then at a yeshivah in Hechingen before attending a *Gymnasium* and the University of Tübingen.

The Dreyfus family in Alsace is, in contrast, an interesting example of gradual acculturation over three generations. The grandfather, Jacob, spoke only Yiddish. His son Raphael, though born a French citizen, had a rudimentary *heder* education but learned German and some French for business purposes: French contracts had to be read to him in German for him to catch all of the details. Raphael's children, including Alfred, grew up speaking French and had formal educations.

Among the intellectuals who experienced rapid acculturation were also some who apostasized. The earliest and most infamous instances were in Berlin. Berlin *salonnières*, for example, highly intelligent and accomplished women, played an important role in the city's culture at the turn of the nineteenth century, in part because Jews constituted a large portion of the capital's haute bourgeoisie. Dorothea Mendelssohn, Henriette de Lemos Herz and Rachel Levin Varnhagen married non-Jewish intellectuals and converted to Christianity.

Jewish men with intellectual or academic ambitions were similarly susceptible to conversion. Eduard Gans (1798–1839) was the scion of a family of Court Jews. A disciple of the philosopher Hegel, he helped found the academic study of Judaism, *Wissenschaft des Judentums*, while a student at the University of Berlin. A distinguished student of the history of jurisprudence, Gans wanted an academic appointment. He applied, and in an infamous ruling that came to be known as the *lex Gans*, the Prussian government decided that under the 1812 emancipation edict, Jews were ineligible for academic appointments. In response to this ruling, Gans reportedly quipped, "I belong to the most unfortunate group of people which is hated for being uneducated and persecuted for attempting to educate itself." Gans subsequently converted and was appointed to a chair in Berlin.

Not all conversions were opportunistic; some were the result of genuine conviction. The Ratisbonne brothers hailed from a distinguished Strasbourg family. Theodore (1802–1884), who was trained as a lawyer, came under the influence of the Catholic philosopher Louis Bautain, converted in 1827 and became a priest. The younger brother, Alphonse (1814–1884), vehemently rejected Theodore's conversion. But during a trip through Rome in 1842, Alphonse had a vision of the Virgin Mary, converted, joined the Jesuits and with his brother founded an order, Notre Dame de Zion, to evangelize among the Jews.

Some intellectuals baptized as children remained obsessed, in one way or another, with their Jewish heritage. Benjamin Disraeli (1804–1881) was the son of a Sephardi Jew in London who, having advocated reforms in Judaism to no effect, had his son baptized. The future prime minister mythologized his Jewish heritage, exploring it in a number of novels and exploiting it for political purposes. Karl Marx (1818–1883) converted as a child—his father was a lawyer who had been appointed to a civil-service position under the French occupation and stood to lose his appointment under the restoration if he did not convert. Marx disparaged Jews in his correspondence, and in 1844, in a debate over Jewish emancipation in Germany wrote a famous essay, "On the Jewish Problem," in which he identified Judaism with capitalism and argued that true emancipation was "the emancipation of society from Judaism."

A pattern of intellectuals who abandoned Judaism only to return to it later in life also developed. The poet Heinrich Heine, among the founders of the academic study of Judaism, converted in 1825 in the hope of a civil-service position. He deemed baptism his "ticket of admission to European culture." But near the end of his life he returned to Jewish themes, writing a series of poems with the title "Hebrew Melodies," and contended to a friend that "I make no secret of my Judaism, to which I have not returned, because I never left it." Moses Hess (1812–1875) was an early socialist thinker associated with Karl Marx and Friedrich Engels who had grown up in a fully observant home and acquired his secular learning as an autodidact. He rediscovered the Jews during the Italian risorgimento, the nineteenth-century movement for political unity, and in *Rome and Jerusalem* of 1862 argued that national liberation in general, and the national rehabilitation of the Jews in particular, was necessary to the emancipation of humankind.

As a concomitant of the emancipation process, a variegated bourgeois culture emerged in Western and Central Europe embracing a range of experiences and relationships to Judaism. These developments, however influential for the future, in fact affected only a minority of world Jewry; the majority lived under very different circumstances.

THE TWO EASTS

The nineteenth century opened a great divide in world Jewry between the emancipated communities and the unemancipated or "backward" communities. The "backward" Jews in fact constituted the vast majority in the nineteenth century and were concentrated in the two Easts: Eastern Europe and the Orient.

The Jews of Eastern Europe, who numbered 1 million or more, saw their status change dramatically in the closing decades of the eighteenth century when the map of Eastern Europe was redrawn.

For centuries, the Polish-Lithuanian Kingdom—which was then the largest kingdom in continental Europe, extending some 800 miles across the European plain from the Dnieper River in the east to the Baltic Sea in the west—had been a haven for Jews, whether in flight from Crusaders in the Rhineland, from persecution during the time of the Black Plague or from expulsions during the Reformation or Counter-Reformation eras.

The Jews served that primarily agrarian society of peasants and gentry as a middle class. They lived in towns and villages where they leased various economic privileges from the gentry (the arrenda system)—whether the management of estates and the sale of its products, or the right to distill and sell liquor—that allowed them to link the rural and urban economies and to promote local and regional trade. In addition, the Jews were an important source of artisanal labor. Although usually excluded from the urban guilds, Jewish artisans often lived in private towns developed by the gentry as sources of revenue. In fact, the Jews' economic and political existence as a whole was largely dependent on the gentry.

Polish-Lithuanian Jewish life was highly developed. The autonomous community reached something of a zenith in the supraregional organization known as the Council of Four Lands, founded in 1580, and taking its name from four provinces in Poland, Russia and Lithuania. The council met annually and had paid officials at its disposal to negotiate with political authorities and to collect taxes in the far-flung communities. The area was also a seat of rabbinic learning, boasting numerous talmudic academies and famous scholars.

The problems that beset the Polish-Lithuanian Kingdom also impinged on the Jews. The kingdom became virtually ungovernable in the course of the eighteenth century because of mounting economic problems and centrifugal political pressures. Similarly, as a result of wars and economic dislocation, the council fell deeper into debt as the eighteenth century progressed. It became increasingly harder to assess and collect taxes, and eventually the council could no longer fulfill its designated functions. Poland-Lithuania's ambitious and better-organized absolutist neighbors—Prussia, Russia and the Habsburg monarchy—began to partition the kingdom in 1772 and finished the task in 1793 and 1795. The Polish Lithuanian-Kingdom, itself on the verge of dissolution, dissolved the council in 1764–65.

One of the most significant developments in the life of East European Jewry in the eighteenth century was the religious movement known as Hasidism. In

The Synagogue of Lancut, Galicia, by Zygmunt Vogel (late eighteenth century).

contrast to the movements of religious *renewal* stimulated by emancipation and acculturation in Western and Central Europe in the nineteenth century, Hasidism was a movement of religious *revival* grounded in a new experience of the divine.

Hasidism emerged from the mystical culture that pervaded East European Jewry. Mysticism not only complemented and informed talmudic study, which was the premier intellectual discipline, but also enjoyed a life of its own. Mysticism had fueled the messianic expectations attached about 1666 to the claims of the false messiah Shabbetai Zvi. The failure of that movement left circles of mystical preachers and enthusiasts with unfulfilled messianic yearnings. Hasidism arose as a means to neutralize those yearnings by giving them a viable form.

The founder of Hasidism, Israel Baal Shem Tov (1700–1760), known by the acronym the Besht, was a healer, exorcist and amulet maker who distinguished himself from other mystical enthusiasts by the intensity of his mystical experiences, the nature of which are apparent in a letter he wrote in 1746:

> I went up stage after stage until I entered the palace of the Messiah where Messiah studies Torah with all the Tannaites and the Zaddikim and I became aware of very great rejoicing of which I did not know the meaning and I thought that it might be because of my decease from this world [in his ecstasy]. But later it was intimated to me that I was not yet to die, for they in heaven enjoy it when I perform acts of mystical unification on earth by meditating on their teachings. But the true nature of this rejoicing I do not know to this very day. And I asked Messiah: when will he come and he answered.
>
> By this you shall know it: when your doctrine [his way of teaching] will be widely known and revealed throughout the world and what I taught you will be divulged outwards from your own resources. And they too will be able to perform acts of meditative unification and ascents like you. And then all the husks [powers of evil] will perish and the time of salvation will have come. And I was bewildered because of this answer and I was aggrieved by the enormous length of time until this would be possible.

The letter also provides evidence of the neutralization of messianic yearning through Hasidism: the Messiah's arrival was to be deferred to a distant future and made dependent on the dissemination of the Besht's teachings.

Hasidism aimed to revive Judaism by injecting the ecstasy of mystical experience into daily practice and observance. It emphasized intensity and concentration in prayer (*kavanah*) over study, and by positing the immanence of God in the world offered the possibility of continuous attachment to the divine in everyday life (*devekut*). Hasidism also introduced its own version of kosher slaughtering and used the Sephardi, rather than the Ashkenazi, liturgy.

Although the Besht had a following, Hasidism became a movement only after his death. Dov Baer of Mizhirech (d. 1772), with the aid of the first written formulation of Hasidism, Jacob Joseph's *Toledot Ya'akov Yosef* of 1780, introduced the distinctive Hasidic way of life centered on the institution of the charismatic leader or tzaddik, a righteous man. The tzaddik was a settled leader with a court who served his followers by mediating with God: he performed the required mystical acts of contemplation and unification on behalf of his community. An abundance of tzaddikim emerged, ending centralized leadership of the movement and resulting in the foundation of numerous dynasties, with sons succeeding fathers.

Hasidism became an established sect with a self-defined way of life. It did not go unopposed. Its practices represented a repudiation of the core values of rabbinic culture—which is to say, study—and the institution of the tzaddik posed a challenge to rabbinic authority. The eminent scholar Elijah Ben Solomon Zalman, the Gaon of Vilna (1720–1797), pronounced the first ban against Hasidism in 1772 and a number of others followed in the next three decades. The Hasidim replied with bans of their own. There were also denunciations to the political authorities and arrests. The antagonists to Hasidism, the Mitnaggedim (meaning "opponents"), came to be identified by their attitude to the movement. With time, the bitter differences lessened. At its inception during the period from 1770 to 1800, Hasidism appeared to be a heresy that challenged accepted practice and belief; in the social and political configuration of the nineteenth century, it would become a potential ally against new foes.

The partitions of the Polish-Lithuanian Kingdom in the late eighteenth century divided the land among Austria, Prussia and Russia, bringing the bulk of Eastern Jewry under the control of tsarist Russia. Until that time, the tsars had deliberately excluded Jews from their realm, but they now had to devise a policy to deal with large numbers of Jews. In the waning years of the kingdom, the *Sejm* (parliament) had debated the status of the Jews, with some prominent political figures advocating emancipation. Russian policymakers, aware of these debates and also of the emancipation process in Western and Central Europe, vacillated over the next century, until 1881, between policies that promoted an emancipation contract requiring that regeneration precede the granting of rights and policies aimed at social control and repression.

The initial policies under Catherine II, which were designed to deal with the 20,000 or so Jews included in the first partition of 1772, confirmed the Jews' existing privileges for the convenience of collecting taxes, but only in the areas where they already lived; Poles were accorded privileges wherever they chose to reside. The first government reports, however, largely drawn from consultations with merchant groups, depicted the Jews as exploiters and cheats who lorded it over peasant and gentry. A further decree in 1791 closed specific areas to Jews, thus introducing the foundations of residence restrictions.

With the second and third partitions, Catherine's government ruled over an additional 300,000 Jews and attempted to resettle and integrate them into an urban middle class. To encourage the Jews to leave rural areas for towns and cities, the liquor licenses that provided a livelihood were revoked. In response to protests, this decision was reversed, but a note that would become familiar in Russian policy had thereby been sounded: Jews were to be removed from the countryside because of their allegedly pernicious influence on the peasantry. The first effort at comprehensive legislation, the 1804 Statutes Concerning the Organization of Jews, issued under Tsar Alexander I, reiterated this theme: "Numerous complaints have been submitted to us regarding the abuse and exploitation of native farmers and laborers in those provinces in which the Jews are permitted to reside. . . .The following regulations are in accord both with our concern with the true happiness of the Jews and with the needs of the principal inhabitants of those provinces."

The legislation promised "maximum liberties, minimum restrictions," but its overall intent was to manage the Jews by reforming them and only later offering rights. The statute opened all educational institutions to the Jews and required that they learn a vernacular language (Russian, German or Polish) for use in their official transactions, and also allowed them to engage in all occupations. It nevertheless continued the practice of restricting where they could reside, and denying liquor licenses.

A turn for the worse came with Tsar Nicholas I. His first effort was to use the army as a means of social control. Jews had formerly paid a special tax that exempted them, as members of the Merchants' Guild, from conscription. In the legislation of August 26, 1827, they were made eligible for conscription. Moreover, juvenile conscripts, or "cantonists," were to be drafted from the age of twelve and educated in military schools before serving a twenty-five-year term in the army. The purpose of this legislation was to separate Jewish youths from family and religion and to assimilate them into Russian culture; youngsters already exposed to such influence or employed productively—whether studying in Russian schools, apprenticed to Russian artisans or engaged in agriculture—were exempt from conscription. The spectacle of conscripts being marched off for years of hard service horrified Jews and gentiles alike. Of the 40,000 or 50,000 drafted under this legislation, many converted under duress and abuse. The policy had additional repercussions.

The burden of fulfilling the quota for conscription was placed on the Jewish communities themselves. In the decision whose sons should serve, the rich were pitted against the poor, the powerless against the powerful. Indeed, the situation deteriorated to the point that the communities dispatched kidnappers (*khappers*) to seize eligible youths. The result was a breakdown of communal solidarity and a delegitimation of the Jewish authorities.

Nicholas I in 1835 altered the earlier residence restrictions, instituting a delineated Pale of Settlement, an area of some 1 million square kilometers extending from the Baltic to the Black Sea, within which Jews were permitted to live. They were allowed to reside elsewhere only under special circumstances, or with express permission. The Pale of Settlement was to remain intact until the February Revolution of 1917.

The alteration between repression and emancipation can be seen in Nicholas I's efforts to use education as a means of reform. Two of Nicholas' ministers, Uvarov and Kiselev, tried to follow the Central European example of making education a prerequisite for rights. The educational reforms legislated in 1804 had had little effect. In the 1840s, the Russian state sponsored a system of schools and rabbinical seminaries to train a new generation of teachers, rabbis and leaders. But the stick was never far from the carrot: were students to leave these institutions, they would be eligible for conscription. These institutions made education available to a limited number of Jews. They also created an institutional basis for a new Jewish intelligentsia.

The high point of emancipatory legislation came in the reign of Alexander II, from 1855 to 1881, which saw a general policy of liberalization, including the emancipation of the peasants in 1861. Some western border provinces were opened to Jews in 1858; in 1859 the wealthiest Jewish merchants (the first guild) were allowed to travel into the interior; in 1861 Jews holding academic degrees were deemed eligible for the civil service; in 1865 artisans were allowed to live outside the Pale; and in 1864 Jews were permitted to become lawyers and judges. These measures raised hopes of a full emancipation, but the hopes were not to be realized. The emancipation contract broke down because there was a heavy-handed emphasis on regeneration without a reciprocal grant of rights.

Tsarist policy toward the Jews did not lead to emancipation, but it did play a major role in Jewish intellectual life. The Haskalah in Eastern Europe had developed in intimate relationship to the state. The initial stage of Haskalah in the East, at the turn of the nineteenth century, was similar to that in Central Europe early in the eighteenth century: the effort to renew internal Jewish traditions made possible an engagement with European culture and science. One finds such connections in the work of Elijah the Gaon of Vilna and in that of the talmudist and scientist Baruch Schick (1744–1808). Although these deep interests in scholarship were unusual, they did not set their adherents apart from the mainstream Jewish culture of the time.

The Haskalah became a discernible movement in Russia in the 1820s when it began to gain state sponsorship, which first took the form of a subvention for *Testimony in Israel*. In this 1828 work, Isaac Ber Levinsohn (1788–1860), a distinguished Russian Hebrew author, advocated the major principles of the Haskalah: orderly education without corporal punishment; study of the vernacular and science as well as Jewish texts; and a shift in occupations, especially to agriculture. In other works, he also suggested an end to distinctive Jewish clothing and a democratic restructuring of the community.

The emergence of the Haskalah led to a realignment of Eastern European Jewry. The Haskalah aroused opposition among both the Hasidim and the Mitnaggedim. The Russian government in 1843 convened a major conference on education, which representatives of the three groups were invited—indeed, pressed—to attend. The meetings were intended to win over the entire community to the government's policy of introducing modern education for the Jews. The result was that the Hasidim and Mitnaggedim began to unite in opposition to the Haskalah and the government, who appeared to be allied.

The government's turn to education provided proponents of the Haskalah with the institutional basis for its development. As a result of Uvarov's policies, the government opened seventy-one schools by 1855 and in addition founded two seminaries, at Vilna and Zhitomir, to train modern rabbis who would have a secular as well as a traditional education. These institutions offered the Maskilim employment as teachers and inspectors and solidified the image of the alliance between the Haskalah and the government.

The founding of the seminaries had the additional consequence of developing two competing rabbinates. The government began to require that appointees to rabbinical posts be graduates of the "Crown" seminaries. Although such rabbis were appointed to the vacant posts, the communities themselves clandestinely

He Looked and Was Hurt, by Maurice Minkowski, 1910. These traditional Jews in Eastern Europe are touched by the new ideas associated with the Haskalah. That some of younger students are clean-shaven is a sign of the times.

appointed a rabbi of their own choosing, usually one untouched by the Haskalah. The result was a rabbinate that had government approval alongside the rabbinate that actually served the community.

The alliance between the Haskalah and the Russian government was celebrated in its literature. An 1866 poem by Judah Löb Gordon (1830–1892), "Awake My People," which became the clarion call of the Haskalah and provided its motto, "Be a man abroad and a Jew at home," is a striking example.

> Awaken, my people! How long will you slumber?
> The night has passed, the sun shines bright.
> Awake, lift up your eyes, look around you—
> Acknowledge, I pray you, your time and place . . .
>
> Every man of understanding should try to gain knowledge;
> Let others learn all manner of arts and crafts;
> Those who are brave should serve in the army;
> The farmers should buy ploughs and fields.
>
> To the treasury of the state bring your strength,
> Take your share of its possessions, its bounty.

Be a man abroad and a Jew at home,
A brother to your countrymen and a servant to your king. . . .

Yet there were cracks in this apparent alliance, because of fundamental differences. The Haskalah criticized traditional Jewish life in order to reform and renew it. The government, in contrast, saw education as a means to lead the Jews beyond Judaism to European culture and, eventually, Christianity. In addition, the government was suspicious of any group or groups advocating reforms—its natural sympathies lay with the politically quiescent and obedient.

One can see this tension in the work of the Haskalah proponent Mordecai Aaron Günzburg (1795–1846). Günzburg translated historical and geographical works into Hebrew, advocated the study of the vernacular and also promoted the adoption of modern business methods. Though thoroughly loyal to the Russian government, he found that he had to make concessions to get his books published because of the government's suspicions.

One of the Haskalah's enduring achievements was the development, beginning in the 1860s, of a Hebrew- and a Russian-language press that played the same role as the press in Western and Central Europe. The newspapers' influence far exceeded the recorded number of subscribers: one paper circulated among many readers, and the ideas so made current helped shape public opinion.

Another of the Haskalah's contributions to the spread of Hebrew in a secular context was the emergence of an imaginative literature. Following the publication in 1853 of the first Hebrew novel, *Love of Zion* by Abraham Mapu (1808–1867), many books of prose and poetry appeared.

The Haskalah was not an isolated theoretical movement or one whose influence was limited to government-sponsored institutions. Where favorable circumstances prevailed, the Haskalah became the ideological expression of a way of life. This was the case in at least two cities at different times.

From the first partition in 1772 until about 1810, the Byelorussian town of Shklov was a center of both commerce and culture. The Jews of Shklov enjoyed the fruits of both: an early Haskalah emerged, which successfully combined rabbinic learning with the European Enlightenment. It addressed the cultural and political situation of the Jews while also commanding the respect, and assent, of the rabbis. Shklov became something of an ideal for the Maskilim in Russia.

The frontier Black Sea port of Odessa was a city of merchants organized along ethnic lines. In the course of the nineteenth century, Jewish residents developed schools and synagogues, newspapers and printing presses, embodying the principles of the Haskalah, thereby making it the ideology of a middle-class merchant community. In this port city, free of the constraints of the past, Eastern Europe's equivalent of the port Jew was able to flourish.

The history of the Jews in the Russian empire was influenced indirectly by Western and Central Europe, inasmuch as emancipation and related developments served as a model. By contrast, the history of the Jews of the Orient, comprising the Middle East (Levant) and North Africa (Maghreb), was altered by the direct intervention of the emancipated Jews of Western and Central Europe and, of course, of the imperialist powers. The Russian empire would not brook foreign intervention on behalf of a minority like the Jews, but in the Ottoman Empire such intervention was commonplace.

At the beginning of the nineteenth century, the Jewish population of the Ottoman Empire, perhaps numbering 150,000, was in general economic and social decline. In the sixteenth and seventeenth centuries, the Sephardi immigrants had been vital to the Ottoman economy because of their knowledge of European languages and trade routes, medicine and warfare. In the nineteenth century, they lost their advantage as other minority groups learned those skills and usurped their position. As one nineteenth-century European traveler wrote:

> Little by little . . . the taste for study and letters was lost among the Jews of Turkey. When the Greeks, following their example, began to study the languages of Europe, the fear of being supplanted by them, instead of stimulating their ardor, struck them with a kind of apathy, and they saw themselves gradually dispossessed of their positions as interpreters and other lucrative functions which they had occupied at the Sublime Porte [the sultan's government] and in the chanceries. Later even the humbler jobs which they had retained, whether in the customs or finances of the Empire or in the households of the Pashas, were taken from them by the Armenians. While the other communities, Christians and Muslim, familiarized themselves more and more with the languages and affairs of Europe, they continued to remain stationary and, with apparent indifference, saw their riches pass into the hands of their rivals.

The Jews' situation began to change in the nineteenth century with European intervention in and dismemberment of the empire of the so-called sick man of Europe. Russia, England and France claimed jurisdiction over their Christian coreligionists, which led to a system of "capitulations" whereby the Ottoman government transferred jurisdiction over the wealthiest and most powerful merchants to foreign governments. The European powers exerted pressure for tolerance and an end to the second-class *dhimma* status of non-Muslims. At the same time, they also dismembered the empire (Algeria came under the control of France, 1830; Aden of England, 1839; Egypt of England, 1882; Tunisia of France, 1883).

In response to these pressures, the Ottoman Empire undertook reforms to shore up its authority (the Tanzimat), which, among other measures, extended equal rights to the religious minorities, ending their inferior *dhimma* status (the Khatt-i Humayun, 1856). These changes also benefited the Jews. British and French Jews interceded with their governments and the Sublime Porte to guarantee that these rights applied to Jews as well.

The most far-reaching reforms came from direct Jewish intervention. The Tanzimat reform did not include the notion of a unified citizenship whose development would have entailed a national system of education; instead, education was left untouched and in the hands of the ethnic-religious minorities.

It was in education that the Jews of Western and Central Europe found a field of action. The Alliance Israélite Universelle aimed to provide Oriental Jewry with the regeneration that, according to the ideology of emancipation, was held to be the foundation of citizenship. Beginning in Tetouan, Morocco, in 1862, the alliance created a network of elementary schools whose purpose was to restore to Oriental Jewry "the feeling of being men" by teaching them vernacular languages,

An Alliance Israélite School in Constantine (Algeria), 1895.

vocational skills and secular subjects such as science and mathematics. To staff these schools, the alliance founded in 1867 a teachers' college in Paris, the Ecole Normale Israélite Orientale, which gifted Oriental Jewish children attended with the eventual objective of returning to serve their communities. By 1900 the alliance had succeeded in founding some 100 schools that enrolled 26,000 students.

The alliance could not have succeeded in establishing the schools without the cooperation of local elites and at least the tacit approval of the authorities. In Istanbul, Abraham Camondo (1785–1873), a banker known as "the Rothschild of the East" who held Austrian citizenship, played a leading role in founding the first European-style school for boys in 1854. When the alliance was formed, he served as president of the local committee and helped gain government sanction for its activities throughout the empire. Camondo considered the alliance the means to help "the Jews of the East, who are so backward in civilization and for whom only education can open the path to progress."

The Jews also experienced the results of direct European imperialism. The French occupation of Algeria in 1830 led to the shaping of a secular European state in which Jews were fully emancipated by the Crémieux decree of 1870.

The Jews of the two Easts and the Jews of Western and Central Europe had parted ways in the course of the nineteenth century. Developments at the end of the century were to bring these diverse communities face to face.

THE SECOND TRANSFORMATION

The Jews' integration into Europe began with migration, and their subsequent transformation was propelled by the rise of liberal bourgeois society. At the close of the nineteenth century, European Jewry began a second transformation, which also started with migration and this time was encouraged by the beginnings of mass society—explosive population growth, the rise of an industrial working class and the reshaping of the political and social order.

The westward migration of the seventeenth and eighteenth centuries that had introduced new patterns into Jewish life was a trickle compared with the flood of migrants at the end of the nineteenth century. The population of Europe had grown dramatically in the course of the nineteenth century, from approximately 180 million in 1800 to some 490 million by 1914. The number of European Jews had increased equally rapidly, reaching about 8 million by 1900. In the forty years from 1880 to the outbreak of the First World War, some 2 or 2.5 million of these Jews were involved in a "great migration" that would shift the demographic center of world Jewry. In 1880 eighty percent of world Jewry lived in Europe; by 1914 the percentage dropped to sixty-five and by 1939 to about fifty-eight.

The majority of migrants were from Eastern Europe, principally Russia, where the Jewish population had grown to about 5 million in the course of the century. Such an increase would have put pressure on the economy under the best of circumstances, and the circumstances in tsarist Russia were far from the best. The Russian economy expanded slowly and unevenly. The Jews remained restricted to the Pale of Settlement, so that population growth had to be absorbed in an even more limited economy. Moreover, although earlier in the nineteenth century tsarist policy toward the Jews had sometimes favored emancipation, sometimes repression, when the tsarist government confronted industrialization and social unrest at the end of the century, its response was to veer perilously in the direction of repression. The assassination of Tsar Alexander II by nihilists in 1881 was the turning point. Two sorts of discrimination followed.

The first was the pogroms. After the assassination, which was blamed on the Jews, violent mobs attacked them and their property in more than 100 communities. In 1903 the most violent incident to date occurred in Kishinev, where at least 100 people were killed. And in the aftermath of the 1905 Revolution, there were also outbreaks of violence against Jews, most notably in Odessa. Many contemporaries thought that the pogroms were state policy, but in reality the central authorities were alarmed by such extreme and unlawful acts. Local or regional officials were often the ones who either condoned or cooperated in the events.

In 1912–13 the local government in Kiev embarked on a blood libel trial. Although all evidence indicated that the gory death of a young boy was the work of a gang of thieves, a Jew by the name of Mendel Beilis was accused of having perpetrated the crime for ritual purposes. The chief prosecutor tried to put Judaism and the Jewish "race" on trial by calling "expert" witnesses who would make the case for ritual murder. Public opinion was outraged: a *New York Times* editorial saw this trial as part of tsarist Russia's "stupid war on the Jews." Beilis was acquitted.

The second sort of discrimination was embodied in the legal measures that strangled the economic development of the Pale of Settlement. While the "hot" pogroms destroyed lives and property, instilling feelings of fear and insecurity, the "cold" pogroms plunged large numbers of Jews into poverty. The May Laws of 1882, which were justified as a response to the "Jewish exploitation" allegedly responsible for social unrest, further contracted the Pale of Settlement by prohibiting Jews from residing or purchasing real estate in villages and rural areas and reduced the range of legitimate economic activity by effectively ending what remained of the Jews' link between rural and urban economies. In addition, Jews were prohibited from engaging in commerce on Sundays, adding the burden of a second enforced day of rest.

These measures, which began to reverse the emancipatory legislation passed during the reign of Alexander II, were reinforced by quotas that further limited the Jews' economic options. A five percent quota, for example, was placed on Jews employed as army doctors. In the secondary schools, a ceiling of ten percent of Jewish students was established in 1887 inside the Pale and five percent outside it. In 1891 some 20,000 Jews were expelled from Moscow without advance notice or provision for their resettlement elsewhere.

Jews responded in various ways to their opportunities being increasingly circumscribed. Students seeking an education went abroad, with the result that there were colonies of Russian Jewish students at some major German (Berlin, Heidelberg) and Swiss (Berne) universities. Jews also tried to make the most of the available economic circumstances, integrating vertically by cooperating in the production, distribution and marketing of goods—particularly consumer goods such as alcohol, beer, tobacco, sugar, salt and matches—in order to create as many jobs as possible for themselves as well as to circumvent discrimination and the cumbersome Russian system.

Another response was migration, which also took numerous forms. Within the Pale, workers and merchants moved from the older settlements of the north and northwest to the less settled areas of the south and southwest. There was also a pattern of urbanization over a period of a generation or two, with a first move from a small town to a larger one followed by a move to a city. Warsaw, for example, became a major magnet, its Jewish population increasing from some 89,000 in 1870 to more than 300,000 by 1910.

Russian Jews also moved within Europe, where they encountered Jewish communities in transition. The process of embourgeoisement was reaching its culmination. Major urban communities were taking shape. Berlin Jewry numbered 18,953 in 1860, doubled in the next decade and by 1910 reached 144,007. At the same time the three-generational pattern that produced large numbers of Jewish professionals (lawyers, doctors, journalists, professors) became apparent. Like the Dreyfus family, as we have seen, the family of Sigmund Freud (1856–1939) was another case in point: two generations earlier, they had been Hasidic. His father abandoned religious belief and Moravia for Vienna, where the young Sigmund was the first in the family to attend university. An important

Sigmund Freud (1856–1939).

feature of the closing decades of the century was the disproportionately high Jewish attendance rate at the universities.

The reception of the Eastern European immigrants was in part a function of the nature of the community they joined as well as the legal conditions that prevailed.

Vienna was essentially a new community that grew as a result of the grant of emancipation in 1867 (when the Habsburg Empire became the Dual Monarchy of the Austro-Hungarian Empire). Until then, the Jews of Vienna had been a small elite: government regulations had admitted only the wealthy. This elite community had maintained its unity with a decorous modern Orthodox liturgy, the "Vienna rite," developed by the preacher Isaac Noah Mannheimer (1793–1865) and the cantor Solomon Sulzer (1804–1890).

On the eve of emancipation in 1860, about 6,217 Jews lived in Vienna. The number reached 40,227 in 1870 and 146,926 by 1900. The majority of immigrants to Vienna came from Galicia, the southwestern portion of the Polish-Lithuanian Kingdom that the Habsburgs had annexed during the partitions and that remained the most economically undeveloped region of the empire. Vienna attracted migrants from the periphery because of its economic and educational advantages.

Immigrants created new patterns of solidarity, concentrating in the same districts of the city: comprising only nine percent of Vienna's population, they were a third or more of the residents of one district, Leopoldstadt, and a fifth of two others, Alsegrund and Inner City. They also clustered in a new sort of occupation: salaried white-collar employment for private companies—clerks, salesmen or company agents were virtually all Jewish; non-Jewish white-collar workers were primarily municipal or imperial civil servants. The Jews' acculturation as a group was evident in the attendance of their children at institutions of secondary education in numbers far exceeding their proportion of the population: some thirty percent of all *Gymnasium* students were Jewish, and as high as fifty percent in some institutions. Jews treated these institutions as avenues of social mobility (non-Jews generally regarded them as means to confirm already attained social status).

The immigrants to Germany found a far less hospitable environment: geography and government policy combined to heighten tensions between "natives" and "newcomers" by simultaneously impelling and impeding the newcomers' integration into the native community.

The fact that Germany shared borders with Russia and the Austro-Hungarian Empire, and kept those borders open for trade and seasonal laborers, meant that it was the center of transmigration for the vast majority of the 2 to 2.5 million Jewish migrants. This circumstance advantaged certain enterprises. At the end of the nineteenth century, Germany's shipping industry was growing rapidly because of the importation of American grain, so there was an economic need to fill the ships on their westward journey. Albert Ballin, the managing director of the Hamburg-Amerika Line, devised the idea of making the space available to emigrants. His company cooperated with the German government to create special facilities for a vast human traffic, including border stations for delousing, sealed railcars to transport the emigrants directly from the border to the ports of Hamburg and Bremen and special barracks at the ports for temporary housing. The line advertised extensively in Eastern Europe, circulating handbills and opening ticket offices.

The German government's policy toward the newcomers sharpened the conflict between them and the native-born. The East European Jewish immigrants seemed to threaten the emancipation contract on which the ink was hardly dry: they represented the past from which German Jews had dissociated themselves through education and embourgeoisement. And because naturalization was under the aegis of individual states, the absence of uniform regulations made the process more difficult for applicants. The immigrants, who numbered some 100,000 in the period from 1870 to 1930 and were mostly merchants from the Austro-Hungarian Empire, especially Galicia, were subject to expulsion without the protection of due process, and Prussia indeed expelled migrants repeatedly in the 1880s.

As a consequence, immigrants dispersed, trying to blend inconspicuously into the native Jewish community. Still, they were a risk to that community: the immigrants were predominantly male, but among German Jewry there were more women of marriageable age than men. If a German Jewish woman married an immigrant, she forfeited her citizenship and was also subject to expulsion. The immigrants thus posed a legal as well as a symbolic threat to German Jewry's emancipation, resulting in social tension and ostracism.

In England, the native Jewish community of some 60,000 in 1880 was swamped by the 150,000 immigrants arriving between 1880 and 1914. The native born made every effort to stem the tide of immigration. Chief Rabbi Nathan Adler placed notices in the Eastern European press stating that England was inhospitable to immigrants. The Board of Guardians, the leaders of the English Jewish community, allocated funds to buy the immigrants' fare to continue on to the U.S. or to return to Russia.

Immigrants to England, mostly artisans from Russia, concentrated in the "sweated trades"—ready-made clothing, boots and shoes—and settled in the least desirable districts of the industrial cities of London (the East End), Manchester (Redbank) and Leeds. Spurned by native-born Jews and the English working class, the immigrants established their own network of synagogues, clubs, mutual-aid societies and other associations.

The native Jewish community tried to speed the immigrants' "anglicization," hoping to make them respectable by "ironing out the ghetto bend." The native community organized the Poor Jews' Temporary Shelter and Boys Clubs and, with Rothschild support, even built some housing. Samuel Montagu (1832–1911), founder of one of London's most important private banks, helped organize a Federation of Synagogues.

The absorption of the immigrants was far from smooth, however, as witnessed by the famous court case of 1904 in which the chief rabbi's authority to rule on matters of *kashrut* was questioned by the rabbis recently arrived from Eastern Europe but in the end upheld through a tenuous compromise.

It is worth noting that there was a migration of Oriental Jews concomitant with the European one. Jews moved from stagnant economies to dynamic ones, which usually meant those under European influence. Large numbers of Jews moved to Egypt, where British influence had stimulated the economy; there were more graduates of the Damascus Alliance school in Cairo than in Damascus. Algeria, being under French rule, attracted large numbers of Jews for similar reasons.

The migration in the Levant and Maghreb was also a form of urbanization. The Jewish population of Beirut jumped from 500 in 1856 to 5,000 in 1914, and the Jewish population in Algiers doubled between 1880 and 1900.

Oriental Jews also migrated to other parts of the world. Iraqi Jews moved to Shanghai and India. Venezuela and Brazil offered appealing economic opportunities to others. And some Oriental Jews engaged in the textile trade moved to Manchester.

The vast majority of emigrants from Europe had as their destination the United States, the "promised land" or *goldene medina*, which was destined to become a new center of Jewish life. The numbers who came to America made that influx unlike any other: some 2 million Jews between 1880 and 1914, with an additional half million from 1914 to 1924. Until this "great migration," American Jewry was a minor community of some quarter million, but one with an important difference: American Jews enjoyed political equality without having to undergo an emancipation process or to obtain special legislation.

The first Jews to come to North America, in 1654, were a boatload of twenty-three port Jews—namely, Sephardim who had served the Dutch West India company in Recife, Brazil, until they were expelled during the Portuguese conquest (there were also port Jews in a number of Caribbean islands—Surinam and Curaçao, Barbados and Jamaica). Although Peter Stuyvesant, the governor of New Amsterdam, reluctantly admitted the immigrants at the Dutch West India Company's insistence, they were automatically granted the "civil and political liberties" that Jews enjoyed in Holland, as has been discussed. The only restriction they suffered was a prohibition on public religious observance.

Rights survived in the British colonies. The Plantation Act of 1740 made a special provision so that Jews who qualified through seven years' residence in the colonies could also become "his Majesty's natural born subjects." The early republic extended them in Thomas Jefferson's Virginia Act of 1785—"our civil rights have no dependence on our religious opinions"—and in Article VI of the Constitution, 1789, which also opened political office—"no religious test shall ever be required as a qualification to any office or public trust under the United States." The only restrictions were for political office in two states: Maryland first accorded that right in 1826, and New Hampshire delayed until 1877.

From the outset, the American Jewish community was centered on the synagogue. Belonging to the community was entirely voluntary, and there was no organized structure with powers of taxation or coercion. With the establishment of a second synagogue in Philadelphia in 1795 (the first dated from 1773), the potentially monopolistic practice of one community/one synagogue was avoided. Moreover, with independence from Britain, democracy became an integral part of synagogue life, as can be seen in the preamble to the new constitution of Congregation Shearith Israel, New York, in 1790:

> Whereas in free states all power originates and is derived from the people, who always retain every right necessary for their well being individually, and for the better ascertaining those rights with more precision and explicitly, form a declaration or bill of those rights. . . .
>
> Therefore we, the professors of the Divine Law, members of this holy congregation of Shearith Israel, in the city of New York, conceive it our duty to make this declaration of our rights and privileges.

The Jews of colonial America, who numbered about 2,500, were an urban group in an agrarian society. Clustering in the seaport towns of New York, Newport and Philadelphia in the north, and Charleston and Savannah in the south, they were largely shopkeepers and merchants who belonged to the "urban frontier," trading European and West Indian consumer goods (molasses, rum, sugar, dyewoods) for American foods and forest products.

This community grew with the immigration of some 50,000 Jews from Central Europe (Bavaria, Bohemia, Moravia) in the second quarter of the nineteenth century. Coming with the wave of Central European and Scandinavian immigration that populated the Ohio River Valley and much of the Midwest, and bringing with them some commercial experience, these Jews dispersed throughout the Midwest and the West as peddlers and petty retail traders, making goods available on the frontier. Traders reached Louisville, Kentucky, by the 1830s, Texas by the 1840s and California in the 1850s.

Settling in urban centers, often near water routes, the traders maintained the pattern typical of an urban group in an agrarian society: in 1877 sixty-five percent of American Jews lived in the country's ten largest cities, whereas only ten percent of the general population did. In the period from 1825 to 1860, when New York's population tripled to 800,000, its Jewish population increased from 500 to 40,000.

These traders experienced tremendous social mobility as they made the transition, often in a generation or less, from itinerant trade to retail stores, from retail to wholesale, and in some cases continued on to banking and finance. Marcus Goldman (1821–1904), an immigrant from Bavaria, went to Philadelphia in 1848 and worked as a peddler for two years. He opened a men's clothing store, which prospered, and in 1867 founded the merchant bank Goldman, Sachs & Co. Meyer Guggenheim (1828–1905), who arrived in New York in 1848 from Switzerland, initially peddled shoestrings, lace, safety pins, needles and stove polish in the mining areas of Pennsylvania. Realizing that housewives wanted a better grade of stove polish, he began to manufacture his own and traveled by train and horse to sell it. In 1852 he opened a wholesale store in Philadelphia. He eventually went on to build an empire in mining and investment banking.

The Judaism of this community was decidedly Reform, indeed far more radical than Reform in Europe, being encouraged by the community's voluntary structure that enabled each congregation to go its own way. Reform emerged as the prevailing practice, not because of the pressure of emancipation but because

Levi Strauss made a fortune selling his "patent riveted clothing." This photograph of the firm's staff in front of the premises at 14–16 Battery Street, San Francisco, was taken about 1880.

it adapted more easily to the surrounding respectable middle-class Protestant culture. European, and specifically German, Reform served as a model to be reshaped to American needs.

Reform began at Congregation Beth Elohim in Charleston in 1824, originally an Orthodox synagogue founded in 1749, in the form of an English-language sermon and liturgy (the latter significantly abbreviated). Organ music was part of the service. Reform's practice spread in the 1840s and 1850s, as educated laymen and trained rabbis arrived from Europe (Max Lilienthal, 1845; Isaac Mayer Wise, 1846; David Einhorn, 1855), and congregations were formed (Har Sinai, Baltimore, 1842; Emanuel, New York, 1845; Sinai, Chicago, 1858). The dominant and perhaps representative figure of Reform was Isaac Mayer Wise (1819–1900), whose program for the Americanization of Judaism included a uniform prayer book and the founding of a rabbinical school. Wise succeeded in both these respects. The Union Prayer Book, published in 1857, offered a distinctly American rite. The Union of American Hebrew Congregations, organized in Cincinnati in 1873, was intended as an umbrella organization for all Jews. Wise

Not all immigrants made their fortune. Ready for the Sabbath eve in a coal cellar, Ludlow Street, New York, c. 1890.

became the first president of Hebrew Union College, founded in Cincinnati as the American rabbinical school.

The Pittsburgh Platform (1885), which was adopted by the Conference of Reform Rabbis at its founding meeting in 1889, voiced the essential beliefs of this Reform Judaism. It maintained that Judaism was a tolerant religion ("We recognize in every religion an attempt to grasp the Infinite One") that was grounded not in authority ("We accept as binding only the moral laws and maintain only such ceremonies as elevate and sanctify our lives") but in liberty and freedom. Judaism was a religion ("We consider ourselves no longer a nation but a religious community") whose adherents had no expectation of restoration to Palestine but who saw their "mission" as the pursuit of social justice.

The great migration irrevocably changed the nature of American Jewry. A small, acculturated community that understood itself primarily as a religious entity was now faced with an enormous influx of unacculturated, Yiddish-speaking, largely proletarian immigrants who saw themselves and Judaism very differently.

Immigration heightened American Jewry's urban character. Jews were ten percent of New York's population in 1880; in 1915 they were a third of the total. Moreover, they constituted as much as seventy percent of four Manhattan wards, some more densely populated than the most populous areas of Bombay. These were the infamous "noisy, foul-smelling, diseased and hungry" tenements of the Lower East Side, which usually lacked proper light, ventilation and sanitation.

The Jewish immigrants were an important component of the industrial labor force. They were part of a larger migration from eastern (Poland and Russia) and southern (Italy, the Balkans) Europe that the United States welcomed as a source of industrial labor. The Jews who chose to move to America were drawn heavily from the young, urban, artisan proletariat. Although Jews were only ten percent of the overall immigration in the period from 1880 to 1914, they constituted about a quarter of the skilled industrial workers. They consequently played a key role in particular industries, especially the manufacture of clothing.

The ready-made clothing industry that was booming in the late nineteenth century was concentrated in New York City and largely owned by Central European Jews of the earlier wave of immigration (eighty percent of retail; ninety percent of wholesale). Since so many Jews had been trained and worked in the needle trades in Eastern Europe, they now flocked to these jobs. In 1897 seventy-five percent of the 66,500 clothing-industry workers in Manhattan were Jewish, as were eighty percent of the 15,000 cloakmakers.

Laboring in the mass-production clothing industry required long and taxing hours. In the slack season, workers averaged between sixty-six and seventy hours a week; in high season they worked as many as nineteen hours a day. The method of production varied: in the family system, the father, usually the master tailor, did the skilled work with the sewing machine, while the wife and children basted and prepared buttonholes; in the sweatshop system, a contractor hired workers who often lived and worked in his tenement apartment; and in the inside shop system, the manufacturer had his own factory. In none of them was the workplace clean or safe, as this contemporary description of a sweatshop attests:

> Up two flights of stairs, three, four with new smells of cabbage, of onions, of frying fish, on every landing, whirring sewing machines behind closed doors betraying what goes on within. . . . Five men and a woman, two young girls, not fifteen, and a boy who says unasked that he is fifteen and lies in saying it, are at the machines sewing knickerbockers, "knee-pants" in the Ludlow Street dialect. The floor is littered ankle-deep with half-sewn garments. In the alcove, on a couch of many dozens of "pants" ready for the finisher, a bare legged baby with pinched face is asleep. A fence of piled-up clothing keeps him from rolling off on the floor. The faces, hands, and arms to elbows of everyone in the room are black with the color of the cloth on which they are working.

The inside shops, usually located in lofts, were also firetraps. At the Triangle Waist Company, on March 25, 1911, for example, a fire killed 146 workers who were unable to escape because the doors were locked.

As a result of their involvement in these occupations, the Jews were instrumental in the development and growth of the trade union movement. The unions, including the Amalgamated Clothing Workers (1891), the International Ladies Garment Workers Union (1900), the United Cloth, Hat and Capmakers' Union (1901) and the International Fur Workers' Union (1913), claimed the achievement of an enlightened trade unionism that saw strikes and arbitration as means to improve the workers' conditions.

In the Great Revolt of 1910, some 60,000 cloakmakers in New York struck for eight weeks for better wages and working conditions. The strike went to an arbitration board that reached an important settlement involving higher wages and fewer hours, the creation of a preferential union shop and a joint union-management board of sanitation control, as well as the establishment of a standing grievance committee and an arbitration board. That same year, a four-month strike by 8,000 workers in Chicago against Hart, Schaffner and Marx, the largest men's clothing manufacturer in the world, resulted in a similar settlement.

Native-born Jews exhibited the same ambivalence toward newcomers that had been the case in Europe: they preferred that East European immigrants not come in such vast numbers, yet once the migration was under way they aided the immigrants and fostered their Americanization. Numerous charities came to the aid of immigrants as they made their way to the U.S. (especially the Hebrew Emigrant Aid Society, 1882) and once they had arrived (B'nai B'rith, United Hebrew Charities). Mount Sinai Hospital in New York treated more patients free of charge than any other private institution in the city.

The tensions did not disappear. Jacob Schiff (1847–1920), who was head of the banking firm Kuhn, Loeb and Company, and for many years the unofficial leader of American Jewry, thought the concentration of large numbers of immigrant Jews in the cities of the eastern seaboard could have a potentially detrimental effect on American Jews. He therefore proposed to disperse the immigrants to other parts of the country by having them enter through the port of Galveston. His Galveston Plan diverted some 10,000 immigrants to the southwestern states between 1907 and 1914.

The "uptown" Jews also attempted to mediate between themselves and the "downtown" immigrants. In 1908 a group of notables established the Kehillah, which aspired to be a unified structure for all the Jews of New York City with appropriate offices to administer the affairs (education, social welfare) of the entire community. Though conceived in the progressive spirit of "constructive social engineering," the Kehillah failed in 1922 because the immigrants resisted losing their own organizations and also suspected the organizers' motives—that the Kehillah was a means for the uptown Jews to retain power.

The immigrants had indeed created a vast network of organizations covering a broad range of activities. These organizations included hometown groups (*landsmannshaften*), which often began as synagogues and grew to become benevolent societies; communal charities, including the Hebrew Sheltering Society (1890) and the Hebrew Free Loan Society (1892), hospitals such as Beth Israel (1889) and Jewish Maternity (1906) and religious schools.

The immigrants' independence was also evident in their relationship to Judaism. Many Orthodox Jews from Eastern Europe felt that America was not the land of opportunity (*goldene medina*) but rather the land of impurity (*trayfa medina*) that would rob them of their piety more effectively than had any developments in Europe. As Moses Weinberger (1854–1940), an Orthodox Jewish writer living in New York, put it in 1887: "Yes, how awesome is the strength of America! In a single year it transforms 'Rachel the wife of Reb Jacob' into 'Mrs. Jacobs,' and 'Reb Baruch the cobbler and shoemaker' into 'Mr. Benet Shoe Manufacturer.' The Enlightenments of Berlin and Europe put together did not accomplish as much in half a century."

Other Eastern European Jews were willing to make accommodations but without going as far as Reform. Many of these Jews found a home at the Jewish Theological Seminary, established in 1885, which presented itself as an alternative to Hebrew Union College.

> The necessity has been made manifest for associated and organized effort on the part of the Jews of America faithful to Mosaic Law and ancestral traditions, for the purpose of keeping alive the true Judaic spirit; in particular by the establishment of a seminary where the Bible shall be impartially taught and rabbinical literature faithfully expounded, and more especially where youths, desirous of entering the ministry, may be thoroughly grounded in Jewish knowledge and inspired by the precept and example of their instructors with the love of the Hebrew language and a spirit of devotion and fidelity to the Jewish Law.

The immigrants also created a flourishing Yiddish culture of printed matter, theater and music whose chief emblem was the newspaper *The Jewish Daily Forward* (*Vorwerts*), which had the largest circulation of any foreign-language daily in the country. This ethnic Jewishness, or *Yiddishkeit*, was far removed from the Judaism of American Reform.

To gain a better understanding of these differences, however, we must look more closely at the ideological changes that belonged to the Jews' second transformation.

REMAKING THE JEWS AND JUDAISM AGAIN

The beginnings of mass society changed the nature of European politics and ideology. The "social question"—the future of the lower and working classes—became one of the burning issues of the day. As this group slowly gained influence, mass political parties with an interest in collective issues formed, and politics ceased to be the affair of notables. The ideology of Left and Right that had defined European politics since the French Revolution now broadened and radicalized, with socialisms to the left of liberalism, and authoritarian and imperialist politics to the right of the old conservatism. Bourgeois society started to give way to a mass society informed by post-liberal beliefs.

This new configuration also produced the "Jewish question." To be sure, there had been hostility to the Jews throughout the nineteenth century from all parts of the political spectrum. Conservatives had raised objections to Jewish emancipation as part of their rejection of liberalism or the French Revolution, and these views were reinforced by romantic notions of the organic nation or *Volk*. Early socialists opposed Jewish emancipation. Charles Fourier saw Jews as obstacles to a communitarian society, and Karl Marx saw them as the very incarnation of capitalism. Many liberals had been ambivalent, fearing that the Jews did not and could not qualify for citizenship. In addition, traditional Christian, often clerical, antagonism to the Jews also played a significant role. Moreover, these views were not renounced with the achievement of emancipation but eventually fed a fundamentally new perspective on the Jews.

The "Jewish question" became linked to the "social question." By the 1870s liberalism had largely achieved its agenda of constitutional monarchy, national unification, political participation of the propertied classes and a free market economy. The Jews had been among liberalism's chief beneficiaries, with emancipation serving, as we have seen, as the great enabling event. A new breed of post-liberal politicians began to single out the Jews' economic and social success. By holding the Jews responsible for the liberal order and all of its ills, these politicians transformed the Jews from the beneficiaries of liberalism into its symbols and creators. An important ingredient in this process was racial thinking. A consequence was that antisemitism supplied a bridge to post-liberal politics.

The term *antisemitism* was coined in 1879 by the German journalist Wilhelm Marr to denote an opposition to the Jews based on "race" rather than religion. Racial thinking had emerged in the course of the nineteenth century as a theory of history and society. It posited that humankind was divided into unchanging and recognizable natural types, which explained the moral behavior and mental outlook of individuals as well as groups. Moreover, racial thinkers offered racial purity as an explanation for the rise and decline of nations as well as for the position of social classes. At the end of the century, social Darwinist notions radicalized racial thinking with the idea of the "survival of the fittest": an inevitable war between so-called races became part of the racists' vision.

Racial thinkers at the end of the century began to pose the "Jewish question" in terms of "aryan" versus "semite." As the French writer Edouard Drumont put it in 1886, "Semite and Aryan represent two distinct races which are irremediably hostile to each other, whose antagonism has filled the world in the past and will disturb it even more in the future."

In Germany in the 1880s, antisemitism gained visibility with the emergence of Adolph Stöcker's Berlin Movement. Stöcker, the preacher at the Berlin royal court, attempted to attract workers and the petite bourgeoisie by offering an amalgam of Christian social ethics, social reform and antisemitism, as evidenced in his infamous speech, "What We Demand of Modern Jewry" (1879): "Israel must renounce its ambition to become master of Germany. . . . The social abuses which are caused by Jewry must be eradicated by wise legislation. . . . Either we succeed in this and Germany will rise again, or the cancer from which we suffer will spread further. In that event our whole future is threatened and the German spirit will become Judaized. The German economy will become impoverished. These are our slogans: A return to a Germanic rule in law and business, a return to the Christian faith." Stöcker, who used the new means of inciting public opinion, such as rallies in working-class neighborhoods, won the intermittent backing of the chancellor. Bismarck used Stöcker and his antisemitism to break the alliance with the liberals that had brought him to power and to form a new one with the conservatives. Antisemitism also gained legitimacy from the opinions of other intellectuals like the nationalist historian at the University of Berlin, Heinrich Treitschke, who appealed in 1880 for an immediate end to the immigration of Eastern European Jews: "the multitudes of pants-selling youths from the inexhaustible cradle of Poland, whose children and grandchildren are to be the future rulers of Germany's exchanges and Germany's press. This immigration grows visibly in numbers and the question becomes more and more serious how this alien nation can be assimilated."

In the 1890s a new breed of racist politicians such as Ernst Henrici and Otto Boeckl embraced antisemitism as the key to a larger program of political and social reform. These politicians founded new parties that reached the height of their appeal to the electorate in 1893, when they garnered, of the available 7 million votes, one-quarter of a million.

In Austria, antisemitism served Georg von Schoenerer as a means to move from an initial liberalism to a pan-Germanism, which in the Linz Program, his 1885 political platform, asserted that "the removal of Jewish influence from all sections of public life is indispensable for carrying out reforms." In 1897 Karl Lueger became mayor of Vienna, the highest elected office in the Austro-Hungarian Empire, on an antisemitic platform that mobilized new sections of the populace beyond those who embraced liberalism. Once he was in office, his opportunistic antisemitism translated into a municipal socialism that aimed to extend the benefits of urban life (utilities, trams, labor exchanges, saving banks) to the laboring classes. Lueger was a master orator, and the young Adolf Hitler, who came of age in Lueger's Vienna, learned much from him.

France witnessed stirrings of antisemitism in the 1880s and 1890s. Edouard Drumont's scathing attack on the "Jewish conspiracy," *La France Juive,* became a best-seller in 1886; and in 1890 the Merchants' Antisemitic Association was formed in Paris, followed in 1894 by a Students' Anti-Semitic League. The Dreyfus Affair symbolically pitted the "old France" (the army, the Church) against the "new" (the ideas of 1789, the republic). During the affair, there was violence against Jews in some seventy different towns, and in 1898 twenty-two municipal politicians were elected on antisemitic platforms. Dreyfus' eventual exoneration testified to the resilience of the concept of emancipation.

In the decades prior to the First World War, antisemitism became part of European political discourse. The parties and politicians who espoused it were political failures: they won some votes but never enough, or they did not hold office long enough, to limit or abrogate emancipation. Nonetheless, they succeeded in making antisemitism into a kind of cultural code that, inextricably linked to authoritarianism, imperialism, racism and antimodernism, purported to address all the ills of mass society, which is why the social democratic leader August Bebel called antisemitism the "socialism of fools." Nevertheless, this cultural code ominously began to permeate society through social clubs, student fraternities and other organizations, eventually leading to the marginalization of Jews.

The same developments that engendered the new mass politics and antisemitism also reshaped Jewish politics. During the heyday of liberalism in the nineteenth century, Jews participated in local and national politics, defending the particular cause of emancipation but also the larger liberalism on which it depended. In Germany, Johann Jacoby (1805–1877) and Gabriel Riesser (1806–1863), Eduard Lasker (1829–1884) and Ludwig Bamberger (1823–1899) were politicians of national reputation, and many other Jews held office at state and local levels. The rise of antisemitism in the 1880s and 1890s made it difficult for Jews to stand for national office and also propelled Jewish politics in a new direction.

In response to the new political antisemitism in Germany, Jews for the first time organized into a political-interest group. The initial reaction of German Jewish leaders had been either to ignore antisemitism in the hope that it would disappear or to allow non-Jews to offer a defense, which is what occurred with the establishment in 1891, by Christian liberal politicians and notables, of the Association for Defense against Antisemitism. Two developments showed the weakness of this strategy. The antisemitic parties flourished, and there were a number of ritual murder charges in Central Europe. At the same time, the growth of interest groups like the Agrarian League, formed in 1893, introduced new political options.

In 1893 young university-educated activists founded the Central Association of German Citizens of the Jewish Faith. Many of them had encountered antisemitism at the universities. Most of the founders were lawyers, and the organization featured a legal department that used libel suits to take antisemitic politicians to court and put them behind bars. The organization also distributed informational literature to correct the antisemites' allegations. The organization grew steadily: from some 5,000 individual members and 39 corporate members in 1896, it had by 1916 enrolled 40,000 persons and through corporate affiliation a total of some 200,000 members (or two-fifths of German Jewry).

The Central Association represented a liberal solution to the "Jewish question": as an organized interest group, it defended the Jews' place in the larger society as full citizens while affirming their right to maintain their specific identity as Jews. A similar organization, the Austrian-Israelite Union, had been founded in the Austro-Hungarian Empire in 1882.

The chief rival of organized liberalism was Zionism, which became a political movement in 1897 with the convening of the First Zionist Congress at Basel, Switzerland. Zionism was a post-emancipation phenomenon in the sense that it declared emancipation a failure. As the cultural critic and Zionist luminary Max Nordau (1849–1943) noted, "Jewish misery has two forms, the material and the moral." In the Zionist view, Eastern European Jews suffered from poverty and want, while those in Western and Central Europe suffered from spiritual disfigurement or, as Ahad Ha-Am (1856–1927), the Hebrew essayist and theorist of cultural Zionism phrased it, "slavery within freedom." In addition, the Zionists understood antisemitism to be endemic to Jewish life in the Diaspora.

Contrary to the emancipationists' position that Judaism was a religion alone, Zionists asserted the nationhood of the Jews, proposing the Jewish return to the Land of Israel by secular political means. Theodor Herzl (1860–1904), the founder of political Zionism who made precisely such a proposal in his 1896 pamphlet, *The Jews' State*, in particular sought to gain a charter from the European powers and the Ottoman Empire that would give international recognition to the Jews' legal right to a homeland in Palestine. Herzl devoted himself to the quest for a charter, first seeking the backing of the major Jewish philanthropists and then convening the Zionist Congress as a means to strengthen his claims. Zionism was a child of its times: it engaged in the diplomacy of imperialism and was one of many flourishing nationalisms in the Austro-Hungarian Empire at the turn of the twentieth century.

The conflict between liberalism and Zionism was another that sharpened the encounter between natives and newcomers. In Germany, newcomers deprived of citizenship were nonetheless allowed to vote in communal elections because they paid community (*Gemeinde*) taxes. The Eastern European immigrants were often

Zionists who then allied with the Orthodox to try to oust the liberals. Their efforts resulted in a number of bitter battles in which the natives unsuccessfully tried to disenfranchise the immigrants (for example, at Duisburg in 1912).

In England, similar disagreements arose as successful or "alrightnik" immigrants who were elected to the Board of Deputies of British Jews tried to press the Zionist cause against the opposition of the emancipationist Anglo-Jewish elite.

Nonetheless, prior to the First World War, Zionism in Western and Central Europe remained the movement of a minority within a minority. To be sure, Zionism often attracted gifted persons, especially intellectuals like the philosopher Martin Buber (1878–1965), for whom it offered a Jewish version of the neoromantic rebellion against bourgeois life. In Western and Central Europe, it was a movement at the fringes that played a small, if incontrovertibly growing, role in Jewish life.

In Eastern Europe, the mounting discrimination against Jews and such social changes as urbanization and the growth of industry combined to politicize the Jewish masses. The first to organize were the socialists and Zionists.

The Jewish socialist movement, known as the Bund, took shape in 1897. Tsarist Russia was a hotbed of political agitation in the closing decades of the century. The Jews were a particularly receptive audience because of their position vis-à-vis the government and the economy; indeed, the high concentration of literate Jewish artisans employed in small shops in cities like Warsaw and Lodz

Members of the Bund, together with Russian and Polish Social Democrats, honor the victims of a pogrom in Vilna, 1905.

made them an agitator's dream. Agitation began in the 1880s, with intellectuals such as A. S. Liebermann (1844–1880) addressing the Jewish workers in Russian. Gradually this agitation developed from a socialism among the Jews to a Jewish socialism that recognized the distinct position of the Jews in Russia, their claims to minority rights and Yiddish as their language.

When the Bund was founded, it was the earliest and best-organized section of the Russian socialist movement, whose first party was established a year later, in 1898. The Bund was in fact to be a major constituent of the entire movement. It had some 35,000 members in 1903, which was a considerable number, given that it was illegal, like all parties in Russia at the time.

The Bund's attraction for Jews was manifold. It addressed the specific needs of the workers and also offered a solution to the so-called Jewish problem, positing that antisemitism was a product of capitalism that would disappear with the creation of a socialist society. The Bund also began to play a direct role in Jewish life: during the pogroms of 1903–05, for example, the Bund organized self-defense units.

Zionism in Eastern Europe antedated Herzl. The Lovers of Zion was organized in 1884 at the Kattowicz Conference, with the objective of unifying all Zionist bodies. It was primarily a philanthropic organization designed to support colonization in Palestine. Enlisting both secular and religious figures, it had as nominal leader Leon Pinsker (1821–1891), whose famous pamphlet of 1882 was titled *Autoemanzipation (Self-Emancipation)*. While the Lovers of Zion struggled to support a small number of colonists, it did prepare the ground by recruiting youth for the movement.

Starting with the Bilu (a Hebrew acronym meaning "O House of Jacob, Come Let Us Go Forth," Isaiah 2:5), the first modern Zionist pioneering movement, the youthful cadres of Zionism were recruited primarily in Eastern Europe. The Second Aliyah (immigration of the Jews to Israel) of 1905 brought to Palestine many of the leaders of the Yishuv (the Jewish community in Israel) as well as of the future State of Israel, including David Ben-Gurion (1888–1973). These groups injected socialism into Zionism, developing numerous socialist-Zionist parties. In Palestine, they developed the pioneer ideal (*Halutziut*) of Jewish labor creating a Jewish homeland that inspired all forms of Labor Zionism. In the Zionist Congress, proponents encouraged the tendency known as "practical" Zionism, which emphasized piecemeal colonization and reclamation of the land over Herzl's "political" search for a charter. Cultural Zionism, associated with Ahad Ha-Am, which viewed Palestine as a spiritual center that would revive the waning life of the Jews, also emanated from Eastern Europe and had a major impact on the shape of Zionism.

The Jewish Liberals, nationalists desiring both civil emancipation and minority rights, were perhaps more successful at the time than their socialist or Zionist rivals. They organized as a political group as a result of the new freedoms introduced by the Revolution of 1905 and participated fully in Russian parliamentary politics, cooperating with the Russian Liberals (*Kadets*) as well as taking part in the politics of the Jewish community. The restrictions on parliamentary life in the period after the Revolution of 1905 led the Liberals to turn to "organic work"—that is, the restructuring of Jewish education and economic life. The

Liberals were so successful that they set the political agenda for their competitors, especially the Zionists.

Eastern European immigrants to America brought in their baggage the seeds of ideologies that flourished in the soil of the New World. Trade unionism was far more successful in America than in Eastern Europe and consequently served as a model and inspiration for the Bund, so that there was a reciprocal relationship between socialist Europe and America. The immigrants in America also created political parties of the kind that were beginning to appear in Europe (Jewish Socialists, 1887; Jewish Socialist Federation, 1912) but, even more important, fraternal and social organizations that had a clearly articulated cultural program. The Workmen's Circle, established in 1900, at its height had more than 60,000 members in some 400 branches. It sponsored afternoon schools and summer programs that promoted a secular, politically "progressive" Yiddish education, as some of the points of an educational program demonstrate:

> To acquaint [the children] with the life of the worker and of the broad Jewish masses in America and other countries.
>
> To acquaint [the children] with the history of the Jewish people and with episodes in general history of the struggle for freedom. . . .
>
> To develop within [the children] idealism and the striving to perform noble acts, which are necessary for every child of the oppressed class in making his way through life towards a better order.

Zionism, despite the sentiments of many of the immigrants, played a negligible role in America during the great migration. In 1914, for example, the Federation of American Zionists had a membership of approximately 12,000 out of some 2.5 million Jews. All of this would change very quickly with the outbreak of the First World War.

CONCLUSION

The First World War was a watershed in European history, marking the end of the era of liberalism. With the collapse of four empires—the Austro-Hungarian Empire, tsarist Russia, the German Reich and the Ottoman Empire—the map of Europe was redrawn, the forces of mass society that had been held in check during the fin de siècle came into their own and an ominous political order emerged. Yet the war also paradoxically created conditions that seemed to hold great promise for the Jews.

One historian has written that "the war was a calamity for the world at large; for the Jews it was a disaster of stupendous proportions." The war's immediate effect was to devastate numerous Jewish communities. The worst destruction was in Galicia, an area that contained more than 1 million Jews. Russian armies invaded Galicia and were repulsed six times. As a result, there were in excess of 400,000 Jewish refugees, many of whom moved to the interior of the Austro-Hungarian

Empire, especially Vienna, where they were treated as a burden by communities already stretched by wartime shortages of food and medicine.

Russian Jewry in the westernmost parts of the Pale of Settlement also suffered. In the face of defeat, the tsarist government began to expel the Jews as an unreliable population. Some 600,000 were expelled under the worst possible conditions: they were given only a few hours' notice and no provisions were made either for transportation or for the sick, disabled and pregnant. Had the government's plans not been foiled by the rapid advance of the German armies, some 2 million Jews would have been affected.

Just as the war made the United States a key player in European politics, it gave American Jewry a role in European Jewish affairs. Since the United States remained neutral until 1917, American Jewry could aid Jewish refugees in all the belligerent countries. The Joint Distribution Committee of American Funds for the Relief of Jewish War Sufferers was established in 1914 under the leadership of the banker Felix M. Warburg (1871–1937). It brought together Jewish organizations from all points on the political spectrum, and in fact succeeded in raising some $20 million during the war years. The committee cooperated with its European counterparts, such as the Vienna branch of the Alliance Israélite Universelle and the Jewish Committee for the Relief of War Sufferers in Petrograd, in distributing food, medicine and other necessities.

The war also encouraged the creation of an organization for all of American Jewry. Until the war, the German Jewish elite had kept the reins of leadership through the American Jewish Committee (founded in 1906), which was an American equivalent of the Alliance Israélite Universelle: "The Committee . . . was organized to prevent the infraction of the civil and religious rights of the Jews, and to alleviate the consequences of persecution." Eastern European immigrants, who now constituted some eighty percent of the 3 million Jews in America, felt excluded from power and wanted a democratic organization that would welcome their participation. The American Jewish Congress was founded in March 1916. Louis Brandeis (1856–1941), a Supreme Court Justice and Zionist leader, argued that only an American Jewry united in a democratic body would be able to obtain equal rights for their brethren in postwar Europe. The first congress convened in December 1918.

The war's end also promised a new era with the potential to fulfill the dreams of all the competing Jewish political parties and persuasions. The February Revolution of 1917 had brought emancipation to the Jews of Russia. The Provisional Government that came to power in March 1917 abolished on April 2 all restrictions based on religion and national origin, thus sweeping away the Pale of Settlement and all the other discriminatory laws pertaining to the Jews. With the Bolshevik seizure of power in November, the dreams of a socialist society free of discrimination and devoted to the welfare of all its members seemed within reach. Jewish socialists in Russia and throughout the world foresaw with the death of capitalist society the end of antisemitism and the Jews' anomalous position.

The war and its immediate aftermath also resulted in an enduring association in the popular mind of Jews with left-wing revolution. The second figure and fiery orator of the Russian Revolution, as well as the architect of the Red Army, Leon

Trotsky (1879–1940), was of Jewish descent, as were four of the twenty-four members of the Central Committee, including the first president, Jacob Sverdlov (1885–1919), and the president of the Comintern or Third International, Grigori Zinoviev (1883–1936). So, too, were the leaders of the brief revolution in Hungary, Béla Kun (1886–1939), the even briefer revolt of the Spartacus League (the nucleus of the German Communist Party) in Berlin, Rosa Luxemburg (1870–1919), and some of the leading figures of the revolution in Munich, like the playwright and poet Ernst Toller (1893–1939).

The Balfour Declaration of November 2, 1917, provided the Zionist movement with the charter that Herzl had envisioned. The British government made the pronouncement that it "view[ed] with favour the establishment in Palestine of a national home for the Jewish people," because it fitted with immediate war needs as well as Britain's postwar aims of securing a foothold in the Mideast. Whatever the underlying motives, the declaration electrified the Zionist movement because, as the World Zionist Organization London Bureau declared, "what has been a beautiful ideal . . . has now been given the possibility of becoming a reality." Moreover, the Balfour Declaration had teeth, since it coincided with the British conquest of Palestine.

The abdication of Kaiser Wilhelm II in 1918 raised hopes for a true democracy that would include the complete realization of emancipation. In Wilhelmine Germany, Jews had enjoyed full legal emancipation but suffered from discrimination in certain key areas such as the judiciary and the diplomatic and officer corps. The Weimar Republic (1919–33), with a democratic constitution, promised an end to all such administrative discrimination.

The postwar settlement at Versailles also realized the program of national minority rights advocated by Russian Liberals and autonomists, Bundists and Zionists. The Fourteen Points, promulgated by the American president Woodrow Wilson, recognized the twin rights of national self-determination and democracy, but in Eastern and East Central Europe these were difficult to achieve because of the significant minority populations, including Jews, who were spread throughout the area. The American Jewish Congress was founded to promote emancipation and especially national minority rights in Central and Eastern Europe, as well as to secure and protect Jewish rights in Palestine. Its delegation led the way, in cooperation with delegations from the affected areas and from the other victorious powers, France and England, in pressing the case at Versailles. They were successful, and the treaty establishing an independent Poland included guarantees of national minority rights for the non-Polish minorities who constituted one-third of the country. That treaty became a model for similar guarantees by other countries, including Greece, Czechoslovakia, Romania and Yugoslavia.

Postwar events of course disappointed the wartime expectations. The British gained the Mandate over Palestine from the League of Nations on the strength of the Balfour Declaration, but then found it increasingly convenient to repudiate the declaration's intent in the face of rising Arab opposition to increased Jewish immigration. The Weimar Republic did offer Jews the full participation they had been denied during the Reich, but the republic's growing political and economic difficulties overshadowed those gains. And Poland demonstrated that the national minority rights guaranteed in a treaty were a dead letter if the government had no intention of honoring them. Nowhere was the discrepancy between expectations and reality greater than in the Soviet Union.

Whatever benefits the Soviet Union offered individual Jews, they came at the expense of collective Jewish life and Judaism. With the disappearance of the Pale's boundaries and the transformation of the economy, the Jews experienced rapid urbanization and occupational shifts. They moved into the interior of Russia, which had been closed to them throughout the tsarist period, in large numbers, so that by 1939 Moscow, for example, contained some 400,000 Jews, making it the largest concentration in a single European city. Jews also moved into civil service and professional positions in large numbers because the universities were now open to them. In addition, Jewish workers shifted from commerce and artisanry into industrial work. By 1935 there may have been as many as 1.1 million Jewish industrial workers. Jews were also prominent in Soviet culture, including such figures as the writers Isaac Babel (1894–1941?) and Boris Pasternak (1890–1960) and the filmmaker Sergei Eisenstein (1898–1948).

Sovietization increasingly entailed the destruction of national minority and religious culture. In the 1920s the Bolsheviks attempted to gain control of society by dismantling all competing institutions. "Jewish Sections" (*Yevsektstia*) were formed, and competing political parties outlawed (Zionism in 1922) or coopted (the Bund in 1921). Jewish life briefly flowered in the 1920s, when culture was conceived as being "socialist in content, national in form." Yiddish publishing and schools flourished, and Yiddish was used in the courts and in Soviets where Jews constituted over fifty percent of the population. When Joseph Stalin consolidated power and turned against the "right deviation" of nationalism after 1928, these institutions came under attack and were slowly if inexorably dissolved. The Jewish leaders of the revolution and during the early Soviet period were murdered almost to a man in the great purges of 1936 to 1938. By 1939 Jewish life in all forms had essentially been forced underground.

The period from 1648 to 1918, then, saw the integration of the Jews into the modern world, an integration that brought to fruition myriad ideologies and ways of being a Jew, many of which continue to shape Jewish life today.

6

The Darkest Hour

Michael R. Marrus

With the benefit of hindsight, we can see the thirty years from 1918 to 1948 as fatefully dominated for the Jewish people by two powerful political movements, one external and one internal: antisemitism and Zionism.

As we saw in the previous chapter, both these movements, though they have roots extending back into the ancient world, emerged in the light of day in concrete and explicit form toward the close of the nineteenth century. Different though they are from one another, both represent a reaction against integrating the Jewish minorities into the surrounding society. For the antisemites, the Jews represented an alien and indeed nightmarishly menacing presence within Europe. For the Zionists, who were reacting in part against the threat of antisemitism, the only hope of survival for the Jewish people lay in a return to the ancient homeland and the resumption of national autonomy.

The upheavals caused by the First World War and its aftermath provided a boost to both movements. The next two chapters trace the momentous and highly charged events that followed. The stories they tell are dramatically different, though they cover a similar timespan and there are significant points of contact between them. Their geographical focus is different too. We begin with the struggle of the Jews in Europe for their very existence.

Opposite: Charred prayer books, from a synagogue burned during the *Kristallnacht* pogrom, November 9, 1938.

Europe on the Eve of World War II, with some reference points for the Holocaust

Political boundaries as of 1936

S. DANIEL / STARSHELL MAPS, 1997

"Hitler and his cronies have already enslaved more than a fifth of the human race," David Ben-Gurion told a British Labour Party convention in October 1942. "More than a third of the Jewish people are in Nazi concentration camps, tens of thousands are put to death in the darkness of forests, on the roads, and in closed vans, and the rest are abandoned to starvation, plagues, disease, forced labor, and the desecration of their humanity and their Judaism." Filled with grief and foreboding, and with access to the flood of information that reached the western media in the summer and autumn of 1942 about the massacre of European Jewry, the leader of Palestinian Jewry still could not fully comprehend what we now refer to as the Holocaust. Uncertain about reports of the death camps, gas chambers, Europe-wide deportations and systematic mass murder, Ben-Gurion described "concentration camps," and put the Jewish catastrophe in the context of enslavement rather than systematic mass killing. Vaguely sensing that this was a Jewish calamity of biblical proportions, the Zionist veteran nevertheless spoke of millions of Jews who would be left in Europe *after* the war was over. Like so many others, some friends of the Jews, some their enemies and some simply indifferent or unconcerned, Ben-Gurion found it hard to contemplate the unprecedented, bitter, astounding truth. And even when comprehended, it was extraordinarily difficult to articulate. This was indeed the darkest hour in the modern history of the Jews, and one of the greatest trials faced by any people, at any time. Jews pondered then, and ponder still, how it happened, and what it meant to them.

DEFINING A "JEWISH PROBLEM"

The historian George Mosse, himself a refugee from Nazism, is fond of asking how people would respond to the following question: "If you were deposited in the Europe of the 1890s, and knew nothing of its subsequent history, but were nevertheless told that one country would slaughter Jews on an unheard-of scale, which would you suppose it to be?" Knowing the Europe of the day—the racist antisemitism and antisemitic riots of the Dreyfus Affair come immediately to mind—most people would choose France, he argued. Another candidate, I would add, would be tsarist Russia, site of dreadful pogroms—organized, popular massacres of Jews, sanctioned by the authorities—beginning in the early 1880s. The point is that, looking forward, whatever one may say of the state of its anti-Jewish culture or rhetoric, Germany would probably not have seemed headed for a murderous, continent-wide assault on Jews. Certainly German Jews at the time would not have thought so. How, then, did a "Jewish problem" come to be identified in Germany, and how did it develop such terrible consequences?

Opposition to Jews spread during the last quarter of the nineteenth century in Germany with particular intensity, some would argue, following the period of economic downturn, slowed growth and periodic stagnation beginning in 1873 and lasting until 1896—sometimes referred to as the "Great Depression" of the nineteenth century. During this era of dislocation and rapid change, anti-Jewish

Antisemitic propaganda: the world Jewish conspiracy.

rhetoric became part of the public discourse in Imperial Germany, with politicians and intellectuals stigmatizing Jews as the source of whatever they found wrong in German society. Many Germans feared and resisted the rapid and wide-ranging transformation associated with the emergence of a modern, industrial society: typically, in this scenario, the decline of handicrafts, the weakening hold of religion, rapid urbanization, democratization, the erosion of traditional culture and many other perceived ills of modernity were blamed on the people who seemingly were its outstanding beneficiaries—the Jews. As the famous German historian Heinrich von Treitschke observed in 1879, "The instinct of the masses has . . . clearly recognized a great danger, a serious sore spot of the new German national life; the current word 'the German Jewish question' is more than an empty phrase."

By the end of the nineteenth century, dislike of Jews was a widely shared sentiment, surfacing periodically in government, national and local associations, the civil service, educational and cultural institutions. Anti-Jewish opinions were particularly strong on the Right, in circles championing militant nationalism, imperial expansion, racism, anti-socialism, militarism, and calling for a strong, authoritarian government. Yet at the same time, as so many German Jews appreciated, and as Jews from other countries understood, the outlook for Jews in Germany was not entirely bleak. Not everyone espoused the anti-Jewish cause. Many Germans had no idea what they thought about Jews, and could not have cared less about them. Others, notably liberals and social democrats, resisted the calls to limit Jewish rights or exclude Jews from civil society. Germany was, after all, a *Rechtsstaat*, a law-abiding society, in which civilized standards prevailed. So thought many East European Jews, for example, when their villages were occupied by the German troops during the First World War; and so many German Jews insisted, when they proclaimed their Jewishness fully compatible with their feeling for their German homeland. Some went even further, believing in a special German Jewish symbiosis. "We German Jews are in a particularly favorable position," wrote the great Kantian philosopher of Marburg, Hermann Cohen (1842–1918), "since we were able to influence the rest of world Jewry in the spirit of our German culture . . . and our religious reforms. Our own intellectuals have expressed the synthesis of Jewish messianism and German humanism, and we are trying to impart these values to our brethren outside Germany."

Hermann Cohen expressed these views in 1915, in the midst of a dreadful war in which Jews patriotically supported the national cause. But as with practically everything else, the First World War made matters worse. Antisemitism found a new degree of legitimacy in many quarters, in Germany as in many other countries. In the coarse, brutalized public rhetoric of the day, there was more than a hint of the impact of the Great War, with its terrible loss of life, its new thresholds of destruction and its seeming lesson of the futility of liberal politics. Postwar

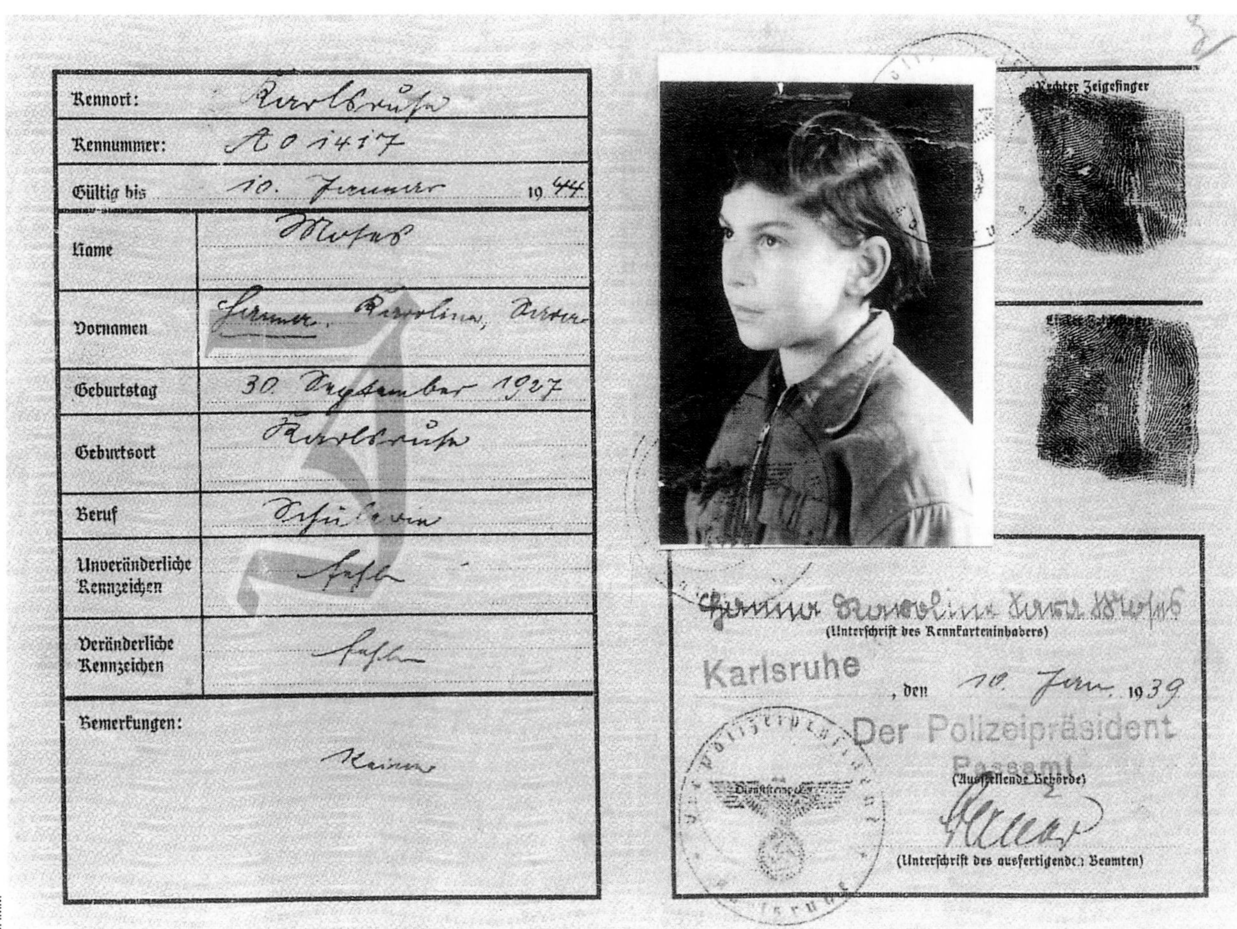

Kennort: Karlsruhe

Kennummer: A 01417

Gültig bis 10. Januar 1944

Name

Vornamen

Geburtstag 30. Dezember 1927

Geburtsort Karlsruhe

Beruf Schülerin

Unveränderliche Kennzeichen fehlen

Veränderliche Kennzeichen fehlen

Bemerkungen: Keine

Rechter Zeigefinger

Linker Zeigefinger

(Unterschrift des Kennkarteninhabers)

Karlsruhe, den 10. Jan. 1939

Der Polizeipräsident Passamt

(Ausstellende Behörde)

(Unterschrift des ausfertigenden Beamten)

USHMM

Identity card of an eleven-year-old German child stamped with the letter J for Jude (Jew).

TATE GALLERY, LONDON/ART RESOURCE

Kristallnacht, by Mordecai Ardon (1959). On the night of November 9–10, 1938, hundreds of synagogues in Germany were destroyed, and Jewish scrolls and books were burned. Hardly a finger was raised to help the victims. This was a key moment in the early stages of the Nazi war against the Jews (see page 259). The painter, Ardon (1896–1992), studied at the Bauhaus, and left Germany in 1933 for Palestine. This is part of a larger composition titled *Missa Dura: The Knight, Kristallnacht, House No. 5.*

KULTURGESCHICHTLICHES MUSEUM, OSNABRUCK

Self-Portrait with Jewish Identity Card, by Felix Nussbaum (1904–1944?). Nussbaum, who had embarked on a successful career as an artist in Berlin, fled Germany in 1933 and lived in Belgium. After the German invasion of Belgium, he was interned in camps in southern France. He escaped and went into hiding in Belgium, but in 1943 he and his wife were recaptured and sent to Auschwitz, where they are believed to have died in 1944.

USHMM

Untitled portrait by Gert H. Wollheim (1894–1974). Born near Dresden, Wollheim studied in Weimar before serving in the German army in the First World War. In 1933, when the Nazis were elected to government, he fled to Paris, and during the German occupation he was interned in various camps and eventually went into hiding. After the war, he immigrated to the United States. This drawing is one of a number made in the camp of Gurs in the Pyrenees (where Nussbaum, too, was briefly interned).

WILLIAM L. GROSS COLLECTION/RAMAT AVIV

Theodor Herzl, the founder of political Zionism, surrounded by stylized scenes of labor on the land (color lithograph, Vienna, 1925). Romantic Zionist iconography of this kind has a history going back to the beginning of the movement. Herzl, who was only forty-four years old when he died in 1904, became a kind of patron saint, whose image appeared in a wide range of contexts.

Opposite: Jaffa Orange Groves, by Nahum Gutman (1926). Like Rubin, Gutman (1898–1980) was a student at the Bezalel School in 1912, and like him he spent some years in Europe before returning to Palestine in 1926. Gutman, unlike Rubin, had lived his childhood years under the fierce Middle Eastern sun, and he had a close relationship with the landscape of the Land of Israel, which enchanted him. *Jaffa Orange Groves* invokes a number of contrasts, both visual and conceptual, such as that between the traditional Arab figures and the progress represented by the railway train in the background.

COLLECTION AYALA ZACKS ABRAMOU, JERUSALEM/ISRAEL MUSEUM

Left: The Beginnings of Tel Aviv, by Reuven Rubin (1912). Born in Romania, Reuven Rubin (1893–1974) was accepted in 1912 by the newly founded Bezalel School of Arts and Crafts in Jerusalem. He stayed for only a year before leaving for Paris, but he returned to Palestine in 1922 and eventually became one of Israel's best-known painters. *The Beginnings of Tel Aviv* captures the infancy of the new Jewish city on the sand dunes, a stone's throw from the ancient Arab city of Jaffa but resolutely seeking a character and personality of its own.

ISRAEL MUSEUM

THE HEBREW UNIVERSITY OF JERUSALEM

The Opening of the Hebrew University, by Leopold Pilichowski. Lord Balfour is speaking, and seated behind him on the rostrum are the Sephardi and Ashkenazi chief rabbis of Palestine, General Allenby, the high commissioner Sir Herbert Samuel, Dr. Chaim Weizmann, and the chief rabbi of the British Empire, Dr. Joseph Hertz. (The artist himself can be seen in the foreground.) The inauguration of the university on April 1, 1925, was a big step forward for Hebrew culture in the Land of Israel.

Germany in particular was a deeply troubled society. Much of the population failed to come to terms with the catastrophic defeat the country had suffered at the hands of the western Allies. From its inception, the democratic regime established at Weimar was besieged, attacked by nationalist and communist extremists, and with indifferent support in major national institutions such as the army and civil service. Demobilized soldiers, many of them scarred psychologically by the war, adrift in a society for which they had sacrificed prodigiously, and which they felt had betrayed them, hungered for scapegoats. Jews, over half a million strong and about one percent of the total population, were increasingly singled out.

Still, Germany was by no means the most dangerous place for Jews. Throughout East Central Europe, much larger numbers of Jews also faced hostile populations, unchecked by parliaments, the rule of law or liberal traditions. In Poland, Hungary and Romania, where liberal and democratic restraints on antisemitism appeared much weaker than in Germany and Western European countries, the Jews were marginalized and sometimes attacked, particularly in times of economic hardship. With the advent of international economic crisis at the beginning of the 1930s, antipathies rose to the surface, and violence and persecution appeared to be real possibilities. The Zionist Revisionist leader Vladimir (Zeev) Jabotinsky (1880–1940), sometimes credited with remarkable prescience regarding the coming catastrophe, felt that East European troubles would soon overwhelm the difficulties Jews faced in Germany, even under Hitler.

Liberal democracy, to which so many Jews felt they owed both their emancipation and their astonishing success in Western societies, came under increasing attack as economic depression spread worldwide in the early 1930s. Some, though by no means all, of its challengers included hatred of the Jews in their political inventories. Antisemitism rose dramatically in the decade before the outbreak of the Second World War—everywhere there were Jews, and even in some places where there were hardly any at all. In Poland, anti-Jewish forces surged following the death of the authoritarian marshal Jozef Pilsudski in 1935. In France, anti-Jewish opinion rose to a fever pitch in 1936, with the election of the Popular Front government, headed by the socialist and Jewish prime minister Léon Blum (1872–1950). Even in North America, this was a time of unprecedented, publicly expressed anti-Jewish feeling. But most strikingly it was in Germany, with the accession to power of Adolf Hitler and his Nazi Party in January 1933, that antisemitism was legitimized and became a government priority.

Nazi antisemitism was inseparable from Hitler, who, as the Führer of the National Socialist German Workers' Party, demanded unquestioning loyalty to himself and to his worldview. Although the Führer was utterly obsessed by Jews, returning to them constantly in his hate-filled public rhetoric and in his private ruminations, his antisemitism was conventional and unoriginal. In a crude perversion of the Darwinian worldview, Hitler saw the world as an arena in which peoples forever engaged in ruthless competition with one another. And in this contest, he believed the Jews to be at the very center of the historical process; they were the great enemies of Germany—ubiquitous, powerful agents of decomposition, disease and demoralization, working to undermine German and other societies, wherever they were to be found. Returning again and again to the Jews, he most commonly referred to them using expressions of parasitology. Eberhard Jäckel, editor of Hitler's writings, sums up the Führer's references to Jews in his autobiographical *Mein Kampf*: "The Jew is a maggot in a rotting corpse; he is a plague worse than the Black Death of former times; a germ carrier of the worst sort; mankind's eternal germ of disunion; the drone which insinuates its way into the rest of mankind; the spider that slowly sucks the people's blood out of its pores; the pack of rats fighting bloodily among themselves; the parasite in the body of other peoples; the typical parasite; a sponger who, like a harmful bacillus, continues to spread; the eternal bloodsucker; the people's parasite; the people's vampire."

This yellow star was imposed on Jews in France in the spring of 1942.

From the start, Hitler was the driving force of antisemitism within the Nazi movement, constantly pressing his hatreds on his followers and the wider public. Hitler stood out in this sphere, as in so many others, for his ruthlessness, his fanaticism, and his unrivaled capacity to energize his German following with his hate-filled obsessions. Even if his ideas were conventional, his impact was extraordinary. Indeed, part of Hitler's genius was his capacity to activate widely held perceptions, to whip up crowds to flights of enthusiasm and to present himself credibly as the vehicle for the resolution of broadly perceived national problems. Something, he proclaimed insistently, would have to be done about the Jews.

Did the rise of Hitler and the Nazis signify from the very beginning the mass murder that they launched during the course of the war? Nazi rhetoric during the so-called *Kampfzeit*, the decade or so of ceaseless campaigning for support and power in Germany, fairly reeked of antisemitism and incitement to take drastic action against the Jews. Yet despite their sometimes bloodcurdling speechifying, the Nazis failed to define any concrete program or course of action. Were the Jews to be expelled? Imprisoned? Removed from economic life? Or merely face restrictions in daily life? Articles and speeches can be found to support all of these. The Jews, Hitler raged, had to be removed, pitilessly isolated, annihilated, subjected to "the most severe methods of fighting." In all probability, he was not sure of the course to follow, and in this sphere, as in foreign policy, to mention a similar case, his exhortations indicated a general direction but hardly constituted a detailed blueprint for action. What is plain enough is that Hitler set the course, and that he was determined to act.

In power from January 30, 1933, the Nazis proceeded cautiously at first, fearful of upsetting some elements of the German establishment by moving too violently, and equally cautious about economic repercussions, both at home and abroad, of too rapid a dispossession of the Jews. What happened, to be sure, was bad enough. In a seemingly uncoordinated fashion, the Nazi leadership promoted a boycott of Jewish businesses, a removal of Jews from the army and civil service and exclusion of Jews from parks, public transportation, theaters, cinemas, swimming pools and resorts. In 1935 the Nuremberg Laws took away the Jews' citizenship and defined the Jews by race—providing the basis for their further marginalization in German society. Individual Jews were humiliated, harassed, beaten, robbed and thrown into concentration camps, originally established to punish opponents of the regime. From 1937 the state moved to confiscate Jewish property. Nazi policy also favored Jewish emigration—to the point that the government even worked out a scheme, known as the *Haavara* ("transfer") Agreement, whereby Berlin facilitated some Jews' departures to Palestine, taking a small portion of their property with them. On the surface, there were signs of restraint: some Nazi persecution during this period had a legal cast, such that many Jews convinced themselves, at various points, that things would only go so far and no further.

Nineteen thirty-eight marked a radicalization—in Jewish policy as well as in other spheres. Benefiting now from economic recovery and having solidified their hold on power in Germany, the Nazis purged many of their conservative followers, and made bold, aggressive moves on the European chessboard. March 1938 saw the *Anschluss*, bringing Austria, and 200,000 Austrian Jews, into the framework of the Reich. September saw the Munich crisis, with first the Sudetenland, and later the Czech part of Czechoslovakia delivered up to a blustering, threatening Hitler. In November, using the pretext of the assassination of a German diplomat in Paris by a distraught young Jewish refugee, the Nazis provoked a riotous outbreak against the Jews, known historically as *Kristallnacht*, the night when synagogues were set on fire and broken glass from the windows of shops owned by Jews littered streets throughout the entire country. Thereafter, the Nazis assigned an even higher priority to Jewish emigration, in effect forcing Jews to

Kristallnacht, November 9, 1938: in one night, hundreds of synagogues all over Germany were burned down, shops and homes were attacked and Jews were killed on the streets by "Aryan" Germans. The success of the pogrom relied on the indifference of the populace and the local authorities. Here, the fire brigade leaves a synagogue to burn, while preventing the blaze from spreading to an adjacent house.

leave. Before *Kristallnacht*, about 150,000 Jews had fled Germany; afterward, another 150,000 were able to emigrate, the principal obstacle being that there were fewer and fewer places that would accept Jews. Put otherwise, between 1933 and 1939, about half of German Jewry and two-thirds of the Austrian Jewish population managed to flee—many of these, however, to be engulfed by Nazism once again as German territory expanded during the war.

On the eve of the Second World War, European Jewry was plainly in crisis. German Jews had become desperate. Against the expectations of many, Hitler and the Nazis had not proved a passing phenomenon; persecution of the Jews in the Reich had not abated but, rather, intensified; moreover, antipathy toward Jews had spread within the democratic countries during the Depression years, further diminishing prospects for asylum. Remembering her childhood in a little village in the Rhineland, the anthropologist Frances Henry recalls that many Jews were literally confined to their homes. "When people did visit each other, the content of their conversation almost always revolved around questions of strategy." The main issues were who was leaving, where were they going and what others might do. Many Jews found themselves stateless, having lost their German nationality through the actions of the Nazi government or because of the absorption of their country into the expanding German Reich. And as stateless persons, Jews had even fewer prospects for refuge than before: without some citizenship, they found that countries that might have accorded temporary asylum refused to do so, for stateless persons could not be easily sent back whence they came. A fifth of German Jewry was more or less dependent on welfare. Because they were unable to take any of their property with them, their prospects for emigration were even more reduced. Moreover, not only German Jews were at issue. Throughout East Central Europe, where the future of Jewish communities numbering several million was at stake, right-wing governments pounded the Jews economically, restricted their rights and threatened them with even more drastic actions. Many from those countries also sought refuge abroad.

Internationally, no relief appeared. The League of Nations proved impotent. The conference of western representatives that met in the agreeable French resort of Evian-les-Bains in July 1938, called at the behest of the American president, Franklin Delano Roosevelt, made a few impractical recommendations and offered no specific havens. Jewish critics pointed out that Evian was *naive* spelled backward. Well-meaning visionaries proposed a variety of resettlement schemes—mentioning Alaska, South American countries and even some exotic options, such as the island of Madagascar or various locations in Africa. None of these were taken seriously by the international community, however, and none proved practicable. For those in flight, Jewish homelessness was underscored as a worldwide issue. One obvious destination was Palestine, where the British Mandate had, since the end of the First World War, involved a commitment to the establishment of a "Jewish National Home." Following the Arab revolt that began in 1936, however, the British were increasingly ill-disposed to accept Jewish immigrants. Britain's Peel Commission of 1937 sought to determine whether Palestine was ready for constitutional change. In their subsequent white paper of May 1939, the British set an annual quota of 10,000 Jews to enter Palestine for the next five years, plus another 25,000 refugees. After that, there would be no more Jews allowed, except with the agreement of the Arabs. (As it turned out, the British accepted even fewer than these.) On the high seas, ships with Jewish refugees pathetically sought refuge somewhere, usually in vain—Havana, New York, Tel Aviv or wherever. Jewish appeals fell on deaf ears. One after another, countries that had accepted Jews now imposed restrictions. "Shall all come in?" asked a headline in the London *Daily Express* in March 1938. In one country after another, the answer was a resounding no. "The world," the Zionist spokesman Chaim Weizmann (1874–1952) had told the Peel Commission, "is divided into places where [the Jews] cannot live and places where they may not enter."

"Today I will once more be a prophet," Hitler menacingly told the Reichstag on January 30, 1939. "If the international Jewish financiers outside Europe should succeed in plunging the nations once more into a world war, then the result will not be the bolshevization of the earth, and thus the victory of Jewry, but the annihilation of the Jewish race in Europe." In retrospect, Hitler's words may seem to refer directly to the Europe-wide annihilation organized in the last three years of the war. Seen from the vantage point of the German conquest of Poland in 1939, however, the Germans' intentions were much less easy to decipher and their objectives for Jews much less clear. The war in the east began with a *Blitzkrieg* attack on September 1, and concluded less than a month later, with the Germans and the Soviets dividing Poland between them. In occupation, the German policymakers undertook the first moves in the achievement of a central goal of Nazism—the construction of the new *Lebensraum*, or living space, in the east. Jewish policy was one of their preoccupations, but fitted within their program for the transformation of newly conquered territory.

Committed to the renewal and "purification" of the German race, the Nazis embarked on a grandiose project of reordering the ethnographic map of Eastern Europe, moved by racist ideology and the urge to subjugate other peoples. Having partitioned Poland with their Soviet allies, they divided their own Polish territory into two: the northern and western parts, including Danzig, West Prussia, Posen and Eastern Upper Silesia, were incorporated into the Reich; the rest, known as the *Generalgouvernement*, was placed under the authority of a German governor, Hans Frank, responsible directly to Hitler. The incorporated territories were to be subject to the most ruthless Germanization, to be purged of any other national presence; the *Generalgouvernement*, for the time being at least, was to become a dumping ground for the unwanted—the place where Jewish and Polish deportees would be dispatched, and that would be exploited ruthlessly for the greater good of the Reich. Polish national culture was to be eradicated; the Polish leadership was to be massacred and dispossessed. At the same time, the Nazis wanted to gather ethnic Germans or *Volksdeutsche* from wherever they were to be found in what had once been Poland and farther east, settling them in the newly conquered territories as the bearers of the new Germanic order. To take charge of this vast process, overseeing the uprooting and resettlement of literally millions of people, Hitler appointed Heinrich Himmler, head of the Schutzstaffel (SS) and master of the huge police apparatus known as the Central Office for Reich Security (Reichssicherheitshauptamt, or RSHA), to head a new agency, the Reich

Commission for the Consolidation of Germandom (Reichskommissariat für die Festigung des deutschen Volkstums, or RKFDV). This vast reordering of peoples, declared Himmler, was "one of the most essential goals to be established in the German East." "We either win over the good blood we can use for ourselves . . . or else we destroy that blood. For us, the end of this war will mean an open road to the East. . . . It means that we shall push the borders of our German race 500 kilometers to the East."

During the months following the German victory in Poland, Nazi Jewish policy fitted within the framework of this wider objective. The Jews were the most detested inhabitants Germans met in the occupied lands, and there is no doubt they wanted to be rid of them. On September 21, 1939, even before the fighting in Poland ended, Himmler's lieutenant, Reinhard Heydrich, head of the RSHA, told officials in the occupied territories to concentrate the Jews from the countryside into the larger cities in preparation for an as-yet-undefined "final aim." Initial plans called for sending a million Jews into Hans Frank's *Generalgouvernement*—600,000 from the incorporated territories and the rest from the Reich, ridding the latter almost entirely of its Jews. Heydrich also called for the establishment of councils of Jewish elders (Jüdische Ältestenräte) in each Jewish community, "to be made fully responsible," as his directive put it, "for the exact and punctual execution of all directives issued or yet to be issued."

Unexpectedly for Berlin, the war continued, since the British and French were unwilling to sue for peace on the Führer's terms. Hitler and Himmler were therefore too preoccupied with war making to put much energy into their objectives for Eastern Europe. Instead, while the attention of the Nazi leadership was riveted on strategic objectives, occupation officials busied themselves with harassing the newly conquered populations, moving Poles and Jews about, crushing independent expressions of Polish nationality and preparing to settle *Volksdeutsche* in their new homes. Without a clear priority, Nazi policy during this period seems confused and sometimes contradictory. At first, the Germans focused on deporting the Jews from the incorporated territories. Then they discovered that it better suited their objectives to remove the Poles first of all, since the latter occupied homesteads that could be turned over to ethnic Germans. In practice, German moves were poorly prepared, poorly organized and poorly coordinated. Officials quarreled with one another. Military and civilian chieftains fought for jurisdiction and set their own policies.

In Poland, occupation officials had speculated about the way to deal with the Jews virtually from the beginning of the war. For nearly two years, the ground kept shifting under Jewish policy because there were other priorities, because officials grossly underestimated the effort needed for vast population transfers, because of the distraction of war and because of uncertainty among decision makers, who lacked a final push from the Führer himself. At the local level, German officials improvised, awaiting the directions on Jewish policy from Berlin. Following Heydrich's direction, they concentrated the Jews, uprooting tens of thousands. Throughout occupied Poland, the German authorities ordered the Jews into ghettos, usually in the poorest and most run-down neighborhoods, where they were packed together and subjected to periodic roundups, forcible labor drafts and occasional massacres. In the Incorporated Territories, officials closed off the ghetto of Lodz in April 1940, forcing 164,000 Jews into a small portion of the city, cut by two major thoroughfares. The huge ghetto of Warsaw, with more than 350,000 people, representing some thirty percent of the city's population, was sealed in mid-November. Terrorizing and harassing the Jewish inhabitants, the Germans robbed the Jews of their remaining valuables and cut food supplies drastically. Local authorities imposed a battery of restrictions on their movements, severed their links with the surrounding society, set curfews and in one case after another sealed the ghettos from the rest of the towns or cities where they were established. After a time no one could leave—except those rounded up for slave labor and, occasionally, the dead. Within the ghettos, overcrowding and the other effects of ghettoization led to starvation and disease. In a severely weakened population, typhus, tuberculosis and dysentery took a heavy toll. Ultimately, at least a half a million Jews who died in the Holocaust perished in this way—without ever having seen a German concentration camp, gas chamber or firing squad.

With the final aim still undefined, local occupation authorities debated what to do with the Jews. Some believed they had sufficient warrant to reduce the Jewish population through the most savage policies—terrorizing and robbing the stunned population, imposing ever-more-impossible demands to hand over the pathetically few remaining valuables. Others, however, wanted to turn the ghettos into workshops for the Reich and for the occupation forces. The latter encouraged the establishment of ghetto workshops, productive enterprises inside and outside the ghetto walls, and the identification of Jewish skilled laborers to serve the German war machine.

In Lodz and then in Warsaw, the military came to set the tone in 1941, heaping new hardships on the Jews in doing so, but nevertheless suggesting to the inhabitants that there was some sense behind their victimization: through work, many Jews came to believe, the ghetto might persist, and most of its inhabitants, as a result, would survive. Some German administrators resisted the dispatch of Jews into major population centers, fearing attendant problems such as the spread of disease and the damage that huge movements of Jews would do to the occupation regime and to economic productivity. The following July, Friedrich Übelhör, in charge of the ghetto of Lodz, urged that the ghetto was too valuable in economic terms to be made to "disappear." Wehrmacht commanders also lamented, on occasion, the killing of Jews who could be more properly engaged in war production. Until the implementation of the Final Solution, such objections on the part of German officials could be heard respectfully.

Distracted by the continuation of the fighting, middle-echelon Nazi officials gave some thought to the goals for the Jews, although the Führer's own thoughts seem to have been elsewhere, and as a result there was no definitive resolution. One possibility, as we have seen, was to dispatch all unwanted Jews to the *Generalgouvernement*. The governor, Hans Frank, however, developing ambitions of his own, objected to his domain being turned into the dumping ground of the Third Reich. Registering his protests in Berlin, Frank had obtained in March 1940 a promise from Hermann Göring, Hitler's chief lieutenant, that deportation convoys of Jews heading his way would be, for a time, suspended.

For a while, during 1939 and 1940, German planners identified a desolate, marshy region in the Lublin district of Poland, not far from the city of Radom and near the town of Nisko, west of the San River, as a colony for Jews, intending, in all likelihood, that the Jews who survived this "colony" would eventually be pushed even farther to the east. Adolf Eichmann, the SS colonel who had helped organize the Jewish departure from Vienna in the wake of *Anschluss*, was put in charge of the deportations for this so-called Nisko Plan. As many as 60,000 Jews may actually have been sent to the Nisko sites—utterly unprepared, and with practically nothing available for them. The results were catastrophic, leading to recrimination within the German apparatus, pitting the SS against the civil administration.

Another more ambitious project concerned the French island of Madagascar, in the Indian Ocean, off the east coast of Africa. Madagascar had been bruited about ever since the 1930s as a possible destination for unwanted Jews, and at various points both the Polish and French governments had entertained this suggestion. The project reemerged in 1940, following the defeat of France. From the standpoint of Berlin, the surrender of France solved most of the problems involved in using the island for this purpose, and the prospective surrender of Great Britain opened up the possibility of using the sea lanes for deportation convoys of Jews. As often happened with the Nazi apparatus, various arms of the state made independent plans for a matter of high ideological importance for the regime. The SS was involved, of course, seeing the settlement of the Jewish question as the kind of racial engineering project that it specialized in; but the Foreign Office also drafted plans, emphasizing the Europe-wide nature of the problem and the thickets of diplomacy that would have to be cut through in order to achieve this objective. In every case, however, the prospect for the Jews in the Madagascar colony, as with the Nisko Plan, was grim. Many, if not most, were to die at one point or another in the establishment of these settlements. Few would survive for long. As in the ghettos of Poland, starvation and disease were key elements in the Final Solution.

TOWARD THE FINAL SOLUTION

Energized, as the Nazis certainly were in the years when they were flushed with success, to think in terms of finality, of a resolution once and for all, German planners used various phrases to address the Jewish "problem" they had identified. The term "Final Solution," or *Endlösung*, may have first appeared in Nazi terminology in June 1940, in the context of the search for a "territorial Final Solution" (*territoriale Endlösung*), such as that contemplated in the Nisko or Madagascar Plans. During 1939 and 1940, Berlin offered little guidance: the clarification and the launching of such a Final Solution would have to await the end of the war. Instructing his SS units during the conquest of Poland, Reinhard Heydrich referred to a "final goal" (*Endziel*) of Jewish policy, which "would require extended periods of time." He also spoke of "planned overall measures," which were to be kept "strictly secret." Comprehensive action was anticipated, it seems evident, but there is no precise indication of what those "measures" might involve beyond the vast population shifts that we have already discussed.

Military success, both against Poland and against western countries in the spring and summer of 1940, brought ever more Jews under Nazi rule. But as long as the fighting continued, the final goal or solution had to be postponed. As a result, tensions over the Jewish question mounted within the German bureaucracy. The Nisko and Madagascar Plans proved unrealizable. In Poland, as we have seen, occupation officials clashed with one another, some proposing to put the Jews to work, and others wanting to extract from them all remaining wealth and let attrition wreak its terrible toll. The army fought with the SS over the issue, with the former often wanting to harness Jews to the war effort, the latter preferring the finish them off. Occupation officials did not always welcome the dispatch of Jews to the newly established ghettos. Hitler himself, according to some reports, was uncertain. "If [I] only knew where one could put several million Jews," the Führer is supposed to have mused to high-ranking Nazis in February 1941. Nazi Jewish policy, he may have felt, was at an impasse, or even worse.

In the end, the breakthrough occurred in the context of Barbarossa, the attack on the Soviet Union that began on June 22, 1941. As with so many other aspects of Nazism, with Barbarossa a new line was crossed. During the spring of 1941, planning directives for the attack indicated killing on a hitherto unprecedented scale. The war against the "Jewish-Bolshevist system," Hitler promised, was to be a *Vernichtungskrieg*, a war of annihilation, on a scale of importance that would cast into the shade all other wars. In March, Field Marshal Wilhelm Keitel passed along an order from Hitler about "the final struggle that will have to be carried out between two opposing political systems." The new campaign involved "special tasks," it was made clear, for Reichsführer SS Heinrich Himmler, whose authority to act behind the battle lines in this respect was to be untrammeled. The murderous nature of these "special tasks" became clear as planning proceeded. Four Einsatzgruppen, motorized units of the SS intended to follow in the wake of the Wehrmacht, were assigned to various regions, from the Baltic in the north to the Black Sea in the south; these units in turn were divided into several Einsatzkommandos, instructed to carry out the slaughter. Addressing (in one of many such speeches given at the time) military units of the SS in Stettin (near Poland's northwestern border), Himmler set the reckoning with the Jews into its ideological context. Barbarossa, he explained, was

> an ideological battle and a struggle of races. Here in this struggle stands National Socialism: an ideology based on the value of our Germanic, Nordic blood. Here stands a world as we have conceived it: beautiful, decent, socially equal, that perhaps, in a few instances, is still burdened by shortcomings, but as a whole, a happy, beautiful world of culture; this is what our Germany is like. On the other side stands a population of 180 million, a mixture of races, whose very names are unpronounceable, and whose physique is such that one can shoot them down without pity and compassion. These animals, that torture and ill-treat every prisoner from our side . . . these people have been welded by the Jews into one religion, one ideology, that is called Bolshevism, with the task: now that we have Russia, half of Asia, a part of Europe, now we will overwhelm Germany and the whole world.

To the Nazis, the war to the death against Bolshevism was part and parcel of a final coming to terms with the Jews.

Murder began with the opening attacks, and within a short time the targets of this orgy of open-air shootings extended from Communist leaders, Jewish men and other undesirables to include entire Jewish communities—men, women and children. During the early weeks of the conflict, Himmler poured SS troops eastward to assist the Einsatzgruppen in their grisly task; in the second half of July, he further reinforced the murder squads by adding auxiliaries from the Baltic countries and the Ukraine and units of Order Police (Ordnungspolizei) to SS command. Wehrmacht units, too, were involved: not only did they provide logistical support for the killing units, but they occasionally perpetrated massacres themselves. In the latter part of the summer, tens of thousands of killers fanned across Soviet territory, slaughtering Jews as they went. For the most part, the killings were carried out by old-fashioned shooting parties: the Jews were herded together and then marched to a place where they were made to dig their own graves and forced to undress. Then they were shot. Occasionally, the murderers used gas vans—vehicles specially rigged so that exhaust fumes entered closed compartments where the victims were asphyxiated—in an effort to carry out the killings more efficiently and to relieve the psychological burden on the killers.

German police shooting Jews in occupied Ukraine, 1942.

Increasingly, and sometimes under the pretext of conducting antipartisan warfare, the killers turned to the Jewish elderly, women and small children. Accounts of these massacres poured into Berlin: Einsatzgruppe A in the north reported the total killed in the Baltic countries and White Russia between July 23 and October 15 as 135,567; Einsatzgruppe B noted 45,467 murdered up to mid-November; and so on. Referring to one of the most infamous slaughters of the Holocaust, Einsatzgruppe C reported that 33,771 Jews from Kiev were "executed" in a ravine called Babi Yar outside the city. "Money, valuables, underwear and clothing were confiscated and placed in part at the disposal of the National Socialist People's Welfare for the use of *Volksdeutsche* and in part given to the city's administrative authorities for the use of the needy population." In all, it has been estimated, the Jewish victims of these mobile killing operations, extending over many months, numbered about 2.2 million.

As German troops pushed eastward, bringing the expected victory tantalizingly close, the Final Solution was put back on track. On July 31, in the flush of success of the *Blitzkrieg* then under way, Hitler's confidant Hermann Göring wrote to Reinhard Heydrich, Himmler's deputy and RSHA chief, who had been put in charge of Jewish emigration at the beginning of 1939. Göring commissioned Heydrich "to carry out all necessary preparations with regard to organizational, substantive, and financial viewpoints for a total solution [*Gesamtlösung*] of the Jewish question in the German sphere of influence in Europe." So far as one can tell, the precise character of this "total solution" was still being resolved. A month later Hitler held back, insisting to Heydrich and to the propaganda minister, Joseph Goebbels, that deportations from the Reich could not begin until the end of the war. Yet something new was in the air. What is particularly significant about the July 31 communication is the scope of the Nazi determination: at issue in Göring's mind, and presumably also Hitler's, were not only the Jews of Germany and the newly conquered territories of the Soviet Union but those in all of German-dominated Europe as well.

What was to be done with the Jews of an entire continent? Sometime in the late summer or early autumn of 1941, it seems likely, Hitler determined to move beyond his vague notions of a solution via attrition, expulsion or a transfer of Jews into Soviet territory, "to the East." Up to that point, official German policy had been to favor emigration; and where they imposed restrictions, the explanation was that priority was being given to the departure of Jews from the Reich itself. Then, on October 23, Himmler issued an order extending to the farthest corners of the Nazi empire: henceforth, there would be no Jewish emigration from anywhere in Nazi-controlled Europe. At the end of the following month, invitations went out to a coordinating conference on Jewish policy, inviting high-ranking Nazi officials associated with Jewish matters to a meeting in a Berlin suburb to plan deportations of Jews from every part of Europe. About this time, work began on the first of the death camps, Belzec and Chelmno, where hundreds of thousands of Jews would die, killed by poison gas.

On January 20, 1942, Reinhard Heydrich called the Wannsee Conference to order. More than a dozen specialists attended, representing the principal state agencies involved with the Jewish question. Adolf Eichmann kept the minutes. To

The construction of the gas chamber and crematorium II at Auschwitz-Birkenau (photo taken by the SS, 1943).

the assembled guests, Heydrich announced that he had been appointed Plenipotentiary for the Preparation of the Final Solution of the European Jewish Question—thereby underscoring not only his own authority but the new Europe-wide scope of the plans that were now discussed. Emigration, he continued, was no longer an approved policy; instead, he mentioned an "evacuation of the Jews to the East." What was to happen then? The minutes were not explicit on this point, but they indicated clearly that something very ominous was in the offing: "even now practical experience is being gathered that is of major significance in view of the coming final solution of the Jewish question." Eleven million Jews were involved—and the record noted not only the Jews of the *Generalgouvernement* (estimated at 2,284,000), pre-1938 Germany (131,800) and other major European centers, but also the Jews of England (330,000), Switzerland (18,000), Ireland (4,000), Finland (2,300) and even Albania (200). A gigantic process of "evacuation" was about to get under way. And although details had still to be worked out, the broad direction was plain enough: the Final Solution was about to begin.

Months passed before the Nazis refined the machinery of destruction, organizing the vast process of identifying Jews, robbing them of their property, rounding them up, clearing the ghettos where some of them had been forced to live, scheduling deportation convoys and dispatching the victims to camps equipped to kill vast numbers and dispose of their remains. During this period, there was still much trial and error as the Germans groped toward the most efficient methods of killing. Unquestionably, the apocalyptic context of the war in the east facilitated the Nazis' ghastly project: Germans were repeatedly admonished that the "war of destruction" then under way was a struggle to the death against barbaric forces, justifying the most cruel and unbridled measures. But the Final Solution also drew on the Nazis' experience with the killing of other persons deemed inferior, the so-called euthanasia program that had been launched at the beginning of the war and expanded significantly since then.

Systematic mass killing as a solution to a Nazi-defined problem began not with the Jews but with little children, those who lived, as many eugenicists understood it, a "life unworthy of life," and who were targeted by Nazi ideology in its fundamental commitment to the purification of the race. Although the Nazis had devoted government attention since 1933 to the problem of the handicapped, prewar public policy focused on various restrictions and even sterilization, determined by specially designated hereditary health courts. Based on eugenics theories, the idea was to improve the quality of the race through selective breeding and the elimination of the unfit. Between 325,000 and 350,000 Germans, it has been calculated, were subjected to forcible sterilization by radiation or surgery in the pursuit of these goals. Killing on a large scale, however, had to await the war. Beginning with handicapped infants and small children under the age of three, the wartime massacres extended to adults, and were organized by a central office located in a confiscated Jewish villa at number 4 Tiergarten Strasse—hence the name of the program, Operation T4, or simply T4. Utilizing six killing centers in Germany and Austria, this program pioneered the use of gas vans, gas chambers and an organizational infrastructure that took charge of everything from identifying and rounding up the victims to burning their corpses afterward. The entire process, as with the Final Solution, was shrouded in secrecy. Word of the killings leaked out, however, and was the object of some protest in 1941, prompting Hitler to issue an order to stop them in August. Murder on a large scale nevertheless continued, within Germany, in the conquered territories of Poland and in Nazi concentration camps, eventually claiming the lives of more than 100,000 victims.

Although many details of the Final Solution still had to be resolved in 1941 and 1942, the Nazi hierarchy was able to draw on the very considerable body of experience with mass murder that had been generated by the "euthanasia" campaign. Deportations, deceptions, as well as the apparatus of mass killing, were all modeled on the previous campaign against "life unworthy of life." During the winter of 1941–42, in preparation for the killing of Jews, teams of T4 specialists visited Poland to contribute their expertise. Indeed, Operation Reinhard, the murder of the Jews of the *Generalgouvernement* in Belzec, Sobibor and Treblinka, was turned over almost entirely to T4 men. Extending from March 1942 to November of the following year, this operation eventually claimed the lives of 1.7 million Jews, mostly in the camps of Belzec, Treblinka and Sobibor. At least ninety veterans of euthanasia killing worked under the authority of SS Obergruppenführer Odilo Globocnik, SS commander in Lublin, and Christian Wirth, a senior alumnus of the T4 program.

THE FINAL SOLUTION SPREADS ACROSS EUROPE

Killing operations throughout Europe did not function as a single well-coordinated process. Rather, murder on a vast scale became part of the rhythm of things from the inception of the Barbarossa campaign, assuming a variety of forms, gradually extending to include various countries and carried out under numerous commands. Unquestionably, the inspiration came from Berlin, and so did the coordination of deportations. But the implementation involved plenty of improvisation, fits and starts, experimentation, and occasional inconsistencies in policy toward the victims. The long run, however, was clear. This was the showdown that had long been promised. "World Jewry will suffer a great catastrophe at the same time as Bolshevism," Goebbels confided to his diary a few weeks after the Wannsee Conference. "The Führer once more expressed his determination to clean up the Jews in Europe pitilessly. There must be no squeamish sentimentalism about it. The Jews have deserved the catastrophe that has now overtaken them. Their destruction will go hand in hand with the destruction of our enemies. We must hasten this process with cold ruthlessness. We shall thereby render an inestimable service to a humanity tormented for thousands of years by the Jews."

On Soviet territory, as we have seen, there was an orgy of killing during the summer and autumn of 1941. That year, the death toll of Jews, hitherto about 100,000 for the entire period from the Nazis' seizure of power until the end of 1940, soared to 1.1 million. Nineteen forty-two was the most ferocious year of the Final Solution—with an estimated 2.7 million Jews murdered, close to half of all of those killed during the Holocaust. (Thereafter, 1.2 million or more were killed from 1943 to the end of the war.) Nineteen forty-two was also the year when "the machinery of destruction," as the dean of Holocaust historians, Raul Hilberg, refers to it, was finally set in place and functioned on a Europe-wide scale. The task was complex and required the cooperation of many different agencies and vast numbers of officials. The main point, however, is that the Nazis found their way through. Occasionally inefficient and sometimes improvising chains of command, stopping and starting, depending sometimes on others, the German leadership taught itself how to kill on a previously unheard of scale. And so the murders continued, to the very end of the war.

On Polish and Soviet territory, the implementation of the Final Solution meant the liquidation of the ghettos established in 1940 and 1941, and the murder of those Jews who had managed to survive to that point. Often referred to as "resettlements," this meant savage operations, beginning with smaller ghettos and moving toward the larger population centers. "Resettlement" itself took time, requiring considerable organization and preparation. In consequence, the process was uneven and involved enlisting substantial numbers of helpers to assist the German forces. Thousands of auxiliaries from Belorussia, the former Baltic states and the Ukraine took part in ghetto clearances and attendant massacres. In Bessarabia and southern Ukraine, the Germans received help from their Romanian allies, who operated in liaison with the southernmost Einsatzgruppe D. Roundups, deportations and shootings proceeded furiously in 1942, but because local conditions sometimes determined the timing, there were cases of communities surviving into 1943 and even 1944, with pathetic remnants remaining alive, often protected for a time because their labor was deemed necessary for the war effort. Whether the Jews were dispatched to camps for killing, as was usually the case in Poland, or shot on the spot, as in much of Soviet territory, these clearances were utterly devastating, leaving only small numbers of survivors.

Throughout Central and East Central Europe, the Germans sought to bring a disparate group of states within the framework of the Final Solution. Satellites and allies of the Reich, these societies each responded differently to the imprecations from Berlin, and the results varied substantially, owing to the degree of independence of the countries in question, their strategic importance and the size of the local Jewish population. Slovakia and Croatia were small, weak and largely subservient puppet states, with a significant local anti-Jewish climate. Hungary and Romania were far more important countries to the Germans, and far more independent as allies of the Third Reich. There, too, antisemitism was an integral part of the local culture. Bulgaria was an exception: on the periphery of the Nazi empire, it kept out of the war against the Soviets, and managed to keep the Germans at arm's length when it came to the Final Solution.

In each case, the indigenous authorities moved against the Jewish population in the early part of the war, defining Jews, passing laws against them, confiscating their property and separating them from the surrounding society. In every case except Bulgaria, local politicians drew on powerful antisemitic forces that had deep roots in the indigenous societies. Both Jozef Tiso, the Slovakian leader, and Ante Pavelic, who headed the government in Croatia, were eager to purge their societies of the Jews. The military leaders of Hungary and Romania, Admiral Miklós Horthy and Marshal Ion Antonescu respectively, similarly set a tone of aggressive antisemitism, which in the cases of those two countries was exported to territories seized in the campaigns of 1941. The Germans encouraged these moves but took no direct part in launching and administering local anti-Jewish programs. In each case, as well, the governments in place faced even more radical antisemitic elements at home, encouraged by Berlin, which demanded even more violent action against the Jews. Vojtek Tuka and the Hlinka Guard played this role in Slovakia, as did the Arrow Cross in Hungary, the Iron Guard in Romania and the Ratnisi in Bulgaria.

Throughout the region, German demands for Jews became insistent in 1942 and 1943. Applying pressure, the Germans used the language of forced labor; by this time, however, horrific reports from Poland suggested a quite different objective—mass murder, on a genocidal scale. Croatia provided the fewest obstacles, with close to a third of the Jewish population already murdered by the end of 1941 in the course of the vicious war fought by the Ustasha regime against Jews, Serbs, Gypsies and others. In Slovakia, the Vatican representative relayed details of systematic extermination to Tiso, a Catholic priest, and may well been responsible for the suspension of deportations in October 1942. In Romania and Bulgaria, while the local authorities continued to punish their own Jewish citizens, they nevertheless resisted German demands to dispatch their nationals to be murdered. Hungary also resisted, despite the strenuous case that Hitler made to the regent, Admiral Horthy, in a personal meeting at Schloss Klessheim, near Salzburg, in April 1943. "The Jewish question is being solved least satisfactorily by the Hungarians, Goebbels noted in his diary on May 8. "The Hungarian state is permeated with Jews, and the Führer did not succeed during his talk with Horthy in convincing the latter of the necessity of more stringent measures. Horthy himself, of course, is badly tangled up with the Jews through his family, and will continue to resist every effort to tackle the Jewish problem aggressively. He gave a number of humanitarian counterarguments which of course don't apply at all to this situation. You just cannot talk humanitarianism when dealing with Jews. Jews must be defeated."

Each of these regimes singled out Jews who were not of the dominant nationality. The Bulgarians yielded up to the Germans the Jews of Macedonia and Thrace, newly acquired territories being subjected to intense Bulgarianization. The Hungarians massacred Jews at Novi Sad (Ujvidék) in former Yugoslavia, at Kamenets-Podolsk, in Ukrainian territory, and elsewhere. The Romanians slaughtered Yiddish-speaking Jews on a spectacular scale in the conquest of Bessarabia, during the Barbarossa attack on the Soviets, and in extensive killings in the Crimea and southern Ukraine as the war spread farther east. Bucharest also established its own killing grounds in Ukrainian territory, in the newly acquired province of Transnistria, between the rivers Bug and Dniester, where the total numbers of victims numbered in the many tens of thousands.

Western Europe, under Nazi occupation since 1940, was also targeted for the Final Solution in 1942. Meeting in Berlin in June, SS Jewish experts from Paris, Brussels and the Hague assembled in Eichmann's office to work out details. Later that summer, after careful preparation, the Germans dispatched freight trains from western transit camps carrying their miserable cargo, usually 1,000 Jews a convoy, to death camps in Poland where almost all of the victims were to be murdered. Continuing intermittently until the advance of the Allied troops in 1944 made the deportations impossible, these convoys carried away nearly 235,000 men, women and children to the gas chambers.

In Western Europe, there were far fewer Jews than in the East, and those targeted for destruction were often more extensively integrated into the surrounding society than was the case in Poland or Russia. Consequently, the task was much more complex, and often required the assistance of collaborationist governments and sympathetic elements among the local population. For two years, most of these Jews had suffered varying degrees of discrimination and the confiscation of property, but unlike their co-religionists in Eastern Europe, they were not subjected to mass uprooting, ghettoization and random slaughter. Although circumstances varied, they survived—fearfully, with great hardship, but often with hope that the worst had passed.

With their manpower resources stretched thin and with their energies focused on the war in the East, the Germans preferred overwhelmingly to leave the task of persecuting and keeping tabs on the Jews to local authorities. And generally speaking, they did not disappoint the occupying forces. Everywhere, too, foreign Jews—refugees from Nazism who had fled Hitler either before the war or in the wake of the *Blitzkrieg* of 1940—were less secure than Jewish citizens of the various Western European countries. Local authorities treated them far worse than the others, as a rule, and the proportion of those deported among them was greater. In Belgium, Norway and the Netherlands, local officials and police took charge of much of the anti-Jewish regulation. In France, the situation was different: following an armistice agreement in June 1940, the Germans occupied only the northern three-fifths of the country and allowed a collaborationist French government, headquartered in Vichy, an important measure of autonomy.

From Vichy, and under the authority of the head of state, Marshal Philippe Pétain, French politicians and bureaucrats initiated a wide-ranging antisemitic program in 1940 and carried it out on their own. Assuming anti-Jewish policy as a French priority, Vichy poured enormous energy into antisemitic legislation. In early 1942, according to the government-appointed head of Vichy's anti-Jewish bureau, measures involved in the confiscation of Jewish property, or "aryanization," involved eighteen different French laws, eighteen implementation directives for metropolitan France, thirteen for Algeria, five for the colonies, plus a number of special decrees—altogether sixty-seven texts, with 397 articles. And this for aryanization alone! Driven by their antisemitic priorities and hoping thereby to win credit with the occupation and ease the Germans out of their control over French affairs, the French government, headed after April 1942 by the wily centrist politician Pierre Laval, played an important role in the deportations as well. In this case, the role of the local police was crucial: without their help, it seems clear, the Germans would not have been able to round up and deport some 76,000 Jews.

There were important exceptions to the general pattern in the case of two countries, Denmark and Italy. In each, thousands of Jews were saved. In the Danish case, it is important to underscore how different were the circumstances of occupation from those of other Western European countries. For more than three years after surrendering in 1940, practically without firing a shot, Denmark was considered by Nazi administrators to be the "model protectorate," suffering only minor inconveniences of occupation in exchange for economic cooperation with the Reich. A German political crackdown on Danish society came in the second half of 1943, in response to a rising tide of resistance everywhere, and the battering received by the Reich at the hands of the Red Army and Allied aerial bombardment. As part of the new wave of repression, the Germans set out to rid Denmark of its small community of 8,000 Jews. In October, just before the scheduled deportation, news of the impending roundup was leaked to Jewish leaders—possibly by a disaffected operative within the German hierarchy. Thereafter, in a remarkable rescue, elements of the Danish resistance and ordinary seafarers spirited the Jews—the entire Jewish population, except for a few hundred people—across a narrow stretch of water to a welcoming haven in Sweden. Due in part to divisions within the German administration, to the Jewish concentration in Copenhagen, to the fact that deportation did not threaten until late in the war and to the opportunity afforded by neighboring Sweden, the Danish rescue is nevertheless one of the few instances during the history of the Holocaust of massive intervention in favor of the Jews.

In the Italian case, a close ally of the Reich utterly failed to achieve the level of anti-Jewish enthusiasm demanded by the Nazis. Although it is true that Italy adopted a rigorous antisemitic program in 1938, a policy engineered by Mussolini as part of his rapprochement with the Reich, antisemitic feeling never profoundly affected Italian society. Persecution of the Jews in Italy, though serious, was qualified by extensive exceptions, widespread indifference to the official anti-Jewish goals of Fascism and an important degree of corruption. With the advent of the war, a serious gulf opened up between the Germans' anti-Jewish priorities and the attitude of the Italians. The Italians' dislike of their German allies, based on Italian distrust of notions of Aryan supremacy and the thinly disguised sense of superiority championed by Nazi racism, plus a widespread war-weariness, discredited German Jewish policy even further. Not only in Italy itself but wherever the Italian forces found themselves as an occupying force in control of Jews—in France, in Croatia, in Greece and even here and there in Soviet territory—Italian soldiers, police and officials mitigated the effects of anti-Jewish regulations and refused to implement the Final Solution. In some cases, the Italians even established havens for Jews—sanctuaries, guarded by *carabinieri*, which Jews in the south of France, for example, desperately sought to reach in order to find refuge from the Vichy police.

The Danish and Italian cases raise interesting questions about Nazi priorities when it came to the Jews. In Denmark, there are indications that the Germans were fully aware of the impending departure of the Jews for Sweden; certainly, they showed no inclination to patrol the open stretch of water used by small vessels to ferry the Jews to Sweden. In the Italian case, although high-ranking Germans remonstrated with Rome on the Jewish issue, Hitler seems to have been unwilling or unable to bring Mussolini to heel on the matter. Perhaps this was due to the Führer's tenacious respect for the Duce, chronologically his senior as the first European Fascist. Possibly the Nazis calculated that there were too few Jews at stake or that they had other priorities to press with the Italians. In any event, thanks to both Denmark and Italy, substantial numbers of Jews were able to escape—only for a time, in the Italian case, for the Fascist protection vanished after the precipitate surrender of the Italians to the Allies in September 1943, the collapse of the Fascist regime and its replacement by the Salò Republic, a puppet state completely under German control.

THE JEWISH ORDEAL

One of the most durable generalizations about the Jewish response to the Nazi onslaught arose, in the first instance, from Jewish wartime polemics: the Jews, it was said by young radicals, trying to goad their co-religionists to revolt against the Nazis in the ghettos of Eastern Europe, went to their deaths "like sheep to the slaughter." This contention has been torn loose from its context of the most desperate circumstances imaginable: communities terrorized by periodic German raids, murdering sometimes at random; entire Jewish populations weakened by hunger, disease, cold and homelessness; and victims sealed off from news of the struggle against Germany and even from detailed information about local condi-

A Jewish family leaving Memel in 1939, when the city was annexed by Germany.

tions. "Sheep to the slaughter," it has been contended, fitted a traditional pattern of Jewish passivity in the face of powerful external forces, or a Jewish preference for manipulative politics that sought to win favors from the powerful by anticipating their demands and complying fully with their orders. This argument, however, is a poor indication of the extraordinary range of Jewish responses, including the most heroic, across more than a decade of persecution, upheaval and mass murder.

German Jews were the first to respond to Nazi persecution, beginning immediately following Hitler's becoming chancellor in January 1933. Overwhelmingly middle class, well assimilated into German society for the most part, these Jews were a highly patriotic, thoroughly integrated and relatively prosperous segment of the national community. As such, they found Nazism a particularly shattering experience, challenging some of the fundamental assumptions on which their life in Germany had rested. Like most liberals in Germany and abroad, many expected that the crisis would soon pass. Certainly there was a degree of self-delusion, based on an understandable reluctance to conclude the worst. "They could not possibly believe," the Berlin lawyer Benno Cohn testified about his co-religionists, "that this cultured German nation, the one which was the most cultured of all the peoples of the world since time immemorial, would resort to such iniquitous things."

To emigrate or not to emigrate? German Jews passionately advanced different viewpoints during the first five years or so under Nazism. Definitely not, said the banker Max Warburg in 1933, determined to defend his family's banking firm "like a fortress," as he later put it. Although Warburg was convinced that Jews were about to undergo a period of suffering, as he later explained, "It was my firm belief that this period would be limited in duration." Emphatically yes, said others who also claimed to have the long view. "What good is it to stay and to wait for the slowly coming ruin?" one émigré remembered the argument that was presented. "Is it not far better to go and to build up a new existence somewhere else in the world, before our strength is crippled by the everlasting strain on our nerves, on our souls? Is not our children's future more important than a fruitless holding out against Nazi cruelties and prejudices?"

From the start, while some decided to flee abroad, they often saw their emigration as temporary. Many traveled to neighboring countries such as France, Belgium or the Netherlands, expecting to return home in a short time, as soon as Hitler was overthrown. In the early years, some championed emigration without any sense of urgency, maintaining that there was plenty of time to leave. After consultation with Max Warburg, a British Zionist group produced a memorandum on emigration in 1935, envisioning departures over a four-year period of Jews aged seventeen to thirty-five, ultimately reducing German Jewry by half. Through the mid-1930s, German Jews debated the direction to be taken in newly energized Jewish vocational training centers. Some saw these ventures as emergency preparation for leaving Germany; others insisted on a long-term restructuring of Jewish life in which vocational training played only one role. And until the end of 1937, a large proportion of German Jewry insisted that there was a long-term future for Jews in Germany.

Not all German Jews were demoralized. Responding to the boycott in April 1933 in a manner that seems utterly unrealistic today, Robert Weltsch (1891–1982), editor of the Zionist *Jüdische Rundschau*, told German Jews to "wear the yellow badge with pride." "The Jewish answer is clear. It is the brief sentence spoken by the prophet Jonah: *Ivri anokhi*, I am a Hebrew. Yes, a Jew. The affirmation of our Jewishness—this is the moral significance of what is happening today." Weltsch's electrifying admonition echoed, as many German Jews answered persecution with a vigorous Jewish self-assertion. Responding to a program organized by the Nazi-approved representative body, the Reichsvertretung der deutschen Juden, German Jews maintained and extended an impressive network of cultural institutions—schools, adult education, vocational training, theater, music and religious institutions. As often in the history of the Holocaust, hope remained alive among the Jews.

Following the *Anschluss* of March 1938, the Munich crisis in September, and then the riots of *Kristallnacht* in November of that year, the Jewish mood shifted radically. With their businesses plundered and their livelihood taken away, many who once hesitated now sought desperately to escape. Jews frantically applied for the documents necessary to leave, to gain access to some country, to pass through others and to find asylum somewhere. Huge queues formed outside diplomatic offices in Vienna, Berlin and other German cities. These quests involved heartrending difficulties and often ended in frustration, as the possibility to enter countries abroad vanished to practically nothing. Those who remained behind sheltered as best they could under the wing of official Jewish organizations, encouraged by the Nazis as a means of controlling the remaining Jews and supervising the liquidation of the Jewish community. This became the task of the Nazi-approved National Union of Jews in Germany, or Reichsvereinigung, organized by the Jews themselves in 1939 as a way of coordinating the remaining communal activities and supervised by the Ministry of the Interior—in practice, the police apparatus of the SS. Even the most optimistic came to see how bleak was the future for Jews in Germany, and how fragile were the support systems that still remained to them.

War brought increased menace and misery, extended to more than 2 million Jews in territories occupied by the Wehrmacht in 1939. During their advance into Poland, Jews had a foretaste of the nightmare to come. Defenseless civilians were mowed down at random. Jews were packed into synagogues, which were locked and set on fire. Everywhere, Jews were rounded up to clear rubble, dig ditches, repair damaged buildings and roads. Thousands were humiliated, degraded and then shot. Then, as with masses of Poles, Jews were assembled with bundles and told to march. For some two years following the German attack on Poland, hundreds of thousands of Jews were uprooted—moved from the countryside to cities, dumped into the *Generalgouvernement*, forced into ghettos—a calamitous process of population upheaval the effects of which were only overshadowed by the Final Solution that came later. These Jews were also periodically massacred, starved, terrorized, degraded, despoiled, ravaged by disease and cold and subjected to innumerable indignities.

The Jews who survived the first onslaught were progressively herded into ghettos, urban prisons calling to mind the residential restrictions of the Middle Ages. An escapee from the Warsaw Ghetto, Toshia Bialer, described the process:

> Try to picture one-third of a large city's population moving through the streets in an endless stream, pushing, wheeling, dragging all their belongings from every part of the city to one small section, crowding one another more and more as they converged. . . . In the ghetto, as some of us had begun to call it, half ironically and in jest, there was appalling chaos. Thousands of people were rushing around at the last minute trying to find a place to stay. Everything was already filled up but still they kept coming and somehow more room was found. The narrow, crooked streets of the most dilapidated section of Warsaw were crowded with pushcarts, their owners going from house to house asking the inevitable question: Have you room? The sidewalks were covered with their belongings. Children wandered, lost and crying, parents ran hither and yon seeking them, their cries drowned in the tremendous hubbub of half a million uprooted people.

More than 160,000 Jews were packed into the ghetto of Lodz, where there were 31,721 apartments, most of them with a single room. Of these, only 725 had running water. No electricity could be used between eight in the evening and six in the morning. The Germans cut food supplies to below starvation levels, encouraging smuggling and black marketeering as a way of draining the Jews' remaining wealth. Starvation and typhus followed quickly. Weakened by hunger and disease, the ghettoized Jews presented a shocking picture to visitors, such as Jan Karski (b. 1914), an emissary from the Polish underground who managed to slip into the Warsaw Ghetto in 1942. "These were still living people, if you could call them such," Karski wrote. "For apart from their skin, eyes, and voice there was nothing human left in these palpitating figures. Everywhere there was hunger, misery, the atrocious stench of decomposing bodies, the pitiful moans of dying children, the desperate cries and gasps of a people struggling for life against all odds."

As elsewhere in dealing with defeated peoples, occupation officials sought to have Jews govern their own communities, assume the burdens of office and assist in carrying out German plans. Sometimes the Germans simply ordered Jews to take charge; sometimes they volunteered. Communities debated the issue of whether Jews had the right to enter into a relationship with the occupation. In Kovno, community leaders pleaded with Elchanan Elkes (1875–1944), a physician and leading Zionist, to become chairman of the German-defined governing body and protect the community as best he could. To an assembly of the community, Rabbi Jacob Schmuckler appealed to Elkes to take up the post: "It has

Jews in the Warsaw Ghetto, photographed by a German soldier in the summer of 1941.

fallen to your part to accept duties of unequaled difficulty, but at the same time it is also a great privilege and a deed of charity, and you do not have the right to escape from it; stand at our head, defend us, you shall be with us and we will all be with you, until we arrive at the great day of salvation." The result, here as elsewhere, was the establishment of a Jewish-led Jewish Council, or Judenrat, an institution shaped to fit different circumstances of occupation and patterns of Jewish population throughout Nazi-occupied Europe.

Germans and their auxiliaries occasionally appeared inside the ghettos—to regulate, to terrorize, to gather forced laborers or exact punishment. But increasingly, Jews found themselves in a palpably Jewish environment—isolated from non-Jewish contacts and progressively sealed off from communication with the rest of the world. A Jewish press was the vehicle for communication, Yiddish was the language of the street and the crowds that snaked through the packed neighborhoods were entirely made up of Jews. In a Jewish idiom, individuals struggled to protect and nurture what life remained to them. Memoirs and diaries report the mood of the ghetto, where emotions extended from resignation, despair, depression, grief, anguish and humiliation, to anger, optimism, defiance, piety and determination. Periodically, the ghettos were swept by rumors, endemic in a world of near isolation, that Göring or Hitler had been assassinated, that an armistice was close, that the Wehrmacht might collapse before the Red Army. Elated by such rumors, the Jews could also be plunged into despair by others. Via underground channels, news reached them about killings, the camps from which no one returned and the fate of the deportees. Even when informed about the Nazis' murderous operations, many Jews refused to accept the bitter truth: some continued to believe, almost until the end, the stories that "resettlement" meant work camps rather than certain death.

Made responsible for a wide array of communal activities—including health, sanitation, food supplies, housing, law and order and culture—the councils spawned bureaucracies, filled with persons whose jobs provided fragile elements of security accorded to those in office. The councils organized Jewish police forces, uniformed with armbands or other signs of authority, and sometimes armed with truncheons. Amid misery and death, ghetto administrations supported a wide array of welfare agencies—soup kitchens, shelters, hospitals, orphanages and old people's homes. And they also ministered to the ghetto's cultural life. In Vilna, there was a Children's and Youth Club, which organized special projects every Sunday, a History Circle, a Literary Circle, theater groups, a symphony orchestra and many other activities. "For April [1942] fourteen events in the theater are being planned," reads one report from the ghetto administration. "Because of the small number of events in March (only Saturdays and Sundays) there was no free performance. In April one free performance is being planned for the Brigadiers Council and one free concert for the Social Welfare."

Many heads of the Jewish Councils sensed, almost from the start, that their role was to salvage what little they could from a catastrophic situation—and that their range of options was very narrow. An example, heading the Judenrat of the huge ghetto of Warsaw, was the engineer Adam Czerniakow (1880–1942), whose agonizing ambivalence about his tasks is known to us because of his remarkable diary, covering almost three years, which survived the war. Ordered to form a ruling council by the Gestapo, Czerniakow took office in October 1939 and remained in place until his suicide in July 1942, when faced with the Germans' demand for deportees from the ghetto. Like so many of his counterparts, Czerniakow spent his time in office interceding with the Germans to obtain concessions, alleviate shortages and postpone or reduce the impact of calamitous regulations. Progressively worn down by his task and by the countless frustrations and humiliations it involved, he recorded his personal reactions—often in pedantic detail. "Today I took 2 headache powders, another pain reliever, and a sedative, but my head is still splitting," Czerniakow wrote less than a week before swallowing cyanide and ending his life. "I am trying not to let the smile leave my face." What pushed him over the edge was the Germans' demand that he help in a massive roundup of Warsaw Jews, including little children, for dispatch to the Treblinka death camp in the summer of 1942.

For Czerniakow in 1942, and for many Judenrat leaders who found themselves in similar circumstances, almost anything had to be tolerated to prevent—or postpone—the liquidation of the ghetto. But ultimately, the Warsaw leader seems to have realized, all of his efforts only served to assist the Germans to do just that. Czerniakow was not alone in ending his life; other heads of Judenräte did so as well. Some were deposed by the Germans, when the latter sensed recalcitrance in carrying out the dreadful deportations of 1942 and after. Still others were engulfed by the very process they had tried to contain and were deported with their fellow Jews, the last remnants of the ghettos they had once ruled.

Some were less prescient. At the other end of the spectrum, some Judenrat leaders convinced themselves of their own omniscience in dealing with the occupation authorities. Adapting to the bizarre circumstances of the Nazis' declared priorities, Chaim Rumkowski (1877–1944) in Lodz and Jacob Gens (1905–1943) in Vilna convinced themselves that they alone could save the Jews in their care. Both concluded that the Germans' goals were ultimately rational, and hence that their respective ghettos could be saved if the Jews worked hard enough, becoming indispensable for Hitler's war machine. Each developed a messianic complex, intoxicated with the idea that he was the sole agent of Jewish salvation for his community. Consumed by the endless process of bargaining with their German overlords, they believed that lives depended on their every move. Both became autocrats, with extraordinary illusions about their own achievements; both inflated their own self-image to megalomaniac proportions, shored up by institutions that glorified their administrations. Rumkowski's picture appeared on ghetto currency and stamps; he traveled about the ghetto in a horse-drawn carriage, and he was widely known as King Chaim. Somewhat less flamboyant, Gens built a powerful administration that served him unconditionally. The justification, both insisted, was that Jews were being saved.

Saved, of course, only for a time. Relentlessly, the Germans asserted their murderous priorities. The Germans had a keen sense of how to manipulate their victims and their leaders, tantalizing them with suggestions of advantage and bullying them into serving their wider objectives. Reducing the ghettos, occupation officials called whenever possible on the Jews themselves to provide contingents of deportees and assemble Jews for their final journeys. This was the final, bitter task of the Judenräte—although the leaders never knew for certain that the Germans had in mind the destruction of the entire ghetto population. Commonly, Jewish Councils publicized the orders for Jews to report at some central location to be transported out of the ghetto. Jewish leaders helped disseminate the fictitious explanation that Jews were being deported to "work camps" or "resettled" to some other location. Jewish police helped preserve order, or round up those who were called.

As the Germans saw it, the Jewish leaders were naturally cringing, obsequious and self-interested. Having bludgeoned the Judenräte into subservience, occupation officials saw in Jewish compliance a confirmation of their fundamental prejudices. For Jews in the ghetto, opinions about Jewish leadership were mixed: some condemned those in charge for their self-interestedness and complicity in the carrying out of the Germans' designs; others sympathized with the leaders and believed they were doing their best. As for the leaders themselves, it is hard to peer into their consciences. Sometimes their words are too terrible to contemplate. In September 1942, Chaim Rumkowski addressed a large assembly in the ghetto of Lodz. He told them of the pressures he faced, ruminated on his options and then announced his horrifying choice:

> I was given an order yesterday evening to deport some 20,000 Jews out of the ghetto. [I was also told that] if I refused, "We shall do it ourselves." The question arose: Should we comply and do it, or should we leave it for others to do? We were not, however, motivated by the thought of how many would be lost, but by the consideration of how many it would be possible to save. We all, myself and my closest associates, have come to the conclusion that despite the horrible responsibility, we have to accept the evil order. I have to perform this bloody operation myself; I simply must cut off limbs to save the body! I have to take away the children, because others will also be taken, God forbid (a terrible outcry from the assembled people followed these words). . . . I did not come to console you today. And I did not come to quiet you down either, but to reveal to you the whole woeful, torturing truth. I came like a robber to rob your dearest ones from your very hearts! With all my might I strove to repeal this evil order. And as it has been impossible to rescind it, I have tried to make it milder. Only yesterday, I ordered the registration of children nine years of age, because I have endeavored to save children of at least this single aged group, from nine to ten. But they did not relent, and I have succeeded only in saving the ten-year-olds.

Lodz was no exception, in the end. As the Red Army drew close in the spring of 1944, deportation convoys emptied the ghetto during the summer. On one of the last trains, on August 30, Rumkowski himself, together with his family, was dispatched to Auschwitz to be murdered.

Quite different was the experience of the Jews in Western and Central Europe, for until their internment in camps or deportation "to the East," as it was said, they often lived in close proximity to their non-Jewish neighbors, sometimes even remaining part of the communities where they had once enjoyed free lives. As in Eastern Europe, there was much diversity of experience. Some Jews were clearly outsiders and found themselves singled out for persecution. Refugees from Hitler, or foreigners who had arrived sometime before the war, they were by far the most vulnerable: speaking the local language poorly or with a heavy accent, they could be easily identified; they generally had few, if any, non-Jewish relatives or associates, and fewer resources to help them to blend into the surrounding society and escape detection. Invariably, these Jews suffered disproportionately: they were the first to be interned, the most victimized during the period of persecution and were rounded up and deported in greater proportions than their native-born counterparts.

As in Eastern Europe, there were Jewish Councils, although in the absence of ghettoization these organizations had far less to do with the government of Jewish communities than their counterparts in Poland or Russia. Their role remains controversial, however. Established by the Germans, or in the case of France by the collaborationist government of Vichy, these organizations became the transmission belts for persecution and control, and may eventually have facilitated the roundup and deportation of the Jews. As in Eastern Europe, Jewish leaders argued about legitimizing and participating in these bodies; and the fact that some were uneasy at the time has fueled criticism of council members ever since. As a rule, the leadership came from a high-minded, well-established and thoroughly acculturated elite, personally courageous if not always politically astute. In Germany, the Reichsvereinigung, established in 1939, worked hard to facilitate Jewish emigration and protect the minimal conditions of life for German Jews, certainly not seen as contrary to Jewish interests at the time. Rabbi Leo Baeck, the president of the Reichsvereinigung, could have spoken for many Judenrat leaders when in 1939 he declared his commitment to remain at his post. "I shall be the last to leave. . . . As long as a minyan exists in Berlin, here is my place . . . until the last Jew is saved."

No doubt some of the Jewish leadership engaged in wishful thinking. Intensely patriotic and deeply conservative, many of these leaders were incapable of making the radical break with past assumptions about the Jews' acceptance in the societies where they found themselves. Raymond-Raoul Lambert, head of the Vichy-organized Union Générale des Israélites de France (UGIF), wrote constantly in his diary, as if to convince himself, that the best policy was to "hold on and hold out." Lambert, who was murdered in Auschwitz in 1943, persistently attempted to pry favors loose from the Vichy establishment whose culture he shared and whose social language he spoke. For him, the participation of the French government and police in the roundup and deportation of the Jews beginning in mid-1942 came as a crushing blow. Yet at the same time, the UGIF, as the Reichsvereinigung and other such bodies, provided a cover for genuinely oppositional activity—some would even say Jewish resistance. France is the classic case, for in that country some of the UGIF agencies, with the knowledge of Lambert himself, secretly worked to hide Jewish children, smuggle people to safety and help those on the run. As the deadly character of the Final Solution revealed itself, this kind of work became more extensive. Unfortunately, by then it was often too late.

East or west, the Germans' plans for the Jews pointed increasingly, in 1942, to a handful of death camps in Poland to which Jews were transported from every corner of Europe, in a process of killing that has become emblematic of the Holocaust. At the time, few of the deportees had any idea what was happening to them. With people of all ages and conditions of health packed into freight cars, these transports were themselves lethal: without food, water or sanitary facilities, stifling in the summer heat, freezing in the winter, shunted off to spur lines to wait as other transports passed through, the trains took several days to reach their destination. Many Jews died en route. At their arrival, usually at night, they faced new horrors: doors flung open, brilliant lights, barking dogs, shouts, beatings and a process the Germans called "selections." Drawing on the fittest of these stunned deportees for slave labor, camp authorities forced entire convoys to pass before an SS doctor, who with a gesture to the right or the left determined who should live, for a time, and who should be killed immediately. Most fell into the second category. As if on an assembly line, the Jews were then moved from station to station, told to undress, to put their clothing together and rush to "showers," which in reality were gas chambers. Only at this point did many of the victims realize that they were about to be murdered.

Varying in size and design, the gas chambers killed masses of Jews in short periods of time, with a methodology constantly adjusted to achieve the most efficient results. Experiments in killing using poison gas occurred in the latter part of 1941—first in Chelmno, in western Poland, not far from Lodz, and also in Auschwitz, near Kattowice, originally a camp for Polish prisoners, later expanded with a subcamp of Birkenau intended for Soviet prisoners of war. Jews of the *Generalgouvernement*, as we have seen, were put to death in Belzec, Sobibor and Treblinka, staffed from the beginning with experienced killers from the "euthanasia" campaign. As often with murder, the greatest technical challenge was disposing of the bodies—a problem the Germans never satisfactorily resolved. At first, corpses were buried in mass graves. Then they were burned in open pits. Jews were enlisted to do the work. Invariably, there were problems: it was too difficult to keep up with the supply of bodies, the stench was too great, open fires an invitation to aerial attack and so forth. At the Auschwitz-Birkenau complex, the killers refined their methods, installing specially designed crematory ovens adjacent to huge gas chambers to constitute massive killing units, four of which were eventually built and put into use in 1943 and 1944. Although subject to frequent malfunction, these refinements turned out to be the apotheosis of the killing system—at Birkenau killing more than 12,000 persons a day and disposing of their bodies as well.

When people entered the camps, their individual suffering overwhelmed their sense of collective identity. Jews of every walk of life, with every kind and degree of Jewish identity, with every possible religious and political commitment and speaking many different languages, were swept into the maelstrom. Those who remained alive, usually for a short time, were as if removed from the historical process. Seemingly by design—that is, in addition to their gratuitous cruelty—the Nazis set out to obliterate every distinguishing feature or quality of their victims—not only their collective identity as Jews, but their individual identities and sense of self. Stripped of practically every element of self-definition—with their heads shaved, their clothing replaced by prison garb, and in the case of Auschwitz

A Jewish girl photographed in Auschwitz.

with a number tattooed on their forearms—the Jews assumed the dehumanized form created by Nazi antisemitic ideology.

It is difficult to imagine this bizarre society of inmates, an essential ingredient of which was a struggle for life that ended so often in failure. A few things are clear. Of all those in Nazi camps—criminals, political prisoners, Slavs, Soviets, Gypsies, Jehovah's Witnesses, homosexuals and others—Jews remained at the very bottom of the system of punishment and degradation. Survival depended on many things, including possibly the way inmates were able to make connections with fellow prisoners. But most of all, survival depended on luck—escaping the eye of an SS guard, negotiating an indoor work assignment, knowing the right language at the right time, having a badly needed skill or whatever. As best they could, Jews struggled against the Nazis' attempt to reduce them to total dependency and passivity, to what were called *Muselmänner* in the camp jargon, taken from an alleged Muslim belief in fatalism. But nothing was a guarantee of survival, as the fate of hundreds of thousands attests. In all, it has been estimated, as many as half of the Jews killed in the Holocaust died in these camps. These include tens of thousands worked to death at slave labor—starved, beaten, frozen, abused and packed together without proper shelter or proper sanitation; desperately diminished and humiliated before they expired; toiling sometimes uselessly and without any reference to skills they might have had.

JEWISH RESISTANCE

Reference to the painful struggle of persons in camps brings us to the wider issue of Jewish resistance, a difficult subject, in part because of problems of definition, and in part because this theme is so closely intertwined with issues of Jewish self-esteem and postwar Jewish identity. A few generalizations apply across the entire field. Most important, as with the general resistance to Nazism, resistance was an affair of minorities, usually very tiny minorities. Resisters of any sort constituted a minuscule proportion of the societies menaced by Nazism during the Second World War, and the Jewish profile simply fits that of other resistance populations—disproportionately young, idealistic and often politically mobilized before the war. Measured in conventional military terms, their impact on the war against Nazism was slight. Among the Jews, resisters were most frequently embedded in civilian communities—full of dependants, living barely at subsistence levels, with the very old and very young, without military training, equipment or supplies, and often with only the most slender links to the outside. As historians of resistance know well, in such conditions even the most determined and seemingly qualified fighters were unable to do much. An obvious case in point is Soviet prisoners of war. Of some 5.7 million captured, about 3.3 million perished, most of them shot, starved, beaten or worked to death—young men of military age and training, hardened by combat and used to a chain of command. These unfortunates were subjected to many of the same horrors as the Jews—and all of this without any significant resistance at all.

Another obvious point is that resistance was multifarious, including not only armed conflict but a broad spectrum of organized opposition, extending from intelligence gathering through smuggling, caregiving under the most dire conditions, encouraging noncompliance with German or other decrees, public assertions of defiance, rescue missions, sabotage and so forth. Jewish circumstances in Europe were so varied that we can find numerous instances of all of these. What really counts, in determining when these should qualify as *Jewish* resistance, is an assessment of the motivation of the Jews in question. Did those who smuggled food into ghettos, painstakingly forged identity documents, published clandestine newspapers or built secret shelters stocked with food intend by their actions to strike a blow at the Nazi apparatus? And did those who did such things, usually at great risk, consider that they were acting in some sense as Jews? If so, it seems reasonable to say that their acts were Jewish resistance.

A third observation is that Jewish resistance, like all others, should be understood as a function of time. Resistance of any sort requires time—time to plan, to organize, to recruit participants, to study the enemy's weak points, to prepare weapons and supplies and to win allies—not to mention time to make mistakes. As any student of resistance appreciates, resisters required time in abundance, so that behind every act of opposition there stood hours, days, weeks or months of patient and often boring but utterly necessary activity. Yet for the Jews, time was often scarce—a result of the way they were singled out, often from the first moment of occupation, for massive terror and victimization. Here is where Jewish resistance seems distinct: cut off as they were in ghettos, or isolated from the surrounding society by a wall of regulation, Jews lacked both the time and means to resist. Practically all of their effort was poured into a daily struggle for existence, finding the means to feed oneself and dependants, working crushing hours of forced labor, scurrying to and fro to meet the demands of the Germans or their helpers.

Under these circumstances, it is not surprising that so much Jewish resistance activity was devoted to sustaining the Jews' precarious physical existence. Despite variations across Europe, the simple effort to stay alive often required extraordinary, ingenious, risk-filled, heroic work. In Warsaw, in defiance of German regulations, Jewish doctors organized a public health service designed to subvert systematically the Nazis' intentions and keep Jews alive. In the forests of Belorussia and Volhynia, thousands of fugitive Jews found refuge in the so-called family camps, clusters of dependants guarded by Jewish partisans. For these, the enemy was not only the Germans and their auxiliaries but also the seasons, hostile populations and rival bands of partisans. In France, Jewish aid workers, mostly women, organized intricate networks to place Jewish children in the care of willing households. This required meticulous planning, diplomacy and often the continuing provision of material aid. In the Netherlands, young Zionist pioneer groups, organized under the aegis of prewar political affiliations, took charge of smuggling Jews to safety across much of occupied Europe to a collection point in Spain.

Jews in each of these circumstances burned with commitment to the struggle against Nazism. To them, resistance meant the assertion of some sort of Jewish political will, addressing fellow Jews, the Germans, the surrounding societies, the Allies or even future generations. Groups of resisters conveyed different messages. Common to them all, however, was a refusal to submit, to allow the Germans to break the Jewish spirit. "Preserve dignity in adversity!" urged the educator Janusz Korczak (c.1875–1942) in an appeal to the Jews of Warsaw on behalf of the children in his care. Emmanuel Ringelblum (1900–1944), another unconventional Warsaw Jewish resister, had the idea of striking out at the Germans by communicating to the outside world. He organized an underground research and intelligence group, which took the code name Oneg Shabbat, or OS, devoted to collecting information about the ordeal of the Warsaw Ghetto. In June 1942, after hearing a BBC radio broadcast on the ordeal of Polish Jewry, Ringelblum considered that he and his comrades had won a great victory over the Nazis. "The O.S. group has fulfilled a great historical mission," he wrote. This involved the smuggling out of Poland of information, partially supplied by Oneg Shabbat, detailing what the Jews had suffered. Oneg Shabbat, he felt, "has alarmed the world to our fate, and perhaps saved hundreds of thousands of Polish Jews from extermination. . . . I do not know who of our group will survive, who will be deemed worthy to work through our collected material. But one thing is clear to all of us. Our toils and tribulations, our devotion and our constant terror, have not been in vain. We have struck the enemy a hard blow. . . . We have revealed his Satanic plan to annihilate Polish Jewry, a plan he wished to complete in silence."

Tragically, Ringelblum's assessment was wrong. Thousands of Polish Jews were not saved as a result of Oneg Shabbat. The enemy was not "struck . . . a hard blow." Oneg Shabbat was not the first to reveal the Nazis' plans to annihilate Polish Jewry, although no one could gainsay their efforts. Smuggled to the West at great costs, their facts were often simply not believed. That theirs was a work of courageous resistance, however, echoing to this day as a challenge to Nazism, seems beyond dispute.

Against tremendous odds, Jews managed on a few occasions to mount an armed resistance to the Nazis, and it is worth looking at some specific instances, not only because of their intrinsic importance but also for the light they cast on the extraordinary difficulties faced by Jews. Across Europe, when resistance organizations pondered an armed assault on the Nazi occupation, they had to weigh the terrible costs involved in massive reprisals and repression. Characteristically, resisters agonized over the right moment to strike, and usually decided to wait until they had the greatest prospect of success—often determined to be on the moment of liberation, just when the Nazi yoke was about to be overthrown through conventional warfare. With Jews, these calculations simply could not apply. Because Jewish communities often faced a massive onslaught virtually from the first moment of occupation, because Jewish resisters lacked the time to plan and prepare, because they were so often cut off from outside, without allies, weapons or support, and finally because their communities were weakened by starvation and disease, the Jews scarcely ever had the luxury to wait for the "right" moment to strike. In the few instances where it actually occurred, therefore, their armed resistance was, as one recent work puts it, "the war of the doomed."

In the most famous case, the revolt of the ghetto of Warsaw in the spring of 1943, about 1,000 insurgents mounted an uprising against the Germans, using painstakingly assembled and crudely manufactured weapons—a veritable United Nations of light firearms, Molotov cocktails and the like. At the time of the uprising, the Jewish population was a mere remnant—about eighty percent of the Jews having died from ghetto conditions or having been carried away to the death camp of Treblinka during the previous summer. As was often the case in Jewish communities, particularly in Eastern Europe, proposals for armed resistance came from militant political activists from a Zionist or Bundist background. These young men and women came from a political culture committed to a drastic alteration of the existing political assumptions. Ideologically sophisticated, used to camaraderie and collective action, they shared a utopian vision—a socialist society in the case of the Bundists, and a Jewish nation in Palestine in the case of the Zionists. Both had a historical view that placed their struggle against the Germans

A group of Jewish partisans from Vilna, photographed at the liberation of the city. Among them is the Hebrew poet Abba Kovner, who later wrote about his experiences fighting in the Rudniki forests.

in the context of Jewish victimization and self-assertion. But because they took ideology so desperately seriously, it was hard for the various groups to work with one another. In Warsaw, it took months for the insurgents to come together in September 1942 under the banner of the Jewish Fighting Organization, headed by the leader of one of the Zionist factions, Mordecai Aneliewicz.

Having reached the point, in the spring of 1943, when activists considered that the end of the ghetto could not be far away, the insurgents decided that they had nothing to lose. Beginning their uprising with an assault on Jewish police, the Warsaw Ghetto fighters took on the Germans in a struggle they realized they could not win and one that was in some sense to speak for history. The point of it all was to demonstrate to the wider world that Jews could fight back. "The dream of my life has risen to become a fact," wrote Aneliewicz in his last letter. "Self-defense in the ghetto will have been a reality. Jewish armed resistance and revenge are facts. I have been a witness to the magnificent, heroic fighting of Jewish men of battle." Battling the well-equipped German fighters commanded by SS Brigadeführer Jürgen Stroop, the insurgents held out for more than a month against armored vehicles, aircraft, flame throwers, machine guns and infantry. Stroop claimed only sixteen of his men were killed. The Jews achieved far more than this, however. The Warsaw Ghetto uprising was the first armed urban revolt against the Nazis anywhere in occupied Europe. It was, as Aneliewicz intended, a signal of Jewish resistance—to the Germans, to Jews elsewhere, inside and outside Nazi-occupied Europe and to future generations, inspiring pride and in some cases emulation.

In a few other ghettos, in Jewish partisan groups that managed to survive in the forests of Lithuania, Belorussia and the Ukraine, Jews clashed with the Germans and their helpers. Almost always the shots fired or bombs exploded were intended, as in Warsaw, to defend the honor of the Jewish people at least as much as to achieve practical results. These were desperate revolts, usually waged without any expectation that the insurgents would live to see the end of the war. Remarkably, in a handful of cases, there were even revolts in the death camps, where the Germans were able to bring crushing force immediately to bear against pitifully armed inmates. Such uprisings occurred in Sobibor and Treblinka in August and October 1943, and Birkenau in October 1944—the result of painstaking planning and preparation by those who understood that they had no chance to survive. There were a few other cases, and in all likelihood others we will never know of, where not only were all the insurgents killed but no record of what they achieved has ever seen the light of day.

REACTIONS

How much was known about what was happening to the Jews of Europe during the Holocaust? Historians, participants and survivors of these events have long debated this question, which is fundamental to any discussion of how individual persons, groups and societies reacted to the Jews' agonies. The basic answer seems to be that although there was considerable information available, what was known and understood varied considerably with time, place and the particular people one has in mind. During the prewar period, persecution was public knowledge—on display daily, discussed in the press and relayed by thousands of witnesses. *Kristallnacht*, for example, was reported immediately and in full detail in the western press, and was widely condemned internationally. And although Hitler's government was certainly concerned with adverse publicity, it made no effort to keep its punishment of the Jews from the public eye.

With the outbreak of war, however, and with the Nazis' quest for a Final Solution, new strictures applied. From the start of the killing, the Nazi leadership cloaked murderous operations in secrecy, fearful of the consequences should information leak out. The Germans' communications on the subject of the Final Solution were studded with euphemisms—the term *Final Solution* itself, of course, but also *Sonderbehandlung* ("special treatment," sometimes abbreviated as SB), *Umsiedlung* (resettlement) and many others. High-ranking Nazis knew that they were not to refer directly to killings. Lower-level perpetrators were literally sworn to secrecy. SS men engaged in the massacres of Operation Reinhard, for example, had to sign a special form "as a person with special duties in the execution of tasks in the evacuation of Jews." In this they agreed not to pass on information, take photographs and so on—even after they had left the service. In a lengthy speech to SS leaders in Posen in October 1943, Himmler mentioned "the evacuation of the Jews, the extermination of the Jewish people" as a weighty matter that one could never speak about publicly. Ordinary Germans, he indicated, had really no idea what such things really involved.

That said, the efforts to hide the killing clearly failed, just as they failed with the killing of the physically handicapped and mentally ill. From the start, news leaked into the public domain, not only in occupied Europe, where it was transmitted both as rumor and increasingly reliable fragments of information, but also in the world outside, relayed by underground organizations, numerous eyewitnesses and escapees, to find its way into the news media of the day. To be sure, no one at the time grasped the broader picture with the clarity that is possible today. In a famous communication to London and Washington in August 1942, Gerhard Riegner, a young lawyer of German Jewish background who represented the World Jewish Congress in Geneva, relayed reports of "a plan to exterminate all Jews from Germany and German controlled areas in Europe." Wrong in particulars, Riegner's telegram revealed with chilling accuracy the essential, Europe-wide program then under way, to murder the Jews. Some months later, in response to Riegner's telegram and to the flood of reports that accumulated in the second half of 1942, the Allied governments simultaneously issued a statement outlining the extermination of European Jews:

> From all the occupied countries Jews are being transported in conditions of appalling horror and brutality to Eastern Europe. In Poland, which has been made the principal Nazi slaughterhouse, the ghettos established by the German invader are being systematically emptied of all Jews except for a few highly skilled workers required for war industries. None of those taken away are ever heard of again. The able-bodied are slowly worked to death in labor camps. The infirm are left to die of exposure and

> starvation or are deliberately massacred in mass executions. The number of victims of these bloody cruelties is reckoned in many hundreds of thousands of entirely innocent men, women and children.

For those who wanted to know, information was certainly available.

The problem, of course, is that not everyone *did* want to know. In Allied countries, many received information skeptically, treating it as unsubstantiated rumor, to be discounted just as rumors of atrocities during the First World War, sometimes colored by wartime propaganda, ought to have been discounted. Some found accounts too horrible to be believed, beyond the scope of anything known or experienced, and quite simply unbelievable. When Jan Karski told the Supreme Court justice Felix Frankfurter (1882–1965) about the ghettos, the death camps and the slaughter in the East, the distinguished American Jewish jurist responded, "I can't believe you." As Frankfurter later explained, "I did not say this young man is lying. I said I cannot believe him. There is a difference."

Inside the Nazi empire, the degree of knowledge varied considerably. In Hitler's immediate entourage, people certainly knew of mass murder on a gigantic scale. "Beginning with Lublin," the propaganda minister Joseph Goebbels wrote in his diary on March 27, 1942, "the Jews under the General Government are now being evacuated eastward. The procedure is pretty barbaric and is not to be described here more definitely. Not much will remain of the Jews." The leaders of German allies—Mussolini, Admiral Horthy of Hungary, Marshal Antonescu of Romania, President Tiso of Slovakia—certainly knew as well, without necessarily having a grasp of details. Collaborators—Marshal Philippe Pétain and Pierre Laval in France, for example, together with their high-ranking associates—knew that deported Jews were going to meet a ghastly end, and knew enough to adopt an anodyne cover story to hide the truth. For masses of ordinary Germans, French, Hungarians and so forth, matters are less clear. Official propaganda persuaded many. It not only presented a more palatable image of the Reich, but it was also more hopeful, more in keeping with people's aversion to personal risks or troubled consciences—or with the Jews' hopes of remaining alive.

Across Europe, Jews held different views. Some certainly knew of mass killing, and some had a sense that this was happening on a Europe-wide scale. Yet there are also indications of deception, or self-deception. Jews living in Soviet territory engulfed by the Germans in 1941 had fewer illusions than those in Poland, who had experienced a gradual escalation of murderous assaults. Jews in the West, of course, had access to warnings about mass murder broadcast by the BBC. But Georges Wellers, a French Jew involved in resistance work, believed he was going to a work camp when he was deported from France to Auschwitz in 1944. Non-Jews knew enough to avoid the subject. Even when reports of the murders were at hand, many understood that talk about Jews could be dangerous. More often than not, people found it easiest to cut themselves off from Jews, to ignore them whenever possible.

Antisemitism also shaped reactions. In Germany, SS operatives reported periodic bursts of popular approval of what people understood was happening to Jews—preexisting "static hatred," as one opponent of the Nazis put it, transformed under some conditions into "dynamic hatred." French prefects told their superiors that the deportation of Jews "to the East" was well received in some quarters. Jews were unpopular, particularly foreign Jews, and the cover story that outsiders were being sent back where they came from had an unquestioned currency. Throughout Eastern Europe, the Germans fanned ancient hatreds and suspicions of Jews. In Poland, a long tradition of antipathy rested on a virtual consensus to the effect that Jews were not Poles and that they were agents of the Soviet Union. Built on half-truths, and fed by anti-Jewish preoccupations within the Catholic Church, Polish antisemitism surfaced regularly as Jews were being carted off by the Germans and slaughtered in camps. "A large proportion of Polish society," Jan Karski reported to the Polish government in exile, appreciated German policy toward the Jews.

Could anything have been done to help? Jewish appeals for aid reached the West from the beginning of the war, and Jews abroad attempted to respond. However, as the example of Frankfurter suggests, Jewish bystanders also failed to grasp the essence of the terrible news. Their unbelief and uncertainty were sometimes compounded by fears for relatives under Nazi occupation and a paralyzing feeling of powerlessness that prompted many either to put the issue out of their minds or to repress its significance. Moreover, in no democratic country did Jews have much impact politically, and nowhere were they able to influence government priorities, except perhaps at the very end of the war. American Jewry, about 4.8 million strong at the beginning of the war, was far from a powerful, cohesive force. Many feared that any effort on behalf of European Jews would simply stir opposition to Jews at home without achieving anything abroad. No real "Jewish lobby" existed before the war in the United States, and Jews found it difficult to mobilize one even as their needs increased dramatically.

Following a well-established pattern of Jewish philanthropy, Jews dispatched financial aid to beleaguered Jewish communities through channels provided by an important U.S.–based charity, the American Jewish Joint Distribution Committee, known as the Joint, which managed to deliver aid, for a time, to Jews in desperate need. Most of these channels became blocked at the end of 1941, when the United States entered the war. Thereafter, the possibilities seemed very few. As information about the Nazi horrors accumulated, American Jews struggled against factional and organizational obstacles to common action. Itself divided, the Zionist movement grew more powerful, and its arguments in favor of a Jewish national home (not always defined) seemed increasingly convincing. There were some achievements in 1944, as we shall see, but Jewish critics felt these were "too little, too late." Practically speaking, however, this may have been all the political situation allowed.

The Jewish community of Palestine, known as the Yishuv, was about half a million strong during the war—to which were added about 50,000 immigrants, mostly refugees, of whom 16,500 came illegally, smuggled into the country in a process known as Aliyah Bet. Overwhelmingly of Ashkenazi origins, these Palestinian Jews were closely linked to their brethren in Europe by family ties, and they followed the terrible events in Europe with great apprehension. Yet even here, as suggested by Ben-Gurion's statement that began this chapter, Jews

No escape: the SS *St. Louis* in Havana harbor, May–June 1939. The ship had left Hamburg carrying nearly 1,000 Jewish refugees, all with valid documents allowing them to land in Cuba. Once it arrived, only a handful were allowed off. The rest were sent back to Europe.

found the appalling truth hard to grasp. Even in the Yishuv, there was reluctance to believe and a slowness to appreciate the magnitude of the destruction. In any event, as a poor and struggling outpost of Jewish life, the Yishuv was hardly in a position to do much for the Jews of occupied Europe. Living precariously until the German commander Erwin Rommel's Afrika Korps was defeated at El-Alamein in Egypt between October 23 and November 4, 1942, Palestinian Jewry had to look to its own defenses against the Germans in the first part of the war. Thereafter, Palestinian Jews attempted to provide what aid they could. Yet in a depressingly familiar pattern of the powerless, these Jews fought among themselves over priorities and rescue possibilities. Like Jews elsewhere, those in Palestine were divided and impotent.

Among other bystanders, indifference remained the most commonly identifiable reaction to the persecution and murder of European Jews. The prewar reluctance to receive Jewish refugees, accentuated during the late 1930s just as the pressure on Jews in Germany and Eastern Europe intensified, continued as the conflict in Europe raged. With the outbreak of war, the flow of refugees slowed to a trickle. Still, more than 71,000 Jews managed to flee the Greater German Reich between September 1939 and the end of 1941. What is striking is how, in addition to the practical difficulties involved in flight—slipping through the net of Nazi regulations and harassment, finding the resources with which to emigrate and obtaining passage on one of the few passenger ships on the high seas—receiving countries imposed formidable obstacles. Neutral countries used for transit, like Spain and Portugal, protected themselves with thickets of exclusionary regulations. Switzerland and Sweden, feeling vulnerable to Germany, particularly in the early part of the war, practically closed their borders. Under Japanese military control, the port of Shanghai received a flood of refugees in the period immediately before the war, but wartime conditions ended the possibility of overseas passage. Meanwhile, the British used warships to prevent Jews from landing on the coast of Palestine. And the United States and other democratic countries raised barriers to Jewish refugees even higher than in the prewar period. In Washington, it is ironic that Franklin Delano Roosevelt was the one who might have made a difference. The president, revered and even idolized by American Jews, had done more than any previous occupant of the White House to bring Jews into the mainstream of government decision making. Yet FDR, knowing that antisemitism remained a powerful presence in the United States, and appreciating the force of indifference among the American public to the fate of the Jews in Europe, acted with characteristic caution. Realizing that responding to Jewish demands meant trouble politically, the president refused to take any political risks to come to their aid and seems to have kept the issue out of his mind.

The shadow of indifference—and sometimes distraction by other concerns—extended across many governments and institutions, and is part of the lugubrious history recorded here. Here are three examples, which in each case shows the importance of particular considerations. First, the Geneva-based International Committee of the Red Cross (ICRC) jealously guarded its neutrality, and on a few extraordinary occasions managed to turn a blind eye to atrocities against Jews in the camp of Terezin and even in Auschwitz itself. Deeply conservative in the definition of its mandate, the ICRC feared that any public appeal would jeopardize its capacity to carry out its statutory tasks. For most of the war, any action on behalf of the Jews seemed likely to be a "mission impossible." Consequently, the ICRC barely tried. In the case of the Vatican, the pope repeatedly disappointed those who appealed to the Holy See explicitly to condemn the murder of European Jewry. As with the Red Cross, the need to preserve neutrality and thereby achieve a higher good was a major preoccupation—something that Pius XII believed in passionately, and defended even against Catholic groups that appealed to him to take a more partisan line on their behalf against the Nazis. In this case, the higher good included protecting Catholics and Catholic interests within the Nazi empire, preventing the spread of Communism and preserving the Catholic Church itself. Third, the Soviets, self-proclaimed enemies of Fascism, rejected the idea of receiving refugees from Hitler, with the exception of a handful of politically useful leaders. Worse, Moscow dispatched hundreds of thousands of Jews to far-flung corners of its empire, taking great care, as a major propaganda theme, not to accentuate the particular suffering of Jews among other Soviet citizens. And there was never any question of Soviet participation in rescue efforts directed at Nazi-held territory, despite the Russians' proximity to the death camps in Poland. Antisemitic traditions, alive and well in the Soviet political culture, played a role in Stalin's callousness and deep suspicion of Jewish motives. To be sure, callousness, suspicion and much worse characterized Soviet policies toward all sorts of groups; attitudes to the Jews, in this case, paralleled responses to any group or nationality understood not to share the goals of the Soviet leadership.

Until mid-1943, the issue of the war remained substantially in doubt. European neutrals feared that German domination of Europe might last indefinitely and attuned their policies toward Jews accordingly. At the same time, Allied powers strained every effort to pursue their war effort, and spurned practically all appeals to divert energies to challenge Nazi genocide. They did agree to issue warnings, however, and from 1942 Allied leaders repeatedly spoke of postwar retribution for wartime atrocities. In November 1943, following a meeting of foreign ministers in Moscow, Stalin, Churchill and Roosevelt released a declaration promising international proceedings to punish war criminals after the defeat of Hitler. Meeting in Bermuda in the spring of 1943, the British and Americans deftly parried appeals to extend possibilities for refuge and assistance to Jews.

Indifference was not the whole story, however. Across Europe, tens of thousands of individual citizens provided substantial help to Jews trying to escape the Final Solution. Often spontaneously, people in every country where Jews lived, in every possible circumstance, including the most dangerous, risked their lives and sometimes those of their families so that Jews might survive. In France, where three-quarters of the Jews escaped deportation, largely interspersed with the general population, virtually every one was aided at one point or another by a non-Jewish person—who gave shelter, supplied food, misled authorities, provided crucial information, guided Jews to safety or whatever. Sometimes help was minor, although that, too, could make the difference between life and death. In the Netherlands, where 105,000 of a Jewish population of 140,000 were carried off, many thousands went underground—or "under water," as the local expression had it. According to Dutch researchers, as many as 25,000 Dutch men and women may have worked to hide Jews at one time or another, and at least 2,000 or 3,000 resistance workers were principally involved in finding hiding places, preparing documents and furnishing supplies to Jews attempting to avoid deportation.

Rescuers everywhere took great risks, but these were consistently greatest in

The altar boy marked with an X is a Polish Jew saved from the Nazis and raised as a Christian.

Eastern Europe, where German repression was the most savage, and also where there was plenty of local antisemitic opinion, often stimulated by the occupation regime. Examples abound. Between 15,000 and 20,000 Jews lived in hiding in the "Aryan" side of Warsaw during the life of the ghetto. "Despite the fact that the Polish public was rife with elements that exposed Jews and turned them in to the Nazis, and gangs of Polish extortionists (*szmalcownicy*) were the bane of Jews in hiding or living under false identities," reports Israel Gutman, both survivor and historian, "it is obvious that the concentration of such a large number of fugitives in a single area could not have been possible without the active involvement of a good number of Poles." In Warsaw, as elsewhere, the most effective rescue operations were those in which powerful resistance agencies engaged individual idealism and goodwill. A case in point is the Warsaw-based Council for Aid to Jews, known as Zegota, spawned in the autumn of 1942 by left-of-center political parties with the support of local representatives of the Polish government in exile, or Delegatura.

THE END OF THE HOLOCAUST

During the last year of the war, both perpetrators and victims sought in a final spasm of effort to realize their plans—in the Nazis' case, to murder as many Jews as possible; in the case of the victims and their supporters, to mount rescue on a hitherto unattempted scale. Each side achieved some measure of success.

In mid-1944 the Germans' murderous program focused on Hungary, where up to that point Jews had lived largely untouched by the massacres that raged all around. The Hungarian authorities counted 825,000 persons as Jews in 1944, including many who were in fact non-Jews and many who came from territory under Romanian control in 1939. All Jews were persecuted by the Hungarian authorities, and many of the men had been drafted into labor battalions in which they had suffered grievously. But as we have seen, the Hungarian leadership, proud and defensive of their sovereignty, resisted giving in to German demands to add the Jews of Hungary to the Final Solution. Then, in March 1944, fearing that the Hungarian government might successfully negotiate a separate peace with the western Allies, the Germans swept across the border to occupy the country. With them came SS Jewish specialists, headed by Adolf Eichmann, determined to make short work of the Jews.

Supported by the German-imposed Hungarian government led by General Döme Sztójay and the Hungarian gendarmerie, Eichmann and his SS organized massive deportations during May, June and the first week of July. More than 437,000 Jews were dispatched to Auschwitz in just over two months in a catastrophic sweep. Then, on July 7, in response to protests from around the world, and fearing the aerial bombardment of Budapest, Horthy ordered the trains to halt. Two months later, the Germans took the final step to eliminate Hungarian independence: they arrested Horthy and set up a pro-Nazi regime headed by Ferenc Szalasi and his Arrow Cross fanatics. For the Jews who had survived to this point, the result was a new round of persecution, robbery and mayhem.

Thousands were killed, and others forced onto the road—this time on foot, to camps in the Reich. In the chaos of those weeks, with the Russians coming closer, Hungarian zealots in power and the Germans deeply divided and pulling in different directions, there were some extraordinary rescue efforts, successfully saving the lives of thousands. The Swedish businessman Raoul Wallenberg (b. 1912), acting with the support of American authorities, bluffed and negotiated on behalf of terrified Jews, using Swedish protective passports. Others also provided help—the International Committee of the Red Cross, the Swiss and Spanish embassies and representatives of the Catholic Church.

Even as Hungarian Jewry was being carried to Auschwitz to be murdered, large-scale rescue possibilities were being pursued—or rejected—in London, Washington and some less likely locations closer to the scene of the crime. Linked specifically to the Hungarian drama, Jewish representatives engaged in complex negotiations with high-ranking German authorities based in Budapest, for nothing less than the suspension of the killing of European Jews. Negotiations of this sort had a history extending back to the late 1930s, when German emissaries, acting with the full approval of Berlin, proposed to facilitate the departure of Jews from the Reich in exchange for various considerations, usually cash payments to Germany—valuable transfers, which would come from Western countries and would be provided by what the Nazis often referred to as "international Jewry," a mythical construct, but which in their minds meant a genuinely powerful force of great wealth and influence.

In 1944 Jewish leaders in Budapest believed that they were resuming discussions first undertaken by Slovakian Jews, headed by a social worker, Gizi Fleischmann (1897–1944), and an Orthodox rabbi, Michael Dow Ber Weismandel (1903–1956). During the last days of 1942, the latter had negotiated for some time with Eichmann's representative in Bratislava, Dieter Wisliceny. For a time the Slovakian deportations were suspended, and some Jews came to believe that these negotiations had been responsible. Now, almost two years later, Wisliceny showed up in Budapest and tempted desperate Jewish representatives with the idea that huge numbers of Jews might be saved. Taking over negotiations himself, Eichmann gave the Jews reason to believe that all the Jews of Hungary might be allowed passage to the West, in exchange for 10,000 trucks and other war materiel. With German permission, this offer was carried to the attention of the Allies by a Jewish emissary, Joel Brand (1907–1964), who flew to Istanbul together with a mysterious comrade, Bandi Grosz, in all likelihood a German operative. Notwithstanding Jewish appeals, however, the British firmly rejected the offer. Most British officials were deeply skeptical of the entire business. But it was none other than the prime minister, Winston Churchill, otherwise highly sympathetic to the Jewish plight, who set the tone of adamant refusal to bargain with the Nazis: "There should . . . in my opinion be no negotiations of any kind on this subject," he wrote to his foreign minister, Anthony Eden, on July 11. "Declarations should be made in public, so that everyone connected with it will be hunted down and put to death."

To the Jews in Budapest, the apparent failure of the Brand mission was devastating. Eager to keep discussions alive, one of the Hungarian Jewish rescue advocates, Rudolf Kastner, pursued various plans for the release of Jews through tortuous discussions—which gathered steam remarkably on the German side as news from the battlefronts became progressively worse. In the last months of the war, a handful of Jews and Germans were carrying on several lines of discussion. Jews who survived have sharply disputed the intentions of the Germans involved, who included Himmler himself and his entourage. Their motivations remain unclear. Were high-ranking Germans seeking a personal alibi? Were the discussions an opening démarche in an effort to make peace with the West? Was the entire process a ruse? Uncertainty remains. There is also some dispute about the Jewish side, with accusations of self-interest and attempts to save friends and relatives, although here opinions may have muted somewhat with the passage of time. The most recent evaluation suggests that although the Jewish negotiators may have lacked sophistication and may have overestimated their capacity to bargain on a grand scale, they negotiated in good faith, with the best interests of their communities at heart. And their achievements—several thousand lives saved—were after all not negligible.

During the last months of the war, appeals of all sorts rained on Washington and London. In early 1944, responding to pressure at home, Roosevelt agreed to the establishment of the War Refugee Board, mandated to evacuate those in danger and find ways of providing relief and assistance. After much hesitation, the British established a Jewish fighting force, drawn from Palestinian Jewish volunteers, which eventually saw action in Italy. The British also agreed to arm and train a few Jewish parachutists—a proposal that ended in disaster with the capture and execution of the Jewish commandos. Both the British and the Americans refused to carry out one idea—bombing the rail approaches to Auschwitz or the camp itself. Pressed on Allied decision makers by some Jewish representatives, the idea was not universally supported by Jews, and was probably not believed to be technically feasible. As it turned out, the results of the proposal would have been largely symbolic, given the limited technical capacity of Allied air power for such a mission, the proven German ability to repair rail lines quickly and the fact that the proposal came too late, in any event, to assist Hungarian Jews.

In the end, what brought the Final Solution to a halt was the pursuit of war by the Allies, and most particularly the advance of the Red Army into the East European killing grounds of the Third Reich. In January 1945, Himmler issued an order to evacuate the camps in Eastern Europe and move the inmates westward, out of territory about to be swallowed by the Soviets. Thereby began the final ordeal of Jews in the Holocaust—death marches, which probably claimed the lives of more than 100,000. The pattern was largely the same: survivors of work and death camps, racked by hunger and disease, clad in rags and without adequate provisions, forced on the roads in long columns, harassed and attacked by German guards. Periodically their numbers were "thinned out" in massacres, sometimes ordered by commanding officers, but sometimes not.

As the end drew near, the Germans redoubled their efforts not only to punish Jews but also to hide traces of the crime—as if murder on this scale could ever be hidden. For many months, crews had labored on the sites of some of the camps—

notably Belzec, Sobibor, Treblinka—returning the sites of mass murder to their pastoral origins. In some cases, the Germans' timing failed: Auschwitz and Majdanek were captured by the Russians practically intact, replete with evidence of the most terrible things done to Jews and others. The Germans also moved the dead, or the almost dead, westward by rail, out of the path of the Russian armies. In this way Jews ended up in camps throughout Germany, transported there shortly before the end, in what was for many the last journey of their lives.

To the very end, the killing continued. Although individual perpetrators broke ranks and some even abandoned the anti-Jewish crusade, the weeks before the collapse were among the most dangerous for Jews who had survived in Nazi captivity to that point. Certainly, in the immediate entourage of the Führer, there was no reprieve. On April 29, the day before committing suicide, Hitler penned a final testament defining his priorities for the new government that was to follow his death: "Above all else," he concluded this document, "uphold the racial laws in all their severity, and mercilessly resist the universal poisoner of all nations, international Jewry."

The events outlined in this chapter cost the lives of between 5 and 6 million Jews—two-thirds of the Jews of Europe and one-third of the Jewish people worldwide. For many survivors, their ordeal continued even after the end of the war. The few hundred thousand survivors in the camps liberated by the Allies, of all nationalities, backgrounds and religions, were stunned and disoriented at the moment of liberation, emaciated and often gravely ill. In the full glare of the world's publicity, the skeletal victims seemed scarcely human. Despite the efforts of the soldiers who first reached them, they died by the tens of thousands even after liberation. Liberators were shocked, outraged and then sometimes disgusted by what they found. At the same time, tens of thousands of Jews emerged from hiding, sometimes uncertain what to do next. In Eastern Europe, conflicts erupted when Jews sought to return to their homes and reclaim their property. What they found was a graveyard of Jewry and a persistence of old antipathies. Poland, where most of the Jews had perished, was in a state of near civil war, with savage hatreds of all sorts coming to the boil. In the town of Kielce, south of Radom, there was a pogrom on July 4, 1946, with Jews being accused of ritual murder: forty-one Jews were killed and another fifty injured. In Western Europe, violence was not the problem, but understanding and restitution certainly were lacking; governments and societies, and even sometimes the established Jewish organizations, seemed reluctant to acknowledge the special victimization that had been the lot of the relatively few Jews who returned home from deportation. In Central Europe, many Jewish survivors remained behind barbed wire, unwilling to return to countries from which they had been deported during the war and unable to go elsewhere. This was an old pattern. Restrictive immigration policies in the West took several years to be undone. Conflict erupted, too, in Palestine, where the British resisted Jewish demands for statehood and the lifting of barriers to Jewish immigration.

The darkest hour of Jewish history underlay all of these events. So, too, did a particular legacy of the Holocaust, the Jews' bitter sense that in a perilous world, they remained a people ultimately alone. "The most extreme agony," wrote the psychologist Bruno Bettelheim, a Jewish survivor of Buchenwald and Dachau, "is to feel that one has been utterly forsaken." Many Jews felt that way, and that feeling endured when the war was finished. Still, the darkest hour was over. Contending with it was another matter.

Survivors.

7

"To Be a Free Nation..."

Derek J. Penslar

"To be a free nation in our own land": these words of the Israeli national anthem, "Hatikvah," encapsulate the Zionist dream.

Of all the different national solutions to the "Jewish problem," it was Zionism alone that succeeded in the long run in capturing the imagination and commitment of sufficient Jews, and significantly placed non-Jews, to be able to achieve its aim. The declaration of independence of the new state of Israel in May 1948 decisively inaugurated a new phase in Jewish history.

Opposite: **David Ben-Gurion reads Israel's Declaration of Independence, May 14, 1948.**

In August of 1897, some 200 Jews gathered in Basel, Switzerland, to attend a congress devoted to the creation of a Jewish homeland in Palestine.* After the end of the congress, its convener, the Viennese journalist and playwright Theodor Herzl, wrote in his diary, "In Basel I created the Jewish State. Were I to say this aloud I would be greeted by universal laughter. But perhaps five years hence, in any case, certainly fifty years hence, everyone will perceive it."

*A note on terminology: The names people choose to describe a place can carry heavy political connotations, especially so in the history of Zionism and the Arab-Israeli conflict. In this section, when I use the term *Palestine*, I mean to describe a geographic region that, since Roman times, has been known to much of the world by that name. I also use the word *Palestine* when discussing the perspective of Palestinians and other Arabs. I employ the terms *Holy Land* and *Land of Israel* when discussing traditional Jewish perceptions of the region. *The Holy Land* is also used with reference to Christian sensibilities. Finally, up to the declaration of Israel's statehood in 1948, Palestine's Jewish community was known in Hebrew as the Yishuv ("settlement"), and I use this term throughout the text.

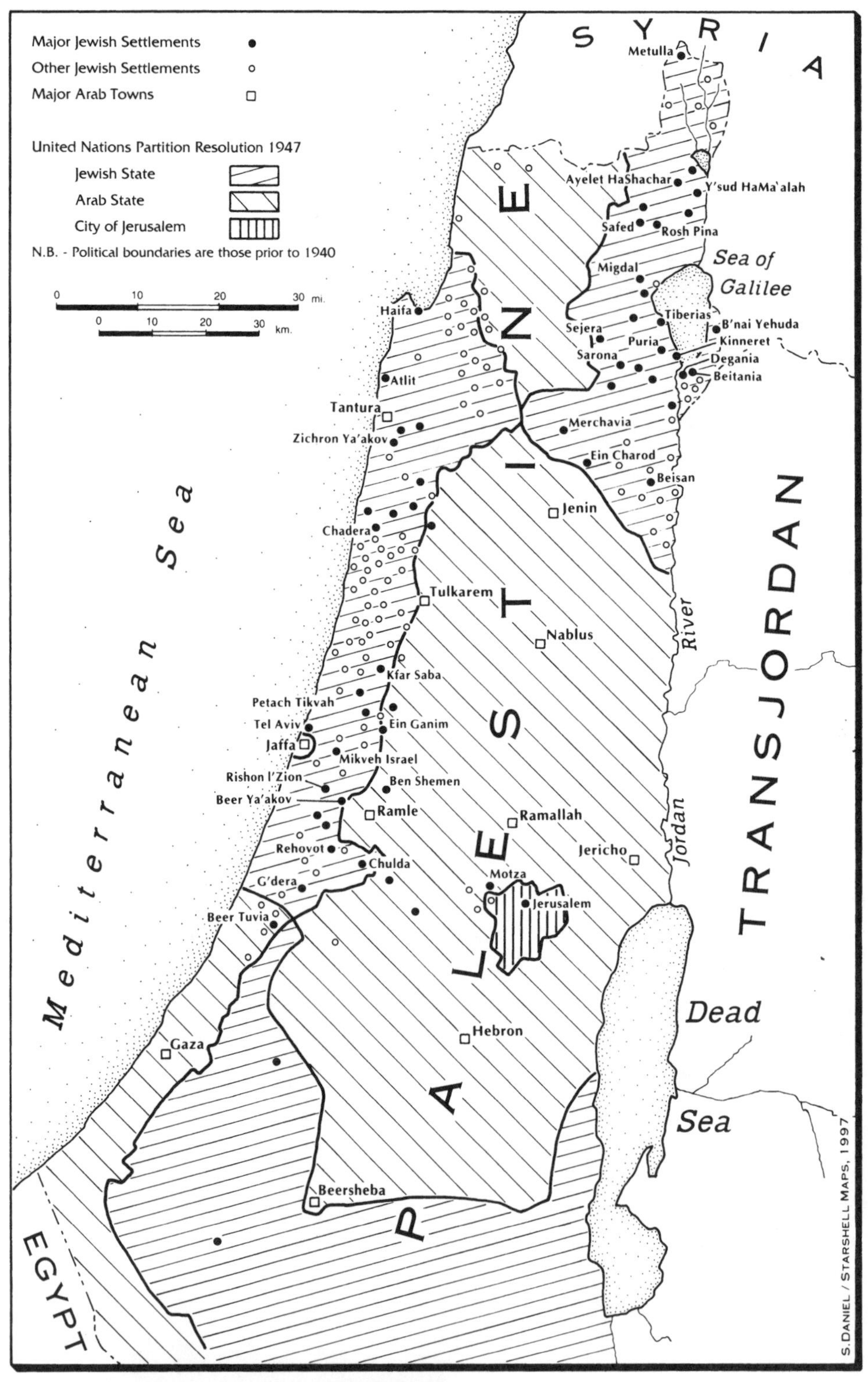

The Birth of Israel

Today, Herzl's words are more likely to provoke awe than scorn, for it was precisely a half century after he penned these lines that the United Nations approved the creation of a Jewish state in part of Palestine. Yet there is more than a touch of theatrical exaggeration in Herzl's statement. By the time he convened the first Zionist Congress, the Zionist movement had flourished for almost two decades, and intensive Jewish activity to regenerate the Land of Israel had begun earlier still, in the middle of the nineteenth century. Moreover, Herzl's Zionist activity might have left no historical mark whatsoever had it not been for a fortuitous combination of forceful Zionist leadership, Jewish financial and physical sacrifice, Great Power intrigue and supportive international public opinion during the five decades between the modest assembly at Basel and Israel's achievement of statehood.

THE ORIGINS OF JEWISH NATIONALISM

The Zionist movement represented both a continuation of, and a revolt against, traditional Jewish ties to the Land of Israel. For a period of almost two millennia, between the destruction of the Second Temple in 70 C.E. and the nineteenth century, rabbis conceived of the Holy Land as central to Jewish life as an object of prayer, devotion and pilgrimage, but not of purposeful colonization. The Holy Land was seen as a sacred relic to be lamented but left in ruins; any attempt to people the land with Jews en masse would be considered a sacrilege, a violation of God's express wish to punish them through destruction and exile. Only in the age of the Messiah would the Jewish commonwealth, along with the Temple and its sacrificial service, be restored.

This stance allowed for, and indeed commanded, support for small communities of Jewish pietists and mystics in the Holy Land. A network of emissaries transmitted funds between the Diaspora and the pilgrim-scholars of Palestine's Jewish community, the Yishuv. These emissaries also brought news from the Yishuv back to the Diaspora. Reports from Palestine, combined with the copious material in the Bible and Talmud about Palestine's landscape, flora and fauna, helped Diaspora Jews to form vivid images of the Holy Land in their minds. The Land of Israel was a mythic, but concrete and central, component of Jewish collective consciousness.

At first glance, it would seem that the Haskalah (Jewish Enlightenment) and Reform movements among nineteenth-century European Jews weakened much of this traditional attachment to the Land of Israel. After all, the general tendency of Jews in Western and Central Europe was to adopt the culture of the country in which they lived and to consider that land not merely a temporary host but rather a true homeland. Among some Reform congregations in Germany, prayers for the return of Jews to the Land of Israel and the restoration of the Temple were deleted from the service. But ironically, the major intellectual movements among nineteenth-century European Jews, along with the increasing social and economic mobility that they enjoyed, in some ways strengthened Jewish bonds with the Land of Israel, although the nature of these bonds underwent considerable change.

Central to the Haskalah was the notion that Jews needed to undergo a process of transformation in order to render them acceptable to gentile society. Jews were to obtain a modern Western education, and the poor among them were to be channeled out of peddling and moneylending and into respectable occupations like crafts and agriculture. Progressive Jewish leaders believed that this transformation should take place not only in Europe but in the Holy Land as well. The poverty and backwardness of the Yishuv disturbed European Jewish leaders and stimulated them to engage in intense philanthropic activity on behalf of Palestinian Jewry.

In the nineteenth century, there was no political unit called Palestine. What Jews called the Land of Israel was part of the Ottoman Empire and was divided into administrative districts ruled out of Jerusalem and Beirut. In 1880 there were some 25,000 Jews (out of a total population of 450,000) in the area equivalent to today's Israel, West Bank and Gaza. Two-thirds of the Jews lived in Jerusalem; most of the rest were divided among three other ancient Jewish holy cities: Safed, Tiberias and Hebron. Approximately half of the members of the Yishuv were Sephardim, whose ancestors had immigrated centuries before. The other half were Ashkenazim, immigrants from Central and Eastern Europe, who had begun to arrive at the end of the 1700s. The Ashkenazim were deeply traditional, and for some, pietist and mystical motivations drove them to the Land of Israel. But for most, grinding poverty played at least as great a role in their decision to move. The Yishuv's population, then, was both deeply Orthodox and wretchedly poor, dependent on charity from abroad for survival and engaged primarily in the study of sacred texts rather than a remunerative livelihood.

For Western European Jews, this situation evoked not only compassion but also a degree of embarrassment. From the middle of the nineteenth century, the Holy Land became increasingly visible to gentile European observers, thanks to the expansion of Great Power interests in the region on the one hand, and tourism by members of the growing European bourgeoisie on the other.

The Anglo-Jewish financier and philanthropist Sir Moses Montefiore (1784–1885) was among the first to try to regenerate the Yishuv into a productive society. Beginning in 1839, he established a number of agricultural and artisanal projects, none of which was terribly successful, but they attracted great international interest. In 1842 the German Reform rabbi Ludwig Philippson (1811–1889) called for an international Jewish philanthropic union to assist Palestinian Jewry. The American Jewish leader Isaac Leeser (1806–1868) held similar views. In the decades that followed, Jerusalem became home to modern Jewish schools and hospitals, and in 1870 the French-Jewish Alliance Israélite Universelle established an agricultural school near Jaffa. Major Jewish organizations in Europe and the United States supported a simultaneous cutting of charity to the Yishuv and the promotion of a modern educational and economic infrastructure for the Jews of Palestine.

Jewish activists for Palestine in the mid to late nineteenth century were not Zionists. They did not think of the Jews as a nation, and they did not envision a Jewish state. But their actions represent a necessary first step toward the unfolding of Zionism. Taking the Yishuv's fate into their own hands, Jewish philanthropists broke with the traditional view of the Land of Israel as an untouchable, sacred ruin. They fostered international Jewish solidarity through a program of concerted activity to regenerate the Holy Land.

Many Orthodox Jews in Palestine opposed this new type of philanthropic work. They feared that it would take power away from their rabbinical leaders and threaten a way of life based on Torah study and isolation from modern society. But a cluster of traditionalist Jews wholeheartedly supported the philanthropic activities in Palestine. For example, the rabbis Yehuda Alkalai (1798–1878) and Zvi Hirsch Kalischer (1795–1874) were important influences behind the Alliance Israélite Universelle's work in Palestine. These rabbis were more than philanthropists, however; they were mystics, convinced that settling Jews as farmers on the soil of the Holy Land would usher in the days of the Messiah. Breaking with the standard Orthodox view that the return to Palestine can occur only *after* the Messiah has arrived, Kalischer wrote: "If the Almighty would suddenly appear, one day in the future, through undeniable miracles, this would be no trial. What straining of our faith would there be in the face of the miracles and wonders attending a clear heavenly command to go up and inherit the land and enjoy its good fruit? Under such circumstances what fool would not go there . . . ? Only a natural beginning of the Redemption is a true test of those who initiate it . . . . Jewish farming [will] be a spur to the ultimate Messianic Redemption. As we bring redemption to the land in a 'this worldly' way, the rays of heavenly deliverance will gradually appear."

Kalischer's and Alkalai's fervor was fanned not only by Jewish mysticism but also by the nationalist sentiment that swept through Europe at the time. Both men lived in lands where stateless peoples struggled to establish their national identity. Kalischer lived among the Poles, and Alkalai among various Balkan peoples who sought to break away from the Ottoman Empire. "The spirit of the times," Alkalai wrote, "summons every [people] to reclaim its sovereignty and raise up its language; so too does it demand of us that we reestablish [Zion], the center of our life, and raise up our holy language and revive it." Kalischer and Alkalai used the struggling nations as an example for the Jews to follow, but the two rabbis were themselves not Jewish nationalists. They conceived of Jewry as a religiously defined entity, and their goal was not a normal national life for the Jews but rather the onset of the messianic era.

The first thinker to apply European nationalist ideas to the Jews in a secular sense was Moses Hess (1812–1875). A prominent socialist in Germany and France, Hess in midlife grew weary of international socialism and focused on Jewish affairs. Unlike well-meaning philanthropists, who identified the "Jewish problem" with poverty, or Orthodox activists, who considered the decline of religious observance and study the greatest catastrophe to befall the Jews, Hess concentrated on antisemitism, which, he claimed, would always prevent Jewish integration into European society. The solution was migration to Palestine. Hess laid these views out in his 1862 book, *Rome and Jerusalem*. Rome here symbolized Italy, whose recent successful war against Austria had ushered in the era of Italian unification. Like Italy, wrote Hess, so would the Jewish nation, if allowed to determine its own destiny, live in peace, flourish culturally and contribute to world civilization as a whole.

Hess's call for a restored Jewish homeland in the Land of Israel received little support. But there were also less explicit signs of growing nationalist feeling among Jewish intellectuals in Europe. At the time that Hess published his book, the German Jew Heinrich Graetz (1817–1891) was writing an eleven-volume history of the Jews, a work of great literary beauty as well as scholarship, which glorified Jewish achievement, and by implication peoplehood, throughout time. (Graetz's work was similar to that of nationalist historians throughout Europe at the time.) A further step was taken in the 1870s, when the Russian Jew Perez Smolenskin (1842–1885) proclaimed that the Jews were a spiritual nation united by the Torah. At that time another Russian Jew, Eliezer Ben-Yehuda (1858–1922), wrote that spiritual nationalism needed to be rooted in land and language—and so in 1881 he moved to Palestine, where he devoted the rest of his life to the revival of the Hebrew language.

In many other ways as well, that year marked the first great turning point in the history of Zionism. The pogroms in Russia embittered Eastern European "enlightened" Jews, dashing their hopes for integration into Russian society and pushing them toward full-blown Jewish nationalism. The result was a flowering of Jewish nationalist groups, known as Hovevei Tziyon (Lovers of Zion*). These groups sprang up not only in Russia but also in Romania, where antisemitism and governmental persecution were as strong as in Russia. There were Lovers of Zion throughout Western Europe as well.

They were organized into a loose federation by an assimilated Russian ophthalmologist, Leon Pinsker, whom the pogroms had galvanized into Jewish political activity. Pinsker's pamphlet *Auto-Emancipation,* written in 1882, argued that Jew hatred was imbedded in society and was the natural product of the Jews' ghostly existence as an uprooted, stateless people. Europe had been proved unable to emancipate the Jews, so the Jews were now obliged to emancipate themselves by selecting a territory outside Europe and colonizing it. Although Pinsker himself was not single-mindedly focused on Jewish acquisition of territory in the Land of Israel, such was the sentiment of the overwhelming majority of the Lovers of Zion. (Thus it is no surprise that the word *Zionism* was coined by an active member of the Lovers of Zion in Vienna, Nathan Birnbaum [1864–1937], in the early 1890s.)

The Lovers of Zion longed to see the Land of Israel colonized by productive Jewish farmers, craftsmen and tradesmen. They envisioned robust children, their faces free of fear, chattering in the language of the Bible and imbibing a modern Hebrew culture. There was much room for Jewish observance in the Lovers of Zion's envisioned utopia, but it was to be based on the principles of the Haskalah; Judaism, like the society of the Yishuv, was to be enlightened and modernized along the lines of nineteenth-century middle-class values. The Lovers of Zion rarely articulated a concrete political program, however, and they lacked the means to attain their goals. The groups had little money and even less expertise. Their activity was hampered by Russian law, which prohibited political organiza-

*I discuss many organizations in this section. Whenever possible, I have translated the names of these organizations into English. Sometimes, when there is no clear English equivalent, I leave the name in Hebrew.

tions. The legal restrictions did much to account for the small size of the Lovers of Zion network, which numbered only about 15,000 in the 1880s.

But the movement also had a strictly limited appeal. Most Orthodox Jews shunned it, largely because they saw, rightly enough, the Lovers of Zion as latter-day Maskilim seeking to alter the Jews' traditional ways of learning and living. Poor Jewish workers were far more likely to find solace in Jewish socialist organizations advocating revolutionary change within Russia than they were to find it in Zionist cells supporting a trickle of emigration to a far-off land. Wealthy Jews who still aspired to assimilate into the general society had little reason to become passionate Zionists. Thus the Lovers of Zion were limited to middle-class Jews, sympathetic to tradition but not beholden to it. It was a respectable group, but not a mass movement. This would change with the advent of Theodor Herzl.

THEODOR HERZL

Theodor Herzl was the greatest Jewish leader of the early twentieth century. Although active in Zionist affairs only during the last decade of his brief life, Herzl forged the poorly organized Zionist movement into a state-building force known as the World Zionist Organization. He won scores of thousands of adherents to Zionism and stimulated interest among the European Great Powers for what would otherwise have been dismissed as a foolhardy project. An enormously complex person, Herzl was gifted with mesmerizing charisma, a quick mind and organizational genius, yet he was also racked by frustrated ambition, insecurity and anxiety. Like most great leaders, he had faults as grand as his virtues.

Herzl was born into a prosperous Budapest family that had cast off much of the Jewish observance central to traditional Jewish life. Herzl's father, a businessman from Galicia, labored so that his son could become immersed in the dominant German culture of the Habsburg Empire and enjoy a prestigious career. As a child, Herzl displayed a strong aesthetic sense, which his parents encouraged through private lessons of all kinds. While still in his teens, Herzl began to write plays. The heroes of these plays were usually young aristocrats struggling to lead lives of beauty and honor in a corrupt bourgeois world. These heroes were the alter ego of Herzl himself, who longed to be an aristocrat but felt trapped by his Jewish and middle-class origins.

As a student, Herzl cultivated an aristocratic manner and strove to be accepted into Austrian youth culture. He dressed impeccably, joined a fraternity and participated in innumerable drinking parties. When he wrote in his diary about Jewish matters (he kept a voluminous diary throughout his life), he at first wrote approvingly of intermarriage as a means of eliminating Jewish separatism once and for all. He was disturbed, however, by the outbreak of antisemitism in Austria in the early 1880s, and when his fraternity embraced a raucous antisemitism, he resigned in a huff.

At the age of twenty-four, he received a doctorate in law from the University of Vienna and went to work for various governmental courts. Within three years after beginning work, Herzl had decided to devote himself full-time to writing. A number of his plays were produced, all of them mediocre, but he did establish himself as a contributor to the cultural supplements to Austrian newspapers. Herzl's career was assured in 1892, when he became the Paris correspondent for one of Vienna's most prestigious newspapers, the *Neue Freie Presse*.

About 1890 Herzl began to read deeply in the literature on antisemitism. He often wrote of antisemitic incidents in Paris in his newspaper columns. Herzl toyed with two possible solutions to this growing "Jewish problem." First, he considered Jewish conversions en masse to Christianity. In keeping with his theatrical bent, Herzl envisioned a spectacular massive baptismal ceremony in front of St. Stephen's Cathedral in Vienna, with the pope himself in attendance. Herzl then pondered the Jews' growing affinities for socialism, which promised to overthrow the capitalist economic system, and with it the Jewish occupational concentration in commerce and finance that fueled antisemitism. Neither of these alternatives, conversion or socialism, truly satisfied Herzl. Conversion, no matter how one finessed the issue, was a betrayal of one's heritage and so a blow to personal honor, something that Herzl held dear. And the other vehicle of assimilation, revolutionary socialism, could not help alarming this high-living aesthete, who was attached to property and the comfort it bestowed.

In 1894 and 1895, Herzl became increasingly obsessed with antisemitism. He wrote a tragic play called *Out of the Ghetto*, in which a brave Jewish attorney, defender of the poor, is killed in a duel by a despicable Christian aristocrat. Shortly after finishing the play, he attended synagogue services for the first time

A Zionist committee meeting in a Vienna café; Theodor Herzl is seated at rear-center table.

in many years. And then came the trial in Paris of the Jewish captain Alfred Dreyfus, falsely accused of treason, and the object of a massive antisemitic movement throughout France. Herzl, who covered the trial for the *Neue Freie Presse*, claimed in later years that the Dreyfus Affair turned him into a Zionist. Such a claim suited Herzl's penchant for melodrama; the truth is that Herzl's shock over the antisemitic frenzy surrounding the Dreyfus trial was only the culmination of years of reflection on the Jewish problem and of attempts to find solutions to it, which in the end did not satisfy him. France, the most liberal and enlightened land on the continent of Europe, had shown itself to be unwilling to treat its Jews fairly. What solution was left but the mass transfer of Jews to a new land?

Herzl turned to one of the world's wealthiest Jews, the railroad magnate and philanthropist Baron Maurice de Hirsch (1831–1896), with a proposal for mass immigration. The baron's noncommittal reply led Herzl to write a pamphlet, *The Jewish State*, for general distribution throughout the Jewish world. In this work, and in his subsequent writings, Herzl used his journalistic gifts to offer a vivid description of his envisioned Jewish state and a convincing account of the means by which it was to be achieved.

Underneath Herzl's sober prose lay deep-seated powers of fantasy and an ability to appeal to the irrational yearnings of his Jewish readers. Herzl attributed the survival of the Jewish people to their sheer willpower, manifested in their collective beliefs. For thousands of years, those beliefs had centered on the Jewish religion; now, in what Herzl believed to be an age dominated by secular values and national patriotism, the Jewish state would inspire world Jewry. Herzl was the child of the age of mass politics, when charismatic orators like Vienna's mayor, Karl Lueger, won over crowds of voters through huge meetings, demonstrations and festivals. Herzl adopted the same tactics, but whereas Lueger and other street politicians used antisemitism to win popular support, Herzl organized a mass movement to combat Jew hatred through the construction of a Jewish homeland. Herzl appealed to emotion because it was the only resource that his prospective audience possessed. "Great things," he wrote, "need no firm foundation. . . . Perhaps I can found the Jewish State without any firm anchorage. The secret lies in movement." One of his most popular sayings about Zionism was that "if you wish it, it is no dream." Zionism for Herzl represented an act of will that could transcend everyday reality and create a new world.

At the same time, we cannot help being struck by the rational, democratic and progressive quality of the nation-building institutions that Herzl founded. The World Zionist Organization (ZO) was embodied in its annual (later biennial) congress, an assembly elected by all who paid a token annual fee. From 1898, women were allowed to vote for the congress (this at a time when New Zealand was the only country in the world with national female suffrage). The ZO executive was fully responsible to the congress; so were the ZO's bank, the Jewish Colonial Trust, and the Jewish National Fund, which was dedicated to land purchase in Palestine. The congress accommodated sundry factions or parties, ranging from Orthodox to secular-liberal to socialist.

Looking beyond Herzl's actions to his long-range vision for the future, we can see that Herzl's writings and speeches call for a liberal utopia, with economic justice, free education and an advanced welfare system. Political leadership would be exercised by an elite selected by merit alone. The state would have no demagogy, no chauvinism and no war. Perhaps Herzl was willing to adopt the illiberal political tactics of his enemies, but he did so to attain a goal that was quintessentially liberal.

Herzl's assimilated origins, and his willingness to consider mass conversion and other means of wiping out the Jews as a distinctive presence in European culture, have led some critics to dismiss his Zionism as superficial, an expression of frustration over antisemitism, and nothing more. But throughout the modern world, ethnic minorities and colonized peoples from Ireland to Indochina have produced great leaders steeped in the culture of the state that dominated their people, who began their lives in the service of that state and turned to nationalism when they hit a glass ceiling of discrimination against their kind.

POLITICAL ZIONISM AND ITS OPPONENTS

The ZO was a political body whose executive and legislature functioned as a provisional government for the Jewish people. As president of the ZO, Herzl conceived of himself as having the same purview as any head of government: the mobilization of support and the satisfaction of the popular will on the one hand, and the representation of Zionist interests to the international community on the other. Those interests demanded the acquisition of Palestine, a land under Ottoman Turkish rule and a center of intrigue for the European Great Powers. Herzl considered it his chief task, therefore, to negotiate with Ottoman and European officials in order to win a charter, an internationally recognized authorization for Jewish colonization and self-rule in Palestine.

Antisemitic fantasies played an important role in the thinking of Herzl's negotiating partners. The German emperor, Wilhelm II, believed that the Jews were so rich as to be able to resuscitate the ailing Ottoman Empire. Germany had extensive economic interests in the region, which was falling increasingly under the control of Germany's rivals, France and England. Wilhelm flirted with the idea of making Palestine a German protectorate and handing it to the Zionists, thus simultaneously promoting German imperialism and ridding Europe of the Jews, whom Wilhelm despised. In his dealings with the Turks, Herzl made use of these fantasies, offering to pay off the Turks' enormous imperial debt in exchange for the charter.

Herzl's schemes, however, collapsed, partly because he could not mobilize anywhere near the funds required. What is more, the Turkish authorities perceived Zionism as a planned invasion by foreigners who would serve as a wedge for even greater European intervention in the empire's internal affairs. Most important, the sultan, who also bore the title of caliph, or leader, of the Islamic world, could not countenance a massive Jewish presence in a land that, since the Christian Crusaders had been driven out centuries before, had been especially dear to Islam.

Neither Herzl nor any of his negotiating partners took the sensibilities of Palestine's Arabs into consideration. For the Ottoman and European leaders alike, the fate of Palestine, like that of all territories under their control, was to be decided by war and diplomacy, not plebiscites. At the time Arab nationalism was in its infancy, and a specifically Palestinian nationalism did not yet exist. Herzl was well aware that Palestine had hundreds of thousands of Arabs, but he perceived them as a backward population that would enjoy vast educational and technological benefits from the Zionist presence. (In Herzl's utopian novel *Old-New Land*, the one Arab character speaks flawless German and has fully assimilated European culture.) Given the era in which he lived, it would have been remarkable indeed had Herzl foreseen Arab claims on Palestine.

About the turn of the century, some Eastern European Zionists with socialist inclinations expressed concern about the Palestinian Arabs not as fellow claimants to the land but as competitors with Jewish workers. Nahman Syrkin (1867–1924), the father of socialist Zionism, claimed that the availability of plentiful and cheap Arab labor would impede the formation of a Jewish working class, and with it of the Jewish national home. Thus the Jewish homeland could only be constructed if it replaced the market economy, in which Arab labor would always have the advantage, with a socialist regime.

Syrkin's ideas would resonate in the Yishuv in the coming decades. At the turn of the century, however, it was doubtful if the Jews would ever be allowed to create any kind of modern society in Palestine, capitalist or socialist. As Herzl's political negotiations proved fruitless and the prospect of obtaining Palestine dimmed, the persecution of Eastern European Jewry reached new heights, culminating in the dreadful pogrom in Kishinev, Bessarabia, in May 1903. The month before, the British colonial secretary, Joseph Chamberlain, had proposed to Herzl that the Zionists colonize British East Africa (today part of Kenya). With a heavy heart, Herzl brought what came mistakenly to be known as the "Uganda proposal" to that year's Zionist Congress. Although the Uganda scheme never materialized, it is significant because it unleashed a torrent of opposition that points to the deep factionalism that ran through the early Zionist movement.

From the start, Herzl's single-minded devotion to diplomacy irritated many of the Lovers of Zion, who favored a variety of measures that they dubbed "practical Zionism" and opposed to Herzl's "political Zionism." Practical Zionism entailed any measure of immediate, visible benefit, from settlement activity in Palestine to various forms of political and cultural activity in the Diaspora. For Eastern European Zionists who were steeped in the Jewish tradition and Hebrew language, the prospect of nation-building in any other land but Palestine was ludicrous and proved Herzl's political Zionism to be spiritually bankrupt.

Herzl's greatest critic was Asher Ginsberg, who took the pen name Ahad Ha-Am ("One of the people"). Born into a wealthy Hasidic family in the Ukraine, Ahad Ha-Am received a strictly Orthodox education. As a youth, he taught himself Russian and German, clandestinely read modern literature and, in his twenties, lost faith in traditional Judaism. He devoted his life to the creation of a new Jewish culture, based on the Hebrew language, the study of Jewish history and folklore and, most important, the tie to a revived national home in Palestine.

Unlike Herzl, Ahad Ha-Am did not believe that Palestine could or should become a home for masses of persecuted Jews. Rather than try to solve the physical "problem of the Jews," Zionism should take on the spiritual "problem of Judaism," which in the modern world had devolved into fossilized Orthodoxy or vapid liberalism. Zionism should mold the Yishuv into a small, model community, economically healthy and intellectually vibrant, a source of inspiration to the vast majority of Jews who would continue to live in the Diaspora.

Ahad Ha-Am was a meek, retiring man, lacking Herzl's overt charisma and political genius. But in his own quiet way he was a great leader, though he led by example rather than organization building, and by hinted wishes rather than express commands. (His pen name may have literally meant "one of the people," but in classical Hebrew the term could also mean its opposite—"the king himself.") Moreover, Ahad Ha-Am was, like Herzl, a revolutionary, though on a different plane. Ahad Ha-Am—and even more so, his young admirers in the Zionist movement—challenged Jewish Orthodoxy in a way that Herzl did not. Herzl sought to make common cause with the leading Orthodox rabbis, and although many opposed him, others were willing to cooperate with Herzl out of a desire to alleviate Jewish misery. Such was the spirit of the Mizrachi, or religious Zionist, party within the ZO, founded in 1902. The Mizrachi had an easier time dealing with an assimilationist like Herzl, who cared only about the acquisition of a Jewish homeland, than with deeply engaged and literate Jews like Ahad Ha-Am,

A souvenir postcard, designed by E. M. Lilien, from the Fifth Zionist Congress, 1901.

who sought to develop an alternative to traditional Judaism. The notion of Uganda as a provisional haven was actually less of a problem for the Mizrachi than it was for the cultural Zionists, whose project for Jewish renewal depended on contact with the Land of Israel and a revived Hebrew language.

The Uganda controversy provoked rancor and even violence. (Max Nordau, Herzl's closest ally in the Zionist leadership, was shot at by a deranged opponent of the proposal.) Herzl, despite his impressive appearance, had always been a frail man, and the strains of leading so riven a movement hastened his untimely death at the age of forty-four. But the institutions that he built survived him, even as lesser men assumed executive authority. By the eve of the First World War, more than 200,000 Jews paid the Zionist shekel, making the ZO the largest Jewish organization in the world. During the decade following Herzl's death, the ZO adopted what was called a "synthetic" policy, which combined diplomatic activity, cultural work in the Diaspora and settlement work in Palestine. It established a Palestine Office in Jaffa, thus adding the ZO to an array of philanthropies, pioneers and visionaries all seeking to breathe new life into the Yishuv.

THE SEEDS OF THE JEWISH NATIONAL HOME

The face of the Yishuv began to change in the early 1880s. Between 1882 and 1903, its population more than doubled, as some 30,000 Jews immigrated to Palestine. They were part of a much larger wave of migrants that, over the same period, brought a half million Jews from Eastern Europe and Russia to the United States. Why did such a small number go to Palestine? The economic backwardness of the land and the many restrictions that the Ottoman authorities placed on settlement by foreigners were enough to put off all but the most idealistic immigrants. Indeed, except for the occasional poor soul who could not afford passage to the United States and so opted for the cheaper fare to Palestine, most of the 30,000 who did come were idealists of one sort or another—devout Orthodox Jews or, for the first time in the history of the Yishuv, avowed Zionists determined to create a flourishing national community in the Land of Israel.

This wave came to be known as Zionist settlement's First Aliyah, literally "ascent," the term used in the Bible to describe the uphill journey from the Palestinian lowlands to Jerusalem, and, by extension, from the Diaspora to the Land of Israel. Positing a clear break between the Zionist immigrants and the Orthodox Yishuv, the former called their community the "New Yishuv" and critically dubbed the existing one the "Old Yishuv." Most of the Zionists in the First Aliyah were religiously observant, but their approach to observance differed radically from that of the Old Yishuv. The Old Yishuv saw itself as a static community of pilgrim-scholars, depending on foreign charity or eking out a livelihood to support its spiritual labor of Torah study. The Zionists, on the other hand, saw themselves as an avant-garde, preparing the way for future waves of immigration, and laying the foundations for a revived Hebrew culture. Thus tensions between the Old and the New Yishuv ran high. For example, the Hebrew linguist Eliezer

A pioneer family at Yesud Ha-Ma'alah, a First Aliyah colony, c. 1898.

Ben-Yehuda (1858–1922) so despaired of the Jerusalem rabbinate's grip over the Yishuv's cultural life that he supported the Uganda proposal as a way of distancing the Jews from Orthodox domination.

Four-fifths of the members of the First Aliyah settled in Palestine's cities. They strengthened the Jewish presence in the traditional "holy cities" of Hebron, Tiberias and Safed, and in Jerusalem they created a number of new neighborhoods beyond the walls of the Old City. Their most original urban creation was in Jaffa, where they established business enterprises and modern schools. Even more striking was the decision of some 5,000 Romanian, Russian and Polish Jews to settle on the land and earn a livelihood through agriculture. These rural pioneers were by and large middle-class and middle-aged men and their families. There was a famous exception—the Biluim, a group of several dozen youths from Kharkov, whose idealism and political vision captured the imagination of generations of Zionists. They failed as farmers, however, and the older Jewish settlers rarely did better. Most of the First Aliyah's agricultural colonies would have perished had they not been financially sustained by Baron Edmond de Rothschild (1845–1934), a scion of the Paris branch of the great banking family.

Rothschild was the sort of Jewish philanthropist who was not overtly Zionist but deeply committed to improved circumstances for the Jews and the revival of the Holy Land. Under his supervision (and that of the Jewish Colonization Association, to whom he entrusted his Palestinian operations in 1900), the agricultural settlements flourished, but they were dependent on Arab labor. This was so partly because there was not a sizable and capable Jewish labor force in the land at the time. But it was also true that the Jewish colonists frequently preferred Arab over Jewish workers, who demanded a higher wage and better working conditions.

The lack of a Jewish labor force was not the only limitation of the First Aliyah. The immigrants also lacked a clear political vision and organizational skills. And despite the best of intentions, they did not succeed in making Hebrew into a modern vernacular; they spoke a mixture of Yiddish, French and Russian instead.

Solutions to these shortcomings came from members of the Second Aliyah (1904–14). This wave was brought on by the pogroms and upheaval during the years surrounding the Russian Revolution of 1905. Persecuted and impoverished, more than 1.5 million Jews left Eastern Europe over this period. Thirty-five thousand Jews went to Palestine (more than eighty percent male) and only a fraction of these remained in the country for more than a few years. In large measure, the Second Aliyah was similar to the first: a mix of traditionally pious Jews and middle-class Zionists, who flocked to the Yishuv's cities and fostered their modernization. (A group of bourgeois Zionists founded the city of Tel Aviv in 1909.) What was truly exceptional about the Second Aliyah was a cluster of some 2,000 to 3,000 young people steeped in Russian revolutionary and Zionist ideology. This core of the Second Aliyah included the State of Israel's founders, such as David Ben-Gurion, Berl Katznelson (1887–1944) and Yizhak Ben-Zvi (1884–1963), as well as a host of political, cultural and military leaders of the Yishuv and future state. The accomplishments of this core of pioneers are all the more remarkable when one considers their youth—most were still adolescents on arrival in Palestine—and near-total lack of experience in public affairs.

These pioneers considered their move to Palestine to be a dual revolution, against both their own background and the gentile world. They had mainly grown up Orthodox and Yiddish speaking, but they identified Orthodoxy with passivity and Yiddish with moral disfigurement. Thus they became aggressively secular, struggled to speak Hebrew and, beginning a practice that would exist in Israel until the most recent past, Hebraized their names. (Ben-Gurion had been Gruen, and Ben-Zvi had been Shimshelevich). After abandoning Jewish observance, some of the pioneers had become involved in Russian revolutionary movements, which promised to overthrow the oppressive tsarist regime and put an end to class and ethnic conflict. But the antisemitism ingrained in the Russian Left and its failures to effect substantive change drove the pioneers to Zionism and Palestine.

The pioneers may have rejected Eastern Europe, but they brought its political ideologies and operating methods with them. They immediately went to work founding political "parties," small groups of at most a few hundred members. The first party, the Young Worker (Ha-Po'el Ha-Tza'ir), denied any connection with Marxist socialism, but it was nonetheless revolutionary in its call for the conquest of the labor market by Jews and the establishment throughout the Yishuv of a vigorous Jewish working class. The Young Worker was associated with the teachings of A. D. Gordon (1856–1922), a middle-aged mystic, a sort of Zionist Tolstoy, who waxed eloquent about the psychically uplifting effects of physical labor. A second party, Workers of Zion (Po'alei Tziyon), was the Palestinian branch of an international federation of socialist-Zionist societies. The Workers of Zion adhered to a Marxist view that the Jewish state would emerge out of a class conflict between capitalists and proletarian laborers in the Yishuv. The party believed its mission was to organize the Yishuv's working class and prepare it for an eventual socialist revolution. This way of thinking appealed to some of the pioneers, who wished to see themselves as part of a process of international revolution and not parochially focused on Jewish liberation alone.

Eastern European political ideologies also help account for one of the Second

Aliyah's greatest achievements, the agricultural collective settlement first known as a kvutzah and later as a kibbutz. The pioneers who worked in the First Aliyah colonies often lived communally. Communal living was the child of necessity, given the workers' desperate poverty. But the pioneers' hostility to private property, and their willingness to sacrifice what little they had for the common good, strengthened the commitment to communal living. This ideal was extended in 1908, when a group of pioneers coaxed the manager of the colony Sejera, in the Jezreel Valley, to let them farm a tract of land collectively for a year. The next year, the experiment was tried again, this time on land bought by the Jewish National Fund, near the Sea of Galilee. Named Degania, this kvutzah, or collective, flourished, and it became a model for other collectives founded in years to come.

The collectives were valuable to the Zionist workers' parties because they hired only Jewish laborers. In a pure market economy, Jewish labor could never compete against that of the Arabs, but the collectives operated along socialist lines and were built on land owned by the ZO. The pioneers' aim of creating a Jewish polity and the imperative to create a functioning Jewish working class led them to demand a separation of Jews and Arabs.

The Arab presence also stimulated the pioneers to develop military capabilities. Attacks on Jewish property by Arab criminals were common. Even without the Arabs, these impassioned youth would have been attracted by the idea of wielding force, because as revolutionaries they had come to believe that no political movement could succeed without a military arm. Moreover, some of the pioneers had taken part in Jewish self-defense activity during pogroms in Russia, and they carried their experience and expectations with them to Palestine. The pioneers assumed that attacks on Jewish property or statements of opposition to Zionism were motivated by antisemitism of the type that the Jews had encountered in Europe. Determined not to let the Yishuv suffer the humiliations heaped on Diaspora Jewry, a handful of workers in Jaffa established in 1907 a secret military society, Bar Giora. Two years later, the Yishuv's first paramilitary body, the Guard (Ha-Shomer), was founded to defend the Jewish colonies, first in the Galilee, and then in the country as a whole.

By 1914 there were some 85,000 Jews in Palestine. The pioneers of the Second Aliyah had introduced the political, economic and military structures that would characterize the New Yishuv during the interwar period. But these achievements, however impressive, were fragile when compared with the power of Palestine's current master, the Ottoman Empire, to crush the Yishuv, or that of Britain, Palestine's future master, to present Zionism with undreamed-of possibilities. And the voice of Palestine's half million Arabs was only beginning to be heard.

CHAIM WEIZMANN AND THE BALFOUR DECLARATION

The First World War brought chaos to the Yishuv. The Ottoman authorities, long suspicious of foreign nationals on Palestinian soil, turned their wrath first against the Jewish citizens of Russia, one of the Turks' wartime foes. But soon even citizens of the Turks' allies, Germany and Austria, were subject to expulsion. Tens of thousands of Jews were exiled from or fled the country. Those who stayed faced the threat of forced labor or military service. Turkish oppression, combined with the effects of a British naval blockade, caused the deaths of thousands from hunger or disease. By the end of the war, the Yishuv had been reduced to some 55,000; that the number did not plummet further still was because of heroic philanthropic action by American Jewry.

The Zionist movement, caught between the alliance of England, France and Russia on the one hand, and of Germany, the Habsburg Empire and the Ottoman Empire on the other, frantically sought neutral ground. ZO headquarters moved to Copenhagen; the JNF set up shop in the Hague. American neutrality during the first three years of the war did much to enable the transfer of American Jewish contributions to the Yishuv. Nonetheless, it was in England, the most powerful country in the Triple Entente and home to the sleepiest of Zionist movements before the war, that wartime political Zionism flourished. This was because of a fortuitous overlapping of Zionist and British diplomatic interests in the ailing Ottoman Empire.

All the European Great Powers had strategic and economic interests in the Ottoman Empire. Since the 1870s, the empire had been disintegrating; by 1914 it had lost virtually all of its European possessions to independence movements and had granted extensive European influence, amounting to total control, over many of its territories in the Middle East. Statesmen throughout Europe assumed that the world war would finish off the empire, whose future division became a major issue in wartime diplomacy. The most aggressive diplomatic maneuvers over Palestine came from France and England. The French wanted to protect their North African empire and their hegemony in Lebanon. The British sought the greatest possible control over the eastern Mediterranean, starting point of the land routes to British zones of influence in Mesopotamia and of the sea lanes to India, the jewel in the British colonial crown. Since sea traffic to India depended on the Suez Canal, the British wished to hold the territories on either side of it—Egypt to the west, and the Sinai and at least some portions of Palestine to the east. Early in the war, British diplomats simultaneously pursued two somewhat contradictory strategies to meet this goal.

An Israeli stamp commemorating Chaim Weizmann and the fiftieth anniversary of the Balfour Declaration.

On the one hand, they sought an alliance with Arabs against the Ottoman Turks. They chose as their partner Husayn, patriarch of a distinguished Hashemite family—that is, one claiming descent from the ancestors of the prophet Muhammad. Husayn was emir of the Hijaz, an area in western Arabia that included the Islamic holy cities of Mecca and Medina. In a series of letters in 1915, the British high commissioner in Egypt, Henry McMahon, promised Husayn British support for an independent state that would encompass most of the Arab Middle East. In return, the house of Husayn would organize Arab guerrilla warfare against the Ottoman Turks. Husayn kept his end of the bargain, and in 1916 an Arab force led by Husayn's son Feysal began a series of military operations, including harrying Turkish supply lines in Arabia and seizing the port of Aqaba.

The second British strategy, however, complicated England's ability to keep its word to Husayn. In the year of the onset of the Arabs' guerrilla war against the Turks, a secret agreement between Mark Sykes, a British cabinet official, and Charles Georges-Picot, a French diplomat, called for France and Britain to divide the Middle East between them after the war. Some parts would be under direct Allied control, and others under a less invasive form of influence, so Arab independence in certain areas was possible, but not in the fashion envisioned in the Husayn-McMahon correspondence.

And what of Palestine? Husayn assumed that it would be his; the wording of McMahon's correspondence on this issue was obscure and still arouses controversy. And the Sykes-Picot agreement assumed that Palestine would be administered by a condominium of European powers. Moreover, there were voices in the British cabinet that favored a protectorate over Palestine as the best means of safeguarding the Suez Canal. In such a scenario, the Zionists emerged as a possible client that would serve British interests. Thus it occurred that an early proposal for a pro-Zionist declaration by Britain was drawn up by Lucien Wolf (1857–1930), a non-Zionist Jew who headed the Conjoint Committee of the Board of Deputies of British Jews and the Anglo-Jewish Association, and who was motivated primarily by British patriotism.

In 1916 and 1917, even officials who had not previously championed a post-war Zionist protectorate measured the worth of a public declaration of support for Zionist aims. The key here was a vastly exaggerated opinion of Jewish political and economic power, particularly in the United States and Russia. The British prime minister, David Lloyd George, believed that American Jewry could push the United States into the war. When America did enter the war in April 1917, the prime minister hoped that Jewish public opinion would hasten that country's mobilization. After Russia's February Revolution, it was commonly believed among British ruling circles that Jews controlled the Kerensky government and would determine whether Russia would stay in the war. There was fear that Germany might sway international Jewry over to the Triple Alliance by making a pro-Zionist declaration of its own. Even France, Britain's ally, was seen as a rival for Zionist affections, because its foreign ministry communicated support for Zionist aims in June of 1917.

Strategic interests and the desire to manipulate public opinion, however, are only part of the story of the wartime relationship between Britain and Zionism. There were many forces, in both the British government and the Zionist movement itself, that opposed a close relationship between the two, and it would take outstanding Zionist leadership to overcome those forces. Through happenstance, such a leader emerged from an unlikely place: a chemistry laboratory at the University of Manchester. The chemist was Chaim Weizmann.

Weizmann represented something of a cross between the two great rivals in the pre-1914 Zionist movement, Herzl and Ahad Ha-Am. Like Ahad Ha-Am, Weizmann was a product of Eastern Europe and steeped in traditional Jewish culture. The son of a timber merchant, Weizmann grew up in a village near Pinsk, where he acquired a thorough Jewish education. Owing to quotas in Russian universities that severely restricted the admission of Jews, Weizmann, like many other talented young Russian Jews, moved west for his higher education. While studying in Berlin, he became involved in Zionist affairs, and developed strong sympathies for the cultural emphasis of Ahad Ha-Am. Throughout his Zionist career, Weizmann would be passionately devoted to educational and cultural issues, such as the founding of a Hebrew university. And yet, although critical of Herzl's exclusive focus on diplomacy, Weizmann soon developed a flair for political organization and a taste for hobnobbing with world leaders. These traits emerged soon after he moved to England in 1904 and began teaching and research at Manchester. He became active in British Zionism, joined the ZO executive and at the 1907 Zionist Congress delivered an influential speech advocating a "synthesis" of Herzlian political Zionism and its Ahad Ha-Amian counterpart.

During the First World War, Weizmann came into his own as a leader, with most of Herzl's virtues and only a few of his faults. Possessed of great charisma and personal charm, speaking flawless but exotically accented English, Weizmann deeply impressed the members of the British upper crust. He disarmed antisemites by bluntly accepting the truth of some of their opinions and then demonstrating how Zionism would rid the Jews of those traits that his interlocutors found objectionable. When speaking with devout Christians, Weizmann invoked the biblical landscape and the common Judeo-Christian veneration for the Holy Land. Such sentiments reinforced, and did not contradict, the pragmatic political reasoning that supported his cause. Weizmann played on the British impression of extensive Jewish international political and journalistic influence. "Weizmann is ready," one official excitedly wrote, "to start an active pro-Ally propaganda campaign throughout the world."

Like Herzl, Weizmann achieved fame for his pre- and extra-Zionist activity, and this fame gave him entrée to the highest circles of government. But whereas Herzl had been merely a successful journalist, Weizmann was an accomplished chemist, whose formula for the production of acetone, an ingredient used in the manufacture of explosives, substantially assisted the British war effort and greatly enhanced his influence in governmental circles. This recognition from the outside world in turn heightened Weizmann's influence among Zionists.

Yet for all of Weizmann's commitment to the Zionist movement, he, like Herzl, stood above it. Both men appealed to the masses but were uncomfortable with them; both preferred "vertical alliances" with powerful leaders over the machinery of politics. Both men took great risks, representing themselves to world leaders as spokesmen for all Zionists, even for world Jewry, when at times they spoke only for themselves. Early in the war, Weizmann took it on himself to pursue an alliance between Zionism and Britain despite the ZO's official stance of neutrality and Weizmann's own relatively humble position in the movement. (Even after he was elected head of the English Zionist Federation in 1917, Weizmann had no real authorization for his contacts with the British government.) Many Zionists feared that a statement of British support for Zionism would endanger the Yishuv, which was at the mercy of Britain's enemy, the Turks.

What's more, Britain was allied with Russia, a country universally loathed by Zionists. A connection with Britain meant support for Russia, something that most Zionists found unconscionable, at least until the February Revolution, which brought Jewish emancipation.

Weizmann also had to overcome considerable British governmental opposition to a declaration of support of Zionist aims in Palestine. Sir Edwin Montagu (1879–1924), the secretary of state for India and the only Jew in Lloyd George's cabinet, opposed such a move; he may have been motivated by assimilationist yearnings, legitimate reasons of state or a mixture of the two. Other officials inclined to be sympathetic, like the foreign secretary, James Balfour, questioned the worth and morality of a declaration of support for the Zionists but not for the Ottoman Empire's other stateless peoples, such as the Arabs or Armenians.

Weizmann and his advisers worked the British cabinet through its moments of doubt; the two groups collaborated on the formulation of the official statement, known as the Balfour Declaration, which was formally sent to Walter, second Lord Rothschild (1868–1937), then president of the English Zionist Federation, on November 2, 1917. In part, the letter read: "His Majesty's Government view with favour the establishment in Palestine of a national home for the Jewish people and will use their best endeavours to facilitate the achievement of this object, it being clearly understood that nothing shall be done which may prejudice the civil and religious rights of existing non-Jewish communities in Palestine, or the rights and political status enjoyed by Jews in any other country."

The document's reference to "a" rather than "the" national home and its cautious invocation of the rights of non-Jews in Palestine do not detract from the magnitude of Chaim Weizmann's accomplishment. Here was, apparently, the charter that Herzl had coveted but that had eluded his grasp. The world's greatest colonial power had pledged itself to nurture the Zionist project in Palestine.

THE BRITISH IN PALESTINE IN THE 1920s

As part of the general Allied campaign against the Turks, and Britain's specific desire to hold Palestine in the postwar division of the Ottoman Empire, the British army invaded Palestine in October of 1917. By Hanukkah, Jerusalem had been taken, and the entire land was under British control by September of the following year. Palestine remained under military administration until 1920, when, at the San Remo conference, the Allied powers formally divided former Ottoman territories between France and Britain, with the former receiving Lebanon and Syria and the latter Palestine and Iraq. The Allies and the newly formed League of Nations spoke of these dependencies as "mandates," that is, charges on the Great Powers who were obliged to guide them toward eventual political independence. This language reflected the ideology of the American president, Woodrow Wilson, who saw in the wartime collapse of the great multinational empires—German, Austro-Hungarian and Ottoman—a victory for national self-determination.

Despite the Balfour Declaration and wartime promises to Husayn, the British government had its own interests, not the goal of national self-determination, in mind as it drew up the borders of mandatory Palestine. The Zionists, seeking to maximize the economic capacity of their national home, envisioned a Palestine that would include the fertile land east of the Jordan River and the sources of the Jordan in southern Lebanon and the Golan Heights. The British, on the other hand, did not need to reach so far north in order to fulfill the strategic goal of protecting Egypt, and policymakers in London did not wish to clash with French interests in Syria. As to the territory east of the Jordan River, although the British Mandate for Palestine included what is today's Kingdom of Jordan, from the beginning it had a separate status. During the war, much of this territory passed into the hands of the Hashemite military forces moving north from Arabia. In 1921 the vast and thinly populated area was closed to Jewish settlement, and the British formally offered it to Husayn's son Abdullah. In 1923 Transjordan was proclaimed an autonomous entity.

The creation of Transjordan was designed to satisfy the territorial ambitions of a princely Arab house, not the nationalist yearnings of ordinary Arabs. The same was true for the creation of the Kingdom of Iraq. In 1920 a group of Arab nationalists in Damascus proclaimed an independent Syrian kingdom with Husayn's son Feysal as ruler. French military forces intervened and expelled Feysal, whom the British compensated by seating him on the throne of mandatory Iraq.

The British felt a certain admiration for the house of Husayn, which exuded an aristocratic aura and embodied the stereotype of the noble Bedouin warrior. British attitudes toward the Palestinian Arabs, however, were more mixed. British officials had close relations with Palestinian Arab clerics and notables, and there were many well-intentioned British civil servants who labored to improve the educational and living standards of the Palestinians, particularly the peasantry. But the British also tended to see Palestinians as corrupt and backward

Rural Palestinian laborer.

Levantines rather than true Arabs—true Arabs being sons of the desert, like the house of Husayn.

British policy in Palestine was driven by a mixture of sympathy and antipathy toward both sides, as well as an overriding concern with British imperial interests in the Middle East. The Occupied Enemy Territorial Administration, the military administration in Palestine up to 1920, had a decidedly pro-Arab orientation, and its leaders worked against the spirit and letter of the Balfour Declaration. There were sharp clashes between the OETA and the Zionist Commission, the proto-governmental body established along with the British conquest of Palestine. The commission, assuming that the Balfour Declaration had given it a green light, put forward concrete proposals for the establishment of a Jewish commonwealth, only to have those proposals rebuffed. There were also tensions between the OETA and the Jewish battalions in the British army that had engaged in the 1918 campaign, many of whose members remained in Palestine after the war. Widespread agreement in London indicated that the military administration did not do enough to prevent or control Arab rioting that swept through Jerusalem in April of 1920. The OETA's coldness to the Zionists, however, had less to do with a respect for Palestinian Arab national rights than a recognition that Arab hostility to Zionism was a potentially destabilizing force and could threaten British interests in the region. Moreover, the Bolshevik Revolution, along with the influence of Bolshevism over Zionists entering Palestine during the immediate postwar years, fanned fears that the Yishuv was becoming a Soviet fifth column. This stance did not last, however; in July 1920, a pro-Zionist wind blew into Palestine when the military administration was replaced by civilian colonial rule. The first high commissioner for Palestine was Sir Herbert Samuel (1870–1963), a Jew and committed Zionist, who intended to fulfill the terms of the Balfour Declaration but was also sympathetic to the sentiments of the Palestinian Arabs.

Samuel's first steps as high commissioner prove just how difficult a task lay before him. He opened the doors to Jewish immigration, which jumped from 1,800 in 1919 to over 8,000 in 1920 and 1921. But the surge of Jews into Palestine, occurring at the same time as the overthrow of Feysal's kingdom in Damascus, enraged Palestinian Arabs. In May of 1921, Arabs rioted in Jaffa and the nearby colonies, killing dozens of Jews. Samuel tried to placate Arab opinion by temporarily suspending Jewish immigration, and in the following year, the colonial secretary, Winston Churchill, produced a governmental white paper that both reaffirmed the Balfour Declaration and denied that Palestine was to become an entirely Jewish land. The white paper also tied Jewish immigration to the economic capacity of the land to successfully absorb it. These statements pleased the Zionists far more than the Arabs. The Arabs wanted the Balfour Declaration rescinded and would accept nothing less. The Zionists, on the other hand, agreed with Samuel that the Jewish immigrant pool should become smaller and more selective. The Yishuv was too weak to absorb large numbers of immigrants, and the ZO did not have the resources to create work for them. Although the Zionists resented British control over the immigration process and wanted it for themselves, during the early 1920s a policy of selective immigration actually advanced Zionist interests.

Throughout the decade, the Mandate benefited the Zionists in other, unplanned, ways. The structure of government in Palestine rather than the intentions of the governors was the key factor here. Since the Jews in Palestine tended to be better educated and more likely to have a command of English than the Arabs, Jews had more bureaucratic know-how and access to the high commissioner's ear. As attorney general between 1920 and 1931, the Zionist Norman Bentwich (1883–1971) exerted considerable influence. The Zionists also benefited from the refusal by Palestinian Arab leaders to serve on a joint Jewish-Palestinian Legislative Council. Arabs would not sit on a body that operated within the framework of the Balfour Declaration. This stance makes sense, given the Arab position that Palestine was theirs, and that an offer by a usurper to share power was by definition illegitimate. As a result of this rejection, however, the Arabs were deprived of an important arena to air their views. Unable to forge Jewish-Arab cooperation, the British encouraged each people to form its own semiautonomous governing body, where the Zionists' higher levels of political and organizational experience was evident.

In the sphere of economics, no less than in politics, the British administration played an essential role in the development of the Jewish national home. And here, too, much of the benefit that the British brought the Yishuv was unintentional. The British built Palestine's infrastructure: its railroads, roads, communications lines and first deepwater harbor, at Haifa. They did this to promote effective military administration, not the growth of the Yishuv. At the same time, the Yishuv's economy depended on British expenditures. Public-works projects provided employment to hundreds of young Zionist workers who came to Palestine after the First World War. The construction of the new Haifa harbor, completed in 1933, was carried out largely by Jews. The Yishuv's agricultural exports were fostered by Palestine's integration into the broader economic structure of the British colonial empire. Finally, although afforestation work in Palestine is most commonly associated with the Jewish National Fund, the mandatory administration engaged in this as well.

True, the British did little to foster the development of the Yishuv, which in large measure took care of itself. ZO expenditures for each Yishuv resident were twice those of the mandatory government. There were also many British policies that worked against Zionist interests. The British denied the Zionists access to much state-owned land, as in the Beisan Valley, where the British attempted to establish a class of independent Arab cultivators. But throughout the decade, the British did allow a nearly constant stream of Jewish immigration (despite constant Arab opposition), tolerated most Jewish land purchases and encouraged the development of autonomous political and economic institutions in the Yishuv.

These were necessary preconditions, but they were far from sufficient ones. The British allowed the Zionists to establish a toehold in the country, but it required vast amounts of labor and money to turn that toehold into a polity. Unlike other modern national movements, which seek independence for a native people resisting imperial or colonial rule, Zionism required the buildup of a critical mass of Jews in Palestine and the construction of a national economy before independence could even be considered. Other national movements, including that of the Palestinian Arabs, featured a large peasantry that held the land, produced enough food to sustain itself and provided a labor force for cities and industry. The Zionists, however, had no peasantry, and, paradoxically, set out to invent one among one of the world's most urbanized peoples. Finally, the Zionist movement, unlike nationalist movements among indigenous peoples, required forceful leadership throughout the world, not only in the Jewish homeland but in the Diaspora as well.

BUILDING THE JEWISH NATIONAL HOME

Before the war, the ZO had been headquartered in Central Europe; after 1918, with the Allied victory and the award of mandatory Palestine to England, it divided its administration between London and Jerusalem. At the same time, the United States, with its 4.5 million Jews and booming economy, became Zionism's chief funding source. Confident in the giving potential of American Jewry, Weizmann in 1920 launched a $150 million campaign for what was called the Foundation Fund—a massive instrument that would finance the construction of the Jewish national home. Weizmann's expectations, however, were exaggerated: eight years later, the Foundation Fund had raised barely $20 million. Equally important, Weizmann early on faced a challenge to his leadership from a faction of American Zionists led by the Supreme Court justice Louis Brandeis (1856–1941). It was a challenge that would haunt Weizmann, in one form or another, for a full decade.

Brandeis was an American Herzl—assimilated, imbued with liberal and progressive sentiments and convinced that Zionism was as much a project of social engineering as of political machination. But whereas Herzl had suppressed his own social vision in the interests of obtaining Great Power recognition for Zionism, Brandeis saw the Balfour Declaration as having satisfied the goals of political Zionism. In his view, priority could now be given to building a new society. Weizmann interpreted Herzl's legacy differently: he believed that Zionism's political project had just begun. To Weizmann, the ZO was a provisional government, its officers were politicians and its Foundation Fund was a national treasury. This view was shared by the leaders of the Yishuv's workers' movement, which drew on public funds for wages and inventory on the collective agricultural settlements. Brandeis sympathized with the ideals of the workers, but not with their methods. He saw ZO as a business corporation, which should not be squandering money on potentially lucrative projects like agricultural settlement. Its job was to attract private investment and judiciously use public funds for unambiguously nonprofit undertakings such as education.

Brandeis was defeated both within the ranks of the Zionist Organization of America and the ZO, but his businesslike spirit lived on in the negotiations leading up to the expansion of the Jewish Agency in 1929. The British Mandate had called on world Jewry to create a "Jewish Agency" to promote the development of the Jewish national home. At first, the ZO was designated as this agency, but Weizmann envisioned a vast increase in the agency's resources and scope, should

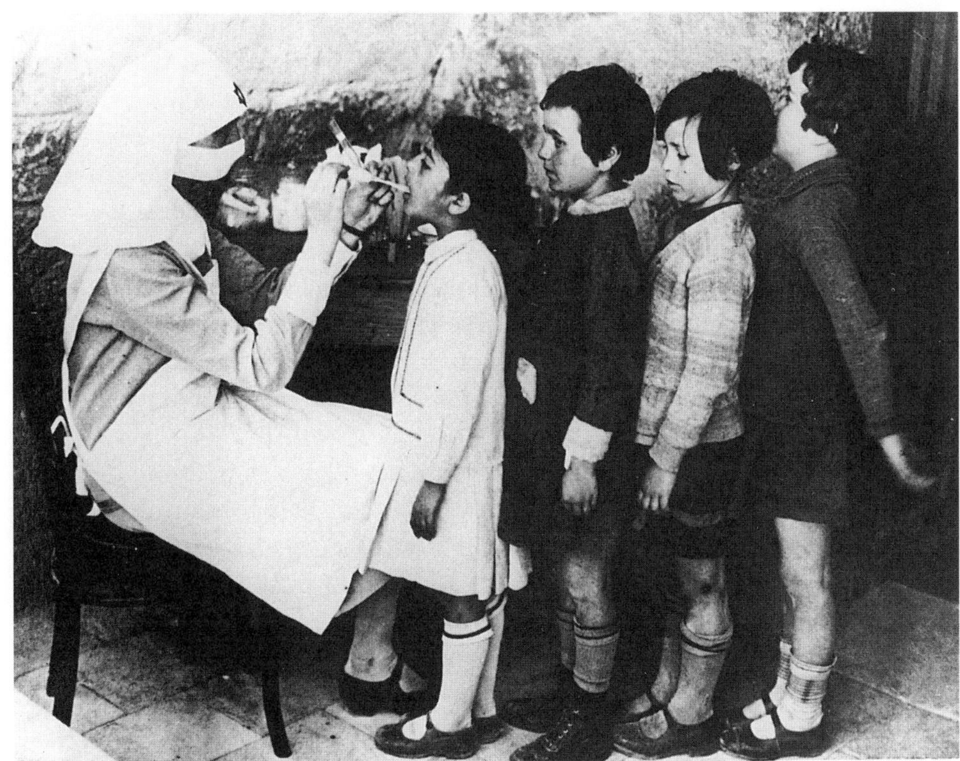

A nurse from the Hadassah medical unit examining young girls in Jerusalem, 1920s. Hadassah was an organization of American Zionist women that provided health care to both Jews and non-Jews in Palestine.

it include wealthy non-Zionist Jews. Throughout the 1920s, Weizmann tried to coax America's most prominent Jewish philanthropists into offering substantive support for the Jewish national home, only to be frustrated by Brandeisian rhetoric. American Jewish leaders like the attorney Louis Marshall (1856–1929) and the financier Felix Warburg (1871–1937) demanded strict accountability and the placement of experts, not politicians, in positions of authority. In 1927, at a time when the Yishuv wallowed in economic depression, a cost-cutting regime briefly took hold of the ZO and cut its ties to the workers' movement. In 1929 Weizmann finally won the allegiance of such men to an expanded Jewish Agency, whose twin executives in London and Jerusalem would henceforth serve as the principal nexus between world Jewry and the Yishuv.

Contrary to the Americans' expectations, however, the Jewish Agency, and particularly its Jerusalem Executive, quickly took on the trappings of government. This was largely the doing of the Yishuv's workers' movement, which possessed unshakable political ambition and was the leading political force in the Jewish national home. From the outset, representatives of the Yishuv's workers' movement sat on the Jewish Agency Jerusalem Executive, and when David Ben-Gurion became chair of that body in 1935, he effectively became the prime minister of a Zionist provisional government. By that time, workers' parties commanded the support of some forty percent of the Yishuv electorate, and they dominated the Yishuv's representative National Assembly and that assembly's executive, the National Council.

Labor Zionism's rise to dominance in the Yishuv was the result of two forces: the molding of socialist ideology into a form compatible with Zionist ideals, and the construction of a formidable political machine. The former enabled the latter. Already by 1914 the Workers of Zion party had begun to lose its Marxist tinge. The Yishuv's working class was so frail, and the challenges of building a nation so great, that socialist Zionists could not afford to take a purely adversarial stance toward the ZO and the Yishuv's bourgeoisie. In a land as poor as Palestine, capital was not the worker's enemy, as it was in the highly industrialized West, but rather his only hope for a livelihood. Moreover, for those hardy few who had immigrated to Palestine and successfully made a stand there, Zionism meant far more than a small component in a process of international socialist revolution. The Bolshevik Revolution entranced many of the Workers of Zion not for its impact on the world as a whole but for the lessons it taught about the attainment of hegemony in Palestine.

Thus in 1919 Ben-Gurion effectively pushed the Workers of Zion into dissolution by melding the party with a group of independent activists to form a new party, Unity of Labor (Ahdut Ha-'Avodah). Most of the leaders of the new party, including Berl Katznelson and Yitzhak Tabenkin (1887–1971), came from the independents. The party's name reflected wishful thinking, however, for it faced stiff opposition within the Yishuv labor movement. The Young Worker, the more romantic and purely nationalist of the prewar parties, remained suspicious of Unity of Labor because of the latter's continuing lip service to the principle of class struggle. And a surge of support for a solidly Marxist approach came from thousands of socialist youth who arrived with Zionism's Third Aliyah, which occurred between 1919 and 1923.

Many of these young people took part in what they called the Labor Brigade (Gedud Ha-'Avodah), a mobile and revolutionary community of workers. The brigade's collectivist spirit manifested itself in communes among the road builders and urban laborers, as well as the creation in 1924 of a new form of communal settlement, the kibbutz, which was much larger and economically more varied than the prewar kvutzah. In time, the Labor Brigade collapsed, a victim of exhaustion, rivalry with Unity of Labor and the ideological factionalism that is so common among movements on both extremes of the political spectrum.

Like Marxism, the agrarian orientation of the early pioneers was also subject to compromise. During the 1920s, two-thirds of the members of the Zionist labor parties and trade unions were urban workers. The kibbutzim quickly established themselves as an enclave within the labor movement, with their own interests and champions, competing for scarce resources with the urban workers and their party bosses. One political party, the extreme leftist Young Guard (Ha-Shomer Ha-Tza'ir), did commit itself entirely to the kibbutz ideal, but this case was exceptional.

Although true unity within Labor Zionism remained unattainable, the movement consolidated itself into a formidable political force with the creation in 1930 of Mapai (an acronym for the Land of Israel Workers' Party). This party melded the Young Worker into the ranks of Unity of Labor. The result was a complete retreat from the concept of class struggle. This retreat was elegantly defended by Chaim Arlosoroff (1899–1933), a brilliant theoretician in the Young Worker, and by Ben-Gurion himself, who wrote in 1929 that the interests of the Jewish worker are not identical with those of the Jewish nation as a whole. The Yishuv, Ben-

Gurion acknowledged, depended on private capital. (Over three-fourths of capital imports during the Mandate period came from private sources.) At the same time, Ben-Gurion argued, the labor movement had an obligation and unique ability to lead the nation toward independence, and he favored a strong public sector as a guiding and regulating economic force. The centralization of power, both political and economic, was an essential vehicle for the realization of Zionist aims.

In this spirit, Ben-Gurion favored the expansion of the power of the Histadrut, a national trade union that had been founded in 1920. Although there was widespread support in the Zionist labor movement for such a union, opinions differed as to its relationship with the political parties. Staunch Marxists from the Third Aliyah wanted to see a clear separation between a party, whose chief function was to plot revolution, and a trade union, which had the more humble task of improving the workers' present circumstances. But Ben-Gurion, as secretary of both Mapai and the Histadrut, sought to meld the two and to extend the latter's purview from representing employees to being its own employer and producer. Through its Workers' Bank and a variety of enterprises, the Histadrut had by 1930 become the hegemonic economic force in the Yishuv.

There was far more to the Histadrut than economics. It was a vast educational organization, running schools, youth movements and cultural centers throughout the Yishuv. Moreover, it strongly influenced gender relations and the role of women in the workplace. The Histadrut's Women's Workers' Council both encouraged women's involvement in public life and set limits on the nature of that involvement. At first the WWC had a strongly feminist leadership that championed the rights of the woman worker, but from the late 1920s the organization retreated to a focus on social-welfare activities such as day care and women's vocational education. Similar developments occurred among the kibbutzim, about one-fifth of whose population was female by the mid-1920s. On the one hand, women enjoyed legal and social freedoms in the collective settlements that they had not known in Europe. On the other hand, women were, by and large, kept out of the kibbutzim's productive branches, such as agriculture, and concentrated instead in the nursery, laundry and dining hall. Kibbutz ideology claimed that a truly socialist spirit could be inculcated only in children raised collectively. At the same time, both the men and women among the pioneers believed in the superiority of breast-feeding and of the importance of maternal child care.

Although the Yishuv's labor movement was in many ways pragmatic, and in some quite conventional, it nonetheless embodied tremendous passion and revolutionary spirit. This was a movement of the young, of thousands of idealistic adolescents, burning with Zionist fervor and dreams of social justice. There was no small element of generational revolt in the labor movement, whose youth movements in Central and Eastern Europe attracted rebels against their parents' values—whether Orthodox, middle class or assimilationist.

These sentiments were powerfully expressed by the poet Uri Zvi Greenberg (1894–1981), a Galician Jew from a Hasidic background who immigrated to Palestine in 1924, worked as a rural laborer and became involved in the leftist edge of the labor movement before turning to the far right. In his poem "At Your Feet, Jerusalem," he wrote:

Father raged, mother cried, and the white bed was orphaned.
We brought you blood and fingers, love and sinew, unburdened
Shoulders to bear the Hebrew globe with its heavy troubles.
And all our dreams and all our wishes we gave up
So that we may be poor laborers in the wasteland . . .
And we demand no compensation for our destruction
We who cover the swamps with dead bodies,
As hands drive into them the eucalyptus trees.

The concept of pioneering entailed self-realization through sacrifice to the collective, transcendence through the material improvement of the land, elevation of the spirit through hard physical labor. Labor Zionism, combining the secular messianism of the Marxist Left with traditional Jewish yearnings to sanctify the world, created a substitute religion. One of the labor movement's most influential poets, Avraham Shlonsky (1900–1973), made these sentiments explicit:

Dress me, good mother, in a glorious coat of many colors
And with dawn lead me to toil.
My land wraps itself in light like a prayer-shawl.
Houses are placed like frontlets
And hand-paved roads glide like the straps of *tefilin*.

Not all Jews in the Yishuv, of course, hearkened to the call of Greenberg and Shlonsky. Although young pioneers continued to stream into Palestine throughout the 1920s and 1930s, the bulk of Jewish immigrants were what the British authorities called "capitalists," that is, middle-class Jews possessed of at least modest means. Between 1924 and 1939, some 300,000 Jewish immigrants reached Palestine. During the 1920s, the immigrants of what is called the Fourth Aliyah came largely from Poland, whose 3 million Jews encountered severe economic instability and discrimination in the postwar era. The United States' adoption in 1924 of extremely low immigration quotas enhanced Palestine's appeal for persons who had frequently not been committed Zionists. The general deterioration of Jewish life throughout Central and Eastern Europe during the 1930s, coupled with the Nazi rise to power in 1933, accounts for the massive influx of the Fifth Aliyah.

Whereas the Second and Third Aliyot gave the Yishuv its political leadership and laid out the framework for its public sector, the Fourth and Fifth Aliyot made that public sector viable and created a vibrant private counterpart. As in the previous waves of immigration, so now did approximately three-fourths of the newcomers settle in urban areas. Tel Aviv's population, not even 4,000 in 1921, was 135,000 by 1935. By that same year, Jerusalem had 70,000 Jews, and Haifa 40,000. Those immigrants who chose the countryside expanded both the network of collective settlements and the capitalist plantation colonies, which made handsome profits through the export of citrus fruits. Industrial development rapidly quickened; the number of Jewish industrial workers increased sixfold between 1921 and 1936. The largest industrial enterprises were the Palestine Electric Company and the Palestine Potash Company, which extracted minerals from the Dead Sea.

A Jewish New Year greeting card depicting Polish Jews emigrating to Palestine.

There were fields in addition to business in which the newcomers were pioneers. Approximately a quarter of the Fifth Aliyah came from Germany, and these immigrants generally possessed a high level of education and professional expertise. The German Jews included physicians, lawyers, economists, scientists and scholars of all sorts. German Jews figured disproportionately in the teaching staff of the Yishuv's high schools, and even more so in the Hebrew University of Jerusalem, founded in 1925. Under the guidance of the likes of the historian Fritz (Yitzhak) Baer (1888–1980) and Gerhard (Gershom) Scholem (1897–1982), the study of Judaism was moved out of the yeshivah, where it could not be viewed from a distance, and also out of the gentile university, where it could be viewed only from a distance. Instead, Baer and Scholem created a secular and nationalist environment in which Judaica scholarship could strive to be both sympathetic and critical.

At the Hebrew University of Jerusalem, cafés in Tel Aviv and in kibbutz dining halls, a new Hebrew culture was forged. It was not a Middle Eastern culture, but rather a European and Jewish compound, transfigured by the encounter with the Middle Eastern landscape. As the poet Leah Goldberg (1911–1970) wrote, for the newcomers of Tel Aviv, "pure winter nights, rainy, overseas summer nights" and the "darkened mornings of world capitals" gave way to "the language of a strange land . . . thrust into the desert-wind-day like the blade of a cold knife." What united this new culture, besides its language, was an overwhelmingly secular outlook. The immigrants were mostly nonreligious, thus overwhelming the anti-Zionist, ultra-Orthodox Jews of the Old Yishuv. The ultra-Orthodox looked on the secular, Zionist and quasi-socialist New Yishuv with deep suspicion, even contempt. Moreover, ten to fifteen percent of the Jewish immigrants during the interwar period associated with political parties that were both Orthodox and Zionist. These parties had to find creative ways of reconciling themselves to the secular New Yishuv.

Many of the Yishuv's ultra-Orthodox Jews were organized in a political party called Agudat Yisrael, which was part of an international Orthodox federation that had been founded in 1912. Immediately after the war, the ultra-Orthodox agreed to take part in elections for the Yishuv's National Assembly. Constituting half the Yishuv's population at the time, the ultra-Orthodox counted on winning control over the body. But a disappointing electoral performance, followed by the waves of secular immigration that came in the 1920s, caused Agudat Yisrael to secede formally from the Yishuv's political structure and function as an entirely separate body.

Agudat Yisrael's anti-Zionist stand softened over time. Riots in the Yishuv in 1929, and the perils facing European Jewry throughout the following decade, created feelings of mutual need and solidarity. But ultra-Orthodox rabbis in Jerusalem continued to dismiss Zionism as the work of Satan, the greatest instance of idolatry since the time of the Golden Calf. This condemnation applied to secular and religious Zionism alike. The latter was seen an expression of colossal hubris, because it attempted to initiate the divine redemption of the Jews. What's more, by endorsing the physical revival of the Land of Israel, religious Zionists tainted this most holy of lands with worldly, material concerns.

Religious Zionists rejected these accusations. The perilous conditions of Jewish life in interwar Europe strengthened the old argument of the religious Zionist party, the Mizrachi, that Zionism represented a rescue operation in which secular and religious Jews had to join forces. An offshoot of the Mizrachi, the Mizrachi Worker (Ha-Po'el Ha-Mizrachi), shared many of Labor Zionism's social goals and worked within the framework of the Histadrut. For both the Mizrachi and the Mizrachi Worker, the Yishuv was unique, both for its geographic location in the Land of Israel and for its burgeoning Jewish community. It was the mission of religious Zionists to infuse the Yishuv with Torah values and prepare the way for a state administered, to the greatest extent possible, according to the laws and principles of the Torah.

An even more dynamic approach came from Avraham Yitzhak Kook (1865–1935), who in 1921 was appointed the first chief Ashkenazi rabbi of Palestine. As a young man, Kook was hostile to secular Jewish nationalism, but he venerated Herzl as the "Messiah ben Joseph," a figure who, according to Jewish tradition, will pave the way for Jewish salvation but is doomed to die in battle. Later in life, he applied similar logic to the secular Labor Zionists, whom he likened to Herod the Great, a great sinner, yet the man chosen by God to transform the Second Temple into a magnificent structure. For Kook, the Zionist movement represented the beginning of a process of divine redemption, and the Labor Zionists were God's unwitting vehicles for the realization of his plan.

Although Labor Zionists did not share Kook's views, they did welcome the possibility of a meeting of minds between Labor and religious Zionist interests. At the 1935 Zionist Congress, Mapai drew Mizrachi into a coalition government by offering support for Sabbath closings in the Yishuv. This was the basis for decades of coalition and compromise with Orthodox political parties. On the eve of Israeli statehood, the Jewish Agency Executive agreed to allow rabbinic control over Sabbath closings, dietary regulation and matters of "personal status," such as marriage and divorce. Thus, although tensions between secular and Orthodox Jews in the Yishuv could never be fully resolved, they could at least be managed, because of the overarching goals that virtually all its inhabitants shared.

There was no commonality of interest, however, between the Yishuv and the Palestinian Arabs, whose national movement viewed the Yishuv with increasing alarm and anger, and which began, at the end of the 1920s, to take matters into its own hands.

TOWARD ARAB-JEWISH CONFRONTATION

At the end of the First World War, there were some 600,000 Arabs in Palestine; thirty years later, they numbered well over 1 million. This rapid population growth was mostly due to a sharp drop in infant mortality, caused by improvements in health care and a rising standard of living under the Mandate. British and Jewish expenditures stimulated the formation of a prosperous Palestinian merchant class, which built beautiful residential neighborhoods such as Talbiye and Baqa in Jerusalem. The cities also became home to an Arab working class, with about 100,000 wage laborers by 1939. In the countryside, Palestine's landowning notables prospered as they sold produce to the Jews and, even more important, to markets abroad. Among the peasants, a traditional fear of authority curbed their willingness to make use of British-funded schools and assistance programs. The peasantry did benefit from employment in the old Rothschild colonies and other privately owned Jewish agricultural settlements. (These continued to hire Arabs, despite the Labor Zionists' strenuous efforts to stop this practice.) Moreover, many peasants moved into the cities, feeding the urban labor force. The dynamic character of the Palestinian economy attracted some illegal Arab immigration from neighboring lands. This phenomenon, however, has been exaggerated by pro-Zionist writers seeking to delegitimize Palestinian nationalism by denying the existence of an indigenous Palestinian Arab people.

Palestinian political life under the Mandate differed markedly from that of the Zionists. Whereas the latter centered on parties that mobilized the entire New Yishuv, the former consisted of associations of powerful landowning and mercantile families. These associations did little to organize or inform the Arab peasantry or urban proletariat. In the 1930s, Palestinians founded what were called parties, but these organizations were for the most part gatherings of notables around a powerful family, such as the Husaynis or Nashashibis of Jerusalem. The poverty and traditionalism of Palestine's rural populace, along with the aristocratic outlook of the elite, hampered the development of the modern machine politics that characterized the Yishuv. Arab political life was further complicated by divisions between the Muslim majority and the Christian minority, itself divided into many denominations.

Whereas the Zionists' most effective political institution was a secular political party, its Palestinian counterpart was a religious council. In the early 1920s, at the time when the British created the chief rabbinate, they also established a Supreme Muslim Council and appointed as its president Amin al-Husayni, a man with deep Islamic learning and strong Arab nationalist sentiments. Amin al-Husayni was also declared chief Islamic judge and mufti of Jerusalem. (The latter title was traditionally more honorific than substantive.) Owing to the power vacuum in Palestinian political life, as well as the religious sensibilities of most of Palestine's Muslims, the SMC operated in a far wider sphere than the chief rabbinate. The SMC became an important site for the expression of Palestinian nationalist feeling.

Palestinian nationalism defined itself largely in terms of opposition to Zionism. To be sure, even without Zionism, a Palestinian nationalism would still have developed, just as Arab nationalism took on specifically Egyptian, Syrian and Iraqi forms. Throughout the Middle East, and not only in Palestine, Arab nationalism was shaped by a paradoxical combination of resistance to European rule and the use of the colonial regional divisions as a sort of container into which nationalist ideology flowed like water. Throughout the Middle East, Zionism was seen as the most aggressive form of European imperialism because it was believed to seek not merely subordination of the Arabs but also their expropriation from a land holy to Muslim and Christian Arabs alike. In Palestine, however, Zionism had a particularly galvanizing effect, creating a sense of shame over Arab weakness on the one hand, and of mortal danger on the other.

As we saw earlier, violent demonstrations by Arabs against colonial rule and Zionism occurred in March 1920 and May 1921. Throughout the 1920s, Zionists responded to this opposition in two ways. Labor Zionists attributed Arab hostility to a minority of powerful landowners who used the language of nationalism to maintain their economic domination over the impoverished Palestinian peasantry. In this view, most Arabs, if allowed to view Zionism objectively, would see it as a source of social and economic liberation. At the same time, Labor and the ZO stuck to a policy of a dogged "creation of facts," that is, steady immigration, settlement and land purchase that would someday produce a Jewish majority, a fait accompli with which the Arabs would have no choice but to live in peace.

The Zionist project depended on the acquisition of land. Arable land in Palestine was scarce and fetched high prices, especially as demand skyrocketed during the 1920s. Until the mid-1930s, the ZO did not have the means to engage in extensive land purchase. In 1936, JNF purchases accounted for little more than one-fourth of the land held by Jews, but by 1947 that proportion had climbed to one-half. The rest of the Jewish purchases were made by private persons or the Jewish Colonization Association, a non-Zionist philanthropy. The Arab sellers were, during the 1920s, mostly wealthy absentee estate owners who had been hurt financially by the First World War and needed capital to maintain their aristocratic lifestyles. During the 1930s, economic difficulties in Palestine caused an increasing number of local estate owners as well as some small-holding peasants to trade in their land for cash.

Land bought by the JNF normally went for various forms of collective settlement such as the kibbutz and *moshav*, a small-holders' cooperative village. These were the forms of settlement supported by the Yishuv's labor movement, whose ties to the ZO provoked charges of favoritism from middle-class Jews who wanted help setting up private farms and citrus plantations. But the ZO's land-policy experts reasoned that the kibbutz and moshav were the perfect targets for public funds. They promoted all of Zionism's most hallowed national goals: they hired only Jews, provided agricultural training and staked out the borders of the Jewish state in the making.

Zionist land purchases are a source of great controversy. Critics of Zionism claim that these purchases expropriated the land of thousands of Palestinian Arabs. To be sure, landlessness among Palestinian villagers was a serious social problem during the interwar period. Zionist activity no doubt contributed to the problem. In 1920, for example, the ZO bought a large portion of the Jezreel Valley from an absentee landowner, and as a condition of the sale some 8,000 Arab tenants were required to leave their holdings. That said, peasant landlessness was a common phenomenon throughout the Middle East at the time, as the region began to urbanize and develop industry, thus drawing peasants away from the countryside and to the cities. In Syria and Egypt as well as among Arab estate owners in Palestine, capitalist forms of agriculture replaced peasants with hired labor, thus creating a landless proletariat. Further, critics of Zionism actually weaken their case by bringing in a second, contradictory argument, which seeks to delegitimize Zionism by pointing out that Zionist purchases amounted to only a minuscule portion of Palestine—in 1947, 6.6 percent of the entire territory, and 12 percent of its arable land. These limited holdings make it difficult to attribute to the Zionists primary responsibility for the plight of the Palestinian peasantry.

Regardless of economic reality, Palestinians perceived the Zionists as invaders. They were loathed both as Europeans, the hated supermen who held the Arab world hostage, and as Jews, members of a lower-caste religion. This latter reason made Arabs susceptible to propaganda, issued by the SMC, that Jews wished to take over Jerusalem's Temple Mount and destroy the Al-Aqsa mosque. Zionist efforts throughout the 1920s to buy up the property surrounding the Western Wall of the Temple Mount appeared to confirm Muslim suspicions. Moreover, the wall itself was a source of contention. According to Muslim tradition, the Prophet Muhammad tethered his horse, 'al-Buraq, at the wall before his mysterious Night Journey. The Muslim religious authority that controlled the wall allowed Jews very limited access to it. A chair for an old Jewish man to sit on while praying, or a screen to divide male from female worshipers, was considered a first step toward a foreign takeover of Jerusalem.

In 1928 attempts by Jews to make minor changes in the status quo at the wall prompted angry protests from Amin al-Husayni. British support for Amin al-Husayni's position infuriated the Zionists. Tensions over the wall escalated throughout the next year; an expansion of JNF activity and the establishment of the expanded Jewish Agency exacerbated Arab anxieties. In August of 1929, a demonstration by right-wing Zionist youth at the wall touched off mass panic among Arabs, who rioted throughout Palestine, killing 133 Jews, including 70 in the ancient community of Hebron. One hundred sixteen Arabs were killed, mostly by British forces. To this day it is not clear whether the violence was entirely spontaneous. Amin al-Husayni did call on the faithful to stop the rioting, although his inflammatory rhetoric had done much to provoke it.

Shortly after the riots, two British governmental commissions toured Palestine, and their recommendations were incorporated into a white paper issued in 1930 by the colonial secretary, Lord Passfield. The white paper was highly sympathetic to the Arabs, attributing their landlessness and unemployment to Jewish land purchase and the economic policies of the Histadrut. The white paper recommended a sharp curtailing of Jewish land purchase and immigration. This finding was harshly criticized by not only the ZO but also by key British officials and politicians. In 1931 the British prime minister, Ramsay MacDonald, wrote Weizmann a letter that effectively undermined much of the content of the Passfield white paper. Despite this victory, the Zionists' position was now quite different from what it had been earlier in the decade. Arab opposition to the growth of the Jewish national home had become militant, and the British were recognizing the impossibility of implementing the Balfour Declaration without alienating Palestine's Arab majority. These two problems would only intensify during the 1930s.

Palestinian Arab militancy grew in response to the Fifth Aliyah and to the maturation of Arab nationalist movements in other lands. Palestinian Arab leaders complained that they were being made to pay for European antisemitism and the rest of the world's reluctance to take Jewish refugees. Hoping to be able to block further Jewish immigration, they accepted a renewed British attempt to establish a joint Legislative Council, but the Zionists rejected it, knowing that such a body would work against their interests. When, in the wake of demonstrations in Egypt and Syria in late 1935, the British and French agreed to advance the countries toward independence, Palestinian nationalists concluded that militancy was required to promote their cause. In April 1936, the Palestinians formed an Arab Higher Committee, with representatives of five of the major Palestinian political parties, and headed by Amin al-Husayni. The AHC proclaimed a general strike, a tax revolt against the British authorities and a boycott of British goods. Armed assaults against Jewish settlements soon followed. The Palestinian Arab Revolt had begun.

The Arab Revolt was both a traditional peasant rebellion and a modern nationalist uprising. The peasantry found a hero in a Haifa-based sheikh, Izz al-Din al-Qassam, leader of a band of brigands opposed to the Palestinian landowning elite. (Al-Qassam's death at the hands of the British in 1935 turned him into a martyr, whose name would echo in the 1990s, in the Hamas movement's Al-Qassam brigades.) The Palestinians had no centralized army, but rather a number of militias, the most important of which was commanded by Abd al-Qadir al-Husayni, later a major figure in the 1948 war. There was also a multinational Arab army, led by a career officer in the Iraqi army, Fawzi al-Din al-Qawuqji, but mutual suspicions between the Palestinians and his forces frustrated his efforts.

The revolt entered a lull in November 1936 but started up again in the fall of 1937. Between then and January 1939, Palestine fell into near anarchy, as Arab bands murdered British officials, Jews and rival Arabs, and the British responded with massive force. In 1938 alone, some 1,700 Arabs and 290 Jews were killed. By the time the British had finally put down the revolt, war with the British and internecine bloodshed had decimated the Palestinian Arab leadership. The AHC had disbanded, and Amin al-Husayni had fled abroad to escape arrest.

The Arab Revolt brought British officials to despise Palestinian nationalism,

Rioting in Jaffa during the Palestinian Arab Revolt, 1936.

but they could not ignore it. The British could not simply withdraw from Palestine, nor could they hand it to the Zionists. Events in Europe forced them to formulate an alternative solution.

The rise of Fascist Italy and Germany posed a direct threat to British imperial interests in the Middle East. Benito Mussolini had clear designs on North Africa, and Adolf Hitler presented Nazi Germany to the Arabs as an ally and example, a model of a vanquished nation, "humiliated" by the West, which had, against all odds, risen to greatness. Hitler's antisemitism, which struck a responsive chord in Arabs hostile to Zionism, enhanced the attractiveness of the Nazi state. Faced with the growing likelihood of war, Britain had to retain good relations with the Arab world, home to the Suez Canal, thousands of British troops and oil—vital for a mechanized army. Thus the British began to consider a way out of the Palestinian quagmire that would leave them on solid ground.

In 1937 Palestine hosted yet another royal investigative commission, this time headed by Lord Peel, former secretary of state for India. The commission recommended dividing Palestine into Jewish and Arab states. The Arab state, which would be united with Transjordan, would be the larger of the two, consisting of central Palestine's hill country (today's West Bank), the Gaza Strip and the Negev. The Jewish state would consist of a coastal strip and most of the Galilee. The corridor linking Jaffa with Jerusalem, as well as these two cities, would remain in British hands.

The only Middle Eastern party supportive of the partition proposal was Transjordan's emir Abdullah, who coveted the moderately fertile West Bank for his desert territory. The Arab Higher Committee rejected not only the specific proposal but the very concept of partition. Not only did the AHC deny a Jewish claim to any part of Palestine, but it also would not countenance the proposed transfer of hundreds of thousands of Arabs who lived within the borders of the proposed Jewish state to its Arab counterpart.

The Zionist reaction was more complex. Weizmann supported the proposed borders, and Arthur Ruppin (1876–1943), the ZO's leading settlement expert, advocated an even smaller Jewish state to lessen the number of Arabs within it. Yet the consensus was that the proposed Jewish state would be too small to be economically viable, defensible and capable of absorbing mass immigration. Within this consensus, however, there was a split between those who accepted partition in principle and those who rejected any sort of division of Palestine.

The former view was that of the majority; at the 1937 Zionist Congress, the delegates rejected the Peel Proposal but authorized the Zionist leadership to continue negotiations with the British within the framework of a partition agreement. The latter view was held by right-wing and religious Zionists, who argued that the Land of Israel in its entirety was an inalienable possession of the Jews. There were also left-wing Zionists who rejected partition, but for quite different reasons. The kibbutz movement leader Yitzhak Tabenkin argued that a small Jewish polity would become a garrison state, militaristic and chauvinistic, and that only a state in all of Palestine would be secure enough to devote its resources to the spread of socialism and the kibbutz ideal.

As the Peel Proposal wilted, the Arab Revolt flared up again with renewed vigor. The near certainty of a new world war, and the strategic significance of the Middle East for British interests, led to the abandonment of partition and a search for a solution acceptable to the Arabs. In May 1939, after an acrimonious conference of Jewish and Arab leaders in London, the colonial secretary Malcom MacDonald (son of Ramsay) issued a white paper proclaiming that Palestine would, in ten years' time, become an independent state. During this transition period, Jewish land purchase would be highly restricted and immigration would be limited to 75,000, thus leveling off the Yishuv at about a half-million people. The Arabs, who numbered 1 million at the time, would clearly be the dominant force in such a state, although the white paper spoke of the future state as "binational," with some sharing of political power between the two peoples.

Arab leaders dismissed the white paper for its allowance of any further Jewish immigration and land purchase, the ten-year delay in the attainment of statehood and the power-sharing arrangements. Amin al-Husayni was particularly piqued because the British had denied him any part in the deliberations leading up to the issuing of the white paper. In 1940 he changed his mind and accepted the white paper, but he was rebuffed by the British, who did not consider him a viable negotiating partner.

Zionist reactions to the white paper were even more bitter. Instead of a state, the Jews were being offered, or so it seemed to them, a ghetto surrounded by powerful and hostile gentiles. Ben-Gurion, writing on behalf of the Jewish Agency, threatened to unleash a Jewish revolt against British rule. The great alliance between Zionism and Britain, forged by Weizmann during the First World War, appeared to have collapsed as Europe approached its Second. The age of diplomatic Zionism had ended; the era of militant Zionism had begun.

MILITANT ZIONISM

From its inception, the Zionist movement embraced an ideal of courage and physical strength. Zionists perceived the Jews as having been rendered feeble and passive by centuries of life as a ghettoized people. The answer, according to Herzl's ally Max Nordau, was a "muscular Jewry" (*Muskeljudentum*), strong and self-confident. For Nordau and his Central European peers, being "muscular" entailed being physically fit, successful at sports and gymnastics and, perhaps most important, knowing how to wield a rapier in order to fight a duel, still a common form of defending personal honor at the time. Herzl's heart leaped when, during his 1898 visit to Palestine, he was greeted at a First Aliyah village by young Jewish horsemen, riding tall in the saddle, with bodies hardened by labor and faces bronzed by the sun.

The rhetoric about "muscular Jewry" was not militant; it idealized physical prowess but rarely led to thinking about, let alone employing, deadly force. For a Jew in early-twentieth-century Central Europe, self-defense meant guarding one's dignity against antisemitic taunts, not one's life and property against rioting hordes. In Eastern Europe, however, the situation was far grimmer, and in the early 1900s young Jews took up arms to defend themselves against pogroms. As we saw in our earlier discussion of the Second Aliyah, some of the pioneers brought to Palestine the militant posture that they had acquired in Eastern Europe. The Guard, the armed band of pioneers that defended the Zionist settlements, was a response to both the Yishuv's genuine security needs and its members' yearnings to feel strong and empowered.

In the Zionist labor movement, armed force had little psychological appeal unless it was connected with the pioneering values of settlement and farming. The link between the two was fixed in March 1920, at the settlement of Tel Hai in the upper Galilee. During the First World War, members of the Guard had moved to this remote and strategically vital area in order to claim it for the Yishuv. They remained in the area even when, after the war, public order collapsed and marauders attacked the settlements at will. On March 1, Tel Hai was invaded; eight Jews died, including Joseph Trumpeldor (1880–1920), a decorated Russian army officer who had helped form the first Jewish unit in the British army. Trumpeldor was the Yishuv's first true military hero, and in death he became a universally venerated martyr. Right-wing Zionists emphasized his militaristic side, while Labor Zionists depicted him as a farmer who held a gun only to protect his fields.

Labor Zionism claimed a monopoly on the use of force. After the war, the Guard disbanded, and a national militia, the Haganah, was organized under the aegis of the Histadrut. At first quite modest in scope, the Haganah expanded in the wake of the 1929 riots, and even more so in response to the Arab Revolt of 1936–39. The Haganah was placed under the authority of the Jewish Agency, whose leadership overlapped considerably with that of Mapai and the Histadrut. The Haganah grew in size, procured weapons from abroad and began to manufacture them at home. These activities were at times clandestine, but occasionally quite open, for during the Arab Revolt the British trained and collaborated with Haganah field squads in raids against Arab villages.

The possibility of a partition of Palestine into Jewish and Arab states stimulated the Haganah to create a new kind of settlement called "Tower and Stockade." Established in areas far from the coastal population centers, these communal settlements originated with nothing more than a watchtower and a fence, both erected in a single night. This was a new kind of kibbutz, valued not so much for its social equality or use of Jewish labor so much as its ability to stake out and defend the borders of the future state.

Thus, pioneering values became subordinate to strategic considerations. Still, the Labor Zionist leadership claimed to adhere to polices of what it called "restraint" and "purity of arms" in its dealings with the Arabs, and insisted that the gradual construction of a Labor Zionist commonwealth remained the surest means of overcoming Arab hostility. When Zionist militancy was cut off from this optimistic worldview, the result was a quite different political ideology, Revisionist Zionism.

If Labor Zionism was the product of a political machine, Revisionist Zionism was the work of one charismatic leader, Vladimir (Zeev) Jabotinsky. Born in 1880 in Odessa, Jabotinsky had minimal exposure to Judaism as a child, but escalating antisemitism pushed him toward Zionism while he was in his early twenties. Like Herzl, Jabotinsky was an accomplished journalist and writer and a mesmerizing speaker. Jabotinsky was by far, however, Herzl's intellectual superior; he was fluent in at least six languages and became, despite his assimilated upbringing, an accomplished Hebrew writer, poet and translator. Jabotinsky's literary genius coexisted with a profound will to power and a belief that Zionism's political needs, above all else, required immediate attention. In this sense, Jabotinsky might be thought to resemble Herzl, and Jabotinsky himself claimed to be the authentic successor to the founder of political Zionism. Yet Jabotinsky was far more rigid in his views and enamored of militarism than the somewhat capricious and utopian founder of the ZO.

During the First World War, Jabotinsky made a clear choice to favor Britain as the future guardian of the Middle East. He worked with Trumpeldor to organize the Jewish military forces in the British army, served therein and, after the war, organized the first Haganah activity in the Yishuv. At first an ally of Weizmann, Jabotinsky by the early 1920s had grown harshly critical of Weizmann's cautious, diplomatic style. He demanded that the ZO hold Britain accountable to fulfill the promises inherent in the Balfour Declaration, which he interpreted as allowing unrestricted Jewish immigration and moving quickly toward the declaration of a Jewish state in all of Palestine (including Transjordan). This maximalist program became the watchword of Betar, a militant Zionist youth group founded in Lithuania in 1923, and of the World Union of Zionist Revisionists, founded in 1925.

For several years, the Revisionists enjoyed growing support within the ZO. In the elections for the 1931 Zionist Congress, Revisionists won twenty-one percent of the vote, as opposed to Labor's twenty-nine percent. In 1933, however, the

Revisionists faltered, in part because of the assassination earlier that year of Mapai leader Chaim Arlosoroff. Right-wing extremists were tried for the killing, which tarnished the Revisionists' image considerably. Angered by this and other setbacks, Jabotinsky and most of his Revisionist followers in 1935 seceded from the ZO and founded a New Zionist Organization. It claimed to represent some 710,000 voters, as opposed to 1,200,000 ZO members in that year.

Jabotinsky's aggressive, unyielding stand endeared him to many Diaspora Jews, particularly in Eastern Europe. He spoke to the psychological needs of Jews fearful of antisemitism and frustrated by the slow pace of Zionist nation building, who had internalized the right-wing nationalist ideologies of the lands in which they lived. Unlike the Labor Zionist leaders, Jabotinsky spent most of the interwar period in Europe—until 1930 by choice, and thereafter because the British, blaming the 1929 riots on Revisionist incitement, denied him entrance into Palestine. Jabotinsky sensed the strength of antisemitism and predicted that a great catastrophe would soon befall European Jewry if they did not emigrate en masse. (Jabotinsky's admirers claim that he predicted the Holocaust, but this is not so; he envisioned economic ruin and sporadic violence.) He sensed, and shared in, Eastern European Jews' longings for self-respect, and through his spellbinding rhetoric he painted an appealing picture of an armed, disciplined nation afraid of nothing.

There was more to Jabotinsky's worldview, however, than a yearning for land, dignity and power. His political ideology included a profound hostility to socialism and to Labor Zionism. Although he had flirted with socialism as a youth, Jabotinsky came to reject it as a totalitarian force that stifles individual development, psychic as well as economic. Whereas the Labor Zionists wanted to transform the Jews into laboring slaves, argued Jabotinsky, Revisionism glorified the Jews as heroic entrepreneurs. Jabotinsky accused Labor Zionism of fomenting class conflict, to which he counterposed the ideal of a national unity transcending class interest.

Revisionist political ideology was riven with contradictions. Jabotinsky claimed to favor limited state intervention in people's economic affairs, yet at the same time he called for nationalized land ownership and compulsory, binding labor arbitration. He claimed to be a classical liberal, supportive of civil liberty and democracy and hostile to authoritarianism, yet he glorified militarism. Jabotinsky's Zionist critics called him a Fascist, as did Benito Mussolini, though the Italian dictator meant it as a compliment. Jabotinsky's thinking certainly possessed Fascist elements. More important, the Revisionist leader was unwilling or unable to control those of his followers who toed an outright Fascist line.

The Revisionists in Palestine tended more to extremism than their counterparts in the Diaspora. The Revisionists were never powerful in the Yishuv; Labor had too strong a grip on power, and the middle-class parties failed to mobilize themselves effectively. This lack of access to power encouraged the growth of an underground mentality, a self-image as a minuscule group that had to employ violence to make itself heard. Moreover, Jabotinsky's enforced absence from Palestine deprived the Yishuv Revisionists of a possibly moderating influence. Instead, Revisionism was led by the likes of Abba Ahimeir (1898–1962), a historian, educator and former Labor Zionist, who in 1932 founded a group known as the League of Thugs (Brit ha-Biryonim). This small group disrupted lectures on Arab-Jewish reconciliation at the Hebrew University, attacked the German consulate in Jerusalem and was implicated in the assassination of Arlosoroff. Ahimeir was a visceral anti-communist and romantic nationalist; he exalted force and openly admired Fascist regimes. The League of Thugs was little more than a cell, but the Revisionist youth group, Betar, mobilized sizable numbers to protest the Histadrut's monopoly over employment and collective bargaining. During the early 1930s, violent clashes erupted between Histadrut members and Betar strike-breakers at workplaces and in the streets. In these altercations, Labor and Revisionist forces alike displayed considerable brutality. Both sides condoned the use of force; all the major European political movements that influenced interwar Zionism—Bolshevism, Fascism and Eastern European authoritarianism—considered violence to be the continuation of politics by other means.

The difference between Labor and Revisionism was not that the former was pacific and the latter aggressive, but rather that Labor did a better job of controlling its members and regulating the use of force. The Haganah, as we have seen, was an arm first of the Histadrut and then the Labor-dominated Jewish Agency. By the late 1930s, the Haganah numbered some 20,000 members and had a well-organized national command structure. Revisionism, on the other hand, never possessed such authority over a military group. In 1931 Haganah members who opposed Labor control over the militia seceded, forming a Haganah B. Although the organization grew to some 2,500 within a few years, and many of those members had Revisionist leanings, few of Haganah B's commanders were directly tied to Betar or the Revisionist party. Haganah B's leader, Avraham Tehomi (1903–1991), was not subordinate to Jabotinsky, and Tehomi took the initiative to reunite Haganah B with its parent in 1937. About 1,000 Haganah B members rejected this agreement, and they founded a new militia known by its acronym, Etzel. (It was also called the Irgun.) Even this rump militia, however, was not under Jabotinsky's direct authority.

To be sure, Labor Zionism experienced its share of factionalism. In 1935 Ben-Gurion and Jabotinsky negotiated a series of accords to put an end to the conflict between their forces, but in a plebiscite a majority of Histadrut members angrily rejected the agreement. Socialist purists and opponents of Ben-Gurion's machine politics were a constant source of friction, and there formed within Mapai a Faction B, which in 1944 seceded to form its own party. Throughout the 1930s and 1940s, Mapai's struggle with its leftist opponents was at least as fierce as its conflict with Revisionism. Yet despite it all, Mapai held sufficient control over its members and the Zionist national institutions to lead the Yishuv into statehood. Revisionist Zionism, on the other hand, may have glorified force, but as of 1939 it wielded little.

Jabotinsky's worldview assumed an intimate connection between Zionism and Great Britain, which, he believed, could be convinced that its imperial interests would best be served by one-sidedly promoting the interests of Palestine's Jewish population. Weizmann, although less strident, maintained that there was no alternative to a continued attachment to and support of Britain. Thus the issuing of the MacDonald white paper and the outbreak of world war in 1939 confronted the entire Zionist movement with a dreadful dilemma: whether to undermine "perfidious Albion" for having forsaken the Jewish national home, or to join forces with her against the greatest enemy the Jews had ever known.

THE SECOND WORLD WAR, THE HOLOCAUST AND THE YISHUV

As in 1914, so in 1939 did Palestine become part of a Middle Eastern theater of war between the Great Powers. The German-Italian Axis vied with an alliance of Britain, France and, after June 1941, Russia for control over a vast territory from North Africa into Central Asia. Unlike the previous conflict, where the Allies gained Arab goodwill by encouraging them to rebel against their rulers, this time around the Allies themselves were the rulers, and thus liable to be perceived as the enemy. In order to maintain Arab goodwill, the British imposed harsh immigration restrictions on Palestine. Whereas the 1939 white paper had allowed for 75,000 Jews to enter over five years, only about 50,000 immigrated to Palestine between 1939 and 1945, and at least 16,000 of them were smuggled in by sea by the Haganah, the Revisionists and other Jewish groups. The British authorities were zealous in their attempts to prevent ships laden with Jewish refugees from entering Palestine. These efforts led to great tragedies, such as that of the *Struma*, which in February 1942 foundered at sea, killing all but 1 of the 768 on board.

Despite their coldness to the suffering of Eastern European Jewry, the British did much during the war to develop the economic and military infrastructure of the Yishuv. This occurred in response to British self-interest, not a change of heart toward Zionism. Palestine's central location in the Middle Eastern theater made it an industrial and commercial hub, and many Yishuv industries were placed on a war footing. (Textile factories, for example, were put to work making uniforms.) Moreover, the Yishuv, with its educated and skilled population, much of which had military training, was a valuable manpower reservoir for the British army.

Despite initial attempts to suppress the Haganah and imprison its commanders, the British military realized that the militia was needed in the increasingly desperate battle against the Axis in the Middle East. In the spring of 1941, there was a meeting of minds between the Haganah, which wanted to beef up its forces in preparation for an Axis invasion of Palestine, and the British, who needed reconnaissance specialists for the upcoming Allied invasion of Vichy Syria. The result was the formation of the Yishuv's first permanently mobilized military force, the Palmach. (The Palmach operated within the framework of the Haganah and was responsible to the Haganah national command.) Palmach members served with distinction in Syria and Libya. The British also made use of Irgun members. In May 1941, the Irgun commander David Raziel (1911–1941) died while fighting against an anti-British revolt in Iraq.

The Zionists responded enthusiastically to the British call for military support. The Jewish Agency, the Haganah and the Irgun proclaimed support for the

A poster urging Palestinian Jews to enlist in the British armed forces during the Second World War.

British struggle against Nazism. The Zionists not only saw Hitler as a common enemy, but they also believed that assistance to the British would result, after the war, in the rescinding of the 1939 white paper. To this latter end, Weizmann demanded the formation of a separate Jewish army within the Allied forces. The British had no qualms about integrating conscripts from the Yishuv into the British army, and they created de facto Jewish battalions in Palestine, but the formation of a Jewish Brigade was delayed until 1944. More frustrating, the British attempted to disband the Palmach and suppress the Haganah after the Axis threat to Egypt and Palestine passed with the defeat of Nazi commander Rommel's North African forces at El-Alamein in late 1942.

During the first three years of the war, the Yishuv leadership feared for the very existence of the Jewish national home. Yishuv residents anxiously followed the Axis' eastward advance from North Africa. Italian bombers attacked Tel Aviv and Haifa, killing more than 100 Jews and Arabs. After the threat to the Yishuv passed, daily life became calm for the first time since the mid-1930s. Not only was the economy strong, but there were few clashes with Palestinian Arabs during the war years. There were several reasons for this lull in the Zionist-Palestinian conflict. Like the Jews, the Arabs benefited economically from the war. Moreover, the Palestinian leadership had been left in disarray after the Arab Revolt. In the resulting power vacuum, a relatively modern and moderate political party, Istiqlal (Independence), gained influence. Finally, there was a general feeling that regardless of the outcome, the postwar environment would favor the Arabs.

Early in the war, there was much hope among the Palestinian Arabs for an Axis victory. Amin al-Husayni strove to assist the Axis; in 1941 he met with both Mussolini and Hitler, and he asked the latter for a declaration of support for Palestinian national rights not dissimilar to the Balfour Declaration. A "Hitler Declaration" was not forthcoming, however, because the Nazi dictator saw no reason to irritate his Vichy and Italian allies, who had Middle Eastern interests of their own. Although Hitler did little for the Palestinians, Amin al-Husayni did the Nazis some service, living in Berlin from 1942 on, broadcasting anti-British propaganda into the Arab world and mobilizing Arab and Balkan Muslims into the Axis armies. Ever since the war, Zionists have branded Amin al-Husayni a war criminal, directly involved in the Holocaust. But although he was certainly a virulent antisemite, Amin rarely attempted, let alone succeeded at, influencing Nazi Jewish policy.

The relationship of the Yishuv leadership to the Holocaust is also a highly controversial and emotional subject. From the 1950s to this day, many historians and writers in Israel have argued that the leaders of the Jerusalem Jewish Agency Executive and the major Labor Zionist institutions did not give their all to try to thwart the Nazi genocide. The Yishuv leadership should have done more, it is argued, to publicize the Holocaust in the international arena, promote immigration and engage in rescue operations. Ben-Gurion in particular has been criticized for coldness toward the suffering of European Jewry and for insisting that any rescue activity conducted by the Jewish Agency be coordinated with the British.

These accusations, however understandable from a psychological point of view, do not hold up under objective scrutiny. As mentioned above, until late 1942 the Yishuv's main preoccupation was its own survival. By then, the Nazis' killing machinery had been operating for well over a year, and as many as two-thirds of the Holocaust's victims were already dead. Moreover, there is little that the half-million residents of the Yishuv could have done to rescue substantial numbers of Jews trapped in Nazi-occupied Europe. Critiques of Zionist behavior during the Holocaust rest on an exaggerated assessment of Jewish organizational and military power.

Ben-Gurion believed that the Jewish Agency's limited funds should be allocated for the strengthening of the Yishuv, not engaging in European missions of dubious value. When, in 1944, he authorized the dropping of Haganah paratroopers in Eastern Europe, he had in mind not rescue but rather public relations. He hoped this dangerous mission's volunteers, the most famous of whom was the young Hungarian Zionist Hanna Szenes (1921–1944) would convince Holocaust survivors of the Zionist movement's concern for them and win their allegiance in the postwar struggle for statehood. Indeed, an explicit concept of imminent statehood drove Ben-Gurion and his allies in the final years of the war, and this concept owed its birth in part to the Holocaust.

In May 1942, the Zionist Organization of America convened an emergency conference at New York's Biltmore Hotel. Believing that as many as one-fourth of European Jewry might not survive the war (the real figure was closer to two-thirds), the conference demanded immediate Jewish sovereignty in all of Palestine. Nothing less was acceptable for a people that had suffered so grievously and that so desperately needed a homeland to house the postwar refugees. This rejection of partition and demand for statehood represented a triumph for Ben-Gurion and the American Zionist leader Abba Hillel Silver (1893–1963) against the aging Chaim Weizmann. Weizmann continued to negotiate with the British for a favorable partition agreement, but in 1944 the Jewish Agency and the Yishuv's National Assembly firmly declared their rejection of anything less than statehood in the entirety of Palestine.

In that same year the Irgun called for a revolt against the British presence in Palestine. The Irgun had grown during the war owing to an influx of Jewish soldiers who had fled Nazi-occupied Poland, enlisted in the Allied armed forces and been shipped to Palestine. With some 2,000 members, the Irgun launched a number of attacks, some lethal, against British installations in Palestine. Its new commander was Menahem Begin (1913–1992), former leader of Betar in Poland, and a longtime opponent of Jabotinsky's emphasis on diplomacy and condemnation of terrorism. Under Begin's command, the Irgun broke ties with the Revisionist New Zionist Organization. Even further removed from Jabotinsky's worldview and the Revisionist movement was a splinter group, led by the Irgun commander Avraham Stern (1907–1942), which as early as 1940 had declared itself unwilling to suspend hostile operations against the British. For eighteen months, the "Stern Gang" attacked British officials and supported itself through criminal activity, including the robbery of the Histadrut's Workers' Bank. Stern was killed by the British in 1942, but in the following year some of his followers created a new underground movement known as Lehi, an acronym for Lohame Herut Israel, Warriors for the Freedom of Israel. Its leaders were Yitzhak Jezrnitsky (Shamir) (b. 1915) and Nathan Friedman (Yellin-Mor) (1913–1980). Lehi believed that all means, including assassination, had to be employed to expel the British. Such thinking led in November 1944 to the assassination of Lord Moyne, the British minister-resident in Cairo, by two members of a local Lehi cell.

Lehi's ideology was a strange brew of fascism and communism, racism and universalism. The worldview of Lehi members differed considerably, and the one thing that united them was a veneration of violence and a boundless hostility to British rule. But there were some among the Lehi intellectuals who resisted not only British rule in Palestine but Western European imperialism as a whole, along with the capitalist economic system that underpinned it. They claimed to be the allies of all oppressed peoples and states, be they the Arabs, the Soviet Union or even Nazi Germany, a "proletarian nation" fighting for its place in the sun. Inspired by their bard, the poet Yonatan Ratosh (1891–1965), Lehi favored what came to be known as an ideology of "Canaanism." Canaanism claimed that in antiquity, a pagan and universalist Hebrew culture infused the ancient Middle East. According to Ratosh, today's Canaanites stood ready to revive the decrepit contemporary Middle East with their neo-Hebrew culture. This worldview was actually anti-Zionist, because it rejected any notion of a mission to or ties with the Jews of the Diaspora.

Lehi's ideology was eccentric and its acts of violence spectacular. But for Ben-Gurion, the Irgun was the greater threat, both because it was larger and because he mistakenly saw it as the military arm of his political rivals, the Revisionists. Thus the Haganah focused on the Irgun when, in the wake of the Moyne assassination, it collaborated with the British in their crackdown against the Jewish underground organizations.

Although the Irgun and Lehi were minority movements, the Yishuv as a whole was radicalized by the experience of the Second World War. Unlike the previous war, which left the Yishuv weakened, the Yishuv was this time economically and militarily invigorated by conflict. And the Holocaust inspired the international Zionist movement and the Yishuv leadership in the subsequent battle for Jewish statehood.

THE STRUGGLE FOR PALESTINE

Nothing could be done to bring back the 6 million dead. The Zionists' attention turned to the living, particularly the million Jews remaining in the former Nazi empire. In 1947 some 250,000 Jewish refugees crowded the Displaced Persons camps that the Allies had set up in Germany and Austria. The Zionist leadership claimed that Palestine was the only logical destination for the refugees. The Zionists demanded the immediate admission of 100,000 DPs, and in August 1945 the American president, Harry S Truman, publicly endorsed this proposal.

Truman's attitudes toward Zionism were conditioned by many factors. He had genuine sympathy for Zionism and a humanitarian concern for the misery of the Holocaust survivors. This concern coexisted with unease about flooding America with the refugees, who could become welfare cases or form a communist fifth column. Moreover, as Truman was well aware, American Jews wielded considerable political clout; they constituted three percent of the electorate at the time, and they were well organized and politically active. Truman wished to check the expansion of the Soviet Union's influence in the Middle East, and Palestine was a possible source of conflict between the two superpowers. Working against these considerations, however, was the view, championed by the State Department, that Arab goodwill was essential to promote and defend America's Middle Eastern interests.

Britain, too, wished to maintain close relations with the Arab world, though unlike the wealthy and powerful United States, Britain now had to deal with the Arabs more as a partner than as a patron. Bled white by the war, Britain could no longer afford a massive Middle Eastern military presence; it vacated Egypt and India and watched nervously as Soviet influence grew in Iran. Britain still had considerable oil interests in the Persian Gulf and was determined to retain control over the Suez Canal, which it hoped to protect by maintaining a military force in Palestine's Negev desert. Thus the British foreign minister, Ernest Bevin, saw little benefit in a pro-Zionist position. Bevin's Labor party had hewed to a strongly pro-Zionist line during the war, but that was because the party had been in opposition and was looking for electoral support. When elected to office at the end of the war, Labor reversed its position to reflect the dictates of *raison d'état*.

Britain's pursuit of its own best interests appeared to the Zionists as betrayal. Despairing of diplomatic solutions, the Haganah in October 1945 joined forces with the Irgun and Lehi in attacks against British targets in Palestine. Lehi focused on murdering British soldiers. The Irgun did this occasionally, but it, like the Haganah, concentrated on destroying trains and military installations. The most audacious attack was the destruction in July 1946 of the British military headquarters at Jerusalem's King David Hotel. This operation was performed by the Irgun, but the Haganah played a role in planning the attack.

In addition to engaging in guerrilla warfare at home, the Haganah and the Irgun made heroic efforts to smuggle Jews from Europe to Palestine. Between 1945 and 1948, some 70,000 illegal immigrants attempted to reach Palestine by

Jewish illegal immigrants to Palestine, deported to Cyprus and interned in a detention camp in 1946.

ship; almost all the ships were intercepted by the British and their passengers interned. About half of the refugees were allowed to enter Palestine, but their numbers were counted against the monthly quotas for legal immigration. Although the illegal immigration movement accomplished little, it had great psychological impact as a symbol of the Yishuv's determination to take matters into its own hands. More important, the spectacle of ships being boarded by British soldiers and their passengers forcibly interned on Cyprus created a groundswell of international public support for Zionism.

International pressure, and the escalating toll from the Zionist guerrilla war, pushed Bevin in February 1947 to turn the Palestine matter over to the jurisdiction of the United Nations. An additional factor behind Bevin's move was ongoing Palestinian resistance. The Palestine Arab party, the vehicle of the Husayni clan, was reestablished in 1944. After the war, the Arab Higher Committee, which linked the various Palestinian parties, was reconstituted. At a conference in London in early 1947, Arab representatives forcefully demanded Palestinian independence and an immediate end to Jewish immigration. The Zionists had retreated from their wartime opposition to partition and now favored a division of the land, but there was still no common ground between Zionist and Palestinian demands.

The UN's Special Committee on Palestine, like the Peel Commission a decade earlier, recommended partition. This time around, though, the Jewish state would gain the virtually empty Negev, and the Arab state would hold much of the Galilee, which had a large Arab population. The Zionists accepted the proposal, although they were distressed by the loss of the Galilee and of Jerusalem, which would be placed under international trusteeship. The Arab states led what appeared to be a sufficiently large opposition to defeat the proposal within the General Assembly. Yet when it was put to a vote on November 29, 1947, it received just over the required two-thirds majority (thirty-three for, thirteen against and ten abstentions). American backing was crucial, not only for the one vote it represented but also for the pressure that the United States placed on some of the other countries to follow suit. No less crucial was the support of the Soviet Union, which saw in the Labor-dominated Yishuv a possible socialist ally in its search for a broad Middle Eastern sphere of influence. Finally, the Latin American countries, which voted solidly for partition, appear to have been motivated by a sense of solidarity with a small and historically oppressed people.

A vote for partition, then, meant many things: a bid for Jewish votes, a humanitarian impulse, a search for a client and, finally, a recognition of Zionism as the national liberation movement of the Jewish people.

The partition vote was Zionism's greatest political victory since the Balfour Declaration, almost exactly thirty years before. It marked the final chapter of Chaim Weizmann's illustrious career, which began with negotiations with the British during the First World War and culminated, at the close of the Second, with impassioned appeals to the leaders of Britain's successor superpower, the United States. Like Zionism's first diplomatic triumph, however, this one, too, was incomplete. A recommendation by an international body without coercive power did not automatically result in Jewish statehood. Whereas in 1917 the inhabitants of Palestine were poorly organized and their new colonial master firmly in charge, now the master was enfeebled and preparing to leave, and the Zionists and Arabs were mobilized to escalate the diplomatic struggle for Palestine into a military confrontation.

That conflict took place in two stages. First, there was a war between Jews and Arabs in Palestine between November 1947 and May 1948, when the British formally vacated Palestine, and the state of Israel declared its independence. Then, between May 1948 and January 1949, Israel fought a series of short wars, punctuated by truces, against the armies of five Arab nations, principally Egypt and Jordan, but also Syria, Lebanon and Iraq.

There is perhaps no issue in the history of Zionism more controversial than the 1948 Arab-Israeli war. Arabs and Israelis have always had opposing perspectives on the conflict, and in recent years Israelis have come increasingly to differ with one another as well. In the late 1970s, Israeli archives made their holdings on the 1948 war available to scholars. Scholars began to publish their findings in the mid-1980s, and since then this literature has come to be known as "new" or "revisionist" Israeli history. (The term *revisionist* implies revising earlier-held views and has no link with Jabotinskian Revisionism.) This scholarship tends to be more critical of Israel than earlier treatments of the war by Israeli or pro-Zionist writers. This is the case not merely because some of the documents are incriminating, but also because the younger generation of Israeli historians, like their counterparts throughout the Western world, tend to have a critical, even adversarial, approach to their country's past.

Our understanding of the 1948 war remains limited by the fact that the Arab states' archives are not easily accessible, so we know much more about Israel's behavior than that of her opponents. Moreover, Arab historiography, although capable of harsh criticism of Arab governments, conceives of criticism in a quite different manner than do Israeli scholars. Whereas Israeli historians accuse Zionist leaders of immorality and brutality, their Arab counterparts attack the Arab states for incompetence and corruption. Israeli scholars bemoan the cruelty of their country's victory in 1948, whereas Arabs lament the ignominy of their defeat. One kind of writing is motivated in good part by guilt, the other largely by shame. The account that follows draws on many interpretations of the war, Arab and Israeli, "revisionist" and "conventional."

The first Arab-Israeli war began with the Partition Resolution itself. In the autumn of 1947, the leaders of the Arab states bordering Palestine privately expressed inability to prevent the establishment of a Jewish state should the UN vote for partition. The Palestinian Arab Higher Committee, however, proclaimed confidence in the military option, and on the day after the UN vote, Arab attacks on Jews flared up throughout Palestine. The Zionists, too, felt that military action was essential. Although the Zionists had formally accepted the UN resolution, the partition borders were a strategic nightmare, and the Haganah quickly pushed beyond them to take land in the Galilee, coastal plain and Judaean hills.

By endorsing the Partition Resolution, the Zionists were by implication supporting the creation of a Palestinian state. In fact, the Zionists, British and King Abdullah of Jordan did not welcome such a prospect. Abdullah wanted the land designated for the Palestinian state for his own kingdom, and the British vastly preferred Abdullah, a stable and pro-British monarch, over the anticolonial Palestinian leadership. The Zionists, too, saw in Abdullah a relatively trustworthy neighbor, and suggested that he annex the central Palestinian hill country, the heavily populated heartland of the designated Arab state. Between 1945 and 1948, there were extensive negotiations between Jewish Agency/Mapai officials and Abdullah, but these negotiations produced no formal understandings between the two sides. Abdullah did not clearly sanction the establishment of a Jewish state; nor was there agreement about the ultimate control of much of Palestine's territory, especially Jerusalem. Moreover, had the Arab world accepted the UN resolution, Abdullah would not have dared attempt to prevent its implementation. Abdullah's sensitivity to Arab opinion was demonstrated in 1948, when, bowing to pressure from his cabinet and wishing to maintain his stature in the Arab world, he agreed to lead the multinational Arab force that invaded Palestine in May.

When Abdullah did go to war against Israel, his military goals were unknown and unknowable to his erstwhile negotiating partners. Neither did the Zionist leadership have an accurate understanding of the military strength of his forces, or of those of the other Arab countries. The Zionists assumed that Abdullah's Arab Legion had 25,000 soldiers, when in fact there were 7,400; they anticipated an Arab invasion army of 165,000, but the actual force was less than half that size.

Arab leaders made up for their military limitations with bloodcurdling rhetoric, which the Israelis had no reason not to take seriously.

Moreover, the Zionists had considerable military problems of their own. The Haganah (including its elite unit, the Palmach) could mobilize some 50,000 fighters, but they were for the most part poorly armed and equipped. More important, the Haganah was a militia, not an army, and many of its civilian commanders belonged to Mapam, a party to the left of Mapai. Thus the command structure of the Haganah was not fully responsible to Ben-Gurion. In May, Ben-Gurion dissolved the Haganah national command and created a standing army, called the Israel Defense Force, led by a professional officer corps. At first the Palmach resisted incorporation into the IDF, but within a couple of months it submitted. Ben-Gurion also melded the right-wing underground movements, the Irgun and Lehi, into the IDF. Each of these actions was risky and traumatic. It is one of the great achievements of Israeli history that in the heat of battle the leaders of Israel's military forces chose to subordinate themselves to a civilian commander-in-chief rather than launch a coup or engage in internecine warfare.

The Palestinians outnumbered the Jews by a 2:1 ratio, but the former did not have a credible army, owing to their lack of effective national leaders and institutions. Nonetheless, in late 1947 and early 1948 their militias killed hundreds of Jews in commando raids, sniping and bombing. Arab control of the roads cut off rural settlements from one another and placed Jerusalem under siege. In March 1948, the Haganah formulated a plan to secure the borders of the future Jewish state before the British withdrawal in May, after which, the Zionists feared, there would be a multinational Arab invasion. In this plan (known as Plan D), the securing of roads and Jewish settlements demanded the conquest of the Palestinian villages from which the Arab guerrillas were operating. Expulsion of the villagers was sanctioned if the commanders on the scene deemed it strategically necessary.

This plan was quickly implemented in the Judaean foothills in order to break the siege of Jerusalem. In the battle for the village of Qastel, the most notable Palestinian military leader, Abd el-Qadir al-Husayni, was killed. Palestinian morale was weakened further by the killing of the inhabitants of Deir Yasin, a village on the outskirts of Jerusalem. The Irgun and Lehi perpetrated the operation, but the Jerusalem Haganah command knew and approved of the planned conquest. The Irgun publicized their operation in order to terrify Palestinians into fleeing the country. In order to maximize the effect, an Irgun official on the spot made up a figure of 254 Arabs murdered. (Recent Israeli and Palestinian studies both put the number at 120.) At least some of those Arabs killed were unarmed civilians.

The Irgun's strategy augmented an already sizable wave of Palestinian flight. During the spring of 1948, most of the Arabs of Haifa and Jaffa fled in the face of battle. In these cities the Arabs were neither expelled by the Zionists nor told to leave by the Arab leadership. Expulsions of Arabs occurred later in the year, and in the rural areas that came under the purview of Plan D. The largest single expulsion, involving as many as 100,000 Arabs, occurred with the Israeli conquest of Lydda and Ramle, towns along the Tel Aviv–Jerusalem road and adjacent to the

Jordanian-held West Bank. In general, though, the Israeli army's emphasis appears to have been on conquest rather than depopulation. Christian and Druse villages in the Galilee, which put up less resistance than Muslim ones, were much less likely to be emptied through either flight or expulsion. All told, the number of Palestinian refugees was somewhere between 600,000 and 750,000; most of them went to the West Bank or the Gaza Strip.

Zionist military successes in the spring led Ben-Gurion to believe that the Yishuv should declare independence, even if that meant a multinational Arab invasion. Several members of his government demurred, but the majority supported their chairman. Even Weizmann, known for his moderation, urgently telephoned from New York to say, "Proclaim the State, no matter what happens." On the afternoon of May 14, several hours after England's formal surrender of control over Palestine, Ben-Gurion read the Declaration of Independence from the Tel Aviv Museum. His message was broadcast throughout the country, except for Jerusalem, whose electricity had been disrupted because of the war. In the proclamation, Ben-Gurion encapsulated the history of Zionism from the first Zionist Congress through the Balfour Declaration and Mandate up to the recent world war and near extermination of European Jewry. The Jewish state had been sanctioned not only by the United Nations, the declaration claimed, but also by the "self-evident right of the Jewish people to be a nation, like all other nations, in its own sovereign state."

Thus the Land of Israel became home to the state of Israel. The Yishuv's governing bodies became a provisional executive and legislature. Yet this little nation, with just 600,000 people, was not yet a viable state. The day after the Israeli declaration of independence, armed forces from the bordering Arab states entered Palestine. The Arab leaders had mixed feelings about going to war, but Arab public opinion demanded that the Jewish state be crushed. The battle plans of the Arab armies were poorly coordinated, and they often fought at cross-purposes, yet nonetheless they inflicted heavy losses on the Jewish state, which barely held its own. In June a UN-imposed truce gave Israel the chance to reorganize its army, and an infusion of arms, mainly from Czechoslovakia and France, provided the edge in materiel that they had previously lacked. When the Arabs unilaterally broke the truce in July and attacked, Israel routed its opponents and took land in the western Galilee that the UN had designated for the Arab state. By the beginning of January, Israel had secured the Negev. Ben-Gurion favored entering the West Bank as well, but he was overruled by his cabinet.

Israel emerged from the war with about twenty percent more territory than the UN had allotted it, but it was still among the smallest of states—about 8,000 square miles (the size of New Jersey), and half of that was desert. Even after signing armistice agreements with the bordering nations, Israel remained in a state of constant tension with its neighbors. At a peace conference in Lausanne in 1949, Arab representatives belatedly accepted the principle of partition, but in return for peace treaties they demanded that Israel retreat to the UN Partition boundaries and repatriate the Palestinian refugees. The Israeli government felt that these demands were unrealistic, especially since masses of European Jews were stream-

Theodor Herzl's remains, brought from Vienna to Israel, 1949.

ing into Israel and needed homes, workplaces and farmland. (Israel's population doubled between 1948 and 1951.)

Israel won the 1948 war, but at a terrible price. Five percent of the population was killed or wounded. The wars would continue for decades. They are with us still. The state of Israel that emerged from the battlefield was in many ways different from, even contrary to, Theodor Herzl's vision of a Zionist utopia enjoying the blessings of perpetual peace. But it had the undeniable advantage of being real. Given the circumstances and environment in which the Zionist movement operated, Israel's birth could hardly have been any less traumatic.

Despite all the international political factors that worked to the benefit of Zionism, the state of Israel owed its existence to the commitment and persistence of the international Zionist movement and, even more so, of the Jews in Palestine. The courage of the Yishuv was the product of not only confidence but also a sense of destiny. Like Herzl, the leaders of the young state of Israel combined rationality and vision, calculated action and colossal risk. They were awed to be participating in world-shattering events, but their confidence in the outcome was tinged with apprehension. This conflicted sense of self-assurance and doubt, of the possibility of imminent redemption or cataclysm, was voiced by Israel's greatest poet of the era, Nathan Alterman (1910–1970):

A night of straits, a night of trial.
And you ready and accustomed to trial.
I saw you desperate. I saw you armed.
My brazen remnant.
I saw you and understood how thin is the line

RICHARD LOBELL

The faces of the Jews are varied: what binds them together? Nothing but a sense of belonging to a single people, of sharing a common past and a common future.

RICHARD LOBELL

RICHARD LOBELL

L. CAPPER/TRIP

The public face of the Jewish religion is the synagogue, and at its heart is the sacred scroll of the Torah, which is both a teaching to live by and a holy relic of ancient times, a precious gift from the God whose voice thundered forth at Mount Sinai.

WERNER BRAUN

Judaism has a family face as well: the Jewish home is a "small sanctuary." *Left:* A wedding of Jews from Yemen. *Below left:* A Jewish woman lights candles to welcome the Sabbath. *Below right:* Purim is celebrated with dressing-up and revelry.

E. JAMES/TRIP

WERNER BRAUN

RICHARD LOBELL

"You shall teach them to your children . . ." The teachings of the Torah must be passed on from generation to generation if they are to remain alive. Today's Jews are seeking painfully for the appropriate ways of transmitting Judaism in a rapidly changing world. Some *(above)* opt for traditional methods, and put the emphasis on the male line. Others favor integrated schooling. The progressive movements have given a new role to women as rabbis and teachers *(below)*.

BAITEL-BENIANOUS/PONOPRESSE

JAMES MARSHALL

The Western Wall has changed its character since the reunification of Jerusalem in 1967, from a mournful (and under Jordanian rule, inaccessible) reminder of the lost Temple to a jubilant symbol of national recovery, attracting pilgrims and tourists from all over the world and from many different backgrounds.

RICHARD LOBELL

Holy city of three world faiths, and capital of the modern state of Israel, Jerusalem has captured the imagination and represented the longing of the Jews since ancient times. The Psalmist sang: "As the hills surround Jerusalem, so the Lord encompasses his people for all time." The medieval poet Judah Halevi wrote: "Beautiful heights, joy of the world, city of a great king, for you my soul yearns from the lands of the West." The victorious Israeli troops entered the Old City in 1967 singing the words of Naomi Shemer: "Jerusalem of gold, of copper, of light, I am a harp for all your songs." And after that war, the Jerusalem poet Yehudah Amichai wrote: "A man returning to Jerusalem feels that places which hurt before hurt no more, but everywhere there hangs a faint warning. . . . Jerusalem: the only city in the world where even the dead have voting rights."

RICHARD LOBELL

What does the future hold for the Jewish people? History is full of surprises—like the collapse of the Communist regime in Russia and the revival of Judaism there; like the victory of the few over the many at the time of the Maccabees, commemorated every year in the Hanukkah lights. The numerous problems, political, religious, and cultural, that troubled the Jews in Hellenistic times still haunt them today, as they face a new millennium.

8

The Age of Upheavals

Bernard Wasserstein

The second half of the twentieth century has been for the Jewish people a time of adaptation to new perplexities. The Land of Israel, for so long remote and almost mythical, has recovered its place at the center of the Jewish world. The creation of the Jewish state followed the nightmare of the Nazi years, when the Jewish people were confronted with virtual annihilation in Europe. The traumatic effects of the Nazi mass murders on Jews everywhere remain a central feature of Jewish collective self-consciousness. Israel's existence has been challenged by armed invasion and terrorism, so that the impression persists that the struggle for survival is not yet over.

Meanwhile, in the Diaspora, the process of social integration has come to be seen as a danger, threatening the Jewish minority with destruction through the gentle embrace of assimilation. The Jewish people worry increasingly about their survival as a distinctive entity. In some ways the trials of recent times have toughened the Jewish fiber, even if Jews outside Israel are numerically depleted. But there remains a strong sense of insecurity. Can the Jews, a people who have repeatedly adapted over the centuries to new challenges, cope with the perils and possibilities of modernity?

Opposite: Jews from Yemen arriving in Israel in 1962.

AFTER AUSCHWITZ

The Jewish world in 1945 was in a state of trauma. In the former Ashkenazi heartland in Eastern Europe, pitiful remnants of once-great communities stumbled out of concentration camps and made their way back to what had been their homes. More often than not, these had either been destroyed or occupied by local non-Jews, who now asserted squatters' rights. In Poland, the Ukraine and Slovakia, returning Jews were often greeted with recriminations and sometimes with violence. Even in the Netherlands and France, survivors encountered a general coldness and widespread disbelief in the reality of Nazi horrors.

At first the vestiges of European Jewry stood alone and almost helpless. Family and friends were often dead, neighbors were unsympathetic, if not openly hostile, and governments were indifferent and rarely inclined to offer special assistance to Jews. The only significant source of aid was the American Jewish Joint Distribution Committee, which responded rapidly with large-scale food, medical and other supplies. In the first two years after the war, hundreds of thousands of Jews in Poland, Romania, Hungary and other countries owed their survival primarily to the Joint.

Dependence on such help was greatest among concentration-camp survivors in Germany and Austria, many of whom crowded into so-called Displaced Persons camps in the British and American occupation zones. As political and economic conditions in Eastern Europe deteriorated in the course of late 1945 and 1946, tens of thousands more Jewish refugees from Eastern Europe crowded into these camps.

The influx grew to a flood after a particularly terrible episode in July 1946. At Kielce in Poland, a mob attacked a Jewish community hostel and murdered forty-six Jews. Elsewhere in Poland, hundreds more Jews were killed. The Polish authorities showed little concern to defend the victims. Some soldiers and policemen joined in the violence, and senior churchmen, including the Polish primate, Cardinal Hlond, blamed the Jews rather than the perpetrators for the outbreaks.

The British and American military-occupation authorities were ill equipped to cope with the mass migration westward of Jews from Poland, which was exacerbated by a Soviet decision to allow thousands of Polish Jews who had survived the war in the U.S.S.R. to leave the country. As the Displaced Persons camps became ever more overcrowded, the residents grew increasingly frustrated and resentful. Anger was heightened by some blatant instances of antisemitism by occupation forces, and the refugees' bitterness was fanned by Zionist activists who succeeded in gaining wide support for their cause in the camps.

An Anglo-American Committee of Inquiry into the problems of European Jewry and Palestine reported in April 1946, urging the immediate admission of 100,000 Jews from Europe to Palestine. But the British government would not implement the report. Although the Labour Party, headed by Clement Attlee, which had taken office in July 1945, was committed to support for Zionism, its behavior in government brought it into a head-on conflict with the Yishuv and with the Zionists' Jewish and other supporters around the world.

A STATE IS BORN

The last three years of the British Mandate in Palestine, between 1945 and 1948, were a miserable period of terrorism and counterterrorism by Jewish underground groups and the British authorities, three-way civil war among the Jews, the Arabs and the British and, ultimately, abdication of responsibility by the mandatory government.

Although the British retained formal authority in the country, the imperial power's political and economic weakness accelerated the internationalization of the Palestine problem. The United States administration, spurred by the greater part of the American Jewish community, pressed the British to implement the Anglo-American Committee's report and admit larger numbers of Jewish refugees from Europe into Palestine. The Soviets, too, gave diplomatic support to the Zionists. The Arab states, whose public opinion was aroused increasingly in support of the rights of the Palestinian Arabs, denounced Britain's sponsorship of the Jewish national home and demanded immediate independence for a Palestinian Arab state. With the new importance to Britain of Middle Eastern oil imports, this was pressure that could not be ignored. Britain accordingly continued to restrict Jewish immigration to Palestine and insisted that the country would not become a Jewish state.

The Zionists, however, posed a dramatic challenge to Britain's Palestine policy. Refugee ships, laden with survivors of Hitler's camps, were dispatched toward Palestine by the Zionists from ports in southern Europe. Most were intercepted by the British navy. More than 50,000 of the would-be immigrants, including women and children, were interned behind barbed wire in camps on Cyprus. In the notorious case of the *Exodus 1947*, the British foreign secretary, Ernest Bevin, ordered the ship and its cargo of 4,515 refugees to be sent back to its French port of embarkation; when France refused to readmit the refugees, Bevin ordered them to Hamburg, where they were forcibly disembarked and sent back to a camp. The miserable episode was one of many that poisoned relations between the Zionists and the British and tarnished the British government's reputation for humanity in the eyes of most Jews, particularly in the United States. By 1947 the British government concluded that it could no longer hope to rule the country. The last British high commissioner withdrew ignominiously from Palestine on May 14, 1948. At 4:00 p.m. that day, during a meeting of the National Council convened in Tel Aviv, David Ben-Gurion, the combative socialist-Zionist leader of the Palestinian Jews, announced the creation of the state of Israel:

> The Land of Israel was the birthplace of the Jewish people. Here their spiritual, religious and national identity was formed. Here they achieved independence and created a culture of national and universal significance. Here they wrote and gave the Bible to the world.
>
> Exiled from Palestine, the Jewish people remained faithful to it in all the countries of their dispersion, never ceasing to pray and hope for their return and the restoration of their national freedom. . . .

> We, the members of the National Council, representing the Jewish people in Palestine and the Zionist movement of the world . . . by virtue of the natural and historic right of the Jewish people and of the resolution of the General Assembly of the United Nations, hereby proclaim the establishment of the Jewish state in Palestine, to be called Israel. . . .
>
> With trust in the Rock of Israel, we set our hand to this Declaration . . .

The new state was accorded almost immediate recognition by both the United States and the Soviet Union. Ben-Gurion became the first prime minister and the veteran Zionist statesman Chaim Weizmann was elected to the largely ceremonial role of president.

The restoration of Jewish sovereignty was greeted with a great wave of collective emotion and pride by most (though not all) Jews in the Diaspora. Particularly in the United States they rushed to give financial and other support to Israel. The political influence of American Jewry also made itself felt in the policy making of the Truman administration. In January 1949 the United States government extended a critically needed $100 million credit to Israel.

In 1949 Israel succeeded in registering her victory over her Arab neighbors by securing their signatures to armistice agreements that left her in occupation of a much larger area than had been envisaged by the UN partition plan. No Palestinian state was established. Egypt and Transjordan remained in charge of the segments of Palestine that they had conquered. Jerusalem was partitioned between Israel and Jordan (as the expanded Transjordan was renamed).

Israel failed, however, to translate military victory into diplomatic or political acceptance. The armistice agreements were not followed by peace treaties. Desultory peace talks at Lausanne ground down in stalemate. Israel was regarded as a pariah by all the Arab states; she was subjected to an economic and diplomatic boycott, and *fedayeen* marauders frequently crossed the (largely unmarked) southern borders into Israel, provoking reprisal raids and reinforcing the atmosphere of enmity.

THE INGATHERING

One of the first acts of the new state was to open its borders to free entry by all Jews. The Law of Return, promulgated in 1950, guaranteed that "every Jew has the right to immigrate to the country." Within four years of independence, nearly 700,000 arrived. This huge immigration consisted mainly of refugees from oppression who went there as much because of the push out of their countries of origin as because of the pull of Zion. The two largest elements were European survivors of Hitler's camps and Jews from Arab lands who were compelled to leave their homes by nationalistic Arab regimes.

The Displaced Persons camps emptied rapidly as Jews flocked to Israel. Thousands more secured admission to the United States, Canada and other countries that now, tardily and selectively, opened their doors to Jewish refugee immigration. Those who went to Israel were often the most dependent cases,

A transit camp by the Sea of Galilee, 1951.

Jewish immigration to Israel, 1948–93.

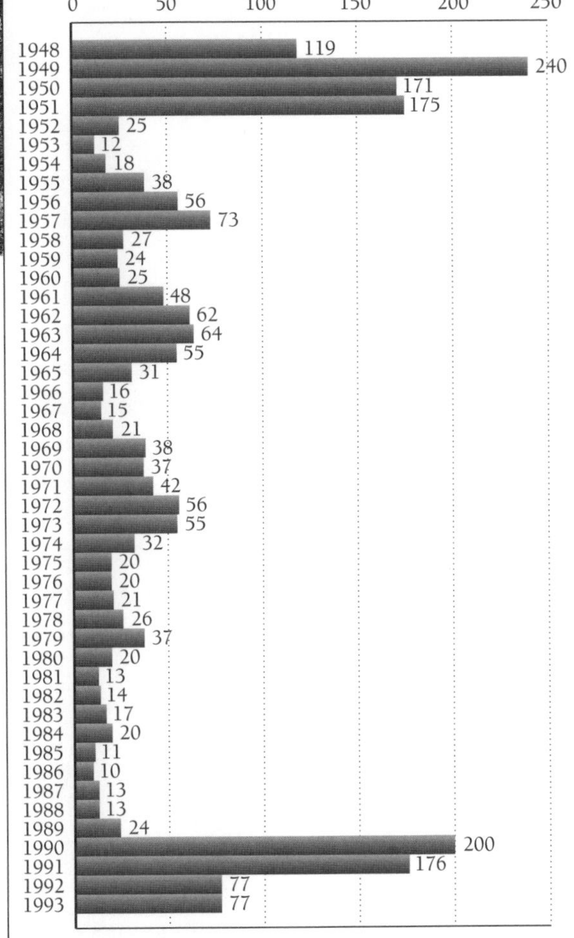

without capital, lacking skills, the young, the old, the sick: Israel took them all. Conditions on arrival in the country were often tough: fighting was still going on and men frequently had to go straight into uniform on arrival; many immigrants had to live for a long time in tent cities (*ma'abarot*). But most adapted to their new surroundings and soon felt at home in what they regarded unreservedly as their own country.

Meanwhile, another wave of immigration was arriving from Arab lands. Most were not originally Zionists by conviction: Zionism had never been strong among Jewish communities in the Arab world. But the fierce hostility to Jews throughout the Arab world generated by the first Arab-Israeli war drove Jews to emigrate in large numbers.

The ancient community of Iraq, heirs to nearly three millennia of Jewish tradition in the land between two rivers, immigrated virtually en masse to Israel. The exodus was technically illegal, although the authorities, eager to see the back of the Jews, winked at their departure. Sometimes, however, there were tragic side effects. The story was told, for example, of the rabbi of Khanaqin, a ninety-four-year-old man, bent double with age, who was arrested on the charge of smuggling Jews out of the country; he died two days later, and his body was returned to his family for burial. Within a few weeks, he was sentenced *in absentia* to four years' hard labor.

In many Arab countries, anti-Jewish riots accelerated the exodus. In Egypt bombs exploded in Jewish-owned department stores: an official explanation attributed one of these explosions to "an aerial torpedo from a Jewish aircraft." In 1947 the Jewish quarter in Aden was attacked by rampaging mobs. Most of the Adeni Jews left for Israel in the following year, though about 1,500 stayed put, trusting in British protection. When Britain finally withdrew from the colony in 1969, they immigrated to Britain.

The departure of Jews from much of the Arab world was organized by Israel in semiclandestine fashion. The most striking example was the isolated Jewish community of Yemen. Between June 1949 and August 1950, almost the entire community, numbering about 45,000 souls, was transported to Israel in planes in what became known as Operation Magic Carpet.

A NEW SOCIETY

In spite of the severe economic hardships of the early years in Israel, the integration of the Ashkenazi Jews was relatively successful. The power structure of the new state was dominated by Jews of Russian and Polish origin. Israeli society and culture remained attuned to European mores, and most of the former Displaced Persons soon felt completely at home.

Less happy was the experience of North African and other non-Ashkenazi Jews who continued to arrive in Israel in large numbers in the course of the 1950s and 1960s. All but 20,000 of the 250,000 Jews in Morocco emigrated in the three decades after 1948. The better-off elites among the Jewries of Morocco and Tunisia, who were francophone in language and culture, preferred to immigrate to France or Canada, while the poorer elements went to Israel. There they were treated with condescension and disdain and directed to settle in so-called development towns in remote areas or in run-down urban neighborhoods that soon became slums. Economic discontent and a feeling that they were second-class citizens erupted into riots in the late 1950s. The social and economic gap between Ashkenazim and the *edot ha-mizrah* (literally, "oriental communities," the category into which all non-Ashkenazi Jews in Israel were often indiscriminately lumped) gradually narrowed; but mutual incomprehension and resentment remained rife.

In the initial phase, the vast cost of integrating refugees from the Displaced Persons camps in Europe and from the Arab lands placed a heavy burden on the country's economy. The Israeli success in absorbing the immigrants was accomplished with the help of donations from world Jewry and reparation payments by West Germany; but it was above all a feat of organization, collective effort and commitment by the Israelis themselves. The austerity, rationing and low living standards of the early years eventually eased, but Israelis remained for several decades one of the most heavily taxed populations in the world.

The new state quickly developed a distinctive style and personality. An authentic Israeli culture flourished, radically different from the culture of the Eastern European shtetl or of the Maghrebi *mellah*. The great socializing engine of compulsory army service accelerated the acquisition of Hebrew and the process of acculturation. Although many of the immigrants from non-European countries had received little education beyond elementary school, and in some cases were illiterate, most soon learned Hebrew. Israel invested heavily in education at all levels. By the 1970s the participation rate in colleges and universities was among the highest in the world. The Hebrew University of Jerusalem, which had opened in 1925, and the Technion in Haifa, established in 1912, were joined by four other universities and many colleges.

The national passion in the young state for archaeology, a self-conscious effort to connect with the distant Jewish dominion in the land, produced some spectacular finds. One of the most notable archaeological ventures was the excavation of Masada, site of the last (ultimately suicidal) resistance to the Roman conquest of Judaea nineteen centuries earlier.

Yet in spite of its social and cultural achievements, Israeli society remained deeply divided: between Left and Right, between Jews and Israeli Arabs (who remained subject to military government that controlled movement and activities

Archaeologists and secularists protesting against a ban on excavations in the City of David in Jerusalem, instigated by the religious faction.

in Arab towns and villages until 1966) and, ominously, between religious and secular Jews. Religious political parties, participants in most Israeli coalition governments, succeeded in embedding certain elements of Jewish religious law in the law of the land. Civil marriage was prohibited; public entertainments (other than radio) and public transportation (other than taxis and a few buses) were prevented from operating on the Sabbath; and periodic disputes arose in the courts over the vexed issue of "who is a Jew?"

Behind such conflicts lay the larger issue of Israel's collective identity. As a large part of the population lost an intimate connection with the Jewish religious past and forged a new secular Israeli character, the question arose: In what sense did they still feel themselves to be Jews? The essential premise of Zionism, the oneness of the Jewish people, was thrown into question as Israelis became (in the outspoken words of one observer in the early 1960s) "Hebrew-speaking gentiles," while, at the same time, the Jews of the Diaspora became ever more assimilated into their countries of residence.

FACING THE PAST

One element in recent historic memory that drew together Jews from Israel and the Diaspora was the Nazi genocide. In the immediate postwar period, many Jews, particularly survivors of Hitler's Europe, found difficulty in coming to terms with the destruction of the greater part of European Jewry. The shock of mass murder took some time to become absorbed into the Jewish collective consciousness. In spite of the long history of antisemitic persecutions in Europe, there was no precedent for such an attempt at all-embracing annihilation of a people.

At first, physical memorials to the murdered Jews were relatively few—apart from plaques on the walls of synagogues and Jewish institutions. In literature and the plastic arts, the theme was largely absent in the early postwar years. A rare exception was *The Diary of Anne Frank*, the affecting record of a young Jewish girl's reflections while in hiding in wartime Amsterdam. It became one of the bestsellers of the 1950s. Translated into many languages and adapted into a stage play and a film, the diary opened the door for many to an appreciation of the realities of Jewish life under Nazi rule. Anne's former home became a shrine visited by millions, both Jewish and non-Jewish.

But it was not until the traumatized numbness began to wear off, half a generation later, that Jewry began to face seriously the full and terrible implications of what had occurred under Hitler's rule.

In the early war-crimes trials conducted by the Allies at Nuremberg in the immediate aftermath of the war, the specifically Jewish nature of the tragedy was subsumed in the larger category of "crimes against humanity." Matters began to change with the capture in 1960 and subsequent trial of the fugitive chief mechanic of the Final Solution, Adolf Eichmann. The Eichmann trial represented a major stage in collective Jewish understanding of the genocide. The seizure of the former Nazi functionary by Israeli agents in Argentina and his clandestine removal to Israel electrified the Jewish world. The Israeli prime minister, Ben-Gurion, determined that the trial be conducted with maximum publicity in order to serve an educational purpose, particularly for young Israelis, compelling them to face the realities of the Jewish experience during the war. This objective was largely realized. The horrors of Nazi atrocities against the Jews, recounted by witness after witness, were forced into the forefront of the Jewish consciousness. Eichmann was hanged in 1962, the only Nazi war criminal (indeed the only person) executed in Israel.

War-crimes trials continued in West Germany until the 1990s, in spite of calls from right-wing elements for a *Schlussstreich* ("drawing of a line"). But many cases were dropped for lack of sufficient evidence. In Eastern Europe, large numbers of war criminals were executed or imprisoned, mainly in the immediate aftermath of the war. Elsewhere the judicial reckoning was more tardy. In the United States, Canada, Britain and France, it was not until the 1980s that public opinion compelled governments to begin prosecution of fugitive Nazi war criminals—with inevitably feeble results.

The mixed outcomes of such trials, from Nuremberg onward, aroused deep feelings among many Jews—and others—who felt that the past was being swept under the rug. The issue of reparations, too, led to bitter debate. Some former victims of the Nazis objected on principle to having any truck with postwar Germany and wished to reject German offers of restitution and reparations as "blood money." But most Jews came round to the view that the Germans should pay compensation to the former owners of confiscated property or to their heirs. Since these, too, had often been murdered, the principle was established that the state of Israel was a collective heir to the Jewish people and should therefore receive compensation. An agreement on reparations was negotiated between the West German government and Jewish representatives headed by Nahum Goldmann(1894–1982), president of the Conference on Jewish Material Claims against Germany. The agreement, signed in Luxemburg in 1952 by German and Jewish representatives, including the Israeli foreign minister, provided for payment by the West German government of more than $800 million, most of it to Israel and the rest to the Claims Conference. Subsequent agreements greatly enlarged the scope of these reparations and provided also for payments to individuals. By 1976 more than $18 billion had been paid by the West German government in restitution and compensation. By contrast, the Communist East German government refused to pay any reparations. Austria similarly disclaimed any responsibility—at least until 1995 when, in a belated gesture of repentance, the Austrian government offered to set aside some (very limited) funds for the purpose. Switzerland waited until 1997 before agreeing under pressure to a full accounting of its actions, as a neutral during the Second World War, in disposing of Nazi assets stolen from Jews.

Meanwhile, the strange phenomenon of what became known as "Holocaust denial" troubled historians and the general public. At one extreme, refusal to accept the truth of the Holocaust (as it came to be known in the English-speaking world) was a deliberately provocative device used by neo-Nazis and other extreme rightists. So long as such groups commanded little public support, their twisting of the historical record could be dismissed. But when their electoral basis expanded, as in the case of the National Front in France in the 1980s and early 1990s, such distortions became more worrying. Similarly, in West Germany in the mid-1980s, a fierce controversy among modern historians, known as the *Historikerstreit*, spilled over into the public domain: the suggestion by some of the historians, notably Ernst Nolte, that Soviet crimes against humanity antedated, exceeded and (he seemed to many to be arguing) to some extent explained or even extenuated Nazi genocide. Such arguments, emanating from a respectable historian, caused widespread outrage.

From the 1960s onward the Holocaust became a central element in Jewish self-understanding. The almost willful amnesia of the postwar years was set aside, and Jewish communities, as if to compensate for their earlier neglect, rushed to memorialize the dead in every possible way, some dignified, others tawdry—all, inevitably and tragically, inadequate in the face of the immensity of the loss. Against this background, world Jewry became ever more closely engaged in helping Israel resist what appeared to be a succession of renewed assaults against the very survival of a Jewish collectivity.

ISRAEL'S SEVEN WARS

The history of Israel's first fifty years was dominated by the struggle against external foes determined on building their strength with a view to a "second round." Following the War of Independence, Israel fought another six wars before her enemies would sign permanent treaties of peace with her.

Israel's second war, the Sinai Campaign, was launched in 1956 after a series of border incidents with Egypt. In October that year, Israel signed a secret treaty with Britain and France in which it was agreed that Israeli forces would move into Sinai while French warplanes provided air cover for Israeli cities. Israel attacked on October 29, and in a lightning campaign, her forces moved south and west to occupy the whole of the Sinai Peninsula within a week. In accordance with their prearranged plan, Britain and France issued an ultimatum to Israel and Egypt, demanding that each withdraw its forces to a distance of ten miles on either side of the Suez Canal. When Egypt rejected the ultimatum, British and French forces moved into the Canal Zone. The United States, however, opposed the Anglo-French invasion and criticized its allies publicly. Pressure in the financial markets threatened the value of sterling, and within a matter of hours the governments in London and Paris called a halt. For Britain and France, their abortive Suez expedition was a humiliation that seemed to mark their demise as world powers.

For Israel, on the other hand, the war had positive results. Her stunning military victory put paid, for a while, to Arab hopes of eliminating her by armed force. Although Prime Minister Ben-Gurion succumbed to American pressure and withdrew Israeli forces from Sinai by March 1957, it was agreed that a United Nations force would be stationed in the peninsula. The UN presence at Sharm el Sheikh on the southern tip of Sinai effectively opened passage through the narrow Straits of Tiran to Israeli shipping to and from the Red Sea port of Eilat. Israel put this opening to the east to good use over the next decade, establishing friendly relations with a number of newly independent states in Africa and Asia.

In the aftermath of the Suez crisis, the anti-Western mood in the Arab world was fanned by Soviet economic and military assistance, particularly to Egypt. Under the leadership of Gamal Abdul Nasser, Egypt provided a focus for the pan-Arab nationalist movement that briefly threatened to unite Israel's neighbors in one colossus. But in 1961 the United Arab Republic, which for three years had bound together Egypt and Syria, collapsed in a welter of mutual recriminations. Yet however disunited they might have been on other issues, the Arab states remained of one mind in their fierce hostility to Israel.

Jubilant Israeli soldiers dance at the Wailing Wall, captured from Jordan in June 1967.

Israel responded by modernizing her armed forces, particularly with the help of France, which supplied new fighter aircraft, and Britain, which supplied reconditioned Second World War tanks. These were put to the test in Israel's third engagement with the Arab states, the Six-Day War of June 1967. The renewed conflict arose from a decision by Nasser in May that year to close the Straits of Tiran to Israeli shipping, a threat that he rendered realistic by ordering the United Nations force in Sinai to leave Egyptian territory. The UN secretary-general, U Thant, immediately complied, and Egyptian troops moved into Sinai. For two weeks a war of words ensued. Israel seemed to many observers to be in mortal peril, and her predicament aroused widespread public sympathy in the West—though no power took action on her behalf. Finally, at dawn on June 5, 1967, Israeli aircraft performed precision bombing raids on military airfields in Egypt, Jordan, Syria and Iraq that effectively knocked out the air forces of those countries. Once again Israeli forces advanced into the Gaza Strip and Sinai, and once again they were victorious within a few days. Meanwhile, the Israelis also moved into the Golan Heights, overlooking the Sea of Galilee, and occupied the whole of the West Bank of the Jordan, including east Jerusalem, which had been under Jordanian control since 1949.

The abrupt transition from apparent threat of destruction to sudden and total victory produced a feeling of collective catharsis throughout the Jewish world. The conquest of the whole of Palestine west of the Jordan, and, in particular, the

Jewish return to ancient holy places, most notably the Western Wall of the Temple Mount in Jerusalem, seemed to some an event of almost messianic proportions. Reunited Jerusalem was declared the eternal capital of Israel, and a large plaza was cleared in front of the Western Wall, which became a national shrine. Over the next quarter of a century, thousands of Jewish settlers established new all-Jewish towns and villages throughout the West Bank as well as in the Gaza Strip.

The years 1967 to 1973 were boom times for Israel. Jewish immigration, sluggish before the Six-Day War, picked up, and for the first time a significant number of immigrants began to arrive from Western Europe and North America. The old socialist-Zionist values and ethos began to relax a little as the culture of consumerism advanced inexorably. A significant vehicle of such change was television, which, in spite of strong opposition from many old-time leaders (including the now-retired Ben-Gurion), was introduced in 1969.

Israel's foreign-policy orientation changed dramatically as a result of the 1967 war. Calling the Jews an "elite people, dominating and self-confident," President Charles de Gaulle of France pronounced his displeasure with Israel's failure to follow his prewar advice not to be the first to engage in hostilities; the flow of arms and other aid from France abruptly halted. The United States, under President Lyndon B. Johnson, stepped into the breach and became Israel's chief arms supplier, economic supporter and diplomatic patron. The election in 1968 of a Republican president, Richard Nixon, who was not beholden to a significant body of Jewish votes, did not change American policy toward Israel. Over the next generation, a bi-partisan consensus in the U.S.A. maintained a firm, albeit unwritten, alliance with Israel in successive crises.

Israel's fourth war followed almost immediately after her 1967 victory. The War of Attrition of 1969–70 was launched by Egypt in an attempt to eject Israel from Sinai. The war on the ground took the form of cannonades across the Suez Canal by the opposing forces stationed on either side, and brief forays by small units into enemy territory (including some adventurous deep-penetration raids by Israel into Egypt). In desperation the Egyptians turned to the U.S.S.R. for support. Advanced Soviet fighter planes were supplied to the Egyptian air force, and for a time Soviet pilots flew missions in planes with Egyptian markings. The danger that this posed of direct superpower involvement marked a serious escalation of the conflict. In the hope of dissuading the Egyptians from continuing the strife, Israel resorted to large-scale air raids over Egypt, whose towns along the edge of the canal were reduced to rubble. In August 1970, Egypt and Israel, both exhausted from the inconclusive warfare, announced a truce.

Efforts over the next three years to secure a diplomatic settlement of the conflict proved unsuccessful. The Israeli government, headed from 1969 by the redoubtable Golda Meir (1898–1978), insisted that it would not withdraw from any occupied territories in advance of peace treaties with its neighbors. Meanwhile, terrorist attacks by followers of the Palestine Liberation Organization, founded in 1964, and its extremist offshoots brought a renewed threat to Israeli civilians—and to Jews and non-Jews in other countries. A wave of hijackings and bomb attacks culminated in 1972 in the seizure of Israeli athletes at the Olympic Games in Munich: eleven were killed in the course of a botched rescue attempt by German paramilitary forces. The Egyptian leader, Anwar Sadat, who had assumed power following the death of Nasser in September 1969, gave some signs of a change in thinking: in 1972 he ordered Soviet advisers out of Egypt and effected a dramatic shift in diplomatic alignment toward friendship with the United States. Sadat even expressed a readiness to make peace with Israel. These moves were not, however, taken seriously in Jerusalem, which maintained an unbending diplomatic stance.

In response, Sadat secretly planned a further round of hostilities in partnership with Syria. The fifth major Arab-Israeli military confrontation, the Yom Kippur War began on October 6, 1973, with a simultaneous onslaught by Egyptian forces across the Suez Canal and by the Syrians on the Golan Heights. The Arab armies succeeded in completely surprising the Israelis, whose forces on the front lines were unusually thin because the date chosen for the attack was the Day of Atonement, the holiest date in the Jewish religious calendar. At two o'clock that afternoon, sirens were heard all over Israel and reservists rushed from synagogues to join their units. This war engaged the largest numbers of tanks, aircraft and troops of all the Arab-Israeli military encounters. Israel eventually succeeded in throwing back the Arab armies and in launching a counteroffensive. Israeli forces crossed the Suez Canal and advanced into the heart of Egypt. On the Syrian front, after savage fighting, the initial Syrian thrust, which had almost broken through into northern Israel, was repelled, and Israeli forces moved close to Damascus. By the time a shaky ceasefire was concluded at the end of October, Israel had achieved victory. But the triumph was costly (more than 2,500 Israelis had been killed in the fighting), the blow to Israeli morale was profound and the reckoning was bitter.

Golda Meir and her defense minister, Moshe Dayan (1915–1981), were compelled to resign in early 1974. The next prime minister, Yitzhak Rabin (1922–1995), belonged to a new generation and was the first head of an Israeli government born in the country. Rabin warned his country that the fat years since 1967 would now be succeeded by a lean period. The 1973 war marked the opening of a major international energy crisis in which the Arab-dominated oil producers' cartel, OPEC, succeeded in tripling the price of petroleum. The Arab deployment of the "oil weapon" against Western powers judged overly sympathetic to Israel seemed to presage a dramatic shift in the balance of power in the Middle East. As Third World countries formerly friendly to Israel broke off relations with her under Arab pressure, the Jewish state now found itself increasingly isolated in international forums. In 1974 the head of the Palestine Liberation Organization, Yasir Arafat, appeared at the podium of the United Nations General Assembly in military fatigues, carrying a barely concealed gun. In November 1975 the assembly passed a resolution declaring Zionism "a form of racism": seventy-five countries (including the Communist bloc, Arab countries and most African and Asian states) voted in favor; thirty-five (mainly Western countries) voted against; and thirty-two abstained. Economic recession and renewed terrorist attacks further darkened the Israeli national mood.

Following the October war, efforts to achieve a diplomatic resolution of the Arab-Israeli conflict were promoted by the United States, under the energetic direction of the secretary of state, Henry Kissinger (a Jew, born in 1923 in

Germany, who had arrived in America as a refugee from Nazism). An international conference, attended by Israel, Egypt and Jordan as well as representatives of the two superpowers, opened at Geneva in December 1973. But it was stillborn: after the initial meeting, it was indefinitely adjourned and never met again. Over the next two years, Kissinger's indefatigable "shuttle diplomacy" secured two "disengagement agreements" between Israel and Egypt in Sinai and one with Syria. These led to limited withdrawals by Israeli forces on both the northern and the southern fronts. But hopes that these agreements might lead to a general political settlement were frustrated.

The mood of disillusionment in Israel since the 1973 war produced a delayed political turnaround in the general elections of May 1977. By the 1970s Jews from Arab lands and their descendants formed nearly half of Israeli society and began to use their numbers to exercise political influence. The Labor movement, which had dominated all Israeli governments since the establishment of the state, was ousted from power by the nationalist Likud bloc headed by the former Irgun commander and veteran right-wing politician Menahem Begin. His Likud movement (a union of his Herut Party with the center-right Liberals) formed a coalition with centrist and religious parties, ending the twenty-nine-year hegemony of the Labor Zionists in Israeli politics. Declaring that his goal was the entrenchment of the Jewish state in the whole of the Land of Israel, including the territories captured in 1967, Begin ordered the acceleration of Jewish settlement in these areas. In a further assertion of Israeli determination to resist pressure for withdrawal, the Golan Heights were formally annexed.

In November 1977, however, a dramatic initiative by President Sadat led to a decisive change in the diplomatic climate. The Egyptian president defied Arab critics by visiting Jerusalem as an official guest. He received a rapturous welcome from the Israeli population, who thronged the streets to welcome their former enemy, almost delirious at the prospect of peace. In a speech to the Israeli parliament, Sadat declared his readiness to make peace. Lengthy negotiations between Israel and Egypt culminated in 1978 in a mammoth session under the auspices of the American president, Jimmy Carter, at Camp David in Maryland. The Camp David agreements, sealed with embraces by the three leaders on the lawn of the White House, led to the signing of a formal peace treaty between Israel and Egypt in 1979. Under the terms of the treaty, Israel withdrew in stages from the whole of the Sinai Peninsula (but not from Gaza) by 1982.

The other Arab "confrontation states" and the Palestine Liberation Organization refused, however, to join in the movement toward reconciliation and bitterly denounced Sadat as a traitor to the Arab cause. Sadat's assassination by Muslim extremists in 1981 did not end the Egyptian government's commitment to peace, which was maintained by his successor, President Hosni Mubarak, but no other Arab leader dared to follow in his footsteps.

In June 1982 the sixth Arab-Israeli war erupted in Lebanon. Officially dubbed by Israel Operation Peace in Galilee, the Israeli invasion of southern Lebanon was masterminded by Begin's hawkish minister of defense, Ariel Sharon (b. 1928). Although Israel achieved rapid mastery in the air over Syrian air power, Israel's ground forces encountered unexpected difficulties on the hilly terrain. Large

Peace at last! Anwar Sadat, Jimmy Carter and Menahem Begin relaxing during the Camp David discussions.

numbers of casualties resulted from their own fire. Altogether the Israelis lost more than 600 men, while causing an estimated 20,000 Arab deaths. Although the Israelis had originally declared that they would proceed no farther than forty kilometers (twenty-five miles) into Lebanon, they ultimately moved into the outskirts of the Lebanese capital, Beirut, aided by their allies among local Christian forces. A massacre by Christians of Palestinians in the Sabra and Shatila refugee camps near Beirut provoked worldwide outrage. The Peace Now movement organized a massive protest demonstration in Tel Aviv, which forced the Israeli government to establish a judicial commission of inquiry. Its report, issued some months later, severely criticized the conduct of Sharon, who was obliged to resign. Begin clung to office until August 1983, but he was a broken man and his government declined into mutually hostile factions.

New elections in 1984 produced indeterminate results and led to the formation of a grand coalition government of the two major parties, Labor and Likud, in which it was agreed that the leaders of each would serve a two-year term. Shimon Peres (b. 1923), who took office first under this rotating arrangement, eventually extracted Israeli forces from the Lebanese morass, though Israel continued to exercise effective control over a narrow strip near the frontier. His successor, Yitzhak Shamir, a former leader of the pre-state terrorist group Lehi, held the government to a more militant course. Settlement activity in the occupied territories was once again promoted with vigor, and terrorist onslaughts brought fierce counterattacks.

The envenomed relationship between Jews and Arabs in the occupied territories gave rise in 1987 to the seventh Arab-Israeli war, the *intifada* (an Arabic word literally signifying "shaking-off"). This uprising of the Arab population in the West Bank and Gaza took the forms of fierce civil unrest, strikes, riots and stonings of Israeli troops and civilians. Guided by the defense minister, Yitzhak Rabin, Israel responded with severe repression, but this proved ineffective in quelling the disturbances and aroused worldwide condemnation.

ZIONISM FULFILLED?

The succession of wars that punctuated Israel's first five decades required immense diversion of national energies and resources. Nearly all men and most women were called up for compulsory army service lasting two or three years, as well as for annual reserve duty. In spite of large-scale aid from the United States, amounting to $3 billion each year from 1973 onward, the proportion of Israeli gross national product devoted to military expenditures was the highest in the world. The human cost of warfare and of terrorism had the melancholy silver lining that Israel became a world leader in rehabilitation of the disabled and a formidable competitor in the paraplegic Olympics.

Such human and material costs notwithstanding, Israel succeeded, in the course of her first five decades, in fulfilling the basic aims of her founders. A focal point of sovereignty had created for the Jewish people an ultimate guarantor of their physical security and a potential for long-term cultural survival. New waves of immigrants from the Soviet Union, Ethiopia and elsewhere attested to the continuing vitality of the dream of an "ingathering of the exiles." As a result, Israel's Jewish population multiplied nearly tenfold between 1948 and the late 1990s. Elsewhere, other Jewish centers stagnated, withered or died.

A NEW BABYLON?

The only Jewish community that, for a time after the Second World War, had some pretensions to centrality in the Jewish world was that of the United States. In 1945 American Jewry suddenly found itself the dominant element in Jewry, the world's largest, richest and most powerful community. At first a little bewildered at the greatness thus thrust on it, American Jewry gradually adapted to its new role. Some American Jews conceived of their community as a kind of new Babylon that would guide the revived Jewry of the national homeland. But this flattering self-conception was eventually shattered by manifestations of Israel's determination to carve out its own destiny.

American Jewry in 1945 still consisted overwhelmingly of first- and second-generation immigrants, products of the great influx from Eastern Europe between the 1880s and the 1920s. By dint of pressure of numbers and growing affluence, the East Europeans and their descendants were beginning to oust the old German Jewish elite from positions of dominance in the community.

Elite bodies such as the American Jewish Committee lost their earlier primacy in Jewish life, and organizations more representative of the Jewish masses acquired greater weight. The Conference of Presidents of Major Jewish Organizations, formed in 1955, henceforth constituted the acknowledged lay leadership of the community.

Jews benefited immensely from the era of economic growth and prosperity in America between 1945 and 1973. Although some pockets of Jewish poverty remained, the average income of American Jews rose well above that of the general population. The social center of gravity of the community moved from the working and lower-middle class to the professional and business upper-middle classes, and many Jews enjoyed considerable affluence.

By 1970 only eleven percent of employed American Jewish males worked in "manual occupations"—compared with fifty-eight percent of the general population. Eighty-seven percent of Jewish males over twenty-five were engaged in white-collar occupations. In large measure, the upward occupational mobility reflected Jewish educational achievement. Eighty percent of American Jews of college age in 1971 were enrolled in higher education as against only forty percent of the population as a whole.

As the Jewish working class declined almost everywhere, Jews moved out of the characteristic old Jewish districts near the center of many cities to more affluent suburbs. Former Yiddish-speaking immigrant areas lost their Jewish flavor. On the Lower East Side of Manhattan, once the heart of Jewish New York, only 20,000 Jews remained in 1982 out of the quarter million who had once lived there. The former office of *Der Tog-Morgen Zhurnal*, one of many Yiddish daily newspapers that had once flourished in the city, became the home of a Chinese noodle factory.

American Jewry was on the move geographically as well as socially—to the west and to the south. Between 1930 and 1979, the proportion of American Jews living in the northeast of the country declined from sixty-eight percent to fifty-eight percent. New York remained the largest urban concentration of Jews in the world; but here, too, a decline was noticeable: the Jewish population of New York City shrank from about 2 million in the 1950s to under 1 million in the 1980s. Many had moved out to nearby suburbs. But others had migrated to Sunbelt states, particularly Florida or California.

Jews now found general acceptance in American society. Old social barriers against them—in banks, universities and clubs, as well as some branches of the legal and medical professions—were dismantled. Formerly "restricted" hotels opened their doors to Jews.

The upward social mobility of American Jews was reflected in political life. Jewish influence in politics arose not so much from their numbers (they never formed more than three percent of the total population) but from other factors. They were heavily concentrated in large states such as New York and Illinois that could swing the electoral college in presidential elections. In a country where the participation rate in general elections was the lowest among major democracies, Jews turned out to vote much more heavily than other groups. And Jews contributed very substantially to finance political campaigns. President Truman's support for the Israeli cause in 1948 was widely attributed to the importance of

American fund-raising for Israel: a United Jewish Appeal poster.

Jewish votes—though he undoubtedly felt a genuine personal sympathy for Zionism.

Jewish political influence was directed to both internal and external objectives. In domestic politics, Jews gave strong support to the civil-rights movement and in general opposed efforts to permit prayers in public schools. In foreign affairs they brought pressure to bear on Congress and on successive administrations of both parties to persuade the Soviet Union to relax restrictions on Jewish emigration.

Most significantly, Jewish lobbying groups such as the America Israel Public Affairs Committee, founded in 1954, exercised significant influence on political leaders in Washington to give diplomatic, economic and military assistance to Israel. Under the Eisenhower administration, between 1953 and 1960, pro-Israel lobbyists met with only limited success. During the Suez crisis of 1956, they were unable to prevent the administration from adopting an unfriendly attitude toward Israel. But the Kennedy administration began to supply advanced weapons to Israel, and after the 1967 war the U.S. became Israel's main arms supplier and also gave strong diplomatic support. When administrations occasionally seemed inclined to adopt a more neutral position between Israel and the Arabs, congressional opinion was rapidly mobilized to persuade the government to revert to a pro-Israel posture. Such lobbying was to be of vital importance in the 1970s. At a critical moment in the 1973 war, American arms supplies were airlifted to Israel, and American nuclear forces were placed on a heightened state of alert as a signal to the Soviet Union to restrain its Arab clients.

Jews had only rarely held major office before the Second World War, save for the occupants of the so-called Jewish seat on the Supreme Court. In the postwar period, several rose to prominent positions in both Republican and Democratic administrations: Henry Kissinger served as secretary of state under presidents Nixon and Ford. Arthur Burns and Alan Greenspan (b. 1926) became chairmen of the Federal Reserve Bank. And Jews became disproportionately numerous in the Senate—some, such as Jacob Javits (1904–1986) of New York, elected by heavily Jewish states, but others representing states with very small Jewish populations. In 1937 a Gallup poll had shown that forty-six percent of Americans would be prepared to vote for a Jewish presidential candidate; by 1978 the figure had risen to eighty-two percent—though neither party actually offered a Jew as candidate for the highest office.

Although the religious *behavior* of American Jews changed significantly in the postwar period, the institutional religious *structure* of American Jewry, with its division into three major groups, Reform, Conservative and Orthodox, underwent little alteration in the late twentieth century.

Reconstructionist Judaism was one of the few attempts to redefine Judaism in a way that rejected the rigid immobility of Orthodoxy yet sought to go beyond selective jettisoning of tradition favored by Reform and Conservative Judaism. The movement's founder, Mordecai M. Kaplan (1881–1983), set out his philosophy in his best-known work, *Judaism as a Civilization*, published in 1934. In this book Kaplan called for the transformation of Judaism from a faith based on supernatural revelation to a religion understood as evolutionary in nature. Salvation was to be attained in this world rather than the next. In his abandonment of belief in a personal God, Kaplan was much more radical even than most Reform thinkers. The Reconstructionist movement never attained the numerical strength of the three main Jewish streams in the U.S., but Kaplan's thought nevertheless had profound influence, particularly on Conservative Judaism.

Within Orthodoxy, the arrival as refugees from Hitler of some Hasidic groups from Eastern Europe bolstered the ultra-Orthodox fringe. Orthodoxy consequently divided between the black-coated ultras and the so-called modern Orthodox, who sought to combine strict religious practice with openness to some modern secular ideas. Yeshiva University in New York was the main intellectual bastion of modern Orthodoxy. Its leaders combined strict religious traditionalism with a readiness to cooperate with other segments of Jewry in the furtherance of objectives of general Jewish interest.

A chief topic of religious controversy was the role of women in the synagogue. The ceremony of bat mitzvah had been initiated by Mordecai Kaplan (the first girl to perform the ceremony was his daughter Judith in 1922). The practice was widely adopted by Reform and Conservative Jews, though only rarely by the Orthodox. Reform Jews were the first to grant women a position of complete equality and to appoint women rabbis. Conservatives, while ready to accept mixed seating in synagogues and to grant women some part in the conduct of services, initially proved more resistant to the idea of women rabbis. Eventually, however, the movement approved the change, and the main Conservative rabbinical training school, the Jewish Theological Seminary in New York, began ordaining women as rabbis.

Another area of vigorous debate was the question of mixed marriages. Until the late 1950s, under ten percent of Jews in the United States married non-Jews. But in the general climate of social assimilation the rate climbed rapidly thereafter, so that by the early 1970s nearly a third of all Jewish marriages involved a non-Jewish spouse. Even more dramatic than the change in practice was the change in *attitudes*. A poll in 1965 showed that eighty-three percent of American Jews disapproved of marriage to non-Jews. Only six years later, the rate of disapproval had shrunk to forty-one percent—and most of these were people over the age of forty-five. The Orthodox and most Conservatives remained strongly opposed to Jewish out-marriage: their rabbis would not officiate at such weddings, mixed couples were barred from synagogue membership and their children from education at Hebrew schools. The Reform movement adopted a more relaxed approach. Many Reform rabbis were prepared to perform marriages between couples in which only one partner was Jewish. Others facilitated matters by arranging for the speedy conversion to Reform Judaism of the non-Jewish spouse. Some saw such conversions as a potential demographic infusion in an era of population decline; but all the evidence suggested that the number of converts to Judaism in mixed marriages was exceeded by the number of Jews in such unions who converted out of Judaism. Overall, only about a quarter of non-Jewish spouses in mixed marriages converted to Judaism. The relatively lax Reform attitude to conversion was fiercely criticized by the Orthodox, who warned that the result was likely to be a divided Jewish people.

In other areas of social concern, too, the Reform movement in the U.S. embraced solutions that were anathema to the more traditionalist streams of Judaism. For example, Reform moved toward acceptance of homosexuality and of civil homosexual unions akin to marriage.

A disturbing trend of the late 1960s was the growth of hostility between Jews and blacks. Jews had been among the foremost supporters of the black civil-rights struggle. But severe tensions arose between the two groups in several major cities. In New York there were ugly conflicts between the largely Jewish teachers' union and militant blacks demanding "community control" of public schools. In formerly Jewish districts, now transformed into black "ghettos," Jewish-owned stores were ransacked by rioting mobs.

Amid the political and social turmoil of the late 1960s and early 1970s, some Jews shifted their political bearings. On the Left, many Jewish students were active in radical movements. Meanwhile, an older generation of ex-leftists coalesced as the "new Right" and found their intellectual voice in the influential monthly *Commentary*, published by the American Jewish Committee and edited by the combative Norman Podhoretz (b. 1930). But its stridently expressed views did not reflect broader American Jewish opinion on most political issues (except Israel). By and large, the unprecedented affluence of Jews in the United States and Canada did not seem to impair their predilection for liberal politics.

DECAY IN THE HEARTLAND

By contrast with the vitality of Jewish life in North America, the former Jewish heartland in Eastern Europe was the stage in the period after 1945 for a tragic sequence of terror, decay and, ultimately, virtual dissolution. The last years of Stalin's rule, between the end of the war and the dictator's death in 1953, were the darkest period in the history of Soviet Jewry. Most remaining Jewish institutions, particularly Yiddish-language schools and newspapers, were closed. The Jewish Anti-Fascist Committee, which, since its foundation in 1941, had functioned as a kind of ersatz representative body for Soviet Jews, was suddenly dissolved in 1948. Yiddish writers were arrested and murdered by the official state apparatus. A campaign against "rootless cosmopolitans" in Soviet literature and cultural life was conducted in terms that indicated that Jews were the main target. The climax of the anti-Jewish terror came in 1952 with the arrest of a number of Moscow doctors, most of them Jews, who were charged with seeking to poison senior Soviet officials. The alleged Doctors' Plot was played up in the Soviet press, and Jewish

Communists abroad were deployed to add their denunciations to the torrent of abuse against the supposed plotters. Ugly rumors spread that Stalin contemplated the exile of the entire Soviet Jewish population to Siberia (along the lines of similar forced movements of other population groups during the war, such as the Volga Germans and the Crimean Tatars).

Stalin's sudden death in March 1953 brought a relaxation in the atmosphere. The doctors were released and charges against them dropped. Some of the Jewish victims of the Stalinist purges were "rehabilitated"—all too often only posthumously. The following decade was marked by an easing of anti-Jewish measures. A small number of Yiddish theatrical and musical performances were permitted. A Yiddish periodical, *Sovyetish Heymland*, began to appear, though its circulation was small—and much of that was sent abroad. But Jewish schools and newspapers were not reopened, hardly any Yiddish books were published and all Jewish institutions remained under party or secret-police control and surveillance. In the early 1960s, a number of Jews were arrested and some executed for so-called economic crimes. Although the practice of Jewish religion was not prohibited, the number of synagogues steadily declined: by 1965 no more than ninety-seven synagogues functioned in the U.S.S.R.—many of these in Georgia and only a very few in the main centers of Jewish settlement in Russia and the Ukraine. A yeshivah functioned in Moscow, but it attracted scarcely any students.

Between 1945 and 1949, the U.S.S.R. gave a measure of diplomatic and practical support to the Zionist movement (in Palestine, that is, not within the Soviet Union itself, where Zionist activity was banned). Viewing Zionism as a vehicle for weakening British imperialism in the Middle East, the Soviets supported the UN partition resolution for Palestine in November 1947; they raced against the U.S. to be first to recognize the new Israeli state in May 1948; and they allowed thousands of Polish Jews in the U.S.S.R. to leave for Poland—and thence for Palestine. The Communist-dominated government of Czechoslovakia supplied arms that played a crucial part in bringing about the Israeli victory in the War of Independence in 1948–49.

But once Israel had come into being and secured its survival, Soviet policy changed. Some suggested that this was a result of the extraordinary reception accorded to the first Israeli minister to the U.S.S.R., Golda Meir. Attending synagogue shortly after her arrival in Moscow in 1949, she was greeted by mass street demonstrations of enthusiastic Jews. Such eruptions were almost unheard of in the Soviet capital and were regarded by the authorities as dangerous signs of independent thinking.

In the Soviet Union, as elsewhere in the Jewish world, the Israeli victory in the 1967 war brought a wave of Jewish exultation and for some a rebirth of Jewish identification. The fact that the Israeli victory had been achieved against clients of the Soviet Union lent a dangerously anti-Soviet edge to this renewed collective consciousness.

In the Communist satellite states of East Central Europe, Jewish populations, already savagely reduced by Hitler, dwindled further as a result of Stalinist persecution, emigration and rapid assimilation. The state seized control of all Jewish religious institutions. Communist antireligious propaganda was pervasive. Most

Jewish secular institutions (including all Jewish political parties, Zionist bodies, most youth movements, schools, theaters and newspapers) were closed, and rigid government direction of those few that remained reduced Jewish life to little more than a dim reflection of its prewar dynamism.

The large Jewish presence among the Communist leadership in many of these countries hurt rather than benefited Jews in general. The hostility to the imposition of communism manifested by the majority of the population throughout the region, particularly Poland, combined with traditional antisemitism, often fanned by the Roman Catholic Church, to produce anti-Jewish violence. The attacks in Poland, Slovakia and elsewhere led to hundreds of Jewish deaths.

Unlike the Soviet Union, the Eastern European satellites permitted Jewish emigration, albeit in fits and starts. As the general conditions of life remained harsh, and as Jews in particular encountered lingering hostility, most of the remaining Jewish population in the region emigrated, mainly to Israel and the United States. By the mid-1960s, only Romania and Hungary still held significant numbers of Jews.

In spite of the disappearance of most Jews from Eastern European societies, the Jewish issue persisted in political discourse, and at times of crisis was repeatedly exploited by populist politicians. In Poland in 1968 and again in the early 1980s the shaky Communist government courted popular support by organizing "anti-Zionist" campaigns. The main victims were the few thousand surviving Jews in Poland, many of them loyal Communists who were dismissed from positions in the bureaucracy, universities and the press. Most immigrated to Western Europe, the United States or Israel. The political crisis in Czechoslovakia in 1968 produced a similar thinly disguised antisemitic campaign sponsored by elements opposed to the reformist Dubcek regime.

In Romania, the idiosyncratic dictatorship of Nicolae Ceausescu negotiated a secret arrangement with Israel whereby Jews were, in effect, ransomed: emigration was permitted in return for payment in dollars per head. The greater part of Romanian Jewry had immigrated to Israel by the time the regime collapsed in December 1989.

In 1971 the Soviet Union surprisingly reversed policy and, for the first time since the 1920s, permitted more than a trickle of Jewish immigration to Israel. There were two main reasons. At one level, the change was a response to the extraordinary quasi-revolt of Zionist activists within the country. At another, it reflected the Soviet leadership's desire to remove an obstacle to the central objective of their foreign policy in this period: détente with the NATO powers. Not all Jews who applied were permitted to leave. In particular, persons who had held jobs with access to what were defined as state secrets, including scientific knowledge that might be of use to the West, were denied emigration permits. Thousands of such people, dismissed from their jobs as unreliable elements, languished in a kind of social limbo. In the West, a great campaign on behalf of these "refuseniks" mobilized broad public support. Some cases, such as those of the ballet dancer Valery Panov (b. 1938) and the imprisoned human-rights activist Anatoly Shcharansky (b. 1948), became international causes célèbres. In the course of the 1970s, nearly a quarter of a million Jews left the U.S.S.R. Most went to Israel, but in the late 1970s a significant number chose to go instead to the U.S., Canada or Australia. This trend greatly alarmed the Israeli government, which took a number of steps to try to curb the so-called drop-out rate among Soviet Jewish refugees arriving in Vienna.

In 1979 the exodus was abruptly curtailed. The movement in the West on behalf of Soviet Jewry appeared to have overplayed its hand by persuading the United States Congress to pass the Jackson-Vanik amendment, linking U.S. trade concessions to the U.S.S.R. to Soviet emigration policy. The Soviet leadership took offense and, with détente ebbing, decided to limit departures. From 1980 to 1986, few Soviet Jews were allowed to leave.

The ascent of Mikhail Gorbachev to supreme power in the Soviet Union in 1985 brought a gradual reopening of the Jewish escape valve. But it was not until December 1989 that truly free emigration of Jews was at last permitted. A great flood surged forth, driven by extreme economic hardship, fear of impending pogroms (none occurred) and apprehension lest the door suddenly close again. Over the next five years, more than half a million Jews arrived in Israel, and another quarter million went to the U.S., Germany and other countries.

The mass migration of Soviet Jews reinvigorated Israeli society. The new immigrants were a highly sophisticated population, rich in skilled workers, scientists and musicians. After some initial difficulties, the Soviet Jews integrated with remarkable speed and relative ease into the Israeli economy—and eventually also into Israeli society.

At the fall of communism in Eastern Europe in 1989, a distinct, often joyous, revival of Jewish life took place. Some tiny communities of Jews, half forgotten in obscure corners of the Communist world, emerged from the shadows. In 1991 370 Jews from Albania, who had survived the harsh terror of the Stalinist regime

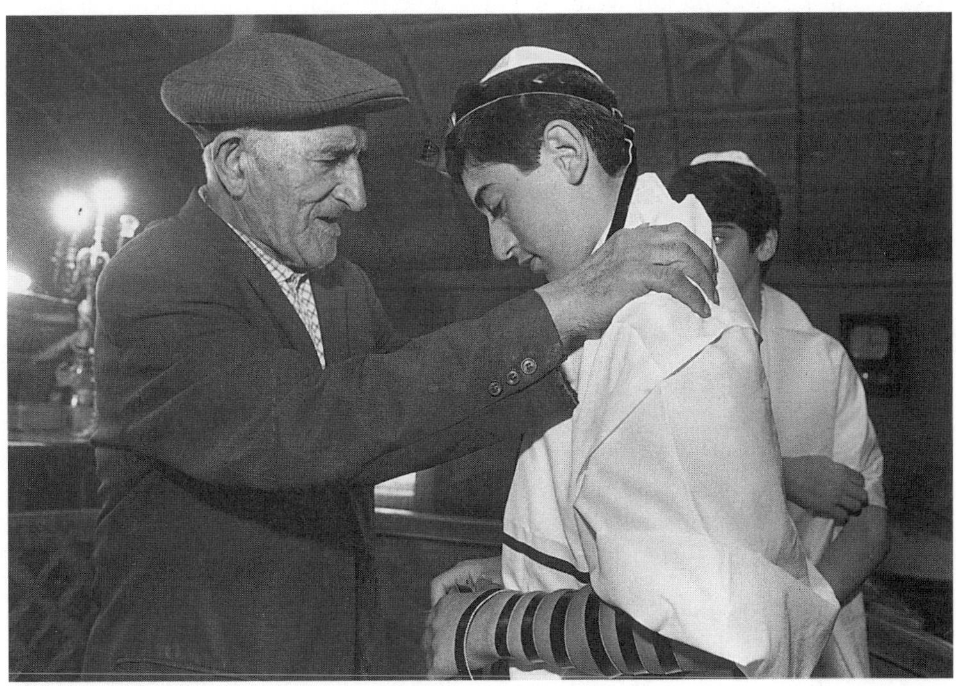

Bar mitzvah in Georgia.

of Enver Hoxha, immigrated to Israel and the United States. Under Hoxha, all religious activity had been banned, and the only surviving forms of Jewish practice, other than private prayer, were observance of the Yom Kippur fast and occasional secret gatherings of Jews in the capital, Tirana, at which sweetmeats had been eaten in honor of dead family members, a Sephardi practice.

In Poland, a tiny core of traditionalist Jews rebuilt Jewish institutions. The Czech Republic retained very few Jews, but its capital, Prague, restored its fine Jewish monuments and became a mecca for Jewish tourism. In Russia, a national coordinating body, the Va'ad, sought to unify the argumentative elements of the reemerging autonomous Jewish communities. A free Jewish press emerged—although the absence of a sufficiently large readership doomed most of the newly founded papers to short lives.

Yet these green shoots did not betoken a rebirth of Jewish life. From every part of Eastern Europe, Jewish emigration quickened and what had once been the great reservoirs of Jewish population in Russia and the Ukraine seemed likely by the end of the century to be virtually empty. In East Central Europe, only Hungary still harbored a Jewish community of any importance (estimates of its size varied between 50,000 and 100,000). But there, as elsewhere, emigration, assimilation and intermarriage cast a shadow over the long-term viability of the community. By the mid-1990s, for the first time since the early modern period, there were more Jews in Western than in Eastern Europe.

RECONSTRUCTION IN WESTERN EUROPE

In contrast with the dismal Jewish predicament in the East, Western European Jews in the postwar period were generally able to establish themselves, as individuals and as communities, in societies where antisemitism was declining and no longer a major threat. The Nazi massacres had radically altered the shape of every significant Jewish community in the region, save that of Britain. But help from American Jewry enabled institutions to be rebuilt and Jewish life to resume.

A new regional pattern emerged. The traditional hegemony of German Jewry had disappeared under the impact of Nazism and could never be restored. Only shattered remnants of German Jewry remained. Most were old people, and many of these survivors immigrated to Israel or the United States after the war. In the postwar period, the communities of Britain and France became the largest and most important in Western Europe.

Anglo Jewry in the decade after the war reached its demographic peak of about 410,000 persons. In the period 1945–48, British Jews had to bear the brunt of an unusual wave of antisemitic feeling that was aroused in Britain by the terrorist exploits of the Jewish extremist underground in Palestine. This soon subsided with the British withdrawal from Palestine in May 1948, and thereafter Jews in Britain settled down happily to a period of growing prosperity and upward social mobility. In Western Europe, as in North America, Jews, once the most urban social group in the world, were reborn as suburbanites. In the East End of

London, former synagogues were turned into mosques for the burgeoning Pakistani immigrant population. New Jewish concentrations formed in suburban districts such as Golders Green or Edgware.

French Jewry, which had lost 75,000 people—a quarter of the community—to the death camps during the war, took several years to recover psychologically from the experience of betrayal by the collaborationist French Vichy government and by many of their fellow citizens. In the mid-1950s, however, the community began to be revitalized by the start of a new emigration of Jews from North Africa, principally Tunisia and Morocco. In 1962 the trickle turned into a torrent, with the arrival of virtually the entire Jewish community of Algeria, who fled the country when it became independent under an Arab nationalist regime. Almost overnight, the Jewish population of France doubled to more than half a million.

The North African Jews changed the face of French Jewry. Many of them, particularly the Tunisians, were more traditional and religious in outlook than their French-born co-religionists. They soon became the dominant element among practicing Jews in France. One of their number, Samuel-René Sirat (b. 1930), became the chief rabbi of France. Others assumed positions of lay leadership, usurping the roles that had been traditionally and almost unquestioningly assumed by the Rothschilds and other members of the wealthy Ashkenazi elite. Provincial communities that had become moribund were regenerated by the new arrivals. New synagogues opened and attendance at services increased. Districts of Paris that had earlier been strongholds of Yiddish-speaking culture such as the Marais and Belleville soon echoed with the accents of Judeo-Arabic. French Jewry in the 1970s exhibited a cultural vitality and a political self-confidence that seemed absent elsewhere on the continent.

With the exception of France, however, the general picture of West European Jewry in the postwar period was one of somnolence and slow but steady decline. The central element was demographic: more Jews died than were being born, a tendency that accelerated from the 1960s onward in almost every country in the region. In Britain, the Jewish population declined to under 300,000 by the early 1990s. The causes were easy to discern: Jews were marrying later and having fewer children. Intermarriage with non-Jews had increased dramatically. By 1996 it was estimated in Britain that nearly half of all young Jews who married or who were "involved in relationships" had non-Jewish partners.

The decline was not only demographic. A number of other indices gave warning signals of a weakening of many forms of Jewish identification. The number of kosher butcher shops shrank as the proportion of Jews adhering to the laws of kashrut diminished. Attendance at synagogue steadily declined, except among the strictly Orthodox. By the 1990s the majority of Jews in most countries seldom attended religious services except on the High Holidays (the Jewish New Year and the Day of Atonement). Sabbath observance, too, declined. Most Jewish shopkeepers opened their stores on the Sabbath. Even among those Jews who attended Sabbath services, many defied the religious law by driving to synagogue; this was often true even in the case of those attending nominally Orthodox services, particularly in Britain.

Yet in spite of the decline in religious practice, Orthodox Judaism remained the primary synagogal form among Western European Jews. By contrast with North America, the advance of Reform Judaism was slow and hesitant. As for middle-of-the-road American Conservatism, its doctrines found few followers in Europe. In Britain in the 1960s, a start in this direction was made with the foundation of what later became known as the Masorti movement, headed by Rabbi Louis Jacobs (b. 1920). A former Orthodox rabbi, he had, in effect, been excommunicated from Orthodoxy as a result of his publication of what were seen as heretical views, in particular his questioning of the literal nature of the biblical account of the revelation on Mount Sinai. But it was not until the 1980s that the movement began to expand, and even then it did not attain anything like the importance of American Conservativism.

From the early 1970s onward, West European Jewry had to come to terms with a new and alarming phenomenon: terrorism. Attacks on Jewish targets took place throughout non-Communist Europe: in Istanbul, Vienna, Rome, Paris, London, Athens, Antwerp and elsewhere. All Jewish institutions found it necessary to take strict security precautions. The two sources of such attacks were the extreme Right and Palestinian Arabs and their sympathizers. Hardly less alarming than the attacks themselves were the often equivocal responses of some elements in surrounding non-Jewish society.

Was this a new and deeply threatening manifestation of antisemitism? Or were European Jews facing something rather different: a savage response to their heightened identification with the cause of Israel? Debate over this issue divided many Jews. Some argued that anti-Zionism was merely a cover for deep-seated antisemitism; others suggested that, on the contrary, anti-Zionism was strengthening antisemitic currents.

In Western Europe, unlike North America, the traditional identification of Jews with liberal causes and the political Left became less pronounced in the late twentieth century. A discernible drift to the Right seemed to reflect the rising socioeconomic status of most Jews. In Britain this was reflected in the 1970s in a shift in Jewish voting patterns away from Labour toward the Conservative Party. In the House of Commons, Conservatives outnumbered Labour members among Jewish MPs by 1983. Margaret Thatcher's Conservative cabinet at one point included five Jewish ministers. In France, Jewish support for the Communist Party remained significant between 1945 and 1958. But the discrediting of Stalinism and Soviet actions in Eastern Europe gradually reduced the attractiveness of communism to French Jewish intellectuals. In general, however, Jews shifted not to the Right but to the moderate socialist Left. Several Jews, mainly socialists, served in senior political office, among them Pierre Mendès France (1907–1982), the most impressive prime minister of the Fourth Republic. In the 1980s Jews gave strong backing to the revived Socialist Party of François Mitterrand—though his Jewish supporters were dismayed toward the end of his presidency in 1994 by revelations of his youthful association with the extreme Right.

One reason for the growing Jewish disenchantment with the European Left was the hostility it evinced toward Israel. This was first felt after the Soviet tilt against Israel in 1949 but became pronounced after the 1967 war and the branding of Israel as a colonialist implant in the Middle East. Israel's invasion of

Lebanon in 1982 cast her once again in the role of imperialist aggressor in the eyes of much of the Left. With the outbreak of the *intifada*, in 1987, a massive chorus of execration descended on Israel. For the Jews in Western Europe, such events brought embarrassment and occasional terrorist violence. But for another major segment of the Jewish people, they brought disaster and wholesale displacement.

JEWS OF MUSLIM LANDS

Each successive phase of the Middle East conflict exacerbated the plight of Jews living in Arab countries. In Egypt, many Jews were arrested during the Suez crisis of 1956. After the war, large numbers departed from the country, leaving only a few hundred, mainly old people.

The Six-Day War brought renewed insecurity to the few remaining Jews in the Arab world. Fifty-seven Syrian Jews were reported to have been killed in anti-Jewish riots. Henceforth Jewish emigration from Syria was forbidden, and the 4,000 Jews still in the country were subjected to curfews and restrictions on education, employment and movement.

In Iraq, similarly, the few thousand remaining Jews, most of them elderly, were treated alternately as showpieces and hostages by the ruling dictatorships. Emigration was forbidden and Jewish leaders were forced to issue ritual denunciations of Zionism. After lengthy secret negotiations, the Jews of Syria were finally permitted in 1993 to apply freely for emigration. Most, including the chief rabbi, seized the opportunity to go, settling either in Israel or the United States.

In Egypt, a large number of young Jewish men were arrested in 1967. On their release, most emigrated. Among those who left was the last chief rabbi of Egypt, Haim Douek (1904?–1974). In Libya, eighteen Jews were killed in rioting, and Jewish property was destroyed or confiscated; before 1948 some 35,000 Jews had lived in Libya; by 1970 none remained.

The little Jewish community of Lebanon found itself a victim of the country's murderous civil war after 1975. In the wake of several kidnappings and murders in the 1980s, most Jews left the country. By the time the civil war died down in 1991, the community, once 7,000 strong, could barely gather a *minyan* (the Jewish prayer quorum of ten adult men) for services.

The only Arab countries in which Jewish communities still flourished, albeit on a greatly reduced scale, were Morocco and Tunisia. In Tunisia in 1967 anti-Jewish disturbances were severely dealt with by the government. President Habib Bourguiba sought strenuously to reassure the Jewish community: in one case he was reported to have gone personally to the airport to persuade a Jewish businessman, M. Bocobza, owner of a distillery, to remain in the country, but to no avail. Jews continued to leave, and the community, which had numbered 105,000 in 1948, dwindled to no more than 2,000 by 1993. On the island of Djerba, once the seat of a 2,000-year-old Jewish community, the yeshivot all closed, as did the Hebrew printing press; by the 1990s the island's fourteen synagogues had become little more than tourist sites.

In Morocco, opposition elements called for a boycott of "everything that smacks of Zionism." The government of King Hassan II, like that of Bourguiba in Tunisia, worked hard to suppress anti-Jewish violence and to assuage Jewish fears, but many of the 50,000 Jews still in the country were unconvinced and emigration continued.

The last remnants of Jewry in the Muslim world disappeared by the 1990s. In Iran in the 1950s and 1960s, the Jewish community, numbering some 80,000, enjoyed the protection of the shah and great prosperity. But the militantly Islamic Iranian revolution of 1979 imperiled its safety. Many Jews were arrested and some executed. In spite of restrictions on Jewish emigration, the greater part of Iranian Jewry left the country in the course of the following decade. Most settled in the United States, particularly in Los Angeles, a few in Germany or Israel.

LATIN AMERICA

Relatively isolated from the main centers of Jewish life, the half million Jews of Latin America shared in the general Diaspora trends toward assimilation and dissolution. In most of the continent, small relatively affluent Jewish communities struggled to maintain their identity but found that Jewishness increasingly came to have little meaning aside from membership in Jewish social clubs and a shared, generally vague, nostalgia for the past. The two largest communities, those of Argentina and Brazil, had difficulty ensuring their own continuity and had to look to the Northern Hemisphere for inspiration and, in some cases, for rabbis.

In Argentina, under the military dictatorship of 1976 to 1982, Jews figured prominently among the *desaparecidos* who were imprisoned, often tortured, sometimes murdered, by the secret police or paramilitary forces. The left-wing Argentine journalist Jacobo Timerman (b. 1923), who later immigrated to Israel, wrote movingly of his own experiences in prison in his best-selling book *Prisoner without a Name, Cell without a Number*. At one point during his incarceration, Timerman was visited by the junta's minister of the interior, and the following Kafkaesque exchange ensued:

Minister: You admitted to being a Zionist and this point was revealed at a meeting of all the generals.

Timerman: But being a Zionist isn't forbidden.

Minister: No, it isn't forbidden but on the other hand it isn't a clearcut issue. Besides, you admitted to it. And the generals are aware of it.

The fall of the military regime eased some of the anxieties of Jews in Argentina, but these were renewed in a terrifying manner in July 1994 when a huge bomb exploded in the headquarters of the main Jewish communal organization in Buenos Aires. Eighty-six people were killed and 150 injured. Iranian terrorists, Palestinian Arab opponents of the Middle East peace process and Argentine extreme rightists were variously suspected, but the perpetrators were never captured.

OUTPOSTS

The more far-flung outposts of the Jewish world disappeared or declined in the postwar period. The Jewish community of India was more than halved as a result of emigration, mainly to Israel. Nearly all the 25,000 Jews in China and the Far East left before or shortly after the victory of the Communists under Mao Tse-tung in 1949. Most of the Jews of Soviet Central Asia immigrated to Israel after 1971.

In Christian Ethiopia, a small Judaizing sect known as Falashas had existed for centuries in virtual isolation from the main currents of the Jewish world. The Marxist revolution of 1974 brought a steady worsening of the Falashas' position. There were reports of mass arrests and the use of torture. Between 1980 and 1985, the Israeli government organized a secret airlift, dubbed Operation Moses, in which about 12,000 Falashas were transported to Israel. Several thousand more followed over the next few years, virtually liquidating the community in Ethiopia. The operation was applauded and hailed as a vindication of Zionist purpose. But the integration of the new arrivals was difficult. The Orthodox religious establishment queried their Jewishness: many were sent to live in caravan parks in remote parts of the country; their children were segregated in special schools; their males were compelled to undergo a humiliating symbolic circumcision; their priests were not recognized as rabbis until they had been reeducated in Orthodox yeshivot. In 1996 the grievances of the Ethiopians in Israel crystallized and erupted into fierce riots when it was revealed that blood that they had donated to the national blood bank had been secretly thrown away for fear of AIDS and other contamination.

The 120,000 Jews of South Africa were unusual among Jewish communities in the strength of their commitment to Judaism as a religion and to Zionism as an ideal. Jewish day schools, most with a Zionist orientation, enrolled a majority of the country's Jewish youth. The envenomed racial conflict in the country troubled many South African Jews. The ascent to power in 1948 of the National Party, which had a history of antisemitic as well as antiblack attitudes, dismayed the Jewish community. Some joined the political opposition. For many years, Helen Suzman (b. 1917) was a lone voice of liberal opinion in the all-white parliament. Others joined the underground Communist Party, whose leader Joe Slovo (1926–1995), a Lithuanian-born Jew, steered it toward close support for the African National Congress.

Although antisemitism was present in several strata of South African society—from the extreme Right of the Afrikaner nationalists to the Pan-Islamic fervor of some Indian Muslims in Natal—it did not represent a serious threat to the survival of the South African Jewish community. Yet Jews in South Africa did not feel safe. So long as the apartheid regime endured, their future seemed bound up with that of the white population in general. As political conflict in the country became ever more embittered in the 1970s and 1980s, however, a trend toward Jewish emigration became visible. Young Jews in particular emigrated in order to avoid military service in defense of a cause with which they felt little sympathy. Most went to the United States, Australia or Britain; some settled in Israel. With the exodus of a significant part of the Jewish population of child-bearing age, there was dark talk of the foreseeable dissolution of the country's Jewish community. The transition from white minority to black majority rule in the early 1990s alleviated some fears but reinforced others. The flow of Jewish emigration continued, and South African Jewry seemed to be following slowly down the path to gentle oblivion that had been traced in miniature a generation earlier by its little northern neighbor, the Jewish community of Rhodesia, now known as Zimbabwe.

Partly as a by-product of emigration from South Africa, Australian Jewry was one of the few Jewish communities in the world that grew in the postwar period. It more than doubled to about 90,000 by the early 1990s. Intermarriage remained low (an estimated 8.5 percent in Melbourne in 1991) and more than half of all Jewish children attended Jewish schools: the Mount Scopus school in Melbourne was the largest in the world.

Within a generation of the end of the Second World War, therefore, almost every part of the Jewish world had been radically transformed. The transformation affected practically all aspects of life: social, economic, demographic, religious and—perhaps most significant, though least noted—cultural.

ORTHODOXY AND COLLECTIVE SURVIVAL

One segment of Jewry that seemed able to maintain and perhaps even increase its numbers was ultra-Orthodoxy. Disdaining the practice of birth control and celebrating large families, the ultra-Orthodox generally succeeded in resisting the forces of assimilation, intermarriage and demographic decline that affected (many would have said afflicted) other Jews. But by the late twentieth century, evidence suggested that the ultra-Orthodox, too, were beginning to practice birth control and to have somewhat smaller families. In any case, they represented only a tiny fraction of Diaspora Jewry as a whole. Concentrated mainly in a few cities—greater New York, Chicago, London, Paris, Antwerp—they maintained their own synagogues, rabbis, educational institutions, kashrut authorities and welfare bodies, insulating themselves not only from the surrounding gentile world but also from much contact with neighboring Jewish communities.

A significant exception to this pattern was the Habad movement, led by Rabbi Menachem Schneerson (1902–1994), of the Hasidic Lubavitch dynasty. From his base in Brooklyn, New York, Schneerson directed a worldwide effort by his followers to proselytize among fellow Jews. Lubavitch emissaries spread far and wide, like Christian missionaries in darkest Africa. They could be found in unlikely locations: Hong Kong, Milan, Oxford and Johannesburg. In areas of large Jewish population concentration, they would set up "mitzvah-mobiles" and accost passersby, encouraging Jewish males to fulfill the commandment of donning *tefillin* (phylacteries) and reciting the daily prayers. As with all Hasidic dynasties, the Lubavitchers greatly revered their leader. Toward the end of his life, however, the hero worship developed into a cult with quasi-messianic overtones.

Moshiach Now signs, often accompanied by a representation of the bearded visage of the *rebbe*, sprouted on buildings, car bumpers, and T-shirts on five continents. After his death, some of his distraught followers even spoke of his imminent rising from the dead.

Most of the ultra-Orthodox remained hostile to Zionism, which they saw as a sacrilegious and presumptuous anticipation by secular Jews of the messianic return to the Land. Those who lived in Israel, particularly in centers such as Jerusalem and Bnei Braq, for the most part accommodated themselves reluctantly to the existence of the Jewish state, supporting their own political parties, particularly the long-established Agudat Yisrael movement and the newer Shas party, the latter catering mainly to Orthodox elements among Jews originating in Arab countries. Using the political clout that these parties gained from the Israeli system of proportional representation and coalition politics, the ultra-Orthodox succeeded in maintaining their own educational system and in winning large-scale financial support for their yeshivot and other institutions. An extreme fringe, known as the Neturei Karta (Guardians of the City), refused to have any truck whatsoever with the Jewish state and even cooperated with the Palestine Liberation Organization—before the Israeli government itself decided to do so.

Lubavitch Hasidim.

Among the ultra-Orthodox outside Israel, the majority opposed Zionism. Most fervent in their rejection were the Satmar Hasidim, based mainly in New York. Some other Hasidic movements, however, looked more favorably on the Zionist enterprise—for example, the Belzer Hasidim, whose leader lived in Israel. Occupying a rather equivocal position in the middle were the followers of the Lubavitcher *rebbe*. They established a village, Kfar Chabad, in Israel, and their leader adopted a militant stance in opposition to Israeli withdrawal from the West Bank area occupied in 1967. But this militancy was based on religious not nationalistic considerations, and Schneerson himself never set foot in the Jewish state.

Among mainstream Orthodox Jews in the Diaspora, support for Israel remained strong. Indeed, Orthodox Jews gave disproportionate support to the more militant elements in Zionism, particularly those calling for the maintenance of Israeli rule over the entire Land of Israel within frontiers set according to their reading of the Bible.

With their strong emphasis on Jewish education, their resistance to many forms of social assimilation (such as intermarriage) and their apparent ability to transmit values down through the generations, the Orthodox minority among Jews seemed the most capable of ensuring some form of group survival in the Diaspora into the next century.

SECULAR JUDAISM?

A few secular Jewish intellectuals and others in the Diaspora believed that a form of Jewish identification could be maintained even in the absence of religious practice or belief. In the immediate postwar period, this often took the form of a fervent Yiddishist secularism, to be found particularly in the United States, France and Argentina. But this virtually disappeared with the decline of the Yiddish language and of the last remnants of the old socialist-nationalist Bund.

Some Jews argued that "Jewish values" continued, even in the secular era, to cement a common identity and provide a basis for collective action. Sometimes this was indeed so: Jews, for instance, reacted with a special intensity to the reappearance in Europe of racial expulsions and killings in the Yugoslav civil war in the early 1990s. At the opening of the National Holocaust Museum in Washington, the Nobel peace laureate Elie Wiesel (b. 1928) uttered an eloquent protest against the world's inaction and seeming indifference to the horrors of racial "cleansing" in the former Yugoslavia.

Occasionally analysts argued that the Jews of the Diaspora were not in danger of losing their identity. They were merely changing, the religious and communal definitions of Jewishness being replaced by a personal affinity that, although looser and less institutionalized, was no less real. So-called marginal Jews, it was suggested, often maintained interest in and links to Jewish causes, most notably Israel. But for many Jews, whether in the Diaspora or in Israel, the concept of Jewishness, divorced from religion, amounted to little more than a thin patina of vaguely remembered customs, jokes, recipes and nostalgic recollections.

A NEW CULTURAL IDENTITY?

Bereft of its spiritual and cultural heart in Eastern Europe, postwar Jewry lived to a large extent on inherited intellectual capital. Few significant thinkers grounded in a profound knowledge of the classical Jewish sources emerged in the postwar period to compare with the giants of the past. Most of those who did achieve distinction were isolated survivors of prewar Jewish culture, such as the religious philosopher Martin Buber, whose thought gained a significant audience among Christians as well as Jews.

Perhaps in consequence, the major intellectual events in the postwar Jewish world were less creative achievements in themselves than rediscoveries and reinterpretations of the past. The attitude was reflected in a poignant story told of a small group of Jewish survivors who were making their way westward a few months after the end of the war from exile in Siberia. When they eventually arrived in their former hometown, a Polish hamlet, they discovered that

> [t]he town was a mass of rubble. They did not find even graves. All their kith and kin had been burned alive in the crematoriums. The synagogue was in ruins. But a stair to the cellar had been saved. Descending that stair these Jews found a few Talmudic volumes, charred and water-soaked but still usable in part. They procured a few tallow-candles and sat down to read a page or two. One came running and cried: "Jews, do you forget that you are running for your lives. The Soviets are closing the frontiers. The American zone is still far off. Flee!" But one of the group waved the messenger aside: "*Shah* [Hush]!" he said gravely. "Be still. *M'darf lernen* [One must study]!"

Much of authentic, internally generated Jewish culture had been murdered by the Nazis with the Jewish communities in the former Jewish heartland of Eastern Europe. One measurable element of cultural decline was the eclipse of Jewish languages. The most important, Yiddish, came close to extinction. The native tongue of some 10 million people in 1939, it suffered shattering blows at the hands of both the Nazis and the Communists. In German-occupied Europe, most Yiddish speakers were murdered during the war. In the Soviet Union, a large part of the Jewish population still spoke Yiddish in the immediate postwar period. The Communist regime had originally favored Yiddish as an allegedly "proletarian" language as against "bourgeois-nationalist" Hebrew. But under Stalin it was virtually proscribed. In the 1959 Soviet census, 410,000 Soviet Jews still declared Yiddish as their native tongue, but the percentage steadily declined in each census thereafter. Nor did Yiddish fare much better elsewhere in the Jewish world. In Israel it remained a victim of the traditionally Hebraizing ideology of Zionism. In the United States its demise accompanied the disappearance of the last generation of immigrants from Europe. By the 1990s the last Yiddish daily newspaper in New York, the *Jewish Daily Forward*, had become a weekly and was publishing an English-language edition. Yiddish literature enjoyed a final popular flowering in the work of Isaac Bashevis Singer (1904–1991), winner of the Nobel Prize for Literature. But it was his tragic destiny to find most of his readers in English translation. By the 1990s Yiddish was spoken as a language of daily discourse only among small groups of the elderly in New York, Montreal, Paris and Buenos Aires, and among ultra-Orthodox communities in Israel, Belgium and the United States. Antwerp, with its strongly Orthodox diamond cutters and dealers, was the last significant Jewish community in Europe whose lingua franca was Yiddish.

Other Jewish languages suffered a similar fate. Ladino, the Judeo-Spanish dialect that had been preserved by Sephardi Jews in the Balkans and the Levant since the expulsions from the Iberian Peninsula at the end of the fifteenth century, was subjected, like Yiddish, to death blows by the Nazis. The Jewish community of Salonica, a Ladino stronghold, was obliterated. In Bulgaria and Turkey, what remained of Ladino culture was snuffed out by nationalistic educational policies aimed at eliminating ethnic particularism, and by large-scale emigration, mainly to Israel. Judeo-Arabic, the dialects of Jewish communities from Casablanca to Baghdad, virtually disappeared as the bulk of these communities, too, moved to

Israel or other non-Arabic-speaking countries. Similarly, the languages spoken by the Jewish mountain peoples of Central Asia, such as the Judeo-Tat of Daghestan, could not survive the move of most of their speakers to Israel.

Efforts to revive Yiddish literature, theater and even film in the postwar period were, with few exceptions, quixotic failures. Hebrew culture in the Diaspora also declined after 1948, as most of those who were seriously interested in it naturally gravitated to Israel. Jewish cultural expression in the Diaspora henceforward was almost invariably through the medium of the language of the gentile majority—English, French or Spanish. In North America, a genre of novels in English depicting (often satirizing) contemporary Jewish society, by writers such as Saul Bellow (b. 1915) (*Herzog*), Bernard Malamud (1914–1986) (*The Fixer*), Philip Roth (b. 1933) (*Portnoy's Complaint*) and Mordecai Richler (b. 1931) (*The Apprenticeship of Duddy Kravitz*) attracted considerable attention. In Britain, playwrights such as Arnold Wesker (b. 1932) (*Chicken Soup with Barley*) and Wolf Mankowitz (b. 1929) (*The Bespoke Overcoat*) and novelists such as Bryan Glanville (b. 1931) (*The Bankrupts*) and Bernice Rubens (b. 1923) (*The Elected Member*) tackled Jewish themes with imaginative insight, as did French Jewish writers such as Albert Cohen (1895–1981) and Marek Halter (b. 1932) and Italians such as Primo Levi (1919–1987) and Giorgio Bassani (b. 1916). But by and large, all these figures thought of themselves primarily as English, French or Italian writers rather than as Jewish ones. In this they resembled most of the German Jewish writers of the interwar period as distinct from the Yiddish storytellers and poets of the previous generation. They seemed to represent an age of transition in which the last sparks of a distinctively Jewish cultural identity in the Diaspora were being extinguished.

One element of hope for Jewish continuity outside Israel was the growth of Jewish education. This took place in several countries and at several levels. Almost everywhere, attendance at the traditional *heder* (late-afternoon or Sunday religious school) declined. But at the same time, concern about standards of public education in several countries stimulated the establishment of large numbers of Jewish day schools, some under the auspices of religious communities, others organized by Zionist groups. In South Africa and Australia, these educated a majority of Jewish children. In North America and Western Europe, the percentage was much smaller, though numbers grew significantly from the 1960s onward. By 1982, 60,000 children were attending Jewish day schools in the New York area alone—an estimated one-fifth of Jewish school-age children. The great majority of these were from Orthodox homes, but the Conservative movement also boasted a number of schools in many cities, some of which attained outstanding results. By 1990 a total of 120,000 Jewish children were enrolled in 800 Jewish day schools in the United States and Canada.

At the level of higher education, too, there was significant expansion. From about 1960 onward, Jewish-studies departments mushroomed in universities in the United States and Canada and later spread also in Western Europe, South Africa and Australia. Over 600 colleges and universities in North America offered such programs by 1990. Some of these were major centers of Jewish scholarship;

Ashkenaz: a festival of new Yiddish culture, Toronto, 1995.

others provided a veneer of ethnic consciousness. For many young Jews, however, such courses provided their first, sometimes their only, serious intellectual encounter with their heritage.

Jewish adult-education programs attracted many, particularly senior citizens. A surge of Jewish book publishing, particularly in the form of translations of works from Hebrew and Yiddish into English, and to a lesser extent French, German and Spanish, rendered the classics of Jewish literature accessible to a new generation that could not read them in the original. Television and computer technology offered new media for such endeavors. After 1967 growing numbers of young Jews chose to spend a year in Israel, either before entering college or as a "junior year abroad." The more Orthodox attended yeshivah; others studied at Israeli universities or participated in work-study programs on kibbutzim.

In spite of all these developments, however, most Diaspora Jews were, in Jewish terms, culturally impoverished by comparison with their parents' and grandparents' generations. A Commission on Jewish Education in North America, conducted over a period of three years by a number of Jewish communal leaders, reported in 1991 that American Jewry was facing a crisis of continuity "of major proportions." Half of Jewish school-age children in the U.S. were receiving no Jewish education at all. The picture was similar elsewhere. Most Jews in the Diaspora received little or no Jewish education, few learned more than the rudiments of Hebrew and knowledge of the Talmud or of Jewish traditional literature was limited to the yeshivah-educated minority. The contrast with the culturally self-sufficient and creative Jewish world of the prewar period was painful.

INCREASED DANGERS FROM WITHIN?

Cultural decline was merely one facet of a broad range of indications that Jewish survival in the Diaspora could not be taken for granted. Almost everywhere outside Israel, the number of Jewish births dropped below the rate necessary for population replacement. A downward trend had been noted in the United States even before the war: it was estimated that the Jewish birthrate there fell by more than one-third between 1920 and 1940—more than double the decline among the white population in general. By the 1960s the decline accelerated alarmingly. An estimate of comparative fertility in the U.S. in the years 1967–69 showed that whereas there were 2,388 births per thousand women in the white population as a whole, among Jewish women the rate was only 1,468 per thousand—pointing to a huge natural decrease in population. In succeeding decades, the Jewish fertility rate declined notably, raising serious concern about Jewish continuity. This trend was by no means limited to the U.S.—Soviet Jewry exhibited strikingly similar negative demographic characteristics. In Western Europe, too, the Jewish fertility rate was reduced. In Britain, for example, Jewish births shrank by about fifteen percent between 1980 and 1993; the trend seemed likely to continue, given the even steeper decline in Jewish marriages—by about twenty-five percent over the same period. In France, the arrival of the North African Jews in the 1950s and 1960s raised the Jewish fertility rate; but as the immigrants assimilated to the social patterns of the native Jewish population, they, too, married late, often outside the faith, and had fewer children.

The National Jewish Population Survey carried out in the United States in 1990 provided the fullest picture of social and religious trends among American Jewry in the late twentieth century. It found that a third of all married Jews in the U.S. had a non-Jewish spouse. More than a quarter of the 5.5 million Jews in the country were living in households that included at least one non-Jewish adult.

REDUCED DANGERS FROM WITHOUT?

The demographic and cultural pressures toward dissolution of the Diaspora were heightened by changes in the environment in which Jews lived. Antisemitism, for centuries the main external threat to Jewry, was replaced in most liberal societies by a more insidious threat to collective identity: philosemitism—or at any rate a benevolently neutral attitude toward Jews. True, antisemitism did not disappear completely and remained present in some form and to some degree almost everywhere. In some countries it was little more than an irritant, in others a major danger. In Communist countries and in much of the Arab world, antisemitic stereotypes, traditions and slogans were frequently drawn on by governments as a convenient propaganda tool. In the former Soviet Union and Eastern Europe after the fall of communism, extreme nationalist groups often sought to mobilize support by means of populist resort to antisemitism.

In Poland in particular, the strong residue of traditional popular antisemitism was fanned by a series of untoward controversies: over the memorialization of the Warsaw Ghetto, over the attempt to establish a nunnery at Auschwitz, and over a series of ill-considered remarks by Polish priests and even by the primate of the Polish church, Cardinal Glemp, that were judged offensive by many Jews. Yet contrary trends were visible at the same time in Polish society, and public-opinion polls registered declining support for antisemitic attitudes. Some Polish intellectuals (including Catholic intellectuals) argued that the nation had to come to terms with the historic reality of its relationship with the Jews who had lived in its midst. Sadly, the debate was perforce conducted largely in the past tense. In a country that before the war had been home to more than 3 million Jews, only about 6,000, mainly elderly people, still survived.

In Western Europe in the early 1990s, extreme rightist parties grew in strength, particularly in Austria, Italy and France; although the xenophobia of such movements was generally directed more against Muslims and other immigrant groups than against Jews, the nativist rhetoric and cultivation of group hatred rang alarm bells for Jews also. In newly reunited Germany, the extreme Right made little headway in conventional electoral politics, but rampaging mobs of neo-Nazi "skinheads" created an atmosphere of anti-immigrant violence in which the country's 50,000 Jewish residents (most of whom were themselves immigrants) felt beleaguered.

In the United States, the Anti-Defamation League of the B'nai B'rith closely monitored anti-Jewish incidents and recorded disturbing evidence of continued antisemitic activity. Much of this was on the lunatic fringe, but some of it merged into the political mainstream—for example, in sections of the Christian Right, which came to acquire a significant influence within the Republican Party in the mid-1990s. Even where such elements were not explicitly antisemitic, their illiberal political agenda aroused discomfort among many Jews and appeared to threaten the transformation of the social climate toward intolerance and the imposition of puritanical values with which few Jews felt an affinity.

Yet, notwithstanding such disturbing phenomena, the essential characteristics of the social environment in which most Diaspora Jews lived by the 1990s were no longer hostile. In the U.S., Canada, France, Britain, Australia and South Africa, the idea of a multicultural society in which minority groups could maintain distinctive traditions, customs and identities had replaced the unicultural or "melting pot" ideologies of previous generations. Public-opinion polls over long periods showed a secular decline in antisemitism. And perhaps most important, the Christian churches, in earlier times powerful engines of antisemitic ideas, had undergone a thoroughgoing reevaluation of their relationship to Judaism and Jews.

This inner accounting by most of the major Christian Churches (except the Orthodox) with their antisemitic doctrinal heritage had begun in the aftermath of the Second World War and, to some extent, as a result of guilty consciences about the conduct of some Christian institutions in the face of the wartime persecution of Jews. The issue came to a head within the Roman Catholic Church in the early 1960s during the debates at the Second Vatican Council, convened by Pope John XXIII. In its last session, in 1965, the council issued a historic declaration, *Nostra*

Pope John Paul II visits Chief Rabbi Elio Toaff at the Rome Synagogue in 1986.

Aetate, acknowledging the Jews as the medium through whom the Church had received the Old Testament and with whom God had concluded his covenant. The declaration called for mutual understanding and respect and adjured that the Jews should "not be presented as rejected or accursed by God." It added that the Church decried "hatred, persecutions, displays of anti-Semitism, directed against Jews at any time and by anyone."

The decisions of the council began a revolutionary process of change within the Catholic Church, in the course of which it discarded its ancient hostility to Judaism and its condemnation of the Jews as a deicide race. Over the next three decades, the old triumphalism yielded to a more humble approach, in which the Church began to acknowledge the evil effects of its earlier hate-filled doctrines. The moving visit to Auschwitz by the Polish pope John Paul II in 1979 and the opening of diplomatic relations between the Vatican and Israel in 1994 were further milestones on the path toward a healing of the antagonism of the Church to the Synagogue.

The major protestant churches, too, including those of Germany, undertook a collective soul-searching, issued declarations accepting guilt for their actions and doctrines in the past and engaged in dialogue with Jews in an effort to construct a new and more healthy relationship.

ALL ZIONISTS NOW?

One form of Jewish political identification strengthened in the postwar period and in many cases became the cement binding Jewish communities together: this was Zionism—or perhaps it would be better defined as pro-Israelism, since most of its adherents, at any rate in the prosperous countries of the West, combined fervent support for the Jewish state with a reluctance to fulfill the primary Zionist commandment of settlement in the Land of Israel.

During the war, Zionism had made great strides among American Jewry. Throughout the crisis in Palestine of the last years of the British Mandate, between 1945 and 1948, the bulk of American Jewry gave strong support to the effort to achieve a Jewish state. Bodies that had once been skeptical of or hostile to Zionism, such as the American Jewish Committee, now modified their views.

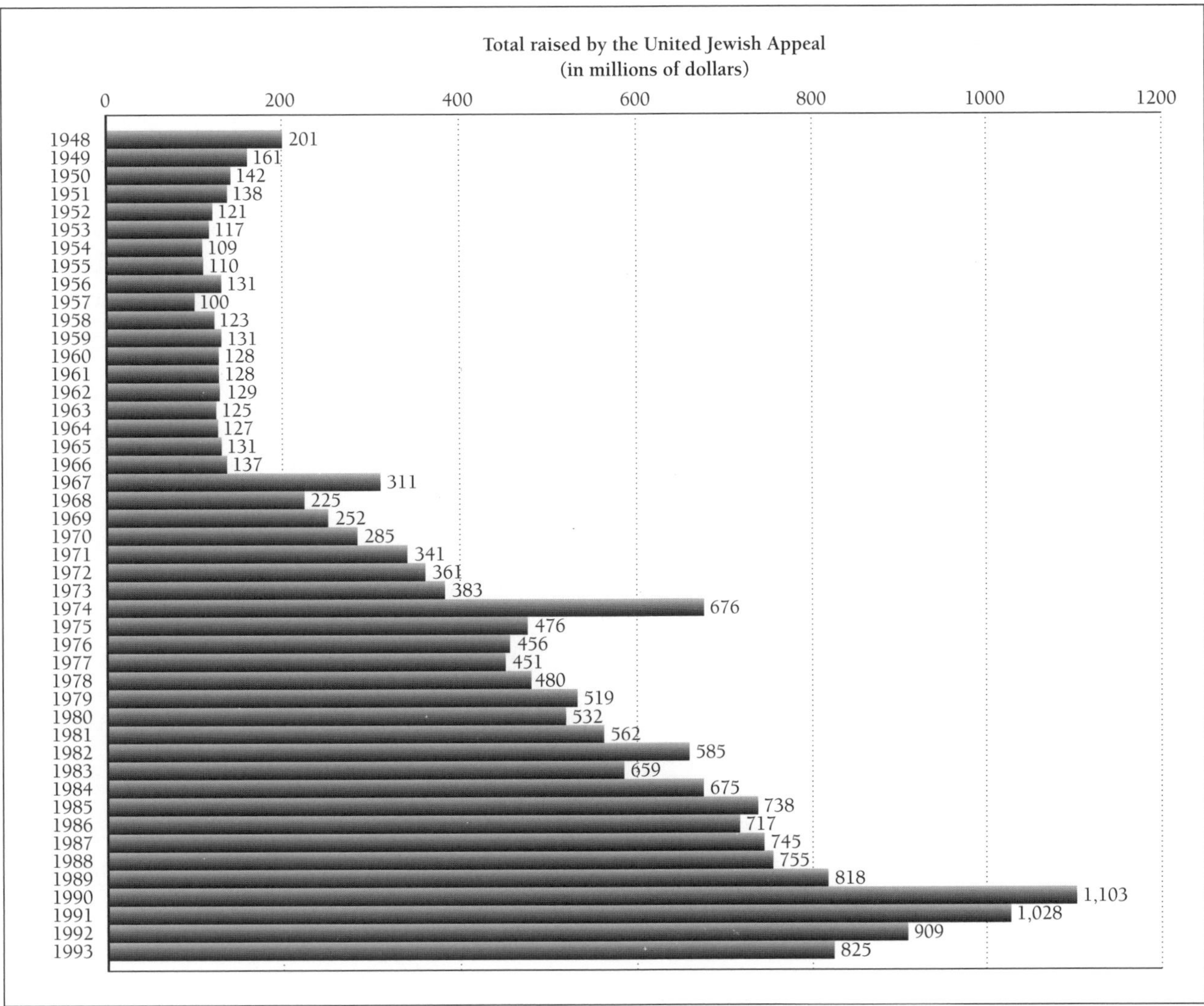

Jewish fund-raising in the U.S.A., 1948–93.

Thereafter, fund-raising for Israel became the single most significant secular activity in Jewish communities. In crisis years such as 1947–48, 1956, 1967 and 1973–74, vast sums were raised to help sustain the Jewish state. In 1973, for example, $383 million was raised by the United Jewish Appeal in the United States.

After 1948 there was much anxious theorizing among Jews about the nature of the Israel-Diaspora relationship. Some argued that with the establishment of Israel, the continued existence of Jewish communities in the dispersion served no function: if Jews wished to maintain their identity, they should move to Israel; otherwise they would—and should—cease to be Jews. But few took this extreme position.

By the 1960s anti-Zionism had become a fringe phenomenon among Diaspora Jews. The establishment leadership in most communities regarded the mobilization of support for Israel as one of their chief functions. Among the Orthodox, only a small fringe of the ultra-Orthodox remained hostile to Israel. Reform Judaism in the United States, whose ideology in earlier times had been opposed to the concept of a Jewish nation, vied with other movements to prove the wholeheartedness of its commitment to Israel; a small minority, organized in the

American Council for Judaism, maintained principled opposition to Zionism—but found themselves virtually cast out of the community as renegades. Even the dwindling band of Jewish Communists faithfully followed the Moscow line and therefore abandoned their opposition to the existence of a Jewish state—though they often criticized its policies violently.

The high point of Diaspora Jewish enthusiasm for Zionism came with the Israeli victory in the 1967 war with Egypt, Jordan and Syria. But the Israeli occupation of large Arab-inhabited territories in that war sowed a seed of doubt.

Was Israel a blessing or a liability for Diaspora Jews? Most argued unhesitatingly that the Jewish state was a boon, straightening Jewish backs everywhere, providing a basis of pride and dignity that had been lacking before. So long as Israel remained generally admired in surrounding gentile societies, such a view was easy to maintain.

With rare exceptions, the bulk of Jewish opinion outside Israel tended to follow closely the Israeli government's line of the moment. Thus, in 1982, for example, more than three-quarters of American Jews were found to approve the view that "Israel is right not to agree to sit down with the PLO because the PLO is a terrorist organization that wants to destroy Israel." But as Israel's image in most western countries changed for the worse, particularly during the *intifada* after 1987, Diaspora Jews began to find the relationship more problematic. In the increasingly complex and variegated Jewish communities of the West, Jews reacted more as individuals than as a unified body. Some criticized Israeli policies, particularly in the territories occupied by Israel in 1967. Others adopted the Israeli cause with a heightened fervor reminiscent of the vicarious nationalism of American Irish and Greeks. The issue came to a head after 1993, with the movement toward reconciliation between Israel and the Palestinian Arabs.

A LAND OF PEACE?

Three events accelerated progress toward Middle East peace. The first was the Gulf War of January 1991, in which the United States, Britain and other European powers joined Saudi Arabia, Egypt and other Arab states in ejecting Iraqi troops who had occupied Kuwait the previous August. Israel remained on the sidelines in this conflict and, under American pressure, refrained from responding to Iraqi missile attacks on her cities. The second catalyst for change was the fall of the Soviet Union in December 1991 and the end of the Cold War. And the third was the election in 1992 of an Israeli Knesset in which, for the first time in the country's history, left-wing parties held a "blocking vote" of 60 out of the 120 seats, thus enabling Labor to form a coalition government, headed by Yitzhak Rabin, that depended neither on the Right nor on the religious parties.

Transgressing a long-held taboo of Israeli diplomacy, Rabin's new government embarked on secret negotiations with the Palestine Liberation Organization, with the Norwegian government acting as a facilitator. The talks eventually produced an agreement (later known as Oslo I) that was sealed on the White House lawn in 1993 with a memorable handshake between the former sworn enemies Yasir Arafat and Yitzhak Rabin. The agreement provided for Israeli withdrawal from the Arab-inhabited areas of Gaza and the West Bank and for the establishment there of a self-governing Palestinian authority. In spite of terrorist attacks by Arab extremists opposed to the accord, its central features were put into effect, and in 1996 the first elections to a Palestinian governing council were held in the areas designated as falling under Palestinian control. Jordan, too, signed a peace treaty with Israel and formalized close and friendly relations. Syria and its tributary, Lebanon, were left isolated in refusal to join the peace process. Syria's dictatorial strongman, Hafez al-Assad, grudgingly opened negotiations with Israel; by 1996 the elements of a settlement seemed within sight (Israeli withdrawal from the Golan Heights in exchange for a full peace treaty), but the parties seemed loath to close the deal.

Peace brought Israel some important diplomatic dividends. African and Asian countries that had cut ties with Israel resumed relations. China and other countries that had hitherto not recognized Israel exchanged ambassadors with her. And some further Arab countries gingerly established low-level representation.

In the meantime, right-wing Israeli hostility to the peace process had grown in intensity. Opposition was particularly strong among Israeli settlers in the occupied areas and their supporters among religious nationalists. In November 1995 a student at the religious-Zionist Bar Ilan University shot Yitzhak Rabin in the back as he left a peace rally in Tel Aviv; he died on the way to hospital. The assassination traumatized the country and aroused deep feeling, not only among Jews, throughout the world. Rabin's funeral was attended by an extraordinary array of world leaders: among them were President Mubarak of Egypt and King Hussein of Jordan, both of whom eulogized their former enemy. Shimon Peres, who succeeded Rabin as prime minister, committed himself and his government to continuing on the path of peace. Progress was endangered by a series of terrorist bomb attacks by militant Islamic opponents of the peace process. Nevertheless, as Israel neared the celebration of its first half century of existence, it seemed, for the first time in its history, that it might find a measure of security as a recognized and accepted element in the region. The election of

The funeral of Yitzhak Rabin, November 6, 1995.

Binyamin Netanyahu as prime minister in 1996 slowed down the process. His right-wing government was openly skeptical about it and sought to renegotiate key elements of the Oslo agreement. Nevertheless, in spite of many setbacks, the historic change in Israeli-Palestinian relations that had begun in 1993 seemed to have acquired a momentum of its own.

AFTER ZIONISM?

By the end of the twentieth century, the balance between Israel and the Diaspora was beginning to shift—in terms of population, of power, of economic weight and, perhaps most significantly, of collective psychology. Diaspora Jews continued to give strong support to Israel: in 1993, an overwhelming majority of American Jews supported the Israeli-Palestinian pact. Yet Zionism was beginning to be seen as a mixed blessing. On the one hand, Israel gave Jewish life a desperately needed focal point; on the other, it drained the Diaspora of money, of committed Jews and of energy.

By the 1990s Jewish communities in North America and elsewhere were beginning to rethink their priorities. Israel, boasting a gross national product comparable to the economies of Western Europe, no longer looked like a charity case. The mass immigration of Soviet Jews to Israel after 1989 boosted charitable giving to Israel for a while. But increasingly the call was heard for greater emphasis to be placed on funding Jewish institutions at home, to bolster Jewish education and to buttress Jewish old-age homes and other bodies adversely affected by the growth in the numbers of the aged and the trend away from the welfare state.

The continuing growth of the Jewish population of Israel and the slow disintegration of American Jewry is likely to have the dramatic result, sometime early in the twenty-first century, that the Jewish state will at last become the home of the largest Jewish community in the world. Indeed, if demographic decline continues in other Diaspora communities, it is conceivable that within a few generations a majority of all self-identifying Jews in the world will live in Israel.

The Jewish world's center of gravity is plainly shifting to Israel. This will necessarily affect the Diaspora Jewish relationship. Some consequences are already becoming apparent. Diaspora Jews are ceasing to view Israel as a poor relative to be treated with a mixture of concern and condescension. Fear, sometimes even paranoia, about survival is shifting from Israel to the Diaspora communities themselves. Increasingly Israel is seen as a rock of solidity to which Jews elsewhere must cling for their collective survival—spiritually, culturally and in terms of mass psychology.

Yet Israel itself is becoming, in the eyes of many beholders, less Jewish. The arrival of the great many mainly secular Russian Jews has tilted the balance against religious elements in Israeli society. Although the ultra-Orthodox minority, with their large numbers of children, maintain their position, they live in an increasingly cocooned world, while the rest of Israeli society, like most Western societies, succumbs to an apparently irreversible process of secularization.

For Jews more than for any other people, the twentieth century has been the most terrible and the most revolutionary of centuries. The challenges that confront them in the twenty-first century are immense: Can they maintain some sort of balance between the Israeli core and the Diaspora periphery? Can they reverse apparently inexorable demographic trends of decline? Can they preserve some form of connection with their traditions amid the assimilatory pressures of liberal societies? Above all, the challenge is one of self-understanding: in what historically authentic sense can they remain Jews in a post-religious age?

Independence Day celebrations in Jerusalem.

Selected Bibliography

Chapter One: Beginnings

Primary sources: the Hebrew Bible (there are innumerable reasonably good commentaries, the most widely available of which are probably those in the Anchor Bible series; many Jewish readers will have ready access to the fine Jewish Publication Society Pentateuch).

The standard edition of the Elephantine Papyri is A. E. Cowley, *Aramaic Papyri of the Fifth Century B.C.* (Oxford: Clarendon Press, 1923).

Any Christian Bible contains the books of the Apocrypha, including 1 and 2 Maccabees, Ben Sira (or Ecclesiasticus) and Judith, and they are also printed separately, as, for example, in the *Oxford Annotated Apocrypha.* The Anchor Bible series once again contains valuable commentaries on the individual apocryphal books. Of special interest are the commentaries on Ben Sira, by A. DiLella, and on 1 and 2 Maccabees, by J. Goldstein. The latter are brilliant but eccentric, and must be used with skepticism.

The Pseudepigrapha, including 1 Enoch, and the fragmentarily preserved Greco-Jewish writers, such as Eupolemus, are conveniently collected, in English translation, in J. H. Charlesworth, ed., *Old Testament Pseudepigrapha* (2 vols., Garden City: Doubleday, 1983–85).

A convenient translation of the main Dead Sea Scrolls is G. Vermes, *The Dead Sea Scrolls in English*, 3d ed. (London: Penguin, 1987).

The best English translation of the works of Josephus is in the Loeb Classical Library series: H. St. J. Thackeray, R. Marcus, A. Wikgren and L. H. Feldman, eds. and trans., *Josephus* (10 vols., Cambridge: Harvard University Press, 1926–65).

Modern Literature

Good introductions to the history of biblical Israel may be found in H. J. Hayes and J. M. Miller, *Israelite and Judaean History* (Philadelphia-London: University of Pennsylvania Press, 1977), and in R. E. Clements, ed., *The World of Ancient Israel: Sociological, Anthropological and Political Perspectives* (Cambridge: Cambridge University Press, 1991); the account of Israelite religion is indebted in part to M. Smith, *Palestinian Parties and Politics That Shaped the Old Testament*, 2d ed. (London: SCM, 1987); the religious implications of Israelite personal names are discussed by J. Tigay, *You Shall Have No Other Gods: Israelite Religion in Light of Hebrew Inscriptions* (Atlanta: Scholars Press, 1986); the several contributors discuss the Elephantine Papyri in the following important collection, which also serves as a good introduction to Judaea under the Persians: W. D. Davies and L. Finkelstein, eds., *The Cambridge History of Judaism*, vol. 1: *Introduction: The Persian Period* (Cambridge: Cambridge University Press, 1984); the standard account of the Persian Empire is now M. Dandamaev and V. Lukonin, *The Culture and Social Institutions of Iran* (Cambridge: Cambridge University Press, 1989).

An up-to-date synthetic account of the role of priests and prophets in pre-Maccabean Jewish society is J. Blenkinsopp, *Sage, Priest, Prophet: Religious and Intellectual Leadership in Ancient Israel* (Louisville: Westminster John Knox, 1995); also valuable is the same author's *Wisdom and Law in the Old Testament* (Oxford: Oxford University Press, 1983); for the problem of Hellenism, the basic general account is now S. Sherwin-White and A. Kuhrt, *From Samarkhand to Sardis: A New Approach to the Seleucid Empire* (London: Duckworth, 1993); the standard, though in some ways idiosyncratic, studies of Hellenism and the Jews are M. Hengel, *Judaism and Hellenism*, 2 vols. (Philadelphia: Fortress Press, 1974) and *Jews, Greeks, and Barbarians* (Philadelphia: Fortress Press, 1980); for some interesting studies of the religious environment in Judaea in the third century B.C.E., see J. H. Charlesworth and J. J. Collins, eds., *Mysteries and Revelations* (Sheffield: JSOT, 1991); an excellent history of Judaea from Alexander the Great through the Maccabean Revolt is V. Tcherikover, *Hellenistic Civilization and the Jews* (Philadelphia: Jewish Publication Society, 1966); the other classic account of the Maccabean Revolt is E. J. Bickerman, *The God of the Maccabees* (Leiden: Brill, 1979); recent scholarship is accessibly summarized in D. Harrington, *The Maccabean Revolt: Anatomy of a Biblical Revolution* (Wilmington: Michael Glazier, 1988).

For the history, literature and religion of the Jews in the period of the revolt and following, the essential reference work is E. Schürer, *The History of the Jewish People in the Age of Jesus Christ*, rev. and ed. G. Vermes and F. Millar, 4 vols. (Edinburgh: T & T Clark, 1973–87); the Hasmonean expansion has been little studied, but a good summary of the issues is provided by S. Cohen, "Religion, Ethnicity, and 'Hellenism' in the Emergence of Jewish Identity in Maccabean Palestine," in P. Bilde, et al., *Religion and Religious Practice in the Seleucid Kingdom* (Aarhus: Aarhus University Press, 1990) 204–23; S. Cohen has also written an excellent survey of post-Maccabean Judaism, containing also a responsible survey of sectarianism, *From the Maccabees to the Mishnah* (Philadelphia: Westminster Press, 1987). It should be pointed out, though, that the legal monopoly on publication of the Dead Sea Scrolls came to an end in the early 1990s. The result has been a flood of publication of scrolls; the state of the study of sectarianism is thus in flux, liable to change day by day.

The most authoritative modern treatments of Herod's reign are in German and Hebrew; a major synthetic account in English has now appeared: P. Richardson, *Herod: King of the Jews and Friend of the Romans* (Columbia: University of South Carolina Press, 1996). English readers may also consult Schürer, E. M. Smallwood, *The Jews under Roman Rule* (Leiden: Brill, 1976), and M. Avi-Yonah and Z. Baras, eds., *The World History of the Jewish People*, vol. 7: *The Herodian Period* (New Brunswick: Rutgers University Press, 1975).

CHAPTER TWO: THE MAKING OF THE DIASPORA

For further information on the various communities, see the following: W. D. Davies and L. Finkelstein, eds., *The Cambridge History of Judaism*, vol. 1: *The Persian Period.* (Cambridge: Cambridge University Press, 1984), 326–400; E. Schürer, *The History of the Jewish People in the Age of Jesus Christ (175 BC–AD 135)*, rev. and ed. by G. Vermes, F. Millar and M. Goodman (vol. III/1, Edinburgh, 1986), 1–176 ("A Geographical Survey"); J. Mélèze Modrzejewski, *The Jews of Egypt from Ramses II to Emperor Hadrian* (Philadelphia and Jerusalem, 1995); P. Trebilco, *Jewish Communities in Asia Minor* (Cambridge, 1991); L. V. Rutgers, *The Jews in Late Ancient Rome* (Leiden: Brill, 1995); Isaiah M. Gafni, *The Jews of Babylonia in the Talmudic Era*, (New Haven, forthcoming).

On further topics relating to the lives of the Jews in the Diaspora, see M. D. Goodman, *Mission and Conversion: Proselytizing in the Religious History of the Roman Empire* (Oxford, 1994); Shaye J. D. Cohen and S. Frerichs, eds., *Diasporas in Antiquity* (Atlanta, 1993); and Lee I. Levine, ed., *The Synagogue in Late Antiquity* (Philadelphia: Jewish Publication Society, 1987).

CHAPTER THREE: A REJECTED PEOPLE

There are several good collections of primary sources on this topic. A full collection of Roman legislation concerning the Jews can be found in Amnon Linder, *The Jews in Roman Imperial Legislation* (Detroit: Wayne State University Press, 1987). A good collection of sources concerning the Church and the Jews is Solomon Grayzel, *The Church and the Jews in the XIIIth Century*, rev. ed. (New York: Hermon Press, 1966), and Solomon Grayzel, *The Church and the Jews in the XIIIth Century*, vol. 2: 1254–1314, ed. Kenneth Stow (New York: The Jewish Theological Seminary, 1989). Documents concerning Ashkenaz: Julius Aronius, *Regesten zur Geschichte der Juden im fränkischen und deutschen Reiche* (Berlin: L. Simion, 1902). Documents concerning Sepharad: Yitzhak Baer, *Die Juden im christlichen Spanien*, 2 vols. (Berlin: Schocken Verlag, 1929-1936). Augustine's concept of the Jews was shaped in his famous *City of God*, trans. H. Bettenson, ed. D. Knowls (Harmondsworth: Penguin, 1972).

Jewish-Christian relations in the first centuries were described by James Parkes, *The Conflict of the Church and the Synagogue* (New York: Atheneum, 1934), and by Marcel Simon, *Versus Israel: A Study of the Relation between Christians and Jews in the Roman Empire (135–425)*, trans. H. McKeating (Oxford: Oxford University Press, 1986).

Salo Baron's history of the Jews is still irreplaceable: *A Social and Religious History of the Jews*, 2d ed. (Philadelphia: Columbia University Press and the Jewish Publication Society, 1952–1983). As for the Jews in the different countries—Spain, Germany, Italy and Byzantium—the best surveys are still Yitzhak Baer, *A History of the Jews in Christian Spain*, trans. Louis Scheffman et al., 2 vols. (Philadelphia: The Jewish Publication Society, 1961–1966); Guido Kisch, *The Jews in Medieval Germany* (New York: Ktav Publication House 1970); Cecil Roth, *A History of the Jews in Italy* (Philadelphia: The Jewish Publication Society, 1946); Andrew Sharf, *Byzantine Jewry* (London: Routledge and Kegan Paul, 1971). Kenneth Stow wrote several important works on Christian attitude toward the Jews. An overall survey is *Alienated Minority: The Jews of Medieval Latin Europe* (Cambridge, Mass.: Harvard University Press, 1994). For the Counter-Reformation Church, see R. Kenneth, *Catholic Thought and Papal Jewry Policy 1555–1593* (New York: The Jewish Theological Seminary, 1977).

Several significant scholarly works have been written in the past two decades on Christian missionary efforts and on Jewish-Christian dialogue and polemics. We mention here David Berger, *The Jewish-Christian Debate in the High Middle Ages* (Philadelphia: The Jewish Publication Society, 1979); Jeremy Cohen, *The Friars and the Jews: The Evolution of Medieval Anti-Judaism* (Ithaca and London: Cornell University Press, 1982); Hyam Maccoby, *Judaism on Trial: Jewish-Christian Disputations in the Middle Ages* (London: Associated University Press, 1982); Robert Chazan, *Daggers of Faith: Thirteenth-Century Christian Missionizing and Jewish Response* (California: University of California Press, 1989). Short summaries of the main Christian polemical works against the Jews are included in Lukyn A. Williams, *Adversus Judaeos: A Bird's-Eye View of Christian Apologie until the Renaissance* (Cambridge: Cambridge University Press, 1935).

The famous story of the first ritual murder accusation (Norwich) is Thomas of Monmouth, *The Life and Miracles of St. William of Norwich*, ed. Augustus Jessopp and Montague Rhodes James (Cambridge: Cambridge University Press, 1896). The mentality that stands in the background of the later blood libels is the theme of R. Po-chia Hsia, *The Myth of Ritual Murder: Jews and Magic in Reformation Germany* (New Haven and London: Yale University Press, 1988). The diabolical image of the Jew was described in a famous book: Joshua Trachtenberg, *The Devil and the Jews: The Medieval Conception of the Jew and Its Relation to Modern Anti-Semitism* (Philadelphia: The Jewish Publication Society, 1943).

Several themes included in the chapter were the topics of notable scholarly books and articles: Robert Chazan, *European Jewry and the First Crusade* (Berkeley: University of California Press, 1987); Solomon Grayzel, "The Papal Bull *Sicut*

Iudeis," in *Studies and Essays in Honor of Abraham A. Neuman*, ed. Meir Ben-Horin, Bernard D. Weinryb, and Solomon Zeitlin (Leiden: Brill, 1962: 243–80); R. I. Moore, *The Formation of a Persecuting Society* (Oxford: Blackwell, 1987).

CHAPTER FOUR:

"MY HEART IS IN THE EAST..."

A small but growing body of literature on the Jews in Muslim lands exists. The best overview can be found in Bernard Lewis, *The Jews of Islam* (Princeton: Princeton University Press, 1985). Lewis clearly presents the attitude of Islam toward other religions in general and the Jews in particular, detailing the discriminatory regulations as well as the positive aspects of intergroup relations. Norman Stillman's *Jews of Arab Lands* (Philadelphia: Jewish Publication Society, 1979) includes a varied collection of primary sources documenting the complex subject of Jewish life in the far-flung Muslim empire.

The richest source of information on medieval Jewry in Muslim lands derives from the horde of documents known as the Cairo Genizah, discovered in an Old Cairo synagogue at the end of the nineteenth century. The master of Genizah research, S. D. Goitein, has produced a monumental five-volume study culled from the tens of thousands of Hebrew and Arabic fragments that he deciphered. His *Mediterranean Society* (Berkeley and Los Angeles: University of California Press, 1967–1988) sheds light on the social, economic, communal and family life of the Jews throughout the Mediterranean. The Genizah material is richest for the tenth and eleventh centuries and sheds most light on Cairene and Tunisian Jewry.

A separate consideration of Muslim Spain (Andalusia) can be found in the absorbing, if sometimes romantic, study of selective aspects of Jewish life in Andalusia in E. Ashtor's *History of the Jews in Muslim Spain* (Philadelphia: Jewish Publication Society, 1973–1984). A useful syntheses of Sephardi history, which includes both Muslim and Christian Spain and the various communities of the Sephardi diaspora after 1492, can be found in *The Jews of Spain* by Jane S. Gerber (New York: Free Press, 1992).

Jewish intellectual life under Islam has been the subject of inquiry since the birth of modern Jewish scholarship in nineteenth-century Europe. Spain and its poetic revolution is the subject of several excellent recent publications. For a fine general survey of the subject of the Golden Age, see Shalom Spiegel's essay "On Medieval Hebrew Poetry," in *The Jews: Their History, Culture and Religion*, ed. Louis Finkelstein, 3d ed. (New York, 1990). Raymond Scheindlin's *Wine, Women and Death: Medieval Hebrew Poems on the Good Life* (Philadelphia: Jewish Publication Society, 1986) and *The Gazelle* (Philadelphia: Jewish Publication Society, 1991) provide masterful translations and commentaries on selected Hebrew secular and religious poetry. Translations of a broader array of poems can be found in T. Carmi's *Penguin Book of Hebrew Verse* (New York: Penguin Books, 1981).

Poetry was only one part of a broader cultural milieu that included the study of medicine, the contemplation of philosophy and an abiding interest in language. The best introduction to Maimonides' writings is Isadore Twersky's *Maimonides Reader* (New York: Behrman House, 1972). Maimonides' epistles are the subject of a fine translation by Abraham Halkin, with a significant introductory essay by David Hartman, in *Crisis and Leadership: The Epistles of Maimonides* (Philadelphia: Jewish Publication Society, 1985). A good edition of Halevi's *Kuzari* is Isaak Heinemann's (Oxford: Oxford University Press, 1947).

Individual regional studies of specific Jewish communities include H. Z. Hirschberg's *History of the Jews in North Africa*, 2 vols. (Leiden: Brill, 1974–1980). For a fine survey of Sephardi Jewry in the Ottoman Balkans, see E. BenBassa and Aron Rodrigue, *The Jews of the Balkans: The Judeo-Spanish Community, 15th to 20th Centuries* (Oxford: Blackwell Publishers, 1995). Cecil Roth's biographies of Don Joseph Nasi and Doña Gracia Mendes (Philadelphia: Jewish Publication Society, 1992) are still useful and highly readable.

The intellectual upheavals attendant on the expulsion from Spain and resettlement in the Ottoman Empire resonate in the classic essay by Solomon Schechter, "Safed in the Sixteenth Century" in his *Studies in Judaism* (Oxford: Oxford University Press, 1970). Highly recommended for its enormous erudition and wealth of data is the biographical history of the messianic movement of Shabbetai Zvi by Gershom Scholom, *Sabbetai Sevi: The Mystical Messiah* (Princeton: Princeton University Press, 1973). Marc D. Angel's *Voices of Exile* (Hoboken, NJ: Ktav Publishing House, 1991) discusses little-known thinkers from the Sephardi diaspora.

CHAPTER FIVE: INTO THE MODERN WORLD

A useful documentary collection for the entire period is Paul Mendes-Flohr and Jehuda Reinharz, eds., *The Jew in the Modern World: A Documentary History*, 2d ed. (New York: Oxford University Press, 1995).

Harbingers: An indispensable introduction to the Jews of early modern Europe (c. 1550–1750) is Jonathan Israel, *European Jewry in the Age of Mercantilism, 1550–1750* (Oxford: Oxford University Press, 1985). For the classic study of the internal structure and development of the Ashkenazi Jewish community, see Jacob Katz, *Tradition and Crisis: Jewish Society at the End of the Middle Ages* (New York: New York University Press, 1993). The port Jews have been evaluated in excellent case studies. For Trieste, see Lois Dubin, "Trieste and Berlin: The Italian Role in the Cultural Politics of the Haskalah," in Jacob Katz ed., *Toward Modernity: The European Jewish Model* (New Brunswick: Rutgers University Press, 1987) 189–224; for London, see Todd Endelman, *The Jews of Georgian England, 1714–1830* (Philadelphia: Jewish Publication Society, 1979); for Bordeaux, see Frances Malino, *The Sephardic Jews of Bordeaux* (Tuscaloosa: University of Alabama Press, 1978). The standard study of Moses Mendelssohn is Alexander Altmann, *Moses Mendelssohn: A Biographical Study* (Tuscaloosa: University of Alabama Press, 1973). For Mendelssohn's Jewish thought, see David Sorkin, *Moses Mendelssohn and the Religious Enlightenment* (Berkeley: University of California Press, 1996).

The First Transformation: The best single volume on the emancipation period is Jacob Katz, *Out of the Ghetto: The Social Background of Jewish Emancipation*,

1770–1870 (New York: Schocken, 1978). For France, see Simon Schwarzfuchs, *Napoleon, the Jews and the Sanhedrin* (London: Routledge and Kegan Paul, 1979); Jay R. Berkovitz, *The Shaping of Jewish Identity in Nineteenth-Century France* (Detroit: Wayne State University Press, 1989); and Paula E. Hyman, *The Emancipation of the Jews of Alsace* (New Haven: Yale University Press, 1991). For England, see M. C. N. Salbstein, *The Emancipation of the Jews in Britain: The Question of the Admission of the Jews to Parliament, 1828–1860* (East Brunswick: Associated University Presses, 1982), and Bill Williams, *The Making of Manchester Jewry, 1740–1875* (Manchester: Manchester University Press, 1976). For Germany, see Reinhard Ruerup, "Jewish Emancipation and Bourgeois Society," *Leo Baeck Institute Yearbook 14* (1969), 67–91, and David Sorkin, *The Transformation of German Jewry, 1780–1840* (New York: Oxford University Press, 1987). For useful biographies, see Frances Malino and David Sorkin, eds., *From East and West: Jews in a Changing Europe, 1750–1870* (Oxford: Blackwell Publishers, 1990).

The Damascus Affair has been studied by Jonathan Frankel, *The Damascus Affair: "Ritual Murder," Politics and the Jews in 1840* (Cambridge: Cambridge University Press, 1997). For the origins of the Alliance Israélite Universelle, see Michael Graetz, *The Jews in Nineteenth-Century France: From the French Revolution to the Alliance Israélite Universelle* (Stanford: Stanford University Press, 1996).

Remaking the Jews and Judaism: Excellent overviews of cultural, social and religious developments are found in two collections of essays: Jacob Katz, ed., *Toward Modernity: The European Jewish Model* (New Brunswick, NJ: Rutgers University Press, 1987), and Jonathan Frankel and Steven J Zipperstein, eds., *Assimilation and Community: The Jews in Nineteenth-Century Europe* (Cambridge: Cambridge University Press, 1992). For religious changes, see Michael Meyer, *Response to Modernity: A History of the Reform Movement in Judaism* (New York: Oxford University Press, 1988). For religious thought, see Ismar Schorsch, *From Text to Context: The Turn to History in Modern Judaism* (Hanover: University Press of New England, 1994). David Cesarani has studied a central example of the press in *The Jewish Chronicle and Anglo-Jewry, 1841–1991* (Cambridge: Cambridge University Press, 1994).

On Jewish intellectuals, see Isaiah Berlin, "Benjamin Disraeli, Karl Marx and the Search for Identity," in *Against the Current: Essays in the History of Ideas* (Oxford: Clarendon Press, 1991); S. S. Prawer, *Heine's Jewish Comedy: A Study of His Portraits of Jews and Judaism* (Oxford: Clarendon Press, 1983); and Michael Meyer, *The Origins of the Modern Jew: Jewish Identity and European Culture in Germany, 1749–1824* (Detroit: Wayne State University Press, 1967).

The two Easts: The history of Eastern European Jewry is surveyed in Salo Baron, *The Russian Jew under Tsars and Soviets*, 2d ed. (New York: Schocken, 1987). For Jewish life in the Polish-Lithuanian Kingdom, see Gershon Hundert, *The Jews in a Polish Private Town: The Case of Opatow in the Eighteenth Century*

(Baltimore: John Hopkins University Press, 1992), and Murray J. Rosman, *The Lords' Jews: Magnate-Jewish Relations in the Polish-Lithuanian Commonwealth in the Eighteenth Century* (Cambridge: Harvard University Press, 1990). For Hasidism, see Gershon Hundert, ed., *Essential Papers on Hasidism: Origins to Present* (New York: New York University Press, 1991), and Moshe Rosman, *Founder of Hasidism: A Quest for the Historical Ba'al Shem Tov* (Berkeley: University of California Press, 1996). On the partitions and early Russian policy, see John Klier, *Russia Gathers Her Jews: The Origins of the "Jewish Question" in Russia, 1771–1825* (De Kalb, Ill.: University of Northern Illinois University Press, 1986). For the development of the Haskalah, see Michael Stanislawski, *Tsar Nicholas I and the Jews: The Transformation of Jewish Society in Russia, 1825–1855* (Philadelphia: Jewish Publication Society, 1983). For the case of Shklov, see David E. Fishman, *Russia's First Modern Jews: The Jews of Shklov* (New York: New York University Press, 1995); for Odessa, see Steven J. Zipperstein, *The Jews of Odessa: A Cultural History, 1794–1881* (Stanford: Stanford University Press, 1986). Michael Stanislawski has studied a major figure of the Haskalah in *For Whom Do I Toil: Judah Leib Gordon and the Crisis of Russian Jewry* (New York: Oxford University Press, 1988).

An introduction to the Jews of North Africa and the Middle East is Norman Stillman, *The Jews of Arab Lands in Modern Times* (Philadelphia: Jewish Publication Society, 1991). Two studies of the Alliance are Aron Rodrigue, *French Jews, Turkish Jews: The Alliance Israélite Universelle and the Politics of Jewish Schooling in Turkey, 1860–1925* (Bloomington: Indiana University Press, 1990), and Michael M. Laskier, *The Alliance Israélite Universelle and the Jewish Communities of Morocco, 1862–1962* (Albany: State University of New York Press, 1983).

The Second Transformation: The changing economic situation of the Jews in Russia has been studied by Arcadius Kahan, *Essays in Jewish Social and Economic History* (Chicago: University of Chicago Press, 1986). For government policy, see Hans Rogger, *Jewish Policies and Right-Wing Politics in Imperial Russia* (London: Macmillan, 1986).

For the encounter between "natives" and "newcomers," see for Germany, Steven Aschheim, *Brothers and Strangers: The East European Jews in German and German Jewish Consciousness, 1800–1923* (Madison: University of Wisconsin Press, 1982) and Jack Wertheimer, *Unwelcome Strangers: East European Jews in Imperial Germany* (New York: Oxford University Press, 1987); for Vienna, Marsha L. Rozenblit, *The Jews of Vienna, 1867–1914* (Albany: State University of New York Press, 1983); for England, David Feldman, *Englishmen and Jews: Social Relations and Political Culture, 1840–1914* (New Haven: Yale University Press, 1994); for France, Paula Hyman, *From Dreyfus to Vichy: The Remaking of French Jewry, 1906–1939* (New York: Columbia University Press, 1979).

For the Jews in America, see the documentary collection, Jacob Rader Marcus, *The Jew in the American World: A Source Book* (Detroit: Wayne State

University Press, 1996). Useful surveys are Nathan Glazer, *American Judaism*, 2d ed. (Chicago: University of Chicago Press, 1972) and Abraham J. Karp, *Haven and Home: A History of the Jews in America* (New York: Schocken, 1985). A solid collection of essays is Jonathan Sarna, *The American Jewish Experience* (New York: Holmes and Meier, 1986).

Remaking the Jews and Judaism again: On the new antisemitism, see Peter Pulzer, *The Rise of Political Anti-Semitism in Germany and Austria*, 2d ed. (London: Peter Halban Publishers, 1988); Shulamit Volkov, "Antisemitism as a Cultural Code," *Leo Baeck Institute Yearbook 23* (1978), 25–45; and Zeev Sternhell, "Roots of Popular Antisemitism in the Third Republic," in Frances Malino and Bernard Wasserstein, eds., *The Jews in Modern France* (Hanover: University Press of New England, 1985), 103–34.

On Jewish liberalism, see Ismar Schorsch, *Jewish Reactions to German Anti-Semitism, 1870–1914* (New York: Columbia University Press, 1972), and Christoph Gassenschmidt, *Jewish Liberal Politics in Tsarist Russia, 1900–1914* (New York: New York University Press, 1995). On Zionism, see Steven Beller, *Herzl* (London: Peter Halban Publishers, 1991), and David Vital, *The Origins of Zionism* (Oxford: Clarendon, 1975). On the Bund, see Henry J. Tobias, *The Jewish Bund in Russia, From Its Origins to 1905* (Stanford: Stanford University Press, 1972), and Jonathan Frankel, *Prophecy and Politics: Socialism, Nationalism and the Russian Jews, 1862–1917* (Cambridge: Cambridge University Press, 1981).

CHAPTER SIX: THE DARKEST HOUR

Since the end of the 1970s, historians have been hard at work investigating all aspects of the European Jewish catastrophe that occurred during the Second World War. I have surveyed the resulting publications in my book, *The Holocaust in History* (New York: American Library, 1987). What follows is a brief selection from a vast literature.

For a generally reliable overview, see Leni Yahil, *Holocaust: The Fate of European Jewry, 1932–1945* (New York: Oxford University Press, 1990). Yehuda Bauer, *The Holocaust in Historical Perspective* (Seattle: University of Washington Press, 1978) puts the event into a broader context, as do Zygmunt Bauman, *Modernity and the Holocaust* (Ithaca, NY: Cornell University Press, 1989), and Michael Burleigh and Wolfgang Wippermann, *The Racial State: Germany 1933–1945* (New York: Cambridge University Press, 1991). Useful as well is Martin Gilbert, *The Macmillan Atlas of the Holocaust* (New York: Macmillan, 1982).

The history of the persecution and murder of European Jewry may be studied from the standpoint of the perpetrators, victims and bystanders. Beginning with the perpetrators, the most important work is Raul Hilberg's classic, *The Destruction of the European Jews*, rev. ed., 3 vols. (New York: Holmes and Meier, 1985), probably the most important single work ever written on the subject. For the background to the Holocaust, looking at the course of persecution in Germany, see Saul Friedländer, *Nazi Germany and the Jews*, vol. I, *The Years of*

Persecution (New York: HarperCollins, 1997); Karl Schleunes, *The Twisted Road to Auschwitz: Nazi Policies toward the Jews, 1933–1939* (Urbana, Ill.: University of Illinois Press, 1970); and Henry Friedlander, *The Origins of Nazi Genocide: From Euthanasia to the Final Solution* (Chapel Hill: University of North Carolina Press, 1995). Christopher Browning's collections of essays, *Fateful Months: Essays on the Emergence of the Final Solution* (New York: Holmes and Meier, 1985) and *The Path to Genocide: Essays on the Launching of the Final Solution* (New York: Cambridge University Press, 1992), offer sophisticated assessments of how Nazi policy evolved to Europe-wide mass murder. Also on this theme, see Gerald Fleming, *Hitler and the Final Solution* (Berkeley: University of California Press, 1987); Richard Breitman, *The Architect of Genocide: Himmler and the Final Solution* (New York: Knopf, 1991); and Christopher Browning, *Ordinary Men: Reserve Police Battalion 101 and the Final Solution in Poland* (New York: HarperCollins, 1992). On the operation of the death camps, see Debórah Dwork and Robert Jan van Pelt, *Auschwitz: A History, 1270 to the Present* (New York: Norton, 1996); Yisrael Gutman and Michael Berenbaum, eds., *Anatomy of the Auschwitz Death Camp* (Bloomington: Indiana University Press, 1994); and Yitzhak Arad, *Belzec, Sobibor, Treblinka: The Operation Reinhard Death Camps* (Bloomington: Indiana University Press, 1987). There are numerous treatments of the role of Germany's allies, vanquished states and collaborationist governments in the murder of European Jews. Among these are Randolph L. Braham, *The Politics of Genocide: The Holocaust in Hungary,* 2 vols. (New York: Columbia University Press, 1981); Michael R. Marrus and Robert O. Paxton, *Vichy France and the Jews* (New York: Basic Books, 1981); Meir Michaelis, *Mussolini and the Jews*, 1922–1945 (New York: Oxford University Press, 1978); Jonathan Steinberg, *All or Nothing: The Axis and the Holocaust 1941–43* (London: Routledge, 1990); Jacob Presser, *The Destruction of the Dutch Jews* (New York: E. P. Dutton, 1969); and Leni Yahil, *The Rescue of Danish Jewry: Test of a Democracy*, trans. M. Gradel (Philadelphia: Jewish Publication Society of America, 1969).

For the victims' experience, the reader is referred in particular to Yisrael Gutman and Cynthia J. Haft, eds., *Patterns of Jewish Leadership in Nazi Europe: Proceedings of the Third Yad Vashem International Historical Conference, Jerusalem, April 4–7, 1977* (Jerusalem: Yad Vashem, 1979), and the rich sampling of survivors' testimony in Martin Gilbert, *The Holocaust: A History of the Jews of Europe During the Second World War* (New York: Holt, Rinehart and Winston, 1985). On particular circumstances, see especially Yisrael Gutman, *The Jews of Warsaw, 1939–1943: Ghetto, Underground and Revolt*, trans. Ina Friedman (Bloomington: Indiana University Press, 1983); Yitzhak Arad, *Ghetto in Flames: The Struggle and Destruction of the Jews of Vilna in the Holocaust* (Jerusalem: Yad Vashem, 1980); and Lucjan Dobroszycki, ed., *The Chronicle of the Lodz Ghetto*, trans. Richard Lourie et al. (New Haven: Yale University Press, 1984). On the Jews' experience of the camps, see Terrence Des Pres, *The Survivor: An Anatomy of Life in the*

Death Camps (New York: Oxford University Press, 1976), and Yisrael Gutman and Avital Saf, eds., *The Nazi Concentration Camps: Structure and Aims, The Image of the Prisoner, The Jews in the Camps*. Proceedings of the Fourth Yad Vashem International Historical Conference, Jerusalem, January 1980 (Jerusalem, Yad Vashem, 1984).

On the bystanders, important treatments of particular subjects include Martin Gilbert, *Auschwitz and the Allies* (New York: Holt, Rinehart and Winston, 1981); Walter Laqueur, *The Terrible Secret: An Investigation into the Suppression of Information about Hitler's "Final Solution"* (New York: Penguin, 1982), Deborah E. Lipstadt, *Beyond Belief: The American Press and the Coming of the Holocaust, 1933–1945* (New York: The Free Press, 1986); and John F. Morley, *Vatican Diplomacy and the Holocaust, 1939–1943* (New York: KTAV, 1980). Among the investigations of individual and collective rescue efforts are Yehuda Bauer, *Jews for Sale? Nazi-Jewish Negotiations, 1933–1945* (New Haven: Yale University Press, 1994); Samuel P. Oliner and Pearl M. Oliner, *The Altruistic Personality: Rescuers of Jews in Nazi Europe* (New York: Free Press, 1988); Nechema Tec, *When Light Pierced the Darkness: Christian Rescue of Jews in Nazi-Occupied Poland* (New York: Oxford University Press, 1986); and Eva Fogelman, *Conscience and Courage: Rescuers of Jews During the Holocaust* (New York: Anchor Books, 1994). For the responses of particular countries and societies, see Irving Abella and Harold Troper, *None Is Too Many: Canada and the Jews of Europe: 1933–1948* (Toronto: Lester and Orpen Dennys, 1982); Henry Feingold, *The Politics of Rescue: The Roosevelt Administration and the Jews, 1938–1945* (New Brunswick, N.J.: Rutgers University Press, 1970); David S. Wyman, *The Abandonment of the Jews: America and the Holocaust, 1941–1945* (New York: Pantheon, 1984); Verne W. Newton, ed., *FDR and the Holocaust* (New York: St. Martin's Press, 1996); Bernard Wasserstein, *Britain and the Jews of Europe, 1939–1945* (London: Oxford University Press, 1979); Chaim Avni, *Spain, Franco, and the Jews*, trans. Emanuel Shimoni (Philadelphia: Jewish Publication Society of America, 1982); Dina Porat, *The Blue and Yellow Stars of David: The Zionist Leadership and the Holocaust, 1939–1945* (Cambridge: Harvard University Press, 1990); and Dalia Ofer, *Escaping the Holocaust: Illegal Immigration to the Land of Israel, 1939–1944* (New York: Oxford University Press, 1990).

Finally, for the aftermath of the Holocaust and its continuing impact, the reader is directed to Leonard Dinnerstein, *America and the Survivors of the Holocaust* (New York: Columbia University Press, 1982); Michael R. Marrus, *The Unwanted: European Refugees in the Twentieth Century* (New York: Oxford University Press, 1985); Deborah Lipstadt, *Denying the Holocaust: The Growing Assault on Truth and Memory* (New York: The Free Press, 1993); James Young, *The Texture of Memory: Holocaust Memorials and Meaning* (New Haven: Yale University Press, 1993); and Edward T. Linenthal, *Preserving Memory: The Struggle to Create America's Holocaust Museum* (New York: Viking, 1995).

CHAPTER SEVEN: "TO BE A FREE NATION..."

There are a number of excellent overviews of the history of Zionism and the origins of the state of Israel: Howard M. Sacher, *A History of Israel from the Rise of Zionism to Our Time*, 2d ed. (1996), and Walter Laqueur, *A History of Zionism* (London: Weidenfeld and Nicolson, 1972), are easily available. Noah Lucas's *Modern History of Israel* (London: Weidenfeld and Nicolson, 1974) is out of print but well worth the search. Mitchell Cohen, *Zion and State: Nation, Class, and the Shaping of Modern Israel* (1992), combines clear synthesis with Marxist analysis. *Essential Papers on Zionism*, eds. Jehuda Reinarz and Anita Shapira (1996), combines classic articles with cutting-edge scholarship on all aspects of Zionist history.

For studies of Zionist thought, two classics still hold the field: Arthur Hertzberg, *The Zionist Idea* (Westport, Conn.: Greenwood Press, 1959), and Ben Halpern, *The Idea of the Jewish State*, 2d ed. (Cambridge: Harvard University Press, 1969). Shlomo Avineri, *The Makings of Modern Zionism: The Intellectual Origins of the Jewish State* (1981), and Gideon Shimoni, *The Zionist Ideology* (1995), add important new perspectives.

There are a number of absorbing biographies of the major figures discussed in this chapter. The most recent biography of Herzl is Ernst Pawel, *The Labyrinth of Exile: A Life of Theodor Herzl* (New York: Farrar, Straus and Giroux, 1989). Herzl's nemesis, Ahad Ha-Am, is the subject of Steven J. Zipperstein's *Elusive Prophet: Ahad Ha-Am and the Origins of Zionism* (1993). Jehuda Reinarz has chronicled Chaim Weizmann's life up to 1925 in two volumes: *Chaim Weizmann: The Making of a Zionist Leader* (1985) and *Chaim Weizmann: The Making of a Statesman* (1993). For biographies of leaders of Labor Zionism, see Shabtai Teveth, *Ben-Gurion: The Burning Ground, 1886–1948* (Boston: Houghton Mifflin, 1987); Anita Shapira, Berl: *The Biography of a Socialist Zionist* (1984) on Berl Katznelson; and Gabriel Sheffer, *Moshe Sharett* (New York: Oxford University Press, 1995). We still do not have a scholarly biography of Jabotinsky, although there is much to be gained from Joseph Schechtman, *Rebel and Statesman: The Life and Times of Vladimir Jabotinsky* (1986), and Shmuel Katz, *Lone Wolf: A Biography of Vladimir (Ze'ev) Jabotinsky* (1996).

The birth and development of Political Zionism through the First World War have been chronicled by David Vital in an outstanding trilogy: *The Origins of Zionism* (Oxford: Clarendon Press, 1975); *Zionism: The Formative Years* (Oxford: Clarendon Press, 1982); and *Zionism: The Crucial Phase* (Oxford: Clarendon Press, 1987). Michael Berkowitz's *Zionism and West European Jewry before the First World War* (1993) offers a cultural-historical counterpart to Vital's political analysis. Conversely, Derek J. Penslar, *Zionism and Technocracy: The Engineering of Jewish Settlement in Palestine, 1870–1918* (Bloomington: Indiana University Press, 1991), focuses on the social and economic history of the Yishuv over the period.

On British interests and relations with the Zionists in Mandatory Palestine, see Christopher Sykes, *Crossroads to Israel, 1917–1948* (London: Collins, 1965); Bernard Wasserstein, *The British in Palestine: The Mandatory Government and the*

Arab-Jewish Conflict, 1917–1929 (London: Royal Historical Society, 1978); and Kenneth Stein, *The Land Question in Palestine, 1917–1939* (Chapel Hill: University of North Carolina Press, 1984). On Jewish nation-building during the 1920s and 1930s, see Henry Near, *The Kibbutz Movement: Origins and Growth, 1909–1939* (Auckland, NZ: Oxford University Press, 1992), and Dan Horowitz and Moshe Lissak, *Origins of the Israeli Polity in Palestine* (Chicago: University of Chicago Press, 1978). Zionist women's history has until recently been a neglected subject; *Pioneers and Homemakers: Jewish Women in Pre-State Israel*, ed. Deborah Bernstein (Albany: State University of New York Press, 1992), is a valuable corrective.

The cultural history of the Yishuv has been sensitively analyzed in Yael Zerubavel, *Recovered Roots: Collective Memory and the Making of Israeli National Tradition* (Chicago: University of Chicago Press, 1995), and Nachman Ben-Yehuda, *The Masada Myth: Collective Memory and Mythmaking in Israel* (Madison: University of Wisconsin Press, 1995). For the institutional and ideological development of the Hebrew University, see David N. Myers, *Re-Inventing the Jewish Past: European Jewish Intellectuals and the Zionist Return to History* (1995). On the revival of modern Hebrew, see Benjamin Harshav's fascinating study, *Language in Time of Revolution* (Berkeley: University of California Press, 1993). Aviezer Ravitzky, *Messianism, Zionism, and Jewish Religious Radicalism* (Chicago: University of Chicago Press, 1996), analyzes the dilemma that Zionism and the creation of Israel have posed for Orthodox Jews.

The origins and course of the Arab-Israeli conflict are concisely discussed in Charles D. Smith, *Palestine and the Arab-Israeli Conflict*, 3d ed. (New York: St. Martin's Press, 1996), and in greater detail in Mark Tessler, *A History of the Israeli-Palestinian Conflict* (Bloomington: Indiana University Press, 1994). Baruch Kimmerling and Joel S. Midgal, *Palestinians: The Making of a People* (Cambridge: Harvard University Press,1993), offers an absorbing and sympathetic account, as does Philip Mattar's biographical study of *The Mufti of Jerusalem: Al-Hajj Amin Al-Hysayni and the Palestinian National Movement* (New York: Columbia University Press, 1988). General histories of Palestinian nationalism include Muhammad Muslih, *The Origins of Palestinian Nationalism* (New York: Columbia University Press, 1988), and two books by Yehoshua Porath: *The Emergence of the Palestinian Arab National Movement, 1918–1929* (1974) and *The Palestinian Arab National Movement, 1929–1939* (1977). Recently, scholars have attempted to combine the history of Palestine's Jews and Arabs into a single analytical framework; see Gershon Shafir, *Land, Labor, and the Origins of the Israeli-Palestinian Conflict, 1882–1914* (Cambridge: Cambridge University Press, 1989), and Zachary Lockman, *Comrades and Enemies: Arab and Jewish Workers in Palestine, 1906–1948* (1996).

The development of Zionist militance is the subject of Anita Shapira, *Land and Power: The Zionist Resort to Force, 1881–1948* (Oxford: Oxford University Press, 1992). This theme also runs through Yehuda Bauer, *From Diplomacy to Resistance: A History of Jewish Palestine 1939–1945* (1970), and Shmuel Dothan, *A Land in the Balance: The Struggle for Palestine, 1918–1948* (Tel Aviv: MOD Publishing House,

Ministry of Defense, 1993). On revisionist Zionism and the right-wing Zionist militias, see, in addition to Dothan, Yaakov Shavit, *Jabotinsky and the Revisionist Movement, 1925–1948* (Ilford, UK: Cass and Company, 1988), and Joseph Heller, *The Stern Gang: Ideology, Politics, and Terror 1940–1949* (Ilford, UK: Cass and Company, 1995). The traumatic impact of the Holocaust on the Zionist movement and the Yishuv is analyzed in Dina Porat, *The Blue and Yellow Stars of David: The Zionist Leadership in Palestine and the Holocaust, 1939–1945* (Cambridge, MA: Harvard University Press, 1990), and Tom Segev, *The Seventh Million: The Israelis and the Holocaust* (New York: Hill and Wang, 1993).

More than any other subject, the 1948 war inflames passions and produces books with radically differing interpretations. For a solidly pro-Israeli presentation, see Nathanel Lorch, *The Edge of the Sword: Israel's War of Independence, 1947–1949* (New York: Hartmore House, 1961). Benny Morris's *The Birth of the Palestinian Refugee Problem, 1947–49* (Cambridge: Cambridge University Press, 1987) was one of the first fruits of the more critical "new Israeli historiography" about the war. Other examples include Avi Shlaim, *The Politics of Partition: King Abdullah, the Zionists, and Palestine, 1921–1951* (New York: Columbia University Press, 1990) and two books by Ilan Pappe: *Britain and the Arab-Zionist Conflict, 1948–1951* (New York: St. Martin's Press, 1988), and *The Making of the Arab-Israeli Conflict, 1947–1951* (London: I. B. Tauris Co., 1992).

CHAPTER EIGHT: THE AGE OF UPHEAVALS

The historiography of postwar Jewry is, in the nature of things, very much a matter of work in progress. Many of the most readily available books are vitiated by tendencies toward propaganda and special pleading. Much of the literature is inadequately researched or lacks historical distance; nevertheless, useful books are available on most aspects of the subject.

General surveys include Barnett Litvinoff, *A Peculiar People: Inside the Jewish World Today* (London: Weidenfeld and Nicolson, 1969), dated but still worth reading. W. D. Rubinstein, *The Left, the Right and the Jews* (London: Croom Helm, 1982) is a vigorously argued analysis of Jewish political attitudes in several countries. Geoffrey Wigoder, *Jewish-Christian Relations since the Second World War* (Manchester: Manchester University Press, 1988) gives a lucid overview of the great change in attitudes toward Jews within the Christian churches.

On the problem of the "displaced persons" and European Jewry in the immediate postwar period, see Yehuda Bauer, *Flight and Rescue: Brichah* (New York: Random House, 1970) and the same author's *Out of the Ashes: The Impact of American Jews on Post-Holocaust European Jewry* (Oxford: Pergamon, 1989). Leonard Dinnerstein, *America and the Survivors of the Holocaust* (New York: Columbia University Press, 1982) is also eye-opening.

The literature on Israel and the Arab-Israeli conflict is vast. A starting point is Itamar Rabinovitch and Jehuda Reinharz, eds., *Israel In the Middle East: Documents and Readings on Society, Politics and Foreign Relations 1948–Present* (New York: Oxford University Press, 1984).

Benjamin Pinkus, *The Jews of the Soviet Union: The History of a National Minority* (Cambridge: Cambridge University Press, 1988) provides a synoptic survey. Robert O. Freedman, ed., *Soviet Jewry in the 1980s: The Politics of Anti-Semitism and Emigration and the Dynamics of Resettlement* (Durham, N. C., Duke University Press, 1989) and Mordechai Altshuler, *Soviet Jewry Since the Second World War: Population and Social Structure* (New York: Greenwood Press, 1987) are both authoritative studies.

American Jewry has spawned a large historical and sociological literature to which the best introduction is Marshall Sklare, *American Jews: A Reader* (New York: Behrman House 1983).

On the revived French Jewish community, see Georges Benguigui et al., *Aspects of French Jewry* (London: Vallentine, Mitchell, 1969). Peter Sichrovsky, *Strangers in Their Own Land: Young Jews in Germany and Austria Today* (London: I. B. Tauris, 1986) provides some insights into a troubled area of postwar Jewish life. On British Jewry, the best overall survey is Geoffrey Alderman, *Modern British Jewry* (Oxford: Oxford University Press, 1993). An older, entertaining discussion is Chaim Bermant, *Troubled Eden: An Anatomy of British Jewry* (London: Vallentine, Mitchell, 1969). David Cesarani, *The Jewish Chronicle and Anglo-Jewry 1841–1991* (Cambridge: Cambridge University Press, 1994) gives a reliable account of the history of the world's oldest Jewish newspaper.

On the final phase of the Jewish presence in the Muslim world, the best introduction is Norman Stillman, *The Jews of Arab Lands in Modern Times* (Philadelphia: Jewish Publication Society of America). Gideon Shimoni, *Jews and Zionism: The South African Experience 1910–1967* (Cape Town: Oxford University Press, 1980) is a soundly researched study.

As for the prospects for Diaspora Jewry, Bernard Wasserstein, *Vanishing Diaspora: The Jews in Europe since 1945* (London: Hamish Hamilton, 1996) reaches pessimistic conclusions, at any rate regarding Europe. David Vital, *The Future of the Jews: A People at the Crossroads?* (Cambridge, Mass.: Harvard University Press, 1990) is a thoughtful essay by a leading contemporary Jewish historian.

INDEX

A page number in italics denotes an illustration.

A

B

C

D

E

F

G

H

I

J

K

L

M

N

O

P

S

T

U

V

W

Y

ACKNOWLEDGMENT OF PICTURE SOURCES

Sources of black-and-white illustrations are as below. For reasons of space, the following abbreviations have been used:

AAA: Ancient Art and Architecture Collection
Art Resource: Art Resource, New York
CZA: Central Zionist Archives, Jerusalem
JTS: Library of the Jewish Theological Seminary of America
USHMM: United States Holocaust Memorial Museum Photo Archives
Yale: Yale University Art Gallery/Dura-Europos Collection

Page 1: Courtesy L. Boussat, Begnins; *7*: Israel Antiquities Authority; *9*: British Museum/118885; *13*: Jewish Museum/Art Resource; *15*: Israel Museum; *27*: Werner Braun; *30*: Israel Museum; *36*: Jane Taylor/Sonia Halliday Photographs; *41*: R. Sheridan/AAA; *46*: Courtesy Holyland Hotel, Jerusalem; *49*: Werner Braun; *52*: Yale; *57*: The Jewish National and University Library; *63*: Courtesy Jewish Museum, London; *64*: Jewish Museum/Art Resource; *69*: Yale; *71*: Israel Antiquities Authority; *74*: Daniel Blatt; *77*: Daniel Blatt; *81*: Yale; *83*: Yale; *86* (left, right): Giraudon/Art Resource; *91*: Alinari/Art Resource; *95*: State Historical Museum, Moscow; *99*: Corbis-Bettmann; *103* (top): Palacio de Lira, Madrid; (bottom): British Museum/Beth Hatefutsoth Photo Archive, Tel Aviv; *107*: Staats und Universitats Bibliothek Hamburg/Sub.cod.heb. 37, 79R; *111*: Biblioteca Medicea Laurenziana, Florence; *118*: Lambeth Palace Library/Ms. 2099, f. 46; *125*: The Granger Collection, New York; *132*: AAA; *136*: Library of Congress/Rosenwald Collection, no. 652; *140*: R. Sheridan/AAA; *145*: Richard Lobell; *151*: Courtesy JTS/ENA 2559, folio 5, side 2; *157*: Reproduced by permission of the Syndics of Cambridge University Library/T-S KS.13; *163*: Courtesy JTS/Shahin's Ardishir and Ezra book/ms. 8270, fol. 95V; *166*: R. Sheridan/AAA; *171*: The Bodleian Library, Oxford/Ms. Hunt 80; *178*: British Library; *183*: Courtesy JTS/Broadside Collection, K56 (Dr1-L110); *184*: Beth Hatefutsoth Photo Archive, courtesy of Yitzhak Einhorn, Tel Aviv; *187*: Courtesy JTS/RB 1697:13 vol. 2; *195*: Courtesy JTS; *198*: Courtesy Permanent Collection, Judah L. Magnes Museum; *202*: British Library; *206*: Jewish Historical Museum, Amsterdam; *212*: Rijksmuseum–Stichting, Amsterdam (*Amsterdam Jews Welcome Bonaparte* by J.A. Lanjendijk, 1808); *222*: Jewish Museum/Art Resource; *225*: Beth Hatefutsoth Photo Archive, Tel Aviv; *230*: Jewish Museum/Art Resource; *233*: Bibliotheque et Archives de L'Alliance Israelite Universelle; *236*: The Granger Collection, New York; *240*: Courtesy Levi Strauss & Co. Archives, San Francisco, CA; *241*: Museum of the City of New York (The Jacob A. Riis Collection #286); *248*: YIVO Institute for Jewish Research; *254*: USHMM; *258*: Wiener Library, London; *260*: Arnold Kramer/USHMM; *261*: Trudy Isenberg/USHMM; *268*: Main Commission for the Investigation of Nazi War Crimes/USHMM; *270*: Yad Vashem/USHMM; *277*: Bibliotheque Historique de la Ville de Paris/USHMM; *280*: Rafael Scharf/USHMM; *286*: USHMM; *289*: Yad Vashem Archives; *294*: Hulton Getty–Keystone/Tony Stone Images; *296*: Yad Vashem Archives; *301*: National Archives/USHMM; *302*: Corbis-Bettmann; *310*: CZA; *314*: CZA; *316*: CZA; *319*: Courtesy Isidore Baum; *323*: CZA; *327*: Courtesy of Hadassah, The Women's Zionist Organization of America, Inc.; *331*: YIVO Institute for Jewish Research; *337*: CZA; *344*: CZA; *348*: CZA; *353*: UPI/Corbis-Bettmann; *354*: Werner Braun; *359*: Werner Braun; *361*: Werner Braun; *365*: Werner Braun; *369*: Jimmy Carter Library; *372*: Courtesy United Jewish Appeal, New York; *377*: Richard Lobell; *385*: Richard Lobell; *389*: Photo by Nir Bareket/Courtesy Ashkenaz; *392*: Mari/Catholic News Service; *395*: Corbis-Bettmann; *397*: Werner Braun.

About the Authors

Nicholas de Lange, General Editor, is Reader in Hebrew and Jewish Studies at the University of Cambridge. His publications include *An Atlas of the Jewish World.*

Seth Schwartz ("Beginnings") is Assistant Professor of History at the Jewish Theological Seminary in New York City.

Oded Irshai ("The Making of the Diaspora") is a professor in the Jewish History Department of the Hebrew University of Jerusalem.

Ora Limor ("A Rejected People") is a professor at the Open University of Israel, where she teaches Medieval History.

Jane S. Gerber ("My Heart Is in the East . . .") is Professor of Jewish History and Director of the Institute for Sephardic Studies at the Graduate School of the City University of New York. Her publications include *The Jews of Spain*, which was awarded the National Jewish Book Award in 1993.

David Sorkin ("Into the Modern World") is the Frances and Laurence Weinstein Professor of Jewish Studies at the University of Wisconsin–Madison. He is the author, most recently, of *Moses Mendelssohn and the Religious Enlightenment.*

Michael R. Marrus ("The Darkest Hour") is Dean of Graduate Studies and Professor of History at the University of Toronto. He is the author of *The Holocaust in History*.

Derek J. Penslar ("To Be a Free Nation . . .") is Associate Professor of History and of Jewish Studies at Indiana University. He is completing a book titled *Shylock's Children: The Jews, Economics, and Ethnic Identity in Modern Europe.*

Bernard Wasserstein ("The Age of Upheavals") is President of the Oxford Centre for Hebrew and Jewish Studies. His most recent book is *Vanishing Diaspora: The Jews in Europe since 1945.*